Tukārām:

Lacking the guile of a mass hypnotizer
I merely extol your name and sing your praise

Not being a miracle worker or a faith healer
Without a train of disciples to boast of

Being the patriarch of no monastery
But a mere shop keeper

No high priest no seer no necromancer no exorcist no witch doctor
Neither the story teller with a grand narrative style
Nor the wretched pandit stewed in dialectics

Not a fool among fools
Wagging a sage beard

There is no voodoo about Tuka—Tuka is like
None of these hell-begotten lunatics

Tukārām Gāthā, Maharashtra Govt. edition 272. The translation is by Arun Kolatkar, in *Poetry India*, vol. 1. The calligraphy on the cover is by R. K. Joshi, Bombay. Joshi does not imitate the handwriting of a pandit, but aims at the somewhat loose, free folkstyle of writing which is supposed to have been that of Tukārām (cp. the facsimile in V. L. Bhave's *Mahārāṣṭra Sārasvat*, Punem, 2nd edn., 1919, facing p. 185).

MYSTICISM IN INDIA

The Poet-Saints of Maharashtra

R. D. Ranade

State University of New York Press
ALBANY

The frontispiece was paid for by a grant from the E. A. Barvoets Fund.

The frontispiece is a photograph of the murte of Bhagawan Nityananda

First published in 1933 by Mr. Anant Vinayak Patwardhan, Poona, under the title *Indian Mysticism: Mysticism in Maharashtra.*

Published by State University of New York Press, Albany

Printed in the United States of America

For information, address State University of New York Press, State University Plaza, Albany, N.Y., 12246

Library of Congress Cataloging in Publication Data

Ranade, Ramchandra Dattatraya.
Mysticism in India.

Reprint. Originally published: Indian mysticism. Poona: [Aryabhushan Press Office, 1933] (History of Indian philosophy; v. 7) With new pref. and foreword.
Bibliography: p. 477
Includes index.
1. Mysticism—Hinduism. 2. Mystics—India—Maharashtra. I. Title.
BL1215.M9R268 1982 294.5'42 82-10458
ISBN 0-87395-669-9
ISBN 0-87395-670-2 (pbk.)

10 9 8 7 6 5 4

PREFACE

In my quest for the ultimate reality, I traveled the length and breadth of India four times. But the region which appealed to me most was Maharashtra. It was not its climate that captivated me, but its spirituality. The lives and works of Jnaneshwar, Tukaram, Eknath, Ramdas, Namdev, Mukundraj, and the other great saints of Maharashtra enchanted me—not just because of their poetic beauty but also because of their spiritual depth. The more I read the works of these saints, the more I recognized them as a complete catalogue of spiritual experience. In them I found expressed even the subtlest inner experiences of Kundalini Yoga or Siddha Yoga, the experiences which were taking place within me through the grace of my Guru, Bhagawan Shree Nityananda.

The literature of these great saints is in verse. It clearly reveals that they were in perfect tune with the rhythmic play of the primordial Shiva. Moreover, the states they describe are completely identical with the teachings of Siddha Yoga. For example, Tukaram's words, *Dehu Hi pandhari atma ha vitthal nandato kevala panduranga*—"The body is holy Pandharpur and the soul is Vithala. Panduranga alone dwells in this shrine" demonstrate the oneness between his state of Para Bhakti (supreme devotion) and the Siddha Yoga teaching, "Meditate on your Self, worship your Self; God dwells within you as you."

Mukundraj also an outstanding figure among these masters, produced two famous works, *Viveksindhu* and *Paramamrit.* They are immortal evidence of his deep insight into the philosophy of Siddha Yoga, and give a detailed description of the spiritual experiences, from the grossest to the subtlest states of awareness, which a seeker has in Siddha meditation by the grace of the Guru. There is an interesting story about Mukundraj and a ruler named Jayatpal, whose capital was located at Ambe-Jogai in the Marathwada region of Maharashtra. Although he had everything which money and royal authority could command, Jayatpal was not happy. He yearned for Self-realization, so whenever a saint came by he would eagerly approach him for a direct experience of the ultimate reality. If he got nothing but words, he would throw the holy man into jail. In this way, quite a few learned Brahmins and holy men were imprisoned by the impetuous king in his quest of Truth. Finally, the day arrived when his wish was to be fulfilled and the sufferings of the poor prisoners were to come to an end.

Mukundraj came by, and the king asked him the same question he had asked all the other saints. Mukundraj replied that he would certainly give the king instantaneous Self-realization. He told Jayatpal to mount a horse. As the king was slipping his feet into the stirrups, Mukundraj struck him with a cane. By that one touch, the master transmitted his spiritual power into the king, awakened his Kundalini, and plunged him into a state of deep *samadhi*. This story is popularly titled: *Rikhab me pav brahma batav*, "Show me God while my foot is still in the stirrup." After this experience the king attained the Supreme and released all the holy men whom he had jailed in his ignorance.

This process of Kundalini awakening by the grace of the Guru is known as *shaktipat*, or the descent of spiritual power. Even in modern times, thousands of seekers all over the world are experiencing spiritual bliss through this process. Gurudev Ranade has done a great service to the world by describing the various ecstatic spiritual experiences mentioned by Mukundraj in his great work *Paramamrit*.

Jnaneshwar has been acknowledged as a king among yogis. Describing the yogic phenomenon of his sister Muktabai's disappearance in a flash of lightning and reappearance in the presence of Saint Gorakumbhar,Jnaneshwar said, "At that moment it appeared as if the deep blue sky had put on a garment of orange and gold; then the Blue Pearl, the core of all Consciousness, began to sparkle." These lines reminded me of my own experience of the Blue Pearl and of the way it had transported me to different worlds.

The addiction of the saints of Maharashtra to the chanting and repetition of the divine name also drew me to that region. I too am addicted to the name. To me, as to them, the name of God does not denote any particular form, but represents the supreme reality behind the animate and inanimate world. The divine name has been called "the unspoken word" by the Upanishads, "uplifting music" by the Vedas, and "king of all words" by the Muslim saints. It is the Pranava, *aum*, the Mother of the three *gunas*, which form the fabric of the universe. The divine name is the nectar of our life; it is our life itself. The great saint Namdev said, "The divine name is the abode of divine consciousness."

When by the grace of the Guru the Kundalini is awakened, it releases the whole range of subtle inner sound. When a seeker glides into the rhythm and melody of those sound waves, he begins to penetrate deeper and deeper within himself and ultimately reaches the very core of his existence—the heart of the Blue Pearl. This happened to me by the grace of my Guru, Bhagawan Nityananda, and it has happened to all saints by the grace of their own Gurus. In fact, the Guru plays the key role in the right understanding of these divine experiences.

The lives and teachings of all realized saints bear witness to the greatness of the Guru—the master who guides them to Self-realization. Saint Ramdas said, "God is so near to you. He is within you, yet you go through life unaware of this. It was my good fortune to meet saints who had realized the Supreme. By their grace I saw God."

This is the unique role of the Guru, the perfected master whose life style and mission are depicted at length in this work. The teachings of such a master emanate from his perfect identity with the supreme Consciousness. His limited individual 'I' has totally merged into the unlimited universal 'I'. His individual self has become one with the universal Self. Being permanently established in the state of "I am That" (*Aham brahmasmi*), his will has become one with the divine will, and he has become the master of all the primordial elements that make up the universe. His words are mantras and materialize as the choicest blessings of God, the supreme reality. The world can neither understand him nor comprehend his actions. Awestruck by his greatness and his command over the elements, people call him a mystic. Nevertheless, for those who understand the subtle causal relationship between the form and the formless, the world and its creator, there is nothing enigmatic about such a being. The great saints of Maharashtra, on whose lives Gurudev Ranade has dwelt at length in this work, fall into this category of mystics. Total lack of ego, born out of unconditional surrender to the Guru; constant awareness of divinity in everything within and without; immense love of God; absolute faith in the power of the divine name; transcendence of both pain and pleasure, profit and loss; and immersion in divine Consciousness as a result of the awakening of the Kundalini by the grace of the Guru are some of the unmistakable features of their lives.

For them, life is a play of consciousness. Their lives fall into a single beautiful pattern, for they are one with That which is unending bliss, That which projects the entire universe on the screen of its own Self without any external aid or material. That is what Kashmir Shaivism calls Paramashiva, the supreme reality. Realization of this supreme reality is the gift of the Guru and of him alone. No ordinary individual could ever fulfill the Guru's role.

As Tukaram Maharaj said, "For Self-realization you must turn to the Guru. Cling to his feet. Only the Guru can make you identical with himself." This process does not involve any particuar length of time; it can happen in an instant. As Tukaram said, the philosophers' stone converts iron into gold, but the Guru converts you into his own divine Self. Tukaram says, "Wordly people are so blind and ignorant that they have forsaken true divinity and have resorted to worshiping imaginary gods."

I am happy that this great study of mysticism in Maharashtra is now being published in the West, and I have no doubt that Western seekers will benefit from this book immensely. The West has begun to accept the understanding that to truly know the mind one must go beyond the mind and that lasting peace can be found only within oneself.

In the words of Tukaram Maharaj: "As I meditated on the Lord, my mind and body were transformed. What can one say about that state? My sense of 'I'-ness has become the Lord. As my mind subsided, it became pure Consciousness, and I saw the entire creation as the Lord's own form. Tukaram says, 'What can I say? There is only one, only one. My only thought is of Him.' "

SWAMI MUKTANANDA

FOREWORD

Maharashtra is one of the principal linguistic and cultural regions of India. It has produced some of the treasures of medieval Indian religious literature as well as some of the leading intellectual figures of modern India. It is thus particularly fitting that R. D. Ranade's *Indian Mysticism: The Poet Saints of Maharashtra* be reprinted as the first volume of a series of books on the religious traditions of Maharashtra. For the subject of the book is some of Maharashtra's medieval religious literary treasures, and its author is one of Maharashtra's modern religious intellectuals.

The book may thus be read as a secondary source or as a primary source. As a secondary source, it remains, half a century after its original publication, the only major study in English of the literature it discusses. As a primary source, it gives revealing insights into the intellectual position of its author.

Jñāneśvara, Nāmadeva, Tukārāma, Ekanātha, Rāmadāsa, and the other saints discussed in this book belong to the great movement of devotional religion (*bhakti*) which spread across India in the medieval period. Their compositions ("writings" would be an imprecise term for many of them) are in Marathi, the vernacular language of Maharashtra. That these poet saints composed in Marathi is in conformity with the ideals of the medieval *bhakti* movement to which they belonged. Whereas Vedic and classical Hindu rituals and texts are the province of Sanskrit-educated Brahmin men, the saints of medieval India proclaimed that the love of God is open to all: not just to those who have learned Sanskrit, not just to Brahmins, and not just to men. Hence, by and large, these saints sang their love of God in the Indian vernaculars, the languages which, in their several regions, could be understood by all members of society. The literature of the medieval *bhakti* movement is thus a number of different literatures belonging to the different linguistic regions of India.[1]

Each of these literatures is further distinguished into different traditions, depending on to which of several gods the authors were more or less exclusively devoted, or to which of several sects devoted to each god they belonged. Except for Rāmadāsa, the saints discussed in this volume belong to a single tradition or sect (*saṃpradāya*), that of the Vārkarīs. The Vārkarīs are devotees of the god Viṭhobā, whose chief temple is in the town of pandharpur in southern Maharashtra. The tradition of the Vārkarīs, which has been described in G. A. Deleury's *The Cult of Viṭobā* (Poona: Deccan College Postgraduate and Research Institute, 1960), is the most popular one in Maharashtra today. Rāmadāsa is also a popular saint in contemporary Maharashtra, and is particularly important to the tradition (*saṃpradāya*) to which Ranade belonged.

For, despite his claim to 'stand for no Sampradāya whatsoever" (p. 20, below), Ranade certainly belonged to one, and after his death he still occupies an important place in it. Ranade was initiated in his youth as a disciple of Bhāūsāheb Umadīkar (Bhāūsāheb Mahārāj, d.1914), who was in turn a disciple of Nārāyan Mahārāj (Nimbargī Mahārāj, d.1885); Nārāyaṇ Mahārāj had connections with both the Liṅgāyat (Vīraśaiva; see p. 18-19, below) and the Nātha (see p. 19, below) sects.[2] In 1933, the year *Indian Mysticism* was first published, Ranade himself succeeded to the spiritual leadership of the *saṃpradāya*;[3] he is still referred to as "Gurudev" ("divine *guru*") by people inside and outside the *saṃpradāya*.

In his academic career, Ranade was known principally as a philosopher. Although he never formulated a philosophical system, it is clear that mysticism played an important role in his philosophical thought as well as in his religious life. Significantly, the original title of this book which was to be part of an eight-volume *History of Indian Philosophy*,[4] was *Indian Mysticism: Mysticism in Maharashtra*. Jñāneśvara, Tukārāma, and the others interested Ranade not primarily as historical persons or as poets, but as mystics. He would have preferred them to be philosophers as well, as he reveals when he characterizes the "mysticism of the Middle Age" in India as showing "a strong, if not even a slightly perverted bias against philosophical endeavour to reach the Absolute" (p. 2-3, below). But, self-conscious philosophers or not, these and other mystics are for Ranade teachers of what others have called the "perennial philosophy." That is, the mystics' experiences have metaphysical implications which are everywhere, ultimately, the same. This sort of theoretical approach to mysticism, once quite prevalent, has been subjected to serious criticism since Ranade's time.[5] But for Ranade it was the basis of his interest in the subject.

In Rānade's own account of his intellectual development,[6] he explains his interest in philosophy as originally subordinate to his religious concerns: "I began a serious study of European philosophy, with the intent of finding in Eastern and Western philosophic thought a justification for the spiritual life." But finally it is the spiritual life which, for Ranade, justifies his philosophy. Matthew Lederle explicates as follows the relationship between mysticism and metaphysics in Ranade's thought:

> For Rānaḍe mysticism could be put into the service of philosophy to make up for the basic incapacity of reason to reach reality. Mystical experience brings in contact with reality and so the experience itself is for the mystic the evidence of its validity. Rānaḍe recognized that this experience had to become objective and universal before it could be a general criterion of true knowledge. He answered, '. . . . it is objective and universal, because all mystics, irrespective of race and creed, talk in the same tongue.' In showing on what all mystics agree he wished to constitute a kind of inductive certitude about the validity of what the mystics say.[7]

A precise identification of Ranade's own metaphysical position, and hence of his version of "what the mystics say," would be difficult; and this is not the place for it. Roughly, his position appears to be a kind of monism which he saw as akin to the *advaita* (non-dualism) of the eighth-century Indian philosopher Śaṅkara.[8] In his Preface the two substantial points on which Ranade finds agreement between "the Mystics of Mahārāshtra" and "the Mystics of the West" are, first, "the Vision of the Self," and, second, "the Identity of the Self and God" (p. v-vii). Ranade's use of the term "God" here indicates the theistic coloring of his brand of monism?[9] this contrasts with the impersonalistic interpretation usually given to Śaṅkara's philosophical system.[10]

Whatever the philosophical position it ultimately served, the "comparative" nature of Ranade's interest in mysticism is evident not only from his Preface but also from his concluding "Bibliographical Note." The "Bibliograhpical Note" also reveals the sources of Ranade's theoretical approach to mysticism: the chief European and American interpreters of mysticism in his day. But, as with Ranade's other works, the *matter* to which his theoretical interest is applied remains Indian. And the matter remains primary. Despite an occasional value judgement,[11] Ranade's chief concern in this book is to present what the saints he writes of said.

For the most part, he allows them to speak for themselves, providing detailed summaries of their principal works. Whatever his interest in finding a unanimity among the mystics of the world, he does not force a superficial similarity upon the saints of Maharashtra. On the contrary, he seeks, through the typology according to which he organizes his book, to point to significant differences among them.

It is for its careful elucidations of the teachings of these saints that Ranade's book retains its value to students of Indian religion. Its renewed availability will, it is to be hoped, stimulate those students to further researches in the religious traditions of Maharashtra.

I am grateful for the helpful advice of Rose Ann Christian, Matthew Lederle, Patrick Olivelle, and Eleanor Zelliot, at various stages in the preparation of this foreword.

ANNE FELDHAUS

Notes

[1]For an excellent brief introduction to the medieval *bhakti* movement, see the Introduction to A. K. Ramanujan's *Speaking of Śiva* (Baltimore: Penguin Books Inc, 1973). For further readings, see Eleanor Zelliot's bibliographical essay, "The Medieval Bhakti Movement in History: An Essay on the Literature in English," in *Hinduism: New Essays in the History of Religions*, ed. Bardwell L. Smith (Leiden: E.J. Brill, 1976), p. 143-168. For a recent survey of scholarship on the articular saints dealt with in this book, see S.G. Tulpule, *Classical Marāṭhī Literature from the Beginning to A.D. 1818* (*A History of Indian Literature*, ed. Jan Gonda, Vol. IX, Fasc. 4) (Wiesbaden: Otto Harrassowitz, 1979).

[2]S.G. Tulpule, *Gurudeva Rā. Da. Rānaḍe: Caritra āṇi Tattvajñāna* (Pune: Venus Prakāśana, 1958; 2nd ed., 1965), p. 83-89.

[3]S.R. Sharma, *Ranade: A Modern Mystic* (Poona, Venus Prakashan, 1961), p. 56f.

[4]The *History* was a collaborative project with S. K. Belvalkar. Of the projected eight volumes, only one other appeared; this was the volume on the Upaniṣads (Vol. II), entitled *The Creative Period* (1927).

[5]One difficulty is that different theorists of this sort come up with different interpretations of the metaphysical implications of the mystics' experiences; more basically, it is difficult to establish that the experiences have metaphysical implications at all. For a bibliography and a brief discussion of philosophical problems involved in interpreting mysticism, see Ronald Hepburn's article "Mysticism, Nature and Assessment of" in *The Encyclopedia of Philosophy*, ed. Paul Edwards

(New York: The Macmillan Company and The Free Press, 1967), Vol. 5, pp. 429-434.

[6]"The Evolution of My Own Thought," in *Contemporary Indian Philosophy*, ed. S. Radhakrishnan and J.H. Muirhead (London: George Allen and Unwin Ltd. 1936; second ed., 1952; third printing, 1958), p. 543.

[7]Matthew Lederle, *Philosophical Trends in Modern Maharāṣṭra* (Bombay: Popular Prakashan, 1976), p. 400-401.

[8]Notice, for instance, his implicit approval of Śaṅkara and disapproval of Rāmānuja and Madhva on p. 15, below. Cf. Lederle, p. 402-405.

[9]See again p. 15, below, on "how theism and pantheism could be reconciled in mysticism."

[10]Ranade reports that one of the experiences which led him to the study of philosophy was hearing the devotional songs of Śaṅkara: this made him "pause and think how a so-called Advaita Philosopher could at the same time make room for devotional songs in his philosophical teaching." (*Contemporary Indian Philosophy*, p. 543.) It may have been his reflections on this question which led Ranade to a more theistic than usual understanding of Śaṅkara's thought.

[11]For instance, his disapproval of sexual elements in religion (p. 5-7, 10-12, 18, etc). For a more sympathetic interpretation of some of the sexual elements in medieval Hinduism, see Edward C. Dimock, Jr., *The Place of the Hidden Moon: Erotic Mysticism in the Vaiṣṇava-Sahajiyā Cult of Bengal* (Chicago: University of Chicago Press, 1966).

RANADE'S ORIGINAL PREFACE

I.

The ineffable and intuitive character of Mystical Experience.

1. Mysticism denotes that attitude of mind which involves a direct, immediate, first-hand intuitive apprehension of God. When Mysticism is understood in this sense, there is no reason why it should be taken to signify any occult or mysterious phenomena as is occasionally done. It is an irony of fate that a word which deserves to signify the highest attitude of which man is capable, namely, a restful and loving contemplation of God, should be taken to signify things which are incomparably low in the scale of being. Mysticism implies a silent enjoyment of God. It is in this sense that mystical experience has often been regarded as ineffable. It is not without reason that Plato in his 7th Epistle, which is now regarded as his own genuine composition, says: "There is no writing of mine on this subject, nor ever shall be. It is not capable of expression like other branches of study . . . . If I thought these things could be adequately written down and stated to the world, what finer occupation could I have had in life than to write what would be of great service to mankind" (341 c-e; *vide* Burnet—Thales to Plato, p. 221). The ineffable character of mystical experience is closely linked with its intuitional character. It has been very often supposed that for mystical experience no separate faculty like Intuition need be requisitioned, but that Intellect, Feeling, and Will might suffice to enable us to have a full experience of God. Now it is a matter of common knowledge that even for heights to be reached in artistic, scientific, or poetic activity, a certain amount of direct, immediate, almost cataclysmic, contact with Reality is required. Far more is this the case in the matter of mystical realisation. It is thus wonderful to see how people like Dean Inge contradict themselves when once they declare that "the process of divine knowledge consists in

calling into activity a faculty which all possess but few use, what we may call the seed of the Deiform nature in the human soul" (*vide* Selbie: Psychology of Religion, p. 257); and yet again that "there is no special organ for the reception of Divine or Spiritual Truth" (Philosophy of Plotinus, I. 5). People, who would otherwise openly side with Intution, yet declare that Intellect alone is sufficient for the reception of Divine knowledge; but their real heart-beat tells us that they believe that not mere Intellect is sufficient, but that a higher faculty is necessary. Intuition, so far from contradicting Intelligence, Feeling, or Will, does penetrate and lie at the back of them all. Intuition would not deny to Mysticism a title to Philosophy if Intellect requires it. As it connotes a determinative Effort towards the acquisition of Reality, it implies a definite, prolonged, and continuous exercise of the Will. Also, Mysticism, *pace* Dr. Inge, necessarily maked place for Emotions in a truly mystical life. It is strange that Dean Inge should fight shy of emotions, and deny to them a place in mystical life, when he says that Mysticism consists only in "seeing God face to face", and that it does not involve "an intensive cultivation of the emotions" (Philosophy of Plotinus, I. 3). We may venture to suggest to the Dean that unless the emotions are purified, and are turned towards the service of God, no "seeing of Him face to face", of which he speaks so enthusiastically, is ever possible. Thus it seems that Intelligence, Will, and Feeling are all necessary in the case of the Mystical endeavour: only Intuition must back them all. It is this combined character of mystical experience, namely, its ineffable and intuitive character, which has served to make all God-aspiring humanity a common and hidden Society, the laws of which are known to themselves if at all. We may even say, that they are known only to God, and not even to them!

II.

2. It is thus that the Mystics of all ages and countries form an eternal Divine Society. There are no racial, no

communal, no national prejudices among them. Time and space have nothing to do with the eternal and infinite character of their mystical experience. It is for this reason that the mystics treated of in this Volume, who form but a cross-section of that Divine Society, yet represent the reality of the Mystic Assembly completely and to the fullest extent. We shall make an endeavour in this Preface first to give a general outline of certain points of comparison between the Mystics treated of in this Volume and the Mystics especially of the Christian world. After having gone into these comparisons, we shall treat in a general way some points in the Psychology and Philosophy of Mysticism, affecting both the Mystics of the East and the West. The greatest of the Mystics treated of in this Volume, namely, Jñāneśvara, has naturally his comparison with such great philosophico-mystical luminaries of the West as Plotinus, Augustine, and Eckhart. Baron Von Hügel has said that there is "a radical inconsistency between the metaphysican and the saint" (Eternal Life, p. 85). But we think that the Baron is wrong when we see such splendid specimens of the combination of Philosophy and Mysticism as in the personalities of the great Mystics we are talking about, Namely, Jñāneśvara, Plotinus, Eckhart, and Augustine. Who will not say that the Jñāneśvarī of the one, and the "Enneads", the "Mystische Schriften", and the "De Civitate Dei' of the other are not embodiments of combined philosophic and mystical wisdom? Secondly, Jñāneśvara may yet again be fitly compared with Dante, whose beatific vision, philosophic imagination, and poet melody are just a counterpart of that greatest of Indian poet-mystics, Jñāneśvara. Thirdly, Jñāneśvara may again be fitly compared with the brilliant St. John of the Cross, whose fulness and variety of mystical experience and whose manner of presenting it stand almost unsurpassed in the literature of Western Mysticism. Of the

The Mystics of Maharashtra and the Mystics of the West: a comparison.

Female Mystics of Mahārāshtra, the three that stand to view at once, namely Muktābāi, Janābāi, and Kānhopātrā naturally have their comparison with such celebrated names as Julian of Norwich, Catherine of Siena, and St. Teresa. It is true that the Female Mystics of Mahārāshtra are more subjective in their temperament, while those of the West are more or less activistic, barring of course such mystics as Madame Guyon; and it is again true that the idea of sexual symbolism in religion is less prominent with the female mystics of Mahārāshtra than it is with their Western compeers. Of the Untouchable Mystics, Chokhāmeḷā, the pariah, naturally stands comparison with Böhme, the shoemaker, with this difference, that while Chokhāmelā does not yield to Böhme in the quality of the heart which makes him touch Reality nearmost, Böhme is certainly superior in so far as the philosophic setting of mysticism is concerned. His doctrines of the Microcosm, Antithesis, and Correspondence have left a deep impression upon Western Thought, and it is not without reason that we count among his disciples such great names as Law, Blake, and Saint Martin. Tukārāma, another type of Mystics in Mahārāshtra, has his comparison, firstly, so far as the personalistic element in mysticism is concerned, with the great Suso, whose joys and fears, griefs and tears, wailings and railings, as well as whose final consummation are exactly like those of his Indian compeer. Then, again, as might be seen by reference to the two chief stages of Tukārāma's mystical experience as described in the later pages of this volume, the dark night of the soul in Tukārāma is followed by a period of fruitful consummation, naturally bringing to mind the two stages through which the great English mystic Bunyan passed from his "Pilgrim's progress' to the "Grace Abounding", from his early "spiritual agonies, inward deaths, and inward hell, to the new divine births that surely follow after these, as after winter follows spring", at which stage, Bunyan saw with the eyes of his soul the beatific vision of Jesus Christ standing at God's right hand. Finally, Tukārāma could be very well paralleled to the brilliant European mystic Dionysius the Areopagite, whose venturesome intimations of the Absolute, description of God as the Divine Dark, and accurate analysis of the mystical and ecstatic consciousness are excellently paralleled by those of the Marāhā Mystic. Finally, that activistic type of Mahārāshtra mystics, namely, Rāmadāsa, has naturally his comparison with European mystics like Pythagoras, Ignatius Loyola, and Ruysbroeck. Rāmadāsa founded an Order of his disciples as Pythagoras founded his. Rāmadāsa had a political colouring to his religious teaching, as Pythagoras even more definitely had in founding his political Order, with this difference, that while Rāmadāsa's Order was backed by the regal power of Śivaji and succeeded, Pythagoras' Order succumbed on account of its over-much political aspirations to found a kingdom. On the other hand, even though mysticism and politics were combined in Rāmadāsa and Ignatius Loyola, with the one the two ran concurrently without the one eclipsing the other, while, with the other, political activity became so absorbing as to throw mystical experience entirely into the back-ground. Finally, Rāmadāsa's teaching on the combination of the active and the spiritual life, that "one should spend one's entire life in strenuous work, and yet again in steady contemplation in a moment" (Dāsabodha, XIX. 8. 29), is beautifully paralleled in the teaching of Ruysbroeck, who tells us that "the most inward man must live his life in these two ways, namely, in work and in rest; in each, he must be whole and undivided, and is perpetually called by God to renew both his rest and his work". Indeed "he is a living and willing instrument of God, with which God works whatsoever He will, and howsoever He will. He is thus strong and courageous in suffering all that God allows to befall him, and is ready alike for contemplation and action" (Adornment, ii. 65).

3. So far we have discussed in a general way how the Mystics of Mahārāshtra stand as compared with the Mystics

of the West. Let us now consider by reference to certain particular passages how the two sets of Mystics inculcate the same mystical teaching. In the first place, so far as the

The Vision of the Self.

Vision of the Self is concerned, let us see how Jñāneśvara on the one hand, and Tauler and Ruysbroeck on the other, describe it in almost identical terms. Jñāneśvara tells us (Mysticism in Mahārāshtra, p. 120) that "when the tree of unreality has been cut down, one is able to see one's Self, one's own form. This is, however, not to be compared to the seeing of the reflection in a mirror; for the reflection in a mirror is simply an other of the seeing man. The vision of the individual Self is as a Spring which may exist in its own fulness even when it does not come up into a Well. When water dries up, the image in it goes back to its prototype; when the pitcher is broken, space mixes with space; when fuel is burnt, fire returns into itself; in a similar way, is the vision of the Self by the Self. This is the Ultimate Being which exists in itself, after reaching which, there is no return". Let us hear what Tauler says: "When through all manner of exercises, the outer man has been converted into the inward man, then the Godhead nakedly descends into the depths of the pure soul, so that the spirit becomes one with Him. Could such a man behold himself, he would see himself so noble that he would fancy himself God, and see himself a thousand times nobler than he is in himself" (Sermon for the Fifteenth Sunday after Trinity). Also let us hear what Ruysbroeck says. "Thanks to the innate Light", says Ruysbroeck, "these interior men, these contemplatives, are wholly changed, and they are united to that very Light, by which they see, and which they see. Thus do contemplatives pursue the eternal Image in Whose Likeness they were fashioned; and they contemplate God and all things in one, in an open Vision bathed in Divine Light" (L'Ornement des Noces Spirituelles, iii. 5). Similar is the teaching of the Upanishads, which tell us that when a man reaches the acme of his spiritual realisation, "he sees his Self, his own form, suffused in a halo of dazzling light" (Maitri Upanishad, II. 1-3). We may have a glimpse from these utterances as to how the great mystics of various ages and climes have an identical teaching about the vision of the Self, which is the acme of their spiritual realisation.

The Identity of Self and God.

4. As regards the identity of Self and God, let us see how Jñāneśvara, St. John of the Cross, and Plotinus again inculcate an identical teaching. "Kṛishṇa and Arjuna," says Jñāneśvara, that is to say, God and the Self, "were like two clean mirrors, placed one against the other, the one reflecting itself infinitely in the other. Arjuna saw hmself along with God in God, and God saw Himself along with Arjuna in Arjuna, and Samjaya saw both of them together! When one mirror is placed against another, which, may we suppose, reflects which?" (M. M., p. 137). St. John of the Cross tells us in his Canticles that "the thread of love binds so closely God and the Soul, and so unites them, that it transforms them and makes them one by love; so that, though in essence different, yet in glory and appearance the soul seems God, and God the Soul" (Cant. xxxi). And, again, "Let me be so transformed in Thy beauty, that, being alike in beauty, we may see ourselves both in Thy beauty; so that one beholding the other, each may see his own beauty in the other, the beauty of both being Thine only, and mine absorbed in it. And thus I shall see Thee in Thy beauty, and my self in Thy beauty, and Thou shalt see me in Thy beauty; for Thy beauty will be my beauty, and so we shall see, each the other, in Thy beauty" (Cant. xxxvi. 3). Also the great Plotinus tells us: "If then a man sees himself become one with the One,—he has in himself a likeness of the One,—and if he passes out of himself as an image to its archetype, he has reached the end of his journey. This may be called the flight of the alone to the Alone" (Enneads, VI. 9. 9-11). According to these

mystics, therefore, the relation of Self and God may be likened to the relation between an image and its prototype, but is never fully represented by it. The union is so close as to defy all expression; but if any analogy is to be found, it may be found in the infinite reflections of one mirror in another when placed over against it, and of this again into the first, as Jñāneśvara tells us, anticipating closely a famous phenomenon in Optics.

The Royal Procession

5. In a curious passage, again, Plotinus, Jñāneśvara and the Upanishads speak the same language about what might be called the Royal Procession. God is here considered as King; and Intelligence, or the Virtues, or the Elements, are considered as his vassals. In the Upanishads we are told how "On the approach of a great king the policemen, magistrates, charioteers, and governors of towns wait upon him with food, and drink, and tents, saying he comes, he approaches, similarly, do all these Elements wait on the conscious Self, saying this Brahman comes, this Brahman approaches; and again, as at the time of the king's departure, the policemen, magistrates, charioteers, and governors of towns gather round him, similarly, do all vital airs gather round the Self at the time of death" (Bṛihadāraṇyaka, IV. 3. 37-38). Plotinus with his favourite theory of the emanation of the Nous from God, of the Soul from the Nous, of Matter from the Soul, tells us how "Intelligence or Nous is a Second God, who shows himself before we can behold the First. The First sits above on Intelligence as on a glorious throne. For it was right that He should be mounted, and that there should be an ineffable beauty to go before Him; as when some great King appears in state, first come those of less degree, then those who are greater and more dignified, then his body-guard who have somewhat of royalty in their show, then those who are honoured next to himself. After all these, the great King himself appears suddenly, and all pray and do obeisance"

(Enneads, V. 5. 3). Jñāneśvara tells us about the march onward of a Mystic who is entering the kingdom of God: "By putting on himself the armour of dispassion, the Mystic mounts the steed of Rājayoga, and by holding the weapon of concentration in the firm grip of his discrimination, he wards off small and great obstacles before him. He goes into the battlefield of life, as the Sun moves into darkness, in order to win the damsel of Liberation. He cuts to pieces the enemies that come in his way, such as egoism, arrogance, desire, passion, and others. . . . . Then all the Virtues come to welcome him as vassals before a king. . . . . At every step as he is marching on the imperial road of spiritual life, the damsels of the psychological States come to receive and worship him. Maidens of the Yogic Stages come and wave lights before him. Powers and Prosperities assemble round him in thousands to see the spectacle, and rain over him showers of flowers, and as he is approaching the true Swarājya, all the three worlds appear to him full of joy" (M.M., pp. 127-128). If we discount a little from these accounts of the Royal Procession the distinction between Self and God, which from the point of view of Mysticism we must, it is curious that the same idea of this victorious procession should have been present to the mind of the Upanishadic Seer, the great Alexandrian mystic, as well as the foremost Saint of Mahārāshtra.

The Ideal Sage.

6. In the matter of the determination of the characteristics of the Ideal Sage, again, there is a very close parallel in the teachings of the Mystics of the East and the West. One of the most celebrated descriptions of the Ideal Saint that occurs in Western literature is in Plotinus, where he describes the Ideal Sage as One without inward difference and without difference from the rest of Being: "Nothing stirred within him; no choler, no concupiscence of the alien was with him when he had gained the summit; not even reason was left, nor any intellection; nay, himself was not present to himself . . . . Even of beauty he is no longer aware, for now he has travelled beyond the beautiful. The very concert of the virtues is over-passed":

. . . . οὐ γάρ τι ἐκινεῖτο παρ' αὐτῷ, οὐ θυμός, οὐκ ἐπιθυμία ἄλλου παρῆν αὐτῷ ἀναβεβηκότι, ἀλλ' οὐδὲ λόγος οὐδε τις νόησις οὐδ' ὅλως αὐτός. . . . . . . οὐδὲ τῶν καλῶν, ἀλλὰ καὶ τὸ καλὸν ἤδη ὑπερθέων, ὑπερβὰς ἤδη καὶ τὸν τῶν ἀρετῶν χορόν. . . . .

In short, Plotinus tells us that his Ideal Sage has passed beyond reason, beyond the beautiful, beyond even the virtues. He tells us, furthermore, that his Sage is entirely "God-possessed: he is poised in the void, and has attained to quiet; in his Being there is no lightest quiver of deviation, no return of consciousness upon itself; utterly stable, he has become as it were the principle of stability" (Enneads, VI. 9. 9-11). If we refer to the Upanishads, we will see that the Ideal Sage is described in identical terms: "For a man to whom all these beings have become the Ātman, what grief, what infatuation, can there possibly be, when he has seen the unity in all things? All his desires have been at an end, because he has attained to the fulfilment of the highest desire, namely the realisation of the Ātman. As drops of water may not adhere to the leaf of a lotus, even so may sin never contaminate . . . . He has attained to eternal tranquillity, because as the Upanishad puts it, he has 'collected' the God-head. All his senses along with the mind and intellect have become motionless on account of the contemplation of the Absolute in the process of Yoga" (Ranade: Constructive Survey of Upanishadic Philosophy, pp. 315-316). We need not cite many illustrations from the Mahārāshtra Saints to see how this doctrine of the Ideal Sage preached by Plotinus is also preached by them. We may only take one of two illustrations from Jñāneśvara and Râmadāsa. Jñāneśvara tells us about his Ideal Sage, that as the result of his devoted concentration on God, "his senses lose their power. His mind remains folded in the heart; the body holds body; breath breath; and activity recoils upon itself; ecstasy is reached, and the object of meditation is gained as soon as he sits for meditation. The mind feels its identity with the Self, and reaches the empire of Bliss by merging its identity in Him" (M.M., pp. 121-122). Rāmadāsa also tells us that "the Ideal Saint is he who has left no desires in him, and has no passion in him; his desires are centered in the Self. He has no reason for logic-chopping, nor does he bear hatred, or jealousy towards others. When he has seen the Self, he has no reason for grief, or infatuation, or fear. God indeed is beyond these, and the Self becomes assimilated to God" (M.M., pp. 394-395).

The Ugly Soul.

7. In the matter of the teaching about the Ugly Soul, again, Plotinus and Jñāneśvara inculcate an identical teaching. Plotinus tells us that "an Ugly soul is intemperate and unjust, full of lusts, full of confusion, fearful through cowardice, envious through meanness, thinking nothing but what is mortal and base, crooked in all its parts, living a life of fleshly passion, and thinking ugliness delightful" (Bigg: Neoplatonism, p. 277). Jñāneśvara's description of the demoniac man is only a perfected commentary on the points urged by Plotinus: "An evil man is he who talks about his own knowledge, and sounds as with a cymbal his own good deeds. As fire may spread through a forest and burn both animate and inanimate objects, similarly, by his actions he is the cause of grief to the whole world. In mind he is full of doubts. He is like a dirty well in a forest on the surface of which there are thorns, and inside there are bones. By his instability he is brother to an ape. His mind roams like an ox that is let loose. He is all the while immersed in sensual pleasures. He knows no humility like an unbending wooden stick. He enters where he ought not to enter. He touches what he in body or mind must not touch. He sees what he ought not to see. He has lost all sense of shame. He is deaf to the censure of others . . . . Harsh as he is, his mind is like the hole of a serpent; his vision is like a discharge of arrows; his speech is like a shower of red-hot coal. He makes a mixture of virtue and sin, and cannot distinguish between their consequences. He opposes the will of God, and lolls in the dung-hill of misery, the very sewage-pit of the world of existence" (M.M., pp. 82-92).

The Sanctuary and the Statues.

8. In a famous passage, again, the two great Saints of the East and the West, Plotinus and Jñāneśvara, inculcate the same teaching about the characterisation of the ecstatic consciousness. Jñāneśvara tells us in a celebrated passage, which we have not incorporated in this volume, but which occurs in a famous Ārati which goes after him, that "when he had entered the Sanctuary, his bodily consciousness was lost. His mind was changed to supermind. All sense of bound-ness was then over. Reason came to a stand-still. Words were metamorphosed into no-words; and he saw his own Self. His eye-lashes ceased to twinkle. Distinction between night and day was gone. The whole universe was a-light, and was filled with the resonance of God. He was merged in an ocean of bliss, and his beatification was ineffable." Let us compare with this account what Plotinus tells us in regard to the Sanctuary. By the "Sanctuary" like jñāneśvara, Plotinus means a state of ecstatic consciousness, and by the "statues" he means the phenomena experienced in the sensuous state. The true mystic is he, says Plotinus, who presses onward to the inmost Sanctuary, leaving behind him the statues in the outer temple: "These are the lesser spectacles'; that other was scarce to be called a spectacle, but another mode of awareness, an ecstasy, a simplifying or enlarging of the Self, an aspiration towards contact, a poise and subtilising of thought to perfect Union; this is the seeing reserved to the Sanctuary" (Enneads, VI. 9. 9-11):

. . . . ἃ δὴ γίνεται δεύτερα θεάματα. τὸ δὲ ἴσως ἦν σύ θέαμα, ἀλλὰ ἄλλος τρόπος τοῦ ἰδεῖν, ἔκστασις καὶ ἅπλωσις καὶ επίδοσις αὐτοῦ καὶ ἔφεσις πρὸς ἁφὴν καὶ στάσις καὶ περινόησις πρὸς ἐφαρμογήν, εἴπερ τις τὸ ἐν τῷ ἀδύτῳ θεάσεται.

We may see by consideration of the passages from Jñāneś-vara and Plotinus how the inmost state of consciousness, namely, Ecstasy, is characterised by them as the Sanctuary, and the outer state of consciousness as the outer temple. Many are those, who, according to these Mystics, enter the outer temple, but few are those who can enter the Sanctuary.

Analogies of Mystical Experience.

9. In the matter of super-sensuous experience which is common to all mystics irrespective of time or clime, we need not dwell here in detail. We need only point out one or two very striking parallels between the experiences of the mystics of the East and the West in this regard. Firstly, in regard to the super-sensuous perception of smell, the saint Nivṛittinātha tells us that the "Experience of God is sweeter than sandal. God is indeed to us more fragrant than jasmine or its manifold varieties. The wish-yielding tree yields whatever we desire, but God is more fragrant than that tree. The light of God to me is fragrance itself, says Nivṛittinātha; life is such a one is enough for me." We may compare this utterance about the fragrance of God in Nivṛittinātha with a similar one in St. John of the Cross: "The Awakening is a movement of the Word in the depth of the soul of such grandeur, authority, and glory, and of such profound sweetness, that all the balsams, all the aromatic herbs and flowers of the world, seem to be mingled and shaken together for the production of that sweetness" (Living Flame, iv. 3). Then, again, in the matter of the Darkness of

God, we have the extreme parallel between the teachings of Jñāneśvara and Angela of Foligno. To quote Jñāneśvara: "One can never too much sing His praises when the dark-complexioned God is seen. It is this same dark Being who lives in the heavens. He is the same as the Ātman. I have seen Him with these eyes. He plays a dark game on a dark night; He manifests Himself as a dark-blue god. The dark-blue colour fills the whole universe. The heavens are merged in that blue light. This blue God lives in our very hearts, says Jñāneśvara" (M.M., pp. 170-171). Compare this utterance with that of Angela of Foligno, when she tells us in her book of Divine Consolations: "Afterwards I did see Him darkly, and this darkness was the greatest blessing that could be imagined, and no thought could conceive aught that would equal this. By that blessing which came with the darkness, ... I was made so sure of God that I can never again doubt but that I do of a certainty possess Him . . . . Unto this most high power of beholding God ineffably through such great darkness was my spirit uplifted but three times only and no more; and although I beheld Him countless times, and always darkly, yet never in such an high manner and through such great darkness" (The New Mediæval Library, pp. 182-183). It is not a mere metaphorical darkness that these mystics are speaking of, but a veritable, mystical, real darkness.

The Value of the Name.

10. Finally, in regard to the value of the Name, the mystics of India are no less insistent upon its efficacy than their compeer mystics of the West. Indeed, if there is any bond of unity more than any other between Hinduism and Christianity in their teaching about the realisation of God, it is their identical insistence on the efficacy of meditation by means of the Name. It is not only in Christianity, however, that the name assumes such gigantic power. Even in the Egyptian and Hebrew religions, we find the same insistence upon the efficacy of the Name.

Dr. Farnell tells us that "the very first Egyptian God Rā effected his own creation by the utterance of his own portentous name, and then created all the things of the universe" (Evolution of Religion, p. 188). Similar again is the attitude of the Hebrews towards the name Yahweh; while Christianity insists that God's name is above everything else: "Hallowed by Thy Name", "the Name that is above every name". It is, however, not merely on the name of God that Christianity insists, but even on the name of Jesus. Even the utterance of the name of Jesus would be as good as the utterance of the name of God. In his "Virtues of the Holy Name of Jesus", Rolle tells us: "O Jesus, verily Thou Whom we call Saviour dost save man, and therefore Jesus is Thy Name. Ah! Ah! that wonderful Name! Ah! That delectable Name! This is the Name that is above all names, without which no man hopes for salvation. Verily, the Name of Jesus is in my mind a joyous song, and heavenly music in mine ear, and in my mouth a honeyed sweetness. Wherefore, no wonder, I love that Name which gives comfort to me in all my anguish." And the "Cloud of Unknowing" says that one might utter any name of God one pleases. Indeed, the shorter it is, the better: "And if thee list have this intent (of union with God) lapped and folden in one word, for thou shouldest have better hold thereupon, take thee but a little word of one syllable: for so it is better than two, for ever the shorter it is the better it accordeth with the work of the Spirit. And such a word is this word God, or this word Love. Choose thee whether thou wilt, or another: as thee list, which that thou likest best of one syllable. And fasten this word to thy heart, so that it never go thence for thing that befalleth. This word shall be thy shield and thy spear whether thou ridest on peace or war. With this word thou shalt beat on this cloud and this darkness above thee. With this word thou shalt smite down all manner of thought under the cloud of forgetting." We need not dwell in detail in this Preface upon the efficacy of the name among the mystics of Mahārāshtra. We may make only a few short excerpts from Jñāneśvara, Rāmadāsa, and Tukārāma in order to see how these mystics have an identical teaching with their compeer mystics of the West in the matter of the value of the Name. Tukārāma tells us: "The sweetness of the Name is indeed indescribable. The tongue soon gets averse to other kinds of flavour; but the flavour of the Name increases every moment. In fact, the sweetness of the Name cannot be known to God Himself. A lotus plant cannot know the fragrance of its flowers, nor can the oyster-shell enjoy its pearls" (M.M., p. 321). Rāmadāsa says: "We should never forget God's Name, whether in happiness or in sorrow. Whenever difficulties overcome us, whenever we are down with the worries of life, we should meditate on the Name of God. By the Name of God are all our difficulties dispelled, and all our calamities swept away. By meditation on God's Name, Prahlāda was saved from dangerous situations. There are a thousand and one Names of God. It matters not which Name we utter. If we only utter it regularly and continuously, Death shall have no power over us. If a man does nothing but only utter the Name of God, God is satisfied and protects His Devotee" (M.M., pp. 399-400). And, again, Jñāneśvara tells us that "by the celebration of God's Name, the Saints have destroyed the *raison d'être* of repentance. The way to the abode of Death has been destroyed. What can restraint restrain now? What can self-control control? By the celebration of God's Name they have put an end to the misery of the world. The whole world has become full of bliss" (M.M., p. 114). By a comparison of the teachings of the mystics of the East and the West about the different topics we have hitherto discussed, we may say that they are in no way the outcome of any imaginable inter-influence. but the consequence of a personal, common, intimate, mystical experience. As Herakleitos says, those that are wakeful have one common world: those that are sleeping, each a different world.

III.

Some General Problems in the Psychology and Philosophy of Mysticism: The Dark Night of the Soul.

11. So far we have made a study in comparisons. Let us now discuss in a general way some of the points of the Psychology and Philosophy of Mysticism which emerge from a consideration of the study of the mystics whose account is embodied in this volume. It is not possible in this short Preface to go into the details of all the points that are worthy of discussion under this head; but we may take the liberty of discussing a few of the more important points. The first point that is worthy of consideration is as to whether what St. John of the Cross calls the Dark Night of the Soul is a necessary ingredient in the perfection of spiritual experience. It is true that persons like Bunyan passed through the Dark Night. It is also true that Plotinus never experienced the Dark Night at all. In a similar way, among the Mystics of Mahārāshtra we may note Tukārāma and Nāmadeva as having fully experienced the Dark Night. Rāmadāsa experienced it just next to them; while Jñāneśvara seems to be almost free from the experience of the Dark Night. In the chief work of Jñāneśvara, the Jñāneśvarī, there is not the slightest touch of this Dark Night. It is only when we come to his Abhaṅgas that we find some of his experience embodied in terms of the Dark Night. On the whole, the question arises, is the Dark Night a *sine quâ non* of the completion of mystical experience; Dean Inge supposes that one may even distrust a mystic who has not passed through the Dark Night (Philosophy of Plotinus, II. 150). According to Delacroix, it seems as if the Dark Night is as necessary to the mystical life as Ecstasy. The Dark Night, he says, condenses the whole vision of things into a negative intuition, as Ecstasy into a positive. The Author of the "Cloud of Unknowing" tells us in a manner which has been seldom surpassed in beauty of emotion that there always hangs a darkness between us and

God: "This darkness and this cloud is betwixt thee and thy God, and telleth thee that thou mayest neither see Him clearly by light of understanding nor feel Him in the sweetness of love. And therefore shape thee to bide in this darkness as long as thou mayest, evermore crying after Him that thou lovest. Then will He sometimes peradventure send out a beam of ghostly light, piercing this Cloud of Unknowing that is betwixt thee and Him; and shew thee some of His privity, the which man may not, nor cannot speak." It seems according to this author that the Dark Night is a necessary feature of spiritual experience; and one of the most helpful suggestions that he gives is when he says that an advancing mystic must abide in darkness as long as he may, ever crying after Him that he loves. In the "Ascent of Mount Carmel", St. John of the Cross tells us that this experience is called Dark Night for three reasons: first, on account of the dark nature of the starting point, namely, the evanescent life of the world; secondly, on account of the dark nature of the road by which one must travel, namely, that of faith; finally, on account of the dark nature of the goal to be reached, which is infinite in its nature. The Dark Night according to St. John of the Cross is thus trebly significant. Tillyard makes a clever suggestion that as, in physical experiment, excess of light becomes darkness, similarly, the Dark Night in mystical experience is caused not by God withdrawing himself, but by the seeker being unable to sustain the brilliance of His vision (Spiritual Exercises, p. 183). If we thus take into account the experiences of the mystics of the world on the subject of the Dark Night, we shall see that most of them, if not all, have passed through this intermediate agonising stage. Rarely a mystic here or a mystic there might not have suffered the full effects of the buffets of misfortune, physical, moral, and mental. On the whole, however, it remains true that the Dark Night is more or less a necessary ingredient, and it seems that mystical healthy-mindedness is never reached, or can never be fully appreciated, unless it is preceded by a mystical sick-mindedness. Carlyle was eminently right when he said that before we pass from the Ever-lasting No to the Ever-lasting Yea, we must necessarily pass through the Centre of Indifference.

The place of Super-sensuous Experience in Mystical Life.

12. A second point that emerges from the consideration of the teachings of the Mystics treated of in this volume in comparison with the Mystics of the West is the nature and value of the Super-sensuous Experience which is enjoyed by them all. We need not discuss here in detail the various items of Super-sensuous Experience which have been treated of in this volume. They are written in such text and capital letters that he who runs by may read. We shall therefore only take account of certain analogues of Super-sensuous Experience which we find among the mystics of the West, and to assess the Eastern and Western experiences together. Eckhart's doctrine of the "Das Fünkelein" which he regarded as the "apex" of spirit, by which the spirit of man was gradually informed with God and became God-like, is famous in the history of Mysticism. Fox's doctrine of the "Inner Light", about which Dr. Hodgkin has remarked that even though that constitutes the fundamental platform of Fox's teaching, yet all the other preachings of Fox were merely logical consequences of that doctrine, such as the disuse of sacraments, the abandonment of liturgy, silent worship, and unpaid ministry, thus proving how mystical experience may lie at the bottom of moral, social, as well as ritualistic teaching. Richard Rolle's famous expression that, in his cases "Calor was changed into Canor", the fire of love into a song of joy, has served to mark him out as one of the greatest of mystics, in whom the apprehension of the divine took the form of Music. Tennyson's "Spiritual City" with all her spire, and gateways in a glory like one pearl—no larger—which he regarded as the goal of all the Saints, is also a very characteristic type of mystical experience. Francis Thompson's "Trumpet-sounds from the hid Battlements of Eternity" is yet again mystical experience in another form. St. John of the Cross's apostrophe to Touch, which penetrates subtilely the very substance of the soul and absorbs it wholly in divine sweetness, is also another very characteristic type of mystical experience, upon which mystics have not dwelt at equal length. "Proclaim it to the world, O my Soul" says St. John of the Cross, "No, proclaim it not, for the world knoweth not the gentle air, neither will it listen to it" (Living Flame, ii. 18-21). In this way does St. John of the Cross throw doubt on the possibility and utility of the expression of this kind of mystical experience before those who do not know. We need not multiply instances to illustrate the different kinds of mystical experience among the Western mystics. We shall only mention here one most characteristic type of experience in St. Paul when he regarded God's grace as a voice speaking articulately in his soul: "I knew a man in Christ above fourteen years ago, (whether in the body, I cannot tell; or whether out of the body, I cannot tell: God knoweth;) such an one caught up to the third heaven. And I knew such a man, (whether in the body, or out of the body, I cannot tell: God knoweth;). How that he was caught up into paradise, and heard unspeakable words, which it is not lawful to utter. Of such an one will I glory: yet of myself I will not glory, but in mine infirmities" (2 Cor. xii. 2-5). St. Paul is too humble to say that it was he who had heard those unspeakable words of which he is speaking. But the fact remains that mystics like him have heard the voice and the words along with St. Paul. The question arises—how shall we explain all these mystical phenomena? Have they any physiological correlations or not? Or are they acts of mere self-hypnotisation? Or have they any objective validity in the sense that they are universal among mystics of all lands? This again is a problem of such great philosophical importance that we cannot afford to discuss it in a rough-shod manner at this place. For that another time and another place will have to be found. But the admonition which St. John of the Cross offers in "Mount Carmel" remains true that we must not allow our minds to be obsessed by these sensations and locutions. The most interior way to God is not these representations or sensations or locutions, but a direct love of God. For, says St. John of the Cross, the fly that touches honey cannot fly: "We must always reject and disregard these representations and sensations . . . . Let such persons learn to disregard these locutions, and to ground their will in humble love; let them practise good works and suffer patiently, imitating the Son of God, and mortifying themselves in all things: This, and not the abundance of interior discourses, is the road unto spiritual good . . . . We must fly from all mystical phenomena, without examining whether they be good or evil. Visions are at best childish toys. The fly that touches honey cannot fly." Mystical phenomena are a necessary accompaniment of mystical life. But what constitutes the essence of mystic realisation is not these mystical phenomena themselves, but an unfaltering, unbending, unending love of God.

Religious Consciousness and Sexual Consciousness.

13. There is one important respect in which the teaching of some of the Saints of Mahārāshtra in connection with the teachings of a few of the prominent Mystics of the West must be considered with some care. It is about the relation of religious consciousness to sexual consciousness. On the whole, the Saints of Mahārāshtra seem to be free from sexual imagery in religion, barring of course a few passages in Jñāneśvara or Chāngadeva or Tukārāma where we find the relation of Soul to God treated as on a par with the relation of the Bride to the Bridegroom. It is also true that Kānhopātrā, like her Hindi compeer Mīrabāī, tried to wed God, in that matter comparing with Catherine of Siena, who wore a pearl-ring

on her finger as a symbol of her marriage with God. The European mystics are, however, in general, far more insistent upon sexual imagery in religion than the mystics of Mahārāshtra. In Jñāneśvara, there is only one small reference in the Jñāneśvarī (M.M., p. 130), where Jñāneśvara speaks about the relation between husband and wife. In one of two of his Abhaṅgas, however, Jñāneśvara brings out this sexual element in fuller detail. In one place, he tells us that he has been thrown away from God in a distant country. The night appears as day, and Jñāneśvara pines that God should not yet visit him. "The cloud is singing and the wind is ringing. The Moon and the Champaka tree have lost their soothing effects. The sandal paste serves only to torment my body. The bed of flowers is regarded as very cool, but it burns me like cinders of fire. The Kokila is proverbially supposed to sing sweet tunes; but in my case, says Jñānadeva, they are increasing my love-pangs. As I look in a mirror, I am unable to see my face. To such a plight has God reduced me" (M.M., p. 169). And again, Chāngedeva tells us that the body is the bride, while the Ātman is the bride-groom; and he describes himself as having been free from care, his body having been delivered over into the hands of the Self. "After the marriage takes place, the Bride-groom will go to his house, and the Bride will be sent with him. I shall remain content, now that I have delivered over the Bride into the hands of the Bride-groom" (M.M., p. 77). In Tukārāma and other saints, the devotee is likewise occasionally depicted as a wistful, sorrowful, longing bride, who pines on account of her separation from her lord. This relation of the bride and the bride-groom is, however, more insistently and more incessantly brought out in the history of European Mysticism. We have authority in some parables and certain expressions of Jesus Christ in regard to such a relationship; Paul in the Rom. vii. 1-4, and more definitely in the Eph. v. 23-33, speaks of the "great mystery" of Christ and the Church as being husband and wife, and tells us that as the husband is the head of the wife, even so is Christ the head of the Church, the husband giving love to his wife and the wife giving reverence in return; one or two passages of the Apocalypse speak also in a like strain about the said relationship; Ruysbroeck regards religious love under the figure of spiritual espousal with the Divine Bride-groom; while the most insistent and the most glaring utterances in regard to such a sexual relationship occur in St. John of the Cross. St. John speaks of "the Touch of the Beloved as setting the heart on fire with love; as if a spark had fallen upon it. Then the will, in an instant, like one roused from sleep burns with the fire of love, longs for God, praises Him and gives Him thanks" (Cant. xxv. 5). The delicious wound which the Bride-groom confers is all the more delicious, as it penetrates the inmost substance of the soul. This burning and this wound are, in St. John's opinion, the highest condition attainable in this life (Living Flame, ii. 9). "In that burn the flame rushes forth and surges vehemently, as in a glowing furnace or forge. The soul feels that the wound it has thus received is sovereignly delicious. It feels its love to grow, strengthen, and refine itself to such a degree as to seem to itself as if seas of fire were in it, filling it with love . . . . . . The soul beholds itself as one immense sea of fire" (Living Flame, 10, 11). St. John of the Cross likewise talks of the deliberate assaults of God upon the soul. "And to make the soul perfect and to raise it above the flesh more and more, he assails it divinely and gloriously, and these assaults are really encounters wherein God penetrates the soul, deifies the very substance of it, and renders it godlike, divine" (Living Flame, i. 34). While the gifts of love which the bride-groom confers upon the soul in the spiritual marriage are inestimable: "The endearing expressions of Divine love which pass so frequently between them are beyond all utterance. The soul is occupied in praising Him and in giving Him thanks, and He in exalting, praising, and thanking the soul" (Cant. xxxiv). We do not suppose that the sexual relationship between the Soul and God has been more abundantly or more passionately brought out anywhere else in the literature of the world. The question arises how it is that these mystics come to regard the relationship between the Self and God as on a par with the relationship between the Bride and the Bride-groom. Is it a morbid pathological condition where the mystics portray their otherwise inexpressible love of the sex? Is it due to what Freud and Jung call the *libido*, which is at the root of every conative and creative activity? Is Schroeder right in supposing that the differential essence of religion is reducible only to a sex ecstasy? We think that none of these explanations would meet the mystic's sexual portrayal of his religious realisation. We have to understand it merely in a sense of an analogy. The only earthly analogy that could be given according to these mystics for the relationship between the soul and God is the relationship between wife and husband: "Tadyathā priyayā striyā samparishvakto na bāhyam kimchana veda nāntaram, evamevāyam purushah prājnenātmanā samparishvakto na bāhyam kimchana veda nāntaram" (Brihadāraṇyaka, IV. 3. 21). This is the only possible explanation, if any could be found. Otherwise, there does not seem to be any justification for the mystic's portrayal of the sexual element in mystical life. The clever psychologist James was absolutely right when he said in his "Varieties of Religious Experience" that religious consciousness and sexual consciousness are as poles apart: "Everything about the two things differs: objects, moods, faculties, and acts; and any general assimilation is simply impossible. In this sense, we may say that the religious life depends just as much upon the spleen, the pancreas, and the kidneys, as on the sexual apparatus" It is impossible to add a hue to the description given by James of the relationship between religious consciousness and sexual consciousness.

The Criterion of the Reality of mystical experience:

(i) The element of Universality.

14. We cannot close this Preface, however, without touching upon a point of vital importance, namely, that of the criterion of the reality of mystical experience. Even though we cannot enter into all the philosophic implications of this criterion, we can at least see in certain respects how this criterion would work. In the first place, as the cumulative experience of the mystics of the East and the West would prove, there is a certain amount of universality in their mystical experience. They have the same teaching about the Name of God, the fire of Devotion, the nature of Self-realisation and so forth, and it is due only to an over-weening superciliousness that certain people would regard the mystics of one country or religion as different from, or superior to, the mystics of other lands or faiths. If all men are equal before God, and if men have got the same "deiform faculty" which enables them to "see God face to face", then there is no meaning in saying that there is a difference between the quality of the God-realisation of some, as apart from the quality of the God-realisation of others. It is true that there may be physical, mental, and temperamental differences, but there is no difference in the quality of their mystical or intuitive realisation. It is this element of universality, which, as Kant contends, would confer upon mystical experience objectivity, necessity, or validity. Sir Henry Jones contends in "A Faith that Enquires" that if religion claims final worth and ultimate truth, then its criterion also must be equally powerful (p. 90). We suppose that the objectivity and necessity conferred by mystical experience is of a higher order than that of any other kind of human experience just because it is "deiform". It is this element of divinity in it that makes it so supremely compelling and valid.

(ii) The Intellectual Aspect.

There is another way of approach to the problem of the criterion of mystical experience. We have pointed out in the opening section of this Preface that mystical life involves a full exercise of the intellect, feeling, and will, and that, in addition, it brings into operation that faculty called Intuition by which one gets directly to the apprehension of Reality. We may say that that kind of mystical experience must be invalid which does not tend to an intellectual clarification of thought. A man whose brain is confused, a man who is labouring under delusions, a man who is likely to suffer from hallucinations, a man who is neurally pathological, can never hope to attain to real mystical experience. The imagination of the mystic must be powerful. He must have a penetrating, accurate, and unfaltering intellect. It is not without reason that great mystics like Śaṅkarāchārya, or Yājñavalkya, or Spinoza, or Plotinus, or Augustine, or St. Paul, or Jñāneśvara produced the great intellectual works that have lived after them. We must say about these works that they enjoy a certain amount of immortality, and they can never perish so long as the world prizes their inner mystic fibre. Accurate intellectual thought, among other things, which will compel philosophical admiration is surely a mark of real mystical experience. It is true, as pointed out above, that there are temperamental differences between mystics, as there are temperamental differences between ordinary men. Not all mystics need be philosophers; not all mystics need lead a life of emotion; not all mystics need be activists; but where-ever true Mysticism is, one of these faculties must predominate; and unless we see in a mystic a full-fledged exercise of at least one of these faculties, we may not say that he is entitled to the name of a Mystic at all. Hence intellectual power and absolute clarity of thought seem to be the first criterion of mystical experience.

(*iii*) The Emotionsl Aspect.

It is occasionally contended by certain writers, as has been pointed out above, that Mysticism has got nothing to do with a life of emotions. If by a life of emotions these people mean a sombre and melancholy, or on the other hand, a buoyant and boisterous sentimentalism, we entirely agree with what these people say. But if they deny to a mystic the possession or use of emotions in their refined, pure, and "deiform" state, we entirely disagree with these writers. In fact, if we take the trouble of reading the account of emotions given by Tukārāma, and Ekanātha in the pages that follow, we may be sure that the life of emotions is a *sine quâ non* of mystical experience. In fact, no mystical experience is possible unless we have a plenitude of finer emotions, all turned to the experience of God. A mystical life so far from being unemotional, is, we must say, supremely emotional; only the emotions ought to be exercised and kept under control by intellect. Otherwise, as we have pointed out above, a mystic would tend either to be an extreme L'Allegro, or on the other hand, an extreme Il Penseroso. The very fine contribution which Ekanātha has made to the psychology of emotions is worthy of consideration at the hands of every student of Mysticism. When Spinoza said that emotions must be transcended in an intellectual love of God, he said most accurately what is needed in a true life of Mysticism.

(*iv*) The Moral Aspect.

Another criterion of the reality of mystical experience is its capacity for the definite moral development of the individual and the society. It has been urged by critics of Mysticism that it tends on the one hand to a life of a-moralism, and on the other, to a life of passivism. Dean Inge has said that those schools of Philosophy which are most in sympathy with Mysticism have been, on the whole, ethically weak; and he instances as a case in point what he calls Oriental Pantheism, — as if it stands in a category apart, — which regards all things as equally divine, and obliterates the distinction between right and wrong (Studies of English Mystics, p. 31). It is to be remembered that he also points out that there are two dangers to which such a mysticism is liable — Antinomianism and Quietism. Antinomianism teaches that he who is led by the spirit can do no wrong, and that the sins of the body cannot stain the soul; while Quietism teaches a life of contentment with anything whatsoever by sitting with folded arms (*Idib.*, pp. 30-31). Now, it is to be remembered that this criticism of Mysticism comes from Dean Inge who is more of a mystic than anything else; and a Mystic saying that Mysticism starves the moral sense is only attempting to throw stones at a glass-house in which he is himself living. On the other hand, we find that a true life of Mysticism teaches a full-fledged morality in the individual, and a life of absolute good to the society. If we just see the very clever and accurate analysis of the different virtues which Jñāneśvara makes in his Jñāneśvarī (M.M., pp. 71-107), we can scarcely find in the world's ethical literature anything which would come up to it in point of excellence of analysis, boldness of thought, or accuracy of portrayal. A Mystic like Jñāneśvara who insists on these virtues can scarcely be regarded as teaching the "effacement of all distinctions between right and wrong". If we go to Plotinus, we find the same perfection of moral virtues in mystical life insisted on. "The vision," he tells us, "is not to be regarded as unfruitful. In this state the perfect soul begets — like God Himself — beautiful thoughts and beautiful virtues" (Enneads, 6. 9. 9). St. Teresa also speaks of the peace, calm, and good fruits in the soul by contemplation on God, and particularly of three graces: "The first is a perception of the greatness of God, which becomes clearer to us as we witness more of it. Secondly, we gain self-knowledge and humility as we see how creatures so base as ourselves in comparison with the Creator of such wonders, have dared to offend Him in the past, or venture to gaze on Him now. The third grace is a contempt of all earthly things unless they are consecrated to the service of so great a God" (The Interior Castle, 6. 5. 12). St. John of the Cross teaches that "in a truly mystical life, a knowledge of God and His attributes overflows into the understanding from the contact with Him and the soul is admitted to a knowledge of the wisdom, graces, gifts and powers of God, whereby it is made so beautiful and rich" (Cant. 14. 16. 24. 2). Rāmadāsa also tells us the same story when he speaks of the moral results produced in a mystic by contemplation on God (M.M., pp. 394-395). Then, again, so far as the utility of the mystic to the Society is concerned, we may almost regard it as a truism of Mysticism that a Mystic who is not of supreme service to the Society is not a Mystic at all. It is true, that here again there are temperamental differences among mystics. One mystic may choose more or less to be of a quietistic, and another more or less of an activistic type. But the fact remains that in either case he is of supreme value to mankind by calling their attention from moment to moment to the perception and greatness of God. Thus Dean Inge's denial of the title of a Mystic to Thomas à Kempis, because the latter teaches Quietism, can hardly be justified. There have been mystics who, like Aristotle's God, have moved the world by their divine contemplation. They might be called what a psychologist calls them men of a world-shaking type. St. Ignatius is a case in point, and James speaks of him assuredly as "one of the most powerfully practical human engines that ever lived. Where, in literature," he asks, "is there a more evidently veracious account, than in St. Teresa, of the formation of a new centre of spiritual energy?" (Varieties of Religious Experience, pp. 413, 414). Plotinus also tells us that "Those who are inspired, those who are possessed, know this much, that within them they have something greater than themselves, even if they do not know what. From what they feel, from what they speak, they have some conception of that which moves them as of something higher than themselves" (Enneads, 5. 3. 14). Rufus Jones narrates how mystics have their consciousness invaded by the inrush of a larger life: "Sometimes they have seemed to push a door into a larger range of being with vastly heightened energy. Their experience has been always one of joy and rapture. In fact, it is probably the highest joy a mortal ever feels. Energy to live by actually does come to them from somewhere. The Universe backs the experience" (Studies in Mystical Religion, p. xxx). Of the mystics treated of in this volume, as we may have ample opportunities to see later on, Rāmadāsa is the type of an activistic saint, illustrating the great power for the good of the world which comes in a mystic by a continuous contemplation on God.

(*v*) The Intuitional Aspect.

Finally, the surest criterion of Mysticism is the validity of the experience as enjoyed by the mystic himself. Before that, there is no appeal; for it, there is no criterion. If he appears to be true to himself, if his whole life is an embodiment of absolute right and truth, if he does not deviate an inch from the path of goodness and virtue, if his whole is dedicated to the contemplation of God and the service of Humanity, if he regards his own mystical advancement as a step towards the realisation of either of these ends, then we do not think that a mystic's search after God and its validity need be much called into question. It is this personal aspect of a mystic's spiritual realisation which stamps it with a peculiar halo and worth. The universality, the intellectualism, the emotionalism, and the moral fervour which we have hitherto talked of are but subservient to this greatest criterion, namely, a first-hand, intimate, intuitive apprehension of God. We need not collect many utterances of the mystics to justify this supreme duty of a mystic to himself. Here in the sensuous state, he sees but dimly; yonder, in ecstatic contemplation, the vision is clear. The criterion which Plotinus affords to us in this connection is of supreme importance:

. . καίτοι ἀμυδρῶς ὁρᾶται ἐκεῖ δὲ καθαρῶς ὁρᾶται. δίδωσι γὰρ τῷ ὁρῶντι ὅρασίν καὶ δὔναμιν εἰς τὸ μᾶλλον ζῆν καὶ μᾶλλον εὐτόνως ζῶντα ὁρᾶν καὶ γενέσθαι δ ὅρᾶ.

"And yet," says Plotinus, "we here see but dimly, yonder the vision is clear. For it gives to the seer the faculty of seeing, and the power for the higher life, the power by living more intensely to see better, and to become what he sees" (Enneads, 6. 6. 18). A mystic's final judge is thus ultimately his own Self!

* * * *

IV.

Relation to the University of Bombay.

15. How the present scheme of the History of Indian Philosophy by the Joint Authors originated, and how it came to be issued "Under the Patronage of University of Bombay", has been fully set forth in our Preface to the Second Volume of this History (the first to see the light of the day), which was issued in December, 1927. With the approval of the Syndicate of the University of Bombay, to whom the typed press copy of this volume was submitted nearly eight years ago, the seventh volume in the original scheme entitled Indian Mysticism was divided into two Parts: the one dealing with Mysticism in Mahārāshṭra, and the other with Mysticism outside Mahārāshṭra, as it was found impossible to compress the really vast material available in one volume of about 500 pages. The press copy as originally submitted to the University has been touched here and there, but in substance it remains unchanged. The Preface of course has been added since, as also the Bibliographical Note, and the Index. As in the case of the

Creative Period (History of Indian Philosophy, Vol. II), so in the case of the present volume, although the authors hold themselves jointly responsible for the whole volume, it is due to both of them to state that practically in this volume all the chapters have been contributed by Prof. Ranade, as the next volume on the Mahābhārata or the Vedānta (Vol. III or Vol. VI of the present History), whichever is prepared first, will be the work entirely of Dr. Belvalkar. After the publication of that volume, our engagement with the University of Bombay for three volumes in the present History will have been fulfilled, and then it would rest entirely with the University to see if they could continue their patronage to the succeeding volumes of this History, but on conditions conceived in quite a different fashion than at present. As events have proved, in fulfilling their engagement with the University of Bombay, the Authors have had to submit not only to great physical and mental exertions, but to extraordinary pecuniary difficulties, but thank God, by His grace they have been able to publish two volumes hitherto, and it is hoped that the third volume also would be brought out at a not very distant date.

Thanks.

16. We have now to express our heartfelt obligations to all those who have helped us in the present concern. We have first to thank very heartily Prof. K. V. Gajendragadkar, M.A., of the Arts College, Nasik, who, as a Research Assistant some years ago under Prof. Ranade, gave continuous and invaluable assistance in the present work. The contribution on the Amṛitānubhava of Jñāneśvara which appears in the present volume (Chapter IV) is due mainly to him. Prof. Gajendragadkar also helped very much in preparing the Index for the press, in collaboration with his colleague Prof. Jog of the Arts College, Nasik, and we are much obliged to these gentlemen for the help they have so readily given. We are also much indebted to Prof. S. V. Dandekar of the Sir Parashurambhau College, Poona, for help in a contribution on the Bhāgawata of Ekanātha which appears in the present volume (Chapter XII). Prof. Ranade had certainly a claim on him, as he was once his student at the Fergusson College, but it is as a friend that in the present case he has worked on a Chapter for which the authors are much obliged to him. Mr. S. K. Dharmadhikari gave great help as a Shorthand Typist throughout the progress of the volume, but the completion of the work was reserved for another stenographer who succeeded him, namely, Mr. H. K. Dharmadhikari of the Commerce Department of the Allahabad University. We thank both these gentlemen for their labours. Mr. Jagannath Raghunath Lele of Nimbal was of continuous and immense assistance in reading out the Sources, on which is based the present volume of Mahārāshtra Mysticism. These Sources were independently published by Rao Saheb V. S. Damle, Retired Mamlatdar, Thalakvadi, Belgaum, in four volumes, entitled Jñāneśvara Vachanāmrita, Santa Vachanāmrita, Tukārāma Vachanāmrita, and Rāmadāsa Vachanāmrita for the Academy of Philosophy and Religion, Poona, a few years ago. The "Index of Sources" in the present volume on Mahārāshṭra Mysticism refers to these Source-Books which have been published by Rao Saheb V. S. Damle.* As regards publication arrangements for this work, we have first to thank very heartily our friend Mr. B. R. Patwardhan, M.A., LL.B., Pleader, Dharwar, who offered a few years ago to advance sufficient money to the Press to enable them to take up the work in hand at once. Even here, the completion of the scheme was reserved for another friend of ours, Mr. S. A. Apte, B.A., LL.B., Government Pleader, Jamkhandi, without whose spiritual solicitude to volunteer enough money to meet the burden of the Volume in every way, the present work would scarcely have seen the light of the day in

*These source books are out of print and no longer available for purchase.

its present form. Mr. A. V. Patwardhan, B.A., Manager, Aryabhushan Press, Poona, who has had ties of various relationship with all of us, and who is publishing the present volume on behalf of Mr. S. A. Apte, is extending to it his fostering care, which concerns not merely its formal publication, but also the administration of its sales with a view to defray out of the sale proceeds the liabilities involved. We have also particularly to mention the help we have received from Prof. N. G. Damle, M.A., of the Fergusson College, Poona, Mr. P. K. Gode, M.A., Secretary, Academy of Philosophy and Religion, Poona, Mr. R. D. Wadekar, M.A., Lecturer in the Bhandarkar Institute, Poona, as well as Mr. S. V. Mhaskar, B.A., formerly State Librarian, Jamkhandi, who have much obliged us by their constant solicitude and unremitting exertions to enable the Volume to see the light of the day as early as was possible. Mr. G. G. Karkhanis, B.A., has also helped in the matter of procuring some hitherto unpublished material on Rāmadāsa, as well as by his constant care concerning the sources of the Jñāneśvarī. We are also much obliged to the Rev. John MacKenzie, M.A., Vice-Chancellor of the University of Bombay, for having looked at the Preface, and made some useful suggestions. We have to thank Shrimant Chief-Saheb of Miraj for having supplied to us the Abhangas of Sāmvatā Māli, who lived some centuries ago at Aranagaon, which is under his jurisdiction. As regards the Bibliographical Note, we must express our obligations heartily to the Rev. Dean Inge, Miss Underhill, and Mr. Fleming, to whose works on Mysticism we are much indebted. It is to be hoped that the present volume would supply the world with a new material for a Philosophy of Mysticism and from a hitherto untrodden territory, namely, that of the religious experience of certain typical representatives of Indian Mysticism. We have also to thank very heartily the University of Bombay for having patiently waited for such a long time for the present volume to see the light of the day. As we have to thank the Bombay University, so we have also to thank the Allahabad University for facilities provided to at least one of the Joint Authors for work connected with this volume. We have to express our gratefulness to Dr. Ganganath Jha, LL.D., Vice-Chancellor of the University of Allahabad, for having done us the honour of extracting a few passages of this book in illustration of his argument in his Kamala Lectures delivered before the University of Calcutta in 1929. We are much beholden to our friend Mr. V. Subrahmanya Iyer B.A., Formerly Registrar, University of Mysore, for the very great care which he bestowed in going through the Chapter on the Jñāneśvarī some years ago, and for having seen the possibility of its teachings being compared with those of a great Vedantic teacher like Shankarāchārya. Finally, we have to express our deepest obligations to the Bangalore Press for having waited patiently for such a long period, and for having carried on the work through thick and thin, and enabled the Authors and Publishers to see that as few imperfections as possible remain in the printed work. It is scarcely necessary for the authors to say in conclusion that a work like this represents a great Sacrifice in which each man brings to the consummation of the Ideal what his individual powers enable him to offer; or else, where each man sings, like the Leibnitzian monad, his own tune, and yet the whole becomes a harmony wonderful, contributing to the glory of God and the relief of man's estate.

CONTENTS.

PART II.

THE AGE OF NAMADEVA: DEMOCRATIC MYSTICISM.

PART III.

The Age of Ekanatha : Synthetic Mysticism.

CHAPTER I.

Introduction: The Development of Indian Mysticism up to the Age of Jnanesvara.

The Mysticism of the Upanishads and the Mysticism of the Middle Age.

1. In the previous volumes of our History of Indian Philosophy, we have traced the development of Indian thought from its very dimmest beginnings in the times of the Ṛig-veda downwards through the great philosophical conflicts of Theism, Pantheism, and Qualified Pantheism to the twilight of the Mysticism of the Middle Age, which being the practical side of philosophy can alone give satisfaction to those who care for philosophy as a way of life. A mystical vein of thought has been present throughout the development of Indian philosophy from the age of the Upanishads downwards; but it assumes an extraordinary importance when we come to the second millennium of the Christian era which sees the birth of the practical spiritual philosophy taught by the Mystics of the various Provinces of India. We have indeed seen that the culmination of Upanishadic philosophy was mystical. But the mysticism of the Upanishads was different from the mysticism of the Middle Age, inasmuch as it was merely the tidal wave of the philosophic reflections of the ancient seers, while the other was the natural outcome of a heart full of piety and devotion, a consciousness of sin and misery, and finally, a desire to assimilate oneself practically to the Divine. The Upanishadic mysticism was a naive philosophical mysticism: the mysticism of the Middle Age was a practical devotional mysticism. The Upanishadic mysticism was not incompatible with queer fancies, strange imaginings, and daring theories about the nature of Reality: the mysticism of the Middle Age was a mysticism which hated all philosophical explanations or philosophical imaginings as useless, when contrasted with the practical appropriation of the Real. The Upanishadic mysticism was the mysticism of men who lived in cloisters far away from the bustle of humanity, and who, if they permitted any company at all, permitted only the company of their disciples. The mysticism of the Middle Age was a mysticism which engrossed itself in the practical upliftment of the human kind, based upon the sure foundation of one's own perfect spiritual development. The Upanishadic mystic did not come forward with the deliberate purpose of mixing with men in order to ameliorate their spiritual condition. The business of the mystic of the Middle Age consisted in mixing with the ordinary run of mankind, with sinners, with pariahs, with women, with people who cared not for the spiritual life, with people who had even mistaken notions about it, with, in fact, everybody who wanted, be it ever so little, to appropriate the Real. In a word, we may say that as we pass from the Upanishadic mysticism to the mysticism of the Middle Age, we see the spiritual life brought from the hidden cloister to the market-place.

The Mysticism of the Bhagvadgita and the Mysticism of the Middle Age.

2. Before, however, mysticism could be brought from being the private possession of the few to be the property of all, it must pass through the intermediate stage of the moral awakening of the people to a sense of duty, which would not be incompatible with philosophical imagination on the one hand and democratisation of mystical experience on the other,—which task indeed was accomplished by the Bhagavadgītā. As is well known, the Bhagavadgītā laid stress on the doing of duty for duty's sake almost in the spirit of the Kantian Categorical Imperative. This is the central thread which strings together all the variegated teachings of the Bhagavadgītā. The doctrine of Immortality which it teaches in the second Chapter, the way of equanimous Yogic endeavour which it inculcates in the fifth, the hope which it holds out for sinners as well as saints, for women as well as men, in the ninth, the superiority which it declares of the way of devotion to the way of mere knowledge in the twelfth, and finally, the universal immanence and omnipotence of God which it proclaims in the last Chapter, supply merely side-issues for the true principle of Moral Conduct which finds its justification in Mystic Realization. The Bhagavadgītā, however, had not yet bade good-bye to philosophical questionings; it had not yet ceased to take into account the philosophical issues raised by the previous systems of philosophy; it had not yet lost hope for reconciling all these philosophical issues in a supreme mystical endeavour. In these respects, the mysticism of the Middle Age offers a contrast to the mysticism of the Bhagavadgītā. Barring a few exceptions here and there, the entire tenor of the mysticism of the Middle Age is for the practical upliftment of humanity, irrespective of any philosophical questionings, and with probably a strong, if not even a slightly perverted, bias against philosophical endeavour to reach the Absolute. We may say, in fact, that as the mysticism of the Bhagavadgītā rests upon a philosophical foundation, the mysticism of the Middle Age rests upon itself, invoking no aid from any philosophical construction whatsoever.

The Personality of Krishna.

3. The personality of Kṛishṇa, which looms largely behind the teachings of the Bhagavadgītā, is indeed a personality which antiquarians and critics have sought in vain to construct from all the available evidence from the times of the Vedas to the times of the Purāṇas. While one view would hold that Kṛishṇa was merely a solar deity, another would regard him merely as a vegetation deity; a third would identify the Kṛishṇa of the Bhagavadgītā with the Kṛishṇa of the Chhāndogya Upanishad on the slender evidence of both being the sons of Devakī, unmindful of any difference between their teachings; a fourth would father upon Kṛishṇaism the influence of Christian belief and practice. To add to these things, we have to note that these critics have been entirely blind to the fact, as a modern scholar has cleverly pointed out, that the Kṛishṇa, the famous prince of the Vṛishṇi family of Mathurā, was the same as Vāsudeva, the founder of "Bhāgavatism", which is also called the Sātvata or the Aikāntika doctrine in the Śāntiparvan. Vāsudevism was indeed no new religion, *pace* Dr. Bhandarkar, as has been contended sometimes. It was merely a new stress on certain old beliefs which had come down from the days of the Vedas. The spring of devotional endeavour which we see issuing out of the mountainous regions of the Veda, being then directed primarily to the personality of Varuṇa, hides itself in the philosophical woodlands of the Upanishads, until, in the days of the Bhagavadgītā, it issues out again, and appears to vision in a clear fashion, with only a new stress on the old way of beliefs. The mystical strain, which is to be found in the Upanishads, is to be found even here in Vāsudevism with a greater emphasis on devotion. That the Vāsudeva doctrine and order existed in the times of Pāṇini is now patent to everybody. The epigraphic evidence afforded by the Besnagar and Ghasuṇḍī inscriptions with even the mention of "Dama, Tyāga and Apramāda"—virtues mentioned by the Bhagavat in the Bhagavadgītā—lends a strong support to, and gives historical justification for, the existence of the

Vāsudeva religion some centuries previous to the Christian era; and the philosophic student would note that as in essence the religion of the Bhagavadgītā does not differ from the religion of the Śāntiparvan, mysticism being the culmination of the teachings of both, it is the same personality of Kṛishṇa which appears likewise as the promulgator of the Bhāgavata doctrine, even though in later times that doctrine fell into the hands of the mythologists, who, not having been able to understand its philosophical and mystical import, tried merely to give it an occult and ritualistic colouring.

Vishnu Occultism: the Pancharatra.

4. This indeed did happen as the Pāñcharātra doctrine came to be formulated and developed. The doctrine has its roots so far back as at the times of the Mahābhārata, though later on it came to be taught as a separate occult doctrine. We are concerned here, however, only with its later theological development, and not with its origin. We have to see how the Pāñcharātra was a system of occult Vishṇu worship. The system derived its name from having contained five different disciplines, namely, Ontology, Liberation, Devotion, Yoga, and Science. Its central occult doctrine was that Divinity was to be looked upon as being fourfold, that Vishṇu manifests himself in the four different forms of Vāsudeva, Sankarshaṇa, Pradyumna, and Aniruddha. These are called the four Vyūhas, that is to say, "disintegrations" of the one Divinity into four different aspects. Now, the supreme Godhead was regarded as possessing six different powers, namely, Jñāna, Aiśvarya, Śakti, Bala, Vīrya and Tejas. These six qualities are to be "shoved off" into three different groups. The first and the fourth constitute the first group and belong to Sankarshaṇa. The second and the fifth constitute the second group and belong to Pradyumna. The third and the sixth constitute the third group and belong to Aniruddha. In fact, it seems that the whole Pāñcharātra scheme was based upon the worship of the Vāsudeva family: Sankarshaṇa was Vāsudeva's brother, Pradyumna his son, Aniruddha his grand-son. Each of these three Vyūhas, with its set of two qualities each, was identical with Vāsudeva in possession of all the six qualities. When, however, we remember that the last three qualities, namely, Bala, Vīrya and Tejas, are merely a reduplication of the third quality, namely Śakti, the sixfold scheme of qualities falls to the ground, and what remains is only the three primary qualities, namely, Jñāna, Aiśvarya, and Śakti. These three belong severally to Sankarshana, Aniruddha, and Pradyumna, and collectively to

Vāsudeva himself. There is also a cosmological sense in which the three last Vyūhas are to be regarded as being related to the first, namely, Vāsudeva. They are a series of emanations, one from another, like one lamp lit from another. From Vāsudeva was born Sankarshaṇa, from Sankarshaṇa, Pradyumna, and from Pradyumna, Aniruddha. This is as much as to say, that from the Self was born the Prakṛiti, from the Prakṛiti, the Mind, and from Mind, Consciousness. Dr. Grierson has put the whole cosmological case of the Pāñcharātras in a lucid fashion: "Vāsudeva first creates Prakṛiti, and passes at the same time into the phase of conditioned spirit, Sankarshaṇa. From the association of Sankarshaṇa with the Prakṛiti, Manas is produced; at the same time Sankarshaṇa passes into the phase of conditioned spirit, known as Pradyumna. From the association of Pradyumna with the Manas springs the Sāmkhya Ahamkāra, and Pradyumna passes into a tertiary phase known as Aniruddha. From Ahamkāra and Aniruddha spring forth the Mahābhūtas." This was how the four Vyūhas came to be endowed with a cosmological significance. Vishṇu, however, whose manifestations all the four Vyūhas are supposed to be, is endowed by the Pāñcharātra doctrine with two more qualities, namely, Nigraha and Anugraha, which, when paraphrased freely, might mean destruction and construction, disappearance and appearance, frown and favour, determinism and grace. The theistic importance of the Pāñcharātra comes in just here that it recognizes the principle of "grace". The grace of the Divinity is compared to a shower of compassion which comes down from heaven: it droppeth as the gentle rain upon the place beneath. The Pāñcharātra rarely uses Advaitic language, and had it not been for the doctrine of the Antaryāmin, which, as Dr. Schrader has pointed out, is its point of contact with Pantheism, it would not have much in common with the Advaitic scheme. It does not support the illusionistic doctrine of the Advaita, and its Occultism is writ large upon its face in its disintegration of the one Divinity into four aspects, which acquire forthwith an equal claim upon the devotion of the worshipper.

Siva Occultism: Tantrism.

5. Correlative to the Vishṇu Occultism of the Pāñcharātra, we have the Siva Occultism of Tāntrism, the sources of which likewise are to be traced as far back as the days of the Mahābhārata. The Śiva Occultism even surpasses Vishṇu Occultism in point of irregularities of belief and practice, which must be regarded evidently as aberrations of mysticism. When we remember the distinction between Mysticism and Occultism, the one given entirely to God-devotion and God-realization, and the other to mere incrustations on these, which inevitably gather round any good thing as time goes on, we shall not wonder at the great aberrations of practice which are illustrated in the development of Tāntrism. Possessing an immense literature as it does, Tāntrism abounds in discussions of Mantra, Yantra and Nyāsa, which are only fortuitous, and therefore unnecessary, elements in the true worship by means of the heart, which alone mysticism commends. Its worship of Liṅga and Yonī, if literally understood, is almost a shame on the system, whatever its redeeming points may be. No doubt, when Tāntrism recognizes Śiva as the embodiment of supreme consciousness, and Śakti as the embodiment of supreme power, both being merely the aspects of that eternal Verity, the Brahman, it preaches a truth which is worth while commending in philosophy. Tāntrism recognizes itself to be the practical counterpart of Advaitism. In that respect, even the great Śaṁkarāchārya may be regarded as a great Tāntrist; and Tāntrism was supposed to be merely the Sādhana counterpart of the doctrine of Monism. It is not its philosophic standpoint which is worth while commenting on in Tāntrism. It is rather its practical part, the part of Sādhana, which, if literally understood, was sure to engender grievous practices, bordering upon immorality and vice. Its fivefold Sādhana, namely, the drinking of wine, the eating of fish, the partaking of flesh, the use of parched cereals, and the act of sexual conjugation, which are regarded by the Tantra as its five chief Makāras, if literally understood, have as much in common with true Mysticism as the South Pole with the North Pole. An attempt is therefore made to justify the Sādhana of the Tāntrists in an allegorical fashion, as has been done, for example, by interpreters like Justice Woodroffe, who say that the five kinds of Sādhana may be represented by the intoxication of knowledge, the surrender of actions to the self, sympathy from a sense of 'mineness' (Mām) with the sins and pleasures of all, the parching of evil actions, and finally, the conjugation of the Kuṇḍalinī in the Mulādhāra Chakra, which is the embodiment of power, with Śiva in the Sahasrāra, which is the embodiment of consciousness. Any belief and practice could thus be made to wear an attractive garb; and wherever, in fact, the fivefold Sādhana was understood in a higher sense, it did certainly not degenerate into corrupt practices. But the generality of mankind are not philosophers, and they could not be expected to understand the philosophic import of the Pañchatattva-sādhana. One could easily understand why an ordinary man would busy himself in the worship of the female as female, and not as the embodiment of the supreme Śakti, and in case one's own wife could not be had for worship, a provision could be made for the worship of the female either in the person of another man's wife, or in that of any virgin whatsoever. When a daughter or a mother could be substituted for one's own wife, the worship would not certainly degenerate into mis-sexual relations; but wherever a woman as woman was to be the object of worship, the generality of mankind could not be supposed to have had that calm vision of things, which would prevent them from mis-using the Tāntric practice. The philosopher indeed could suppose that the worship of the female was intended as a method for checking and controlling one's own evil passions, for the subjugation of the Self in the midst of temptations. But with ordinary men, nature would certainly get the better of belief; hence, the possibility, nay, even the probability of the degeneration of Tāntric practices, as we see illustrated in the Chūḍāchakra and the Snehachakra practices. In Psychology, however, Tāntrism did one good service in the development of Indian thought. It supposed that a man's mind was a vast magazine of powers, and as the universal Consciousness was supposed to be vehicled by the universal Power, so man's consciousness was supposed to be vehicled by the power in the form of mind and body. The unfoldment of such power was the work of Sādhana. A man, in whom Śakti was awakened, differed immensely from the man in whom it was sleeping, and the whole psychological process of the Tāntric Sādhana lay in the awakening of the Kuṇḍalinī. Tāntrism did great service to the development of physiological knowledge when it recognized certain plexuses in the human body such as the Ādhārachakra, the Svādhishṭhānachakra, the Anuhatachakra, and so on, until one reached the Sahasrārachakra in the brain. But on the whole, it may not be far away from the truth to say that Tāntrism would drive true mysticism into occult channels, from which it would not be easy to extricate it, and set it on a right foundation.

The Bhagavata as a Storehouse of Ancient Mysticism.

6. We have hitherto considered the occult movements, both Vaishṇavite and Śaivite, which spring from the days of the Mahābhārata to end in utterly sectarian systems, each of which tries to develop its dogma in its particular way. We shall now consider the mystic movement proper, for which our texts are the Bhāgavata, the Nārada Bhakti-Sūtra and the Śāṇḍilya Bhakti-Sūtra. These three works represent the Mystic development of thought which probably runs side by side with the Occult movement on the one hand, which we have already considered, and the Philosophic movement on the other, which we shall consider a little further. That the Bhāgavata influenced systems of philosophical thought like those of Rāmānuja and Madhva, that it had by that time earned sufficient confidence from the people to be used as a text-book, that it is the repository of the accounts of the greatest mystics from very ancient times, that, though some of its language may be modern, it contains archaisms of expression and diction which may take it back to the early centuries of the Christian era—all these facts make it impossible that the Bhāgavata should have been written, as is sometimes contended, about the 12th century A.D., thus implying unmistakably that it must have been written earlier, *pari passu* with the development of early philosophical systems, so as ultimately, in course of time, to be able to influence later formulations of thought. The Bhāgavata, as we have pointed out, is a repository of the accounts of the Ancient Mystics of India, and if we may seek for some Types of Mystics in the Bhāgavata, we may find a number of such Types, which later on influenced the whole course of the Mystic movement. Dhruva, in the first place, is a child-prince who leaves his kingdom and the world when he is insulted by his step-mother, and who, in the agonies of his insult, seeks the forest where he meets the spiritual teacher who imparts to him the knowledge of the way to God, and who ultimately succeeds in realizing His vision (IV. 8). Prahlāda, the son of the Demon-King, whose love to God stands unvanquished in the midst of difficulties, whose very alphabets are the alphabets of devotion, who escapes the dangers of the fire and the mountain when his earnestness about God is put to the test, supplies another example of a pure and disinterested love to God, so that he is able to say to God when he sees Him—"I am Thy disinterested Devotee. Thou art my disinterested Master. But if Thou wishest to give me any boon at all, bestow upon me this, that no desire should ever spring up within me" (VII. 10). Uddhava is the friend of God, whose love to Him stands the test of time, and of philosophical reasoning (X. 46). Kubjā, the crooked concubine, who conceived apparently a sexual love towards Kṛishṇa, had her own sexuality transformed into pure love, which made her ultimately the Beloved of the Divine (X. 42). Even the Elephant who lifted up his trunk to God when his foot was caught hold of by the great Alligator in the sea, supplies us with another illustration as to how even animals might be saved by devotion, and as to how God might come to their succour in the midst of their afflictions (VII. 2-3). Sudāman, the poor devotee, who has no other present to offer to God except a handful of parched rice, is ultimately rewarded by God who makes him the lord of the City of Gold (X. 80-81). Ajāmila, the perfect sinner, who is merged in sexuality towards a pariah woman, gets liberation merely by uttering the Name of God at the time of his death (VI. 1-2). The sage Ajagara, who lives a life of idle contentment and of unconscious service to others, has derived his virtues from a Serpent and a Bee, whom he regards as his spiritual teachers (VII. 13). Ṛishabhadeva, whose interesting account we meet with in the Bhāgavata, is yet a mystic of a different kind, whose utter carelessness of his body is the supreme mark of his God-realization. We read how, having entrusted to his son Bharata the kingdom of the Earth, he determined to lead a life of holy isolation from the world ; how he began to live like a blind or a deaf or a dumb man ; how he inhabited alike towns and villages, mines and gardens, mountains and forests ; how he never minded however much he might be insulted by people, who threw stones and dung at him, or micturited on his body, or subjected him to all sorts of humiliation ; how in spite of all these things his shining face and his strong-built body, his powerful hands and the smile on his lips, attracted even the women in the royal harems ; how, careless of his body as he was, he discharged his excreta at the very place at which he took his food ; how, nevertheless, his excreta smelt so fragrant that the air within ten miles around became fragrant by its smell ; how he was in sure possession of all the grades of happiness mentioned in the Upanishad ; how ultimately he decided to throw over his body ; how, when he had first let his subtle body go out of his physical body, he went travelling through the Karnāṭaka and other provinces, where, while he was wandering like a lunatic naked and lone, he was caught in the midst of a great fire kindled by the friction of bamboo trees ; and how finally he offered his body in that fire as a holocaust to God (V. 5-6). Avadhūta is yet a mystic of a different type, who learns from his twenty-four Gurus different kinds of virtues, such as Forbearance from the Earth, Luminosity from the Fire, Unfathomableness from the Ocean, Seclusion from a Forest, and so on, until he ultimately synthesizes all these different virtues in his own unique life (XI. 7). Śuka, in whose mouth the philosophico-mystical doctrines of the Bhāgavata are put, is the type of a great mystic who practises the philosophy that he teaches, whose mystical utterances go to constitute the whole of the Bhāgavata, and who sums up his teaching briefly in the 87th chapter of the Xth Skandha of the Bhāgavata, where he points out the necessity of a Spiritual Teacher, of Devotion, and of the Company of the Good for a truly mystical life. Finally, Kṛishṇa himself, who is the hero of the Xth and the XIth Skandhas of the Bhāgavata, who, on account of his great spiritual powers, might be regarded as verily an incarnation of God, whose relation to the Gopīs has been entirely misrepresented and misunderstood, whose teachings in essence do not differ from those advanced in the Bhagavadgītā, who did not spare his own family when arrogance had seized it, who lived a life of action based upon the highest philosophical teaching, and who, when the time of his departure from earthly existence came, offered himself to be shot by a hunter with an arrow, thus making a pretext for passing out of mortal existence, supplies us with the greatest illustration of a Mystic who is at the top of all the other mystics mentioned in the Bhāgavata Purāṇa.

The True Nature of the Relation of the Gopis to Krishna.

7. There has been no greater misunderstanding than that about the spiritual nature of Kṛishṇa, and his relation to the Gopīs. It has been supposed that the Gopīs were filled with sexual passion for Kṛishṇa ; that he primarily satisfied only the sexual instincts of these Gopīs ; that this satisfaction was later given a spiritual turn ; and that, therefore, the true nature of Kṛishṇa's spirituality and his relation to the Gopīs is at bottom sexual. There can be no greater absurdity, or no greater calumny, than is implied in such a view. That eroticism has got anything to do with spiritualism, we utterly deny. It is impossible to see in the sexual relation of man to woman, or of woman to man, any iota of the true nature of spiritual life. When Catherine of Siena and mystics of her type wanted to marry God, when Mīrābāi and Kānhopātrā in later times wedded themselves to God, when Andal, the female Tamil mystic, tried to espouse God, it has been supposed, the erotic instinct implied in such attempts was a partial manifestation of the spiritual love to God. This is an entire calumny on, and a shame to, the true nature of spiritual life. Spirituality is gained not by making common cause with sexuality, but by rising superior to it. That Kṛishṇa ever had any sexual relation with the Gopīs is hard to imagine.

It is a lie invented by later mythologists, who did not understand the true nature of spiritual life. Hence Parīkshit's query, as well as Śuka's justification, about the true nature of Kṛishṇa, are alike illustrations of the *ignoratio elenchi.* Parīkshit truly objects to the holiness of Kṛishṇa, if the latter's sexuality were to be a fact; but the answers which Śuka gives, or is made to give, fall entirely wide of the mark. To Parīkshit's question why Kṛishṇa committed adultery, Śuka gives futile answers. He tells us, in the first place, that all the great gods have committed adultery, thus trying to exonerate Kṛishṇa from the supposed sin. Secondly, he tells us that fire burns all impurities, and that Kṛishṇa's true nature burnt away all sins if he had committed any. Thirdly, he tells us that God must be regarded as being beyond both sin and merit, and that, therefore, the motive of Kṛishṇa was beyond the suspicion of being either meritorious or sinful. Fourthly, he tries to tell us that the conduct of great men need not tally with their words, and thus Kṛishṇa's superior teaching was left unaffected by his practice. Fifthly, he tells us that the actions of a man are all of them results of his *Karman*, and that probably the sexual dalliances of Kṛishṇa were the result of his previous *Karman.* Sixthly, he tries to exculpate Kṛishṇa by saying that by his divine nature he was immanent both in the Gopīs as well as their husbands, and that therefore there was no taint of adultery in his actions. His seventh argument is still more interesting. He tells us that Kṛishṇa by his Māyā produced doubles of these Gopīs before their husbands, and that therefore there was no objection to his enjoying the original Gopīs!—an argument which is foolish on its face, telling us as it does, that God tries to exonerate Himself from His sins by a magical sleight-of-hand. All these arguments are either childish or irrelevant. The only argument of any value that has been advanced to describe the real nature of the relation of the Gopīs to Kṛishṇa is the psychological argument,—that the relation is to be only an allegorical representation of the relation of the senses to the Self,—thus making it evident that any cult of devotion that may be raised upon the sexual nature of the relation of Kṛishṇa to the Gopīs may be raised only on stubble. Finally, we may advance also a mystical explanation of the way in which the Gopīs may be supposed to have enjoyed Kṛishṇa. May it not be possible, that, in their mystical realisation, each of the Gopīs had the vision of the Godhead before her, and that God so divided Himself before all of them, that He seemed to be enjoyed by each and all at the same time? It is granted to women as to men to have a mystical enjoyment of God, and it is as meaningless to speak of God as the bridegroom of a female devotee, as to speak of Him as the bride of a male devotee. There are no sexual relations possible with God, and Eroticism has no place in Mysticism.

The Sandilya Sutra and the Narada Sutra.

8. The Śāṇḍilya and the Nārada Bhakti-Sūtras are, as we have observed, like the Bhāgavata, fundamental works of Indian mysticism. It is not very easy to determine the exact dates of composition of these Sūtras. The Śāṇḍilya Bhakti-Sūtra seems to be older on account of its archaic tone, and is evidently modelled after the pattern of the great philosophical Sūtras. If any internal evidence is of any avail, we may say that even this points to the anteriority of the Śāṇḍilya-Sūtra. The Nārada Bhakti-Sūtra quotes Śāṇḍilya, but the Śāṇḍilya does not quote Nārada. In point of content, however, the Nārada Bhakti-Sūtra surpasses not merely the Śāṇḍilya by its easy eloquence and fervid devotion, but it may even be regarded as one of the best specimens of Bhakti literature that have ever been written. The Śāṇḍilya-Sūtra is more philosophic than the Nārada-Sūtra. It goes into the question of the nature of Brahman and Jīva, their inter-relation, the question of Creation, and so on. The Nārada Bhakti-Sūtra takes a leap immediately into the doctrine of devotion, analyzes its various aspects, and sets a ban against mere philosophical constructions. Both the Śāṇḍilya and the Nārada quote the Bhagavadgītā freely, and in that respect supply us with the connecting link between the Bhagavadgītā on the one hand, and the later Bhakti literature on the other. So far as the teaching of devotion is concerned, we cannot say that there is much distinction between the Śāṇḍilya Bhakti-Sūtra and the Nārada Bhakti-Sūtra. The two are on a par, so far as that doctrine is inculcated. Over and above the general contents of the doctrine of devotion as inculcated in the Nārada, the Śāṇḍilya, however, teaches that Bhakti may be of two kinds—primary and secondary. Secondary Bhakti concerns itself with Ritualism, with Kīrtana, with Dhyāna, with Pūjā, and even with Nāmasmaraṇa. Primary Bhakti, on the other hand, means the up-springing of the pure fount of love in man towards God. When we once taste of this, nothing else matters ; but if we have only secondary devotion, we cannot be supposed to have known the nature of Supreme Devotion.

The Teachings of the Narada Bhakti-Sutra.

9. The Nārada Bhakti-Sūtra begins by defining what Bhakti is. (1) It places on record various definitions of Bhakti advanced by its predecessors, and then gives us what its own definition of Bhakti is. According to Parāśara, we are told, Bhakti consists in the worship of God. According to Garga, it consists of the narration of God's exploits. According to Śāṇḍilya, so Nārada tells us, Bhakti means meditation on the Self. While, Nārada himself holds that Bhakti is the highest love for God, a whole-hearted attachment to God and indifference to other things, a surrender of all actions to God and agony in His forgetfulness. As a matter of fact, however, love's nature, says Nārada, is indescribable. As a dumb man who eats sugar cannot tell of its sweetness, so a man who enjoys the highest fruits of Bhakti cannot describe in words their real nature. (2) Then, secondly, Nārada goes on to discuss the relation of Bhakti to other Ways to God. Between Jñāna and Bhakti, three sorts of opinions are possible. In the first place, it may be maintained that Bhakti is a means to Jñāna, as the Advaitists maintain. Others may maintain that Jñāna and Bhakti are independent and equally useful ways to reach God. And thirdly, it may be maintained that Jñāna is a means to Bhakti, an opinion which Nārada himself endorses. To him Bhakti is not merely the end of all Jñāna, but the end of all *Karman*, and the end of all *Yoga*. In fact, Bhakti should be regarded as an end in itself. It concerns itself with a personal God who likes the humble and hates the boastful. There are no distinctions of caste, or learning, or family, or wealth, or action, possible in Bhakti. (3) Then Nārada goes on to discuss the means to the attainment of Bhakti. What, according to Nārada, are the moral requirements of a man who wishes to be a Bhakta ? He should, in the first place, leave all enjoyments, leave all contact with objects of sense, incessantly meditate on God without wasting a single minute, and always hear of God's qualities. He should give himself up to the study of the Bhaktiśāstras, and should not waste words in vain. He should pray for the grace of the Saints and the grace of God ; and God will appear and bestow upon him spiritual experience in course of time, which, Nārada thinks, can be attained only by God's grace. He should spend his life in serving the good. He should live in solitude, should not care for livelihood, should not hear of women, should not think about wealth, should not associate with thieves. Hypocrisy and arrogance, he should shun as foul dirt. He should cultivate the virtues of non-injury, truth, purity, compassion, and belief in God. He should deliberately set himself to transform his natural emotions, and make them divine. Passion and anger and egoism, he should transform and utilize for the service of God. In fact, a divine transformation of all the natural emotions must take place in him. He should not give himself up to argumentation; for there is no end to argumentation. It is manifold, and cannot be bridled. The devotee should be careless of the censure of others, and should have no anxiety whatsoever while he meditates. (4) Then, Nārada goes on to tell us the various kinds of Bhakti. Firstly, he divides Bhakti into Sāttvika, Rājasa and Tāmasa. He draws upon the three categories of the Bhaktas as given in the Bhagavadgītā, namely, the Ārta, the Jijñāsu and the Arthārthin, and tells us that the Ārta possesses the Sāttvika Bhakti, the Jijñāsu the Rājasa Bhakti, and the Arthārthin the Tāmasa Bhakti, and tells us that the first is superior to the second, and the second superior to the third. One does not know why the Bhakti of the Ārta should be regarded as superior to the Bhakti of the Jijñāsu. Why should we not regard the Bhakti of the Jijñāsu as Sāttvika, and the Bhakti of the Ārta as Rājasa? Nārada has no answer to give. There is yet again another classification of the kinds of Bhakti which Nārada makes. He tells us that it is of eleven kinds. It consists of singing the qualities of God, a desire to see His form, worshipping the image of God, meditation on Him, the service of God, friendship with God, affection towards God, love to God as to a husband, surrender of one's own Self to God, atonement with God, and the agony of separation from God. (5) As regards the criterion of Bhakti, Nārada teaches that it is "Svayampramāṇa": the criterion of Bhakti is in itself. Complete peace and complete happiness are its characteristics. "Anubhava" which is the practical index of Bhakti should increase from moment to moment. It ought to be permanent. It ought to be subtle. While the psycho-physical characteristics of Bhakti are, that it should make the throat choked with love, should make the hair stand on end, and should compel divine tears from meditating eyes. When, therefore, complete happiness and peace are enjoyed, when "Anubhava" is attained, when all the psycho-physical effects are experienced, then alone is true Bhakti generated. They are the criteria of Bhakti. (6) Finally, Nārada tells us what the effects of Bhakti are. It is Bhakti alone which leads to true immortality. It is Bhakti which endows us with complete satisfaction. Bhakti drives away all desires from us. A Bhakta uplifts not merely himself, but others also. He ceases to grieve; he ceases to hate; he feels no enjoyment in other things; he feels no enthusiasm for other things; he becomes intoxicated with love; he remains silent. Spiritual "Epokhē" is the mark of the saint.

The Philosophic Schools and their Influence on Hindi, Bengali and Gujerathi Mysticism.

10. We have hitherto considered two movements, one the Occult, the other the Mystic, which run side by side with each other from the early centuries of the Christian era to almost the end of the first Millennium. *Pari passu* with these, there was yet a third movement, a movement which we may call the Philosophic movement. There are four great representatives of this movement as we have had the occasion to notice in the previous Volumes of this History, namely, Śaṃkara, Rāmānuja, Madhva and Vallabha. Śaṃkarāchārya's system is supposed to be antagonistic to the Bhakti movement, and, to that extent, unmystical. But it must be remembered that Śaṃkara did not neglect Bhakti, but absorbed it into his absolutistic scheme. If Śaṃkara's movement is not mystical in its aim, we do not understand what it is. Rāmānuja, Madhva, and Vallabha, who founded three great schools of philosophic thought, wielded a great influence even up to the end of the fifteenth century, and may all be said to have gone against the Māyā doctrine of Śaṃkara. They made Bhakti the essential element in the Vedāntic scheme, and although Vallabha preached a philosophical monism, Rāmānuja and Madhva could not understand how theism and pantheism could be reconciled in mysticism. It is just this reconciling tendency of mysticism which has been lost sight of by all dogmatic theorisers about theism and pantheism. From the schools of Rāmānuja, Madhva, and Vallabha, sprang forth great Bhakti movements from the 13th century onwards in the various parts of India. It is interesting to note how Rāmānuja's influence dwindled in his birth-land to reappear with greater force in Upper India. Rāmānanda, who was a philosophical descendant of Rāmānuja, quarrelled with his spiritual teacher, and came and settled at Benares. From him, three great mystical schools started up: the first, the school of Tulsidās; the second, the school of Kabīr; and the third, the school of Nābhāji. Kabīr was also influenced by Sufism. Tulsidās was greatly influenced by the historico-mythical story of Rāma. Nābhāji made it his business to chronicle the doings of the great Saints in the Hindi language. From the school of Madhva, arose the great Bengali saint Chaitanya, who was also influenced by his predecessor saints in Bengal, Chaṇḍīdāsa and Vidyāpati. Vallabha exercised a great influence in Gujerath, and Mīrābāi and Narasī Mehtā sprang up under the influence of his teachings. We thus see how from the Philosophical Schools, there arose a Democratical Mysticism which laid stress upon the vernaculars as the media of mystical teaching, as opposed to the Classical Mysticism of ancient times, which had Sanskrit as its language of communication. It was also a democratisation not merely in language, but also in the spirit of teaching, and we see how mysticism became the property of all. It is thus evident how the mystical literature in Hindi, Bengali, and Gujerathi was influenced by the three great schools of Rāmānuja, Madhva, and Vallabha respectively. All these saints we shall have the occasion to notice in great detail in our next Volume.

Christian Influence on the Bhakti Doctrine.

11. We must pause here for a while to consider the question of Christian influence on the development of the Bhakti doctrine in India. Opinions have greatly differed on this subject. According to one opinion, the Indian doctrine of Bhakti is entirely foreign in its origin ; the Indians, according to this opinion, are incapable of Bhakti, and what devotion they came to possess was from the start due to the influence from other lands. A second theory would hold that even though the doctrine of Bhakti in its origins may not be supposed to be un-Indian, its later development was influenced among other things by the worship of the Child-God and the Sucking Mother, and thus, it must be supposed to have been mainly influenced by Christianity; Rāmānuja and Madhva, according to this theory, are supposed to have been influenced by Christian doctrine and practice, especially because, in their native places, it is presumed, there was a great deal of Christian influence. According to a third view, the Indian doctrine of Bhakti is entirely Indian, and it does not allow that either Rāmānuja or Madhva were influenced by Christian doctrine, far less that the Bhakti doctrine was Christian in its origin ; but this view would not deny the possibility, as in the 20th century to-day, of both Hinduism and Christianity influencing each other under certain conditions, both in doctrine and practice. It would suppose that their identical teachings on such important subjects as the value of the Spiritual Teacher, the significance of God's Name, the conflict of Faith and Works, or of Predestination and Grace, are due entirely to their development from within, and to no influence from without. It does not allow that because Śīlāditya, the king of Kanauj, received a party of Syrian Christians in 639 A.D., or even because Akbar received Jesuit missions during his reign, that Christianity influenced the course of thought either of Kabīr or of Tulsidās,

This would be quite as impossible as to suppose that Jñāneśvara himself was influenced by Christianity, simply on the ground, as was once asserted, that the expression "Vaikuṇṭhīche Rāṇive" (the Kingdom of God) occurs in his writings, or that Tukārām was likewise influenced by Christianity by his insistence on the power of sin in man. The feeling of devotion is present in a more or less pronounced fashion throughout all the stages of the progress of humanity from its cradle downwards, and it shall so exist as long as humanity lasts. On this view, we can argue for the early up-springing of the devotional sentiment in all races from within themselves, even though some influence of a kind may not be denied when religious communities mingle together, especially when they have a long contact with each other, a sympathetic imagination, and a genuine desire to learn and to assimilate.

Tamil Mysticism.

12. That the Christian influence has nothing to do with Tāmil Mysticism in its origin, one has merely to open his eyes to discern. Both the Tāmil Śaivites and Vaishṇavites who lived centuries before the age of Rāmānuja, show an utterly innate tendency to Devotion, uninfluenced by any foreign thought or practice. The Tāmil Śaivites seem to have been established in the country in the 6th century A.D., and through a long line of mystics illustrate the inward impulse which rises from man to God. The great lights of Tāmil Śaivite literature are Tirujñānasambandhar who flourished in the 7th century A.D., Appar who flourished in the same century, Tirumūlar who flourished in the 8th century, and finally Māṇikkavāchagar, the man of golden utterances, who flourished in the 9th, and who, in fact, may be said to top the list of the Śaivite mystics. In him we see the upspringing of a natural devotion to God, which through a consciousness of his faults, rises by gradations to the apprehension of the Godhead. In his great poem, he makes us aware, as Dr. Carpenter puts it, of his first joy and exaltation, his subsequent waverings, his later despondencies, his consciousness of faults, his intensive shame, and his final recovery and triumph. The Tāmil Vaishṇavites, who are headed and heralded by the great Āḷvārs, open yet another line of mystical thought, namely, of mysticism through devotion to Vishṇu. If we set aside the impossible chronologies which are generally assigned to these Āḷvārs, we cannot doubt that they also seem equally established in their country along with the Tāmil Śaivites in the 6th century. Nammāḷvār, whose date varies from the 8th to the 10th century in the estimate of critics, has produced works which are reverenced like the Vedas in the whole Tāmil-speaking country. His disciple was Nāthamuni, who lived about 1000 A.D., and who was the collector of the famous four-thousand hymns of the Āḷvārs. The grandson of Nāthamuni was the famous Yāmunāchārya who lived about 1050 A.D., and whose lineal philosophical descendant was the great Rāmānuja, who lived from 1050 to 1135 A.D. Here we have in a brief outline the two great lines of Śaivite and Vaishṇavite mystics in the Tāmil country down to the age of Rāmānuja. Rāmānuja took up his cue from the Vaishṇavite philosophy, and built a system which was intended to cut at the root of both the monistic as well as the dualistic schemes of thought. The predecessors of Rāmānuja, however, were given to devotion more than to philosophy, and they showed the pure love of the aspirant for God-realization, uncontaminated by, or uninfluenced by, philosophical thought.

Canarese Mysticism.

13. Our praise of these saints, however, cannot be entirely unmitigated, for we know how the Rādhākṛishṇa cult had influenced the songs even of these great Vaishṇavite saints. The conception of the relation between the bride and bridegroom as the type of the relation between the saint and God runs through a great deal of this literature, and to that extent vitiates it. Not so the bold and sturdy Vīraśaiva mysticism, which makes an alliance with Advaitic Monism on the one hand, and Moralistic Purism on the other, and which, even though a large part of it is given to an imaginary discussion of the nature of the various Liṅgas, which are, so to say, merely symbolical illustrations of certain psychological conceptions, is yet a philosophy which is well worth a careful study. Basava was only a great reformer who lived at the beginning of the 13th century, and who was the devotee of the image of Samgameśvara at the place where the Malaprabhā and the Kṛishṇā meet. He was preceded by a great number of Siddhas, who are as old as the Tāmil Āḷvārs on the one hand, and the Hindi Nāthas on the other. Nijaguṇaśivayogi who was more of a philosopher than a mystic, Akhaṇḍeśvara who was more of a moralist than a mystic, and Sarpabhūshaṇa who was more of a mystic than either a philosopher or a moralist, are all of them great names in the development of Lingāyat thought. Kanakadāsa, who stands apart somewhat, having sprung from a lowly order of the Hindus, and Purandaradāsa, Jagannāthadāsa, and Vijayadāsa who were full-fledged Vaishṇavite Hindus, must be regarded as supplying us with the development of Vaishṇavism in the Karnāṭaka, which went *pari passu* with the development of Vīraśaiva mysticism. All these are great names, and we must reserve a full treatment of them for our next Volume.

Maratha Mysticism.

14. Our immediate concern in this volume, however, is the consideration of the teachings of the great Marāṭhā saints from the age of Jñānadeva downwards to the age of Rāmadāsa, beginning in fact from the 13th century and ending with the 17th, leaving the consideration of the development of Indian thought in the 18th and 19th centuries for the last Volume of this History. For fear of increasing the bulk of our present volume to an unpardonable extent, we must restrict our attention only to a section of the great mystical community in India, namely, the section of the Marāṭhā Saints. The beginning of the mystical line was effectively made in Mahārāshṭra by Jñānadeva, whose father is supposed to have been a disciple of Śrīpāda Rāmānanda of Benares, or yet again, of Rāmānanda himself. In that case, it would be very interesting to see how not merely the two streams of Kabīr and Tulsidās issued from the fountain-head of Rāmānanda, but even how Marāṭhā mysticism in a way could be traced to the same fountain. But in any case, it is certain that Nivṛittinātha and Jñānadeva came from the spiritual line of the great Gahinīnātha, as is more than once authentically evidenced by the writings of both Nivṛitti and Jñānadeva themselves. That Nivṛittinātha was instructed by Gahinīnātha in spiritual knowledge, that Gahinīnātha derived his spiritual knowledge from Goraksha, and Goraksha from Matsyendra, it is needless to reiterate. The Sampradāya was a Sampradāya of Nāthas. When and how Matsyendranātha and Gorakshanātha actually lived and flourished, it is impossible to determine. But it remains clear that they cannot be unhistorical names. Behind Matsyendranātha, we have mythology, but after Matsyendra, we have history; and it is evident that Jñāneśvara belonged to that great line of the Nāthas, who like the Āḷvārs in the Tāmil country and the Siddhas in the Lingāyat community, successfully laid the foundation of mysticism in Mahārāshṭra through their great representative, Jñāneśvara. It is not without reason that many a later mystic acknowledges that the foundation of that mystical edifice was laid by Jñāneśvara, above which Nāmadeva and other saints later erected the divine sanctuary, of which Tukā became the pinnacle. And while a continuous tradition goes on from Jñāneśvara to Nāmadeva, and from

Nāmadeva to Ekanātha, and from Ekanātha to Tukārāma, Rāmadāsa like Heracleitus stands somewhat apart in his spiritual isolation. His is a new Sampradāya altogether: it is not the Sampradāya of the Vārkarīs. It is for that reason that the Vārkarīs have looked askance at the great spiritual work of Rāmadāsa. But we who stand for no Sampradāya whatsoever, and who, like bees, want to collect spiritual honey wherever it may be found, recognize, from the mystical point of view, no distinction of any kind between the Sampradāya of the Vārkarīs, and the Sampradāya of the Dhārkarīs, the Sampradāya of the Cymbal, or the Sampradāya of the Sword. A little after Jñāneśvara, but contemporaneously with him, Nāmadeva, after being tested and found wanting by the potter Gorā, entered the spiritual line at the hands of Visobā Khechara, who was a disciple of Sopāna, who was himself the disciple of Nivṛitti. Ekanātha was indeed initiated by Janārdana Swāmī, who, as rumour would have it, was initiated by Nṛisimha Sarasvatī, an "avatāra" of Dattātreya himself. But it is to be remembered that Ekanātha, who was the great-grandson of Bhānudāsa, was a great Vārkarī of Paṇḍharī, and moreover, Ekanātha himself tells us that he derived his spiritual illumination from the line of Jñāneśvara. When all these things are taken into account, we cannot say that Ekanātha stands apart from the great spiritual line of Jñāneśvara. Tukārāma, who is perhaps the most well-known among the Marāṭhā saints, derives his spiritual lineage from a Chaitanya line. What connection this line had with the Chaitanya school in Bengal has not yet been discovered. But it is at any rate clear that Tukārāma developed the Vārkarī Sampradāya through a repeated study of the works of Jñāneśvara, Nāmadeva and Ekanātha. Rāmadāsa probably did not come into contact with any of these people for his initiation, and though, as a tradition would have it, while he was yet a boy, he and his brother were taken to Ekanātha who foresaw in them great spiritual giants, he might yet on the whole be said to have struck off a new path altogether. If we re-classify these great mystics of Mahārāshṭra according to the different types of mysticism illustrated in them, they fall into the following groups. Jñāneśvara is the type of an intellectual mystic; Nāmadeva heralds the democratic age; Ekanātha synthesizes the claims of worldly and spiritual life; Tukārāma's mysticism is most personal; while Rāmadāsa is the type of an active saint. A man may become a saint, and yet, as Monsieur Joly has pointed out, he may retain his native temperament. The different types of mystics that we find among the Marāṭhā saints are not a little due to original temperamental differences. Between themselves, these great mystics of Mahārāshṭra have produced a literature, which shall continue to be the wonder of all humanity, which cares at all for an expression of mystical thought in any country without distinction of creed, caste, or race.

PART I.

The Age of Jnanadeva: Intellectual Mysticism.

CHAPTER II.

Jnanadeva: Biographical Introduction.

The Condition of Maharashtra in Jnanadeva's time.

1. The Mahārāshṭra of Jñānadeva's time was a free Mahārāshṭra, yet unmolested by Mahomedan invaders. The kings of Devagiri were all supreme, and among them particularly Jaitrapāḷa, who ruled from 1191 A.D. to 1210 A.D. (Śake 1113-1132). Of the first of these, Mukundarāja has been reported to be probably the spiritual teacher—Mukundarāja, the author of the Paramāmṛita and the Vivekasindhu, and probably the first great writer of note in Marāṭhi literature. In Jñānadeva's time the ruler at Devagiri was the Yādava king Rāmadevarao, who is actually mentioned by name towards the close of the Jñāneśvarī. He was a great patron of learning, as also, it seems, a devotee of the god of Paṇḍharpur, whose shrine he visited and endowed with a munificent sum of money. On the whole, the Mahārāshṭra preceding the days of Jñānadeva was a free, unmolested, and prosperous Mahārāshṭra, where no internecine strife reigned, and where all was unity.

Mukundaraja.

2. We must say a few words about Mukundarāja, the teacher of Jaitrapāḷa, especially because his Paramāmṛita seems to have suggested the title of Anubhavāmṛita (or as it is also otherwise called Amṛitānubhava) to Jñānadeva; and yet again because Mukundarāja was not merely a Vedāntic philosopher, but, as may be gathered from his writings, a mystic also. In his Vivekasindhu II. ii. 34, Mukundarāja traces his spiritual lineage from Ādinātha, his direct spiritual teacher having been Harinātha by name. Mukundarāja tells us in his Vivekasindhu how Harinātha tried to propitiate God Śankara by all sorts of spiritual practices, by utter resignation, by fasting, by concentration, and by every other conceivable remedy to attain to God, and how ultimately, all of a sudden, God Śankara appeared to him in a vision, and endowed him with spiritual illumination. It is true that the language of Mukundarāja's works appears modern, and it is for this reason that doubt has been thrown upon such a great anteriority being assigned to Mukundarāja; but when we remember that ancient works may in course of time be recast into modern form, it need not seem impossible that Mukundarāja's works themselves may also have been recast, and that therefore what modernity there appears in his works is due to the successive shape that the works took after him. As there is, however, an early reference in Mukundarāja's works to the date of composition of the Vivekasindhu, namely, 1188 A.D. (Śake 1110), and as there is a reference also to the king Jaitrapāḷa whose date has been fixed between 1191 to 1210 A.D. (Śake 1113 to 1132), it does not seem impossible that Mukundarāja lived at that early date assigned to him by tradition.

The Paramamrita of Mukundaraja.

3. The Paramāmṛita of Mukundarāja is a work in which was made the first systematic attempt in Marāṭhi for the exposition of the Vedāntic principles. Mukundarāja discusses the nature of the physical body, the subtle body, the causal body, and other such topics. He adds to this intellectual exposition some mystic hints which show that Mukundarāja was not merely a philosopher, but a saint likewise. In the 9th chapter of the work, he tells us in Yogic fashion the practical way to God-attainment, and in the 12th he speaks of the great bliss that arises from spiritual experience. In this latter chapter, he tells us how perspiration, shivering, and other bodily marks characterize the ecstatic state (XII. 1), how bodily egoism vanishes in the contemplation of the Divine, how all sensual desire dwindles to a nullity, how all the senses are filled with joy even when there is no physical enjoyment (XII. 6), how in the palace of Great Bliss one enjoys the woman that makes her appearance in the state of ecstatic realisation (XII. 7), how when both knowledge and not-knowledge are at an end, there is the realisation of the empire of unitive life for the mystic (XII. 8), how by the force of the Great Bliss, no mental state ever dares to intrude upon a mystic's consciousness (XII. 10), and how this Great Bliss can be experienced only by the mystic, while others stare in wonder and sit silent (XII. 13). Mukundarāja tells us furthermore that a mystic never allows others to know his real state (XIII. 11), detailing how he loves all beings, because they are all of them the embodiments of God (XIII. 16), how though a Saint knows the inner hearts of all, he is yet regarded as a lunatic (XIII. 23), and how in the Great Bliss of the ecstatic state he never remembers that he has a world to relieve from the bonds of mortal existence (XIII. 27). With a shrewdness that comes out of spiritual experience, Mukundarāja tells us finally that a mystic should never reveal his inner secret (XIV. 18), for fear that if mystic knowledge were to be cheap among men, people would have an easy chance of deriding the mystic wisdom, assuring us, finally, that he who contemplates the inner meaning of the Paramāmṛita shall turn back from the world and see the vision of his Self (XIV. 25).

King Ramadevarao of Devagiri.

4. As Mukundarāja lived in the time of Jaitrapāḷa so Jñānadeva lived in the time of Rāmadevarao of Devagiri. That this Rāmadevarao was a worshipper of Viṭhoba of Pandharpur, is known from an inscription in the temple of Pandharpur which tells us that he visited that temple in 1276 A.D. (Śake 1198) on the full-moon day of Mārgaśīrsha, and the inscription goes on to tell us that Rāmadevarao was the head of the religious community of Pandharpur. It was during his reign that Jñānadeva composed his Jñāneśvarī in 1290 A.D.(Śake 1212). Two years before Jñānadeva took Samādhi, that is to say, in 1294 A.D. (Śake 1216), Allauddin Khilji had already come over to Ellichpur with the intention of falling upon Devagiri. His forces were immense and powerful, and he was backed up by the Emperor of Delhi, for which reasons Rāmadevarao gave him a large ransom, and saved his kingdom. But, in 1306 A.D. (Śake 1228), Allauddin Khilji sent again against Devagad a large force under Malik Kaphar, and with the help of his thirty-thousand horse Malik Kaphar was able to ransack the whole country of Rāmadevarao and carry him to Delhi, where the latter remained a prisoner for six months, and, returning to his kingdom, died in 1309 A.D. (Śake 1231). The kingdom of Devagiri did not last long thereafter. It was confiscated by the Emperor of Delhi in the year 1318 A.D. (Śake 1240). This tragic end of the dynasty of Rāmadevarao, Jñānadeva did not live to see. So long as Jñānadeva lived, the kingdom of Rāmadevarao enjoyed all prosperity.

The Mahanubhavas.

5. So far about the historical back-ground at the time of Jñānadeva. Let us now turn to the religious back-ground. Here we must take into account two strong forces prevalent before the days of Jñānadeva: the first was the literature and the influence of the Mahānubhāvas, and the other the great Yogic tradition of the Nāthas. As regards the former, it must be remembered that it is a literature which certainly claims our attention, and in brilliance of style certainly paves the way for a later production like the Jñāneśvarī. The Mahānubhāvic conceits are like the conceits of the early Elizabethan writers, and we may say that Jñānadeva stands to the Mahānubhāvas just in the same relation in which Shakespeare stood to the early Elizabethans. Indeed the whole range of Mahānubhāva literature has not yet been brought to light; and what with the discovery of the key to the literature of the Mahānubhāvas which we owe to the late Mr. Rajavade, what with the great trouble which the late Mr. Bhave took in bringing the Mahānubhāva literature to light, and what with the aspirations of the modern Mahānubhāvas themselves to bring their literature into line with the literature of the early great Marāṭhi writers, we may hope that very soon the leading literary works of the Mahānubhāvas will become the property of all. When this happens, we shall be able to see how far Jñānadeva in his great conceits, in his imaginations, in his flights of poetical fancy, in his vocabulary, as well as in his diction, stands related to the Mahānubhāvas; but it may be said at once that the Mahānubhāvic contribution to religion was of a peculiar kind, and that Jñānadeva owed practically little to that tradition. It is true that the Mahānubhāvas made current certain Yogic practices which might have influenced some of the writings of Jñānadeva; but so far as the philosophy of religion is concerned, Jñānadeva goes back to the Upanishads, the Bhagavadgītā, the Bhāgavata (which, by the bye, he also mentions in his great work) and such other early classics. The Mahānubhāvas were hitherto regarded as having disbelieved in the caste system, as having disregarded the teachings of the Vedas, as having felt no necessity for the system of the Āśramas, and as not having recognized any deities except Kṛishṇa. But modern apologists of that sect are announcing that they have ever believed in the caste system; that though they have not recognized the principle of slaughter in Yajña, still they have believed, on the whole, in the Vedas; that they have sanctioned the system of the Āśramas; and that even though they worship Chakradhara as Kṛishṇa, by Chakradhara is not to be understood certainly the man who founded that sect at the beginning of the 11th century. Hence even though they believe in Kṛishṇa, they do not believe in Viṭṭhala. They would recognize no other deities except Kṛishṇa himself. It is probably due to the recognition of this deity that they wear dark-blue clothes. The insinuation, which some critics of Jñāneśvara have made to the effect that the references to the blue colour in his Abhangas are influenced by the Mahānubhāvas, absolutely loses all weight, when we take into consideration the fact that the blue colour referred to by Jñānadeva in his Abhangas is the blue colour of mystic experience, and not the blue colour which is the characteristic of Mahānubhāva costume. And as for the non-worship of any deity except Kṛishṇa, the worship of Kṛishṇa or Viṭṭhala in the

Jñāneśvara school marks that school away from the Mahānubhāva sect. But it cannot be gainsaid that the Mahānubhāvas exercised a great deal of influence in their day, and that Jñānadeva, so far from being merely a partisan or an opponent of them, took a more broad-minded and liberal view, going back to the fountain-head of the Hindu religion.

The Nathas.

6. Another influence this time of the Yogic kind—was afloat in the country before the days of Jñānadeva. We know how Trimbakpant, the great-grandfather of Jñānadeva, was initiated at Āpegaon by Gorakshanātha ; we know how later Gahinīnātha, the disciple of Gorakshanātha, initiated Nivṛittinātha. Gorakshanātha himself was a lineal spiritual descendant of Matsyendranātha, but we do not know whether this latter may be regarded as a historical person. Then again, we do not know anything about the place in which the Nāthas lived. They are claimed by the people in Bengal as having lived in their part of the country ; by the Hindi people as having lived in theirs ; by the Marāṭhi people as having lived in theirs. Thus, for example, the story of Jālandhara and Maināvatī is probably a Bengali story, while in Mahārāshṭra in the District of Satara, there is yet shown a hill sacred to Matsyendranātha, which is called Matsyendragaḍa, and a huge tamarind tree called the Gorakshachiñcha sacred to Goraksha. When Gahinīnātha instructed Nivṛittinātha, we are told that the instruction took place at Brahmagiri near Nasik. It thus seems that Mahārāshṭra disputes with Bengal the honour of being the habitat of the Nāthas. It seems very probable that Gorakshanātha and Gahinīnātha actually existed : that Gahinīnātha was a historical person is proved by his having imparted instruction to Nivṛittinātha and Jñānadeva ; that Gorakshanātha also did likewise exist is proved by some works like Goraksha-Samhitā which go after him and are still extant. All religions thus lose themselves in mystery at their start, and it is only later that they come to the vision of men. Thus was it with the Nātha-sampradāya. The full-fledged fruit of their Sampradāya appeared to view in the great immortal work of Jñānadeva, and it shows what that wisdom was, which Jñānadeva imbibed from his spiritual ancestors. It is also likely that the Nāthas may have been itinerant religious devotees. Thus their appearance in Bengal, in the Hindi-speaking country, as well as in Mahārāshṭra, could be very well explained. What disciples they made is not known. But if they produced one such disciple as Jñānadeva, the whole *raison d'être* of their spiritual life may be said to have been fulfilled.

The Ancestors of Jnanadeva.

7. Trimbakpant is the first well-known ancestor of Jñānadeva. He was, in fact, his great-grandfather. We have referred to the fact that he obtained spiritual initiation at the hands of Gorakshanātha. Bhingarkar produces a document in which Trimbakpant was made the provincial Governor of Bīḍa in 1207 A.D. (Śake 1129) by the king of Devagiri. Bhingarkar also produces another document in which Haripant, the son of Trimbakpant, was made the captain of an army in 1213 A.D. (Śake 1135). The physical lineage of Jñānadeva comes not from Haripant, but from another son of Trimbakpant, namely, Govindpant. Jñānadeva's father, Viṭṭhalpant, was the son of this Govindpant, and it is the story of Viṭṭhalpant which we now proceed to trace.

The Story of Vitthalpant.

8. Viṭṭhalpant inherited from his ancestors the Kulkarniship of Āpegaon, a village situated on the northern bank of the Godāvari, a few miles away from Paiṭhaṇa. He was married to Rakhumābāi, the daughter of Sidhopant, Kulkarni of Āḷandī. It seems Viṭṭhalpant took very much to heart the death of his father Govindpant, and that thereafter he became disgusted with life. From a document produced by Bhingarkar which bears the date 1266 A.D. (Śake 1188), it seems that Viṭṭhalpant with his wife was invited by Sidhopant to live with him, and that he was advised to give up attachment to worldly life only after the obtainment of progeny. Viṭṭhalpant had no children from his wife for a long time, which was another cause of his increasing disgust with the world. One day, with the consent of his wife, he left home and family to live in Benares. He there took orders, and was initiated as a Samnyāsin either by Rāmānanda himself, or by one belonging to his school. There is here a little difference of opinion as to whether Viṭṭhalpant as a Samnyāsin belonged to the Ānanda school or to the Āśrama school. Nābhāji, and therefore Mahīpati, say that he belonged to the Ānanda school. Nāmadeva and Niḷoba relegate Viṭṭhalpant to the Āśrama school. Nāmadeva tells us how Viṭṭhalpant, whom he calls Chaitanyāśrama, later became a house-holder : चैतन्याश्रमवासी । जाहले गृहवासी. In any case, it is certain that while Viṭṭhalpant's spiritual teacher was once travelling from place to place on a spiritual pilgrimage, he got down at Āḷandī, where meeting with Siddheśvarapant and Rakhumābāi, who were pining after the loss of Viṭṭhalpant, he was moved with their heart-felt supplications, and coming to know that Viṭṭhalpant, whom he had made a Samnyāsin, had left behind him a wife to support, promised to send Viṭṭhalpant back as soon as he returned to Benares. Accordingly, when he came to Benares, he sent Viṭṭhalpant to Āḷandī with remonstrations and expostulations to first have progeny from his wife Rakhumābāi by becoming a Gṛihastha again. On his return back to the order of a Gṛihastha, Viṭṭhalpant had from Rakhumābāi four children in succession, all of them, it seems, born at Āpegaon. The names of these were Nivṛittinātha, Jñānadeva, Sopāna and Muktābāi. It is occasionally supposed that these names are merely allegorical representations of the stages of an advancing mystic. But this is a delusion. The whole history of the four children, their actual doings on earth and the Samādhis they have left behind them, give the lie direct to the alleged allegory. The only question is about the dates of birth of these four children, and this we proceed to investigate.

Jnanesvara Chronology.

9. The determination of these dates is a matter of some difficulty, inasmuch as there are two different traditions about their dates. According to one, and the more usually accepted tradition,

Nivṛittinātha was born in 1273 A.D. (Śake 1195), and passed away in 1297 A.D. (Śake 1219) ;

Jñānadeva was born in 1275 A.D. (Śake 1197), and passed away in 1296 A.D. (Śake 1218) ;

Sopāna was born in 1277 A.D. (Śake 1199), and passed away in 1296 A.D. (Śake 1218) ;

Muktābāi was born in 1279 A.D. (Śake 1201), and passed away in 1297 A.D. (Śake 1219).

According to another tradition, the tradition given by Janābai,

Nivṛittinātha was born in 1268 A.D. (Śake 1190) ;

Jñānadeva was born in 1271 A.D. (Śake 1193) ;

Sopāna was born in 1274 A.D. (Śake 1196) ;

Muktābāi was born in 1277 A.D. (Śake 1199).

The matter of immediate interest to us is the determination of the two dates in the case of Jñānadeva. The one historically accredited fact in his life is that he wrote the Jñāneśvarī in 1290 A.D. (Śake 1212). Even here there is another reading which tells us that Jñānadeva wrote the Jñāneśvarī in 1284 A.D. (Śake 1206). But, on the whole, we may say that there is a consensus of agreement in taking the date of the composition of the Jñāneśvarī to be 1290 A.D. (Śake 1212). This date, then, may be said to be a settled fact. As to how long Jñānadeva lived prior to this date and how long after it, we can settle only approximately. To say that Jñānadeva was born in 1275 A.D. (Śake 1197) makes him only fifteen years old at the time of the composition of the Jñāneśvarī; while to say that he was born in 1271 A.D. (Śake 1193) makes him nineteen years old at the time of the composition of the work. Now it does not seem humanly possible that Jñānadeva could have written his great work only when he was fifteen; for a boy of nineteen years of age also to produce such an immortal work is a matter of no small difficulty. But if we were to choose between these two dates only, we had rather say that Jñānadeva was nineteen years old, than that he was only fifteen, at the time of the composition of the work. If, then, Jñānadeva is to be taken as nineteen years of age at the time of the composition of the Jñāneśvarī, his birth-date must be fixed at 1271 A.D. (Śake 1193). This is what Janābāi actually tells us. She tells us that Jñānadeva was born in 1271 A.D. (Śake 1193), and that his brothers and sister were born correspondingly. The Abhanga runs as follows :—

शालिवाहन शके अकराशें नव्वद । नित्रृत्ति आनंद प्रगटले ॥
त्र्याण्णवाचे सालीं ज्ञानदेव प्रगटले । सोपान देखिले शाण्णवांत ॥
नव्याण्णवाचे सालीं मुक्ताई देखिली । जनी ह्मणे केली मात त्यांनीं ॥

It must be remembered that even this Abhanga has got its variant readings, which suit the later chronology of the brothers and sister, but this does not end our difficulties. When did Jñānadeva pass away? According to the tradition which regards Jñānadeva as born in 1275 A.D. (Śake 1197), he is made also to pass away in the year 1296 A.D. (Śake 1218). That Jñānadeva did actually pass away in the year 1296 A.D. (Śake 1218) is attested to by the Abhangas of Nāmadeva, Visobā Khechara, Chokhāmeḷā and Janābāi herself. If then, according to Janābāi's Abhanga, Jñānadeva must be regarded as having passed away in the year 1296 A.D. (Śake 1218), we must adopt one of the three alternatives: either that Jñānadeva lived for twenty-five years from 1271 A.D. to 1296 A.D. (Śake 1193 to 1218)—a fact which contradicts the statement that is made by many men, and particularly by Jñānadeva himself, that he lived only for twenty-two years and that he passed away at twenty-two बालछंदो बावीस जन्में । तोडिलीं भवाब्धींचीं कर्में ॥, or else we must bring back the date of his passing away from 1296 A.D. to 1293 A.D. (from Śake 1218 to 1215), if his life-span of twenty-two years is to be taken as an accredited fact. Hence we see that the determination of the dates of Jñānadeva's birth and passing away offers no small difficulty. This fact, however, remains certain that the Jñāneśvarī was written in

1290 A.D. (Śake 1212) and that that was the central fact of his life.

The Life-Story of Jnanadeva.

10. The other facts of Jñānadeva's life may briefly be told. Jñānadeva along with his brothers and sister, Nivṛitti, Sopāna and Muktābāi, was the offspring of a saint turned house-holder. That brought no small calumny from the orthodox society on these children. The orthodox Brahmins refused to perform the thread ceremony of Jñānadeva and his brothers. Their father Viṭṭhalpant took them to Nasik, where, in order to spend his life in holy activity, he used every day to circumambulate the Brahmagiri near Tryambakeśvara. Once, while he was taking all his children with him on a circular route, a tiger jumped upon them, and in great fear Viṭṭhalpant and his children began to run away. Viṭṭhalpant along with Jñānadeva, Sopāna and Muktābāi was able to return home, but Nivṛittinātha was missing. As Nivṛittinātha was separated from his father and brothers, he went to a cave in Brahmagiri, where it is reported that he met Gainīnātha, (who initiated him in the mystic line), and after a few days returned home. When Viṭṭhalpant actually died we do not know. But it is evident, that after his death, Nivṛittinātha initiated Jñānadeva. The social persecution was yet unabated. The four children, therefore, determined to go to Paiṭhaṇa to obtain a certificate of Śuddhi from the Brahmins of Paiṭhaṇa, which was then regarded as a very orthodox centre. We do not know how much authenticity to attach to the letter of Śuddhi which Hemāḍapant and Bopadeva, the wise men of the day, were instrumental in giving to the four children. It seems that the Brahmins of Paiṭhaṇa must have been struck at the great spiritual learning and intelligence of these boys, and that, therefore, they gave them the required certificate of purification. This incident is supposed to have happened in 1287 A.D. (Śake 1209). After obtaining the certificate of purification, Jñānadeva returned along with his brothers and sister and went to Nevāse, where by his spiritual power he saved Sacchidānanda Bābā from a dangerous illness. This rescue filled Sacchidānanda Bābā with a sense of deep gratitude, and he became a very willing amanuensis for the writing of Jñānadeva's great work, the Jñāneśvarī, which was completed by Jñānadeva at Nevāse. A pillar is still shown at Nevāse where this writing took place. In the Jñāneśvarī, Jñānadeva imagines that Nivṛittinātha is sitting to hear the discourse, and that he is expounding the discourse to an assembly of learned men and saints. Tradition also has it that Nivṛittinātha, not being satisfied with the Jñāneśvarī which is merely a commentary on the Bhagavadgītā, ordered Jñānadeva to write an independent treatise (later known as the Amṛitānubhava), which Jñānadeva accordingly wrote. It seems that Nivṛittinātha and Jñānadeva, along with Sopāna and Muktābāi, later visited Paṇḍharapūr. It was this visit to Paṇḍharapūr about 1293 A.D. (Śake 1215), which made Jñānadeva and Nāmadeva spiritual friends, which filled Jñānadeva with an enthusiasm for the Paṇḍhari Sāmpradāya, of which he later became the first apostle. Jñānadeva and Nāmadeva thereupon have been reported to have wandered throughout the length and breadth of Upper India. They went from Paṇḍharapūr by the Karhāḍa road, which is yet to be seen at Paṇḍharapūr, and then it is said that they went to Delhi and Benares and other places. After having finished the holy places, where they must have met and initiated a number of men into the line of the Saints, they returned to Paṇḍharapūr, probably about 1296 A.D. (Śake 1218) on the eleventh day of the bright half of the month of Kārttika, at the time of the great festival. After having finished the ceremony at Paṇḍharapūr on the full-moon day, Jñānadeva manifested a desire to Nāmadeva to go to Āḷandī, for he said he wanted to pass away from this world. Nāmadeva, along with a number of other great spiritual men, accompanied Jñānadeva and his brothers and sister from Paṇḍharapūr to Āḷandī, where on the eleventh day of the dark half of Kārttika, they kept awake the whole of the night, performing devotions to God. They filled the whole air with spiritual Kīrtanas. Having spent the twelfth day of the month in that manner, Jñānadeva told Nivṛittinātha on the thirteenth day that he would pass away that day. We are told in an Abhanga which is attributed to Jñānadeva himself that Jñānadeva sat performing Kīrtana and meditating on God, and that he passed away in that state:

ज्ञानदेवें घेतलें दान । हृदयीं धरोनियां ध्यान ।
समाधि बैसला निर्वाण । कथा कीर्तन करीतसे ॥

Nivṛittinātha placed a slab on the Samādhi of Jñāneśvara. This incident happened before the temple of Siddheśvara in Āḷandī which is to be seen even to-day. The temple contains an image of Śiva, and it seems Jñānadeva took Samādhi before that temple. The temple of Siddheśvara cannot itself be a Samādhi erected over the bones of another saint—a saint named Siddheśvara. It seems probable that it is a temple dedicated to God Śiva and called the Siddheśvara temple.

The face of Jñānadeva's Samādhi must have been in the direction of the temple of Siddheśvara, that is to say, to the west. This is a contrast with the description which Jñānadeva has given in the Jñāneśvarī that a mystic must pass off with his face turned towards the north. In any case, if God is both to the north and to the west, it matters not in what direction a mystic turns his face at the time of his death. It was even so with Jñānadeva. That he took Samādhi before the temple of Siddheśvara, is an undoubted fact. That this temple of Siddheśvara had been a place of pilgrimage long before Jñānadeva, is also established. That there was even the worship of Viṭṭhala in Āḷandī long before Jñānadeva was born a fact which we shall allude to somewhat later—is also established. Thus did happen that great incident: Jñānadeva passed off at Āḷandī, making Āḷandī one of the greatest places of pilgrimage on earth.

The Works of Jnanadeva.

11. The four great works of Jñānadeva are the Jñāneśvarī, the Amṛitānubhava, the Abhangas, and the Chāṅgadeva Pāsashṭī. Now nobody has doubted that the Jñāneśvarī and the Amṛitānubhava are from the same pen. The language, the ideas, and the vocabulary are so similar that they may be easily recognized as having come from the same pen. If, for example, in the Jñāneśvarī XVII. 3, Jñānadeva praises Nivṛittinātha as being superior to God Śiva ह्मणोनि शिवेसी कांटाळा । गुरुत्वें तूंचि आगळा, in the Amṛitānubhava likewise, he tells us that even Śiva asks an omen from Nivṛittinātha शिवही मुहूर्त पुसे । जया जोशियातें. But some doubt has been thrown upon whether the Abhangas and the Chāṅgadeva Pāsashṭī should be attributed to the same writer. As we shall see later, we have justification enough to say that they come from the same pen. As to whether, however, the Amṛitānubhava was written *after* the Jñāneśvarī or *before* it, opinions differ. According to one opinion, the Amṛitānubhava, even though an independent work, does not possess that high-flown philosophical and mystical sentiment which is the characteristic of the Jñāneśvarī, which, for that reason, is to be regarded as a later production. Prof. Patwardhan, for example, says that "the language, the vocabulary, and the imagery in the Amṛitānubhava are so scanty, poor, and monotonous as compared with that in the Jñānadevī that it may safely be concluded that the Amṛitānubhava preceded the Jñāneśvarī." On the other hand, there is a direct reference in the Amṛitānubhava to the treatment of a certain problem in the Jñāneśvarī, which makes the Amṛitānubhava appear to come later than the Jñāneśvarī. For example, when in the Amṛitānubhava, Jñānadeva says - वैकुंठींचेंनिही सुजाणें । ज्ञानपाशीं सत्त्वगुणें । बांधिजे हें निरूपण । बहु केलें ॥ that omniscient Being of Vaikuṇṭha has described at length how a man is tied by the Sattva quality with the rope of knowledge—which, as readers of the Jñāneśvarī are aware, is a direct reference to the treatment of the problem in that work on the verse in the Bhagavadgītā सुखसंगेन बध्नाति ज्ञानसंगेन चानघ (XIV. 6), we have to suppose that the Amṛitānubhava must have been written later than the Jñāneśvarī.

The Style of Jnanesvari.

12. As regards the style of the Jñāneśvarī, there rarely has been even in other languages another work which shows the same flights of imagination that Jñānadeva shows in his Jñāneśvarī. The employment of analogy at every step in the exposition of any philosophical problem was the most characteristic method in Jñānadeva's time. Wide world-experience is evinced by Jñānadeva at every step : it is really wonderful how at the young age of fifteen or nineteen, such a work should have been composed. Whence could the author have acquired such a vast experience of the world ? The treatment of any problem in the Jñāneśvarī is so lucid, so penetrating, and so full of the fervour of spiritual experience that every reader of it is forced to admit its claim to be regarded as the greatest work in the Marāṭhi language ever written. The Ovi which Jñānadeva employs is a form of the Abhanga itself. In fact, it is from Jñānadeva's Ovi that the Abhanga metre later sprang up. The Ovi of Jñānadeva, however, differs from the Ovi of Ekanātha, inasmuch as the one contains three lines and a half, and the other contains four lines and a half. But Jñānadeva's Ovi is incomparable. As Prof. Patwardhan says : "With Jñānadeva the Ovi trips, it gallops, it dances, it whirls, it ambles, it trots, it runs, it takes long leaps or short jumps, it halts or sweeps along, evolves a hundred and one graces of movement at the master's command. In the music of sound too it reveals a mysterious capacity of manifold evolution. The thrill, the quiver, the thunder, the bellow, the murmur, the grumble—in fact, every shade of sound it wields when occasion demands. It is an instrument that he has only to touch, and it responds to any key high or low, and to any note and tune." As regards the literary value of the work as a whole, we cannot do better than quote the same learned Professor once again : "The Jñānadevī is from the literary side so exquisite, so beautiful, so highly poetic in its metaphors and comparisons, similes and analogical illustrations, so perspicuous and lucid in style, so rich in fantasy, so delightful in its imagery, so lofty in its flights, so sublime in tone, so melodious in word-music, so original in its conceits, so pure in taste......that, notwithstanding the profundity, the recondite nature of the subject, and the inevitable limitations attendant upon the circumstance that the author's main object was to make the original intelligible, rather than add anything new, the reader is simply fascinated, floats rapturously on the crest of the flow, and is lost in the cadence of the rhythm and the sweet insinuating harmonies, till all is thanks-giving and thought is not."

The History of the Text of the Jnanesvari.

13. As regards the text of the Jñāneśvarī, we have to note that even though the actual text dictated to Sacchidānanda Bābā is not available, we have a very close approximation to it in the redaction of the original Jñāneśvarī which Ekanātha undertook in 1584 A.D. (Śake 1506). The incident of the redaction runs as follows. Ekanātha, three hundred years later, once suffered very acutely from a throat disease. While he was thus suffering, Jñānadeva appeared to him in a dream and told him that a root of the Ajāna tree at Āḷandī had encircled his neck, and that, therefore, Ekanātha should go to Āḷandī to extricate it from his neck ; upon which, Ekanātha went to Āḷandī and did as he was directed. The Abhanga which Ekanātha composed at the time of the incident runs as follows :

श्री ज्ञानदेवें येऊनी स्वप्नांत । सांगितली मात मजलागीं ॥ १ ॥

दिव्य तेजःपुंज मदनाचा पुतळा । परब्रह्म केवळ बोलतसे ॥ २ ॥

अजान वृक्षाची मुळी कंठास लागली । येऊनि आळंदीं काढ वेगीं ॥ ३ ॥

ऐसें स्वप्न होतां आलों अलंकापुरीं । तंव नदीमाझारीं देखिलें द्वार ॥ ४ ॥

एकाजनार्दनीं पूर्वपुण्य फळलें । श्रीगुरु भेटले ज्ञानेश्वर ॥ ५ ॥

We are told in this Abhanga that the way to the Samādhi of Jñānadeva was through a hole in the river. What we are at present shown in Āḷandī is the way of entrance to the inside of the Samādhi of Jñānadeva underneath the image of a Bull, situated between the Samādhi of Jñānadeva and the Liṅgam of Siddheśvara. If, therefore, Jñānadeva entered by that hole, it seems that the waters of the Indrāyaṇī at that time were running near the temple, and that the temple was situated in the bed of the river. Anyhow Ekanātha entered by that hole, did as directed, and probably found inspiration for a revision of the Jñāneśvarī when he went to visit that great Saint's shrine. The work which Ekanātha accomplished for the Jñāneśvarī is characterized by Mr. Bhāradvāja as having consisted in "the omitting of some verses, the putting in of new verses, transforming old word-forms and substituting new understandable forms". Now even though there might be some justification in saying that the language of Jñāneśvarī was modernized by Ekanātha, it is not true that Ekanātha took liberty with the verses in the Jñāneśvarī itself. From a remark which Ekanātha has himself left to us to the effect that anybody who would tamper with the text of the Jñāneśvarī by substituting any new verses "would be merely putting a cocoanut-shell in a disc of nectar", it seems that Ekanātha neither omitted any verses nor put in any new verses, but that he only modernized the text and made it accord with the idiom of his time. It is for this reason that Ekanātha's redaction of the Jñāneśvarī has been accepted as authoritative during the whole of the last three centuries. The edition which Rajavade has recently published consists of eighty-eight hundred ninety-six (8896) verses; while Ekanātha's edition consists of exactly nine thousand (9000) verses. Rajavade claims that his edition is even older than that which Ekanātha found and used for preparing a correct text of the Jñāneśvarī in his time. Another attempt was being made by Mr. Madagaonkar for bringing to light what he regarded to be the only correct text of that work. Unfortunately this work has not seen the light of day, although Madagaonkar's earlier edition of the Jñānadevī, which does not differ materially from the text of Ekanātha, is available. As to the actual text Ekanātha used for the improvement of the Jñāneśvarī, we have not yet material enough to judge; but let us hope that during the course of time some new discoveries may enable us to see what text Ekanātha himself used, so that by collating all the early texts available, we may approximate as much as possible to the original text of the Jñāneśvarī.

The Problem of two Jnanadevas.

14. When we come to the consideration of Jñāneśvara's Abhangas, we are landed into a problem which has become the crux of Jñānadeva scholarship during the last half century. Bhāradvāja wrote certain articles in which he tried to prove that the Jñānadeva of the Abhangas was not the same as the Jñānadeva of the Jñāneśvarī, or the Amṛitānubhava. He urges that the author of the Jñāneśvarī lived and died in Āpegaon; and that he was a Śaiva and not a follower of the Paṇḍharī Sāmpradāya. On the other hand, the author of the Abhangas lived and died in Āḷandī; he was under Mahānubhāvic influence, and yet was a devotee of Paṇḍharī. The arguments which he adduces for his position are as follows:

(1) The style, the language and the ideas of the Abhangas and of the Jñāneśvarī are profoundly different.

(2) That the Abhangas contain only Viṭṭhala worship, and that there is no mention of Viṭṭhala, or Viṭṭhala Sāmpradāya, in the Jñāneśvarī.

(3) That in Āpegaon there are two Samādhis joined together, one of which may be said to be that of Jñānadeva; and that in the records of the Kulkarni of that place, we find the entry that a certain land has been dedicated to this Samādhi of Jñānadeva: "ज्ञानदेवाचे समाधीकडे". Let us consider carefully what validity there is for these arguments.

The Linguistic and Ideological Similarity of the Jnanesvari and the Abhangas.

15. The main platform of the contention, that the Jñānadeva of the Abhangas and the Jñānadeva of the Jñāneśvarī are different, is that there is no linguistic or ideological similarity between the Abhangas and the Jñāneśvarī. This is entirely a mis-conception. The fact that the Abhangas now appear to be in a simpler dress than the Jñāneśvarī is due to their having been committed to memory for six centuries past, and then reproduced through memory. This should account for the comparative modernness of the style of the Abhangas. It is for this reason that we might even say that the Amṛitānubhava looks older than the Jñāneśvarī, because the Amṛitānubhava is not so much reproduced or memorized as the Jñāneśvarī itself. This argument from the modernity of style has not been carefully made. When Prof. Patwardhan makes mention of the fact that there is no linguistic similarity between the Abhangas and the Jñāneśvarī, he forgets the entire repertory of old worlds which we find in the Abhangas as in the Jñāneśvarī. Thus, for example, the words साइखेडिया, बिक, पातेजोनि, नीचनवा, बरवंट, बुंथी, गळाळा, संवसाटी and a host of others are common both to the Abhangas and the Jñāneśvarī. He must be a bold man who says that the Abhangas do not contain the peculiar vocabulary of the Jñāneśvarī. The fact that in the Abhangas many words do not appear with the same case-terminations as in the Jñāneśvarī is due to the clothing which these words assumed in course of time having been reproduced from memory. But if we go to the root-words, we shall find that there is a great deal of identity between the Abhangas and the Jñāneśvarī. Nor does the argument from lesser brilliance of the Abhangas in point of ideas as compared with the Jñāneśvarī hold much water. We have no hesitation in saying that the Abhangas are as brilliant in ideas, if not even more, than the Jñāneśvarī. They bespeak the very heart of Jñānadeva. The Abhangas are the emotional garb of Jñānadeva; the Jnāneśvarī is an intellectual garb; and thus we see the heart of Jñānadeva, his personal experience, and his outlook upon the world depicted even more adequately in the Abhangas than in the Jñāneśvarī. To add to this, we have to consider how very similar in ideology the Abhangas and the Jñāneśvarī are. The Abhanga मलयानिळ शीतळु, सुमनाचा परिमळु, गुंफितां नये is entirely reminiscent of a famous passage from the Jñāneśvarī. The Abhanga काय राजयाची कांता भीक मागे is reminiscent of a similar passage in the 12th Chapter of the Jñāneśvarī. The Abhanga कल्पतरुतळवटीं is reminiscent of a similar passage in the ninth Chapter of the Jñāneśvarī. The Abhanga सर्पें दर्दुर धरला रे मुखीं। तंव तेणें माशी तोंडीं धरियेली शेखीं, as well as the Abhanga काम, क्रोध, मद, मत्सराचेनि गुणें। बांधला आपण नेणें भ्रमितु जैसा। किंवा मोहफांसा शुक नाळिके तैसा॥ puts us wholly in mind of similar passages in the Jñāneśvarī. The Abhanga दिसतें परी न हालवें। तें संतातें पुसावें calls our mind to a passage from the Jñāneśvarī XVIII तैसें हारपलें आपणपें फावें। तैं संतातें पाहतां गिंवसावें॥. There is an ideological similarity not merely between the Abhangas and the Jñāneśvarī, but between the Abhangas and the Amṛitānubhava itself. The Abhanga मृगजळाच्या जळीं। चारिशीं जळचरें is entirely reminiscent of the Amṛitānubhava. The Abhanga निशी दिवस दोघे लोपले ते ठायीं। निरंजन ते ठायीं लक्षुनि पहा॥ रवी शशी ज्याचे तेजें प्रकाशले। नवल म्यां देखिलें एक तेथें॥ नारी पुरुष दोघे एकरूपें दिसती। देखणें पारुखे तये ठायीं॥ ज्ञानदेव ह्मणे शिव तेचि शक्ति॥ as well as the Abhanga ज्ञानदेव ह्मणे शिव तेचि शक्ति। पाहतां व्यक्ति व्यक्त नाहीं॥ are an identification Amṛitānubhava-wise of Śiva and Śakti. Also the whole Abhanga कांहीं न करिजे ते तुझी सेवा। कांहीं नव्हेसी तें तूं देवा॥ नेणिजे तें तुझें रूप। जाणिजे तितुकें पाप गा देवा॥ स्तुति ते तुझी निंदा। स्तुतिजोगा नव्हेसी गोविंदा॥ recalls similar utterances from the Amṛitānubhava. After a careful study of this extreme similarity of ideas between the Abhangas and the Jñāneśvarī on the one hand, and the Abhangas and the Amṛitānubhava on the other, nobody will dare to say that they are not from the same pen.

Vitthala-Bhakti in the Jnanesvari.

16. As regards the question that there is no mention of Viṭṭhala and the Viṭṭhala Sāmpradāya in the Jñāneśvarī and that in the Abhangas Viṭṭhala alone is mentioned, we might remember that one most significant fact has escaped the attention of the students of Jñāneśvarī till now. In the twelfth Chapter of the Jñāneśvarī from verse 214 downwards we have a reference to the image of Viṭṭhala holding the Liṅgam of Śiva on the head. The fact that the image of Viṭṭhala at Paṇḍharapūr was said to have held over its head the Liṅgam of Śiva is attested to both by Nivṛittinātha, and later by Rāmadāsa. We read in one of the Abhangas of Nivṛittinātha पुंडलिकाचें भाग्य वर्णावया अमरीं । नाहीं चराचरीं ऐसा कोणी । विष्णुसहित शिव आणिला पंढरीं । भीमातीरीं पेखणें जेणें ॥ and also in Rāmadāsa विठोनें शिरीं वाहिला देवराणा ॥. The passage from the Jñāneśvarī, to which we invite attention, and where there seems to be a direct reference to Viṭṭhala as holding the Liṅgam of Śiva on the head, is as follows:—

मग यावरीही पार्था । माझ्या भजनीं आस्था । तरी तयातें मी माथां । मुकुट करीं ॥ उत्तमासि मस्तक । खालविजे हें काय कौतुक । परी मान करिती तीन्ही लोक । पायवणियां ॥ तरि श्रद्धावस्तूसि आदरू । करितां जाणिजे प्रकारू । जरी होय श्रीगुरू । सदाशिव ॥ परि हें असो आतां । महेशातें वानितां । आत्मस्तुती होतां । संचार असे ॥ ययालागीं हें नोहे । ह्मणितलें रमानाहें । अर्जुना मी वाहे । शिरीं तयातें ॥ (ज्ञा. XII. 214—218.)

This is as much as to say that Śiva who was the greatest devotee of Vishṇu was himself held aloft on his head by Vishṇu in the form of Viṭṭhala. Now as no other image of Vishṇu has been known to have held the Liṅgam of Śiva on its head, there is an unmistakable reference here to the image of Viṭṭhala at Paṇḍharpūr which bears the Liṅgam of Śiva on its head. To add to this, we must remember that Viṭṭhala-Bhakti was prevalent even in Āḷandī about seventy years before the birth of Jñānadeva. There is an inscription in the Maṭha of Hariharendra Swāmi dated 1209 A.D. (Śake 1131), that is, nearly seventy years before the birth of Jñānadeva, where the images of both Viṭṭhala and Rakhumāi are carved on a stone-slab on the pedestal of the Samādhi. This is the earliest reference hitherto found to the prevalent Viṭṭhala Sāmpradāya even in Āḷandī. Moreover, we cannot say that the references to Kṛishṇa and Vishṇu in the Jñāneśvarī are not references to Viṭṭhala. To Jñānadeva as to other devotees of Paṇḍhari, Viṭṭhala and Kṛishṇa are identical. This fact is also symbolized by Rakhumāi who was the wife of Kṛishṇa in his former incarnation being also the wife of Viṭṭhala, by the Gopāḷapura, by the cowherd's and the cow's foot-prints in the sands of the Bhīma being all reminiscences of the Kṛishṇa incarnation. In the Jñāneśvarī we have a reference to Kṛishṇa and Vishṇu in a very famous passage कृष्ण विष्णु हरि गोविंद । या नामाचे निखिल प्रबंध । माजी आत्मचर्चा विशद । उदंड गातीं (Jñāneśvarī, IX. 210). Nor can we say that there is no mention of the Sāmpradāya of Viṭṭhala-Bhakti in the Jñāneśvarī. Though the word Viṭṭhala may not have been mentioned, the word Santa which is amply indicative of the

Viṭṭhala Sāmpradāya is mentioned very often: आत्मज्ञानें चोखडीं । संत हे माझीं रूपडीं ॥ (Jñā., XVIII. 1356), संतातें पाहतां गिवसावें । (Jñā., 18), ज्ञानदेव ह्मणे तुम्हीं संत वोळगावेति आम्हीं । हें पढविलों जी स्वामी निवृत्तिदेवीं (Jñā., XII). This last reference to the Santas unmistakably points out that Nivṛittinātha had taught Jñāneśvara to respect the Santas. Now Santa is almost a technical word in the Viṭṭhala Sāmpradāya, and means any man who is a follower of that Sāmpradāya. Not that the followers of other Sāmpradāyas are not Santas, but the followers of the Vārakarī Sāmpradāya are Santas *par excellence*. Also Jñāṇadeva makes unmistakable reference to the Kīrtana method of the popularization of Bhakti, which is also peculiarly indicative of Viṭṭhala Sāmpradāya: कीर्तनाचेनि नटनाचें । नाशिले व्यवसाय प्रायश्चित्ताचे । जें नांवचि नाहीं पापाचें । ऐसें केलें ॥. From all these references it is evident that we cannot say that Viṭṭhala or Viṭṭhala-Bhakti is not referred to in the Jñāneśvarī itself. Jñānadeva was a very broad-minded and liberal mystic, and to him Śaivism and Vaishnavism were identical, not to speak of the different kinds of Bhakti in Vaishṇavism itself. If Jñānadeva regards even the Liṅgam of Śiva as worthy of being worshipped along with any image of Vishṇu, we cannot say that he made a hard and fast distinction between the worship of Kṛishṇa, and the worship of Viṭṭhala. In the seventeenth Chapter of the Jñāneśvarī in the 204th verse, we read लिंग का प्रतिमा दिठी, which implies according to the author that the Liṅgam or an image of God may be promiscuously worshipped by a devotee. Also in the Jñāneśvarī, XVII. 223, we read that God may be meditated upon either by the Śaivite name or by the Vaishṇavite name: नातरी एकादें नांव । तेंचि शैव कां वैष्णव । वाचे वसे तें वाग्भव । तप जाणावें ॥ (Jñā., 223). We have further a reference to the Ātmaliṅga: तुझी आण वाहणें । तें आत्मलिंगातें शिवणें, not to mention the famous reference to Adhyātma-liṅga in the Jñāneśvarī itself. All these facts unmistakably point out that even in the Jñāneśvarī, Jñānadeva regarded Śaivism and Vaishṇavism as of equal count. This same fact is also attested to in the very famous Abhangas of Jñānadeva where the Liṅgam or the Ātmaliṅga has been described with great mystic fervour. We thus see that both in the Jñāneśvarī and in the Abhangas we have a mention of the worship of the Liṅgam as on a par with the worship of either Kṛishṇa or Viṭṭhala. It matters not to Jñānadeva what deity one worships, provided one worships rightly and earnestly. The fact that he took Samādhi before Siddheśvara, or that Śiva occupies a prominent part in the Amṛitānubhava, is not indicative of Jñānadeva's exclusive partisanship to Śiva worship.

The Samadhi at Apegaon and the Samadhi at Alandi.

17. It has been contended that there is a Samādhi of Jñānadeva at Āpegaon, and that there is a piece of land made over to that Samādhi as recorded in the Daftars of the Kulkarṇi of Āpegaon. The whole history of the existence of the two Samādhis at Āpegaon, one of which is said to be Jñānadeva's, is as follows. There is a joint Samādhi probably erected in honour of two different persons, as there are two different sets of Pādukās on the Samādhi. There are images of Viṭṭhala and Rakhumāi behind the Samādhi. There are two Utsavas of that joint Samādhi ; one from Vaiśākha Vadya 10 to Jyeshṭha Śuddha 1 and the other from Kārttika Vadya 12 to 13 ; of these the more important is the first. It seems probable that one of the Samādhis is erected in honour of an ancestor of Jñānadeva, probably Tryambakapant. Muktābāi tells us that Tryambakapant had such a Samādhi in Āpegaon : भक्त त्र्यंबकपंत मूळ पुरुष आधीं । तयाची समाधि आपेगांवीं ॥. The question is in whose honour the second Samādhi is erected, or the second Utsava is made. The probability is that the second Samādhi belongs to Viṭṭhalapant, or it may even be an imitation Samādhi of Jñānadeva. It is not uncustomary among the Hindus to erect many different Samādhis in honour of the same person at different places, though the original and the most important Samādhi may be at one central place only. Even as there are Samādhis of Jñānadeva at Nānaja and at Pusesavaḷī in the Sātārā District, it is very likely that the residents of Āpegaon may have erected a Samādhi to Jñānadeva at his native place, in order to commemorate the fact of his being a resident of that place. If it be contended that there is an Inām land made over to the Samādhi of Jñānadeva at Āpegaon, it must also be remembered that there are an infinite number of Inām lands made over to the Samādhi of Jñānadeva at Āḷandī. A very important fact which goes against the identification of the second Samādhi at Āpegaon as that of Jñānadeva, who *ex hypothesi* was a Śaiva, is that there are images of Viṭṭhala and Rakhumāi behind the Samādhi at Āpegaon. If it were true that the author of the Jñāneśvarī was only a Śaiva, no images of Viṭṭhala and Rakhumāi could have been erected behind his Samādhi. On the other hand, on this hypothesis, the Jñānadeva of Āḷandī whose Samādhi is before the Liṅgam of Śiva, must himself be regarded for that reason as the author of the Jñāneśvarī. The Utsava that is performed at Āpegaon on Kārttika Vadya 12 and 13 must be merely " in memory of" the Samādhi of the great saint at Āḷandī. Just as a saint's Puṇyatithi may be performed wherever his disciples are, similarly even here, the Puṇyatithi of Jñānadeva, even though he took Samādhi at Āḷandī, may have been customarily performed at Āpegaon. It is evident thus that we need not postulate two different Jñānadevas, one the author of the Jñāneśvarī, and the other, the author of the Abhangas. If this were a fact, we would have to understand that there are two Nivṛittināthas also: one the Nivṛittinātha of the Jñāneśvarī, and the other the Nivṛittinātha of the Abhangas. It would thus follow that two Jñānadevas were born in two different centuries, but in the same place, namely, Āpegaon; that they had brothers of the same name, namely, Nivṛittinātha; that their Samādhis were in two different places, one at Āpegaon, and the other at Āḷandī; and most extraordinarily that the dates of the two Samādhis were so coincidently one, that the two different Utsavas of the two different Jñānadevas were performed on the same day! Moreover, we must remember that the tradition of two different Jñānadevas is entirely unknown to Nāmadeva, Gorā Kumbhāra, Janābāi and other Saints. Ekanātha took the Jñānadeva of Āḷandī to be the real Jñānadeva. The infinite number of pilgrims that have been visiting the shrine of the great saint at Āḷandī for the last six centuries are also evidence of the fact that the Jñānadeva of Āḷandī may be taken to be the real Jñānadeva, and that if there is a Samādhi at Āpegaon, it must be regarded as merely an imitation or a memory Samādhi of Jñānadeva. For all these reasons it is evidently impossible to make a distinction between the Śaivite Jñānadeva of Āpegaon of the thirteenth century, and the Vārakarī Jñānadeva of Āḷandī of the fourteenth century. The hypothesis is gratuitous, and nothing is gained and much is lost in the domain of Jñāneśvara scholarship by that unwarranted hypothesis.

The Passing away of the Brothers and Sister of Jnanadeva.

18. As regards the dates of the Samādhis of the brothers and sister of Jñānadeva, we know that very soon after the date of the Samādhi of Jñānadeva, Sopāna passed away first, and then Muktābāi, and last of all, Nivṛittinātha. Sopāna's Samādhi is at Sāsavaḍa. Muktābāi's Samādhi is at Edalābāda; and Nivṛittinātha's Samādhi is at Tryambakeśvara. There is a beautiful story which tells us that Muktābāi passed away in a flash of lightning while performing a Kīrtana. The story of the disappearance of Muktābāi in the flash of lightning may have been due to such an Abhanga from Jñānadeva as follows:

मोतियांचा चूर फेकिला अंबरीं । विजुचिया परी कीळ झालें ॥
जरी पितांबरें नेसविलें नभा । चैतन्याचा गाभा नीळबिंदु ॥
तळीं वरी पसरे शून्याकार झालें । सर्पाचेंही पिलें नाचूं लागे ॥
कडकडोनि वीज निमाली ठायींचे ठायीं । भेटली मुक्ताई गोरोबाला ॥
ज्ञानदेव ह्मणे कैसी झाली भेट । ओळखिलें अविट आपुलेंपण ॥

" The powder of pearls was thrown in the skies. There was a brilliant flash of lightning. The sky was clothed in beautiful purple. The brilliant blue point began to shine......A serpent's young one began to dance. In a dazzling thunder, the lightning disappeared in itself. Muktābāi met Goroba. In that meeting, says Jñānadeva, Self-knowledge came to be known."

The Personality of Changadeva.

19. Chāṅgadeva, who has been treated along with these four Saints, is a typical example of how a man may take to the life of Haṭhayoga and ultimately finding it barren of spiritual experience, may then take resort to the truly spiritual life. Tradition says that Chāṅgadeva lived for fourteen hundred years, which evidently is an impossibility. The meaning of the statement may only be that there were different Chāṅgadevas of the same name, or there must be the same Chāṅgadeva who got different names in different places which he visited, or that it was a family appellation used by all. Niḷobā tells us in his Abhangas that there were fourteen different names of Chāṅgadeva, which might be a reason why Chāṅgadeva may have been supposed to have lived for fourteen hundred years. It was not uncustomary in ancient times for a wise man to be known by different names. Ātmārāma, the biographer of Rāmadāsa, tells us in his Dāsaviśrāmadhāma that Rāmadāsa was himself known as Vipra, Fakīrajindā, Ramīrāmadāsa and so on. Even so, it might be the case with Chāṅgadeva. Two of the names of Chāṅgadeva especially have been mentioned in the Chāṅgadeva Pāsashṭī : Vateśachāṅgā, and Chakrapānīchāṅgā, which two names then must be identified. Chāṅgadeva may have been known as Vateśachāṅgā after the deity whom he worshipped. It seems that Chāṅgadeva may have acquired certain powers by means of his Haṭhayoga. But, when he met Jñānadeva and others, his arrogance disappeared, and he began to pine after spiritual life. The Chāṅgadeva Pāsashṭī was composed by Jñānadeva just at this time. It embodies an Advaitic advice to Chāṅgadeva. We have shown later that the Chāṅgadeva Pāsashṭī cannot be regarded as a work of the Mahānubhāva Chakradhara, whom

Chandorkar identifies with Chakrapāṇī who is mentioned in the Chāṅgadeva Pāsashṭī. The many similarities between the Chāṅgadeva Pāsashṭī and other works of Jñānadeva point out unmistakably that the Chāṅgadeva Pāsashṭī must have been written by Jñānadeva himself. Just as in the case of the Abhangas, so even here, the similarities between the Chāṅgadeva Pāsashṭī and other works of Jñānadeva are too numerous to be treated with unconcern. A writer has pointed out that for almost every sentence in the Chāṅgadeva Pāsashṭī, we can find a parallel in the other works of Jñānadeva. It seems that Chāṅgadeva was initiated by Muktābāi in the spiritual line. What Muktābāi may have told Chāṅgadeva may be seen from the account of their meeting we have quoted at the end of the present part of the work. Chāṅgadeva died on the Godāvarī in 1305 A.D. (Śake 1227), that is to say, some ten years after Jñānadeva, Muktābāi, and others. He could very well say in pride that he was the culmination of the spiritual knowledge of Nivṛittināatha, Jñānadeva, Sopāna and Muktābāi. In a beautiful Abhanga Chāṅgadeva tells us—

मोतियाचें पाणी रांजण भरिला । पोट भरुनी प्याला ज्ञानदेव ॥
अभ्राची साउली धरोनियां हातीं । गेलासे एकांतीं निवृत्तिदेव ॥
पुष्पाचा परिमळ वेगळा काढिला । तो हार लेइला सोपानदेव ॥
हिऱ्याच्या घुगऱ्या जेवण जेवली । पोट भरुनी घाली मुक्ताबाई ॥
चौघांचें वर्म आलें असे हातां । वटेश्वर स्वतां तये ठायीं ॥

"Jñānadeva drank to his fill the water of pearls; Nivṛittinātha caught in his hands the shade of the clouds; Sopāna decorated himself with the garland of fragrance; Muktābāi fed herself on cooked diamonds; the secret of all four has come to my hands, says Chāṅgadeva."

CHAPTER III.

The Jnanesvari.

Place and Time of the Composition of the Jnanesvari.

1. Jñāneśvara himself gives us the time and place of the composition of the Jñāneśvarī at the end of his work. He tells us that "in the domain of Mahārāshṭra, on the southern bank of the Godāvarī, there is a temple of Mahālayā or Mohinīrāja, famous through all the worlds, and the centre of the life-activity of the world. There Rāmachandra reigns, who is a descendant of Yādava lineage, the support of all arts and sciences, and a just ruler of the world. In his reign was the Gītā dressed in the attire of Marāṭhi by the disciple of Śri Nivṛittinātha who carries back his spiritual lineage to the God Maheśa.... This commentary was written by Jñāneśvara in the Śaka year 1212, Sachhidānanda Bābā having served as a devout amanuensis" (XVIII. 1803-1811). It seems from this that the Jñāneśvarī was written in the year 1290 A.D. Till about three hundred years later the Jñāneśvarī was handed down in MS. form from generation to generation of spiritual aspirants, thus necessitating many changes of reading, and even accretions to and omissions from the original. It was not till Ekanātha took up the work of preparing an authenticated and careful text of the Jñāneśvarī in the Śaka year 1512, corresponding to the year 1590 A.D., that the new era of the study of the Jñāneśvarī might be said to have dawned. Ekanātha tells us with full respect for the author and his work, that he undertook to prepare a correct text of the Jñāneśvarī, because, "even though the work was extremely accurate originally, still it had become spoilt by changes of reading during the interim". It seems that Ekanātha did not tamper with the text at all. He only judiciously substituted correct readings here and there, and thus finally fashioned the work as we have it to-day. Anybody, who adds a verse to the text of the Jñāneśvarī, he says, would be thereby merely "placing a cocoanut-shell in a disc of nectar", implying thereby that nobody should be bold enough to add to the incomparable text of the Jñāneśvarī.

The Spiritual Lineage of Jnanesvara.

2. We also learn from the epilogue to the Jñāneśvarī the spiritual lineage of Jñāneśvara. We cannot say that the account does not contain some mythological elements. Any spiritual lineage, which is carried back to a time where history and memory fail, is bound to suffer from such defects. We are told by Jñāneśvara that "While the spiritual secret was being imparted by Śaṅkara to Pārvatī once upon a time, it caught the ear of Matsyendranātha, who was lying hidden in the bosom of a great fish in the ocean. Matsyendranātha met the broken-limbed Chauraṅgīnātha on the Saptaśṛiṅga mountain, immediately upon which the latter became whole. Then, in order that he might enjoy undisturbed repose, Matsyendranātha gave to Gorakshanātha the power of spreading spiritual knowledge. From Gorakshanātha, the spiritual secret of Śaṅkara descended to Gainīnātha, who seeing that the world had come under the thraldom of evil, communicated it to Nivṛittinātha with this charge 'the spiritual secret, which has come down to us straight from the first teacher Śaṅkara, take thou this, and give succour to those who are afflicted with evil in this world.' Already compassionate as he was, with the super-added weight of this charge of his spiritual teacher, Nivṛittinātha was as much encouraged to action as a cloud during the rainy season; and then, even like the latter, poured forth the stream of spiritual wisdom with the intention of bringing succour to the afflicted. Jñāneśvara was merely like a Chātaka bird catching a few drops of that gracious rain, which are herewith exhibited in the form of this commentary on the Bhagavadgītā" (XVIII. 1751—1763). It is noticeable that Jñāneśvara here gives an account of his spiritual lineage, bringing it down from the age of Śaṅkara through Matsyendranātha and Gorakshanātha to Gainīnātha and Nivṛittinātha, of whom latter he was the immediate disciple. This account could be confirmed by references in other parts of Jñāneśvara's writings, but coming as it does towards the end of his most important work, the Jñāneśvarī, the present reference has a value absolutely beyond parallel.

Jnanesvara's Respect for his Guru.

3. Jñāneśvara is so much possessed by devotion to his Guru that he cannot but give vent to his feelings for his master from time to time. In the first Chapter, he speaks of his master as having enabled him to cross the ocean of existence; as when proper collyrium is administered to one's eyes, they are able to see anything whatsoever, and forthwith any hidden treasure; as when the wish-jewel has come to hand, our desires are all fulfilled; similarly in and through Nivṛittinātha, says Jñāneśvara, all his desires have been fulfilled. As when a tree is watered at the bottom, it goes out to the branches and the foliage; as when a man has taken a bath in the sea, he may be said to have bathed in all the holy waters of the world; as when nectar has once been enjoyed, all the flavours are forthwith enjoyed; similarly, when the Guru has been worshipped, all the desires become fulfilled (I. 22—27).

The Grace of the Guru is competent to all things.

4. Jñāneśvara tells us again in the sixth Chapter that what is difficult of comprehension even by intellect, one may be able to visualise by the light of the grace of Nivṛittināthа. "That which the eye cannot see, he will be able to see without the eye, if only he gets super-consciousness; that which the alchemists vainly seek after, may be found even in iron, provided the Parisa comes to hand; similarly, where there is the grace of the Guru, what cannot be obtained, asks Jñāneśvara? He is rich with the infinite grace of his Guru' (VI. 32—35).

The Power of the Guru is indescribable.

5. Moreover, Jñāneśvara tells us that he cannot adequately praise the greatness of the Guru. Is it possible, he asks, to add lustre to the sun? Is it possible to crown the Kalpataru with flowers? Is it possible to add a scent to camphor? How can the sandal tree be made more fragrant? How can nectar be re-dressed for meals? ....How can one add a hue to the pearl? Or what is the propriety of giving a silver polish to gold? It is better that one should remain silent, and silently bow to the feet of his master (X. 9—15).

Invocations to the Guru.

6. That the Guru is the sole absorbing topic of Jñāneśvara's attention, may also be proved from the way in which he writes many a prologue to his various chapters addressed to the greatness of the Guru. Thus, for example, Chapters 12, 13, 14 and 15 of the Jñāneśvarī all begin with an invocation to the grace of the Guru. In the beginning of the twelfth Chapter we read how Jñāneśvara speaks of the gracious eye of his teacher, making poisonless the fangs of the serpent of sense. How is it possible, he asks, when the grace of the Guru comes down in floods, that the scorching heat of Samsāra may continue to burn one with grief? The grace of the Guru, like a true mother, rears up the spiritual aspirant on the lap of the Ādhāra Śakti, and swings him to and fro in the cradle of the heart; like a true mother, again, the grace of the Guru waves lights of spiritual illumination before the aspirant, and puts on him the ornaments of spiritual gold. The grace of the Guru again rears him on the milk of the 17th Kala, sounds the toy of the Anahata

Nāda, and puts him to sleep in ecstasy. A true lover of the Marāṭhi language as he was, Jñāneśvara finally calls upon the grace of his teacher to fill the domain of the Marāṭhi language with the crop of spiritual knowledge (XII. 1—19). In the beginning of the thirteenth Chapter Jñāneśvara speaks of the praise of his Guru as being the cause of the knowledge of all the sciences, and as so filling his own literary expression that even nectar might be eclipsed by its mellifluity (XIII. 1—5). In the beginning of the fourteenth Chapter he speaks of the vision of the Guru as eclipsing the appearance of the universe, and as making it appear only when it itself recedes in the background. As when the sun shines on the horizon, the moon fades away in the background, similarly when the Guru shines, all the sciences fade away. It is thus that the only adequate way of expressing one's appreciation of the greatness of the Guru is to submit in silence to the feet of the Guru, for the greatness of the Guru can never be adequately praised (XIV. 1—16). Similarly at the beginning of the fifteenth Chapter, Jñāneśvara speaks allegorically of the worship of his Guru. "Let me make my heart the seat for the Guru, and let me place upon it my Guru's feet. Let all my senses sing the chorus of unity, and throw upon the feet of the Guru a handful of flowers of praise. Let me apply to the feet of the Guru a fingerful of sandal ointment, made pure by the consideration of identity. Let me put upon his feet ornaments of spiritual gold...... Let me place upon them the eight-petalled flower of pure joy. Let me burn the essence of egoism, wave the lights of self-annihilation, and cling to the feet of the Guru with the feeling of absorption" (XV. 1—7).

Nivrittinatha, identified with the Sun of Reality.

7. Jñāneśvara is so full of respect for his teacher that he feels that any words of praise that may issue out of him would fall short of the description of the true greatness of Nivṛittināthа. A poor man is so filled with delight by looking at an ocean of nectar that he goes forth to make an offering to it of ordinary vegetables. In that case, what is to be appraised is not the offering of the vegetables itself, but the spirit with which they are offered. When little lights are waved before God, who is an ocean of light, we have only to take into account the spirit in which the lights are waved. A child plays in all manner of ways with its mother, but the mother takes into account only the spirit in which the child is playing. If a small brook carries water to a river, does the river throw it out, simply because it comes from a brook? It is thus that

I approach thee with words of praise, says Jñāneśvara to Nivṛittinātha, and if they are inadequate, it behoves thee only to forgive their puerile simplicity (XVI. 17—30).

The Humility of Jnanesvara.

8. Jñāneśvara is only too conscious of the fact that the work he has written is destined to be one of the greatest works of the world; and yet he never takes to himself the pride and the credit of its composition. We have already alluded to the fact that Jñāneśvara regards himself as a Chātaka bird, in whose up-turned opened bill, the cloud of Nivṛittinātha's grace sends down drops of rain. If a man is fortunate, says Jñāneśvara, even sand can be turned into gold......If it pleases God, even pebbles, put into boiled water, may turn out to be well-prepared rice. When the Guru has accepted the disciple, the whole Samsāra becomes full of joy......In this very wise, was my own ignorance turned to knowledge by the grace of Nivṛittinātha (XV. 18—28). As Jñāneśvara is mindful of the grace of his Guru in the composition of his work, even likewise is he only too cognisant of the fact that the other saints beside his own teacher have also had a share in its production. 'If you teach a parrot', he says to the Saints, 'will it not give out proper words at the right time ?......This plant of spiritual wisdom has been sown by you, O Saints! It now behoves you to rear it up by your considerate attention; then, this plant will flower, and produce fruits of various kinds, and by your kindness, it will be a source of solace to the world......Did not the plant-eating monkeys of the forest go forth to meet the hosts of the king of Laṅkā, simply because they were inspired by the Divine Power of Rāma ? Was not Arjuna, though single-handed, able to conquer the vast hosts of his enemy by the power of Śri Kṛishṇa ? (XI. 17—23.) Finally, Jñāneśvara tells us how he is merely treading the path which was first treaded by the great Vyāsa; how he has been merely putting in the language of Marāṭhi the great words of Vyāsa. If God is pleased with the flowers of Vyāsa, asks Jñāneśvara, would he refuse the little Dūrvās that I may offer to him ? If large elephants come to the shores of an ocean, is a small swan prevented thereby from coming ?......If the swan walks gracefully on earth, does it forbid any other creature from walking ?......If the sky is mirrored in an ocean, could it be prevented from appearing in a small pond ?......It is thus that I am trying to scent the path of Vyāsa, taking the help of the commentators on my journey. Moreover, am I not the disciple of Nivṛittinātha, asks Jñāneśvara, whose power fills the earth, and both animate and inanimate existence? Is it not by his power that the moon tranquils the earth by her nectar-like light? Does not his power fill the lustre of the Sun? That Nivṛittinātha inhabits my heart. It is thus that every new breath of mine is turning into a poem; or what is not the grace of the Guru competent to do? (XVIII. 1708—1735.) Jñāneśvara feels himself to be merely an instrument in the hands of his Guru, to whose real authorship the whole of his work is due.

I. Metaphysics.

The Prakriti and the Purusha.

9. The Jñāneśvarī, being essentially an expositional work, follows the metaphysical lines laid down in its prototype, the Bhagavadgītā. Now as the relation between the Prakṛiti and the Purusha forms one of the most important items of the metaphysics of the Bhagavadgītā, it has also formed one of the foundation-stones of the metaphysics of the Jñāneśvarī. Jñāneśvara reverts from time to time to the description of the Prakṛiti and the Purusha. In the ninth Chapter, he tells us how Ātman is the eternal Spectator while Prakṛiti is the uniform Actor. It is said, says Jñāneśvara, that a town is built by a king; but does it forthwith follow that the king has constructed it with his own hands? As the subjects of a town follow each his own profession, being all presided over by the king, similarly, the Prakṛiti does everything and stands in the background. When the full moon shines on the horizon, the ocean experiences a great flood; but does it follow from this that the moon is put to any trouble? A piece of iron moves merely on account of the vicinity of a magnet; but the magnet itself does not suffer action.........As a lamp, placed in a corner, is the cause neither of action nor of non-action, similarly, I am the eternal spectator, while the beings follow each its own course (IX. 110—129). In the thirteenth Chapter, Jñāneśvara again takes up the problem of the relation of the Prakṛiti and the Purusha, and exhibits it by means of a variety of images. The Purusha, when he informs the body, undergoes the appellation of a self-conscious being. This consciousness is displayed in the body from the very nails of the body to the hair of the head, and is the cause of the flowering of the mind and intellect, as the spring is the cause of flowering in the forest.......The king never knows his army, and yet simply by his order the army is able to overcome enemies......By the simple presence of the Sun, all people go about doing their actions; by simply looking at its young ones is the female tortoise able to nourish them; in a similar manner, the simple presence of the Ātman inside causes the movement of the inanimate body (XIII. 134—141). The thirteenth Chapter is the *locus classicus* of the description of the Prakṛiti and the Purusha. In the Bhagavadgītā, as in the Jñāneśvarī, the Prakṛiti and the Purusha, we are told, are both of them co-born and co-eternal. The Purusha is synonymous of existence, the Prakṛiti of action. The Purusha enjoys both happiness and sorrow, emerging from the good and the bad actions of the Prakṛiti. Un-nameable indeed is the companionship of the Prakṛiti and the Purusha; the female earns, and the male enjoys; the female never comes into contact with the male, and yet the female is able to produce. The Prakṛiti is bodiless, the Purusha is lame and older than the old......The Prakṛiti takes on new shapes every moment, and is made up of form and qualities. She is able to move even the inanimate......She is the mint of sound, the fount and source of all miraculous things; both generation and decay proceed from her; she is verily the infatuating agent; she is the being of the self-born being; she is the form of the formless; she is the quality of the quality-less, the eye of the eyeless, the ear of the earless, the feet of the feetless; in her, indeed, is all the maleness of the other hidden, as the moon is hidden in the darkness of the night; she exists in Him as milk in the udders of a cow, as fire in the wood, as a jewel-lamp inside a cover of cloth. The Purusha loses all his lustre as a vassal king, or as a diseased lion, or as one who is deliberately put to sleep and made to experience a dream; as the face can produce its other in the presence of a mirror, or as a pebble acquires redness in the presence of saffron, similarly does this unborn Purusha acquire the touch of qualities. He stands in the midst of the Prakṛiti as a piece of wood stands motionless in the midst of the Jui plant.........He stands like the Meru on the banks of the river of the Prakṛiti. He is mirrored inside her, but does not move like her. Prakṛiti comes and goes; but he lives as he is. Hence is he the Eternal Ruler of the world (XIII. 958—1224). Finally, Jñāneśvara tells us that what the Sāṃkhyas call Avyakta is the same as Prakṛiti. It is also what the Vedāntins call Māyā. Its nature is Ignorance—the self-forgetfulness of the Self. "The Prakṛiti is verily my house-wife. She is beginningless, and young, of unspeakable qualities. Her form is Not-Being. She is near to those who are sleeping, but away from those who are waking. When I sleep, she awakes; and by the enjoyment of my bare existence, she becomes big with creation. She produces a child from which come forth all the three worlds........Brahmā is the morning of this child, Vishṇu the mid-day, and Śaṅkara the evening. The child plays till the time of the great conflagration, and then it sleeps calmly, and wakes up again at the time of a new cycle" (XIV. 68—117).

The Mutable, the Immutable and the Transcendent.

10. Jñāneśvara takes up also the problem of the Kshara, the Akshara and the Paramātman, like the problem of the Prakṛiti and the Purusha, from the Bhagavadgītā itself, which does not make very clear the distinction between the Kshara, the Akshara and the Paramātman. By Kshara is meant the Mutable, by Akshara the Immutable, and by Paramātman, somehow, the Being that transcends both. Now it is somewhat hard to understand in what sense the Transcendent Being could be distinguished from the Immutable; and yet Jñāneśvara closely follows the Bhagavadgītā in making a distinction between the Immutable and the Transcendent, and in making a Hegelian synthesis of the Mutable and the Immutable into the Transcendent. In this world of Samsāra, says Jñāneśvara, there are two Beings, just as in the heavens reign only light and darkness; there is, however, a third Being who not suffering both these previous Beings, eats them both..... One is blind and lame, the other is well-formed in all his limbs, and the two have come into contact with each other simply because they have come to inhabit the same citadel (XV. 471—477). Of these the Mutable is Matter as well as Individual Spirit, the consciousness which is pent up inside the body. It is all that is small and great, moving and immovable, whatever is apprehended by mind and intellect; what takes on the elemental body; what appears as name and form; what suffers the reign of the qualities;......what we knew as the eight-fold Prakṛiti; what we saw to be divided thirty-six-fold; what we have immediately seen to be the Aśvattha tree;......what seems an image of itself, like that of a lion in a well which forthwith springs upon itself in anger; what thus creates the citadel of form, and goes to sleep in entire obliviscence of its nature, thinking 'the father is mine, the mother is mine, I am white or deformed, the children, wealth, and wife are all mine';......what appears as the flicker of the moonlight in a moving stream, and what thus on account of its connection with the Upādhis appears momentary (XV. 478—501). The Akshara is what appears as the Meru in the midst of all the mountains; what is absolutely formless, as when the ocean dries up, there remain neither any waves nor any water; what appears as Ignorance when the world has set, and when the knowledge of Ātman has not yet been gained; what may be likened to the state of the moon without the slightest streak of light on the new-moon day; what psychologically corresponds to the state of deep sleep; as opposed to the Mutable Being that appears both in the wakeful and the dream states;......what may be regarded as the root of the tree of existence; what does not change, nor is destroyed, and what is thus the best (XV. 502—524). As opposed to both the Mutable and the Immutable is the Transcendent Being, in whom Ignorance is sunk in Knowledge, and Knowledge extinguishes itself like fire; which appears as knowing without an object to be known; which is higher psychologically than the wakeful, the dream, or even the deep-sleep consciousness; which transcends its own bounds like an ocean in floods, and which rolls together all rivulets and rivers as at the time of the final end; which is the scent as intermediate between the nose and the flower; which is Being; which is beyond both the seer and the seen; which is light without there being an object to be illumined; which is ruler without there being anything to be ruled; which is the sound of sound, the taste of taste, the joy of joy, the light of light, the void of voids;......which is like the Sun which does not appear either as night or as day (XV. 526—556).

Body and Soul.

11. When we strip our minds of all such metaphysical conceptions as those of the Prakṛiti and the Purusha, or of the Kshara and the Akshara, what remains of psychological value is the relation of the body and the soul; let us now see what Jñāneśvara says about this relation. The body to Jñāneśvara is simply a complex of the various elements. As a chariot is called a chariot, because it is a complex of the various limbs of the chariot; as an army is called an army, because it is a complex of its various parts; as a sentence is simply a complex of letters; as a lamp is a complex of oil, wick, and fire; similarly the body is a complex of the thirty-six elements (XIII. 151—156). The Soul is as different from the body as the east from the west. The Soul is mirrored in the body as the sun in a lake. The body is subject to the influence of Karman, and rolls on the wheels of death and birth. It is like a piece of butter thrown in the fire of death. It lives for as short a span of time as the fly takes for lifting its wings. Throw it in fire, and it is reduced to ashes; give it to a dog, and it becomes carrion; if it escapes either of these alternatives, it is reduced merely to a mass of worms. On the other hand, the Ātman is pure and eternal and beginningless. He is the all, impartitionable, without any actions, neither short nor long, neither appearance nor non-appearance, neither light nor non-light, neither full nor empty, neither form nor formless, neither joy nor joyless, neither one nor many, neither bound nor absolved......As day follows night and night follows day on the sky, similarly body follows body on the background of this Ātman (XIII. 1095—1124).

Doctrine of Transmigration.

12. The doctrine of transmigration, which Jñāneśvara teaches, is linked closely with the analysis of man's psychological qualities into the Sāttvika, the Rājasa, and the Tāmasa. The Soul of a man, in whom the Sattva quality is augmented, meets a different fortune after death from one in whom either the Rajas or the Tamas qualities are augmented. What, asks Jñāneśvara, happens when the Sattva quality is augmented? The intellect of such a man so fills his being that it oozes out of him as fragrance out of the lotus petals. Discrimination fills all his senses; his very hands and feet become endowed with vision; as the royal swan can discriminate between water and milk, even so the senses of such a man can discriminate between the good and the bad. What must not be heard, the ear itself refuses to hear; what must not be seen, the eye itself refuses to see; what must not be spoken, the tongue itself refuses to speak; as from before a flame darkness runs away, even so from him bad things run away; as in flood-time, a great river flows round about, even so his intellect transcends its own limits in the knowledge of the sciences; as on the full-moon day, the light of the moon spreads about, even so his intellect spreads about in knowledge; all his desires become centred in himself. A stop is put to his activities. His mind becomes disgusted with the objects of sense. When these qualities become augmented in a man, if he happens to meet his death at such a moment,......his new being becomes as full of the Sattva quality as the old, and he takes on a birth among those who pursue knowledge for its own sake. When a king goes to a mountain, does his kingship forthwith diminish? Or when a lamp is taken over to a neighbouring village, does it for that matter cease to be a lamp? (XIV. 205—222.) What happens when the Rajas quality predominates in a man? Such a man becomes over-occupied with his own work, and gives free reins to his senses, as a storm rolls hither and thither; his moral bonds become loosened as a sheep knows not the distinction between the good and the bad. Forthwith, such a man undertakes works which are unworthy of him. He takes into his head to build a great palace, or to perform a great Aśvamedha ceremony; to create new towns; to build new tanks; to foster large forests.........His desire gets such a mastery over him that he wishes to bring the whole world under his feet. When these qualities are augmented in a man, if he happens to meet death, he is bound to come over again to the human kind. Can a beggar, who lives in a king's palace, thereby become a king himself? An ox must needs feed on stumps, even though he might be carried in the procession of a great king. Such a man's action knows no bounds, and he must be always yoked to his work like an ox (XIV. 227—243). What happens when the Tamas quality predominates in a man? The mind of such a man becomes as full of darkness as the night on the new-moon day; he ceases to have any inspiration; thought has no place in his mind; his remembrance seems to have left him for good; indiscrimination fills him through and through; folly reigns supreme in his heart; he takes only to bad actions as the owl sees only at night; things which are shunned, he hugs to his heart; he becomes intoxicated without wine, raves without delirium, becomes infatuated like a madman without love; his mind seems to have taken leave of him, and yet he is not enjoying the super-conscious state......At such a time, if a man were to meet his doom, he is bound to come over again in the Tamas world. The fire, which is flamed, may be extinguished, but the flame continues as ever;...... even so when Tamas is augmented, he becomes incarnate in a beast or a bird, a tree or a worm (XIV. 244—260).

Personal and Impersonal Immortality: Re-incarnation an Illusion.

13. As opposed to this transmigrating process, lies the state of Absolution reached only by the select few who have gone beyond the realm of the Sattva, Rajas and Tamas qualities, and who, by their devotion, have reached identity with God even during this life. About such persons Jñāneśvara tells us that when they have gone to the End, they never return therefrom, as the rivers go to an Ocean from which they never return; as when a puppet of salt becomes wholly absorbed in a vessel of water when it is put inside it, similarly those, who have reached unitive life with God by their superior knowledge, never return again when they have departed from this life. Arjuna, with his inquiring spirit, asks Kṛishṇa at this stage of the argument of Jñāneśvara, "Do these, O God, reach personal, or impersonal, immortality? Granted that they become one with God, and that they never return, do they preserve their individuality or not? If they preserve a separate individuality, to say that they do not return is meaningless; for the bees that reach a flower never become the flower itself; and as the arrows after having reached the target come back again as arrows, even so may these individuals return from their final *habitat.* On the other hand, if there is no barrier between these individuals and God, what is the meaning of saying that these become merged in the other? For they are already identical with Him. How can a weapon turn its edge against itself? In this wise, beings which are identical with Thee, can never be said either to have merged in Thee or to have come back from Thee." To this objection Kṛishṇa replies by saying that the ways in which these individuals return and do not return may be said to be different from each other. If we see with a discerning eye, says Kṛishṇa, then there is seen to be an absolute identity between the individuals and God. If, on the other hand, we look in a cursory way, it seems as if they are different also. It seems Kṛishṇa is here making a distinction between the noumenal and the phenomenal points of view. The waves of an ocean seem different from the body of the ocean, and yet again are identical with it. The ornaments of gold seem different from gold, and yet are identical with it. Thus it happens that from the point of view of knowledge, these individuals are identical with God; it is the point of view of ignorance which regards them as different (XV. 317 —334). From this point of view it is only a step to regard reincarnation an illusion, and Jñāneśvara in a passage boldly takes up the gauntlet. It is the human point of view which tells us, he says, that the Ātman leaves the body, and takes away along with itself the whole company of the senses,...... as the setting Sun carries with him the visions of people, or as wind carries away the fragrance..........It is really the standpoint of indiscrimination which enables one to say so. That the Ātman can re-incarnate, or can enjoy the objects of sense, or can depart from the body, is verily the standpoint of ignorance......If a man is able to see his own reflection in a mirror, does it follow that the man did not exist previously before looking at the mirror? Or if the mirror is taken away and the image disappears, does it follow that the man himself ceases to be? Even likewise we must remember that the Ātman is always Ātman, and the body the body. Those, who have got the vision of discrimination, see the Ātman in this manner. If the sky with all its stars is mirrored in an ocean, the eye of discrimination regards it merely as a reflection, and not as having fallen bodily into the ocean from above. If a pond is filled and is dried up, the Sun remains as he was; even so when body comes and goes, the Ātman remains identical with himself. He is neither increased nor decreased; he is neither the cause of action nor the cause of non-action; such verily is the vision of those who have known the Self (XV. 361—390).

Description of the Asvattha Tree.

14. Like the Prakṛiti and the Purusha, and the Kshara and the Akshara, the Aśvattha itself figures largely in the Jñāneśvarī as in the Bhagavadgītā. Jñāneśvara is at his best in his description of this Tree of Existence. He gives a long description of this tree in its various aspects, and it behoves us to dwell a little at length upon its description. The purpose of the description of the Aśvattha, says Jñāneśvara, is to convince the readers of the unreality of this tree of existence, and thus to fill them with utter dispassion. This tree is entirely unlike other trees, which have all of them roots going downwards and branches wending upwards. It is wonderful, says Jñāneśvara, that this tree grows downwards. This tree fills all that exists, and all that does not exist, as the whole sky is filled with water at the time of the great End. There is neither any fruit of this tree, nor any taster of it; neither any flower nor any smeller of it; its root goes upwards, and yet it is impossible to uproot it (XV. 46—65). Jñāneśvara then proceeds to explain what its upward root is, and how it germinates. The upward root of the tree is that Absolute Existence, which is sound without being heard; which is fragrance without being scented; which is joy without being experienced. What is behind it, is before it; what is before it, is behind it; which, itself unseen, sees without there being any object to be seen;...... which is knowledge without being either knower or known ......which is neither product nor cause; which is neither second nor single; which is alone and to itself (XV. 72—79).

How the Root germinates.

15. The power by which this root germinates is described by Jñāneśvara as Māyā, which emerges from Absolute Existence. What is called Māyā is merely a synonym of non-existence. It is like the description of the children of a barren woman; it is neither being nor not-being, and will not bear reflection for a moment; it is the chest of different elements; it is the sky on which the world-cloud appears; it is a folded cloth of various forms; it is the seed of the tree of existence; it is the curtain on which appears Samsāra; it is the torch of aberrated knowledge;...... it is as when a man may go to sound sleep in himself; it is like the black soot on a lustrous lamp; it is like the false awakening of a lover in his dream by his young beloved, who coaxes him and fills him with passion;........it is the ignorance of self about self; it is the sleep of ignorance, as contrasted with the dream and the wakeful states (XV. 80—90).

The Asvattha, the Type of Unreality.

16. Thus we see that the Aśvattha to Jñāneśvara is the type of unreality. The reason why it is called the Aśvattha, is that it does not stand for the morrow. As a cloud may assume various colours in a moment, or as a flash of lightning has no duration, as water does not cling to a lotus leaf, or as an afflicted man's mind is full of change, similarly does this Aśvattha tree change from moment to moment........People do not see the coming into being and the passing away of this tree of existence, and hence they falsely call it eternal........As cycle succeeds cycle, or as a piece of bamboo succeeds another, or as a part of sugarcandy succeeds another part, as the year that goes is the cause of the year to come, as the water flows past and another quantum of water comes to take its place, similarly this tree of existence, though really non-existent, is yet vainly called real. As many things may take place within the twinkling of an eye; as a wave is really unstationary; as a single eye of the crow moves from socket to socket; ......as a ring, which is made to whirl on the ground, seems as if to have stuck to it on account of its great speed; as a beacon-light which is moved in a circular direction appears like a wheel; even likewise, does this tree of existence come and go, and yet people call it eternal. It is only he who contemplates its infinite speed and knows it to be momentary, ...it is only such a man that may be regarded as having known the Real (XV. 110—141).

The Knowledge of Unreality is the Cause of its Destruction.

17. If the question be asked, "What it is that ultimately lops off this tree of existence?—a tree whose root is placed in the Eternal, and whose branches move down in the world of men,—what it is that puts an end to this vast tree of existence", the answer is simple: to know that it is unreal is to be able to destroy it altogether. A child may be frightened by a pseudo-demon; but does the demon exist for the matter of it? Can one really throw down the castle in the air? Is it possible to break the horn of a hare? Can we pluck the flowers in the skies? The tree itself is unreal; why then should we trouble about rooting it up? It is like the infinite progeny of a barren woman. What is the use of talking about dream-things to a man who is awake?........Can one rear crops on the waters of a mirage? The tree itself is unreal, and to know that it is unreal is sufficient to destroy it (XV. 210—223).

The Origin, the Being, and the End of the Tree of Existence.

18. And people vainly say that this tree has a beginning, an existence, and an end. Really speaking, it has neither come into being, nor does it exist, nor has it really an end. Can we cast the horoscope of the child of a barren woman? Can blueness be predicated about the surface of the sky? Can one really pluck the flowers in the skies? The tree has neither any beginning nor any end. What appears to exist is equally unreal. A river has its source on a mountain, and moves on towards an ocean; but this tree of existence is not like a real river. It is like a vain mirage, which appears, but which does not exist. It is like a rainbow which appears to be of many colours, but in which the colours really do not exist; it has really neither any beginning, nor any end, nor any existence.....This tree can be cut down only by self-knowledge. To go on lopping off the branches of this tree is a vain pursuit. We should lop off its very root by true knowledge. What is the use of collecting sticks for killing a rope-serpent? Why apply balm to a dream-wound? The tree of Ignorance can be lopped off only by Knowledge (XV. 224—254).

A Devout Meditation on God enables one to cross the Flood of Maya.

19. In a sustained metaphor, Jñāneśvara describes how it is possible for a spiritual aspirant to cross the flood of unreality. The stream of Māyā issuing out of the mountain of Brahman first shapes itself in the form of the elements. Then on account of the heavy showers of the qualities, the stream experiences a flood and carries off streamlets of restrained virtues. In that flood there are whirlpools of hate and circles of jealousy. In it, huge fishes in the shape of errors swim to and fro. On the island of sexual enjoyment are thrown over waves of passion, and there many creatures appear to have come together. There are scarcely any pathways through that great water; and it seems impossible that the flood may ever be crossed. Is it not wonderful, asks Jñāneśvara, that every attempt that is made for crossing this flood becomes only a hindrance in the path of crossing it? Those, who are dependent upon their own intellects, try to swim over this flood, and no trace of them remains. Those who are given to over-self-consciousness, sink in the abyss of pride. Those, who try to cross this flood by means of the knowledge of the Vedas, hug to their heart huge pieces of stone, and go entirely into the mouth of the whale of arrogance. Those, who clasp the chest of sacrifice, go only into the recesses of heaven, where no boat of dispassion is available, where no raft of discrimination is to be found, where whatever else may be done becomes a hindrance. If the young one of a deer were to gnaw at a snare, or an ant to cross over the Meru, only then would people cross this stream of Māyā. It is only those who are full of devotion to me, for whom the Guru acts as a steersman, and who take recourse to the raft of Self-realization, for such we may say the flood of Māyā ceases to exist even before they have tried to cross it (VII. 68—98).

God, the Central Reality.

20. We are thus introduced to the central point in Jñāneśvara's mystical theology, namely, devotion to God. Is it not wonderful, he asks, that people should keep repeating that there is no God, when God has filled this world in and out? Is it not their misfortune that makes them say that God is not? That one should fall in a well of nectar and yet try to rid himself out of it: what can we say about such a man except that he is unfortunate? The blind man is moving from place to place for a single morsel of food, and yet he is kicking aside with his foot the wish-jewel that has happened to come in his way, simply because in his blindness he cannot see it (IX. 300—305). If these people were just to open their eyes a little, and look at Nature, they would soon find themselves convinced about God's existence. Do they not see Omnipotence everywhere? And must it not convince them about God's existence? That the sky can envelop everything, or the wind move ceaselessly on, or that the fire should burn, or that rain should quench the ground; that the mountains should not move from their places; that the ocean must not over-reach its bounds; that the earth must bear the burden of all creatures that are on its surface: is not all this due to My Order? The Vedas speak, when I make them speak; the Sun moves, when I make him move; the Prāṇa inhales and exhales, only when I communicate motion to it; it is I, who move the world. It is on account of My order that death envelopes all. All these forces of nature are merely My bondsmen (IX. 280—285). All the names and forms that we see in the world are due to Me; all things exist in Me as waves exist on the bosom of water; and I am in all things as water in all waves. It is only him who submits unconditionally to Me that I relieve from the bonds of birth and death. I am the sole refuge of the supplicants. The Sun sends his image in an ocean as well as in a pond, irrespective of their greatness or smallness. Verily thus am I mirrored in all things (IX. 286—290). Man vainly says that he is the agent of actions. He forgets that he is only an occasional cause. The army which is destined to be killed, is already killed by Me. They are like merely inanimate puppets in a show. The dolls fall down in a confused fashion, as soon as the string that holds them together is taken away (XI. 466—467).

Uselessness of Images and Anthropomorphism.

21. Granted that God exists as the supreme cause of all, how is He to be found out? Can He be found by hunting after perishable images? No, says Jñāneśvara. A man, whose eye is jaundiced, sees everything yellowish, even the moonlight. It is thus that in My pure form they see foibles. A man whose tongue is spoilt on account of fever, regards even milk as a bad poison. In this way, do they regard Me as a 'man', who am not a man. They take merely an external view of Me, which is the result of utter ignorance........As a swan may throw itself into water by trying to catch hold of the reflected stars, thinking that they are jewels; or as a man may gather cinders, thinking that they are precious stones; or as a lion kills himself by throwing himself into a well against his own reflected image; similarly, those who identify Myself with the world, or worldly objects, deceive themselves by pursuing an illusion. Is it possible for a man to get results of nectar by drinking barley-water? Even likewise, do people try to find Me in perishable images, and thus escape My real imperishable nature (IX. 142—152). In this strain does Jñāneśvara condemn all anthropomorphic views of God. People attribute a name to Me, who am nameless; action to Me, who am actionless; bodily functions to Me, who am bodiless; they attribute a colour to Me, who am colourless; quality to One, who is quality-less; hands and feet to One, who is without them; eyes and ears to the eyeless and earless; family to the family-less; form to the formless; Me, who am without clothing, they try to put a clothing on; they put ornaments on Me, who am beyond all ornaments; ....they make Me, who am self-born; they establish Me, who am self-established. Me who cannot come and go, they call upon and relinquish; I am eternally self-made, and yet they regard Me as a child, or a youth, or an old man; for Me, who am without a second, they create a second; for Me, who am without actions, they find actions; I, who never eat, they say, partake of meals;......I, who am the universally immanent Ātman, they say, kill one in anger and support another in love. These and other human qualities which they attribute to Me are themselves embodiment of ignorance. When they see an image before them, they take it to be God incarnate, and when it is broken, they fling it over, saying that it is no God (IX. 156—170).

The Infinite Awe in Creation for God.

22. As a matter of fact, God so fills every nook and cranny of the world that every object must succumb before His infinite omnipotence. When God chooses to show His prowess, the whole world is put in consternation, and with it also the whole host of the gods. "These feel themselves so over-powered by that great lustre," says Arjuna, "that they try to enter into Thy being in great devotion. Fearful, lest Thou might grow wroth with them, they bow down to Thee with their hands folded together. Fallen are we, O God, in an ocean of Ignorance, they say: caught are we in the meshes of senses......Who else except Thee can save us from the fall? They look at Thy great form, and looking, become amazed every moment, and wave their crest-jewels before Thee. They place their folded hands at Thy feet and say, victory, victory to Thee, O God" (XI. 326—336). It is in this manner that God sends an infinite awe throughout the whole of creation.

Vision of Identity.

23. And God is really not different from the world. Originally from a single seed grows the sprout, from the sprout the stem, from the stem the many branches, and from the branches the leaves; after the leaves comes the flower, and from the flower the fruit; and yet when we consider it all, it is only the seed unfolded. In this manner am I identical with the whole world. From Me this world is spread; from the ant to the highest god, there is no being who is without Me. He alone who awakes to this consciousness escapes the dream of difference

(X. 98—118). The wise man is he who sees no difference, but instead sees identity everywhere. If one notices only the difference of names, the difference of actions, and the difference of apparel, he will be born over and over again. From the same creeper are born fruits, longish, crooked, and circular, each with its own use. Thus beings may differ, and yet the same reality inhabit them all......Even when these beings vanish, the Ātman does not vanish; as when the ornaments disappear, gold does not disappear........It is only the man who realizes this, who may be said to have his eye of knowledge opened (XIII. 1059—1080). There is thus no difference between *Natura Naturans* and *Natura Naturata*. Are there not different limbs on the same body, asks Jñāneśvara? Are there not high and low branches on a tree, sprouting from the same seed? I am related to the objects, as waves are related to the sea. The fire and the flame are both of them really the fire. If the world were to hide Me, what shall we say illumines the world? Can the lustre of a jewel hide the jewel? Thus it would be vain to deny the world to find Me; for it is in the world that I am to be found (XIV. 118—128).

God cannot be known.

24. The greatness of God is so infinite that Jñāneśvara has no difficulty in saying that God cannot be known in His entirety. Ages have elapsed, he says, in discussing the nature, the greatness, and the origin of God. As a fœtus in the womb cannot know the age of its mother;......as the sea-animals cannot measure the greatness of the sea; as a fly cannot cross the heaven;...... similarly the sages, and the gods, and all the beings on the earth, being born of Me, cannot know Me. Has descending water ever crossed up the mountain? Much rather would a tree grow up to its roots, than the world born of Me ever hope to know Me (X. 65–69). One, who seeks knowledge on this head, is bound to be ignorant. The sense of plenty is the cause of want......Is there any higher wisdom than can be found in the Vedas? Or, is there one who can talk more glibly than the Śesha? And yet these cannot describe My greatness. Sages like Sanaka have grown mad in searching after Me. There is no sage whose asceticism could be compared to that of Śankara, and yet even he throws away his pride and accepts over his head the water which oozes from My feet. Thus one must throw aside all his greatness; one must forget all his learning; one must become smaller than the smallest thing in the world; only then could he hope to come in My presence. Even the moon ceases to shine before the thousand-rayed Sun ; why should the fire-fly then try to eclipse the greatness of the Sun ? For this reason, one must leave away all the pride of body, and wealth, and virtue, and then seek God (IX. 367—381). The knowledge of the Vedas is incompetent to lead to the knowledge of the Ātman. The Vedas are the cause of happiness and sorrow........ Forget not, therefore, the happiness of Self......As when the Sun has arisen, all the ways are seen ; but is one thereby able to take recourse to all the ways ? In a great flood, when the whole of the earth becomes full of water, one is able to drink only as much as would satisfy his thirst. Thus those, who seek real knowledge, consider the Vedas no doubt, but accept only their teaching about the Eternal (II. 256—263). Only he can hope to know God, who turns his back from the requirements of sense ; ......who rises on the top of the elements, and taking his stand there, looks with his eyes at My own eternal nature in the light of self-illumination. He, who regards Me as prior to the primeval, as the Lord of all beings,......he is like a Parisa among men ; like mercury among all liquids ;......he is the moving image of knowledge ; his limbs are made up of happiness ; his manhood is only a worldly illusion. Senses leave away such a man in fear, as the serpent leaves away a burning sandal tree (X. 72—80). Finally, to know God really is to see Him everywhere ; as when a man wants to collect together the stars, he has only to roll up the sky ; or as when he wishes to take an inventory of the atoms of the universe, he has to lift the globe itself ; similarly, if a man wants to know Me, he must know Me in all My manifestations. As when a man wants to catch hold of the flowers and the fruits and the branches of a tree, he has to pluck its root and take it in his hand ; similarly, when one wants to see My manifestations, he has to see My spotless form. To hunt after the infinite manifestations were a vain pursuit ; hence it would be best that I Myself be apprehended (X. 259—263).

Arjuna's Longing after the Vision of the Universal Atman.

25. There is a point in the Bhagavadgītā which Jñāneśvara in his commentary brings out at great length. The great Transfiguration which Kṛishṇa underwent as described in the eleventh Chapter of the Bhagavadgītā supplies an excellent theme for Jñāneśvara to dwell upon, and to bring into relief the vision of the Universal Ātman. To see God's human form, as Arjuna saw it before him in the person of Kṛishṇa, was but an insignificant matter, as contrasted with his great Transfiguration as

Universal Ātman. Arjuna thus pressed Kṛishṇa to show him His transfigured form. "Would it be possible for me", asked Arjuna, "to see in the outside world the Universal Lord of all?" A boon which no other man had previously asked of Kṛishṇa, Arjuna dared to ask himself. "Granted that my love to Kṛishṇa is of a transcendent order, would it be however in any way greater than that of his spouse? Granted that I have done an amount of service to Kṛishṇa, would it however in any way approach the service of the Great Eagle? Could I be nearer to the heart of Kṛishṇa than the great sages like Sanaka and others? Could I really bear greater love towards Him than His co-mates in the Gokula? ...... And yet if I am afraid to ask Him for this boon of the vision of the Viśvarūpa, my life would be spent in misery." Hence Arjuna dared to ask Him to show him the vision of the Universal Ātman (XI. 28—38). "Would Thou wert to show me," he said, "Thy original form, at whose desire the cycle of worlds comes into being and passes away, show me that original Form from which Thou takest two-handed and four-handed forms to remove the miseries of gods; show me Thy original Form in which after having played the parts of Matsya, Kūrma and others, Thou goest back to Thy original home. Show me the Form which is sung in the Upanishads; which is seen by the Yogins in their hearts; which is the sole inspiration of sages like Sanaka; that Form, which is thus heard, I now wish to see. If Thou wert to grant me a boon, please grant me this" (XI. 81—88).

Visvarupa not seen by Physical Vision, but by Intuitive Vision.

26. Kṛishṇa was thereupon desirous of showing to Arjuna His Viśvarūpa, which He exhibited all of a sudden to his eye, unmindful as to whether Arjuna with his physical eye would be able to see it or not. Kṛishṇa did really show it to him; but Arjuna was yet unprepared. "I have shown you My Viśvarūpa," said Kṛishṇa; "but you have not yet seen it." Arjuna replied that the Viśvarūpa, which would be seen only by intuitive vision and not by physical vision, was as good as unshown to him unless he were endowed with that great intuitive power. "You are making a mirror clean," says Arjuna, "and holding it before a blind man; You are producing a beautiful song, but only before one who is deaf" (XI. 154—159); upon which Kṛishṇa gave him the intuitive vision by means of which he was able to see the Universal Ātman. The darkness of ignorance began to slip away; a flood of light came before the vision of Arjuna; Arjuna was plunged in an ocean of miracles ; his mind sank in wonder ; his intellect and senses ceased to operate ; in wonder he began to see, and the four-handed form which he had seen before him he now saw all about him ; he shut his eyes and saw the form of Kṛishṇa ; he opened his eyes and saw the vision of the Universal Ātman (XI. 176—196). The lustre of the Universal Ātman was so great, the very hosts of heaven were so terrified at that great prospect, Arjuna felt so powerless before the grand power of the Almighty, that he felt as if his very soul was passing out of his body. It was a spectacle of great terror, astonishment, and novelty. Unable to see the infinite lustre of that form, Arjuna prayed to Him : his mind was a mountain of sins ; he asked forgiveness of God, beseeching Him to excuse any derelictions which he may have committed. As when a river brings all kinds of dross to an ocean, does not the ocean receive them all ? "What words I may have spoken through love or mistake, in what way I may have offended against Thy great power, forgive me all, O God," said Arjuna (XI. 555—560). Arjuna fell prostrate before that great Vision, and became full of noble sentiments. His throat was choked, and he besought Him to take him out of the ocean of sins. Does not the father forgive the faults of the son, he asked ; does not a friend draw a veil over the derelictions of his companion ? (XI. 567—574.)

Condemnation of the Fear of Arjuna.

27. Kṛishṇa, in his transfigured form, had hitherto held silence ; but when he saw Arjuna terrified in the extreme, he said to him that it was wonderful that he should show such a great lack of courage. "Thou art ignorant of the great boon that I have conferred on thee by showing thee this vision," said Kṛishṇa, "and thou art prattling like a terror-stricken man......This infinite form of mine, from which all incarnations emanate, has never been hitherto heard or seen by anybody except thee......Thou hast come upon an ocean of nectar, and art afraid of being drowned in it ; thou hast seen a mountain of gold, and sayest that thou dost not want such a great treasure ; thou hast had the wish-jewel in thy hands, and art throwing it because thou feelest it to be a burden ; thou art turning away the wish-cow out of doors, because thou canst not feed her ;........even though this form might be terrific to look at, pin thy faith to this, as a miser keeps his thoughts round his buried treasure ;......thou art afraid because thou hast never seen this form before ; but forget not to exchange love for fear." So saying, Kṛishṇa, for fear of taxing Arjuna's patience too much, took on the human form again (XI. 609—639).

Those who follow the Impersonal, themselves reach the Person.

28. Jñāneśvara employs a number of similes to show how Kṛishṇa took on the human form, because Arjuna was not competent to look at the universal vision. He tells us that Arjuna could not price the jewel to its worth, or was like one, who looking at a fair bride, might say she was not to his taste...... Kṛishṇa took the original gold to pieces in order to make ornaments therefrom. He unloosed the apparel of the universal vision; but because Arjuna was not a good customer for it, He folded it again (XI. 640—646). The internal meaning of such expressions is, Jñāneśvara tells us, that those who are desirous of seeing the Impersonal themselves reach the Person. This is the burden of the twelfth Chapter of the Bhagavadgītā, as also of the Jñāneśvarī, where the question being asked, which of the two is superior, the manifest or the unmanifest, and which of the two aspirants is superior, the devotee or the philosopher, the answer is unmistakably given that the manifest is superior to the unmanifest, and the devotee superior to the philosopher. Kṛishṇa evidently prices a devotee, whose devotion increases day by day as the river in the rainy season. Those who devote all the operations of the mind and senses to Me, says Kṛishṇa, and meditate without distinction of day and night, such devotees I prize more than anything else (XII. 34—39). On the other hand, those who follow the path of the Impersonal, which their mind cannot reach and intellect cannot pierce and sense cannot perceive, which is difficult of contemplation, which does not fall within the purview of the manifest, which exists at all times and in all places, which meditation vainly seeks to reach, which is neither being nor not-being, which neither moves nor stirs, and which is hard to comprehend even by hard penance, even these, ultimately reach My Personal Being, while their penance and asceticism are only vain pursuits, landing them into an ocean of trouble (XII. 40—59).

Characterization of the Absolute.

29. Even though thus for practical purposes Personal Being is proved to be superior to the Impersonal, for logical purposes Jñāneśvara very often sets up the conception of the Absolute as an intellectual ideal: "that which is at once inside and outside; which is far and near; beside which there is no second;........to whose perpetual light, there is no flicker ;......which is immaculate in the beginning, the middle, and the end of existence ; like the sky, which is the same with itself in the morning, mid-day, and the evening ; which itself takes on the names of the Creator, the Preserver, and the Destroyer ; which may be called the Great Void when the qualities have become annihilated ; which illuminates fire ; which inspires the moon ; which is the eye of the sun (XIII. 915—938) ; which has its hands everywhere, because there is nothing outside, which is not occupied by it ; which has its feet everywhere, because there is no place that is not filled by it ; which has its eyes everywhere, because to it all things are always present ; which stands at the head of all ;......which has its face everywhere, because it enjoys all things ; and which, in spite of all these things, may be said to have neither hands nor eyes nor feet and the rest ; but which, because it must be somehow characterized, may be called by these names, just as when a void is to be shown, it is shown in the form of a dot (XIII. 873—889).

The Sun of Absolute Reality.

30. The most celebrated passage, however, in which Jñāneśvara speaks of the Absolute, is when at the beginning of the sixteenth Chapter of the Jñāneśvarī, he compares it to the Sun even like Plato in the Republic, and describes by means of a continued metaphor the Sun of Absolute Reality. How very wonderful is it, asks Jñāneśvara, that while the celestial Sun makes the phenomenal world rise into view, the Sun of Absolute Reality makes the phenomenal world hide its face altogether ? He eats up the stars in the shape of both knowledge and ignorance, and brings on illumination to those who seek Self-knowledge. At the dawn of the spiritual light, the Individual Souls like birds leave their nests on their spiritual pilgrimage. Varying the metaphor, Jñāneśvara speaks of the Individual Souls as bees which were hitherto pent up in the lotuses of the subtle objects, but which, as soon as the Sun of Absolute Reality rose, were suddenly let loose in the light of day. Jñāneśvara compares Intellect and Illumination, reason and gnosis, to a pair of loving Chātaka birds, which, before the spiritual illumination, were crying out for each other in their state of separation, being divided by the river of difference ; but when the Sun of Absolute Reality rose, the pair is brought together, and there is harmony between them...... The Sun of Absolute Reality throws out rays of discrimination, which, falling on the double concave mirror of consciousness, burn to ashes the forests of worldly life. When the rays of the Sun of Absolute Reality fall straight on the Soul, a mirage of occult powers is produced. When the Sun reaches the zenith of spiritual experience, the aspiring Soul feels its identity with the Sun, and its individuality hides itself underneath itself like the shadow of a body at mid-day..... Who is there, the Poet-Saint asks, who has been able to visualize this Sun of Absolute Reality, who is beyond day and night, beyond good and bad, beyond all pairs of opposites, who is like an eternal lamp of light, which burns so miraculously that there is nothing for it to illuminate (XVI. 1—16)?

II. Ethics.

The Seductive Power of the Senses.

31. When we come to discuss the moral teaching of Jñāneśvara, we must remember from the outset that he has as much distrust of the senses as any other mystical philosopher. "The senses are so strong that even those, who are given to the practice of Yoga, and who have acquired all the necessary virtues for the practice of it, those, in fact, who are holding their minds in the hollow of their hands, even these are seduced, as an exorcist is seduced; and when on a higher level of Yoga-practice, new objects of sense are created, and new kinds of power and prosperity open before the practiser of Yoga, these exercise a new charm, and seduce and turn away the mind of the spiritual aspirant, with the result that their practice in Yoga is stopped; such is the great seductive power of the senses" (II. 311—314)!

Catalogue of Virtues: Humility.

32. But more than this current account of the seductive power of the senses, which is common with other moral philosophers, Jñāneśvara's great originality consists in making a very acute and accurate analysis of the various moral virtues. The thirteenth Chapter of the Bhagavadgītā has supplied him with a text where all the necessary virtues of a truly spiritual life have been enumerated. Jñāneśvara draws upon that text and gives us a very full analysis of all the virtues mentioned in that chapter. He employs so many images in order to bring home to the mind of the reader the particular significance of the virtue under consideration, that we may easily regard Jñāneśvara as almost the greatest moral philosopher who has employed the figurative method for the description of the virtues. Moral philosophy would be dry in the absence of this interestive side of exposition; and we shall note presently the great wealth of material that has been employed by Jñāneśvara for the description of the virtues. And first to speak of humility. A humble man is he, says Jñāneśvara, who feels any word of praise as a burden upon him. Even though people may praise him for the qualities which he really possesses, such a man is disturbed, as much as a deer is disturbed when it is surrounded by a hunter; and oppressed, as when a man feels oppressed when he is trying to swim his way through a whirlpool. One should never allow respect to be shown to oneself; one should never so much as be the cause of the praise of one's own particular greatness. A man must feel mortified when people bow down to him; even though he may be as learned as the preceptor of the gods, still he must seek shelter in ignorance; he should hide his cleverness, throw away all his greatness, and show by his actions that he likes to be called an ignorant man! ......"The whole world should mortify me," he should say, "and my relations should leave me"...... He should live so silently that people must not know whether he is living or dead; he should move so silently that people should not know whether he is walking, or is being driven by the wind. "Let my very existence cease," he should say, "let my name and form be hidden; let all beings try to shun me." Such a man retires to solitude every day, and seems to live as if on solitude; he makes friendship with the wind, talks with the sky, and loves the trees in a forest as dearly as his own Self (XIII. 185--202). In another place, also, in the ninth Chapter, Jñāneśvara illustrates this extreme humility of the saint. An humble man is he who regards all existences from the ant to the highest god as identical with his own Self; to him there is nothing great or small; there is no distinction between animate and inanimate; and he regards all things as his own Self. He is forgetful of his own greatness, does not judge about the propriety or impropriety of others' actions, and bows down in modesty when any person whatsoever is mentioned; as water comes down from the top of a mountain and silently moves to the earth, even so, such a man is humble before everybody; as the branches of a tree, which is laden with fruits, are bent down to the earth, even so such a man feels humility before every being (IX. 221—227).

Un-pretentiousness.

33. Then Jñāneśvara goes on to speak about unpretentiousness. An unpretentious man is he who does not bring out his hidden spiritual treasure as a covetous man never brings out his. Even under pain of death, such a man never speaks about his meritorious actions; as a cow which does not give milk hides its own milk; or as a public woman hides her age; or as a rich man hides his wealth when on a journey; or as a noble girl hides her limbs; or as a husbandman hides his crops; similarly, such man never brings out his charity and merit into the broad day-light. He does not worship anybody, nor flatter him; his merit he never lets fly on a highly-raised banner; he is very stingy about his bodily enjoyments; he is very charitable about religious duties; difficulties may press him at home, and yet in charity he competes with the wish-fulfilling heavenly tree;......he is charitable at the right moment, and clever in speaking about self-knowledge; otherwise he looks as if he were a lunatic. The size of a plantain tree looks small, and yet it is rich in fruits which are full of sweetness; a cloud looks as if it may be blown by a wind, but it sends down rain in plenty. By these marks must one know a man who takes pride in unpretentiousness (XIII. 203—217).

Harmlessness.

34. The next virtue that Jñāneśvara goes on to discuss is that of harmlessness. Now harmlessness is of various kinds. It may consist of non-injuriousness either of any organs of the body or of speech or of mind. Jñāneśvara goes on to discuss various kinds of non-injury as thus classified. The ideal sage, according to him, does not even cross a stream for fear of breaking its serenity; he moves as a crane moves slowly on the surface of water, or as a bee moves slowly on a lotus, for fear of disturbing its pollen; the very atoms, he regards, as consisting of life; and therefore he walks softly as if by compassion. The road on which he walks is itself a road of compassion; the direction, in which he walks, is a direction of love; he spreads his life, as it were, below the feet of other beings, in order that he may be a source of happiness to all beings; he treads the earth as softly as when a cat holds its young one in its mouth for fear of injuring them by its teeth (XIII. 241—255). His hands remain motionless as the mind of a sage remains motionless on account of his desires being fulfilled; he does not move his hand for fear of disturbing the wind, or the sky, that lies round about him; far less may we say that he may cause any flies on his body to move away, or any gnats not to enter his eyes, or that he would make an angry face against birds and beasts; he may not even raise a stick; far less may we say that he may wield a weapon; to play joyfully with lotuses in his hands, or to toss garlands of flowers, is to him almost as hard a function as throwing a sling; he raises his hand only to show protection; he stretches his hand only to succour the fallen; he moves his hand only to touch the afflicted; and he does this all so lovingly that even the southern wind might be regarded as harsh when contrasted with his mildness (XIII. 278—290). In a similar way, such a man is harmless even when he sees; he does not look at other things for fear that they may take away his vision of God who is immanent in all things; and yet if he sometimes moves his eyes through internal compassion, he moves them so softly that even the streaks of moonlight may be more palpable than the motions of his eye (XIII. 273—276). The ideal sage is harmless even in speech; his love moves first, and then move the words from his mouth; compassion comes first, and then the words. Is it possible that the words coming from such a man may do injury to any one? He remains silent for fear of breaking the peace of men, for fear of being even so much as the cause of the raising of eyebrows in others; and if, when lovingly requested, he opens his mouth, he is as kind to his hearers as a father and mother; his words sing the mystic sound incarnate ......True and soft, measured and sweet, his words are as it were the waves of nectar. They have once for all taken leave of opposition, argument, force, injury to beings, ridicule, persecution, touch to the quick,......greed, doubt, and deceit (XIII. 261—272). Finally, his mind is as harmless as either his body, or his speech; for his body and his speech would not be harmless, if the mind itself were not already harmless; for it is the seed that is sown in the ground which shows itself as a tree later on; similarly, the mind shows itself in the direction of the senses. Mental impulse has its origin in mind, and then it comes over to speech, or sight, or the motor organs; when the mind's mindness is departed, the senses lose their rigour, as without a wire-puller the dolls cease to throw out their hands and feet; when the sea experiences a tide, the ships are themselves filled with water, similarly the mind makes the senses what it itself is...... If one would want to see what non-injury is, one must go to this man, for he is non-injury incarnate (XIII. 293—313).

Sufferance and Straightforwardness.

35. Sufferance is the next virtue that calls for treatment at Jñāneśvara's hands. It consists in courageously bearing the various kinds of affliction—physical, accidental, mental. Such a man is never tormented under heat, and never shakes under cold, and is not moved by any accident whatsoever; as the earth does not feel that it is over-peopled by the infinite number of beings that range on it, similarly, he is not inconvenienced under the hardship of any duality whatsoever; like an ocean, he gives room within himself to rivers and rivulets of grief, while, finally, he is not conscious that he is suffering from these. This, according to Jñāneśvara, is unconscious sufferance (XIII. 344—351). Coming to straightforwardness, Jñāneśvara speaks of the Sage as being as equable as the sun, with whom persons do not count, or as accommodative as the sky, which gives place to all things inside it; his mind does not change from man to man, nor his conduct; he holds in bonds of friendship the whole world from time immemorial, and he does not know how to distinguish between himself and others; like a full-blossomed lotus, there is no cranny in his heart; his mind is as straight as a downward streak of honey. A straightforward man is the *habitat* of all these marks (XIII. 356—367).

Devotion to Guru.

36. Devotion to Guru is the virtue which has attracted the greatest amount of attention from Jñāneśvara, and Jñāneśvara spares no pains in describing it minutely. As a river should move towards the ocean with all the wealth of its water, or as revelation should finally rest in the Name of God, similarly the devotee is he who resigns all his things to the care of the Guru, and makes himself the temple of devotion; as a woman separated from her husband is only pining after him, similarly, to the devotee's heart, the place where the Guru resides is the only object of attention. When shall I be relieved of my sufferance, he asks, when may I be able to see my Guru? He verily regards a moment spent without the Guru as greater than a world-cycle. When any person brings some news from the Guru, or when the Guru himself sends some word to him, he feels as if a dead man should come to life again; as a poor man should see a great treasure, or a blind man should be restored to his sight, or as a poor beggar may be made to sit on the throne of Indra, similarly when he hears of his Guru, he is filled with great happiness (XIII. 369—383). He also meditates in his heart on the form of his Guru in extreme love; he places the Guru like a motionless star within the circumference of his heart, or within the precincts of his consciousness; and in the temple of beatific joy, he distils the nectar of his meditation on the Guru as the sole object of his worship; or when the sun of illumination has arisen, he fills the basket of his intellect with innumerable flowers of emotion, and worships the Guru with them; or at all the three pure seasons of the day, he burns the incense of his egoism and waves lights of illumination before his Guru.......In short, he makes himself the worshipper, and his Guru the object of worship (XIII. 385—390). Or else, once in a while, he regards his Guru as his mother, and then like a child, he lolls on the lap of his Guru in the enjoyment of the spiritual nectar he has received; or else he regards his Guru as a cow residing at the foot of the tree of illumination, and makes himself the calf; likewise does he make himself a fish, who moves in the waters of the great compassion and love of his teacher; or else he regards himself as a small plant watered by the showers of the grace of his teacher; or he regards himself as the young one of a bird, which, as yet, has neither eyes nor wings, and imagining his Guru as his mother receives his morsel from the other's beak (XIII. 396—403). The devotee must be so full of service to his Guru that, in mere wonder, the Guru may say to him, 'Ask any blessings of me'; and when the Guru becomes thus pleased, the devotee should ask, 'Let me translate myself into thy attendants, my Lord; I should shape myself into all the instruments of thy worship (XIII. 404—408). And so long as the body lasts, the disciple must be full of the spirit of service, and when the body is departing, he should consider that his ashes must be mixed with the earth where stand the feet of his Guru. "The watery portion of my body, I shall dissolve in the place where my Guru is sportively touching the waters; my light, I shall transform into the lamps which are to be waved before my teacher; my Prāṇa, I shall transform into Fans and Chaurīs which serve to please my Guru; the ether inside my heart, I shall dissolve in the place where my Lord lives along with his attendants" (XIII. 431—436). Finally, Jñāneśvara tells us that the devotee himself must become lean in the service of his teacher, and feed on the love of his Guru. He must become the sole receptacle of the instructions of his Guru; he should feel himself of a high lineage on account of his Guru, and must find his nobility in the good actions of his brother-pupils; his sole absorbing topic should be the constant service of his Guru; the line which his Guru lays down for carrying on his spiritual work, he should regard as binding upon him like rules of Castes and Āśramas.......... The Guru must be his place of pilgrimage; the Guru his deity, the Guru his mother and father;........the only thing that ought to fill the mouth of such a devotee, is the Mantra which his Guru has taught him; he should hold no book in his hands which does not contain the words of his master; the water which has touched his Guru's feet, he should regard as superior in spiritual efficacy to the waters of any place of pilgrimage in the world; when he gets a morsel of food which his Guru has thrown before him, he should regard even spiritual ecstasy as insignificant as compared with it; in order that he should enjoy the happiness of atonement, he should accept on his head the dust that is raised when his Guru walks;......when a man becomes full of these qualities, he becomes the sole abode of spiritual realization. Knowledge lives by him; in fact, he is the God of whom Knowledge is the devotee;......and Jñāneśvara goes on to give his personal experience that he has been longing for the service of the Guru as implied in the above statement; he must regard himself fortunate that he is not maimed of body so as to be prevented from engaging in Bhajana; fortunate is he that he is not blind; fortunate is he that he is not lame; fortunate is he that he is not dumb; fortunate is he that he is not idle, for he would have been otherwise uselessly fed; fortunate is he that he is entertaining real love for his master; it is for these reasons, says Jñāneśvara, that he has been nourishing his body in order that he might do spiritual service to his Teacher (XIII. 442—459).

37. Jñāneśvara next goes on to discuss the virtue of purity.

Purity.

A pure man is he whose heart is as lustrous as camphor; or else like a jewel, which is pure inside and outside; just as the Sun himself, who is pure both internally and externally; such a man washes off his bodily sins by good actions, and shines internally by knowledge; in this way, he becomes illuminative on both sides. On the other hand, a man whose mind is not pure, can scarcely be said to be pure even if he does good actions; he is like a dead man adorned with ornaments; or like an ass made to bathe in a place of pilgrimage; or like the bitter Dudhiya fruit anointed externally by raw sugar. Such a man is of as little use as an arch-way built in a deserted place; or as a famished man whose body is anointed with food; or as the Kunkuma mark on the forehead of a husbandless woman. He is like a showy pitcher which contains nothing, even though it may shine externally; or else like a painted fruit whose internal matter is made up of cow-dung; even so, a man who does good actions externally, gets no value, as a wine-bottle immersed in the holy Gang. It is, therefore, that we may say that a man should have internal knowledge, as well as have pure actions; the one takes away the dirt from the inside, the other from the outside; and when purity is produced on both sides, such a man becomes purity incarnate; his holy intentions shine out of him as the lamps in a house of marble. If such a man were to contaminate himself externally with objects of sense, his mind remains pure, and is itself uncontaminated. If a man were to meet persons of the pariah caste on the way, he does not thereby become contaminated himself; or the same youthful woman, who embraces her husband as well as her son, is not affected by passion when she embraces the latter; water has no power to moisten a diamond; sand is not boiled in hot water; similarly his temperament is not contaminated by evil desires. Such a man should be regarded as holy; in him does Knowledge dwell (XIII. 462—484).

Steadfastness.

38. Steadfastness or constancy consists in not allowing the mind to move even a little bit, even though the body may roam from place to place. As an avaricious man who goes to a foreign land, places his mind on his hidden treasure, similarly the mind of a continent man does not move at all. The sky does not move, even though the clouds seem to move; the fixed and constant star is not subject to the revolution of the other stars; the path does not move even though the travellers seem to move; the trees on the way do not come and go; similarly, the mind of a constant man does not move, even though it may be placed in the five-fold elemental existence of change and movement. As the earth is not moved by a storm, so his mind is not moved by calamities; he is not tormented by poverty and misery; he does not shake in fear and in sorrow, and is not afraid when death overtakes his body; his mind does not turn back when affliction, desire, old age, and disease overtake it; censure may come upon him, his life may be in danger, passion and dishonour may overtake him, but his mind does not move even a hair's breadth; the sky may come down, or the earth may rise up to the sky, but his mind knows no movement; an elephant carest a bit when he is attacked with flowers; similarly, a steadfast man does not care when he is blamed with evil words (XIII. 485—498).

Self-Control.

39. Self-control consists in not allowing the mind to obey the behests of the senses. It consists in keeping to the mind, as a spirit keeps to the body which it possesses, or as an armsman keeps to his weapon, or as a stingy man keeps to his treasure, or as a mother keeps to her son, or as a bee keeps to the honey. A man of self-control is afraid lest the ghost of passion may overtake him, or the witch of desire may catch hold of him; he does not allow his mind to move, as a strong husband does not allow his wife to move out; he makes the virtues keep guard at the doorway of mind on the watch-stand of introversion; he pens up his mind in the three Bandhas, famous in Yoga philosophy, or else in the movement of the Prāṇa on the right or lefthand side of the nose; he engages it in meditation quite near to the throne of Samādhi, so that it may reach illumination in course of time (XIII. 502—510).

Dispassion.

40. A dispassionate man does not care for the objects of sense as the tongue has no craving for vomited food, or as one does not embrace the body of a dead man. He does not care for sensual pleasures as one does not care for poison, or as one does not go inside a burning house, or as one does not take lodgment in the cave of a tiger, or as one does not jump into a cauldron of liquid iron, or as one does not rest upon the pillow of a serpent. Such a man has no craving for anything; he is lean of body and takes pride in tranquillity and self-control; he gives himself over to penance and fasting, and it is death to him to enter a busy town; he cares for the practice of Yoga, goes to solitude, and does not care for company; he likes worldly pleasure only as much as one likes to lie on a bed of arrows, or to wallow in mucus, or in mud; he cares as much for heavenly pleasure as one cares for the rotten flesh of a dog. It is only when a man gets such dispassion for the objects of sense that he becomes fit for the enjoyment of spiritual happiness (XIII. 514—523).

Un-Egoism.

41. Un-Egoism consists in doing actions, as if a man were to be addicted to actions, and yet not to take pride for having done those actions. Such a man is quite punctilious in doing his daily duties according to his caste or order, but does not cherish in his heart the thought that he is doing those actions. As wind moves everywhere without any idea, or as the Sun rises without any particular object, as revelation comes of its own accord, or as the Ganges moves without the notion of flowing to any particular place, similarly he acts without any pride. As trees fructify in due season and yet are not conscious of their fructification, similarly, he does actions unconsciously. His egoism is taken away out of his mind and actions, as the central thread may be taken out of a necklace; and as clouds move in the sky unconnected with each other, similarly, his actions are unconnected with his body. As a drunkard does not know what cloth he is wearing, or as a portrait is not conscious of the weapon which it is made to hold in its hand, as an ox may not know what philosophic work it is carrying on its back, similarly, he is not conscious of himself as doing those actions, and therein consists his un-egoism (XIII. 525—534).

Pessimism.

42. Jñāneśvara says that to take a pessimistic view of existence is for some time a necessary step in the realisation of spiritual knowledge. One should contemplate the griefs of birth and death, and old age and disease, before one actually becomes subject to them. One should contemplate one's birth as an abominable condition of existence, seeing that the body is formed out of a bit of mucus, has come out from the passage of urine, and has devoured the sweat of the breasts. One should determine that he should do nothing by means of which he would be subject to this condition again; and before death comes,—may it be even at the end of a cycle,—he should become awake even to-day. For does not a man gird up his loins even on the banks of a river, when he is told that the waters of the river are very deep? Does not a man keep awake when he knows that his guide is a robber? Does not a man take medicine before he meets death? When a man finds himself in a house on fire, it will be useless to dig a well. Just as a man, who has come to contract deadly enmity with a powerful enemy, keeps his sword brandished during all the hours of the day; as a bride, for whose nuptials all the necessary ceremonies are made, is sure to be married; or as a man, about whom it is proclaimed that he will take Samnyāsa, must perforce take Samnyāsa; similarly, one must prepare himself for death even before he meets it. One should live by his own self by averting life with life, and death with death. Moreover, as regards the evils of old age, he should contemplate them even while youth is still on him. To-day the body is fat, but to-morrow it will be like a dried vegetable. To-day these eyes compete with the petals of a lotus, but to-morrow they will be as putrid as a over-ripe 'paḍavala'......"The passages of the fæces and urine will be obstructed, and they will prepare for my death. The world may spit at me. I shall be caught in the clutches of death. My relations will be utterly disgusted with me ....My cough will keep all my neighbours awake, and they may well ask why the old man does not die?" One should keep all this before his mind even in youth, and then one will grow disgusted with life.......One should hear before non-hearing comes. One should move before lameness occurs. One should see while yet vision is not lost. One should talk good words before one becomes dumb. One should do acts of charity before the hands become crippled. In general, one should think about spiritual knowledge, before such a condition befalls and the mind becomes idiotic. As one may make arrangements for his estate before the thieves come to rob one of it, or as one may arrange things in his house while yet the lamp is burning, similarly, one should make arrangements before old age comes. Just as a man may be robbed, if on his way he does not mind the mountains and valleys, or if he does not take hint from the fact that the birds are moving to their nests in the evening; just as a man should take counsel of health before disease overtakes him; or as one may leave a ball of eatables which has fallen into the mouth of a snake; similarly, a man should live in utter detachment, for fear that separation with objects of sense will bring calamity and grief (XIII. 536—590).

Unattachment, and Love of Solitude.

43. An unattached person is he who lives in his body as a guest lives in the house of a host. He has as much desire for a place of residence, as one has for the shade of a tree which one accidentally meets on the road. One should have no craving for union with one's wife, as one has no craving for the shadow which creeps along with the body. Children must be regarded as passengers who accidentally meet, or as cattle which sit under the shade of any tree whatsoever. In the midst of prosperity, such a man lives unattached, as one who only shows the way on a journey without going himself (XIII. 594—598). And he also loves solitude. " He should have a passion for places of pilgrimage, and the holy banks of rivers, forests and groves, which one inhabits for spiritual purposes. He should not come to a busy town, living as he does in caves, the hearts of mountains, and in the precincts of large lakes. He should love solitude and hate all towns" (XIII. 612—614).

God-Devotion.

44. To crown all, he must have God-devotion. He should resolve that there is no object of love greater than God. He should devote his body and speech and mind solely to God's contemplation. " He should come in My near presence and should sit down with Me. As a wife does not feel any difficulty in approaching her husband, similarly, he should approach Me. As the waters of the Ganges keep on moving towards the Ocean, similarly, he keeps on coming to Me. He who becomes one with Me, and yet maintains devotion towards Me, may be said to be Knowledge incarnate" (XIII. 604—611). And what is Knowledge? Knowledge consists in realizing that God alone is; that beyond Him and without Him there is nothing; that the knowledge of this world and of the other world is tantamount to mere ignorance. He alone has attained to Knowledge who becomes fixed in the idea that God alone is real, and all else an illusion. He is like the fixed and constant star in the heavens, who determinately maintains the reality of spiritual knowledge...... What is the use of any other knowledge? Is it not like the lamp in the hand of a blind man? On the other hand, he, who reaches the end in the light of contemplation, holds reality as it were in the hollow of his hands (XIII. 616—632).

Catalogue of Vices.

45. Hitherto we have seen how Jñāneśvara takes an intellectual view of virtue, and how in Socratic fashion he identifies virtue with knowledge. Knowledge to him, in fact, consists, in the manner of the Bhagavadgītā, of the so many virtues which we have hitherto discussed. As he takes an intellectual view of knowledge, he also takes an intellectual view of ignorance. Now ignorance is the absence of knowledge, and therefore means absence or negation of the many virtues which we have hitherto discussed. Following merely a hint thrown out in the text of the Bhagavadgītā—"Ajñānam yadatonyathā"—Jñāneśvara goes into details over a discussion of the negation of virtues, which constitutes ignorance. As contrasted with the various virtues enumerated above, there are a number of vices corresponding to the virtues, each by each; and this Jñāneśvara now goes on to discuss. As when day comes to an end and night begins to have its sway, similarly, when knowledge ceases, ignorance reigns supreme. What now are its marks? An ignorant man is he who lives upon the respect which others pay to him. He expects to be honoured. He is pleased with hospitality. He never descends from his greatness, as one in pride may not descend from the summits of a mountain. On the high tree of speech, he erects an archway of his own merits, as one may raise a broomstick on the top of a temple. He spreads about his knowledge, and sounds as with a cymbal his own good deeds; whatever he does, he does for the sake of fame. And as fire may spread through a forest and burn both animate and inanimate objects, similarly, by his actions, he is the cause of grief to the whole world. What he speaks in jest is more piercing than a powerful and sharp nail. It is more deadly than poison......As dust rises to the top of the sky through a hurricane of wind, similarly, by praise he is inflated and raised. On the other hand, when he hears his censure, he holds down his head, as mud is dropped down by water and dried by wind. His mind is haughty ; in speech he is unrestricted ; in presence he agrees ; in absence he supports another ; his external actions are only as good as the food which a hunter places before a deer ;......or as a pebble enveloped by moss, or as the pungent Nimboḷī fruit which is ripe. He is ashamed of his spiritual teacher. He swerves from devotion to his Guru, and having learned wisdom from his teacher, he behaves arrogantly with him. In his actions and body, he is loose. In mind he is full of doubts. He is like a dirty well in a forest, on the surface of which there are thorns, and inside there are bones. As a hungry dog makes no distinction between what one may take and what one may not take, similarly, for the sake of pelf, he does not recognize persons. Just as the little lion of the village, namely a dog, partakes of pure and impure things together, similarly, he makes no distinction between one woman and another. He is not pained at heart, even if he misses the proper time for daily or ceremonial actions. As a pond becomes dirty as soon as a foot is placed inside it, similarly, his mind is tormented as soon as fear enters it. His mind flows on the waters of desires like a gourd on a flood of water. In such a man, we may say, ignorance reigns; for, by his instability, he is brother to an ape. His mind roams like an ox that is let loose, or like a storm of wind ;......or like a blind elephant that is intoxicated, or like a fire that burns on a mountain. He is immersed all the while in sensual pleasures. To him there is no other occupation except sensual delight. He performs ablutions as soon as he finds a dispassionate man. He approaches sensual objects, as a male ass approaches a she-ass, even though the latter kicks at him and breaks his nose. For the attainment of sensual pleasure, he would throw himself in a place on fire. He regards vices as ornaments. Just as a deer which runs after a mirage until it breaks its head, similarly, from birth to death he runs after sensual objects, and even though defeated in his attainment, he still conceives greater and greater love for them. At first he loved his mother when he was a child. Later on, when he became a youth, his wife was the sole engrossing topic of his attention. In the company of his wife he becomes old, and in his old age his child becomes the sole object of his affection.......In all these cases, he regards the body as soul, and acts likewise. As the worshipper of a deity is possessed as soon as flowers are placed on his head, similarly, he becomes full of pride by his knowledge and youth, and in a supine position he says that there is nobody like him, and that he is omniscient.......As when a flame is burning, the wick is exhausted and along with it the oil, similarly, he burns all his qualities and all his affections, and he is reduced merely to soot. He is like a flame which crackles when water is sprinkled on it, and which is extinguished if a breath is blown against it, but which burns as soon as it catches the slightest piece of grass, which sends out little light but becomes hot even by its littleness. He becomes as inflated as a pariah when crowned, or as the big serpent which swallows a pillar. He knows no humility like the unsuccumbing rolling stick. His heart knows no tears like a stone, and like a bad serpent he does not succumb even to a charmer. He so much believes in life that he cannot imagine that there is death. Like a fish in a small pond of water, he believes that it will never dry up, and therefore feels no necessity for going to a deeper place......But this poor fellow does not know that when a concubine delivers over all that is hers, that is only the cause of ruin; the company of thieves is only the cause of death; to drench a picture in water is to destroy it. As when a man is running to the place of beheadal, death is approaching him at every step, similarly, as life is growing and as happiness is increasing, death is conquering life and destroying it, as salt is being destroyed in water. Old age is sure to come with as much necessity as a cart comes down from a precipice, or a piece of stone descends from the top of a mountain. He is as full of the madness of youth as a small brook is full of water, or as when the buffaloes enter into a deadly quarrel with one another. As an ox may accidently return from a tiger's cavern, and then desire to go back again to it, or as a man may bring a treasure safely for once from a serpent's place,........similarly, he does not imagine that his fortune is accidental, and does not take into account that there is a serpent to guard it. He cannot imagine that in a short time he may be separated from his fortune and be reduced to a plight of misery. By the boasted powers of his youth and the help of his treasure, he resorts to good and bad things together. He enters what he ought not to enter; he walks where he must not walk; he touches what neither body nor mind should touch; he goes where he ought not to go; he sees what he ought not to see;

he eats what must not be eaten ; ....he keeps company which he must avoid ; he goes where he must not go ; he follows a path which he must not follow ; he hears what he must not hear ; he prattles what he must not speak....... His affection is centred in his house, as a bee clings to the new pollen and fragrance of a flower. His wife attracts his attention, as a piece of sugar attracts a fly.......He, whose heart is conquered by a woman, does not know how to benefit his own self. He is not ashamed ; he is deaf to the censure of others ; he worships the heart of his paramour, and dances according to her wishes, as a monkey dances before its master. As a devotee may worship his family deity, similarly, with one-pointed attention, he worships his wife. If anybody were to see her, or if anybody were to oppose her, he feels as if there is going to be an end of the world.......If he loves God, he loves him for the attainment of some end ;......and if he cannot attain to his end as soon as he worships, then he disbelieves, and leaves away his devotion to God as futile. As a villager worships one god after another and with a devotion with which he worshipped the first, he goes to a Guru, who seems to him to be very prosperous, and learns a Mantra from him. He creates an image of his own choice, and places it in the corner of his house, while he himself goes to a place of pilgrimage, and visits temple after temple. He must worship the real god every day, but when he has some end to be fulfilled, he worships his family deity, and when any particular holy occasion comes, he worships quite another. Forgetting that God is at home, he roams to deity after deity, and worships the manes on the occasion of a Śrāddha. With the same devotion with which he must worship God on the Ekādaśī day, he worships the serpent on the Nāgapañċhamī. On the fourth day of the dark half of the month, he worships Durgā. He leaves away his daily and ceremonial duties, and worships the Navachaṇḍī. On Sundays, he distributes food in order to please Bhairava. On Mondays, he runs to a Liṅgam to worship it with Bela leaves. In this way, he tries to please god after god. He worships perpetually without remaining silent for a moment, as a courtesan tries to attract man after man at the doorway of a town. A devotee, who thus runs from deity to deity, may be said to be ignorance incarnate......Such a man takes delight in society, is pleased with the noise of a town, takes pleasure in talking gossip, and when anybody talks to him about the real way to reach God, he creates such a noise that he refuses to hear it. He does not go to the Upanishads. He has no love for Yoga.

His mind has no liking for the Pathway to God. He likes every other subject except the discussion of mystic knowledge. He knows the theory of Karma. He has studied different Purāṇas and learnt them by heart. He is such a great astrologer that he can predict future events. He is skilled in the science of Architecture. He knows the art of cooking. He is an expert in the magic of the Atharva-Veda. His knowledge of the sexual science knows no bounds. He has studied the Bhārata. He is proficient in the knowledge of the Āgamas. He has known all the theories of Ethics. He has studied medicine. In poetics and dramaturgy, there is no man equal to him. He can discuss the topics of the Smṛitis. He knows the art of a magician. He is altogether versed in the Nighaṇṭu. He is clever in the science of Grammar, and has gone very deep in the science of Logic. He knows all these sciences; but he is stark-blind in the science of Self-knowledge...... One should not look at such a man, as one may not look at a child which is born in the constellation of Mūlā and which is the cause of death. The plumage of a peacock is covered all over with eyes, but there is no vision in the eyes; similarly, the knowledge of the various sciences is as nothing when the knowledge of the Self is excluded......The body of such a man is only the seed of ignorance. From such a seed can spring no other plant, or flower, or fruit, except ignorance itself (XIII. 653—842).

Divine Heritage I.

46. The chief excellence of Jñāneśvara as a mystical philosopher lies, as we have seen, in his analysis of the different virtues, and corresponding to them, the different vices in his exposition of the thirteenth Chapter of the Bhagavadgītā. Jñāneśvara recurs again to a similar discussion of virtues and vices in his exposition of the sixteenth Chapter. There we have a division of the two heritages—the divine heritage, and the demoniac heritage. The divine heritage is a heritage of virtues; the demoniac heritage is a heritage of vices. Now, what are the virtues that constitute a divine heritage? Jñāneśvara tells us that the first virtue is fearlessness. It consists in not being afraid of Samsāra, because the egoism in reference to action and non-action has already been killed. It also consists in throwing away all feeling of fear, in the firm belief of the unity of all things and the identification of another with oneself. If water tries to drench salt, the salt itself becomes water. Hence when one has experienced the unity of all things, fear vanishes immediately. The second virtue, namely, purity, consists in keeping the heart as pure as the waters of the Ganges before the onset of the rainy season and after the end of the hot season...... It consists in making the intellect united with God-head, and in keeping the mind unmoved by the senses, as a chaste wife is not moved by the considerations of gain and loss in her separation from her husband at his departure to a distant place. The third virtue, namely, fixity of knowledge, consists in making the mind full of the desire for the attainment of Ātman. It consists in sacrificing the whole of the mind to God as one may throw an offering in fire without any reference to fruit. As a nobly-born person offers the hand of his girl to a person of noble birth without any desire, ...similarly one should become fixed in the knowledge of Yoga without the taint of any desire. Charity consists in sacrificing oneself in mind and wealth to an afflicted man, just as a tree offers itself wholly to a passenger in the street by its shade, or by its flowers, fruits, roots, or leaves. Self-restraint consists in separating the senses from their objects, as water may be cleaned by means of the Nivaḷī seed; it consists in not allowing the objects to influence the senses by giving these latter in the hands of self-control,......in filling all the ten senses with the fire of dispassion, and finally, in making the body succumb to severe duties as incessant as inspiration and expiration. The next virtue, namely, sacrifice, consists in dutifully offering to God whatever is best. When a Brahmin does his caste-duties, and a Śūdra bows down to him, both may be said to be performing sacrifice equally. Everyone can sacrifice in this way by only attending to his proper duties; only he must not be infected with the poison of the fruit of actions. When a ball is struck at the ground, the real intention is not to strike the ground but to catch hold of the ball; when seed is sown in a farm, the real object is not the sowing of the seed, but the rearing of the crops; as, again, a mirror is to be cleaned for enabling one to look at oneself inside it; similarly, one should study the sciences not for their own sake, but for the sake of God. The Brahmin may study the Brahma Sūtras, others may recite a hymn, or sing the name of God. A repetition of any of these things in order to attain to God may be called spiritual practice, which is the next virtue. Finally, by penance is meant emaciation of one's limbs and body for the sake of Self-realization, just as incense is burnt in fire, or gold loses its weight in the process of purification, or the moon wanes in the dark half of the month (XVI. 68—108).

Divine Heritage II.

47. Another set of qualities required for the divine heritage Jñāneśvara now goes on to develop. Straightforwardness consists, according to him, in being good to all beings, as milk is good to a child, or as the soul exists in all beings equally. Non-injury consists in making the body, speech, and mind exist only for the happiness of the world. Jñāneśvara gives us a good analysis of the conception of truth. Truth is as piercing and as mild as the unblown Jasmine flower, or as the light of the Moon which is nevertheless cool. It might be again compared to a medicine, which destroys disease as soon as it is seen, and which is not to the slightest degree pungent to the taste. But such a medicine does not exist, and so truth is incomparable. It is like water which does not pain the eye even though it is put inside it; which, on the other hand, has the power of breaking the precipices of mountains. It ought to be as piercing as iron in dispelling doubts; and in point of being heard it eclipses sweetness itself.......By its sweetness it deceives nobody; and by its straightforwardness it pains nobody. On the other hand, the huntsman's song is sweet to the ear, and yet it is death to the deer. Also, truth must not be like a siren's song, which is sweet to hear, but which, when meditated upon, breaks the heart. Truth is the mother's quality who becomes angry but does not mean ill. Non-anger is that quality of the heart, which, like a stone, upon which water is poured, does not yet sprout like a plant......A serpent's slough may be trodden under foot, and yet it raises no fang. The sky has no flowers even in spring-time. Śuka was never afflicted with passion even though he saw the beautiful form of Rambhā. Even though ghee is poured upon ashes, it does not produce a flame of fire. Sacrifice consists in leaving away all contact with the world, after having killed the egoism of the body by means of the intellect. Tranquillity has an analogue in the destruction of the knower, the knowledge, and the known, all equally, as when the infinite flood of water at the time of the Great End, having eclipsed the existence of the world, makes the spring, the stream, and the ocean, all equally disappear. Goodness is, for example, exhibited by the physician who has no partiality for his or others' people, and whose one desire is to conquer the onset of disease before it passes out of control. When a cow sinks in mud, one does not care whether she is a milch-cow or not; one's only business is to relieve her from suffering. When a man is drowning, people do not care whether he is a Pariah or a Brahmin; their only business is to take him out of water. When a chaste woman has been robbed of her clothes, a good man looks at her only when he has covered her with a cloth. When others' faults leap to the eye, one should cover them and then look at them. We should look at a deity, after we have worshipped it. We should go to a farm, only when the seed has been already sown. We should take the blessings of a guest, only when we have pleased him. Similarly, by one's qualities, one should cover the defects of others, and then look at them. Compassion is like the broad moonlight which sends a cooling influence without considering the great and the small. Compassion is exhibited most by water, which destroys itself in order to maintain the life of grass. Even if one sacrifices oneself wholly by looking at the misery of others, one should consider that one has not yet played one's part completely. He should feel distressed at the misery of others, as when a thorn rushing into the foot makes the whole body ache, and as when the foot is rubbed with cool oil, the coolness goes to the eye, similarly when others become happy, one ought to grow happy. That man is compassion incarnate, whose life is meant merely for the relief of the sufferance of the afflicted, even as water is meant for the quenching of the thirst of those who are thirsty. Uncovetousness is like that of the Sun, who, even though the lotus may follow him, yet does not touch the other's beauty; or like that of the spring, which even though it may be the cause of the entire beauty of the forest, yet does not partake of it; or like that of God Vishṇu, who does not mind even though Lakshmī comes to him with all the Siddhis. The uncovetous man, in short, cares nothing for the enjoyment of the sensual objects of this world or of the next. Softness is like that of the bees when they are touching their hive, or of the sea-animals when they are swimming through waters, or of the birds when they are moving in the sky. The mother has always a soft corner for her child in her heart; the wind from the southern quarter is soft in spring-time; the vision of the beloved is soft to the eyes;......the camphor is soft to the touch, sweet to the taste, fragrant to the nose, brilliant of form, and so would have served as an excellent standard of comparison, could one have partaken of it to one's heart's content. Finally, one must be as soft as ether, which encloses inside all the elements, and yet enters into the smallest of atoms. Bashfulness is like that of the beautiful when affected with white leprosy, or of the nobly-born of whom an evil word is spoken. It consists in the reflection that there is no use in coming to birth and dying from time to time, and in being a corpse even though living. Is it not shameful to be obliged to live in the womb of the mother, where blood and urine and fat and other things make a motley fluid ? To even take on name and form in the shape of a body is most shameful. Finally, absence of fickleness is like that of the doll which ceases to throw out its hands and feet, when once its inner thread is taken away. It consists in reclaiming our senses by conquering the Prāṇa. As when the sun sets, all the rays are absorbed in it, similarly, when the mind is conquered, all the senses become one with it. Hence when the mind and breath have been conquered, all the senses become powerless. In this powerlessness of all the senses consists the constancy of mind (XVI. 113—185).

Divine Heritage III.

48. A third set of moral qualities that come under the divine heritage is discussed in yet another verse of the Bhagavadgītā which now Jñāneśvara tries to expound. Spiritual lustre is that quality which does not allow a man to lessen his courage, when one is trying to reach God by the Yoga method of realization. The Satī does not care for death in fire, because the death is to be met for the sake of her husband. It consists in naturally and determinately following the pathway to God, irrespective of any obstruction from jural or social commandment, or by the hindrances of the so-called Siddhis. Sufferance is absence of pride in having become great by being obliged to suffer evils, as the body which carries the hair on itself does not know that it is so carrying them. Courage is exhibited in withstanding the flood-gates of sensual impulse, or in putting up with any disease that one's misfortune makes one suffer, or in meeting an evil fate. A courageous man stands more boldly than the sage Agastya, even though all these misfortunes may come upon him simultaneously as in a great flood. Just as a small motion of wind dissipates even a lengthy column of smoke in the sky, similarly, a courageous man bears all mental, physical, or accidental evils, and even on occasions of great mental disturbance preserves his absolute equanimity. Purity is like that of a golden pitcher, thoroughly cleansed from the outside, and filled inside with the water of the Ganges. It consists in doing actions without reference to results on the outside, and in maintaining perfect discrimination from the inside. Love towards all is exhibited as by the water of a holy river, which destroys all sin and suffering as it moves on, nourishes the trees on its banks, and ultimately discharges itself into the ocean. As the Sun destroys the blindness of the world, opens temples of lustre, and moves on encircling the universe, similarly the man, who bears love towards all, unloosens those who are bound, helps those who are sunk, and relieves those who suffer and are miserable. Day and night, his primary aim is to achieve the happiness of the human kind, and only secondarily does he care for his own interest, not to speak of any efforts made for the attainment of his end, when that action is sure to bring evil to the world. Finally, absence of pride consists in being bashful of one's greatness as the Ganges, when it descended on the head of Śaṅkara, contracted its volume of water (XVI. 186—206). Jñāneśvara tells us that the twenty-six virtues, which he has hitherto discussed, constitute the entire preparation for entering into the being of God......They are, as it were, the garland of flowers with which the maiden of Deliverance tries to adorn the neck of the Dispassionate; or else they are the twenty-six lights which Gītā, the damsel, waves before Ātman, her husband; or else, again, they are the twenty-six pearls found in the shell of the divine heritage in the ocean of the Bhagavadgītā (XVI. 207—212).

Demoniac Heritage.

49. Jñāneśvara now goes on to discuss the vices which constitute the demoniac heritage. These are, on the whole, six: hypocrisy, pride, arrogance, anger, harshness, and ignorance. Of these, hypocrisy consists in pretending greatness where there is none......If one were to bring to the market-place the learning, which he has imbibed from his teacher, that learning becomes itself a cause of evil. The office of a boat is to carry a man over a flood; but if it be tied to the foot of a man, it will only drown him; similarly, if one were to trumpet one's own meritorious deeds, that itself would become the cause of ruin. Pride is like that of the horse of a professional rider, which regards even the gods' elephant as inferior to it; or like that of the lizard on the thorn, which regards even heaven as inferior to it. The fire, which falls on grass, tries vainly to rise to the sky. The fish in a pond regards the ocean as of no matter. A man feels pride in his wife, or wealth, or learning, or praise, or honour, just as a man of little consequence becomes full of pride by being invited to dinner at another man's house even for a day. It is as if a foolish man should demolish his house, because there is for the while the shadow of a cloud over him; or again, as if one should break open a reservoir of water because he sees a mirage. Arrogance is exhibited by the moth which does not suffer a lamp; or by the fire-fly which tries to eclipse the sun; or by the little Ṭiṭṭibha bird which makes enmity with an ocean. An arrogant man does not suffer even the name of God. He regards his own father as his rival,......which is the sure way to moral ruin. An angry man cannot suffer the happiness of others, which is only the cause of the rise of his passion. When drops of water are poured over boiling oil, it only produces a great noise; a fox suffers deeply when it sees the moon; when the sun rises giving lustre to the whole world, the owl loses its sight; the dawn, which is the cause of happiness to human kind, is greater than death to the thief; milk, drunk by a serpent, becomes only poison; the fire in the bosom of the ocean consumes an amount of water, and yet burns more fiercely; similarly, an angry man becomes all the more angry by not being able to suffer the learning, the wisdom, and the prosperity of other people. A harsh man's mind is like the hole of a serpent; his sight is like a discharge of arrows; his speech is like a shower of fire; and the rest of his actions are as sharp as the edge of a saw. The ignorant man, like a stone, cannot distinguish between cold and heat. Like a man born blind, he does not know the distinction between night and day. He is like the ladle which enters into different fluids, but does not know the taste of any. Not being able to distinguish between a good thing and a bad thing, like a child he puts everything into his mouth. He makes a mixture of virtue and sin, and cannot distinguish their consequences (XVI. 217—252). These six vices constitute the whole demoniac heritage. The fang of a serpent, though small, is yet poisonous. The six vices are like a conjunction of fierce planets in the same zodiac. They are like the sins which gather together near a slanderer. As when a man is dying, he becomes subject to a number of diseases at the same time;...... or when a sheep is departing from life, a scorpion of seven stings may come and sting her; similarly, a man who cultivates these vices, goes down deeper in Samsāra, because he cannot rise to the path of God. He descends down and down, until he is born as the most heinous creature in existence, and is born even in the shape of stones (XVI. 253—263). Those, who oppose the will of God by their demoniac qualities, are born in the most heinous kinds of existences, which are only the dung-hill of misery, or the sewage-pit of the world of existence. They are born like tigers and scorpions, and do not get any food to eat; and suffering unbearable pangs of hunger, they ultimately eat themselves! They burn their bodies by their own poison, like a serpent that is pent up in its own hole. They find no rest even so much as for expiration. For an infinite number of cycles, they continue in these very existences......They are reduced to the state of darkness itself, which adds a deeper hue to the already existing darkness. Sin shudders at them; hell is afraid of them; misery becomes tired of them; dirt becomes more foul by them. Heat burns, and fear runs away at their mention. Evil becomes more evil. Untouchability becomes all the more untouchable......Speech fails at the mention of their evil fate. The mind recoils. What hellish existences have these fools purchased? Why should they have followed the demoniac path, which has led them to such a great fall? (XVI. 407—422.)

Other Miscellaneous Virtues.

50. From the above discussion of the Virtues and Vices, as implied in the discussion of the nature of Knowledge and Ignorance in the thirteenth Chapter, and of the Divine and Demoniac heritages in the sixteenth Chapter, it may be seen that Jñāneśvara excels particularly in his analysis of the moral qualities and their aberrations. Dispersed also throughout his various other Chapters are descriptions of other virtues, which we must not fail to notice. In the second Chapter, he speaks of true intellect as that by which, if it shines ever so little in a man, his whole fear of the worldly existence departs. We must not say that the flame of a lamp is small, as it produces great light; similarly, when true intellect is ever so little, we must say it nevertheless shows great power......The Parisa stone cannot be found like other stones, and even a drop of nectar would be impossible to find even by great accident. Thus the goal of true Intellect is God, just as the goal of the Ganges is the ocean. We may therefore define true Intellect as that which concerns itself with God above anything else whatsoever (II. 237—242). In the sixth Chapter, Jñāneśvara says that dispassion is the necessary condition of the pursuit of God. "Before a man can hope to find God, we must first see whether dispassion has been created in him. Even if a man be of small age, still if he has blossomed in the spring of dispassion, he will not take much time to bear the fruit of God-realization" (VI. 47—50). In the same Chapter, we read also how annihilation of desire itself means the realization of Ātman. "God is not very distant from those who have conquered their hearts, and have stilled their passions. When the dross material in base gold has been driven off, what remains is pure gold itself; similarly, when desire disappears, the Individual Soul becomes Brahman. The ether inside a pitcher that is broken meets the ether in the sky; similarly, when bodily egoism is destroyed, the Individual Soul is Brahman" (VI. 81—84). Then again, in the same Chapter we read further how observation of the mean is a necessary condition of spiritual life. "We must eat food, but take it only in a measured quantity. We must do actions, but in a measured manner. We must speak measured words. We must measure our steps. We may also by measure go to sleep. If we are to keep awake, that also we must do by measure. In this way, when equanimity is produced in the body, great happiness will arise (VI. 349—351). In the twelfth Chapter, Jñāneśvara describes the virtue of equanimity in a very clever way. Such a man knows no unevenness of temper. He is equal to his friends and foes. As a lamp does not think that it must produce light for those to whom it belongs, and create darkness for those to whom it does not belong; as the tree gives the same shade to a man who puts his axe at its root as well as to him who rears it up; as a sugarcane is not sweet to the man who has reared it, and sour to the man who presses it; similarly, the man of equanimity is alike to friend and foe, as well as to honour and dishonour. He is not moved by praise, nor is his mind disturbed by words of censure, like the sky which is not tainted by anything. He tells neither truth nor untruth; but only shuts his lips. He can never be prevented from enjoying the super-conscious ecstatic state. He is pleased with what good befalls him. He is not displeased with loss, as the Ocean does not dry up because there is no rain. He does not resort to any particular place, as the wind has no partiality for any one locality. He deliberately thinks that the whole world is his mansion; in fact, he becomes the All (XII. 197—213).

The Nature of Sacrifice.

51. In the seventeenth Chapter, Jñāneśvara makes particularly two good discussions, namely, of the nature of Sacrifice, and of the nature of Penance. Following the Bhagavadgītā, he recognizes a psychological background to these moral virtues, and says either Sacrifice or Penance may be Sāttvika, Rājasa, and Tāmasa. And first to speak about sacrifice. Sacrifice, in which Rajas predominates, may be disposed off in a word by saying that the aim of such a sacrifice is fame. Likewise we may say that the aim in Tamas-sacrifice is folly. What matters is only that kind of sacrifice in which Sattva predominates. True sacrifice is that in which there is no attachment to the fruit of it, as a truly chaste woman does not allow any scope to her passion, except in the case of her own husband. As when a river has gone to the ocean, it stops moving further ; or as when the Veda had reached the discussion of the Ātman, it stands silent ;......or as when water, when it reaches the root of a tree, reaches its consummation and moves no further ; similarly, in true sacrifice, the sacrificer loses himself in the bare act, and does not think of the fruit. As one can see oneself in a mirror ; or as one can see a jewel in the hand by means of a lamp ; or as when the sun has arisen, one can see the way ; similarly, because it is the command of the Veda, the sacrificer gathers together all the different kinds of material for sacrifice, employs those which are wanted in their particular places,...... and completes the sacrifice without the slightest taint of egoism. The Tulasī plant is reared in a house, but no desire is entertained for its fruit, or flower, or shade. In a similar manner, that kind of sacrifice is alone real in which there is no reference to any fruit whatsoever (XVII. 170—184).

Penance in which Sattva predominates.

52. Like sacrifice, penance is also of three kinds, according as Sattva, or Rajas, or Tamas predominates in it. Now the penance in which Sattva predominates, may be either of body, or of speech, or of mind. Bodily penance is exhibited in going round a number of places of pilgrimage, and thus exercising the feet during all the twenty-four hours. The hands should be devoted to the work of the adornment of temples, and for supplying flowers and incense to the deity. As soon as a Liṅgam or an Image is seen, the body must fall down prostrate like a stick. Also service must be rendered to those who are elders in learning and virtue. Bodily penance also consists in bringing happiness to all those who are suffering from the pains of travel, or from any other difficulties whatsoever. The body should be devoted to the service of the parents, who are holier than any other holy objects. The Guru must particularly be worshipped, who so compassionately bestowed upon us Knowledge, and showed us the way out of the wilderness of Samsāra. The body, which is naturally subject to laziness, must, in the performance of duty, be subjected to the repetitions of good acts. One should bow down to God, supposing that He is in all human beings, take resort to benefaction of others, and have absolute self-control in regard to women. Only at the time of birth must a woman be touched ; further, there should be no contact with any woman whatsoever (XVII. 202—211).

We now turn to the penance of speech. This virtue consists in bringing happiness to another without speaking evil words to him. Just as a philosopher's stone makes an iron ball a ball of gold without reducing its weight; as water goes down in the first instance to the roots of a tree, but incidentally it also helps the grass to grow; similarly, when a man is speaking with one, he should benefit all. Were it possible to find a river of nectar which makes life immortal, we would find that it drove off sin and sorrow as well as supplied sweet drink at the same time......We should speak only when one is spoken to; otherwise we should recite the Vedas, or utter the name of God. The mouth should be verily the abode of the different Vedas, or else should be given to the utterance of the name of God, whether it may belong to the Śaiva school or the Vaishṇava school (XVII. 216—223). Mental penance consists in making the mind atoned to God when all its desires and doubts have been at an end, like a lake which is placid when there are no waves on it, or like the sky in which there are no clouds, or like a garden of sandal trees from which the serpents have run away. It may also be compared to the moon in which the indeterminateness of the Kalās has been at an end, or to a king whose mental anxiety has disappeared, or to the Sea of Milk from which the Mandarāchala mountain has been taken off......Were it possible to find the moon which would have no spots, which would not move, and which was full at all times, it might have been compared to the beauty of such a mind. In it, the striving after dispassion is at an end; the palpitation and shaking have ceased; and what remains is perfect Self-realization. It is for this reason that such a mind does not succumb even to the recital of the Vedas. It has attained its own end, and therefore it has lost its mind-ness, as salt, which, when merged in water, loses its saltness. In such a mind, mental purity exists of itself, as the palm of a hand is naturally hairless. This condition of mind is entitled to the name of mental penance (XVII. 225—236).

Penance in which Rajas predominates.

53. The penance in which Rajas predominates makes one aspire after reaching the pinnacle of greatness. Such a man thinks that the highest honour in the whole world must go to him. He must have the seat of honour at the dinner-time; he should be the sole receptacle of the praise of the world; people in the whole world should make a pilgrimage to him; worshippers of other men should find their ideal in him. Such a man is verily like an old courtezan who still puts ornaments on her body in order to attract the attention of men. That kind of penance, therefore, the aim of which is to acquire wealth or honour, may be called Rājasa penance. When an insect partakes of the milk from the udders of a cow, the cow ceases to give milk, even though she might have just given birth to a calf. A man, who sends his cattle to feed on the crops of his field, shall have nothing left to him from which grain may come. Similarly, that penance in which there is a mere trumpeting of one's effort, becomes utterly useless........Will such an untimely cloud, which fills the sky and which seems to break the heaven by its thunder, continue for a long time to overcast the sky? (XVII. 242—251.)

Penance in which Tamas predominates.

54. The penance in which Tamas predominates is exhibited in foolishly regarding the body as one's enemy; in making it travail in the midst of the five strong fires; or, in fact, in even making an offering of it in fire; in burning resin on the top of the head; in putting one's back on iron pikes;........in famishing the body by swallowing morsels of smoke by placing one's mouth in an inverted position; in resorting to rocks and banks of rivers, which are full to the brim of ice-cold water; and finally, in plucking off portions of flesh from the live body. Such a kind of penance, in which the aim is the destruction or the subjugation of others, may well be illustrated by a stone, which descends at full speed from the top of a mountain, and which, as it is broken into small pieces, breaks also anything that comes in its way; similarly, by giving infinite trouble to oneself, the aim of one who makes such a penance is to bring misery upon those who are otherwise living happily (XVII. 254—262).

Resignation to God.

55. Finally, Jñāneśvara gives us a philosophical account of the virtue of resignation to God in the last Chapter of the Jñāneśvarī. There, he discusses the nature of resignation philosophically rather than morally, and tells us that resignation to God consists in identification with Him. Arjuna may be said to have resigned completely to the will of Kṛishṇa when he became identified with Him. "To know My oneness without the distinction of Self is the meaning of resignation. As when a pitcher is broken, its ether merges in the infinite ether, similarly, be submissive to Me in being united with Me. As gold into gold, or as wave into the ocean, similarly, be thou submissive unto Me..........To say that the devotee has submitted to Me, and that he has retained a separate individuality of his own, is utter folly. Even a bondswoman of an ordinary king becomes equal to him when she tries to please him........To say, on the other hand, that when God is seen, the separate individuality of a person remains,—is it not merely a piece of foolish gibbering?.......When butter-milk is churned out of curds, it can never become curds again. Similarly, when thou hast submitted to Me in unitive life, good and bad shall cease to trouble thee. Iron in its ironness may rust, but when it has become gold on account of a philosopher's stone, dirt shall never spoil it. When fire is churned out of sticks, it shall never become a stick again. When the Sun has arisen, shall darkness reappear? Or when wakefulness comes, shall the illusion of a dream continue to give trouble? When thou hast, therefore, reached unitive life in Me, nothing shall remain outside Me. Think not, therefore, of what may befall thee. For, thy sin and merit shall both be transformed in My being. Thy sin shall be merged in My knowledge, and no trace of it shall remain. ....From this time onwards thou hast become free, O Arjuna! Think but of Me in this light and I shall succour thee. Entertain no anxiety, therefore, and resign thyself to Me in being united with Me" (XVIII. 1398—1416).

The Ideal of the Karma-Yogin.

56. The ideal which Jñāneśvara sets up in the manner of the Bhagavadgītā of the true Karma-Yogin, who reconciles action and actionlessness and reaches actionlessness through action, is explained by him in many places. In the fourth Chapter, he compares the true Karma-Yogin to the Sun, who only seems to move because he rises and sets, but who does not really move. He looks like a man, and yet he is not a man, as the image of the sun is not drowned in water. He sees the world, and sees it not. He does everything, and does it not. He enjoys everything, and has not enjoyed it. He sits in one place, but moves in all places; in fact, he becomes identical with the whole Universe (IV. 99—102). It is to be remembered that in this passage Jñāneśvara speaks of only the apparent motion of the Sun which he really calls stationary. It is a matter of great astronomic interest that this mystic philosopher should have put forth a heliocentric theory at a time when heliocentrism was hardly recognized in Europe. This is, however, by the bye. But, continues Jñāneśvara, the Ideal Sage, even though he may have reached actionlessness, has still to do duty for the sake of others.

As a seeing man walks before a row of the blind, similarly, the sage exhibits the nature of duty to others by practising it himself. How else could the ignorant know the true path, if it were not to be shown to them by such a man? What is, in fact, duty? It is what our elders exhibit to us in their actions. The ordinary run of mankind has only to follow them on the way (III. 155—158). And the ideal sage must remember that even though he himself may have reached the state of actionlessness, still he should not preach the gospel of actionlessness to those who are incompetent to hear it. A child which can hardly suck milk from its mother's breast —how would it be possible for it to eat dainties? Dainties are not for children, O Arjuna. Similarly, those, who are incompetent to do even their own duty, should not be taught the gospel of actionlessness even in sport. To them we should give lessons in good action itself. That alone should be praised before them. The sage must practise it before them. When the sage does such actions merely for the guidance of the generality of the mankind, he will not be bound down by them. Those, who only feign the king and the queen, never really believe that they are either man or woman, and yet they act as if they were so (III. 172—176). The true Karma-Yogin, therefore, must teach the gospel of action to others, even though his heart may have rested in the sabbath of actionlessness.

From Action to Actionlessness.

57. What is the gospel of action that the sage ought to teach? In a famous passage in the eighteenth Chapter, Jñāneśvara tells us that he should tell people that they ought to do all the actions that are necessary for them, like sacrifice, charity, penance, and others. Just as a traveller should never swerve from the path directed to him by the foregoing foot-prints, just as we should not leave the boat unless we have gone to the other bank of the river, just as we should not throw away a plantain-tree before it has given birth to plantains, just as we should not abandon a lamp before we have found out by means of it the thing which has been lost, similarly, until one becomes fixed in the knowledge of the Self, one should not grow indifferent to acts like sacrifice. We must do them with even greater zeal. As excess of speech is rest, similarly excess of action is actionlessness. ......As also when gold is put into the boiling vessel time after time, it loses its dross and becomes pure, similarly, action done with faith destroys Rajas and Tamas, and takes one to pure Sattva. It is for this reason, O Arjuna, that I say that for one, who wants to reach pure Sattva-hood, actions themselves become as holy as places of pilgrimage. A place of pilgrimage wears away one's external impurity; but action wears away internal impurity......As a man who is suffering from thirst in the Marudeśa may find a pond of nectar in that country; or as a drowning man may be saved by the River itself; or as a falling man may be held up by the Earth in pity; or as a dying man get a further release of life from the Lord of Death; or as a diseased man may be relieved of his disease by a poison purified; similarly, a man who is doing actions, may be saved from the effects of action, and become worthy of salvation (XVIII. 149—163).

Works and Realization.

58. We must remember, nevertheless, that there is an eternal difference between works and realization. Jñāneśvara insists from time to time, in the manner of the Bhagavadgītā, on the difference between the doing of actions, and the knowing of God; and he tells us that the one is absolutely insignificant as contrasted with the other. "Those, who by rightful performance of the duties of the Aśramas, become themselves the standards of duty; who by performing sacrifices become an object of praise even for the Vedas;........such sacrificers, who are themselves the embodiment of sacrifice, only incur sin in the name of merit. For, in spite of their knowledge of the three worlds, and in spite of their performance of hundreds of such sacrifices, they leave Me, who am the object of the sacrifice, and hunt after heaven, just as an unfortunate man, sitting under the shade of a wish-tree, may tie and untie his begging satchel........Thus the path to heaven is a meritorious path for those who are ignorant. But those, who know, regard it as an hindrance, and as a ruin. Heavenly happiness is so-called, because it stands contrasted with the misery of hell; while contrasted with either is My spotless Form. When people come to Me, both heaven and hell would be seen to be merely the byways of thieves. One goes to heaven by the sin in the form of merit; while one goes to hell by the sin in the form of sin; while that, which enables one to reach Me, is pure merit. While they live in Me, they are away from Me, and yet they call their actions meritorious. Why should they not lose their tongues for such a lie? They go to heaven only by the sinful merit of not having known Me........ When this merit, however, is exhausted, their Indra-hood comes to an end, and they begin to come down to the world of mortals. As a man who has spent all his money in going to courtezans cannot even so much as touch their door, similarly, the life of the sacrificers becomes shameful, and does not deserve any further description......Thus even though a man may know all the three worlds, he becomes useless if he does not know Me. For he is throwing away the grain to partake of chaff!......Know Me, therefore, and know nothing else, and thou shalt be happy' (IX. 307—334).

Performance of Duty, a Divine Ordinance.

59. There are thus various means suggested from the point of view of action, so that one may ultimately land into the domain of Self-realization. The first means suggested for a riddance from action is the habit of doing our actions, because duty impels us to do them. The consideration of duty, therefore, forms the first justification for action. In the third Chapter of the Jñāneśvarī, we are told that this social duty was first prescribed by God Himself, and this duty was divided according to the requirements of castes and orders. "Do your duty, and the end will take care of itself. Do not go in for any vows or ceremonies. Trouble not yourself by going to places of pilgrimage. Do not deliver yourself to means like Yoga, or to aimful worship, or to charms and incantations. Worship not other deities. Do the sacrifice implied in your duty. Worship your deity with a mind bereft of any consideration of consequences, as a chaste woman worships her lord......If you just follow your duty, then duty will be a wish-cow to you" (III. 85—94). We thus see how the performance of duty as duty is the first way out of the bondage of actions.

Actions should be done without Attachment.

60. A second help, for getting ourselves away from the influence of actions, is that we should do them without any attachment to them. Unattachment seems to supply a second motive for the doing of actions in order that actionlessness might be ultimately secured. We are told by Jñāneśvara in the eighteenth Chapter that we should do acts of great sacrifice, without allowing the egoistic impulse to take possession of us. "He, who goes on a pilgrimage on payment, never prides himself that he is getting the merit of the pilgrimage. By the seal of a powerful king, one may be able to drive the king himself; but one need not therefore pride oneself upon having achieved the result. He who swims by taking the help of the loin-cloth of another, never arrogates to himself the power of swimming on his own account. The sacrificial priest never prides himself upon being the donor in the sacrifice......One should be as regardless of the fruit, as a nurse is about the child of another woman. One does not sprinkle the Pippala tree in order to get its fruit......The boy, who tends the cows, never tends them in order to get milk from them......Similarly, one should always do actions without any attachment. Take this to be My message on the subject of action and actionlessness" (XVIII. 166—176).

Renunciation of the Fruits of Action.

61. A third motive for securing the result of actionlessness in the midst of action is supplied by the absolute renunciation of the fruits of action. "If it be impossible for thee to circumscribe on both sides thy intellect and thy actions by My Self,......at least take resort to self-control, and whenever thou doest any actions, resign the fruits of them. As a tree or a creeper throws away its fruits when it can no longer bear them, similarly, throw away thy actions at the proper time. It does not matter if these actions are not done for the sake of God; let them at least go into the Void. Take thy actions to be as useless as rain on a rock, as sowing in fire, or as a mere dream. Just as one entertains no desire whatsoever about one's daughter, similarly, entertain no desire for actions. As a flame of fire wastes itself in the sky, similarly, let all thy actions go into the Void. It seems, O Arjuna, that this is an easy procedure, but remember that this is the highest of all kinds of Yoga" (XII. 125—134). It seems from this passage that Jñāneśvara advocates the renunciation of actions into mere nothingness, if a man, by his temperament, is not able to resign them in favour of God.

The Offering of Actions to God.

62. The highest motive, however, for the performance of actions in order that actionlessness may be secured is the offering of actions to God. A mere void or nothingness is absolutely insufficient ultimately to give us the result of actionlessness. Jñāneśvara teaches like the Bhagavadgītā that we should offer actions to God, so that in that way only may we secure actionlessness. "All the actions that are done should be delivered over to Me in an attitude of faith. Throw away even the memory of the performance of such actions. Cleanse thy actions, and hand them over to Me. As when seeds are put in fire, they are deprived of the possibility of germination, similarly, both good and bad actions, when they are offered to Me, cease to germinate. As soon as actions have been offered to Me, all considerations of birth and death go away......Wait not for the morrow. Make use at once of this device for actionlessness" (IX. 400—405). In another place, Jñāneśvara tells us again that we should not shut up our senses, or throw away enjoyment, or rid ourselves of the consciousness of our worth. "We may safely perform all our family duties, as well as obey all positive and negative social injunctions. We may be permitted to do all these things. But we must remember that whatever action we are doing mentally, orally, or physically must not be egoistically attributed to ourselves. To do or not to do depends not upon us, but upon God who moves the whole world........Throw thy intellect firmly in Me. Does the chariot take care as to whether it is going on the straight or the crooked path? Whatever thou doest, resign it to Me without thinking as to whether it is great or small. It is only when thou habituatest thyself continually to this temperament that thou, after departing from the body, mightest come to be atoned to Me" (XII. 114—124). Finally, we are told in the last Chapter of the Jñāneśvarī that we should worship the all-pervading God by the flowers of our actions. Thus alone will God be pleased. When He is pleased, He gives us excellence in dispassion as a mark of His grace, by which dispassion, and by severe contemplation on God, all this appears like vomited food. When her lover has gone away, the beloved feels even life to be a burden. In a similar way, all happiness is regarded by such a man as misery itself; and even though one may not have attained to the end, the very concentration on it makes us one with it. Such is the great virtue of this procedure (XVIII. 916—922). We thus see, on the whole, that for securing actionlessness in the midst of action, four kinds of helps are suggested. The first is the performance of an action as a matter of social duty; the second is its performance without any feeling of attachment; the third is the renunciation of its fruit; the fourth and the last is a more positive help, namely, the offering of all actions to God.

The Three-fold Division of the Psychological Temperaments.

63. It has been recognized that the three-fold division of psychological temperaments into the Sāttvika, the Rājasa, and the Tāmasa paves the way for a similar ethical classification and thus for a division of the moral qualities according to these temperaments. Now Jñāneśvara makes an analysis of the upspringing of the Sattva, the Rajas, and the Tamas qualities in man, and tells us in the fourteenth Chapter of the Jñāneśvarī that all the three are born from the eternal background of the Prakṛiti. Just as in the same body there is childhood, manhood, and old age, similarly, there are these three qualities in the same temperament......... Just as before a fish has caught the bait, the fisherman draws his net, similarly, Sattva, the hunter, throws the nets of happiness and knowledge over those who are born with the temperament of Sattva, and catches hold of these as if they were deer to be caught in the net. Then these people flutter with their knowledge, and run on all fours with self-consciousness, and leave away the happiness of Self, which would otherwise have been in the hollow of their hands. These are satisfied by learning, become delighted by the slightest gain, know that they are pleased, and begin to rave in joy. There is no one who is so fortunate as himself, says such a man; there is no man who is so happy; and he becomes full of all the eight emotions arising from Sattva. To add to these things, the ghost of learning possesses him, and unmindful of the fact that he is knowledge himself, he becomes as large as the sky in the consciousness of his intellectual powers (XIV. 139—154). A man with the Rajas temperament is always merged in seeking pleasure, and is ever young in his desires. Just as fire, when smeared over by ghee, passes beyond control, similarly,......the desires of such a man know no bounds, and even though he may be in the possession of a golden mountain, he still tries to push his acquisition further.......If all that one has to-day will be spent, what will he do to-morrow? With these desires, he seeks business after business. What should he eat if he goes to heaven, he asks, and so he performs sacrifice after sacrifice......As the wind at the end of summer-time knows no rest, similarly, his activity knows no rest. He is as fickle as a moving fish, or the side-look of a woman's eye, or the flickering of lightning. With the velocity of these, does he enter into the fire of action (XIV. 161—172). As contrasted with both these, stands the man in whom Tamas predominates. Such a man lives only in ignorance,...... which is merely a spell of indiscretion, a vessel in which the wine of folly is put, a missile to infatuate the whole of mankind. Tamas means sluggishness in all the senses, and foolishness in the mind, which gathers strength from idleness. Such a man merely moves his limbs, has no desire for action, and spends his time merely in yawning. He has open eyes, and yet cannot see. He gets up from his sleep, even though nobody calls him. As a piece of stone, which has fallen down, does not move, similarly he does not move when he once goes to sleep, even though the earth may go down to the nethermost region or rise above the sky. He knows neither right nor wrong. His intellect is given merely to wallow where he is, and he is so fond of sleep that he regards even heaven as inferior to that condition. Let me have the life of a God, he says ; but let me spend it wholly in sleep. When he is even walking by a road, he nods at the slightest move, and goes to sleep. He has no desire even for nectar...... Such a man knows not how to behave ; knows not how to speak......Just as a small fly may vainly try to extinguish by its wing the whole conflagration of a forest, similarly such a man falls to foolish acts of daring ; has courage for actions which he cannot do ; and loves error. In short, a man of the Tamas temperament is bound together by the three ropes of sleep, idleness, and error (XIV. 174—194).

Overthrow of the Thraldom of the Qualities.

64. This is, however, the ordinary routine of the temperament of those who are born with the reign of the qualities in them. Scarcely one among a thousand rises superior to these qualities ; but it is in his absolute transcendence of them, in his liberation from their thraldom, in his identification with the Self, that real absolution lies. Jñāneśvara tells us that as an actor is not deceived by the various parts that he plays, similarly, a man must not be deceived by the power of the qualities. In the midst of these qualities God exists as spring exists in a forest of trees, the cause of the beauty of the garden. As the Sun does not know when the stars set, or how the sun-stone burns, or how the lotuses bloom, or how night disappears, similarly, I exist in all things without getting Myself contaminated with them. It is only he, before whom discrimination dawns in this way, that rises superior to the qualities, and comes to Me......As a river goes to an ocean, so he reaches Me. As a parrot may rise from the iron-bar, and sit freely on the branch of a tree, similarly, he rises from the qualities, and reaches the original Ego. He, who was sleeping and snoring in ignorance, is now awakened to Self-consciousness. The mirror of division has now fallen from his hands, and so he cannot see his temperament in that mirror. The wind of bodily arrogance has now ceased to blow, and the waves and the sea have become one......As the light of a lamp cannot be prevented from going out of a house of glass, as the sea-fire cannot be quenched by the waters of the sea, similarly, his illumination does not suffer by the qualities which come and go. He is like the reflection of the moon in the sky into the waters of the qualities. Even when the qualities possess his body and make it dance, he does not identify himself with them......He does not know even what is going on within his body. When the serpent has thrown away its slough and gone into a nether hole, does it any longer care for its skin? As the fragrance, issuing out of a flower, becomes merged in the sky, does it come back to the lotus from which it came? Similarly, when he has become identified with the Self, he ceases to be influenced by the qualities of the body (XIV. 287—315).

Uprooting of the Tree of Unreality.

65. This is how liberation from the thraldom of the qualities comes about. In another metaphor, Jñāneśvara gives us an insight into the moral process of the destruction of the Aśvattha, the tree of unreality, of which we have already spoken. How is such a man able to uproot this tree of unreality? His intellect becomes filled with dispassion. By that dispassion, he throws away the thraldom of the qualities, as surely as a dog cares not for its vomit......He should take out the sword of dispassion from the scabbard of bodily egoism, hold it lightly in the hands of intuitive vision, and sharpen it on the stone of discrimination until it reaches the sharpness of the identity of Self with God. He should then cleanse it by perfect knowledge; next try its strength by the fist of determination; weigh it by the process of contemplation; until—the wonder of it is—when the sword and the swordsman become one, there shall remain nought to be cut down by the sword. In the light of unitive experience, before that sword of Self-knowledge, the tree of unreality would vanish of itself. Then one need not contemplate whether its roots reach heaven-high, or go hell-deep; whether its branches move upwards or downwards. It will vanish of itself, as the mirage vanishes under moonlight (XV. 255—265).

Destruction of the Moral Vices.

66. We have seen above that the way towards God lies either through an overthrow of the thraldom of the qualities, or the uprooting of the tree of unreality. In a similar way, we are told that it lies in the destruction of the three moral vices, Kāma, Krodha and Lobha (passion, anger, and covetousness), which are compared to the high-way robbers on the way towards God. Where these three gather together, know that evil is destined to prosper. These are the guides of those who want to reach the place of misery. They are an assembly of sins which lead one to the sufferance of hell. One need not take account of the hell called Raurava spoken of in mythology; these are themselves that hell incarnate! They constitute a three-directioned post on the doorway to hell. He who stands in the midst of these, gets honour in the domain of hell......So long as these keep awake in the mind of man, he shall never come to good; never shall one even be able to hear of good. He, who wants to do good to himself, and fears self-destruction, should not go by the way of these vices. Has one been able to cross the sea by binding a huge stone on his back? Has one been able to live by feeding on the deadliest poison? ......It is only when these three leave the mind of man, that he is able to secure the company of the good, and to walk on the path of liberation. Then by the power of the company of the good, and of the knowledge of the sacred books, he is able to cross the woods of life and death, and reach the home of the grace of the Guru, which is always full of the joy of the Self. There he meets the Ātman, who is the greatest among all the objects of love, and forthwith ceases all this bustle of worldly existence (XVI. 424—443)!

III. Mysticism.

The Pathway to God.

67. The description of the way to the Ātman is the sole absorbing topic of mystical writers, and Jñāneśvara spares no pains in describing it from various points of view. The great pathway, says Jñāneśvara, can hardly be expected to be traversed to the very end by any traveller. The great God Śaṅkara himself yet journeys on the path. Whole companies of Yogins have tried to traverse it in the sky, and the pathway could be seen by the footprints of their experiences. They have left off all other sideways, and have gone straight by the way of Self-realization. Great Ṛishīs have walked on this path. Being first novices in the art of Self-realization, they have more or less attained to the goal. God-realizers have become great by having crossed this path. One ceases to be tormented by the appetites of hunger and thirst when one sees this path. One cannot even so much as distinguish between night and day when on the path. Where the travellers on this path place their footprints, the mine of absolution opens of itself. Even if one goes sideways of this path, one goes to heaven. Starting from the east, one does necessarily go to the west; in this determinate fashion is the journey of this path. While the wonder of it is, that as one travels on this path towards the goal, one becomes the goal itself (VI. 152—160).

The Four Avenues to the Pathway.

68. In another place, Jñāneśvara, following the Bhagavadgītā, tells us that there are four avenues to this great pathway. Some people go by the path of knowledge under the influence of the Sāmkhya Philosophy. In the fire of thought they meditate on the problem of the Self and the not-Self, and separating the thirty-six elements, they ultimately fall upon the pure Self. Others there are who by the process of contemplation obtain the vision of the Self within themselves. ......Others there are, who, following the path of Karman, try to reach the Godhead. And yet, finally, there are those who are able to dismiss the darkness of this worldly existence by simply putting their faith in another. They throw away their arrogance, and pin their faith to the words of others, who are able to distinguish the good from the bad, who are filled with pity for their misery, who take away their sorrow, and give happiness instead. What falls from the lips of such people, they listen to with great respect, and try to realize it in their bodily and mental acts.......What words come from them, they throw themselves entirely upon. Even these people, O Arjuna, are able to cross the stream of worldly existence (XIII. 1037--1047). So we see that Bhakti Yoga is here placed absolutely on a par with Sāmkhya Yoga, Dhyāna Yoga, or Karma Yoga, and that a man, who follows the advice of the worthy Guru, is able to reach the Ātman without undergoing the travail of walking on the other avenues.

The Search of God through all Miseries.

69. As misery is the essential feature of life, it follows that whatever miseries may befall a man, he must try always to see God through them. In fact, misery in this life could be relieved only by seeking after God. "How would it be possible that a man might rest in ease, when he is sitting in a boat with a hundred holes? How would it be possible that a man might keep his body bare, when stones are being flung at him? Is it possible for a diseased man to be indifferent to medicine? When fire is burning all round, must not one get away from its midst? Similarly, when the world is full of misery, how would it be possible that a man should not pray to Me? Upon what power do these people count, that they do not try to worship Me? How can they rest content in their homes and in their enjoyments? Of what value would their learning or their age be to them? How can they acquire happiness without worshipping Me? ......Life indeed is a fair where the wares of misery are being spread out, and death is measuring the destinies of men. How can one acquire happiness in such a state? Can one hope to ignite a lamp by blowing through cooled ashes? As one cannot grow immortal by taking the juice out of poisonous roots, so one can never acquire happiness in the miseries of life. Who has ever heard a tale of happiness in this world of mortals? Can one sleep happily on a bed of scorpions? Even the moon of this world is proverbially consumptive. Stars rise in this world only in order to set......In the midst of auspiciousness comes harm. Death is encircling the fœtus in the womb.......If we follow the track of those who have gone before us, we cannot see any returning footprints. The histories and mythologies of this world are merely collections of death-stories. It is wonderful that people should live at ease in such a world!......As a child grows, people rejoice, but they do not know that it is approaching death. Everyday after birth, it is nearing death, and yet in joy these people raise auspicious flags. They cannot even bear the word death, and when people die, they cry after them; but they cannot, in their folly, imagine that whatever is must pass away. Like a frog which is trying to eat a fish even while it is being itself devoured by a serpent, they are trying to increase their avarice every day. Alas, born in this mortal world, O Arjuna, get thyself hastily from it; go by the path of Bhakti, so that thou mayest reach My divine home" (IX. 490--516).

The Attainment of God through any Intense Emotion.

70. Psychologically, it seems that any intense emotion towards God is capable of leading us towards Him. Thus Jñāneśvara tells us that God could be attained either through extreme love, or through extreme fear, or even through extreme hatred. "Those cowherd women thought about Me as a husband, and they reached My form. Kansa, the great demon, entertained mortal fear about Me, and he reached Me. Śiśupāla conceived intense hatred towards Me, and he became one with Me. The Yādavas loved Me as their relative; Vāsudeva loved Me as a child; Nārada, Dhruva, Akrūra, Śuka, and Sanatkumāra loved Me as the supreme object of their devotion, and they all reached Me. I am indeed the sole end to be reached. One may reach Me by any means whatsoever, either by devotion, or by sexual love, or dispassion, or hatred" (IX. 465—470). The purport of this passage is that if we begin by conceiving any intense emotion towards God, as lies in the nature of all intensive emotion, we end by becoming one with the end itself.

Hope for the Sinner.

71. Moreover, Jñāneśvara offers the highest kind of consolation to those who have lived wretched and sinful lives. He gives hope even to the fallen. He tells us that even these, if they but conceive love towards God, have in them the power of reaching God. The sinner, we are told, can and does become a saint. "Even though a man may be quite sinful at first, still by believing in Me, he becomes the best of men, as one, who is dying in an ocean, might just escape death in the waters......No sin is too great to remain undestroyed in a supernal kind of devotion. Thus, if a sinful man just bathes in the waters of repentance, and comes inside the temple to Me with all devotion, his whole lineage becomes pure, and he becomes a man of noble birth. He alone has attained to the end of existence. He has learned all the sciences; he has practised all the penances; he has devoted himself to the practice of the eight-fold Yoga; he has done all actions, provided he has fixed his heart in Me. Having filled all his mental and intellectual impulses in the chest of single-minded devotion, he has thrown it, O Arjuna, in Me. One need not suppose that such a one may become one with God after a while. He has already been in Me. He, who lives in immortality, how can death ever affect him? His mind stands always in My presence, and he verily attains to My likeness. As when a lamp is lighted by a lamp, one cannot distinguish which was the earlier, and which later; similarly, when he has begun to love Me, he has become one with Me, and there is no distinction between us" (IX. 418—428).

The Non-Recognition of Castes in Devotion to God.

72. As all sin is at an end in devotion to God, similarly, all considerations of caste and birth are equally at an end. "Family matters not; one may be even a pariah by birth, or one may even take on the body of a beast. When the Elephant was seized by the Crocodile, and when the Elephant lifted up his trunk towards Me in utter resignation, his beasthood came to an end, and he verily reached Me. People, whose names it is a sin to mention, who have been born in the midst of most sinful kinds of existences, who are the source of vices and folly, and who have been as stupid as stones,—if such people come to love Me with all their heart, if their speech mentions only My words, if their sight enjoys only My vision, if their mind thinks of nothing else except Me, if their ears refuse to hear anything except My name, if their limbs are devoted to the service of no other except Me, if their knowledge has no other object beyond Myself, if their consciousness is given to the contemplation of nothing else except Me, if they find their existence justified only in doing these things, and if in the absence of these they experience mortal pain, if in this manner I become the sole engrossing object of their attention in all ways,—it matters not whether they are born sinful; it matters not whether they have learned no sciences; if thou weighest them against Me, thou shalt find them equal to Me. When characters are imprinted on a piece of leather by royal order, it can purchase anything whatsoever. Gold and silver are of no value unless they are sanctioned by the order of the king. On the other hand, even a piece of leather is superior to them in purchasing power, provided it is sanctioned by the king. In this way if a man's mind and knowledge become filled by My love, he becomes the best of mortals: he is the greatest among those who know. Thus, neither family, nor caste, nor colour, are of any avail in Me. What is wanted is the directing of the mind towards Me. Let a man approach Me with any motive whatsoever; when he has reached Me, everything else becomes nought. We call brooks brooks only so long as they have not reached the waters of the Ganges; but when they once reach the Ganges, they cease to be called brooks. There is a distinction between the Khaira and the Chandana trees only so long as they are not put into fire; but as soon as they are put inside it, they become one with it, and the distinction between them vanishes. Similarly, the Kshatriyas, the Vaiśyas, the Śudras, and Women are so-called only so long as they have not reached Me. But having reached Me, they cease to be distinguished; as salt becomes one with the ocean, even so they become one with Me" (IX. 441—461).

Bhakti, as the only Means for the Attainment of God.

73. Jñāneśvara is indeed the originator of the Bhakti school of thought in Mahārāshṭra, and he tells us that God can be attained by Bhakti alone. "How very often should I tell thee, O Arjuna, if thou longest after Me, worship Me. Care not for the dignity of birth. Mind not the consideration of nobility. Throw away the burden of learning. Cease to be inflated by the beauty of form and youth. If thou hast no devotion towards Me, all this is as good as nought. If the Nimba tree produces an infinite number of Nimba fruits, it becomes only a feast to the crows......If thou servest all kinds of dainty dishes in an earthen pot, and keepest it on the high-way, it becomes useful only for the dogs. He, who has no Bhakti for Me, is only inviting the miseries of existence" (IX. 430—440).

On the other hand, "as the rain that droppeth from above knows no other place except the earth to fall upon, or as the Ganges with all the wealth of her waters searches the ocean and meets it over and over again; similarly, the true devotee with all the riches of his emotions, and with unabated love, enters into My Being, and becomes one with Me. As the ocean of milk is milk all over, whether on the shore or in the middle of the sea, similarly, he should see Me as the supreme object of his love, from the ant onwards through all existences" (XI. 685—690). Jñāneśvara tells us that true devotion means the vision of such an identity through difference. This is indeed a philosophic way of describing the nature of devotion; but it remains true at the same time that this identity must be experienced by the true devotee. "There is difference in the world; but for that reason, knowledge does not become different. There is difference between the limbs in the body, but they all belong to the body. Branches are small and great, and yet they grow on the same tree. The Sun sends an infinite number of rays, but they all belong to the Sun. Thus, in the midst of the difference of individualities, the difference of names, the difference of temperaments, one should know Me as unchanging through all the changes. Whatever one happens to see, and in what place soever he happens to see it, he should regard it all as non-different from Me:......that is indeed the mark of devotion. It is Devotion which surpasses devotion" (IX. 250—261).

The Sensual Life and the Spiritual Life.

74. The first step in the advancement of spiritual life consists in rising from the life of sense to a belief in God and in those who are beloved of God. Jñāneśvara makes Arjuna exclaim in the tenth Chapter that so long as the spiritual impulse was not generated in him, he had no liking for the saints and their words. "Many times before did the sages tell me of Thee, O God; but the reality of their words I now realize, because, I have been the object of Thy grace. The sage Nārada used to come to me very often, and sing Thy glory in these words. But I could not catch the meaning of the words, and listened merely to the song. If the Sun shines in a village of the blind, they can only bask in the sunshine, and not be able to see the light. Similarly, when the divine sage used to sing the knowledge of Ātman to us, I went to him merely for hearing the song, and not for understanding the idea therein. Asita and Devala likewise would talk to me about Thee. But, at that time, my intellect was enveloped in sense. In a miraculous way does the poison of sense make the spiritual life taste bitter, and the bitter objects of sense appear sweet! What of others? The sage Vyāsa himself used to come to the temple, and tell us of Thy glory. But it was all like one who could not see the wish-jewel in darkness, but could recognize it only when the day broke. Similarly, the words of Vyāsa and others, even though they were as valuable as jewels, were neglected by me, O Kṛishṇa! But now that the Sun of your words has arisen, the paths which the former sages had told me of have come to be seen. Their words were verily the seed of knowledge, and they had fallen on the ground of my heart; but they have borne fruit only when Thy grace has descended in showers. The rivers of the words of Nārada and other sages have now become unified in me, who have become their Ocean......Even though my elders had told me often about Thee, I could not know Thee, because Thy grace had not yet descended on me. Hence it is only when a man's fate befriends him that all his efforts become successful......The gardener spares no pains in sprinkling water over plants and trees; but it is only when the spring sets in that they bear fruit......Similarly, all the sciences that we may have studied, or all the Yoga that we may have practised, become successful only when the Guru sends down his grace" (X. 144--172).

The Descent of Grace.

75. How is the grace of the Guru to descend on the disciple? Jñāneśvara tells us that the only way towards receiving his grace is to adore the saints. "They are the temple of knowledge; our service constitutes its threshold; we should take possession of it by resorting to it. We should touch their feet in body and mind and thought. We should do all sorts of service to them with utter absence of egoism, and then they will tell us what we desire. Our mind shall forthwith cease to give rise to conjectures; our intellect shall grow strong in the light of their words;......doubt shall cease; all beings will then be seen as in God; the darkness of infatuation will disappear; the light of knowledge shall shine; and the Guru will send down his grace" (IV. 165--171).

One meets the Guru in the Fulness of Time.

76. Jñāneśvara tells us in a famous passage that one meets the Guru in the fulness of time. We have only to prepare ourselves, and the Guru will find us. "One should regard one's child, wealth, or wife as no more than a vessel of poison. When the intellect has been tormented by the objects of sense, it recoils upon itself, and enters the recesses of the heart. Then one begins to apply his mind directly to the contemplation of Ātman......When the remnant of our actions has been exhausted, and new actions cease to have any fruit,...... in that state of equanimity, the Guru meets us of his own accord; as when the four quarters of the night have been exhausted, the Sun verily meets the eye. By his grace, ignorance ceases as darkness ceases by light......One thus goes beyond the knower and the known, and becomes transformed into knowledge; as when the mirror is taken away from the face, the seer remains without seeing. In that way is actionlessness generated. This indeed constitutes the highest power of man......This power does a man get, when the Guru sends down his grace on him......Rare is the man who has been able to destroy all illusion at the moment at which he hears the words of his Guru;......when his words have fallen on his ear, he has become one with God" (XVIII. 958—991).

The Celebration of God's Name.

77. The means for attaining to this union is, as the upholders of the Bhakti-mārga have pointed out, the celebration of God's Name. "By that celebration, they have destroyed the *raison d'être* of repentance. Sin has been banished out of the world. Self-control and restraint have ceased to have any efficacy. Places of pilgrimage have become of no avail. The way to the abode of Death has been destroyed. What can restraint restrain now? What can self-control control? What can places of pilgrimage purify? There is no impurity which can be taken away. Thus by the celebration of My Name, they have put an end to the misery of the world. The whole world has become full of joy. Such devotees create a dawn without a dawn. They infuse life without nectar. They show God's vision to the eyes of the people without the travail of Yoga. They know no distinction between king and pauper, between great and small. All at once, they have filled the world with happiness. One among many mortals may go to the home of God after his death; but these have brought down God upon earth. They have illumined the whole world by the celebration of My name. In lustre, they are equal to the Sun, and yet they are superior to him, because the Sun sets, and these do not set. The moon is only rarely full; but these are always full. The rain-cloud is generous, but it may cease to rain...... They are right royal like a lion, but full of compassion. On their tongue, My name dances without interruption—the

Name which it would take a thousand births for one to be fortunate enough to utter. I do not live in Vaikuṇṭha; nor do I inhabit the disc of the Sun; I traverse the heart of the Yogins; but before those who celebrate My Name, I am to be always found if I am lost anywhere else. They have become so infatuated with My divine qualities that they have forgotten place and time, and I have been the source of joy to them in their vocation of God-celebration" (IX. 197—209).

The Importance of Practice in Spiritual Life.

78. As apart from this process of the celebration of the Name of God, there is also another process which tries to mingle the meditation on God's name with certain Yogic practices. The Rāja Yoga, if properly carried out, is not contradictory to the Bhakti Yoga, even though the Haṭha Yoga stands in a different category. Hence the devotees very often mingle Rāja Yoga with Bhakti Yoga. "Strengthen thy mind with this practice. Even a lame man can cross the precipice of a mountain by right means. Similarly, by right study, show thy mind the way towards God, and care not whether the body lives or dies. The mind which carries us to different destinies will then win the Ātman as its bride-groom, and the body shall cease to be of any consideration" (VIII. 81—83). There is this value in this kind of Yoga that it enables us to take our mind gradually towards God. "If you cannot deliver your heart immediately to God, then at least do this: think of God at least for a moment during the twenty-four hours of the day. Then every moment that you will spend in the enjoyment of My happiness will be of help to you in taking your mind away from sense. As, when autumn sets in, the river dwindles, similarly, your mind will gradually go out of the bonds of Samsāra; and as, after the full-moon day, the disc of the moon diminishes every day, until it vanishes altogether on the new moon day, similarly, as your heart will go out of the objects of sense and begin to enter into the Being of God, it will gradually end by becoming God. This indeed is what is called the Yoga of practice. There is nothing impossible for this practice. By this practice, some people have been able to move in the skies, others have tamed even tigers and serpents; poison has been digested; the ocean has been crossed; the Vedas have been made to deliver over their entire secret. Hence there is nothing that is impossible for this practice. Do you, therefore, enter into Me by this practice" (XII. 104—113).

Description of Place for Contemplation.

79. We are next told what place one should select for contemplation. "We should select a place, which puts one into such a temper of mind, that one does not like to get up when one has once sat down for meditation, and by looking at which dispassion may become strengthened. It ought to be a place where the saints have meditated on God. It ought to help our feeling of satisfaction, and endow the mind with the backbone of courage......It ought to be a place, by looking at which even the agnostics and deniers of God may be put into a mood of contemplation. Those who cannot stand quiet for a moment, the place should make quiet. Those who roam, it ought to compel to sit down. If dispassion is slumbering, it ought to be awakened by merely looking at the place. Kings should be tempted to resign their kingdoms, and live calmly in meditation in such a place. Even so, those whose minds are full of sexual love should throw it away, as soon as they have looked at such a place........ It ought to be a place where the practisers of Yoga have come together. It must not be contaminated by the dust of the feet of the laity. It should be a place where there are trees, yielding fruits all the year round, and which are sweet like nectar to the very root. At every step we must be able to find water in such a place, even when it is not the rainy season. Springs should be particularly easy of access. The sunlight must appear cool. The wind must be motionless, or blow very slowly. It ought to be a place where no sounds are heard; where beasts of prey do not wander; where there are neither parrots nor bees. Occasionally, there might be some ducks, or swans, or a few Chakravāka birds, or even a cuckoo. Similarly, peacocks may come intermittently to such a place. In such a place, one should find out a monastery, or a temple of Śiva, and there sit for meditation" (VI. 163—174).

The Serpent and the Sound.

80. After sitting for meditation in such a place, one of the earliest effects of success in Yoga would be the awakening of the Kuṇḍalinī. "When the Kuṇḍalinī is awakened and takes possession of the heart, then the unstruck sound begins to be heard. The Kuṇḍalinī begins to be slowly aware of this sound. During the peal of sound, the pictorial representations of the Pranava emerge before consciousness. This requires difference of subject and object. But, it may well be asked how can the subject remain different from the object in this state of contemplation? What then is it that resounds? I forgot, O Arjuna, to tell you that as the wind cannot be destroyed, the very sky begins to have tongues and resounds accordingly. By that unstruck sound, the whole of space becomes filled, and the window at the Brahma-randhra opens of itself" (VI. 274—279).

The Difficulties of the Life of Yoga.

81. Jñāneśvara, however, is not unaware of the difficulties that beset the practitioner of Haṭha Yoga, who goes on meditating without having an iota of devotion in him. Such a man's state he describes in the twelfth Chapter, contrasting it with the fate of a man who follows the path of Bhakti. "Those who spread their motives so as to reach the good of all beings in the supportless unmanifest Absolute, without an iota of devotion, are robbed of all their strength on their way by the allurements of the kingdom of the gods, and of prosperities and prowesses........Thirst kills thirst, and hunger eats up hunger. Their up-stretched hands ceaselessly measure the wind. They clothe themselves in extremes of heat and cold, and live in mansions of rain. This is all verily like entering into fire, O Arjuna. It is what one may call a husband-less Yoga......Those, therefore, who follow this path, have only misery reserved for themselves. If a man who has lost his teeth, were to eat morsels of iron-beads, tell Me whether he will live or die......A lame man must not hope to compete with wind. Similarly, those, who have taken on a body, cannot reach the Absolute. In spite of this, if courageously they begin to wrestle with the sky, they will make themselves the objects of infinite misery. On the other hand, those, O Arjuna, who go by the path of Bhakti, can never experience such hardships on their way to God" (XII. 60—75).

Meditation on God as everywhere.

82. The true Bhakta must find God everywhere, within himself as well as without himself. "Therefore, thou shouldst remember Me always. Whatever thou seest by the eye, or hearest by the ear, or thinkest by the mind, or speakest by the mouth, whatever is internal or external, should be identified with Me, and then thou shalt find that I alone am everywhere and at all times. When such a state is experienced, O Arjuna, one cannot die even when the body departs. Why then do you fear the fight in which you are engaged? If thou resignest thy mind and intellect to Me, then thou shalt certainly come into My Being. If thou entertainest any doubt as to whether this will happen or not happen, then begin practising, and if thou dost not succeed, then say that this is false" (VIII. 75—80). As God is to be identified with every mental experience, similarly, He is to be identified with every objective existence. Did not Arjuna, when he saw the Viśvarūpa, find God everywhere outside him? "Tell me where thou art not, O God! Salutation to Thee, as Thou art in Thyself!" Thus did Arjuna bow down with a passionate heart, and said again, "Salutation, salutation to Thee, O God!" He again looked longingly at the form of God, and said, "Salutation, salutation to Thee, O God!" He saw Him endwise, and his heart was delighted, and he said again, "Salutation, salutation to Thee, O God!" He saw all these beings—movable or immovable—and saw God in them, and said again, "Salutation, salutation to Thee, O God!" He could not remember any words of praise, nor could he afford to remain silent. He was filled with love, and ejaculated in ecstasy "Salutation to Thee O God, who art before me! What use is it to us to consider whether God is before or behind? Salutation to Thee, O God, who art also behind me. Thou standest at my back, and therefore I say that Thou art behind; but really speaking, there is neither before nor behind to Thee. Incompetent that I am to describe Thy various limbs, I say to Thee who comprisest all, Salutation, salutation to Thee, O God!" (XI. 519—532.)

The Atman as Light.

83. Light seems to be one of the chief forms in which God reveals Himself. "That which is older than the sky and which is smaller than the atom; by whose presence the whole world moves; that which gives birth to everything; that by which the world lives; that which surpasses all contemplation; that which even by day-light is as darkness to the physical eye, as the white ant cannot gnaw into fire, nor can darkness enter into light; that, on the other hand, which is as eternal day to the knower; that which contains an infinitude of light-rays, and which knows no setting" (VIII. 87—90), is the description of the photic experience of Jñāneśvara. Jñāneśvara also tells us that God is like a beacon-light of camphor which moves onwards to show the way to the seeking mystic, and which, after the destruction of the darkness of ignorance, shines as eternal day (X. 142—143). In the same way, in the eleventh Chapter, he tells us of the infinite lustre of the Ātman. "The lustre of the body of God was simply indescribable. It was like the combining of the lights of twelve suns at the time of the great conflagration. The thousand celestial suns, that rise at once in the sky, could not have matched the infinite lustre of the Ātman. Had all the lightnings been brought together, had all the fires at the time of the Great End been mingled together, had all the ten great lights been fused into one, it would have been impossible for them to compare with the lustre of the great God. Thus was the greatness of God's light. His lustre shone all around, and I saw it by the grace of the Sage" (XI. 237—241). Is this last to be regarded as a touch of Jñāneśvara's personal experience, though it is put in the mouth of Sañjaya ?

The Atman seen within and without.

84. Jñāneśvara describes the morphic experience of the mystic when he tells us how Arjuna saw the great Form of God. "His mind was tossed by looking at the sublimity of each of His forms, and he could not know whether God was sitting, or standing, or only reclining. He opened his eyes, and saw the whole world full of the Form of God. He shut his eyes, and saw the same thing within himself. He saw an infinite number of faces before him, and as he turned back his gaze, he saw the same faces and hands and feet even in other directions. What wonder that one is able to see God by looking at Him ? It is a wonder that He can be seen without looking at Him. It was really by His grace that He fused within Himself both the vision and the non-vision of Arjuna, and He became the All ; and as Arjuna, who was coming to the shore of one miracle, fell again into the ocean of another miracle. For, the intuitive vision, that was imparted by God, was not like other kinds of vision, which are able to operate only in the light of the Sun, or the lamp" (XI. 226—234). To the vision of Arjuna, the upward and the nether worlds, the sky and the earth and the intermundane region, all ceased to exist, and he saw God everywhere, and he began to exclaim : "Whence have You come, O God ? Art You sitting or standing ? Who was the mother in whose womb You resided ? What indeed is Your measure ? What is Your form and age ? What lies behind You ? What is it that You are standing on ? Considering these things, I see that You are the All. You are Your own support, You belong to none, and You are beginningless. You are neither standing nor sitting, neither long nor short. You are both up and down.... This I saw as I contemplated on Your form" (XI. 271—279).

The Realization of the Self.

85. There is a passage in the Jñāneśvarī where Jñāneśvara is describing the way in which one comes to realize the Self. This description is bound to be a little different from the description of the Viśvarūpa in the eleventh Chapter, because while the subject-matter of the eleventh

Chapter was the vision of the universal Ātman, the subject-matter of the passage in the fifteenth Chapter, which we are now discussing, is the realization of the Self. "When the tree of unreality has been cut down by the sword of Self-knowledge, then......one is able to see one's form, one's own Self. This is, however, not to be compared to the vision of the reflection in a mirror; for the reflection in a mirror is simply an 'other' of the seeing man. The vision of the individual Self is as a Spring which may exist in its own fulness even when it does not come up into a Well. When water dries up, the image goes back to its prototype; when the pitcher is broken, space mixes with space; when fuel is burnt, fire returns into itself; in a similar way is the vision of the Self by the Self......One must see without seeing. One must know without knowing. That is the primary Being from which everything comes......It is for seeing this original Being that seekers have gone by the path of Yoga, after having become disgusted with life, and with the firm determination that they would not return again......They have given over their egoism, and have reached their Original Home. That is this Existence, which exists in itself and for itself, as cold becomes cold by cold, or snow becomes snow by snow, ...after reaching which, there is no return" (XV. 266—283).

The Acme of Happiness.

86. Jñāneśvara tells us very often that he who has realized the happiness of Ātman, ceases to have *ipso facto* any desire for sensual enjoyment. "He, who does not return to the world of sense from his life in Ātman,—there is no wonder that such a man should cease to care for sensual enjoyment. His mind has become full of the happiness of the Self; it does not, therefore, dare to move out of itself to the world of sense. Tell Me, O Arjuna, whether the Chakora bird, which lives upon the rays of the moon on the disc of a lotus-petal, ever goes and kisses the sand? Similarly, he who has enjoyed the happiness of the Self, lives in himself; and there is no wonder that he should leave all sensual enjoyment" (V. 105—108). The same idea is repeated in the twelfth Chapter where we are told that there is nothing comparable to the happiness of the Self, and that therefore sensual enjoyment ceases to have any attraction for the mystic. "He has become the world himself, and therefore all notion of difference vanishes. Similarly, all hatred forthwith ceases. That which really belongs to Him, namely, life in the Self, shall never depart. Hence he does not grieve for the loss of any object, nor has he any craving for any object; for there is nothing outside him. If he, who has thus become realization incarnate, adds to it a devotion towards Me, then there is nothing like him which I would so much love" (XII. 190—196). "He is so engrossed in the happiness of his own Self, that he does not care for any powers that may accrue to him. Living in the beautiful mansion of his own Self, he regards the palace of Indra as useless ; how can he then be satisfied with the hut of a forester ? He, who does not care even for nectar, shall *a fortiori* not care for rice-water. Similarly, he who has enjoyed the happiness of the Self, does not care for any powers ......Regard him alone as having had a firm station in Me, who is content with the knowledge of Self, who feeds on the highest joy, who drives away all egoism, leaves away all passion, becomes the world, and moves in the world" (II. 362—367). Finally, Jñāneśvara puts into the mouth of Arjuna the extollation of the great joy of the Self. "That, of which the gods partook at the time of the great churning, is falsely called Nectar, as contrasted with this great bliss. If that little so-called nectar has such a sweetness, how much more sweet shall this great bliss be ? One need not churn the ocean by the stick of the Mandāra mountain to obtain spiritual joy. It comes of itself to the seeker......It is so powerful in its effects that even at the hearing of it, the worldly existence ceases, and eternity forces itself upon us. All talk about birth and death is at an end. Internally and externally, one begins to be filled with the highest bliss......In addition, God's presence is near, and one is surely able to hear His sweet words" (X. 192—200). That is indeed the acme of happiness for the spiritual seeker.

The Bodily Effects of God-realization.

87. After the discussion of this spiritual happiness which accrues to the spiritual realizer, we must take note of the bodily, mental, and moral effects that are seen in the man who has realized God. And in a discussion of these various effects, we must first take account of the bodily effects of God-realization. Here, we must note that the God-realizer immediately rises superior to the considerations of the body. "Let the body now live or depart. I am the Ātman himself. The serpent, which appears like a rope, is false ; the rope alone is real. The waves on the water are unreal ; the water alone is real. It is not born in the shape of waves, nor is it destroyed in that shape......Similarly, the considerations of body have ceased to exist for the God-realizer, and he does not care when it ceases to be. What path is it necessary for him to find now ? Where and when will he go, if he has become identical with all space and time? Granted, that when the pitcher breaks the space within it mixes with the space outside; does it follow therefrom that there was no space in the pitcher before it broke down? ......Therefore, O Arjuna, practise the path of Yoga; for in that way, you will attain to equanimity; and then let the body live or go in any manner it likes. Thou art ever identical with the Ātman himself" (VIII. 248—257).

The Mental Effects of God-realization.

88. To this indifference to the bodily condition the Yogin has attained by a long practice. Indifference to body is the result of a long process of Yoga, in which, by concentrated mind, he meditated on God, as directed by his spiritual teacher. "As a result of his devoted concentration, he becomes full, inside and outside, of Sāttvika qualities. The strength of his egoism disappears. He forgets the objects of sense. The senses lose their power. The mind remains folded in the heart. In this manner, one should sit on his seat so long as the unitive feeling exists. Then body shall hold body, wind wind,......activity shall recoil upon itself, ecstasy shall be reached, and the object of meditation will be gained immediately that one sits for meditation" (VI. 186—191). And as the body comes under control, the senses and the mind also come under control. "The senses indeed are deceptive, O Arjuna. Does not the tongue regard as unwholesome the medicine which is bitter in taste, but which has the power to strengthen life and avert death? Whatever is really beneficial, the senses always show as unwholesome ......The practice of Yoga, which I told you and which involves the strength of the Āsana, may, if at all, bring the senses under control. It is only when these are brought under control, that the mind is able to find itself. It recoils upon itself, and feels its identity with the Self. When this experience is obtained, one reaches the empire of happiness, and then loses oneself by merging in the Self" (VI. 361—367).

The Moral Effects of God-realization.

89. Let us now turn to the moral characteristics of the God-realizer. "He is firmly fixed in the form of God internally, but behaves like an ordinary man externally. He does not command his senses, nor is he afraid of the objects of sense; and whatever is to be done, he does at the proper time. He does not feel any necessity for training up his sense-organs while doing actions, nor is he affected by their influence. Desire has no power over him. He never becomes infatuated, and is as clean as a lotus-leaf when it is sprinkled with water. He lives in the midst of contacts, and looks like an ordinary man. But he is not affected by them, as the Sun's disc is not affected by the water in which it is reflected. If we look at him in an external way, he looks like an ordinary man; but if we try to determine his real nature, we cannot really know him. It is by these marks that one ought to know the man who has conquered the thraldom of Samsāra" (III. 68—74). We find the characteristics of a God-realizer according to Jñāneśvara in another passage also. In the sixth Chapter, Jñāneśvara tells us that even though such a sage seems to have taken on a body, he is equal, in fact, to the great God, because he has subdued all his senses. "He looks upon a piece of gold which is as large as the mountain Meru, or even an insignificant lump of earth, as of equal count. Again, he looks equally at a price-less jewel, which could not be purchased by the riches of the whole earth, as well as a piece of stone. Whom can he now regard as his brother, or who can be his enemy? He cares equally for all, and obtains the vision of world-unity. He is himself the supreme place of pilgrimage. His very sight is meritorious. In his company, even an infatuated man may enter into the being of God. By his words, religion lives. His look is the cause of the highest prosperity. The happiness of the heavenly world is merely a play to him; and if one were to remember him even accidentally, one may acquire so much merit as to be equal to him" (VI. 92—104). Jñāneśvara elsewhere tells us that "the ideal sage is always like the full moon, and spreads his light on good and bad things equally. His equanimity is unbroken. His compassion for all the beings of the earth is unsurpassed. His mind never undergoes any change. He is never filled by delight on account of something good, nor does he fall a prey to dejection when anything bad occurs. The ideal sage, therefore, is without joy, and without sorrow, and always full of the knowledge of the Self" (II. 297—300).

Metaphorical description of a man who has realized God.

90. In a passage in the fifteenth Chapter of the Jñāneśvarī we have a metaphorical description of the man who has reached Self-realization. "His mind has been deserted by infatuation, as the sky is deserted at the end of the rainy season by the clouds. As the plantains of a plantain-tree, when they grow ripe, fall down of themselves, similarly his actions drop down automatically. As when a tree is on fire, the birds that have perched on it fly off in all directions, similarly, a man who has had the fire of realization kindled in him, is left by all doubts. As iron does not find the 'parisa' stone, nor darkness light, similarly his mind does not know any sense of duality. The sage is a royal swan, who separates the water of the not-Self from the milk of the Self, and feeds upon the latter. He collects together by his spiritual vision the form of the Godhead, which, in the absence of the knowledge of the Self, is dispersed in different directions. His discrimination merges in the determination of the nature of Ātman, as the stream of the Ganges merges in the Ocean. As a mountain on fire cannot give rise to sprouts, similarly, his mind cannot give rise to passions. As the Mandāra mountain, which once served as a churning stick, remained motionless when taken away from the ocean of milk, similarly, his mind does not know the surges of passions. As the full moon is full on all sides, similarly, having realized the Self, he exhibits no deficiency of desire in any quarter" (XV. 284—304).

The crest-jewel of those who know.

91. We have a further description of the marks by which we should know a man who has reached identity with God, in the fourteenth Chapter of the Jñāneśvarī. "The ideal sage is like the Sun who does not know the distinction between the evening, the morning, and the noon. Like the ground on which a battle has taken place, he neither conquers, nor is conquered. He looks as indifferent as a guest called to dinner, or as a post on the cross-way...... Nevertheless, as by the existence of the Sun all actions take place, similarly, by the existence of such a man, the world goes on. The ocean becomes full, the moon-stone oozes, the lotuses blow, but the moon remains silent. The wind comes and goes, and yet the sky is motionless. Similarly, the qualities may come and go, but they do not affect the mind of such a man" (XIV. 320—348). "Happiness and sorrow affect a man only when he lives like a fish in the waters of bodily feelings ......But when he lives in his own Self, happiness is to him on a par with misery. To the pillar in a house, night is as good as day; similarly, to him, who lives in the Self, all dualities are equal. As when a man is sleeping, the serpent is as good as a maiden, similarly, to him who lives in his Self, all opposite qualities are equal......Praise and blame are equal to him, as darkness and flame are equal to the sun. As the sky remains unaffected during all the seasons, similarly no quality does affect his mind......The fruits of his actions have been burnt, because he has been fire incarnate" (XIV. 350—366). "He has a one-pointed devotion towards Me, and therefore he is able to burn the influence of qualities.

What is now one-pointed devotion ?......As the lustre of the jewel is the jewel itself, as the liquidity of water is water, as space is the sky, as sweetness is sugar,......as consolidated ice is the Himālaya mountain, as congealed milk is curds, similarly, the whole world is Myself. Do not, therefore, deny the world to find Me. I include the whole world in Me. Experience such as this means one-pointed devotion, and My devotee has got this one-pointed devotion" (XIV. 372—382). "As a particle of gold becomes one with gold, as a ray of light merges in light,......as pieces of ice constitute the Himālaya mountain, similarly, the individual selves make God. The waves may be small, and yet they are one with the ocean......Experience, such as this, is real devotion" (XIV. 383—388). "This is the acme of all knowledge. This is the goal of all Yoga : as deep may call unto deep, and the two may be connected by incessant showers ; as the image may become one with the original by the contact of light ; similarly, the Self is connected with God......Fire ceases after having burnt the fuel, similarly, knowledge ceases by having destroyed itself. I am not on one side of the ocean, and the devotee on the other. There is a beginningless unity between us......He who knows this is verily the crest-jewel of those who know" (XIV. 389—401).

Description of Mystic Emotions.

92. In a famous passage of the eleventh Chapter, Jñāneśvara gives us an insight into the physical and psychological effects of God-vision. This may be regarded as a description of the Eight pure Emotions famous in the Indian Psychology of Mysticism. "The duality that so long existed between the Self and the world, now ceased to exist. The mind became immediately composed. Internally there was a feeling of joy. On the outside, the strength of the limbs faded away. From top to toe, the aspirant became full of horripilation, as at the beginning of the rainy season the body of a mountain becomes over-spread by grass. Drops of sweat crept over his body, as drops of water creep on the moon-stone when it is touched by the rays of the moon. As an unblown lotus swings to and fro on the surface of water on account of the bee which is enclosed within its petals, similarly, the body of the devotee began to shake on account of the feelings of internal bliss. As particles of camphor drop down when the womb of the camphor-plant is full-blown, similarly, tears of joy trickled down from his eyes. As the sea experiences tide after tide when the moon has arisen, similarly, his mind experienced surge after surge of emotion from time to time. Thus all the eight Sāttvika emotions began to compete in the mind of the mystic, and he sat on the throne of divine joy" (XI. 245—252). This description of Arjuna is, it may easily be seen, applicable *mutatis mutandis* to Jñāneśvara himself.

Competition of the Emotions of Fear and Joy.

93. We must not fail to notice, however, the competition of the feelings of fear and joy in the mind of the advancing mystic, as typically illustrated in the case of Arjuna. When God showed His universal form to Arjuna, his mind was so terror-struck that he said to Kṛishṇa, "I do not care whether this earthly pall lives or goes; but by Thy great power, even my consciousness seems to disappear. My whole body is shaking. My mind is becoming tormented. My intellect is experiencing the panic of losing even its I-ness. My inner Self, which is by nature full of joy, is itself experiencing a feeling of remorse. How terrific is this power of realization, O God! My knowledge has been banished to the other world, and we shall eftsoons cease to exist as pupil and teacher" (XI. 366—370). As contrasted with the feeling of terror, stands the feeling of the joy of union. Fear is experienced on account of the terrificness of the realization; but joy is experienced on account of its novelty and uniqueness. All sense of duality disappears in such a unitive experience, and that is itself the source of infinite bliss. "One does not experience a feeling of difference in such a state, as a bird tastes a fruit as different from itself. In that ecstatic state, a kind of experience arises, which destroys all egoism, and clings fast to bliss. In that state of embrace, the feeling of union arises of itself, as water under water becomes one with water. As, when the wind is lost in the sky, the duality between them disappears, similarly, in that ecstatic embrace, bliss alone survives...... Duality is undoubtedly at an end, but we cannot even call this the state of unitive experience, for there is not even one to experience the state of union" (V. 131—135).

Rare is the man who reaches the end.

94. Jñāneśvara, however, is careful to point out that such a state is to be only rarely experienced, and that it is not the lot of every seeker after spiritual life. In the seventh Chapter, he tells us that rare must be the man who reaches the end. "Out of thousands of men, scarcely one has got resolution enough, and out of many such resolute men, there is rarely one who really comes to know. Just as out of innumerable people in the world, rarely one here and there is selected to be a soldier, and out of such innumerable ones is made an army, but among these there is scarcely one who enjoys the hand of victory when iron is penetrating into his flesh, similarly, in the great flood of devotion, thousands of people enter, but scarcely one reaches the other end of the stream" (VII. 10—13).

Perfection can be attained only gradually.

95. Jñāneśvara is also careful to point out that perfection in mystical life can be attained only gradually. One must not expect to reach the end immediately that one has entered the path. "Granted that all the intellectual preparation is made for the realization of God; granted also that one meets with the Guru, and that he imparts to him the knowledge of the true path; but, is one able to attain to one's original health as soon as one has taken the medicine? Or does it follow that when the sun has arisen, he immediately reaches the zenith? Granted that the field is well-tilled and watered; granted also that the seed that is sown is good of its kind; but it is only in time that a rich harvest could be reaped. Similarly, granted that the true path is known; granted that company with the good is attained; granted that dispassion has been generated, and real discrimination formed; it will however take time to know that the One alone is, namely God, and that all else is nought......To experience the unitive life in Brahman is a matter of only gradual attainment. Even though various kinds of dishes may be served before a hungry man, still he attains to satisfaction only by morsel after morsel. In a similar way, by the help of dispassion if one lights up the lamp of discrimination, that light will enable one ultimately to find out God" (XVIII. 996—1008).

Asymptotic approximation to God.

96. Jñāneśvara further tells us in his final Chapter, which is also the culmination of his philosophy, that one can only make an asymptotic approximation to God instead of becoming God oneself. He employs a series of metaphors to tell us how the life in God is attained, and how in the atonement one reaches God so nearly as to be only just short of Him. "By putting on himself the armour of dispassion, the mystic mounts the steed of Rājayoga, and by holding the weapon of concentration in the firm grip of discrimination, he wards off small and great obstacles before him. He goes into the battle-field of life, as the Sun moves into darkness, in order to win the damsel of Liberation. He cuts to pieces the enemies that come in his way, such as egoism, arrogance, desire, passion, and others.........Then all the virtues come to welcome him as vassals before a king......At every step as he is marching on the imperial road of spiritual life, the damsels of the psychological States come to receive and worship him. Maidens of the Yogic Stages come and wave lights before him. Powers and Prosperities assemble round about him in thousands to see the spectacle, and rain over him showers of flowers, and as he is thus approaching the true Swarājya, all the three worlds appear to him full of joy. Then there is neither enemy nor friend to him. For there is equality all around, and there is neither 'mine' nor 'thine'......Thus, when all the enemies have been conquered and the world is mortified, his Yogic steed begins to take rest. That armour of dispassion, which had clung closely to his body hitherto, he now tries to loosen somewhat, and as there is no other before him, his hand takes back the weapon of concentration; ......and as one in sight of the goal, begins to walk slowly, similarly, by coming in the vicinity of God, he lets loose his practice. As the Ganges loses its speed as it comes near the ocean, as a wife loses her tremor before her husband, as the plantain tree ceases to grow when the plantains become ripe, or as a way entering into a town ends inside it, similarly, as he finds that he comes to realize the Self, he slowly puts aside his weapon of meditation;...... and as the moon on the fourteenth day of the bright half of the month is just short of the size on the full-moon day, as gold of fifteen carats is just short of gold of sixteen carats, and as one can distinguish between the sea and the river by the stillness and motion of their waters, similarly, to that extent only is the difference between God and the God-realizer. He attains to God, falling only just short of His entire Being" (XVIII. 1047—1090).

God, the sole engrossing object of the Saint.

97. We shall now go on to consider the problem of the Communion of the Saint and God as discussed by Jñāneśvara. We are told by Jñāneśvara that the Saint has God alone for his engrossing object. "As he was walking alone in the night of his earthly life, the dawn of the destruction of Karman broke upon him, and after the twilight of the grace of his Guru, he began to experience the early morning-light of Self-knowledge. There, with his eyes, he saw the great vista of equality. At that time, wherever he cast his eye, I was before him; and if he remained silent, there was I also. He could not direct his sight anywhere without seeing Me. Just as when a pitcher is submerged under water, it is filled with water both externally as well as internally, similarly, he is within Me and I am within and beyond him. This is a matter, not of words, but of actual experience, O Arjuna" (VII. 130—134).

The Communion of Saints.

98. It follows from the love that the devotee bears to God, that he bears equal love towards those who bear the same love towards Him. Jñāneśvara, in a passage of the tenth Chapter, describes beautifully the inter-communion of such devotees of God among themselves. "In their hearts, they have become one with Me. I have become their life. By the force of their realization, they have forgotten life and death. By the power of that great illumination, they dance with the happiness of communion. They now give to each other illumination of Self, and nothing else. As two lakes, which are in close proximity to each other, send their waves into one another, and as the mingling waves form as it were a crest-house for them, similarly, the waves of the joy of the two lovers of God mix with each other, and become ornaments of illumination for either. As the Sun may wave lights before the Sun, or as the Moon may embrace the Moon, or as in full equality one stream may mix with another, similarly, the equal love of these Saints makes a happy confluence, on the top of which rise the eight Sāttvika emotions. ......Then by the power of that great happiness, they run out of themselves, and being filled with Me, they begin to proclaim Me to the world. The word, which had passed between pupil and teacher in their privacy, these Saints now proclaim to the whole world like a rumbling cloud. As when the unblown lotus-flower begins to blow out, it cannot contain within itself its own fragrance, and therefore distributes its virtue to king and pauper alike, in that way, they proclaim Me to the whole world, and in the joy of proclamation, they forget the fact of proclaiming, and in that happy forgetfulness, they sink their body and mind" (X. 119—128).

The Devotee is the Beloved: God is the Lover.

99. Jñāneśvara tells us time after time that the devotee is dearer to God than anything or anybody else. "That secret which He did not impart to His father Vasudeva, nor to His mother Devakī, nor even to His brother Baḷibhadra, Kṛishṇa imparted to His devotee, Arjuna. Even His wife Laxmī, who was in such near presence to Him, could not enjoy the happiness of His love. All the power of the love of Kṛishṇa has been made over to Arjuna. The hopes of Sanaka and others had run extraordinarily high ; but even they could not partake of the fulness of that love. The love of God towards Arjuna seems to be incomparable indeed. What merits must he have in store that he deserved such a state?" (IV. 8—11.) We thus see from this passage that the devotee is nearer to the heart of God than anybody else. In one passage of the twelfth Chapter, Jñāneśvara even speaks of God as the lover, and the Devotee as his beloved. This, however, he tells us under the influence of that erotic mysticism, which finds the relation between husband and wife to be the nearest analogue to the relation of God and Devotee. "He who knows no hatred of any being; ......who like the earth neither upholds the good nor discards the evil;......who like water does not assuage the thirst of the cow, nor kill the tiger by becoming poison; who thus has friendship with the whole world and is as it were the fount of pity; who knows no egoism; who has no sense of mine-ness; to whom happiness is as good as sorrow; who in point of sufferance is equal to the earth; who has given contentment a constant abode in his heart; in whose mind the individual Self and the universal Self both live together in close unison; who having achieved the highest stage of Yoga, delivers over his mind and intellect to Me;......he alone, O Arjuna, is the true devotee. He alone is the true Yogin. He alone is truly absolved. The relation between us is the relation between wife and husband......To talk about these things itself brings a sweet infatuation. I would rather have not spoken these words, had not My love made me speak of it! Happy am I that I have reached this happy contentment. As soon as these words were uttered, God Kṛishṇa began to nod in joy" (XII. 144—163).

The office of God for the welfare of the Saint.

100. Jñāneśvara tells us that the office of God is always for the welfare of the Saint. "They who have given themselves over to Me with all their heart like a fœtus in the womb, which knows no activity on its own account; to whom there is nothing higher than Me; who regard Me as their very life; and who worship Me with a constant one-pointed devotion; these themselves become the objects of worship at My hands. At the very moment that they followed Me with all their heart, all their burden of life has fallen upon Me. Whatever they intend to do, I must then Myself accomplish for them, as the mother-bird undertakes every trouble for the life of her young ones. As the mother knows no thirst, nor hunger, and does of her own accord what is good for her child, similarly, I do everything for those who have given over their minds to Me. If they aspire after becoming one with Me, I accomplish it for them. If they want to do Me service, I give them love by which they may do so. Whatever thus they intend in their minds, I gradually begin to make over to them, and whatever I thus make over, I try to consummate in course of time" (IX. 335—342). Jñāneś-vara tells us again in another passage that His devotees need never entertain any anxiety for their material and spiritual welfare. "They are doing duties that are proper for them according to their caste. They obey the law, and discard every thing that is not sanctioned by morality. They deliver their actions to Me, and thus burn their results......The goal of all their bodily, mental, and verbal activity, is I Myself...... They are meditating on My form......With one-pointed devotion, they have sold their mind and body to Me. Tell Me, O Arjuna, what shall I not do for them? ......Is it possible that My devotees be ever troubled by any anxiety for their worldly life? Does the wife of a prince go begging alms?" (XII. 76—85.) In a similar spirit, we are told in the tenth Chapter that God fulfils all the desires of His Saints. "By the plenitude of their love, they have washed off the distinction between night and day, and are enjoying My immaculate happiness......What I now do for them is to make their happiness increase, and turn the gaze of accident from their enjoyment of bliss. As by covering her dear child by the eye of love, the mother runs after it by taking into her hands every play-thing that it wants, and gives it every golden toy that it demands, similarly, I undertake to fulfil the spiritual ambitions of My devotee......My devotee loves Me, and I care only for his one-pointed devotion. Difficult indeed is real love between Devotee and God......I have made over everything to My spouse Lakshmī; but I have withheld from her the knowledge of the Self, which I make over to My devotee" (X. 129—139).

God accepts from his Devotee any offering, howsoever humble.

101. Jñāneśvara tells us how God accepts any object howsoever insignificant that is made over to Him in love by His devotee. "With a love incomparable, when My devotee offers to Me a fruit of any tree whatsoever, or even brings it before Me, I catch hold of it with both My hands, and partake of it without even plucking it from its stem. When My devotee offers to Me a flower by devotion, I should, as a matter of fact, smell it; but I forget smelling, and begin to eat it. What of flowers! If one offers the leaf of a tree—it matters not whether it is a wet leaf—it may even be a dry leaf—I look upon it as covered by the love of My devotee, and as if full of hunger I regard it as sweet as nectar and begin to enjoy it. When even not a leaf is available, water at least is not difficult to find. That can be had at any place without any price, and when My devotee offers it to Me, I regard the offer as greater than that of a palace richer than Vaikuṇṭha, or like that of ornaments richer than the Kaustubha jewel......Thou thyself hast seen, O Arjuna, that I loosened the knots of Sudāman's cloth in order to partake of the parched rice therein. I care only for devotion. There is nothing either great or small to Me. I care only for the spirit in which it is offered. A leaf, a flower, or a fruit is only a cause for worshipping Me: but I am really worshipped by one-pointed love" (IX. 382—396).

The Devotee, the object of God's adoration.

102. In return for the Saint's offer of love to God, "God regards him as the very crest-jewel on His head......He has taken the highest goal of life in his hands, and is traversing the world for giving it over to people in the way of divine love......He is the object of My adoration. I regard him as My head-ornament. I have even prized his kick on My breast. I have made his virtues the ornaments of My speech. I have filled My ears with his fame. I, who am eyeless, take on eyes only in order to see him. I worship him by the sport-lotus in My hand. I have taken on two plus two hands in order to embrace his body......He is the object of My concentration. He is My very deity whom I worship......All My heart is concentrated on him. He is the whole of My treasure. I derive contentment only in his company" (XII. 214—237).

God leads the Devotee onwards in the Spiritual Path.

103. God even endows His devotee with the highest good, namely, the spiritual good. "When I see that he is being tossed on the waves of life and death, and when I see that he is being frightened in the waters of the ocean of existence, I gather together My various forms, and run to his help. I go with a ship to relieve him out of the ocean,—the Names of God constituting the various Boats attached to it. Those, whom I find single, I enable to catch hold of the hem of My garment. Those, who are with a family, I put on a raft. I attach the chest of love to the body of the rest, and bring all of them to the shore of God-union. Even beasts have thus claimed My attention, and have been lifted to the Kingdom of Heaven. Therefore, O Arjuna, there is no cause for any anxiety whatsoever to

My devotees. I come forward to relieve them out of misery. As soon as My devotees have given their hearts to Me, I have taken on Myself the obligation of relieving them. Hence, O King of Devotees, thy only business should be to follow this path of God" (XII. 87—96).

The Devotee, the recipient of particular Grace from God at the time of Death.

104. At the time of death, especially, the devotee is the recipient of particular grace from God. "If thou, O Arjuna, doubtest how My devotee may remember Me at the time of death,—when his senses have been confused, when his life has been plunged in misery, and when all the signs of death have made their presence felt both internally and externally,—if thou doubtest how he should sit for meditation, how he should control his senses, how he should have a heart at all to meditate on God by means of Om, remember that if My devotee has served Me constantly during his life, I become his servant at the time of his death. He has stopped all activities for My sake. He has pent Me up in his heart, and is ever enjoying My presence......He has become Myself, and is yet worshipping Me. When such a man is approaching the time of death, if he remembers Me, and if I do not come to succour him, of what use is his life-long meditation ? If a poor man calls upon Me in poverty of spirit, shall I not go to relieve him out of his misery ? And if My devotee is reduced to the same state as this man, what is the use of his life-long devotion ? Therefore, doubt not, O Arjuna. At the very moment that the devotee remembers Me, I am before him. I cannot bear the burden of his love towards Me. I am his debtor, and he is My creditor ; and for discharging My debt, I serve him personally at the time of his death. For fear that bodily suffering may kill his consciousness, I protect him under the wings of Self-illumination. I spread about him the cool shade of My remembrance, and I bring him towards Me, because his heart has been forever set on Me" (VIII. 120—133).

How one should die in God.

105. And under the consciousness of such protection from God, the devotee should merge his Soul in Him. With a heart concentrated, he should meditate on the immaculate God. "He should sit in the Padma posture with his face towards the north, and being filled internally with the joy of meditation, he should make it his one aim to merge himself in the Form of God......He should prop his heart by inward courage. He should fill his Soul by devotion. He should make himself ready for departing by the power of Yoga, and as the sound of a bell vanishes in the bell, similarly, he should make his Prāṇa vanish through his eye-brows; and as one does not know how or when a lamp, under a pitcher, comes to be extinguished, even so, he should give up the ghost. Such a man is really God himself. He is the highest person, and is My very abode" (VIII. 91—99). "And as ghee which is churned out of milk, cannot become milk any more, similarly, when he reaches Me, there is no return for him......This internal secret I am unfolding to thee, O Arjuna!" (VIII. 202—203).

The Union of Saint and God.

106. In a number of passages of the Jñāneśvarī, we find that Jñāneśvara describes the Union of Saint and God as the culmination of mystical life. Occasionally, he speaks of there being some little difference yet between the two. Elsewhere, he identifies the two altogether. In the seventh Chapter of the Jñāneśvarī, he tells us that even though Saint and God may come together, the Saint remains a Saint and God God. "Even though the devotee may reach union with God, yet he remains a devotee. Even though wind may vanish into space, still when it moves, we see that it is different from space. Otherwise, it would become one with space. Similarly, the saint remains a saint so long as he has to discharge his bodily actions. But by the light of his internal consciousness, he has become one with Me. By the illumination of that knowledge, he knows that he is the Self. Therefore, I also say with great rejoicement that I am he. He, who lives by knowing the mark which is beyond his bodily existence, is not different from it, even though the body may be different" (VII. 114—118). "As the calf of a cow has its heart entirely set on its mother and leaps to it as soon as it sees her, and even as the cow returns the love, in the same manner, with the same intensity with which the devotee loves God, does God return the love of the saint. Having once known Me, the mystic has forgotten to see behind, as the river which reaches the ocean ceases to return. He, whose river of devotion, springing from the recesses of his heart, has reached Me, is my very Soul. He is the real Knower" (VII. 121—126).

Liberation before Death.

107. Elsewhere Jñāneśvara speaks of the absolute identity of Saint and God even before the Saint departs from this life. "The Saint has refused to identify himself with the body, and therefore, he feels no pangs of separation from it when he wants to throw it away; nor does it follow that he reaches Me only after he has thrown off his mortal coil ; for he has been already during his life merged in My Being. He has known his Self as mere moonlight, existing not in itself, but in the moon of Universal Spirit. By having been one with Me in life, after death he also becomes Myself" (VIII. 136—139). "Those who, during life, have worshipped the gods, after death become gods. Those who worship the fathers, merge into the being of the fathers. Those who with motives of sorcery run after minor deities, when death lets down the curtain, merge into these elementals. Those, on the other hand, who see Me with their eyes and hear Me with their ears and think of Me with their minds, who by every limb make salutation to Me, whose merit and charity are done only for My sake, who have Me as their constant object of study, who are filled with My presence in and out, who regard their life as useful only for the attainment of God, who pride themselves upon being the servants of God, whose passion is only the love of God, whose only desire and love are the desire and love of God, who are infatuated by Me, whose sciences make Me the object of their study, whose chants are the chants of God, who in this way make Me the object of all their activities, these, even before death, have already come into My Being. How after death, shall they ever pass out of Me ?" (IX. 355—365.) In this way, we see the absolute identity of the Saint and God even during the life-time of the Saint.

The Practical Way for the attainment of Unitive Life.

108. The practical way for the attainment of this unitive existence in God is described by Jñāneśvara in the eighteenth Chapter. "Fill thy whole inside and outside by My activity. Regard Me as all-encompassing. As wind mixes with space, similarly, in all thy actions mix with Me. Make Me the sole resort of thy mind. Fill thy ears with My praise. Let thy eye fall in love, as on a woman, on the Saints who are My incarnations. Let thy speech live on My names. Let all the actions of thy hand or foot be done solely with reference to Me. Whatever obligations thou conferest upon another, regard them as offerings to Me...... The dislike of beings shall thus depart. I shall be the sole object of thy salutation. Thou shalt come to an eternal life in Me. In the filled world, there shall then be no third except thee and Me. Thou and Myself shall live in absolute union. In a state inexpressible, thou shalt enjoy Me, and I shall enjoy thee. Thy happiness shall thus grow. When a third existence, which obstructs our union, has thus departed, thou art already one with Me......Who shall prevent the wind from filling the sky? Or the wave from reaching the ocean? The difference between thyself and Me, is only on account of thy bodily tenement, and when it is destroyed, thou art Myself already" (XVIII. 1353—1367).

Description of a Unitive Devotee.

109. How does Jñāneśvara describe the external life of such a unitive mystic? "He of whose mind I am the sole occupant, shall, even during sleep, be known for his passionlessness. He has bathed in the river of Self-knowledge. He is filled with contentment after the enjoyment of the full mystical experience. His life is as a sprout to tranquillity......He is, as it were, a pillar of courage. Like a pitcher, he is filled inside and outside with joy ......His very sport is moral......His mind serves as a satchel for Me......His love of Me is ever on the increase ......Duality between him and Me has departed. He has become one with Me, and yet serves Me as an Other" (IX. 186—196). "By the union of knowledge and devotion, he is merged in Me, and has become one with Me......As when a mirror is placed against a mirror, which mirror may be said to reflect which?......He enjoys Me even though he has become one with Me, as a young woman enjoys youth...... In Advaita, there is still Bhakti. This is a matter of experience, and not of words. Whatever, by the influence of previous actions, he speaks or does, it is really I, who do these things for him......As at the time of the Great End, water ceases to flow, being hemmed in on all sides by water, similarly, he is filled everywhere by the Ātman......By becoming one with Me, he ceases to move. That constitutes his pilgrimage to My uniqueness......Whatever he speaks is My praise. Whatever he sees is My vision. I move when he moves. Whatever he does is My worship. Whatever he contemplates is the chant of My prayer. His sleep is ecstasy in Me. As a bracelet is one with gold, so by the power of his devotion he is one with Me. As water is one with waves, or camphor with fragrance, or a jewel with lustre, even so is he one with Me" (XVIII. 1130—1183).

The ecstatic and post-ecstatic states.

110. Jñāneśvara tells us of the great post-ecstatic awakening of such a mystic. "When ignorance has ceased, and sacrificer and sacrifice have become one; when the last act of the sacrifice, namely, the Avabhṛitha ceremony, has been performed in the experience of the Self; he wakes up like a man from his sleep, and says that while he was experiencing a dream, he it was who had manifested himself in all the various forms of the dream ; that the army which he saw, was not an army, but only a manifestation of his own Self" (IX. 244—247). "And when he sits for meditation, he hears the sound of the kettle-drum of victory, and the unique banner of Identity unfurls over him ; and Ecstasy along with her Lord, the Realisation of the Self, is crowned on the throne of Unitive Experience" (IX. 217—218).

A tale of unison brings on unison.

111. The most famous passage, however, in which Jñāneśvara gives us a description of unitive love, is towards the end of the eighteenth Chapter, where Sañjaya is speaking to Dhṛitarāshṭra about the unison of Kṛishṇa and Arjuna, and is so overcome with feelings that he himself becomes one with them. Sañjaya was like a little salt-doll at the confluence of the loves of Kṛishṇa and Arjuna, and became so merged in the waters of the confluence as to be entirely indistinguishable from the love of either. "There is only a difference of names, O Dhṛitarāshṭra, said Sañjaya, between the eastern ocean and the western ocean ; but really speaking, the waters in both are identical. Similarly, there was a difference between Kṛishṇa and Pārtha only so far as their bodies were concerned ; but there was no difference left in their spiritual confluence. Kṛishṇa and Arjuna were like two clean mirrors, placed one against the other, the one reflecting itself infinitely in the other. Arjuna saw himself along with God in God, and God saw Himself along with Arjuna in Arjuna, and Sañjaya saw both of them together! ......Had there been no difference between Kṛishṇa and Arjuna, no question and answer would have been possible for them ; if there was a difference, there would have been no atonement. Sañjaya heard their dialogue, as well as saw their atonement. Kṛishṇa and Arjuna were however identical. When one mirror is placed against another, the difference between the original and the image vanishes. When one mirror is placed before another, which reflects which ? Supposing a Sun arose before the Sun, who is the illuminator, and who is the illumined ? The determination of duality in such an experience would be a failure ; and when two waters have mixed together, if a piece of salt goes to distinguish between them, in a moment's time it becomes mingled with both. So, as Kṛishṇa and Arjuna reached the unitive life, I myself, said Sañjaya, was atoned with them." "While he was speaking thus, he was overcome by extreme emotion, and his consciousness seemed to have departed from him on account of his

Bhāvas. His body was covered with horripilation of hair. He fell motionless, and was full of perspiration, and in a moment's time a shiver passed through his system, which conquered both those manifestations. Tears trickled down his eyes by the blissful touch of unitive life. The tears were not really tears; through them oozed out his spiritual experience. He could contain nothing in himself. His throat was choked, and words failed to come out of his mouth" (XVIII. 1589—1606).

Epilogue.

The Epilogue of the Jnanesvari.

112. In his epilogue to the Jñāneśvari, Jñāneśvara brings in two passages, in one of which he tells us that victory is always with him who is befriended by God; that God's nature being victory itself, victory in any case must accrue to the side where God is present. Dhṛitarāshṭra, the father of the Kauravas, who was anxious to know the result of the fight that was taking place between the Kauravas and the Pāndavas, asked Sañjaya on what side victory would ultimately lie, and Sañjaya had no hesitation in telling him that victory must lie with the side where Lord Kṛishṇa was. "Where there is the moon, there is the moon-light. Where there is the god Śankara, there is his spouse Ambikā. Where there are the saints, there is discrimination. Where the king is, there is the army. Where there is goodness, there is friendship. Where there is fire, there is the burning power. Where there is compassion, there is religion; where there is religion, there is happiness; where there is happiness, there is God. In spring-time, there are groves; in groves, there are flowers; in flowers, there are clusters of bees. Where the Guru is, there is knowledge; in knowledge, there is the vision of the Self; in vision, there is beatification. Where there is fortune, there is enjoyment. Where there is happiness, there is energy. Where there is the Sun, there is light......Where Lord Kṛishṇa is, there is Lakshmī; and where both of them are, there are all the maidens of Lakshmī, namely, the Powers. Kṛishṇa is victory himself, and with the party with which He has sided, victory must ultimately lie. In a place, where Kṛishṇa and His devotee are, the very trees will beat down the wish-trees of heaven; the stones are as jewels; the earth is of gold; through the rivers of that place flows nectar. The prattling of him, whose parents Kṛishṇa and Kamalā are, is equal to the Veda. His very body is divine;......and as the cloud, which is born of the ocean, is more useful to the world than his parent, similarly, Arjuna was more useful to the world than even Kṛishṇa. The touch-stone makes gold of iron, but the world prizes the gold more than the touch-stone. Spiritual teachership is not here called in question. Fire shows itself in the shape of a lamp......That a son should conquer his father is the peculiar wish of the latter. Where Arjuna is, there is victory also, because he is the favourite of God......If thou believest in the words of Vyāsa, then believe in what I say. Where the Lord of Lakshmī is, there is the company of the Saints; there is happiness, and infinite auspiciousness. If this turns out false, then I shall cease to call myself the disciple of Vyāsa. With these thundering words, Sañjaya raised his arm" (XVIII. 1633—1659). The second famous passage in the epilogue of the Jñāneśvarī is the one where Jñāneśvara asks grace from God. "Let the Lord of the Universe be pleased with this literary sacrifice of mine, and being pleased, let Him give me this grace: May the wicked leave their crookedness and have increasing love for good!. Let universal friendship reign among all beings. Let the darkness of evil disappear. Let the sun of True Religion rise in the world. Let all beings obtain what they desire. May the company of the devotees of God, who shower down blessings incessantly, meet the beings on earth! They are verily moving gardens of wish-trees; they are living mines of wish-jewels; they are speaking oceans of nectar. They are moons without any detracting mark; they are suns without any tormenting heat. May all beings be endowed with all happiness, and have incessant devotion to the Primeval Being. Let all those, who live upon this work, have victory in the seen, as well as the unseen! God said to this, 'Amen! this shall come to pass,' and Jñāneśvara became happy by hearing those words" (XVIII. 1794—1802).

CHAPTER IV.

The Amritanubhava.

Jnanadeva's esteem of his work.

1. Jñānadeva expounds his philosophical teaching in this work with such a mastery and wealth of poetic imagery, that it remains to this day one of the greatest philosophical works in Marathi literature. Though Jñānadeva more than once speaks of this work as Anubhavāmṛita (Amt. X. 19, 20, 24, 25, 31), we have yet called it Amṛitānubhava, as this title is more familiar to all. The encomiums which he himself passes on it make it evident what great importance he wanted to attach to this work. He tells us that it is rich in spiritual experience, and that by it people would gain final emancipation in this very life (Amt. X. 19). It is so sweet that even Ambrosia would desire to partake of it (Amt. X. 20). Jñānadeva tells us that he has served to all this dish of spiritual experience in order that the whole world may enjoy a general feast (Amt. X. 24, 31). He declares that the work would be found equally useful for all classes of spiritual aspirants—those who are bound, those who desire for final freedom, as also those who have attained to spiritual perfection (Amt. X. 25). For, in the first place, he thinks that, from the ultimate point of view, there is only a difference of degree and not of kind between these classes of aspirants, as there is a potentiality of spiritual perfection even in those who are bound, and in those who desire for liberation. Thus he asks—Can we from the view point of the Sun say that the Full Moon is different from the Moon of other days? The bloom of youth that expresses itself in a young woman was dormant in her girlhood. Again, with the advent of spring, the trees begin to kiss the sky with their twigs, and they bear flowers and fruits (Amt. X. 21—23); but this is only an actualization of what was potentially present in the trees. Secondly, Jñānadeva declares that all distinction of ability or level between the three classes of spiritual aspirants vanishes as soon as they taste the nectar of spiritual experience presented in this work. He describes the unifying influence of his work in a number of beautiful similes: he tells us that the streams that go to meet the Ganges become themselves the Ganges; the darkness that meets the Sun becomes itself the light of the Sun; we can talk of difference between gold and other metals only so long as the Parisa has not touched the other metals; for then it makes them all pure gold (Amt. X. 26—27).

The Principal Aim of the Work.

2. The principal aim of the work, as Jñāneśvara expresses it, is the extension and diffusion of the Knowledge of God, which he had himself gained through the unlimited magnanimity of his spiritual teacher, to all the people in the world. He tells us that he took to writing this work, simply because he was blessed by his Guru with spiritual bliss not for his own individual enjoyment, but with the express desire that the whole world may be enabled to partake of it; as God endowed the Sun with light not for his own sake, but because he may illumine the whole world. It was not for the Moon's own sake that nectar was given to the Moon; nor does the Sea grant the clouds water for their own use. The light of a Lamp is meant for all......Thus also does Spring enable the trees to bear fruit, and oblige all people (Amt. X. 1—6). Here we find that Jñānadeva is preaching a kind of spiritual altruism, which strongly reminds us of the Parable of the Cave in the Republic, where Plato insists that a true philosopher, who has seen the Spiritual Light outside the Cave, must come inside and tell the shadow-ridden Cave-indwellers that what they are busying themselves with are appearances and not reality. Jñānadeva however tells us with great humility that he has disclosed no new principle, since it is impossible to express in words the Self-luminous, which would have shone even if the work had not been written, and even if he had remained silent (Amt. X. 8—9). Everything is luminous, and there is no secret to be revealed, since the whole universe is completely filled with the one eternal perfect Ātman, who is neither hidden nor manifest (Amt. X. 14—15). Nothing exists, therefore, beyond the one intelligent principle which has been existing from eternity (Amt. X. 16). It is inexpressible, and even the Upanishads can describe it only in negative terms (Amt. X. 18). Jñānadeva, therefore, says that his work is, in fact, an expression of the deepest silence; it is like the picture of a crocodile drawn on the surface of water (Amt. X. 17). This utterance may be taken on the one hand as connoting the impossibility of describing in words the nature of the Ultimate Principle, and on the other, as an expression of the extreme humility that is so characteristic of Jñānadeva.

The Argument of the Work.

3. We shall, in the first place, consider the metaphysical speculations of Jñānadeva, as expressed in this work. We shall see how under the influence of the Sāmkhya system he discusses the nature of the Prakṛiti and the Purusha; how they are related to each other as husband and wife; how the world is created by them; how they are interdependent; how they disappear with the realisation of the real nature of either of them; and how they are united in Brahman which is their substratum. We shall next turn to the description of the nature of the Ātman as given by Jñānadeva under the influence of Vedānta Philosophy. We shall show how the Ātman transcends all expression, and in particular how the Word, useful in reminding us of the real nature of our Self, which we have forgotten through our ignorance, proves, in fact, useless with reference to the Ātman which is self-existent, and which is all-knowledge; while it is also useless in removing ignorance, as ignorance by its very nature has no existence. Next we shall consider the nature of knowledge and ignorance, point out with what keenness Jñānadeva meets the arguments of those who assert the real existence of ignorance in the Ātman, show how he proves definitely that the Ātman is beyond both knowledge and ignorance, and how both of these, being false, only limit the real nature of the Self. Next, we shall see how there exists in this universe nothing but one living intelligent principle, namely, the Brahman or Ātman, and how the world and all phenomenal existence are but vibrations, or manifestations, or the sports of this One without a second. It is the substratum of all existence whatsoever, and by it is everything illuminated. It is this self-luminous self-existent Ātman that presents itself as the world with the triads of the seer, the sight, and the seen, the knower, the knowledge, and the known, and so on, and yet is in fact beyond all these, and absolutely unaffected by them. We shall next pass to the mystical speculations of the Amṛitānubhava, and consider how Jñānadeva shows that this Ātman can be intuitively apprehended, and realised through the grace of a Spiritual Teacher. The significance of the Spiritual Teacher and his real nature form a subject of perennial interest to Jñānadeva, as it does to all other Saints, and we find many pages of the work devoted to this important topic. Finally, we shall briefly notice the nature of supreme devotion to God, as also the condition of one who has attained to final emanicipation in this very life.

Influence of Samkhya and Vedanta on the thought of Jnanadeva.

4. When we come to the discussion of the nature of the Prakṛiti and the Purusha which are also designated as Śiva and Śakti, or God and Goddess, by Jñānadeva, we have to note that the relation between them is likened to that subsisting between husband and wife,—thus clearly showing the influence of Śaivism on the one hand, and that of the dualistic trend of thought of the Sāmkhya on the other. The Prakṛiti is also declared to be nothing but the desire of the Purusha to enjoy himself. It is also contended that both the ideas of the Prakṛiti and the Purusha are interdependent, and the fact that they are but different forms of one living intelligent Brahman argues for their essential unity. This synthesis of the duality is clearly the effect of the influence of the Vedānta on the thought of Jñānadeva. These preliminary remarks will help us to understand the account of the Prakṛiti and the Purusha which Jñānadeva gives in the second chapter of his Amṛitānubhava.

The Prakriti and the Purusha.

5. Jñānadeva regards Prakriti and Purusha, or Śakti and Śiva, as the parents of an infinite number of worlds, who mutually exhibit their essential unity; and he declares that it is very difficult to know what part of either of them is united to the other to make one whole (Amt. I, Sanskrit Verses 4, 3). They are unlimited (Amt. I. 1). They are related to one another as husband and wife, the Purusha himself becoming his beloved, the Prakṛiti, when impelled by a desire to enjoy himself (Amt. I. 2); and so strong is their desire to enjoy themselves that they become one through it, and never allow their unity to be disturbed by anything (Amt. I. 5). So intense and deep is the love between them that they seem as if to swallow up each other, and thus exhibit the world as the sport of their love (Amt. I. 3). What Jñānadeva wants to say is that with the expansion of the Prakṛiti, the Purusha remains concealed and unknown, while with the extension of the Purusha, the Prakṛiti disappears. Thus he tells us that these are the only two inmates of the home of the Universe, and when the Lord (the Purusha) goes to sleep, the Mistress (the Prakṛiti) remains awake, and herself plays the part of both; and that if either of them happens to wake up, the whole house is swallowed up, and nothing is left behind (Amt. I. 13, 14). The Prakṛiti, again, who gives birth to all things living and non-living in the world, herself disappears absolutely when the Purusha wakes up (Amt. I. 37). They mutually serve as mirrors to reflect their own nature (Amt. I. 38), and become objects of enjoyment to one another (Amt. I. 16); and yet both of them vanish as soon as they embrace each other (Amt. I. 47); that is, with the real knowledge of their nature, they cease to be ultimate realities, and become only the manifestations of the one Brahman that underlies them both. Jñānadeva considers Prakṛiti and Purusha to be interdependent, and complementary to each other. Thus, he says that it is only through the God that the other is a Goddess, and it is through her that he is the Lord. The chaste and well-devoted Prakṛiti cannot live without him, while apart from his beloved, the Purusha cannot be called Śiva, nor can he be called the all-doer and the all-enjoyer (Amt. I. 10, 21, 28, 39); thus, these two being relative cannot exist independently of each other. Through their profound love, they live happily not only in the smallest particle, but find the great world too small for them to live in. They treat each other as their very life, and even the most insignificant thing in the world cannot be created without their mutual help (Amt. I. 11—12). On the one hand, the Prakṛiti, blushing at her formless husband, adorns him with the ornaments of names and forms as great as the world itself; and by her miraculous power presents the rich manifold world in Brahman which cannot tolerate even the idea of unity. The Purusha, on the other hand, enhances the growth of his beloved Prakṛiti by contracting himself, as she manifests only the existence of the Purusha in all her manifestations; and he, who assumes the form of a seer through his love for her, suddenly throws himself away in grief when he fails to see his beloved; it is on account of her importunities that he assumes the form of the world, while he is left naked without her, being deprived of the covering of the names and forms created by her (Amt. I. 30—34). Jñānadeva is here giving expression to a very favourite idea of his, that with the expression of the Prakṛiti, the Purusha becomes concealed; while with the knowledge of the real nature of the Purusha, the Prakṛiti vanishes. This reminds us of the Empedoklean idea of Love and Strife, each alternately entering the Sphere and driving away its opposite. What Jñānadeva wants to express here is that as soon as we come to know the real nature of either the Prakṛiti or the Purusha, their dependence on Brahman and their essential unity with it become evident, and we come to regard them as only relative conceptions that point to the one Absolute which underlies them both.

The essential unity of Prakriti and Purusha in Brahman.

6. This leads us to consider the unity of the Prakṛiti and the Purusha in Brahman. We are told by Jñānadeva that both the Prakṛiti and the Purusha live in Brahman and are illuminated by its light, and that from eternity both of them have been living there as one (Amt. I. 8). Both of them melt their forms into the unity of Brahman, though the world that we see by our ignorance is created by the half part of each of them (Amt. I. 15). Jñānadeva further tells us that the duality or difference of male and female is only in name, while in reality the One supreme Brahman in the form of Śiva alone exists. The Prakṛiti and the Purusha together create but one world, as one sound is produced by striking two sticks against each other, or one Vīṇā prepared by means of two bamboo rods; two lips utter but one word, and two eyes give but one vision. The Prakṛiti and the Purusha whose parts are as if intermingled, seem to be two, but are in fact eternally enjoying the unity of the one blissful Ātman (Amt. I. 17—20, 40), and are therefore really one. They cannot be distinguished from one another, as sweetness cannot be distinguished from sugar; again, the sun shines on account of his lustre, but the essence of lustre is nothing but the sun (Amt. 23—25). Śiva and Śakti, the Purusha and the Prakṛiti, are declared to be essentially one, as are air and its motion, or gold and its lustre, or musk and its fragrance, or fire and its heat (Amt. I. 41—42). If day and night were to go together to the abode of the Sun to meet him, the day would vanish along with the night; similarly do the relative conceptions of the Prakṛiti and the Purusha vanish in the unity of Brahman (Amt. I. 43). Though the Purusha and the Prakṛiti seem to be male and female (from the grammatical point of view), yet there is really no difference between them, just as there is no difference in the waters of the Sea (male) and the Ganges (female) when they meet together (Amt. I. 54). Jñānadeva, therefore, bows to Bhūteśa and Bhavāni, the Purusha and the Prakṛiti, in a spirit of unity with them as the ornaments of gold would bow to gold of which they are made (Amt. I. 60, 52). Finally, he declares that having renounced egoism, he has now become one with Śambhu and Śāmbhavī, as a piece of salt becomes one with the sea when it leaves aside its solidity and smallness (Amt. I. 63).

Description of Brahman or Atman.

7. After having shown in the previous section how the Prakriti and the Purusha, being relative conceptions, point to an ultimate principle, call it Brahman or Ātman, which underlies them both, we may now proceed to consider the nature of this ultimate principle. If, as we are told, the Ātman exists independently of everything else, and sees without being seen by anybody, and is ever manifest, how can we talk of him as non-existent, or as lost? The Ātman silently endures the charge of the nihilists who regard him as nothing, for they contradict their own theory in practice, as the assumption of their own existence necessarily presupposes the existence of the Ātman. Can the Ātman be proved as non-existent—the Ātman, who witnesses the sleep which in its dense darkness of ignorance engulfs the gross and the subtle worlds alike, and who is the all-knower, and who cannot be encompassed by what is visible? The Vedas speak about everything, but they have not even mentioned the name of the Ātman, who is beyond all being and non-being. The Sun that illumines all things cannot show us the Ātman; the sky that envelopes all things cannot comprehend the Ātman. Egoism which eagerly embraces as its own every kind of body which is but a conglomeration of bones, leaves aside the Ātman, who is beyond all egoism. The understanding, that grasps all things knowable, falters before this Ātman. The mind, that imagines many things, remains far removed from the Ātman. The senses, that are ever directed to the useless objects of sensual pleasures, like wild cattle feeding on the grass of barren land, absolutely fail to taste the bliss of the Ātman. Is it possible to apprehend in all its totality the Ātman or Brahman that swallows up the world, along with ignorance that created it? It is impossible for any one to see the Brahman, which, being pure knowledge itself, cannot be an object of knowledge even to itself, just as the tongue that tastes all other things cannot taste itself. How could the Ātman be limited by anything else, when it is not limited even by any desire to see itself? Thus all our efforts to determine the nature of the Ātman prove as futile as those of a person who tries to outrun his own shadow. Those, therefore, who describe the Ātman in words or by means of various similes, remain only far removed from him, as they cannot give a real description of the Ātman. The Ātman is not only beyond all words, but also beyond the reach of intellectual apprehension. It is through the Ātman that the individual self is purged away of its ignorance, and can experience the ecstatic, beatific condition. Though the Ātman is the seer, he is not relative to anything seen; for how could there be any act of seeing when there is not in the Ātman even the idea of unity, as unity is only relative to duality (Amt. VII. 104-122)? Thus the ultimate principle, namely the Ātman, is declared to be the all-knower and all-seer; beyond being and not-being; beyond the reach of egoism; beyond the senses, mind, and understanding; baffling all description by means of words; and transcending all perceptual and conceptual knowledge.

Brahman is beyond the three attributes—Existence, Knowledge and Bliss.

8. As regards the nature of Brahman, Jñāneśvara first denies the existence in it of the three attributes, existence, knowledge and bliss, in the sense that they, like the attributes of Spinoza, are incapable of exhaustively determining the nature of Brahman, though they all enter into its nature and are together expressive of Brahman. As lustre, hardness, and yellowness together constitute gold ; or as viscosity, sweetness, and mellifluity together constitute nectar ; or as whiteness, fragrance, and softness are only camphor ; and just as the three qualities in each case mean but one thing, and do not point to the existence of a triad ; similarly the three attributes of Existence, Knowledge, and Bliss involve no triad, but express one Brahman. And as the three qualities of camphor do not exhaust its nature and may therefore be said not to exist in it at all, similarly, the three attributes of Brahman may be declared to be non-existent in Brahman, as they fail to grasp Brahman in its totality (Amt. V. 1, 7). They are only human ways of looking at Brahman, which is absolute and remains unaffected by these ; as we human beings talk of increase or decrease of the Kalās of the Moon from our own point of view, while the Moon is as it is in itself, perfect at all times, and unaffected by our way of looking at it. Similarly Brahman is as it is, and is not affected by our way of determining its nature by means of the three attributes, or their opposites which are implied in them (Amt. V. 8—12). These expressions, however, point to the Absolute before they vanish in it, like the clouds that shower rain, or like the streams that flow into the sea, or like the paths that reach the goal. As a flower fades after giving rise to a fruit, or as a fruit is lost after giving its juice, or as juice vanishes after giving satisfaction ; or, again, as the hand of a sacrificer returns after offering oblations ; or as a sweet tune is lost in the void after awakening pleasurable sensations in the hearers ; or as a mirror disappears after reflecting the face ; similarly, the three terms become lost in silence after manifesting the pure nature of Ātman as the Seer (Amt. V. 20—25). Brahman is beyond all speech, and it is as impossible and futile to speak about it, as to measure one's length by measuring one's shadow by one's own hands (Amt. V. 26—27). Brahman is beyond all relative conceptions, such as existence, intelligence, and happiness ; as also beyond the opposites of these that are implied in them. It is neither existence, nor non-existence, for it is absolute existence ; it is neither

intelligence nor non-intelligence, as it is absolute intelligence; and it is neither happiness nor misery, since it is absolute bliss. It transcends all duality of opposite and relative conceptions, and is absolutely one, though not numerically one (Amt. V. 26—34).

The existence of Brahman proved against the Nihilists.

9. The Sun alone, who is never thrown into the background by any other lustrous body, and who can never be covered by darkness, can bear comparison with Brahman, which is neither darkened by ignorance nor brightened by knowledge. Moreover, it is not conscious of its own condition (Amt. IV. 17—18); for if we were to suppose that Brahman knows itself, this would imply that it was ignorant of its own self for some time, as knowledge is always relative to ignorance; this, however, is absurd (Amt. IV. 23). The mode of existence of Brahman is so unique that both existence and non-existence prove false in its case (Amt. IV. 25). But we cannot say that Brahman does not exist at all; for none has such an experience. Further, Jñānadeva asks, on whose existence can it be proved that Brahman is nothing, and does not exist? Some one's existence is absolutely necessary to prove the existence or non-existence of anything. Brahman's existence is unique, and it exists without existing in any particular way, and without being non-existent (Amt. IV. 26—31). The reason why Brahman is supposed to be non-existent is that it is an object of knowledge neither to itself nor to any one else. Its existence, however, is pure and absolute, and is therefore beyond both existence and non-existence. It exists in its own way, as a man fast asleep in an uninhabited forest exists without being an object to himself or to anybody else (Amt. IV. 32—34). Brahman exists in itself without being conscious of any existence or non-existence (Amt. IV. 37), as the water of a subterranean spring that is not yet tapped, exists in itself perfectly without being an object of experience to anybody (Amt. IV. 39). Thus does the Absolute exist in itself, and is beyond all relative existence and non-existence.

Brahman is indescribable.

10. Jñānadeva speaks of Brahman in the same manner in which Kant speaks of the thing-in-itself, and declares that it remains unknown to all sciences; that it suffers no comparison, and is like itself, as the sun is like the sun, the moon like the moon, or the lamp like itself (Amt. V. 39; VII. 288). It alone can know the mode of its existence, as does an unplanted sugar-plant know the sweetness of its juice; or the sound of an unstruck Vīṇā its own sound; or as the filament and fragrance themselves act as bees to appreciate the fragrance of a flower that has not yet come into being; or again, as food that is not yet cooked can know its own flavour; or as the moon of the 30th day of the month at midday know itself. It is like the beauty that has not yet assumed any form, or like the holiness of a virtuous act before it is performed. The Brahman can be described only if desire, that is dependent on mind, were to grow uncontrollable even before the mind was created. It is like the sound that exists before any musical instrument is constructed; or again it is like fire which having burnt the firewood has returned to itself and lives in itself......The Brahman, in fact, transcends all generality and particularity, and lives, ever enjoying itself. Silence is greatest speech in its case. For all modes of proof proclaim that Brahman cannot be proved, and all illustrations or parables solemnly declare that Brahman cannot be shown. All conceptions and all scientific characterisations vanish before it; efforts prove fruitless, and even experience grows hopeless of verification. Thought along with its determinative quality disappears, and thus proclaims the glory of Brahman like a great warrior, who by his death gains success for his master. Understanding becomes ashamed of its inability to know Brahman......How can words describe Brahman, where experience itself vanishes, along with the subject that experiences and the object that is experienced, where the supreme speech itself disappears, and no trace is found of any sound (Amt. V. 39—63)? Jñānadeva declares that it is as unnecessary to describe Brahman in words, as to wake up one that is awake, or cook food for one who has taken his meals, or to light up a lamp when the sun has risen (Amt. V. 65, 66).

Efficacy of the Word.

11. Jñānadeva now proceeds to discuss the efficacy and the inefficacy of the word, its efficacy as a reminder of Brahman and its inefficacy to reveal the absolute nature of Brahman, as well as to destroy Ignorance which does not exist. First, he begins by praising the importance of the Word, and tells us that we regain a thing that is lost in forgetfulness when we are reminded of it by Word. The Word is therefore glorious and famous as a reminder (Amt. V. 67, 68). Jñānadeva extols the great utility of the Word, and asks if it does not serve as a mirror, which by reflecting the individual Self, makes him vividly realise his own Self, and thus reminds him of his real formless nature which he has forgotten through ignorance. But this wonderful mirror is different from other ordinary mirrors, inasmuch as it enables not only the seeing, but even the blind to see their reflections in it. The Word is declared to be, like the lustrous sun, the glory of the family of the Unmanifest. Through it does the sky come to be what it is, and possess the quality that it does. Though the Word is invisible like a 'sky-flower', it gives rise to the fruit of the world. It is a torch-bearer that lights the path of action, and tells us what ought to be done, and what ought not be done. It is a judge that decides between bondage and freedom. When it pleads for Avidya, it makes the world, which is the result of ignorance, appear as if it was real. It works as a magician, and it is on account of its spell that Śiva comes to be limited, and thinks himself as an embodied Self; while it is also through the Word that the individual Self comes to realise his own real nature. The Word cannot be compared to the Sun, because the latter shines only by destroying the night which is its opposite, while the former supports both the opposite paths of action and actionlessness at the same time. Jñānadeva says that it is impossible to describe adequately the innumerable excellent qualities that the Word possesses, since it sacrifices its own life for the knowledge of the Ātman.

The inefficacy of the Word to reveal the absolute nature of the Atman.

12. Jñānadeva, however, shows that the Word, though famous as a reminder, is yet absolutely useless in the case of the Ātman, first because the self-conceived Ātman, that is all-knowledge, stands in no need of any obligation of being reminded by means of Word (Amt. VI. 12, 13); and secondly, because it is foolish to suppose that the Word can show Ātman to himself by destroying Ignorance, which by its very nature has no existence whatsoever (Amt. VI. 20). The Word is futile both ways, since it can neither destroy ignorance that is non-existent, nor reveal the Ātman that is all-knowledge and self-existent; it is therefore useless like a lamp lit up at midday which can neither destroy darkness which does not exist at that time, nor light the Sun that is self-refulgent. Thus being fruitless both ways, the Word vanishes like a stream that is lost in the waters of the deluge (Amt. VI. 96—98). Now the Word is useless in the case of the Ātman, because there is neither memory nor forgetfulness in him, and nothing else exists besides the Ātman. How could the Absolute remember or forget itself? Can the tongue taste itself?

The Ātman or the Absolute is pure knowledge, and beyond the relative conceptions of memory and forgetfulness (Amt. VI. 14—15). It is simply a contradiction to suppose that the Word can gain greatness by enabling the all-knowing Ātman to experience himself. For this is as impossible as that one should marry oneself, or that the Sun should light itself or eclipse itself, or that the sky should enter into itself, or the sea flow into itself; or again that fruit should bear fruit, or that fragrance should scent itself, or that fire should burn itself. Again, it is as impossible that the all-knowing Ātman should be enabled to know himself, as that sandal should smear itself, or that colour should be coloured, or that a pearl should adorn itself by a pearl; or again, as the eye should see itself, or as a mirror reflect itself, or a knife cut itself. The Ātman that is self-evident and self-existent stands in no need of proof by Word. It is therefore groundless to believe that the Word can gain greatness by enabling the Ātman to enjoy himself (Amt. VI. 75—95).

Inability of the Word to destroy Ignorance, which does not exist.

13. Then, again, the Word is equally useless with reference to Ignorance which it is supposed to destroy. Since Ignorance by its very nature is non-existent, like the son of a barren woman, there is no object left for logic to destroy. Ignorance is as unreal as a rainbow; and if the rainbow were real as it seems to be, what archer would apply a string to it, and discharge arrows? It is as impossible for Word to destroy ignorance as for the sage Agastya to drink up a mirage. Again, if Avidyā were such a thing as to be destroyed by Word, then why should not fire easily burn the imaginary city in the sky? It is as futile to try to destroy Ignorance by Word as by means of a lamp to see the Sun; for Ignorance is unsubstantial like a shadow, and disappears like a dream in wakefulness. Ignorance is false like the ornaments created by the spell of a magician, which can neither enrich a poor man when he possesses them, nor impoverish him when he is deprived of them. Eating of imaginary sweet cakes leaves a man without food. The soil on which a mirage appears is not moistened. If, therefore, Ignorance were real as it seems, men would have been drenched by the rain painted in a picture; fields would have been moistened, and tanks filled by it. What necessity would there be to prepare ink if one were able to write by mixing up darkness? Ignorance is as illusory as the blueness of the sky; and as the very word Avidyā itself declares, it does not exist......If Ignorance were something positive, thought would have determined its nature. But it is by its very nature non-existent, as has been shown in various ways; nothing is left therefore for the Word to destroy. It is as vain to try to destroy Ignorance by logic, as to slap the void, or embrace the sky, or kiss one's reflection. One who yet entertains a desire to destroy this Avidyā may leisurely take off the skin of the sky, or milk the nipple of a he-goat,........or by crushing a yawn take out juice from it, and mixing it with indolence, pour it into the throat of a headless body. He may turn the direction of the flow of a stream, or prepare a rope from wind. He may beat a bugbear, bind in a garment his own reflection, or comb the hairs on his palm. He may pluck the sky-flowers, and break with ease the horns of a hare. He may gather soot from a lustrous jewel, and marry with ease the child of a barren woman; he may nourish the Chakora birds of the nether world with the nectar-like rays of the new moon, and may catch with ease the aquatic animals in a mirage (Amt. VI. 24—54)! Jñānadeva repeatedly declares that Avidyā does not exist at all, that its non-existence is self-evident, and that it is simply meaningless to say that the Word destroys it (Amt. VI. 43, 55, 68). In fact, the Word would destroy itself, if it tries to explain the meaning of Ignorance (Amt. VI. 71). Jñānadeva concludes, therefore, that the Word, which is the very life of Knowledge and Ignorance, vanishes along with them in the Ātman, as the world vanishes in the deluge, or the cloudy day vanishes when the clouds pass away (Amt. VI. 102, 103).

Nature and Relation of Avidya and Vidya.

14. Jñānadeva next turns to the consideration of the relation of Avidyā and Vidyā, and tells us that with the destruction of Avidyā are destroyed the four kinds of speech which are so intimately connected with it, as hands and feet disappear along with the death of the body; or as the subtle senses depart along with the mind; or as the rays disappear along with the Sun; or again as the dream vanishes before the sleep comes to an end. Jñānadeva holds that from the ashes of the Avidyā, that is destroyed, arises, as from those of a Phœnix, the Vidyā, and the four kinds of speech are again revived as philosophical sciences, and they continue to live, as the iron that is burnt lives as Rasāyana, or as the burnt fuel lives as fire, or as the salt that is dissolved in water lives as taste, or as sleep that is destroyed lives as wakefulness (Amt. III. 2—7). As Vibhūti lives in the form of white lustre even when its particles are brushed away, or as camphor lives in the form of fragrance even when it is dissolved in water, or as the waters of a stream, that has run off, live in the form of moisture in the soil, similarly does the Avidyā that is destroyed continue to live in the form of Vidyā (Amt. III. 27—29, 31). Avidyā, therefore, whether living or dead, limits the Ātman either with bondage or liberation; for when living it binds the individual Self with false knowledge about himself, and even when dead it remains as the knowledge of the real nature of the Ātman, which is also equally a limitation to the Ātman; thus it acts like sleep which by its presence creates dreams, and which while departing points to the existence of wakefulness (Amt. III. 11, 9—10). Thus, Avidyā is declared to be the cause of both bondage and freedom, as is sleep the cause of dreams and wakefulness. Jñānadeva maintains that both the conceptions of Bondage and Freedom, as results of Ignorance and Knowledge, are relative and false; since Freedom itself is a sort of Bondage in the case of the Ātman who is beyond them both (Amt. III. 12). Even the knowledge 'I am the Ātman' is itself a limitation to the Ātman, because it is relative to Ignorance; while the Ātman is beyond both knowledge and ignorance, and is of the nature of pure and absolute knowledge. Real emancipation is attainable, only when this relative knowledge of the Ātman also vanishes (Amt. III. 23, 24). It is, therefore, as foolish to suppose that the Ātman, who is absolute knowledge, stands in need of any sort of knowledge in order to know himself, as to think that the Sun requires another Sun for the spread of his light; and it is as ridiculous to say that the Ātman is delighted by his knowledge, as to say that a man who has lost himself wanders over various countries to find himself, and that he is delighted when after a number of days he comes to know that he is himself (Amt. III. 19—22). The final result of all this discussion is that both Knowledge and Ignorance are proved to be obstructions in the way of the realisation of the Ātman, and we are told that both of them should therefore be sublated.

Knowledge that is relative to Ignorance is itself destroyed in Brahman.

15. Now Knowledge, that destroys Ignorance and its effects, is itself destroyed, as the fire in its efforts to burn camphor burns itself, or as the silkworm in confining itself in the cocoon and shutting up the outlet by means of earth kills itself, or as a thief, who enters into a sack and fastens himself in it, gets bound by himself (Amt. IV. 2, 5, 4). Knowledge that thus destroys Ignorance increases till it entirely destroys itself (Amt. IV. 10); but before its final disappearance it grows in size for a moment like the light of a lamp whose oil and wick are exhausted. Thus its increase is only indicative of its final destruction. Knowledge lives only for a moment to be finally destroyed like the Jasmine buds that bloom into flowers only to fade away just the next moment; or like the ripples that rise only to be instantly merged in water; or like the lightning that flashes and disappears at the same moment (Amt. IV. 10, 6—9). Knowledge, that shines by destroying Ignorance, is itself swallowed up by Absolute Knowledge (Amt. IV. 14), which leaves no distinction between Knowledge and Ignorance, as the Sun that fills the whole universe leaves no room for any distinction between light and darkness (Amt. IV. 11—12). Jñānadeva declares that Knowledge and Ignorance are like twins that resemble each other, and that Knowledge is therefore itself a kind of Ignorance (Amt. VII. 6). But for knowledge, the very name of Ignorance would never have been heard (Amt. VII. 1); for Ignorance is as illusory as the horses in a picture, which cannot be used for war (Amt. VII. 4). It is great only in itself, as a dream and darkness are great in themselves (Amt. VII. 3). It is as vain to search for it in real Knowledge, as to seek for the waves of a mirage in Moonlight (Amt. VII. 5).

Jnanadeva's arguments against the Ajnanavadins.

16. The nature of Ignorance and Knowledge is further expounded by Jñānadeva in his subtle and forensic attack against the Ajñānavādins, who argue for the existence of Ignorance in the Ātman. Jñānadeva asks, if Ignorance really lives in real Knowledge, which is the Ātman, why does it not make the Ātman ignorant, since it is the nature of Ignorance to befool a thing in which it exists (Amt. VII. 8, 9)? Jñanadeva subtly argues that if Ignorance exists, it must by its very nature cover everything; and since it cannot know itself, there will be nothing to recognise and prove its existence; on the other hand, if it does not make ignorant the thing in which it exists, it will be no Ignorance at all. Thus, he says that when Ignorance by its existence has rendered the one knowing Absolute ignorant, nothing will exist but Ignorance; and asks 'who would then know that Ignorance exists?' Ignorance cannot know itself, as a proof cannot prove itself; one has therefore to keep silent in this case (Amt. VII. 14, 11—13). Ignorance therefore vanishes since it does not know itself (Amt. VII. 17). On the other hand, it is as meaningless to designate as Ignorance what does not make ignorant the Ātman in which it exists, as to call a cataract that which does not impair the eyesight, or to name as fire that which does not burn, or to posit as darkness that which does not destroy light, or to designate as sleep what does not disturb wakefulness, or to entitle as night what does not diminish the day. It is, therefore, vain to say that Ignorance exists in the Ātman and yet the Ātman remains all-knowing (Amt. VI. 19—23). Again, thought makes it evident that it is merely an unjust distortion of facts to suppose that Ignorance, the cause of worldly existence, exists in the Ātman (Amt. VII. 24). For, how can the two diametrically opposite things like the densely dark ignorance and the refulgent knowing Ātman exist together? Ignorance and Ātman will live together, only if sleep and wakefulness, forgetfulness and memory, can exist together; or if cold and heat can travel together; or if darkness can envelope the rays of the Sun; or if night and day can stay together at the same place; or if death and life can be twins to one another. It is therefore mere nonsense to say that the Ātman and its opposite live together (Amt. VII. 24—30). It is also wrong to suppose that Ignorance can exist in the Ātman when the latter exists in its absolute unmodified condition, as fire does in wood before two pieces of it are rubbed together (Amt. VII. 58, 59). For this cannot be proved; and this also involves a contradiction in including in the Ātman its opposite. Further, how can the Ātman, which cannot suffer even to be called by its name, and which is not even conscious of itself, have any resemblance to Ignorance and be united with it (Amt. VII. 60, 64)? It is as futile to try to remove ignorance from the Ātman as to clean a mirror that is not yet made (Amt. VII. 62). In spite of all this, if one persists in saying that Ignorance exists in the Ātman, which is beyond all being and non-being, we may admit, says Jñānadeva, that it exists, if the non-being of a jar that is broken to a thousand pieces can exist, or if the all-killing death itself be killed, or if sleep be asleep, or if fainting itself faint away, or if darkness fall into a dark well, or if the sky can be turned into a whip and sounded, or if poison can be administered to a dead man, or if letters that are not written can be erased away (Amt. VII. 66—70). It is as false to say that Ignorance exists as to say that a barren woman gives birth to a child, or that burnt seeds grow; for nothing exists except the Absolute (Amt. VII. 71, 72). It is as foolish to try to find out in pure intelligence the ignorance which is entirely its opposite, as to wake up hurriedly in order to catch sleep (Amt. VII. 73—76). Think in whatever way we may, we cannot find any existence of Ignorance (Amt. VII. 77). And it is as vain to trace its existence as to erect a meeting-hall using the hare's horns as pillars, illuminate it with the rays of the new moon, adorn the children of a barren woman with sky-flowers, or give to them the ghee of a tortoise taking the sky as a measure-glass (Amt. VII. 80-83). That 'Ignorance does not exist' forms, so to say, the burden of Jñānadeva's discussion, and he concludes that Ignorance can exist neither in the Ātman nor independently of the Ātman, as a living fish made of salt can neither exist in water, nor separately from it (Amt. VII. 35—39). Its existence is therefore both ways absolutely illusory (Amt. VII. 40).

A logical discussion of the nature of Ignorance.

17. Jñānadeva next proceeds to make a logical discussion of the nature of ignorance. He contends that ignorance must be either directly apprehended, or logically inferred. It is not directly apprehended, first because all Pramāṇas like Pratyaksha are the results of ignorance, though not ignorance itself, as the sprout and creeper are results of the seed, though not seed itself, or as good or bad dreams are the offspring of sleep, though not sleep itself. These Pramāṇas, therefore, as the effect of ignorance, cannot certainly apprehend Ignorance (Amt. VII. 47), as they are themselves Ignorance on account of the identity of cause and effect (Amt. VII. 51). Ignorance and its effect are the same as the dream and the witness thereof are of the same nature (Amt. VII. 49). Secondly, on the same principle the senses, that are also effects of Ignorance, cannot perceive it (Amt. VII. 48), as raw sugar cannot taste itself, or as collyrium cannot besmear itself (Amt. VII. 50). Thus the very fact that Ignorance cannot stand the test of any Pramāṇa proves that it is false, and that there is no difference between it and the sky-flower (Amt. VII. 55, 54, 53). For how can ignorance be called real, when it is neither a cause of anything, nor does it produce any effect? It is therefore evident that ignorance is incapable of direct apprehension since it is neither cause nor effect of anything, which alone are directly perceived (Amt. 56—57). As to the second alternative, that Ignorance can be logically inferred, the Ajñānavādins contend that the very fact that there is this vast world shows that Ignorance exists as its cause, and though it is not directly seen, it may be safely inferred from this, its effect; as from the fact that the trees are fresh and green, it may be inferred with certainty that their roots are taking water, though the ground round about the trees may be apparently quite dry; or as the existence of sleep can be inferred from the dreams, though the man who enjoys the sleep is not conscious of it at that time (Amt. VII. 91–94). Ignorance, therefore, though not directly visible is certainly inferrible (Amt. VII. 90). Jñānadeva replies to this contention that the world which the Ajñānavādins declare to be the result of Ignorance is in fact an extension of the all-knowing and self-luminous Ātman, who presents himself as the visible world, and who himself assumes the function of a seer (Amt. VII. 87). We shall discuss in detail the views of Jñānadeva about the nature of the world in one of the sections that follow. It is sufficient to note here that he declares that to regard the world, which is really a form of the Ātman who is absolute knowledge, as but a flood of ignorance, is as foolish as to call the light of the Sun darkness (Amt. VII. 100, 95). Are we to call a thing collyrium, which makes all other things brighter and whiter than the moon? The world, which is in fact supreme Light, may be regarded as a result of Ignorance, only if water can perform the function of fire......Can ambrosia ever produce poison? (Amt. VII. 86—99.) Similarly, the world, which, as the sport of the Ātman, proceeds from the Ātman, who is all knowledge, cannot be anything but knowledge. If one were to call such a world Ignorance, Jñānadeva says that he knows not of what nature Knowledge would be; for whatever exists is the Ātman (Amt. VII. 101). It is therefore unjust to call the Ātman (who exists also as the world) Ignorance. But, says Jñānadeva, if the Ajñānavādins persist in calling what illumines the world Ignorance, he could regard it only as a mode of expressing truth in a contradictory manner, as what enables a man to see an underground store of wealth may be called collyrium, or as an idol made of gold may be called Kālikā. In reality, all existence is illumined by the refulgent One, and it is on account of him that knowledge knows, and sight sees, and the world exists as his form. It is simply foolish to point out to this world as ignorance (Amt. 269–274). If one were to place fire inside a box made of lac, the box will be immediately reduced to fire (Amt. VII. 276), and there will be inside and outside the box nothing but fire; similarly, there is one Ātman shining inside and outside the world. The world is thus a vibration of the Ātman, and if the Ajñānavādins call it Ignorance, we may regard them as having gone mad (Amt. VII. 277). Jñānadeva regrets that nobody recognises the fact that the very term 'Ignorance' and the statement 'Ignorance exists' become intelligible only through Knowledge (Amt. VII. 279, 18). He declares, therefore, that Ignorance which is not anything and which does not know itself, is proved to be non-existent by all Pramāṇas; and since it has no effect, it cannot be said to exist; while its non-existence is self-evident (Amt. VII. 102, 103). Finally, Jñānadeva criticises the argument adduced in favour of the existence of Ignorance, that from the fact that Ignorance is the cause of the knowledge of the world, it may be inferred that Ignorance exists. Jñānadeva points out that this would make knowledge a quality of ignorance, which is as absurd as to suppose that pearls are produced from soot, or a lamp lighted by ashes. Pure illumination would be produced by dark ignorance, only if flames were to be proceeded from the moon, or stones from the subtle sky, or deadly poison from nectar. It is wrong to suppose that knowledge proceeds from ignorance; for with the appearance of knowledge ignorance is destroyed, and pure knowledge alone ultimately remains (Amt. VII. 282–287). There is, therefore, no difference between the world that is illumined, and the Ātman that illumines it: they are one. Jñānadeva thus forces his opponent, the Ajñānavādin, to confess his mistake, and regard the whole world as but an illumination of the Absolute (Amt. VII. 289).

The Sphurtivada.

18. We may now turn to the consideration of Jñānadeva's theory about the world, since it forms his original contribution to philosophic thought. He regards the world as not in any way different from the Absolute, but as a manifestation of Him, a sport of the one supreme intelligent Ātman. Nothing exists but Brahman, which alone shines forth as the world. We are told that when there arises a desire in the supreme Ātman to see himself, he himself becomes the manifold world, an object to himself, and thus comes to see himself as the visible world (Amt. 129, 131, 156). Thus the Ātman, who is beyond all triads, and of the nature of pure light, expands himself as the world. The supreme Intelligence alone underlies all the objects of the world, that are ever changing and assuming different forms; it is so rich that it wears every moment new apparels in the form of the objects of the world. And as the Ātman regards the objects once created as stale and worn out, he presents to his vision ever fresh and new objects. Jñānadeva remarks that it is the Absolute that itself appears as the knowing Subjects, that vary with the variation of the Objects that are known (Amt. 123–128). But though Brahman itself becomes the visible world, and being itself its seer, enjoys it, its unity is not in the least disturbed by it, as the unity of the original face is not disturbed though it is reflected in a mirror, or as the standing posture of an excellent horse which sleeps while standing is not disturbed even when it wakes up. Just as water plays with itself by assuming the form of waves, the Absolute is playing with itself by becoming the world. Is any difference created in fire, when it wears the garlands of flames ? There is no duality between the Sun and his rays, when he is surrounded by the rays. The unity of the moon is not disturbed, even when enveloped by the moon-light. The lotus remains one, even when it blooms into a thousand petals......Even when there are spread on a loom a number of threads, there is to be found in them nothing but thread. Similarly, there is no difference in the Absolute, when it presents itself either as the seer of the world, or as the world that it sees ; for it is the Absolute alone that becomes both. Thus, the unity of the Ātman is not lost even when he comes to fill the whole universe......If the eye had been able to see the world without opening its lids, or if the seed of a Bunyan tree had been able to produce the full-grown tree without breaking itself, then it could have been illustrated how the unity of Brahman expands itself into the manifold world (Amt. VII. 132—149). On the other hand, when the Ātman ceases to desire to see himself, and thus present himself as the world, he can do so easily, for then he would remain what he is by nature (Amt. VII. 173). He would then rest in himself, as sight remains absorbed in itself when the eyes are closed, or as a tortoise draws within itself its feet, or as on the new-moon day all the sixteen Kalās rest in the moon (Amt. VII. 150—153). It is the Absolute, which, by its mere winking, presents itself as the particular world, and which, after destroying this world, returns to its absolute condition (Amt. VII. 183). As all that exists is but the Absolute, how can there be any subject to see, or any object to be seen (Amt. VII. 155) ? Yet as the visible world that is seen, and the seer who sees, eternally follow from the Absolute, they are eternal and are not newly created, just as the sky and the void, air and touch, light and brightness, that ever live together are not newly united to each other. The Absolute that shines as the universe sees the universe, but it also sees the non-existence of the universe when the latter vanishes ; for it ever continues in its own seeing condition in spite of the existence or non-existence of the universe. It is ever seeing itself in whatever condition it may be, for there is no difference between the Absolute and the World, as there is none in the whiteness of the moon and that of camphor. There is no reason to suppose that the Absolute and the World are two different entities, and that the one sees the other; for it is the Absolute alone that sees itself in the form of the World. The intelligent Absolute ever sees itself, and stands in need of no other entity to see itself, just as a jewel does not require any other thing to cover it with brilliant lustre. It is as impossible that the Absolute should see itself through some other entity, as that the sandal should be surrounded by some other scent, or that camphor should be made white by something else ......As a lamp is wholly filled with light, so is the universe entirely filled with the supreme Intelligence, which is for ever throbbing. And the seeing and the non-seeing of the Brahman are like darkness and light in the case of the moon, which, being really unaffected by these, ever lives in its own original unmodified condition (Amt. VII. 157—172). The seer and the seen, being relative to each other, destroy each other, as camphor that is put into fire vanishes along with fire; and the Absolute that is beyond them both remains as the reality of both, as a zero alone remains when one is subtracted from one, or as water alone remains, destroying all distinction between the eastern and the western seas, when these latter mix together (Amt. VII. 175—181). The natural condition of the Absolute lies between the destruction of the seer and the seen and a new revival of them, as water remains in its natural state when the wave that has arisen vanishes and a new one has not yet arisen, or as we are really ourselves when our sleep ends and we are not yet fully awake; it is like the state of the sky when the day ends and the night has not yet set in (Amt. VII. 185—189). Since the Absolute alone exists in all things, how could there be any seeing and not-seeing, which imply duality? The seeing and not seeing that are relative and dependent on the Absolute thus destroy each other (Amt. VII. 200). The Ātman is not proved to be false even when he is not manifested by Māyā, but remains what he is, as the face remains as it is, whether it is reflected in a mirror or not (Amt. VII. 215, 219). On the other hand, Māyā owes its reality to the Ātman, as a lamp that is lighted by a person proves the existence of the person (Amt. VII, 231—233). Nothing else therefore exists except the Ātman, whether he appears as the world, or its seer, as there is nothing else but the waters of the Ganges, whether it is in itself or flows into the sea, or as the ghee remains what it is, whether it is in a solid or liquid condition......Keenest thought, therefore, makes it evident that both the seer and the seen are false; for if nothing exists except the one Ātman, that is pulsating everywhere, how can there be any subject that may see, or any object that may be seen? It is as useless to say that it sees itself, as to pour waves into water, or to mix light with light, or to serve satisfaction to satisfaction, or to crown the fire with flames (Amt. VII. 234—249). The Ātman is thus declared to be inexpressible in words, and forms no object either for knowledge or for experience (Amt. VII. 252). The richness of the Ātman is incomparable, since it becomes the world without losing its unity; it could have been compared to the Sun, if his rays had not gone out of himself (Amt. VII. 257—264). The sport of the Ātman is unparalleled, and all that we can say about it is that it is like itself. There is neither any waste nor any diminution in the light of the Ātman in presenting himself as the World, which the Ātman enjoys with great rapidity (Amt. VII. 267), thus partaking of incomparable sovereignty within himself (Amt. VII. 268).

Significance of the Spiritual Teacher in the mystic life.

19. We now pass on to discuss the significance of the Spiritual Teacher as described in the Amṛitānubhava. Jñānadeva's love for his Guru is profound, and absolutely unbounded, and though he praises him with all the wealth of his poetic genius, heaping similes over similes and metaphors over metaphors, he yet declares that he is absolutely incapable of adequately describing the greatness of his Guru. He devotes the whole of the second chapter of the Amṛitānubhava to a description of his Spiritual Teacher, Nivṛitti. He dwells on the significance of the name Nivṛitti, and tells us that the glory of the name Nivṛitti lies in its implying absolute actionlessness, without the slightest touch of action (Amt. II. 79). We are further told that he is called Nivṛitti though there is no Pravṛitti in the Ātman, which he is supposed to destroy, as the Sun is called the enemy of darkness, even though there is no darkness which presents itself as his opponent (Amt. II. 33, 34). He regards Nivṛittinātha as verily a god who is indestructible, indescribable, unborn, absolute, and of the nature of pure bliss (Amt. Sansk. 1—2). Jñānadeva bows to his Guru Nivṛitti, who, he says, by killing the elephant in the form of Māyā, offers him a dish of the pearls taken from its temples (Amt. II. 2). The spiritual teacher is as it were a spring to the garden of an aspirant's endeavours for self-realisation, and though formless is, as it were, the form of mercy incarnate (Amt. II. 1). He makes no distinction of great and small in distributing the wealth of final emancipation. As for his power, he surpasses even the greatness of Śiva. He is as it were a mirror in which the individual Self sees the bliss of Ātman. It is through his grace that the scattered Kalās of the Moon of spiritual knowledge are brought together. All the efforts of the spiritual aspirant to realise the Ātman cease when he once meets a spiritual teacher who renders him actionless, as the Ganges becomes motionless and steady when it meets the sea......The grace of the Guru is declared to be verily the Sun, with whose rise vanishes the darkness of ignorance, and the blessed day of self-realisation dawns. Bathed in the waters of his Guru's grace, the individual Self becomes so pure that he comes to regard even Śiva as impure, and would not allow the latter to touch him (Amt. II. 5—11, 14). The spiritual aspirant gains the ripe fruit of self-realisation only when he implicitly acts according to the orders of his spiritual teacher (Amt. II. 17). It is out of the light of the Guru that the moon and the stars are created, and it is through his light alone that the Sun shines (Amt. II. 23). He is a priest whom even Śiva, distressed by the limitations of his body, asks for that auspicious day when he may regain his pristine condition of bliss (Amt. II. 24). The spiritual teacher is beyond all inference, and beyond all modes of proof; he is indescribable in words, which become silent in his oneness which tolerates no duality (Amt. II. 27—28). How can he, who is beyond the reach of all form and sight (Amt. II. 50), be an object for our praise or salutation? Thus, when we go to fall at the feet of the Guru, he does not present himself as an object worthy of salutation; as the Sun is not the cause of his own rise (Amt. II. 44). Not only does he not become an object of salutation, but he even leaves no trace of the person who goes to salute him (Amt. II. 47); for the latter is also made to realise that he is like the former really the Ātman. Jñānadeva tells us that when he went to salute his Master, he found that the object of salutation vanished along with the saluter, as camphor and fire both vanish when they are brought near one another, or as a husband, who in a dream goes to see his wife, is destroyed along with the wife as soon as he awakes (Amt. II. 52, 53). The spiritual teacher is therefore beyond the triad of saluter, salutation, and salutee; and Jñānadeva in his hopelessness to describe him calls him the greatest mystery possible (Amt. II. 37). One cannot love him without being lost to his bodily self, and there remains no difference between master and pupil (Amt. II. 39). The words 'master and disciple,' therefore, mean but one thing, and the master alone lives in both (Amt. II. 61).

Description of One who has realized the Self.

20. Jñānadeva next proceeds to describe the unitive experience of one who has realised Brahman. We are told that the enjoyer and the object of enjoyment, the seer and the object of sight, become merged in the mystic realisation of Brahman, which is one unbroken whole; it is as if fragrance were to become a nose and smell itself, or a sound to become an ear and hear itself, or a mirror to become an eye and see itself (Amt. IX. 1). The knower of Brahman retains his unity in the midst of diversity as a Ṡevantī flower remains one even though it blooms into a thousand petals (Amt. IX. 8). The unity of Brahman is running through all apparent manifold objects of sense, and when the senses go to catch hold of their objects, they are lost along with their objects in the one Brahman which alone remains (Amt. IX. 15—16); for it is this Brahman which itself becomes both the senses and their objects. As the hand that tries to catch the waves finds nothing but water; or as camphor presents itself as touch to the hand, as a white object to the eye, and as a fragrant thing to the tongue; similarly to the wise, one Brahman alone vibrates as the sensible manifold (Amt. IX. 12—14). To him all apparent differences vanish, as the parts that we see in a sugarcane are lost in its juice; no trace of multiplicity is to be found in him, even though his senses may enjoy their objects (Amt. IX. 17, 18). Thus his supreme silence is undisturbed, even though he may speak of all objects that he comes across; and he remains actionless, even when he performs many actions (Amt. IX. 20—21). He remains unique like the Sun who goes to embrace darkness with his thousand rays (Amt. IX. 23).

Nature of Supreme Devotion.

21. The attitude to reality of such a person may be characterised as Advaita-Bhakti, or Unitive Devotion. The eight-fold Yoga is as lustreless before it as the Moon is by day. Here the consciousness of the body absolutely disappears, and all actions are performed with the internal conviction that everything is the Ātman. The unity of the Ātman underlies the apparent multiplicity, implied in the actions of such a knower of Brahman; and the greater the number of the actions performed, the greater does the unity grow. In the case of such a person, the enjoyment of the objects of sense is itself superior to beatitude, for in the home of Supreme Devotion the worshipper and the object of worship are so mixed together as to become absolutely one. In this case, therefore, action and actionlessness become equal, as there is nothing to be achieved by action, nor is there anything to be lost by non-action. This state of Supreme Devotion, that the knower of the Ātman enjoys, is simply unique, as it is beyond both memory and forgetfulness. His sweet will forms the moral code, and his free actions the highest ecstasy. Here, God Himself becomes the devotee ; the goal itself becomes the way ; and the whole universe itself becomes solitude. Now God can be the devotee, and the devotee God. And if a desire arises in God to enjoy the relation of master and servant, he himself becomes both, and thus exhibits this relation. In Supreme Devotion, therefore, the devotee has nothing but God even for his material of worship. Here it may be said that God worships God with God. And Jñānadeva does not think this to be impossible : for he tells us that from the same rock are carved the idols of God, the temple, and God's attendants, which seem to be different, and are yet one (Amt. IX. 26—43). As the devotee is really God Śiva, he, as it were, worships God even when he does not worship ; and it is as unnecessary to ask him to worship, as to ask the flame of a lamp to wear the garment of light, or the moon to cover itself with moonlight (Amt. IX. 48, 45—46). In Brahman, therefore, action and actionlessness are both destroyed, and devotion and non-devotion occupy the same position. The description of Brahman, therefore, which we find in the Upanishads, becomes a censure, and censure itself becomes the highest praise ; and in fact, both praise and censure are reduced to silence. It is wonderful that in Supreme Devotion walking and sitting in one place both become the same thing. The sport of the knower of Brahman in his unitive life is really incomparable, but may be likened if at all to that of a ball, which falls down, rebounds again, and thus plays with itself (Amt. IX. 57).

Personal Experience of Jnanadeva.

22. Finally, we may briefly notice the personal mystical experience of Jñānadeva which he declares to have attained through the grace of his Guru, Nivṛitti. He tells us that he is made really his own self by his Guru, who has placed him beyond the reach of both knowledge and ignorance ; that through his grace he became so great that he could not contain himself within himself ; that he is not limited even by Ātman-hood ; that he cannot be limited even by self-consciousness, because it is relative to a consciousness of not-self ; and finally that though he is of the nature of final emancipation itself, this creates no duality in him. Jñānadeva says that there has yet been created no word that would describe him, no sight that would see him. There is no wonder, therefore, that he remains neither concealed nor manifest; and the real mode of his existence is rarely known to any one. Jñānadeva proclaims that he has been placed by Nivṛitti in a condition that cannot be described by words (Amt. VIII. 1—8). Knowledge and ignorance, that are relative to each other, both vanish in that condition; as both husband and wife would perish, if, in their endeavour to exchange themselves, they were to cut each other's throat (Amt. VIII. 10, 14). Thus swallowing up both the darkness of ignorance and the light of knowledge, the intelligent Ātman, who is verily the Sun of Reality, shines in all his brilliance in the Chidākāśa (Amt. VIII. 19). Jñānadeva exultantly proclaims that he has been made the sole sovereign of the kingdom of supreme bliss by the grace of his Guru; and though he is really one with his Guru, it is becoming the love of the latter that he should be addressed as his Master's own (Amt. IX. 64—66).

CHAPTER V.

The Abhangas of Nivritti, Jnanadeva, Sopana, Muktabai, and Changadeva.

The Abhanga and the Religious Lyric.

1. We have hitherto seen the contribution which Jñāneśvara has made to the Philosophy of Religion by his exposition of the principles of the Bhagavadgītā in his Jñāneśvarī as well as by his independent reflections on philosophico-religious matters in the Amṛitānubhava. We have now to pass through the Abhaṅga literature—a literature which corresponds closely to the religious Lyric in English literature. We see the up-rise of this kind of literature in the days of Nivṛitti, Jñānadeva, and their contemporaries. The first greatest writer, however, of note in the Abhaṅga literature is Jñāneśvara. The Abhaṅgas are an outpouring of the heart, especially in the matter of the relation of the Soul to God. Use is made no doubt of Abhaṅga literature in the matter of reflection on, and criticism of, social customs. But the main purpose of Abhaṅga literature is to express the innermost feelings of the heart. Nāmadeva, who came immediately after Jñānadeva, brought it to greater perfection still; while Tukārāma was the pinnacle of the writers of Abhaṅgas, inasmuch as personal religion reached its acme with Tukārāma. After Tukārāma, there have been reverberations of this kind of literature even among later writers; but the greatness of Tukārāma does not reappear in them. Our present purpose, however, is to take notice of the contribution that was made by Nivṛitti and others to personal religion. We shall discuss first the contribution that was made by Nivṛitti. We shall then pass on to the Abhaṅgas of Jñāneśvara; and then we shall proceed to the teachings of Sopāna, Muktābāi, and Chāngadeva. When we have considered the reflections on personal religion by these writers, this part of the work will come to a close.

Nivrittinatha.

The teaching of Nivrittinatha.

2. To begin with the Abhaṅgas of Nivṛittinātha. Nivṛittinātha compares Saṃsāra to a tree in the manner of the Bhagavadgītā, and tells us that this Tree of Existence could not be uprooted without the grace of the Guru, that it has neither shade nor foliage, and yet that it exercises power everywhere in the world (Abg. 2). By the grace of the Guru, says Nivṛittināṭha, he is able to visualise the Ātman who lives in all things (Abg. 3). Only him should we call our Guru, who is able to show God directly to our sight; him we should hand over all our wealth and mind and body, and take from him the Ātman for whom we aspire (Abg. 4). God shows Himself to a devotee, only if this latter possesses good emotions and desires (Abg. 8). One should verily shut one's ears, when other people are being censured or dispraised for nothing. One should shut up one's mouth, and in a mystical manner meditate on God (Abg. 10). One should never hear one's praise. One should entirely merge one's consciousness in the being of God (Abg. 11). As a sun might rise at night, similarly, this Ātman shines forth by the grace of the Guru (Abg. 22). Narratives of this God are more fragrant than the sandal tree itself. The fragrance of God indeed surpasses the fragrance of the sweetest flowers like Jāi, Jui, and Mogarā (Abg. 27). God's sweet sound emerges out of the warf and woof of breath (Abg. 29). God is indeed the Moon, after whom we pant like a Chakora bird, or of whom we are like rays. We live in the body; God is outside the body. Nivṛittināṭha says that like a Chātaka bird, he looks up to the heaven for God (Abg. 32). There is no special time when God may reveal Himself. We are able to see God always, and at all times (Abg. 36). When we have seen God, all this world vanishes from us. We are unable to see the moon, and the sun, and the stars. We are unable to see the earth and the sky. Every nook and cranny of the universe becomes filled with God (Abg. 37). The whole world indeed becomes God, and there remains no distinction between God and Devotee. As an ocean waxes and wanes, so is the distinction between Devotee and God (Abg. 43).

Jnanadeva.

The teaching of Jnanadeva.

3. Jñāneśvara tells us that we should lead a life of utter ignorance about all things except God. The knowledge of God is devotion, and the knowledge of God is realisation (Abg. 2). Being born in this world, we lead a life of enmity towards ourselves. To say that the body is ours, or the children or the wife or the wealth is ours, is not to know that all these are in the hands of Death. We bind ourselves to these things like a parrot which sits upon an iron bar, falsely fastening itself to it (Abg. 5). As a crane falsely meditates, its object of desire being a fish, similarly, we falsely take resort to penance in a forest, when we are thinking about a woman. There is no use lashing the body until we have conquered our mind (Abg. 7). We need not bid good-bye to a house-holder's life, nor need we bid good-bye to the actions that are consequent thereupon. The real secret of God-knowledge lies elsewhere. So long as our spiritual teacher has not favoured us with his grace, so long our mind shall not become composed (Abg. 11). The spiritual teacher is verily the King of all the Saints. Him we may call an ocean of happiness, or a mine of love, or a mountain of courage, or the source of dispassion. The spiritual teacher is an invariable protector of his disciple. Like a wish-tree, he yields all desires to a devotee. He punishes the wicked, and destroys all sin (Abg. 12). The Name, upon which he asks us to meditate, puts an end to all knowledge, as it puts an end to ignorance (Abg. 16). When Prahlāda uttered the name of God, God came to his rescue. God's name is indeed the best and holiest of all things. It is God's name which came to the succour of Dhruva, of Gajendra, of Ajāmila, of Vālmīki (Abg. 18). Mountains of sin shall perish in an instant at the utterance of the name of God (Abg. 20). There is neither time nor season for the utterance of God's name (Abg. 24). The devotees of God feed upon the nectar of His name. The Yogins find it a source of eternal life (Abg. 25). If we meditate intensely on the Name of God within, God shall take pity upon us. Jñāneśvara silently counts this rosary of God's name within himself (Abg. 27), and is therefore able to see the universe wholly filled with God (Abg. 28). The Saints, says Jñāneśvara, are as untouched by happenings, as the Sun's disc is untouched by the sky (Abg. 30). When one meets a Saint, one feels as if one is endowed with four hands. After meeting the Saints, all the toil of life ceases. What the Saints are able to confer is more valuable than a wish-tree, or a touch-stone, or a wish-jewel (Abg. 31). As a penniless man should get at a treasure, or as a dead man should come to life again, or as a calf might meet its mother from which it is separated, similarly, one is filled with joy at the meeting of these Saints (Abg. 33). When the Saints back up a devotee, nothing shall be wanting to him. Does the wife of a King, asks Jñāneśvara, go on begging alms ? Or, does a man, who sits under a wish-tree, ever lack anything (Abg. 35) ?

The Pain of God.

4. In these utterances of Jñānadeva, we do not yet find his heart panting for God. It is generally supposed that Jñānadeva's mind did not suffer any torment in its search after God. But there are a few utterances in his Abhangas, from which we can see that Jñānadeva's mind was like that of Nāmadeva and Tukārāma in later times, panting after the attainment of God. Jñānadeva weeps that God being so near to him, he should not yet be able to see Him. "As a thirsty man pines after water, so do I pine after Thee", says Jñānadeva (Abg. 37). "I am all the while a-thinking as to how I might come to possess a woollen garment. My garment has been already torn to pieces. I have neither money with me, nor have I the capacity to undergo physical trouble. I am suffering from cold, as I have no external garment with which I might clothe myself. Nobody except God can give me that garment" says Jñāneśvara (Abg. 38). In another place, like a beloved pining after her lover, Jñāneśvara tells us, that he has been thrown away from God in a distant country. The night appears as day, and he pines that God should not yet visit him, even though his heart has been set so much on Him (Abg. 39). "The cloud is singing and the wind is ringing. The Moon and the Champaka tree have lost all their soothing effects without God. The sandal paste serves only to torment my body. They say that the bed of flowers is very cool; but yet it is burning me like cinders of fire. The Kokila is proverbially supposed to sing sweet tunes; but in my case, says Jñānadeva, they are increasing my love-pangs. As I begin to look in a mirror, says Jñāneśvara, I am unable to see my face. To such a plight, God has reduced me" (Abg. 40). Jñāneśvara wonders that God should be seen at all places, and yet he should be unable to hold converse with God. Whatever he hears through his ears, and sees with his eyes, is only a divine manifestation. The Personal and the Impersonal are merely an illusion created by God. Sufficient unto me is the evil of my existence, says Jñāneśvara. My existence fills me only with shame. Let Thy will be done, says Jñāneśvara, for my supplications are all useless (Abg. 41). Finally, Jñāneśvara tells us that as deep was calling unto deep, and the waters of the Jumna were in a tempestuous torment, the eyes of the whole world were set upon the form of God, and God would deceive the world by showing himself in a personal vision, and yet not holding converse with his devotee (Abg. 42).

Mystic Progress by the grace of Nivritti.

5. Jñāneśvara attributes his entire progress in the mystical life to the grace of Nivṛitti. "I was a blind man and a lame man, and illusion had encircled me. My hands and feet were unable to work. Then I saw Nivṛitti, who initiated me into spiritual knowledge by seating me under a tree and dispelling all ignorance. Blessed be the spiritual wisdom of Nivṛitti. Blessed be the Name of God. The fruit of my actions is at an end; my doubt is dispelled; all my desires have been fulfilled. I shall never now move sense-ward. I shall sing the praises of the Lord. My wishes have ended, because I have been living under the Wish-Tree. My anxieties are at an end, because I am feeding on nectar. My mind is engrossed forever in divine joy. All sufferings, along with herds of sin, have now passed away.... ....Ātmanic wisdom has been realised; the secret of the Vedas has been unfolded;......the pitcher has been broken; the bonds have been dissolved; Self-hood has come to an end by the spiritual wisdom of the Teacher;......Buddhi and Bodha have been united (*cf.* Jñāneśvarī, 16th Chapter)...... eyes have been created in eyes; the body has become heavenly. In all directions there is spiritual bliss. Everything now appears to me to be Brahman. My teacher Nivṛitti has dispelled my blindness, has endowed me with sight, has put the collyrium of God in my eyes, and has immersed me in the Ganges of knowledge," says Jñānadeva (Abg. 43).

6. Jñānadeva's mystical experience is very rich and varied.

Colour experience.

We shall begin first by a consideration of the various colours that a mystic is supposed to see. Jñānadeva tells us that "the abode of God is the thousand-petalled cavity in the brain, where is the source of spiritual bliss. One sees the red, the white, the blue and the yellow colours, and sees these with a pure vision. I need not tell you much," says Jñānadeva, "you already know these things. You understand these things, and remain silent" (Abg. 45). Jñānadeva tells us that the mystic sees a perpetual spiritual show. "One sees the black, the blue, and the tawny colours. The eye is lost in the eye. Let now the blue colour remain firm in the mind ......In the eye one is able to see pure light, and one can see it even while living in the body" (Abg. 46). The dark-blue colour is very much insisted upon by Jñāneśvara. God also manifests Himself in a dark-blue shape (Abg. 47). "The dark-complexioned husband is the source of bliss......He has filled my inside and outside," says Jñānadeva (Abg. 48). "It is impossible to take measure of Him. One cannot remember Him too often. One can never too much sing His praises when the dark-complexioned God is seen" (Abg. 49). It is this same dark-complexioned Being who lives in the heavens. He is the same as Ātman. I have seen Him with these eyes, says Jñānadeva, where He remains imperishable as ever

(Abg. 50). He plays a dark game on a dark night; he manifests himself as a dark-blue god (Abg. 51). The dark-blue colour fills the whole universe. The dark-blue being sees the dark-blue Person (Abg. 52). The blue light spreads everywhere. The heavens are merged in that blue light. The blue God lives in our very hearts, says Jñānadeva (Abg. 53).

Form experience.

7. Next to the experience of colour, comes the experience of forms, which are the objects of a mystic's vision on his spiritual journey. Of these the pearl constitutes the first kind of experience. "Beautiful indeed is that pearl which sheds light through all its different eight sides" (Abg. 57). "The pearl ornament is indeed a source of bliss......It cannot be had in the market. It cannot be had in a city. It can be had only by the force of concentration" (Abg. 58). "Priceless indeed is that jewel which thou hast attained. Dost thou not know that it is the source of the Godhead? It cannot perish. It cannot be fathomed. It need not be protected from a robber......That imperishable Jewel has been attained by me, says Jñānadeva, through the instruction of my Spiritual Teacher" (Abg. 56). Then Jñānadeva describes the experience of circles. "What work indeed has he accomplished who has not investigated the nature of the circle? He has been inflated with ignorance and has lived like an ass ......It is only when the circle has been investigated that God comes to be found. The mellifluous experience is hard to be spoken of. The first circle is of a white colour. In the midst of it is a dazzling circle. The still inner circle is of a red colour, and the final circle is blue......Until this circle is investigated all else is ignorance......I have spoken about it to you by the grace of Nivritti" (Abg. 59). Jñānadeva tells us further on that inside the palace of these circles is the form of God (Abg. 60). "This circle is indeed a void. What appears, is a void; what sees, is a void; when the void and the non-void are both lost, there is the form of the Self" (Abg. 61). Next comes the vision of the eye. "By the eye is the eye to be seen, and it is indeed the end of the void. It shines forth like a dark-blue circle. In it rests the light form of God" (Abg. 62). It is the Eye of all eyes. It is the Blue of all the blues (Abg. 64). "Now my eye tries to penetrate my eye. The eye sees the eye in the eye. The eye was verily shown to Jñānadeva by Nivritti, and he saw the eye in all places" (Abg. 63). Finally, Jñānadeva describes the experience of the vision of the Liṅga. "I have indeed seen the Liṅga, and have become as expansive as it is. It moves not, nor has it any form or qualities. In my body, I have seen this Liṅgam of light, and have embraced it without hands" (Abg. 65). Jñānadeva describes in a beautiful way how the whole Universe is like a Liṅgam. "I have seen the Liṅga" says he, "whose basin is the heaven, whose water-line is the ocean; which is as fixed as the Śesha; which is the support of all the three worlds; which fills the whole Universe; on which the clouds pour water; which is worshipped by means of flowers in the form of the stars; to which the offering of the moon as of a fruit is to be made; before which the sun is waved as a light; to whom the individual Self is to be offered as an oblation. I have worshipped it with ecstatic bliss. I have meditated upon that Liṅgam of light in my heart," says Jñānadeva (Abg. 66).

Light experience.

8. Next to morphic experiences, come the experiences of light. Jñānadeva tells us that the whole world is filled by incomparable light. "Interest merges in interest; love throbs; I have seen the intensive form of God. He is full of sound and light......The dawn breaks, and the light of the Sun spreads forth......By the spiritual instruction of Nivṛitti, Jñānadeva has attained to spiritual wisdom" (Abg. 73). "Jñānadeva sometimes speaks of the moonlight which shines without the moon ......God, the cause of all the universe, appears there as subtle and as small as an atom. Viṭṭhala is indeed personal and impersonal" (Abg. 71). "Even the sun's light is inferior to the light of the Ātman. In God, indeed, there is neither day nor light. Beyond all duality Jñānadeva has seen the eye, and nothing can stand in comparison to it" (Abg. 70). God is indeed seen in the super-conscious state... His light is greater than the light of the moon and the sun. This Self-experience is known only to those who have learned it from their spiritual master (Abg. 69). And is it not wonderful, asks Jñānadeva, that the sun should shine by night, and the moon by day? Contrary to all experiences is this. There is neither rising nor setting in Ātman. He is his own mirror. Only the man of experience knows, says Jñānadeva, and Saints became pleased by that sign (Abg. 72). "That light is indeed seen in the thousand-petalled lotus where there is neither name nor form" (Abg. 68); "and it is wonderful that that light is neither hot nor cold" (Abg. 67); "and beyond indeed that light is God who remains transcendent" (Abg. 104).

Sound experience.

9. Jñānadeva's experience of sound is not expressed with the same fulness with which his colour experience or form experience or light experience are expressed. Indeed, in the Jñāneśvarī, he has spoken of the sound which fills the whole universe, telling us that a mystic does not know whence it comes, and whither it goes. In his Abhaṅgas he does make mention of that unstruck sound which is heard in the process of mystic contemplation, and Jñānadeva tells us that beyond it is the light of God (Abg. 74). Jñānadeva is also careful to describe the signs of approaching death. "When a man shuts his ears and does not hear the sound, he should know that he is going to die in nine days' time. When he looks at his brows and does not see them, he shall live only for seven days. By rubbing the eye, if he is not able to see the circle, he will live only for five days. When he does not see the tip of his nose, on that day he will pass out of life. This indeed is the mark of a Saint, says Jñānadeva, and one may realise this at the time of his death" (Abg. 75).

God can be attained in all states of consciousness.

10. The experience of God can be attained in all the states of consciousness—in the waking state, in the dream state, in the deep-sleep state, as well as in the super-conscious state. When all these states become alike, then God is attained. Jñānadeva employs an allegory to tell us how God is to be experienced in all these states. The Waking State is personified and is made to say that she heard the voice of God in the courtyard, and saw Him with her own eyes. The Dream State and the Deep-Sleep State say that they are full of love towards God, and when they will realise God, then the cymbals will be sounded. The Super-conscious State is made to say that everything that belonged to her was taken away by God, and she was made to remain deeply silent (Abg. 84). Elsewhere also Jñānadeva tells us how in all the different states of consciousness—in the waking state, in the dream-state, and in the deep-sleep state,—his mind was full of the bliss of God (Abg. 83). In fact, God's bliss, according to Jñānadeva, could be attained in all states of consciousness.

Experience of Bliss.

11. Jñānadeva expresses variously the attainment of bliss consequent on communion with God. "As I went to see God, my intellect stood motionless, and as I saw Him, I became Himself......As a dumb man cannot express the sweetness of nectar, so also I cannot express my internal bliss. God keeps awake in me, says Jñānadeva, and the Saints became pleased by this sign" (Abg. 79). This same silent communion with God Jñānadeva expresses in many other places. "Throughout all my experiences, I have been overwhelmed with silence. What shall I do if I cannot speak a word? Nivṛitti showed me the God in my heart, and I have been enjoying each day a new aspect of Him" (Abg. 76). "As I heard of God's qualities, my eager heart ran to meet Him. My body and mind and speech became transfixed. In all eagerness, my hands were lifted up. But as I saw the form of God, they remained motionless as it were. My eyes refused to wink, and I remained one with what I saw" (Abg. 88). "I have been satiated by the enjoyment of Divine experience, and I have been nodding from time after time. I have lost all desires; I have grown careless of my body. *Meum* and *Tuum* have disappeared from me. I became merged in God, and the bliss was witnessed by all" (Abg. 81). "God indeed fills the inside and the outside, and as one goes to embrace Him, one becomes identified with Him. God cannot be warded off, even if one wills. Self-hood is at an end. As desire runs after God, God hides Himself. In a moment's time, however, He shows Himself, when all the desires remain tranquil" (Abg. 92).

The final experience of the Self.

12. What is this Self-vision of which Jñānadeva speaks? Jñānadeva characterises it in various different formulæ. "I have seen the God unobtainable by the Yogins," he says, "and my heart's desire is not satisfied, even though I have been seeing Him for all time. I have seen the God of gods. My doubt is at an end. Duality has disappeared. I have indeed seen God in various forms and under various descriptions" (Abg. 77). Contrasted with this attitude of assurance, is also the attitude of submission to the Divine will. Jñānadeva is aware that God's nature cannot be entirely understood. "The cool south wind cannot be made to drop like water from a piece of cloth. The fragrance of flowers cannot be tied by a string. The Lord of all can neither be called great nor small. Who can know His nature? The lustre of pearls cannot be made to fill a pitcher of water. The sky cannot be enveloped. The pupil in the eye cannot be separated from the eye......The quarrel between God and his spouse cannot be made up. Hence, Jñānadeva meekly submits to the will of God" (Abg. 93). Jñānadeva is a past master in the Yogic vision of God, and he sees God in the immaculate region above the different plexuses. God appears neither as male nor as female (Abg. 85). Both night and day are lost in God. Both the moon and the sun derive their light from Him. He appears as the unity of man and woman, and Śiva and Śakti are both merged in Him (Abg. 86). As Jñānadeva sees God, he finds Him in all directions,

"He lights the lamp of experience, and the same vision appears to him in all the ten different quarters" (Abg. 87). God indeed fills not merely the whole outside, but also the entire inside of Jñānadeva. As Jñānadeva sees Him, he becomes merged in Him. "His mind becomes infatuated. Forgetfulness becomes remembrance. The whole world seems to be lost in God" (Abg. 89). "That beautiful form of God infatuates him as he sees it. He sees his own form present everywhere" (Abg. 80). "He sees the mirror of form without form. The seer vanishes. Everywhere God is present. There is neither any rising, nor any setting of God. God alone is, and He enjoys His own happiness in His unitive experience. The invisible Husband keeps awake on his bed without there being any partaker of it" (Abg. 91). This is what is meant by Self-vision. In order to attain to this, the body has first to be delivered over. "God is indeed seen as a full-grown sandal tree, or as a full-blossomed Aśvattha. Jñānadeva bids adieu to all phenomenal existence. True bliss is to be found only in Self-vision" (Abg. 94). As Jñānadeva began to see himself, he was lost in himself. His mind remained cheated. God was inside, God was outside. He himself appeared to him as God. Nivṛitti had really killed his separate individuality (Abg. 95). Jñānadeva even supposed that in his ecstatic experience, he was one with his teacher Nivṛitti (Abg. 97), not to speak of his identity with God. God was his, and he was God's. This unity had naturally come about. God was himself, and he was God. Ignorant they, who did not know this unity (Abg. 98). He had seen God without the eye, and touched Him without the hand (Abg. 99). He had embraced him without a body (Abg. 101). Jñānadeva is anxious that God should speak a word with him, now that He has presented Himself before him. He is on the point of calling God cruel (Abg. 102). But God indeed is able to satisfy all the desires of Jñānadeva. He, on whose forehead a thousand moons shine, whose eyes are as beautiful as a lotus, and who has a constant smile on His lips, begins to move before Jñānadeva, and nods before him. He stands up, and moves his hands, and speaks words in confidence from time to time, thus fulfilling all the desires of Jñānadeva (Abg. 103). "This is indeed the end of the Abhaṅgas of Jñānadeva. In this wise is the super-conscious state to be reached. Nivṛitti alone knows the final cause of the Abhaṅgas. A fool does not deserve to know this spiritual instruction: hence, he is unworthy of entering into this shrine of knowledge" (Abg. 105).

Sopana, Muktabai and Changadeva.

The teaching of Sopana, Muktabai and Changadeva.

13. The Abhaṅgas of Sopāna, Muktābāi and Chāṅgadeva approximate to the Abhaṅgas of Jñānadeva neither in quality nor in quantity. Yet mystical experience in them is entirely unmistakable. Sopāna tells us, that he, who contemplates upon the name of God, shall never come again to experience the turmoil of life after life (Abg. 1). He tells us that the distinction between sacred and not-sacred, which people make, is entirely foolish. The only sacred thing in this world is God, and the not-sacred thing is the mind of the unbeliever. Sopāna, having given himself over to God incessantly, is an exemplar of sacredness (Abg. 2). He also tells us that he forgot all joys and sorrows in the Name of God (Abg. 4), and that as soon as the sound of the devotees fell upon the ears of God, He came forth to receive them (Abg. 5).

Muktābāi tells us that she was leading merely a blind-fold life ; but she was awakened to spiritual consciousness by the grace of Nivṛitti (Abg. 1). She compares the grace of Nivṛitti to the bank of a river, across which, and by the help of which, she was able to swim to her goal (Abg. 2). She tells us also in a mystical fashion that "she saw an ant floating in the sky, and that this ant was able to devour the Sun. A great wonder it was, she says, that a barren woman gave birth to a child. The scorpion went to the nether world, and there the serpent fell at its feet. A fly was delivered, and gave birth to a kite. At these experiences, says Muktābāi, she laughed" (Abg. 4). She asks us, who has been able to see the moon-light by day, and the hot sun-light by night (Abg. 5) ? She tells us that as the trees in a forest become fragrant by a sandal tree, which is in the midst of them, similarly, people begin to love God when there is a devotee in the midst of them (Abg. 6). Muktābāi's advice to Chāṅgadeva is remarkable for its candour, and its grasp of truth. "Turn back from the stream of life", she tells him ; "for if you were to go across the current, you will be swept away. The water of the river of life runs with great force, and it throws down even the greatest of swimmers. Life indeed is transient, and you must not allow it to waste. Think of the internal sign, says Muktābāi to Chāṅgadeva. For, it is the grace of God that would enable you to cross the stream of life" (Abg. 7). Muktābāi also tells Chāṅgadeva to speak words of silence (Abg. 9). She advises him to sleep the sleep of ecstasy, wherein the unstruck sound is heard, the mind is regulated by the thread of breath, and a state is enjoyed which is beyond both sleep and consciousness (Abg. 10). "In that state," says Muktābāi, "the bride-groom will come from the womb of the bride, and as the bride-groom comes out, the bride will vanish from before him, and there will be no limit to the happiness that may be enjoyed" (Abg. 12).

Chāṅgadeva, who was taught the secret of spiritual life by Muktābāi, tells us in his Abhaṅgas that the body is the bride, while the Ātman is the bride-groom (Abg. 4). After the marriage takes place, the bride-groom will go to his house, and the bride will be sent with him. "I shall now remain content," says Chāṅgadeva, "once that I have delivered over the bride into the hands of the bride-groom" (Abg. 5). Like Muktābāi herself, Chāṅgadeva tells us that "the sky has been enveloped by an ant, and there a great wonder took place. It was one gnat which enveloped the whole Universe" (Abg. 7). "As from a sound-machine, words come out, and there is yet no person who is visible, similarly, the flute is playing all day, says Chāṅgadeva, and its sound has filled the whole Universe. Chāṅgadeva, who merged himself in this all-enveloping sound, became God by meditating on God" (Abg. 10).

CHAPTER VI.

General Review.

General Review of the Period.

1. Of the three great works of Jñānadeva, the Jñāneśvarī, the Amṛitānubhava and the Abhaṅgas, it is evident that the Amṛitānubhava is, on the whole, a philosophical work, the Abhaṅgas a mystical work, while the Jñāneśvarī contains both philosophy and mysticism. We have characterised Jñānadeva's mysticism as intellectual mysticism, because it is rooted in the firm philosophical groundings of the Bhagavadgītā. His Commentary on the Bhagavadgītā may be regarded as evidently the greatest of the Commentaries that exist on that immortal poem. This may be evident from the copious citations that we have given in our exposition of the Jñāneśvarī from that great work. The world will await the day when the whole of the Jñāneśvarī may be translated into English, and thus be made available to the world of scholars. But our selections, representative as they are, will sufficiently show the greatness of Jñānadeva's vision. On the ethical side, especially, the Jñāneśvarī excels almost any great work on moral philosophy. Its analysis of the different virtues is acute and profound. The philosophical grounding of Jñānadeva, as evidenced in the Jñāneśvarī, is more or less of the Advaitic kind, though occasionally here and there some concession is made to the other schools of the Vedānta. Sir Ramakrishna Bhandarkar once expressed his great inability to understand how the Maratha Saints could reconcile Advaitism with Bhakti. It is exactly this reconciliation which is made in Mysticism generally, and more particularly in the Mysticism of the Mahārāshtra school which is worth while noting. The philosophical foundation of the Amṛitānubhava is somewhat in a different line. There we see how Jñānadeva is under the influence of the philosophy of the Śiva-sūtras when he refers to such terms as Piṇḍa, Pada, Śiva, and Śakti. It will be an interesting study when Gorakshnātha's and other Nāthas' works are discovered to see how much Jñānadeva owes to that school. But it is evident, as we see in Amṛitānubhava III. 16, that Jñānadeva had come definitely under the influence of the Śiva-sūtra philosophy: आणि ज्ञान बंधु ऐसें । शिवसूत्राचेनि मिषें । ह्मणितलें असे । सदाशिवें. Then again, we have to take into account the way in which Jñānadeva argues against the Māyā doctrine as ordinarily understood, and it is wonderful, as Pandit Pānduranga Śarma has pointed out, how Jñānadeva uses the very same arguments against the Māyā doctrine as Rāmānuja had used in the Śrībhāshya. But we must not suppose that Jñānadeva was not a believer in the Māyā doctrine in its ethical and mystical aspects. Metaphysically, no doubt he advances the Sphūrtivāda in the Amṛitānubhava : as light may come from a jewel, so the world comes from God, and the world is to the same extent real as the light is. This does not bespeak the utter unreality of the world according to Jñānadeva. Ethically and mystically, however, we know how in his Jñāneśvarī he cries aloft :—

आतां महदादि हे माझी माया । उतरोनियां धनंजया ।
मी होइजे हें आया । कैसेंनि ये ॥....॥
येथ एक नवलावो । जो जो कीजे तरणोपावो ।
तो तो अपावो । होय तें ऐक ॥. ..॥
पाडस वागुर करांडी । कां मुंगी मेरू वोलांडी ।
तरी मायेची पैलथडी । देखती जीव ॥
येथ एकचि लीला तरले । जे सर्वभावें मज भजले ।
तयां ऐलीच थडीं सरलें । मायाजळ ॥ Jñā. VII. 68–97.

Jñānadeva points out unmistakably the unreality of existence in this mortal world, and he calls the minds of the people back to the spiritual life which alone is the true reality. This Reality could be attained through devotion. Jñānadeva's philosophy preserves both the oneness and the manyness of experience. His spiritual Mysticism reconciles both Monism and Pluralism. "Not in the Monism of Śaṁkarāchārya, nor in the Dualism that is quite satisfied to remain two, but in the spiritual experience that transcends and includes them both, is peace to be found" (Macnicol). It is not our business here to enter into a philosophical discussion of the nature of Mysticism. But we may say that it does not regard the duality of devotion and the unity of mystical experience as contradictory of each other. It was thus that Jñānadeva and Nivṛittinātha and Sopāna and the rest could start by Bhakti to end in Unitive Experience. Farquhar fitly calls Jñānadeva the "Coryphæus" of the whole Bhakti movement of the Maratha country. When Jñānadeva had once laid the intellectual foundations of mysticism, the superstructure which the other Saints raised was a matter of not very great difficulty. Nivṛittinātha must have been a great Saint indeed a Saint who could have a disciple like Jñānadeva. Sopāna, Jñānadeva has praised immensely. Muktābāi, the young sister of the three brother saints, was perhaps the greatest of the Indian mystical poetesses. Chāṅgadeva, who comes at the end of the line, is a sublime illustration of the insufficiency of the life of mere Yogic power before a truly mystical attainment of God.

PART II.

The Age of Namadeva: Democratic Mysticism.

CHAPTER VII.

Biographical Introduction.

A short History of Vitthala Sampradaya.

1. When we come to the age of Nāmadeva, we come upon an age which is filled with the echoes of the Sāmpradāya of Viṭṭhala. The great saint Jñānadeva lived only for a short time to be able to spread during his life-time the Sāmpradāya of Viṭṭhala far and wide. The work, which had been begun by Jñānadeva, was continued by Nāmadeva, who, though he was born at the same time as Jñānadeva, lived for more than half a century after him, during which period he became the pillar of the Viṭṭhala Sāmpradāya at Pandharpur. It was in his time most especially that Pandharpur gained its great importance. It is true that the shrine of Viṭṭhala at Pandharpur was erected even before the days of Jñānadeva and Nāmadeva. It is probable that Puṇḍalīka was the first great high priest of the God of Pandharpur. As to where and when this saint actually lived we have not any records to determine. It seems, however, that Puṇḍalīka was a Canarese saint, and the temple which is built in his memory is on the sands of the Bhīmā. As to whether this temple of Puṇḍalīka is to be regarded as a Samādhi of Puṇḍalīka, or merely a temple erected to his memory, we have again no evidence to determine. It is, however, to be noted that that temple contains a Lingam of Śiva, and even here, as in the case of Jñānadeva, we have to remember that Puṇḍalīka, who was one of the greatest of the devotees of Viṭṭhala, had a Liṇgam of Śiva erected in memory of him. In fact, all these saints of Pandharpur knew no distinction between Śaivism and Vaishnavism. As Dr. P. R. Bhandarkar has cleverly pointed out, the epithet, Pāṇḍuraṇga, the "white-limbed" God, which is really the name of Śiva, is here transferred to Viṭṭhala, just to show that there is ultimately no difference between Śaivism and Vaishnavism. We have already seen in the Chapter on Jñāneśvara that the earliest inscription of Viṭṭhala and Rakhumāī is to be found in Āḷandī, dated 1209 A.D. (Śake 1131). Later in chronology to this is the inscription of 1237 A.D. (Śake 1159) in the temple of Viṭhoba in Pandharpur itself, where we read that a certain king, called Someśvara, had conquered the kings round about his territory, and had encamped in the year 1237 A.D. (Śake 1159) in a town called "Paṇḍarige" on the banks of the Bhīmarathī, where Puṇḍalīka was being lovingly remembered by people as a great sage. The next inscription is of the date

1273 A.D. (Śake 1195) from that temple itself, which records that in that year the temple of Viṭṭhala was being rebuilt, and that during the period from 1273 A.D. to 1277 A.D. (Śake 1195—1199) funds were being collected in order to raise a suitable temple to the God. In this inscription, the names of those who contributed to the rebuilding of the temple are mentioned, most prominently among whom are the names of Hemāḍapant, the minister of Ramdevrao Jādhava, and of the King Ramdevrao Jādhava himself, who visited the temple in 1276 A.D. (Śake 1198), and gave the temple a very large subsidy. It would seem therefore that the Sāmpradāya of Viṭṭhala at Pandharpur was prevalent even before the time of Jñānadeva and Nāmadeva, and that after Pundalīka the greatest saints in the history of Sāmpradāya were Jñānadeva and Nāmadeva themselves. Pilgrims from all parts of the country flocked to Pandharpur from Gujerath, Karnatak, the Telugu and Tamil Districts, as well as from the Marāṭhā Province. The Kīrtana, as a method of spreading the gospel of these saints, seems to have originated in the necessity of making their spiritual ideas clear to the many pilgrims who were flocking to Pandharpur, and it seems, to a certain extent, Jñānadeva himself, and after him Nāmadeva, were the greatest of the early Kīrtana-performers, or singers of the praise of God.

Jnanadeva and Namadeva as Contemporaries.

2. That Jñānadeva and Nāmadeva were contemporaries, that they went together on a pilgrimage from Pandharpur, that they were brothers in a spiritual Sāmpradāya, are facts too well-grounded, and not mere myths to be disturbed by sceptical considerations. The fact that there is a difference of language between the Jñāneśvarī and the Abhaṅgas of Nāmadeva is not an argument to prove any difference of time between the two great saints. The originals of Nāmadeva's Abhaṅgas are not preserved. They have undergone successive changes, as they were recited and have been handed over from mouth to mouth. All these facts account for the modernness of Nāmadeva's style. For that very same reason, for which the Abhaṅgas of Jñānadeva are separated, for example from the Jñāneśvari by these critics, would they separate the Abhaṅgas of Nāmadeva in time from the writings of Jñānadeva. But the considerations we have adduced above will convince our readers that there is justification enough for the modernness of Nāmadeva's style. Moreover, the fact must not be lost sight of, that there might be a difference of style from individual to individual. This consideration also will justify us in not separating Nāmadeva from Jñānadeva in time. According to Bhāradvāja's proposition, Jñānadeva, the author of the Abhaṅgas, was contemporaneous with Nāmadeva. But, as we have established in our last Chapter that the Jñānadeva of the Abhaṅgas is not a different Jñānadeva from the Jñānadeva of the Jñāneśvarī, the supposition that Nāmadeva was a contemporary of the Jñānadeva of the Abhaṅgas loses all meaning. Nor can Bhāradvāja's argument that the reference in Nāmadeva to the Mahomedan invasions, and the absence of it in the Jñāneśvarī, be an argument for the difference in time between Jñānadeva and Nāmadeva. As we have shown in our introduction to the age of Jñānadeva, Allauddin Khilji invaded the Deccan in 1294 A.D. (Śake 1216), that is to say, about two years before Jñānadeva passed away; while, as we shall see later on, Nāmadeva's death took place in 1350 A.D. (Śake 1272). Thus there is clearly a difference of fifty-four years between the dates of Jñānadeva's and Nāmadeva's passing away. During this half century, it is not impossible that the invasions of the Mahomedans had made great impression upon the minds of the Marāṭhās; and hence it is no wonder that Nāmadeva refers to these invasions in his Abhaṅgas; while we can see from the very same fact why Jñānadeva could not have referred to them. The only sense in which we can say that Nāmadeva was later than Jñānadeva is this: not that Nāmadeva was separated from Jñānadeva in time by over a century as some critics would have it, but that even though they were born about the same time, Nāmadeva outlived Jñānadeva by over half a century. It is only in this sense that we may say that Nāmadeva was later than Jñānadeva; while, the fact that they lived and moved together could be seen not merely from the account of their travels given in the Tīrthāvaḷī of Nāmadeva which nobody has hitherto dared to regard as mythical, but also from the many references in Nāmadeva to Jñānadeva, as well as from the references in Jñānadeva to Nāmadeva, whom he declares to be verily 'the illumination of the world'.

A sketch of Namadeva's life.

3. From an Abhaṅga written by Nāmadeva himself, it seems that Nāmadeva was born in 1270 A.D. (Śake 1192), that is, a few years before Jñānadeva. Nāmadeva tells us that a certain Brahmin, Bābāji by name, had cast his horoscope, foretelling that Nāmadeva would compose a hundred crores of Abhaṅgas (Abg. 1). In another of his Abhaṅgas, we read that his father Dāmāśeta was a tailor by caste, and lived in Narasingpur. The same Abhaṅga tells us that Nāmadeva led a very lawless life in the beginning of his career. We are told that he was a marauder, and a way-layer, who once upon a time killed eighty-four horsemen, and when he had gone to visit the temple of Āmvaḍhyā, as was his usual custom, he saw a woman rebuking her child which was crying because it had nothing to eat; and when Nāmadeva inquired, she told him that she was made a widow, and the child an orphan, on account of her husband being killed among the eighty-four horsemen by a certain way-layer; upon which Nāmadeva's heart was touched to the quick, and he went inside the temple and in the fury of repentance, he struck his neck with a scythe, and let loose streams of blood on the Deity. The worshippers of the temple saw that horrible deed, asked him the reason why he was doing it, and turned him out of the temple. He went to Pandharpur and determined to lead a holy and pious life. Thus it was by the tears that were shed by a woman whom in his lawlessness he had made a widow, that he was suddenly converted from an evil life, and he then determined to lead the life of a saint. He used to visit the temple at Pandharpur and fall prostrate before God. After some years of repentance and devotion to God, he came to realise the nature of God. The story goes that when Jñānadeva, Gorā Kumbhāra, and other saints had once gathered together at Pandharpur, Gorā began to test which of the "pots" that had gathered there were ripe, and which were unbaked; and he ultimately found that Nāmadeva was entirely an unbaked pot. This story we shall give later in detail in the very words of Nāmadeva. Here we have made a reference to it just to give completeness to the life-story of Nāmadeva at this stage. Nāmadeva felt very sorry, and finding that he was the only unbaked pot in the whole assembly of saints, determined to find a Guru, through whom he might know the way to spiritual life. He went to Visobā Khechara, some say at Bārsi, while others say at Āmvaḍhyā, where Nāmadeva was convinced by Visobā Khechara of the Omnipresence of God, and was initiated by him into the spiritual life. Thereupon, Nāmadeva became worthy of the company of the Saints at Pandharpur. Many stories are told of the way in which Nāmadeva led a perfectly spiritual life. While he was once eating a piece of bread, a dog appeared before him, and ran away with the piece. Nāmadeva pursued it with a pot of curds, praying that it should partake of the curds also. This story shows how Nāmadeva began to see God in every creature. There are all kinds of miracles told about Nāmadeva, especially while he and

Jñānadeva had gone on their famous pilgrimage. Janābāī tells us how once upon a time Nāmadeva by his power saved Pandharpur from the ravages of a great flood. Nāmadeva's house in Pandharpur is still shown. There is still the image of Keśirāja in that house. Before the great image in the temple at Pandharpur, Nāmadeva danced in spiritual ecstasy. He was probably the greatest of the early Kīrtana-performers. He developed the Sāmpradāya of Panḍharī, as no other single saint ever did. There were a number of other Saints in his time at Pandharpur, and they all formed a happy spiritual company. It seems that Nāmadeva died in 1350 A.D. (Śake 1272), that is, about fifty-four years later than Jñānadeva. The passing away of Jñānadeva must have been a very severe blow to Nāmadeva. Jñānadeva and Nāmadeva represent the intellectual and the emotional sides of spiritual life. According to some, Visobā's spiritual teacher was Sopāna, and according to others Jñānadeva. If the latter be true, then Jñānadeva happens to be the teacher's teacher of Nāmadeva. Nāmadeva is buried at the great door of the temple of Viṭhoba. Nāmadeva and Chokhāmelā stand face to face before the front door of the temple. The priests in Viṭhoba's temple say that the bones of the Nāmadeva who was buried at the front door are the bones of a Brahmin Nāmadeva, about whom we shall speak presently, and not of the tailor Nāmadeva. But this does not seem to be established. For, the Brahmin Nāmadeva who was otherwise called Vishnudāsa Nāmā does not seem to be so great a saint as to deserve the honour of being buried in the very front of the temple of Viṭhoba. On the other hand, the tailor Nāmadeva, who is one of the greatest of the saints that ever lived, may be regarded as rightly deserving that honour. Whether the other members of Nāmadeva's family were alike buried near the front door is questionable. But we can definitely take the "Pāyarī" which is known at present as "Nāmadeva's Pāyarī" before the great door of the temple, as the Samādhi of the great saint.

Namadeva and Vishnudasanama.

4. An authentic collection of Nāmadeva's Abhaṅgas has yet to be made. Indeed this matter is one of insuperable difficulty, inasmuch as the Abhaṅgas of the Tailor Nāmadeva and the Abhaṅgas of the Brahmin Nāmadeva are hopelessly mixed. The only possible criterion of the separation of the Abhaṅgas of the one from those of the other, is that the latter probably invariably calls himself Vishṇudāsanāmā. It is evident that the latter, who came after the earlier Nāmadeva by a couple of centuries, had justification for calling his Abhaṅgas as those of Vishnudāsanāmā, to distinguish them from the Abhaṅgas of Nāmadeva. The earlier Nāmadeva, if he ever called himself Vishṇudāsanāmā, called himself so, only in the sense that he was a devotee of God. The later Nāmadeva, when he calls himself Vishṇudāsanāmā, uses the term as an appellation. There are other criteria also. The criteria of brilliance of imagination, of simplicity of style, the comparative oldness of vocabulary, and such others, must be systematically applied, and some day, we hope, an authentic collection of the great Nāmadeva's Abhaṅgas will be made. We have said that there is a difference of a couple of centuries between the earlier Nāmadeva, who was a tailor, and the later Nāmadeva who was a Brahmin. Mr. Bhave has shown that the date of the later Nāmadeva should be taken as 1578 A.D. (Śake 1500). In any case, his Abhaṅgas cannot command the originality and the spontaneity of the Abhaṅgas of the earlier Nāmadeva. It is probably a confusion of these two Nāmadevas, which lies at the bottom of transferring even the earlier Nāmadeva to about a century or two later, and many critics have fallen a prey to it. As Pandit Panduraṅgaśarma has shown, the earlier Nāmadeva's exploits are referred to in Narasī Mehtā's "Haramālā", A.D. 1413 (Samvat 1470). This means that Nāmadeva's name must have been a classical one at the time when Narasī Mehtā wrote the work. Moreover, the eighty Abhaṅgas of Nāmadeva in the Granthasaheb of the Sikhs must be attributed to the earlier Nāmadeva. In our account of the teachings of the earlier and the later Nāmadevas, we have tried as best we can to separate their Abhaṅgas by the tests we have referred to; but our conclusions at this stage could only be provisional. It is only when the tests we have referred to have been applied severely, and the Abhaṅgas thus separated into two different groups, that we shall ultimately be able to say that our conclusions are final.

Gora, the Potter.

5. Of the contemporary saints of Nāmadeva, Gorā, the potter, evidently takes the first place. He was born in 1267 A.D. (Śake 1189), three years before Nāmadeva, and about eight years before Jñānadeva. As he was the eldest of the contemporary saints, he was called 'Uncle Gorā'. He lived at Teraḍhokī. As we have seen, he was given the work of testing the spirituality of Nāmadeva by Jñānadeva and others. He was present at the Jñānadeva-Nāmadeva pilgrimage, and was respected by all his contemporaries. The story goes that he was so filled with God-devotion that he once did not know that he had trampled his child in clay under his feet, while he was dancing in joy. But by God's grace the child was saved.

Visoba Khechara.

6. Visobā Khechara, who is next in importance as being the teacher of Nāmadeva, has been supposed to have lived either at Āmvaḍhyā or Bārsi. He was called Khechara in contempt by Muktābāī and Jñānadeva, as he did not at first believe in them. But, having later come to know their spiritual greatness, he became their disciple. While Nāmadeva went to meet him, he had placed his feet upon a Liṇgam of Śiva, and when Nāmadeva rebuked him for having insulted the deity, Visobā asked him to place his feet elsewhere, where also as the story goes, there sprang up a Liṇgam of Śiva under his feet. This only means that Visobā convinced Nāmadeva of the omnipresence of God. He also accompanied Jñānadeva and Nāmadeva in their pilgrimage. He died at Bārsi on Śrāvaṇa Śuddha Ekādaśī, 1309 A.D. (Śake 1231).

Samvata, the Gardener.

7. The third of the great contemporary saints of Nāmadeva, was Sāmvatā, the gardener of Araṇagaon. Araṇagaon is a village three miles from Modanimba Station, B. L. Railway, and is under Miraj jurisdiction. His garden and well are shown even to-day. Sāmvatā could see God in everything, before Nāmadeva could. He was also present in the Jñānadeva-Nāmadeva pilgrimage. He died on Āshaḍha Vadya Chaturdaśī, 1295 A.D. (Śake 1217). His Samādhi is at Araṇagaon. This is a very well-built building, much of the expenses of which have been defrayed by the gardener community of Bombay and Poona. One of the Brahmin Bhaktas of Sāmvatā has been buried before him. Araṇagaon is worth while a visit.

Narahari, the Goldsmith.

8. Narahari, the goldsmith, was at first an inhabitant of Devagiri, and then he came to Pandharpur. He was a great devotee of Śiva, and could not appreciate Vitthala-Bhakti at first. It seems that on account of the influence exercised by Jñānadeva and others, he came into the Bhāgavata line. A story is also told how he came to recognise the identity of Śiva and Vishṇu. He died in 1313 A.D. (Śake 1235).

Chokha, the Untouchable.

9. Chokhā, the untouchable, was a resident of Mangalveḍhā. Mangalveḍhā is now a Taluka under the State of Sangli and is well worth a visit on account of the many antiquarian relics there. Chokhā was a great devotee of the God of Pandharpur, and being of the outcast community, could only pray to God from outside the temple at Pandharpur. But God Viṭhoba loved him none the less. He had a son called Karmā, and a sister called Nirmalā. He was also present in the Jñānadeva-Nāmadeva pilgrimage. While he was at work on the parapet at Mangalveḍhā, the wall fell down on him, and he died with the other workers under the wall in 1338 A.D. (Śake 1260). The devotees of Pandharpur wanted to bring the bones of Chokhā to Pandharpur. But they could not know how to distinguish his bones from those of others. So they prayed to Nāmadeva to tell them how they could separate the bones of Chokhā from those of the rest. Nāmadeva told them to pick up only those bones from the ruins, from which was audible the name of Viṭṭhala, and the story goes that the bones were thus separated and brought to Pandharpur. This story only shows that devotion to the Name of God had penetrated to the very bones of Chokhā, and that even though his physical body was dead, the inert matter of which his body was composed could still be a witness to the presence of God. Chokhā's bones were carried to Pandharpur, and can even to-day be seen placed in a Samādhi before the front-door of the temple just opposite to the place where Nāmadeva's bones have been placed.

Janabai, the Maid.

10. Janābāī, who is the next in the order of seniority, was a maid-servant of Nāmadeva. While only a girl, she was handed over to the care of Dāmāśeta by her father, and she spent her life in doing menial service at Nāmadeva's house, and in singing the praises of God. She was the greatest of the female disciples of Nāmadeva, as Veṇubāī and Akkā were the greatest of the female disciples of Rāmadāsa. As regards her place among the female saints of Mahārāshṭra, we may say that she was the greatest of them, barring only the sister of Jñānadeva, namely, Muktābāī. Her Abhaṅgas show a fervour, in which she is certainly influenced by the great devotion of Nāmadeva. We also owe to her certain Abhaṅgas which enable us to discuss the historical position of Nāmadeva and other saints.

Sena, the Barber.

11. Senā, the barber, was in the service of the king of Bedar. He was so given to God-devotion, that he once gave no heed to the king's invitation for shaving, while he was engaged in meditation. He lived about the year 1448 A.D. (Śake 1370), and could say that he could show God to others as in a mirror.

Kanhopatra, the Dancing Girl.

12. Kanhopātrā was a very beautiful daughter of Śyāmā, a dancing woman in Mangalveḍhā. She said that she would marry only him whose beauty equalled hers. She found the beauty only in the God of Pandharpur, and remained there as Viṭhoba's worshipper. The king of Bedar once sent for the beautiful Kanhopātrā. She implored God to save her, but when the messengers insisted upon taking her to the king of Bedar, she decided to give up the ghost rather than go to the king of Bedar. The dead body was thus laid at the feet of God, and she was buried to the south of the temple. A strange tree has sprung up on the place where she was buried. This tree still remains, and is worshipped by all pilgrims. She seems to have lived about 1468 A.D. (Śake 1390). With this biographical introduction to Nāmadeva and his contemporary saints, let us now turn to a survey of their teachings as gathered from their various writings.

CHAPTER VIII.

The Abhangas of Namadeva and Contemporary Saints.

The Heart-rendings of Namadeva.

1. The great characteristic of the Abhaṅgas of Nāmadeva is the manner in which we see always how his heart pants for God. Like Tukārāma at a later date, Nāmadeva also experienced much heart-rending for the attainment of God. This state has been characterised in Western Mysticism as "the Dark Night of the Soul". We will see how, in the case of Nāmadeva, this state was experienced partially. Later, we will see how Tukārāma experienced it fully. We may say that Nāmadeva in this respect approaches Tukārāma more than Jñānadeva. "As a bee's heart might be set upon the fragrance of a flower, or as a fly might take resort to honey, similarly does my mind cling to God," says Nāmadeva (Abg. 11). "I am called lordless, lordless; but Thou art called the Lord. I am called fallen, fallen; but Thou art called the reliever of the fallen. Poor, poor, do they call me; but they call Thee the reliever of the poor in heart. They call me afflicted, afflicted; but they call Thee one who wouldst relieve people of their afflictions. If Thou wert not to listen to me, says Nāmadeva, would it not be a matter of shame?" (Abg. 13). In this world, there is nobody else except Thee for whom I care, or who cares for me (Abg. 14). This little Samsāra has had the power to conceal Thee, who art all-encompassing. Thou obligest me to cling to Samsāra, and thus bringest to me the treachery of my Lord. I have now come to know Thy wiles, says Nāmadeva; I shall take any measures I will (Abg. 16). If the moon were to satisfy the desires of the Chakora, would her light be diminished for the obligation? (Abg. 18.) If a cloud were to quench the thirst of a Chātaka bird, would his greatness be thereby lessened? (Abg. 19.) Thou art my bird, I am Thy young one. Thou art my deer, I am Thy cub (Abg. 20). If the mother-bird moves out of her nest in the morning, its young ones keep looking out for her. Similarly, does my mind look out for Thee, my Lord (Abg. 22). If a child falls into a fire, its mother comes to its succour with an overpowered heart. If a fire envelopes a forest, the mother-deer is afflicted for its young one. In a similar way, says Nāmadeva, Thou must care for me (Abg. 23). When I consider that, at the end of my life, I shall have to depart alone; when I think that my mother who bore me in her womb for nine months will cruelly stand aside;

when I find the futility of the affection which sisters and brothers bear towards me ; when I find that children and wife shall stay away when my body will be burning upon the funeral pile ; when I contemplate how friends and relatives shall leave me in the cemetery and walk away ; I then begin to shed tears ; my throat chokes ; I find that darkness reigns everywhere ; my only resort is Thy feet, says Nāmadeva (Abg. 24). I contemplate an immolation of myself at Thy feet. The river of desire, however, carries me away. I cannot be rescued from the river by any other swimmer except Thee ; hence, throw Thyself into the river with Thy apparel to rescue me. The necklace of the nine jewels of devotion has been submerged in the river. The gourds of courage and discrimination have been broken to pieces. Faith, the rope by which one might swim out, has been sundered in twain. The great fish plying into the waters, namely Anger, is intent upon carrying me to the bottom of the river. Thou shouldst swiftly leap into the river to take me out, says Nāmadeva (Abg. 28). With tears in the eyes and with out-stretched hands, Nāmadeva is looking out for his Lord (Abg. 30). Shameless as he is, with his life-breath centred in his throat, he has been thinking about Thee night and day (Abg. 31). The three fires of the physical, metaphysical, and accidental evils, have been burning fiercely before me. When wouldst Thou rain from heaven, O Cloud of Mercy ? I have been caught in the flames of grief and infatuation. The wild conflagration of anxiety has spread all round. I am going to the bottom of the river and coming up again. Unless Thou, O Cloud of Mercy, run to my succour, my life-breath will depart from me (Abg. 32). Thou shouldst not consider my merit. I am an ocean of sin incarnate. From top to toe, I have committed sins innumerable (Abg. 35). Do you think that I shall grow weary, and go away from your presence, feeling that you would not come ? The rope of my life I shall bind to Thy feet, and shall bring Thee to me at pleasure. It is best therefore that Thou shouldst see me of Thy own accord (Abg. 36). I shall spread the meshes of my love and catch Thee alive. I shall make my heart a prison for Thee, and shall intern Thee inside. I shall beat Thee with the voice of Self-identity, and Thou shalt surely ask for compassion (Abg. 37). Thy generosity has been falsely praised. Thou givest only when Thou hast taken away (Abg. 40). The great Bali threw his body at Thy feet, and then Thou hadst compassion on him. Thy devotees have sacrificed their lives for Thy sake. Thou shouldst not forget that it is these devotees that have brought name to

Thee (Abg. 41). If a king leaves away his wife, does she not rule over the world? If the son of an Emperor has committed a fault, is it possible that any other man might bring him to book? We may possess as many faults as we like, and yet our faults are in the Lord (Abg. 44). We shall speak such words as will make God nod in joy. Love shall fill every part of our body, and our mouth will utter the name of God. We shall dance in the performance of Kīrtana, shall light the lamp of knowledge in this world, and live in a place which is beyond the highest. All power has come to me, says Nāmadeva, on account of the gift of my Spiritual Teacher (Abg. 47).

Namadeva's Insistence on the Name of God.

2. Among all the Saints of Mahārāshṭra, we find a perpetual insistence on the significance and efficacy of the Name of God; and of all these saints, we may say, Nāmadeva's insistence upon the Name is the strongest. "If I were to leave meditation on Thy feet even for a while," says Nāmadeva, "my life-breath will vanish instantly. If there were a cessation to the utterance of the name ,of God in my mouth, my tongue will split a thousand-fold. If my eyes were not to see Thy beautiful form, they would come out forcibly from their sockets" (Abg. 49). Through mystical experience, through devotion, through deceipt, through the torments of Samsāra, let the name of God always dance upon the tongue (Abg. 51). There is neither time nor season for the meditation of God. There is neither a high caste nor low in His meditation. He who is the Ocean of love and pity shall come to the succour of all (Abg. 54). The great Śiva was tormented by the poison called Hālāhala, and yet his body became cool when he meditated on God. In the eighteen Purāṇas, says Nāmadeva, the only remedy narrated is the utterance of the Name of God (Abg. 55). The Pāṇḍavas, even though they were enveloped in a house of fire, were saved because they meditated on the name of God. The cow-herds could not be burnt by fire, because they held God in their hearts. Hanumān could not be burnt by fire, because he meditated on the name of Rāma. Fire had no power over Prahlāda, because he constantly uttered the name of God. Sītā was not burnt by fire, because she set her heart upon Raghunātha. The home of Bibhīshaṇa was saved in the holocaust at Laṅkā, says Nāmadeva, because he meditated on the name of God (Abg. 59). The coverings of untruth, which envelop a man's words, shall never depart except through a meditation on God (Abg. 61).

The Name of God is the Form of God, and the Form of God is the Name of God. There is no other remedy except the Name of God, says Nāmadeva, and anybody who says there is another is a fool (Abg. 64). God may remain concealed; but He cannot conceal His name. When we have once uttered His name, He cannot escape from us (Abg. 66). Let the body live or depart, fix your mind upon God. I shall never leave Thy feet, says Nāmadeva, shall keep Thy Name in my mouth, and set my heart aflame with Thy love. I only implore Thee, says Nāmadeva, that Thou shouldst fulfil my resolve (Abg. 67). To be in Samsāra is even a pleasure, when the mind is once set upon God (Abg. 68). Poor Brahmins do not know the secret of realisation. God can be attained by meditation on His name only. I implore the young and the old, says Nāmadeva, to cling fast to the Name of God. In all your religious ceremonies, you should think only of God, and nothing else (Abg. 72). They paint the pictures of the sun or the moon, but they cannot paint the picture of light. They can put on the apparel of a Samnyāsin, but they cannot imitate his dispassion. They may perform a Kīrtana, says Nāmadeva, but they will miss the nature of God-love (Abg. 75). With a Vīṇā in my hand, and with the name of God in my mouth, I shall stand up in the temple of God. I shall renounce all food and water, and shall think of nothing but God. I shall forget my mother, or father, or wife, or children. I shall lose all bodily consciousness, and merge it in the Name of God, says Nāmadeva (Abg. 77). If, in such a condition, Death comes to devour me, I shall sing and dance in joy. My only wish is, says Nāmadeva, that I should serve Thee from life to life (Abg. 80).

Reflections on Social Matters.

3. We have said in a foregoing chapter that one of the uses to which the Abhaṅga was put was for reflection on social matters, as it was also for the purpose of personal devotion. Nāmadeva very often makes use of his Abhaṅgas to discourse on social topics. He tells us that it is impossible that the pursuit of God can be coupled with a life of Samsāra. If it had been possible, he tells us, for a man to find God while he was pursuing Samsāra, then Sanaka and others would not have grown mad after God. If it had been possible for him to see God while carrying on the duties of a house-holder, the great Śuka would not have gone to the forest to seek God. Had it been possible for people to find God in their homes, they would not have left them to find out God. Nāmadeva says that he has left away all these things, and is approaching God in utter submission (Abg. 83). Then, again, he tells us that our one goal should be the vision of God, whatever pursuit we might be undertaking. Children send a kite into the sky with a rope in their hands; but their attention is upon the kite, and not upon the rope. A woman from Gujerath goes with pitcher piled upon pitcher, moving her hands freely, but her attention is riveted upon the pitchers. An unchaste woman has her heart always set upon her lover. A thief sets his heart upon other people's gold. A covetous man has his attention ever directed towards his treasure. We may carry on any pursuit, says Nāmadeva, provided we always think of God (Abg. 85). Then, again, he tells us that it is the consideration of the belly which is paramount with all people in the world. The belly, which is scarcely larger than a span's length, is yet so powerful, says Nāmadeva. It prevents us from treading in the way of the saints. The belly is our mother; the belly our father; the belly our sister and brother. Nāmadeva looks at his belly and asks how long it is going to have sway over him (Abg. 87). We should always think of death, says Nāmadeva, in whatever pursuit we might be engaged. As when a thief is being carried to the hanging place, death is approaching him at every step; as when a man is plying his axe at the root of a tree, its life is diminishing every moment; similarly, whatever we may be doing, we must suppose that death is always approaching us (Abg. 90). Moreover, Nāmadeva tells us that we should be supremely indifferent to dualities like good and evil. All objects of sense should be as indifferent to us, as either a serpent or a beautiful maiden is to a man who has gone to sleep. We should regard dung and gold, or a jewel or a stone, as of equal value. Let the sky come and envelop us, or let cinders be poured on our head, we should not allow our life in Ātman to be disturbed. You may praise us or censure us, says Nāmadeva, we shall always live in the joy of God (Abg. 91). People forget, says Nāmadeva, that their bodily miseries are due to the sins they have committed. Nobody should expect a sweet fruit when he sows a sour seed. From an Arka tree, plantains shall never come out. A pestle can never be bent to the form of an arrow. One may pound stones as he pleases, but never will any juice come out of it. We should not grow wroth with our fate, says Nāmadeva: we should ask ourselves what we have done (Abg. 92). Then, again, Nāmadeva tells us that to pin our faith upon stone-images is a vain pursuit. A stone god and an illusory devotee can never satisfy each other. Such gods have been broken to pieces by the Turks, or have been flung in water, and yet they do not cry. Show me not such deities of iron, says Nāmadeva to God (Abg. 94). Is it not wonderful, asks Nāmadeva, that people should give up the animate, and hold the inanimate as superior to it? They pluck a living Tulsi plant, and with it worship an inanimate stone. They pluck the leaves of Bela, and throw them in numbers upon a liṅgam of Śiva. They kill a living ram, and say they are performing the Soma sacrifice. They besmear a stone with red lead, and children and women fall prostrate before it. The performance of an Agnihotra means death to the Kuśa grass and the Pimpala sticks. People worship a serpent made of mud, but they take cudgels against a living serpent. All these pursuits are vain, says Nāmadeva: the only pursuit of value is the utterance of the Name of God (Abg. 95). Then, Nāmadeva tells us that a beautiful woman is the cause of sorrow, and an ugly woman the cause of happiness; for the one incites love, while the other does not (Abgs. 100, 101). Contact with other women, says Nāmadeva, is the sure cause of ruin. In that way did Rāvaṇa die. In that way was Bhasmāsura reduced to ashes. In that way the Moon became consumptive. In that way, Indra had his body covered with a thousand holes (Abg. 102). It is only then, says Nāmadeva, that we may talk of dispassionateness, when we are not attacked by the arrows of a woman's eyes. It is only then, says Nāmadeva, that we may talk of Self-knowledge, when anger and love do not spring up within us. It is only then, says Nāmadeva, that we may talk of absence of egoism, when our self is not censured (Abg. 103). Finally, Nāmadeva tells us how it is difficult to find the following pairs together: gold and fragrance, diamond and softness, a Yogin and purity; a talking god, a moving wish-tree, and a milch-elephant; a rich man with compassion, a tiger with mercy, and fire with coolness; a beautiful woman who is chaste, a hearer who is attentive, and a preacher who knows; a Kshatriya who is grave, a sandal tree covered with flowers, and a handsome man who is virtuous. Nāmadeva tells us that it is impossible to find such pairs in life (Abg. 106).

The Characteristics of Saints.

4. The characteristics of the Saints, says Nāmadeva, are manifold. Him alone we may call a saint, says Nāmadeva, who sees God in all beings; who looks upon gold as a clod of earth; who looks upon a jewel as a mere stone; who has driven out of his heart anger and passion; who harbours peace and forgiveness in his mind;

whose speech is given merely to the utterance of God's name (Abg. 108). As trees do not know honour and dishonour, as they are equal to those who worship them and those who cut them, similarly, the saints in their supreme courage look upon honour and dishonour alike (Abg. 109). That is the supreme Law of Saint-hood, says Nāmadeva, which regards as necessary a perfect belief in the efficacy of God's name, and which requires us to eradicate all our other desires (Abg. 110). He alone, we may say, has reached ecstasy, who looks upon honour and dishonour alike. He alone is the beloved of God, who looks upon friend and enemy alike. He alone is the king of Yogins who looks upon gold and a portion of mud with equal eye. Such a one is a great purifying power, and makes all the three worlds pure by his presence (Abg. 111). The very gods worship the water of his feet. A mere remembrance of him puts an end to all sin (Abg. 114). Nāmadeva tells us that a Saint is a spiritual washerman. He applies the soap of illumination, washes on the slab of tranquillity, purifies in the river of knowledge, and takes away the spots of sin (Abg. 115). Fie upon that place, says Nāmadeva, where there is no company of the saints. Fie upon that wealth and progeny, which is not given to the worship of the saints. Fie upon that thought and life, wherein there is no worship of God. Fie upon that song, and fie upon that learning, which is not given to the name of God. Fie upon that life which does not make God its sole aim (Abg. 120). There is one way, says Nāmadeva, to reach God, namely, that we should go and take resort with the saints ; for when we have worshipped the saints, we shall certainly see God. God always serves His saints, and holds aloft His yellow garment to protect His devotees from sun (Abg. 121). If we cling to the feet of the saints, says Nāmadeva, we shall be relieved of all suffering. If we serve at their door, we shall be relieved of all infatuation. If we partake of their " prasāda ", our life-span shall increase. The saints are an ocean of mercy, says Nāmadeva, and they bestow upon us knowledge, devotion, and love (Abg. 122). Those who have seen God, says Nāmadeva, lose all sense of false shame. For them exist no duties of caste and colour. They are forever filled with the joy of unitive life. We should ask of only one favour from God ; namely, that we should be the pollen on the feet of such saints (Abg. 124). He alone is a Saint, says Nāmadeva, who is able to show God. How fortunate am I, he exclaims, that I have been able to see Him in the company of such Saints (Abg. 125) ! Without the favour of these Saints, the secret of spiritual life does not reach our hands. The names of God are various; but unless the saints confer favour upon us, we shall not know how to meditate on the name of God (Abg. 127). We can take hold of a ray of light and walk thereon to heaven; but we cannot know the full significance of the company of the saints. We can go to the nether world and cross the highest ocean; but we cannot know the value of the company of the saints (Abg. 128). A Chātaka bird shall not ask for all kinds of water; the waters on the surface of the earth have no value for it. A Cuckoo shall not sing at all times; it will sing only when the spring sets in. A Peacock shall not dance before anybody and everybody; it is only when the rain-cloud is rumbling, that it will begin to dance. The Eagle can say that it shall serve nobody except God; similarly, Nāmadeva implores God not to make him dependent upon anybody except Him (Abg. 130). Finally, says Nāmadeva, there have been various types of men who have played the game of spiritual life. Is it not wonderful that where there was nothing, the form of God began to take shape? That which was formless in a while became formful. One Brahmin child ran away from the game to hide itself for twelve years in a forest. A six-faced boy took shelter in a mountain. A four-faced youth called Nārāyaṇa was a stalwart player. Hanumān was a wise man among these stalwart players, for he did not give himself up to the life of sex. One Gopāla, born in the family of the Yādavas, played his game in manifold ways: ultimately he killed all, threw away the sport, and himself went away. Myriads of such players have there been, says Nāmadeva (Abg. 134); but we should play the game which would suit us best.

The Spiritual Experience of Namadeva.

5. Nāmadeva supposes that the faculty of God-realisation is a God-given gift. A cow gives birth to a calf in a forest: who sends the calf, asks Nāmadeva, to the udders of the cow? Who teaches the young one of a serpent the art of biting? A Mogarā flower stands of itself at the top of the creeper: who teaches it to be fragrant? Even if we manure a bitter gourd-creeper with sugar and milk, it makes the fruits of the gourd more bitter still. A sugar-cane shall never leave its sweetness, if it is cut to pieces, or even if it is swallowed. Similarly, says Nāmadeva, the faculty of realising God is a native faculty, and by that alone will one be able to realise God (Abg. 135). When we have once seen God, it matters little to what place we go. As soon as we remember God, God shall be near us (Abg. 137). We shall forget our hunger and thirst in the pleasure of God's Name. God, who is the source of immortality, is in the heart of

Nāmadeva, and Nāmadeva therefore enjoys continued beatification (Abg. 139). There is only one favour that we should ask of God: that we should always think of Him in our heart; that we should always utter His name by our mouth; that we should always see Him with our eyes; that our hands should worship only Him; that our head be placed always at His feet; that our ears should only hear of God's exploits; that He should show Himself always to our right and to our left, before and after, and at the end of our life. We should ask God of no other favour except this (Abg. 140). As Nāmadeva began to see God, he found Him in all corners, and in all directions (Abg. 141). God's form can be seen even by a blind man, and a dumb man can communicate even in a deaf man's ears the knowledge of God. An ant shall devour the whole universe by its mouth, says Nāmadeva. Only we shall have to verify all these things in our own experience (Abg. 142). When the Unstruck Sound springs out of the thousand-petalled lotus and when God's name is uttered, sins shall depart and hide themselves in a cavern. Keep yourself awake in the meditation on God. Your sins will depart at the utterance of God's name, and God will give you a secure lodgment in His abode (Abg. 143). In another place, also, Nāmadeva speaks of sins being destroyed by God's name. A single utterance of the name of God creates panic among sins. As soon as God's name is uttered, the divine recorder ceases to record. God Himself comes forth to receive His devotee with materials of worship. If this were to turn out false, says Nāmadeva, then may his head be cut off from his body (Abg. 144). Indeed, Nāmadeva tells us how God is filled with happiness at the singing of His praise. As we sit down and sing the praise of God, God stands before us. As in devotion we stand up and call on the name of God, God dances before us. God indeed loves his Kīrtana so much that He forthwith comes to the succour of His devotees in the midst of difficulties (Abg. 145). We have experienced joy, says Nāmadeva, a thousand-fold of what we have witnessed in the Divali holidays. There has been a waving of lights in every house, and we have seen God Vitthala with our eyes. His presence has filled us with joy. Utter now the name of God. As the Lord of Nāmadeva came, the very gods were filled with delight (Abg. 146). Nāmadeva in one place describes his experience when he saw God. Light as brilliant as that of a thousand Suns shone forth at once from the heavens. The saints told Nāmadeva that God was coming. God indeed did come to Nāmadeva as a cow goes to its calf. All the ten quarters were filled by the inroads of the Eagle. A garland of flowers was released from the neck of God, and came to the earth. God's disc moved with Him in order to protect His devotee. God lifted up Nāmadeva with both of His hands, and clasped him to His bosom (Abg. 147). He alone, says Nāmadeva, can be awake who has a determined faith in the words of his teacher. What lamp can we light in order to see our Self ? He, who gives light to the sun and the moon, cannot Himself be seen by any other light. There is neither east nor west in Him; neither north nor south. As an ocean at the time of the Great End might fill the universe, similarly, God fills the universe for one who has experienced Him (Abg. 148). And as such a one goes to the sleep of ecstasy, the twelve and sixteen damsels wave the fans before him. The devotee keeps awake in Self-illumination. Trumpets sound forth. Untold varieties of unstruck sound emerge. There is then neither sleep nor dream. The very Sun and the Moon set before that Illumination (Abg. 149). It is only God who can know the love of His devotee in this manner. He always does reside with His devotee. Nāmadeva tells us that he was so filled with God-experience, that he thought that he was God, and that God was himself (Abg. 150).

The Teachings of Gora.

6. Gorā, the potter, who tested the spirituality of the Saints at the time of Jñānadeva and Nāmadeva, found, it is well known, that Nāmadeva was an unbaked pot. But when Nāmadeva came to know the real secret of spiritual life, Gorā Kumbhāra was satisfied, and told him that thenceforth there was no distinction between him and Nāmadeva. He told Nāmadeva that his own Form had been fixed in his eye, and that all his realisation was centred in the pupil of his eyes (Abg. 1). Gorā also tells us that as he began to look at the sky, he felt as if happiness had gone to meet happiness (Abg. 2). He tells us furthermore that he heard the unstruck sound, and that it was proclaiming the voice of victory. The very Vedas describe the nature of God as neither this nor that, and stand motionless before this perpetual sound. Gorā, the potter, advises Nāmadeva to continually partake of this ambrosial juice of ecstasy (Abg. 3). The Potter also tells us that in the contemplation of God, he felt as if he had gone mad. He tells us how he had lost all sense of body. By the primeval form of God having taken possession of him, he felt as if he was possessed by a spirit. Henceforth, it was impossible for him to be besmeared with the mud of action, or even with virtue or sin. He lived, he tells us, as one who was emancipated even during life—a Jīvanmukta (Abg. 4). We also know from Gorā that his mind became mute, and that the bliss of experience transcended all bounds. The eyes, unable to see their object, turned upon themselves, and remained motionless. Gorā tells us that one can enjoy the bliss of experience only in mystic silence (Abg. 5). Just as a dumb man cannot express the sweetness of the sugar he is eating, similarly, by our bliss we enjoy bliss, and in that way attain to emancipation even during life. Finally, he warns us not to let the world know of this state. They do not deserve, says Gorā, to be taught the secret of spiritual life (Abg. 6).

The Teachings of Visoba.

7. Visobā, the teacher of Nāmadeva, tells Nāmadeva, that if he boasts that he has seen God, it is merely false knowledge. It would not be possible for any one to meet God until one's egoism is at an end (Abg. 1). Our bliss is with ourselves; it does not lie in any external object. If we possess merely discrimination and dispassion, the way is open for us to know God (Abg. 2). By the contemplation of God, mountains of sins shall be reduced to ashes. By the contemplation of God, the evils of Samsāra shall come to an end. Visobā advises Nāmadeva that he should consider himself fortunate if he obtains the clue to this spiritual pathway (Abg. 3). Finally, we learn from Khechara that for him all land and water, all stones and trees, beings from the very ant to the highest Being, seemed to have been filled with God. The whole world is God, says Khechara to Nāmadeva. He uttered these words in Nāmadeva's ears, placed his hand upon the head of Nāmadeva, relieved him from the duality of existence, and brought him to oneness with himself. Visobā, who was mad with joy, tells us how it was from Jñānadeva that he had himself received spiritual illumination, and how he communicated the secret of his spiritual life to Nāmadeva (Abg. 4).

The Teachings of Samvata.

8. Sāmvatā, the gardener, was so filled with the presence of God that he found Him all-pervading in the garden where he was working all his life. Garlic, Chilly, and Onion are all my God. The water-bag, the rope, and the well are all enveloped by my God. Sāmvatā is cultivating a garden and has placed his head on the feet of Viṭṭhala. The one supplication that he makes to God is that He should relieve him of Samsāra. The only thing he asks of God, says Sāmvatā, is that He should bereave him of all his progeny (Abg. 1). Very well it was, that I was born in a low caste, and very well it is that I have not attained to greatness. Had I been born a Brāhmaṇa, I would have given myself over to rituals and ceremonies. Placed as I am, I have neither ablutions to make, nor Sandhyā to perform. Born in a low caste, I can only ask for Thy compassion, says Sāmvatā (Abg. 2). Sāmvatā furthermore tells us that we should behave alike in pleasure and sorrow. One day we may ride an elephant, or move through a palanquin; another, we may walk barefooted. One day there may be no corn at home to live upon; another, wealth may be so plentiful that one may not know where to preserve it. One day the God of Death may come and we may go to the cemetery; another, our spiritual teacher might take compassion on us, and the Father of Sāmvatā may show Himself to him (Abg. 4). Sāmvatā also tells us as to how his eyes had once been full-blown, and his hands out-stretched, and how his heart was full of humility. At that time, Jñānadeva and Nāmadeva were passing by his garden. But God went inside the garden, placed His hand upon the head of Sāmvatā, brought him to his senses, and with His four hands embraced him. At that time, Sāmvatā requested God to sit by him, so that he might worship Him (Abg. 5). Finally, he has as much belief in the efficacy of the Name as the other Saints. He tells us that by the power of God's name, one may bid good-bye to all feeling of fear, and deal a blow on the head of Death. By the power of God's name, one can bring God from heaven to earth, and sing and dance in His praise. Sāmvatā thus implores all people to follow the path of Bhakti: for God is surely attained by Bhakti, says Sāmvatā (Abg. 6).

The Teachings of Narahari.

9. Narahari, the goldsmith, is so convinced about the unreality of the world that he regards it as merely a picture drawn upon a wall. As children build houses of stone and then throw them down, similarly, do people engage themselves in worldly life, and then take leave of it (Abg. 1). He tells us that his waywardness was controlled only by his Guru. As an elephant may be controlled by an Ankuśa, as a terrible tiger may be pent up within a cage as the poison of a serpent can be controlled by means of a Mantra or the root of a tree, similarly, Narahari was brought under control by Gaibinātha (Abg. 2). The unstruck sound is forever sounding in my ears, and my mind has been captivated by it. By means of the unstruck sound, think always upon God, and meditate upon Him in your heart. That will endow you with true love of God, and show you His pathway, as it did Narahari (Abg. 4). Finally, we learn from Narahari how he carried on his business of a goldsmith even in his spiritual life. Narahari calls himself a goldsmith who deals in the name of God. He makes his body the melting vessel of the soul, which is the gold therein. In the matrix of the three Gunas, he pours the juice of God. Hammer in hand, he breaks to pieces anger and passion. With the scissors of discrimination, he cuts away the golden leaf of the name of God. With the balance of illumination, he weighs the name of God. He bears the sack of gold on his shoulders, and carries it to the other end of the stream. Narahari, the goldsmith, who is a devotee of God, gives himself night and day to the contemplation of God's name (Abg. 5).

The Teachings of Chokha.

10. Chokhā, the untouchable, tells God that people say to him, "get away, get away". How, then, would it be possible for him to meet Him (Abg. 1)? He implores God to have compassion on him, and to come to him at no slow pace. The worshippers of the temple beat me for no fault of mine. They asked me how it was that I came by the garland on the bosom of the Deity. They abused me and said, that I had polluted God. I am verily a dog at Thy door, says Chokhā; send me not away to another man's door (Abg. 2). Chokhā is convinced that the real Pandharī is his own body, that his soul is the deity Vitthala therein. Tranquillity plays the part of Rukmiṇī, says Chokhā. Contemplating God in this fashion, he says, he clings to the feet of God (Abg. 3). He tells us that a sugar-cane may be crooked, and yet its juice is not crooked. A bow may be curved, and yet the arrow is not curved. A river may have windings, and yet the water has no windings. Chokhā may be untouchable, but his heart is not untouchable (Abg. 4). He tells us, furthermore, that if God were to endow him with a son, he should endow him with one who would become a saint. If God were to endow him with a daughter, she should be like either Mirābāī or Muktābāī. If it would not please God to give him offspring in this manner, it would be much better that He should take all offspring from him (Abg. 5). Chokhā tells us that while we are engaged in the Name of God, we need have no cause for fear, or anxiety. The most wicked persons on the earth should come to this place to get themselves purified, says Chokhā, and sounds his drum (Abg. 6). Chokhā and his wife were sure of the presence of God within their house. Chokhā tells us that God had come to his house to partake of dinner with him. He spreads before Him various kinds of sweet dishes, and requests Him to take His meals with him (Abg. 7). The wife of Chokhā tells God that even though the food that she gives Him is not worthy of Him, yet He may be gracious enough to partake of it to His heart's content. She asks God whether He did not partake of the fluid rice in the house of Vidura, and whether He was not satisfied with merely a leaf of the vegetable which Draupadī had given Him. Similarly, she implores Him to take His meals with them (Abg. 8).

The Teachings of Janabai.

11. Janābāī's place among the spiritual poetesses of Mahārāshṭra is just next to that of Muktābāī. As Muktābāī derived her poetic inspiration from Jñānadeva, similarly, Janābāī derived hers from Nāmadeva. She tells us that as a fly in the vanity of pleasure falls upon the flame of a lamp, similarly, people in this life fall upon sensual pleasures in order to kill themselves. In this life, we should live as if we were the shadows of our body (Abg. 2). We should surpass the earth in forgiveness, be milder than butter, and lighter than a flower (Abg. 3). The weapon of a warrior, the treasure of a miser, the pearl on the temples of an elephant, the hood of a serpent, the nails of a lion, the breasts of a chaste woman, these shall never come to our hands. Similarly, unless we take leave of all egoism, God shall not come to our hands (Abg. 4). The only source of happiness in this life is betaking oneself to the Spiritual Teacher. We should hand him over all our wealth and body and mind, and take from him in exchange the form of God. This will not come to our vision without the grace of the Spiritual Teacher. It is already inside us ; but we do not know that this is so. We wave a rosary of beads, and mutter numbers of prayers ; but He who makes us wave the rosary, and inspires us with the saying of prayers, Him we do not know even though He is inside our hearts. He alone is the Spiritual Teacher, says Janābāī, who can show the Ātman directly to our vision (Abg. 5). Bhakti is indeed like a pit of cinders, or like a deep place in a river which is hard to approach. It is like a morsel of poison, or like the sharp edge of a sword. To be a real Bhakta, says Janābāī, is as difficult as any of the above things (Abg. 6). As a bird may go to roam in the sky and still think of its young one, or as a mother may be engaged in the house-hold duties and yet may think of her child, or as a she-monkey may leap from tree to tree and yet may clasp its young one to her bosom, similarly, says Janābāī, we should always think of Vitthala. Occasionally, she grows wroth with Viṭṭhala, and even goes to the length of abusing Him. Viṭhyā, Viṭhyā, Thou art the spoilt child of the Primeval Māyā. Thy wife has become a courtesan. Thy body is dead. Janābāī stands in the court-yard of her house, and abuses Thee right and left (Abg. 10). It is only when we pen Viṭṭhala within the prison of our heart, enchain Him with the power of the Name, beat Him with the lash of Self-identity, that Viṭṭhala will cry piteously, and ask to be discharged for life (Abg. 11). Occasionally, Janābāī tells us that it was on account of the company of Nāmadeva that she was able to know Viṭṭhala. As in the company of the bride-groom, people get dishes of all kinds, similarly, in the company of Nāmadeva, Janābāī has earned God (Abg. 12). First, there is a red circle, says Janābāī, above which there is a white one, beyond that is a dark-blue circle, and finally there is a full blue circle. Janābāī is greatly struck, she tells us, by hearing the unstruck sound (Abg. 13). She is entirely unable to describe the great flame of light which shines before her (Abg. 14). As she looks at God, she sees Him to her right and left, above and below, and in all quarters (Abg. 16). The form of God came upon Janābāī like a flood, by looking at which, Janābāī unconsciously shut her eyes (Abg. 17). Her weariness departed, her sin and torment were at an end. Where there is the Name of God, there can happen no calamity (Abg. 18). Janābāī tells us that a great miracle took place in the company of her Guru. The camphor was burnt, and no soot came out of it; the sugar was sown, and the sugar-cane was taken out; the ear became the eye; an old woman was married to a child husband. This was the great wonder, she says, which she saw with her eyes, and which she could not explain (Abg. 20). Whatever desires she had harboured in her heart were fulfilled by God. He finally gave her a place in His own abode (Abg. 21). As the form of God became firmly fixed in Janābāī's mind, her bodily condition changed. Passion and attachment took leave of her. As Janābāī began to see, she saw that God Viṭṭhala was standing at her door (Abg. 22). She tells us that she ate God, and drank God; that she slept on God; that she gave God and took God; that God was here, and God was there; that there was no place which was not filled by God, either inside or outside (Abg. 23). As she began to sweep the floor of Nāmadeva's house, God came and took the refuse in a basket. He became so infatuated, that He began to do even mean work for her (Abg. 25). As God danced on mud with the potter Gorā, as He talked with Kabīra while the latter was weaving cloth, as He drove away the cows and buffaloes of the untouchable Chokhā, similarly, He now began to grind in the company of Janābāī, seeing which, she tells us, even the gods were pleased (Abg. 26). He who is befriended by God, becomes an object of favour for the whole world. God sees that such a devotee lacks nothing, and He takes on Himself the duty of protecting him in calamities. He does not stay away from His devotee even for a single moment, and on critical occasions, invariably lends His helping hand (Abg. 30).

The Teachings of Sena.

12. Senā, the barber, has no compromise with the evil-doers. He tells us that we should by all means dishonour the wicked, deal kicks to them, and drive them away. He who lives in the company of wicked men, says Senā, lives in perdition (Abg. 1). Like other saints, he also believes in the great efficacy of the Name. One does not require to inhale smoke, or to sit in the midst of the five fires. One has merely to make his mind calm, and with a concentrated attention sing the praises of God (Abg. 2). There is no other remedy except this, says Senā. God will surely come, and relieve His devotee. He makes no consideration of caste or quality. He runs at once to the cause of those who love Him (Abg. 3). One need not go to mountains and forests. If one goes to the forest, he would be deceived, as Vibhāṇḍaka was deceived by a damsel. Knowing this, Senā sat where he was, and sent his submission to God (Abg. 4). He implores God to relieve him of his sins. I am a great evil-doer, says Senā. I have harboured passion and anger; I have not cared for the company of the good; nor have I meditated on God. I have censured those who have believed in God. I have entertained passion for wealth. Senā is a statue of sin incarnate, and bends in submission before God (Abg. 5). Blessed am I, he tells us, that I have seen Thy feet. All my previous merit has borne its fruit (Abg. 7). To-day is a day of gold, says Senā, that he has seen the Saints (Abg. 9). The child of the powerful is itself powerful. All our sins will be forgiven us by our Father. Senā sits under the shade of the wish-tree, and bears compassion towards all (Abg. 10). Senā describes how he was given to the art of shaving even in spiritual life. We are greatly skilled in the art of shaving, says Senā. We show the mirror of discrimination, and use the pinches of dispassion. We apply the water of tranquillity to the head, and screw out the hair of egotism. We take away the nails of passion, and are a support to all the four castes, says Senā (Abg. 11). In two of his Abhaṅgas, Senā informs us that he departed from this life at midday on the 12th of the dark half of Srāvaṇa (Abgs. 12, 13).

The Teachings of Kanhopatra.

13. Kānhopātrā, the beautiful daughter of a dancing woman of Maṅgaḷavedhā, tells us that it is bad pursuit to follow the path of sensual pleasure. Indra's body became verily perforated; Bhasmāsura was reduced to ashes; the Moon bears the sinful spots on her body; Rāvaṇa lost his life, because he gave himself to carnal pleasure (Abg. 1). I am verily an outcast, says Kānhopātrā. I do not know the rules of conduct. I only know how to approach Thee in submission (Abg. 2). Thou callest Thyself the reliever of the fallen. Why dost Thou not lift me up? I have once called myself Thine. If I am now obliged to call myself another's, on whom would the blame rest? If a jackal were to take away the food of a lion, who would be blamed, asks Kānhopātrā (Abg. 3)? This Abhaṅga she probably composed when she was invited by the Mahomedan king of Bedar to visit his court. When she saw the image of Viṭṭhala, she says, it seemed as if her spiritual merit had reached its consummation. Happy am I, she says, that I have seen Thy feet (Abg. 4). The very God of Death would be terrified if we utter the Name of God. Ajāmeḷa, Vālmīki, and even a Courtesan have been lifted up by the Name of God. Kānhopātrā tells us that she wears the garland of God's Names (Abg. 5).

CHAPTER IX.

General Review.

There are certain characteristics which mark off the saints of this period from the saints who belong either to the earlier or the later period in the development of Mahārāshṭra Mysticism. In the first place, these mystics are cosmopolitans. They recognise a spiritual democracy all round. Prof. W. B. Patwardhan has well described the democracy of the Bhakti school, as represented in Nāmadeva and his contemporaries: "The gates of the Bhakti school were ever open. Whoever entered was hailed as a brother—nay more—was honoured as a saint. He was addressed as a 'Santa'. All were 'Santas' that gathered round and under the Garuḍaṭakā, the flag with the eagle blazoned on it, with Ṭāḷa or cymbals in hand, and the name of Viṭṭhala on the tongue. The very atmosphere was sacred and holy. The breath of Heaven played freely, and all were equal there. Love—true—genuine—pure love admits not of high and low, rich and poor; all is one and equal. All separatist tendencies vanished; the haughty isolation of Pride, of Heredity, of Tradition melted away, and all were but men, human, weak, frail, feeble, lame, and blind, calling on the same strength, seeking the same love, hoping the same hope, dreaming the same dream, and seeing the same vision. Before Viṭhobā or Dattātreya, or Nāganātha—call him by any name—all were equal. Age and sex, caste and class, breathed not in this equalising air. In the joy of Love, in the bliss of the service of the Lord, in the dance round the Flag of devotion—all were inspired with the same fire; they ate of the same dish, drank of the same well, bathed in the same Chandrabhāgā or Krishṇā or Godā or Bāṇagangā, lay on the same sands, and waked to the same dawn. For five successive centuries, Mahārāshṭra was the abode of that noblest and truest of all Democracies, the Democracy of the Bhakti school." In the second place, all these saints are characterised by a contrition of the heart, by the helplessness of human endeavour to reach unaided the majesty of God, by a sense of sinfulness inherent to human nature, by the necessity of finding out a Guru who may relieve them from the sufferings of the world, and finally, by the phenomena of conversion almost in every individual case. Each saint indeed has an individuality of his own even in his spiritual development. In the third place, it seems as if the mystics of this period show an all-absorbing love of God, which would not allow a rightful performance of one's duties before God-absorption. It is true that these saints show that God could be realised in any walk of life; but they also show that God is a very jealous God, who would not allow any love to be given to any other object beside Himself. The tailor, the barber, the maid-servant, the gardener, the sweeper, the potter, the goldsmith, even the nautch-girl, could all realise God in their different stations of life. But as to whether they could continue in a rightful performance of their duties in the state of God-realisation is a different question. It seems that these saints gave themselves up to God-love, and forgot everything else before it. The conflict between a rightful performance of duty and an all-absorbing love of God has existed at all times and in all countries. But it seems that the saints of this period inclined the beam in the latter rather than in the former direction, and exhibited the all-absorbing character of God-realisation. God indeed is an all-devourer, and it seems from the example of these saints that He devours also the performance of one's own natural duties. The saints of the age we shall consider in our next section show rather the opposite tendency, namely, the tendency of making compatible the love of God and the rightful performance of Duty. Janārdana Swāmī was a saint, while he was yet a fighter. Ekanātha was a saint, while he was yet a householder. We shall see as we proceed to consider the lives and teachings of these saints in the next part of this work how this conflict is resolved in a synthetic performance of Duty in the midst of God-realisation.

PART III.

The Age of Ekanatha : Synthetic Mysticism.

CHAPTER X.

Biographical Introduction: Bhanudasa, Janardana Swami and Ekanatha.

Bhanudasa.

1. Bhānudāsa, the great-grandfather of Ekanātha, was born at Paithana in 1448 A.D. (Śake 1370). His son was Chakrapāṇi. Chakrapāṇi's son was Sūryanārāyaṇa, and Sūryanārāyana's son was Ekanātha. Bhānudāsa was a Deśastha Brahmin, and was probably a contemporary of the saint Dāmājipant. This latter saint must have lived either about 1458 A.D. (Śake 1380), or about 1468 A.D. to 1475 A.D. (Śake 1390 to 1397), the two dates of the dire famine in the Deccan. Bhānudāsa himself must have experienced this famine. When he was about ten years of age, Bhānudāsa was rebuked by his father for mischievous conduct. He, therefore, went to a desolate temple outside Paiṭhaṇa, remained there for seven days, and worshipped the God Sun, for which he was called Bhānu-dāsa. Bhānudāsa is reported to have brought back the image of Viṭṭhala from Hampi, where Krishnarāya had taken it. The Abhaṅga which Bhānudāsa composed at this critical moment of his life at Vijayanagar might well be taken as a motto of God-love by all Saints :—

जरी हें आकाश वर पडों पाहे । ब्रह्मगोळ भंगा जाय ।
वडवानळ त्रिभुवन खाय । तरी मी तुझीच वास पाहीन गा विठोबा ॥

From the temple of Vijayaviṭṭhala at Hampi whose remains could be seen even to-day, we do not know definitely whether Kṛishṇarāya had actually taken the image of Viṭṭhala to that place, or whether he had merely erected a building where he might later carry the image from Pandharapūr and establish it finally. At present the temple of Vijayaviṭṭhala presents a desolate, though an architectural, appearance. It is a good temple without any image inside it, though it is known by the name of "Vijayavitthala" temple. It is not unlikely, that, as Pandharapūr must have suffered from the ravages of the Mahomedans, the image of Viṭhoba of Pandharapūr was in danger of being ill-handled by the invaders, and hence a Hindu king like Kṛishnarāya, the king of Vijayanagar, might have thought it fit to take away the image from a zone of danger to a place where it might be safely lodged ; and it is not unlikely, again, that he might have handed the image back to a Saint like Bhānudāsa, when there was no longer any danger of its being ill-handled by the Mahomedans. In any case, it seems that the bringing back of the idol, from Vijayanagar to Paṇḍharapūr was the great achievement of the life of Bhānudāsa. With Bhānudāsa and his successors, the third epoch of the development of the Sāmpradāya of Paṇḍharapūr began. The first was evidently that of Jñānadeva ; the second of Nāmadeva and his contemporary saints ; the third of Bhānudāsa and his successors, Janārdana Swāmī, and Ekanātha. Bhānudāsa is reported to have entered Samādhi in 1513 A.D. (Śake 1435).

Janardana Swami.

2. Janārdana Swāmī, the teacher of Ekanātha, was born in 1504 A.D. (Śake 1426) at Chaḷisgaon. He was a Deśastha Brahmin by birth. He tells us how he led an immoral life at the beginning, and how he was later converted from that life to a spiritual life by the grace of Nṛisimha-sarasvatī whom he met under the Audumbara tree at Ankalakop on the river of Kṛishṇā. This place could be met with even to-day in the Satārā District. Nṛisimhasarasvati was a very great saint. The three sacred places which are known after him are Narasobāvāḍī, Audumbara, and Gaṇagāpūr. When this Saint was at Ankalakop, Janārdanaswāmī went to see him, and was initiated by him into the spiritual life. He was later appointed Killedāra of Devagaḍa by a Mahomedan king. He was a statesman also. He devoted himself to the service of God, while he was doing his worldly duties. He was a type for Ekanātha Swāmī for a combination of worldly and spiritual life. He was respected by the Mahomedans and the Hindus alike, and every Thursday which was sacred to the God of Janārdana Swāmī was proclaimed a holiday at Devagaḍa by the order of the Mahomedan king. Janārdana Swāmī died in 1575 A.D. (Śake 1497) at Devagaḍa or Daulatābad, where his Samādhi could be seen even to-day inside a cave on the hill.

Date of Ekanatha.

3. The dates of Ekanātha's birth vary. Messrs. Sahasrabuddhe and Bhāve took the date of Ekanātha's birth to be 1548 A.D. (Śake 1470). Mr. Pāngārakar in his earlier edition of his Life of Ekanātha, took it to be 1528 A.D. (Śake 1450), while in the second edition, he modified this to 1533 A.D. (Śake 1455), which Mr. Bhāve later accepted. Similarly about the date of Ekanātha's passing away. It was long taken to be 1609 A.D. (Śake 1531), for example, by Mr. Sahasrabuddhe. But Mr. Pāngārakar has shown it to be 1599 A.D. (Śake 1521). It thus seems that there is yet some difference of opinion about the exact dates of the birth and death of Ekanātha. On the whole, we may say that the period from 1533 A.D. to 1599 A.D. (Śake 1455 to 1521) may be taken as the most probable period of the life of Ekanātha. Ekanātha thus seems to have passed away at the age of sixty-six.

Ekanatha's Life.

4. Ekanātha was born at Paiṭhaṇa of Sūryanārāyana and Rukmiṇībāī, both of whom unfortunately died while Ekanātha was yet a baby. Hence Ekanātha was brought up by his grandfather and grandmother. He was of a very calm disposition, and was devoted to God from his very childhood. He had a very keen intellect, and was fond of reading stories and mythologies and the lives of the Saints. He was also given to meditate on the stories he had heard in a temple of Śiva outside Paiṭhaṇa. Once upon a time, while he was only twelve, he heard a voice saying that there lived a saint called Janārdanapant on Devagaḍa, and that he should get himself initiated by him. Ekanātha thereupon went to Devagaḍa of his own accord, without taking the permission of his guardians. The date of the first meeting of Ekanātha and Janārdana Swāmī was formerly given by Mr. Pāngārakar to be 1540 A.D. (Śake 1462); but with a change in his date about Ekanātha's birth, he has also altered the date of Ekanātha's first meeting with his Guru to 1545 A.D. (Śake 1467). In any case, it seems that Ekanātha went to Janārdana Swāmī while he was yet only twelve. He devoted himself to an absolutely disinterested service of his Spiritual Teacher. He studied the Jñāneśvarī, and the Amṛitānubhava with Janārdana Swāmī. He was once asked by Janārdana Swāmī to examine certain accounts, when he was very glad to find that his disciple had after a long vigil detected the error which he was seeking. Ekanātha was instructed by Janārdana Swāmī to perform a like subtle meditation on God on a hill behind Devagaḍa. Ekanātha lived with his spiritual teacher for six years, during which period Ekanātha attained to God-vision. While Janārdana Swāmī was once engaged in meditation, the enemy raided Devagaḍa, but Ekanātha successfully warded off the attack by putting on the coat-of-mail of Janārdana Swāmī. Later, Ekanātha was ordered by Janārdana Swāmī to go on a pilgrimage, and after returning, to go to Paiṭhaṇa, meet his own grandfather and grandmother, marry, and live a householder's life while also leading a life of meditation. Ekanātha successfully did all these things. On his return from the pilgrimage, he was married to a girl from Bijapur called Girijābāī. Ekanātha's married life never stood in the way of his devotion. It is true that he tells us in his Chirañjīvapada that one should not sit among women, one should not look at women, one should not get himself shampooed by women, one should not speak with women, one should not allow the company of women in solitude (30—31). But he also tells us that this rule applies to other women beside one's own wife. One should never give these a place in one's presence. One should never have anything to do with these, and even while one's own wife is concerned, one should call, and touch, and speak to her only as much as is necessary. But we should never allow our mind to be filled with the idea of even our own wife (33—34). The rule of Ekanātha's life was the rule of moderation. His daily spiritual routine was regularly and strictly practised. He rose up at the same hour, devoted himself to spiritual pursuits at the same hour, and went to rest at the same hour. After having got up before dawn and spent some time in spiritual meditation, he would go to the river to bathe in the waters, and after return devote himself to the reading of the Bhāgavata and the Bhagavadgītā ; then receive guests for his midday meals ; then in the afternoon deliver a discourse on the Bhāgavata or the Jñāneśvarī ; spend his time in meditation in the evening ; then perform a Kīrtana at night, and after that go to rest. This was the constant rule of his life, which he never allowed to break. His life was a manifestation as to how a man of real God-realisation should live in worldly life. His patience, his tranquillity, his angerlessness, his sense of equality all around were beyond description. His behaviour with a Mahomedan who spat on his body successively as he was returning from his river bath, his feeding of the untouchables on a Śrāddha occasion, his giving the draught of the holy waters of the Godāvarī which he was bringing to an ass, his purification and spiritual upliftment of a concubine, the reception which he gave to thieves when they broke into his house, his raising of an untouchable boy and carrying him to his mother, his calm and silent behaviour with his son Haripandit who was intoxicated with knowledge and who scarcely knew at first the value of spiritual life, are all indications of the way in which a man of perfect realisation should live in the world. While he was thus pursuing his spiritual life in the midst of worldly life, he once suffered from a throat-disease, as we have pointed out in our Jñānadeva chapter, and was told in his dream by

Jñānadeva that the disease would disappear only when he had taken away the root of the Ajāna tree which had encircled his neck in the Samādhi at Āḷandī; whereupon Ekanātha tells us that he went to Āḷandī, took away the root as directed, and found an inspiration for the reform of the text of the Jñāneśvarī, which he successfully achieved in 1584 A.D. (Śake 1506). Ekanātha has benefited the world as much by his own independent works as by his editing of the text of the Jñāneśvarī. Ekanātha took Samādhi at Paiṭhaṇa in 1599 A.D. (Śake 1521) without allowing any break to occur in his daily spiritual routine, which was the greatest test of his constancy of purpose and the reality and value of spiritual life.

Ekanatha's Works.

5. Ekanātha's literary work was great and voluminous. He has left behind a vast amount of spiritual literature. His commentary on the 11th chapter of the Bhāgavata is his most classical production. Next in order of merit is his Bhāvārtha Rāmāyaṇa which, Ekanātha tells us, he was inspired to write. Ekanātha left it at the 44th chapter of the Yuddhakāṇḍa, and Gāvabā, one of his disciples, later finished it. The Marriage of Rukmiṇī is also another of Ekanātha's great works, showing the very pure love of Rukmiṇī for Kṛishṇa, and *vice versa*. The Abhaṅgas of Ekanātha are also of established value, inasmuch as they constitute a peculiarly original contribution to spiritual life. Other works and commentaries are expositions; but in his Abhaṅgas Ekanātha pours out his heart. There are a number of other minor works of Ekanātha, for example, his commentary on Chatuhślokī Bhāgavata, Svātmasukha, and such others. In our exposition of Ekanātha, we shall concern ourselves especially with two of his productions which are alone relevant for our purpose as giving us the philosophical and mystical teachings of Ekanātha, namely, the commentary on the Bhāgavata, and his Abhaṅgas. Other works are mainly expository, and do not contain the requisite philosophical or mystical interest; so we concern ourselves with only those that are significant for our purpose. Ekanātha is a past master in depicting the emotional side of poetry. Prof. Patwardhan has given very acutely Ekanātha's descriptions of the various sentiments in his Wilson Philological Lectures. For example, we can read in Patwardhan how Ekanātha describes the love sentiment, or the heroic spirit, or pathos, or yet terror, and such other cognate emotions. Ekanātha is not merely a saint, but also a poet of a very high order, which fact has contributed in no small measure to his popularity as a great teacher of religion.

CHAPTER XI.

The Abhangas of Bhanudasa, Janardana Swami and Ekanatha.

The Abhangas of Bhanudasa.

1. Bhānudāsa, the great-grandfather of Ekanātha, tells us that he knows of no other code of conduct and no other mode of thought than that of uttering the Name of God (Abg. 1). He says that Paṇḍharapūr is a mine of rubies. Those, who come to this place may take howsoever much they like, yet the treasure remains the same as it was. God Viṭṭhala himself is like a well-set ruby, says Bhānudāsa (Abg. 2). When Bhānudāsa was taken to the gallows, because he was reported to have stolen the necklace of God, he is said to have composed some very pathetic Abhaṅgas. How long are you going to test my devotion, asks Bhānudāsa? My breath is choked in my throat. Torments of all kinds are befalling me, and my mind is submerged in grief. There seems to be no remedy to this situation, except to fall in submission before Thee. Fulfil my desires, says Bhānudāsa, and endow me with real happiness (Abg. 5). Even if the sky were to fall over my head, if the world were to break into pieces, and if the universe were to be devoured by the sea-fire, I will still wait for Thee, says Bhānudāsa. I believe in the efficacy of Thy name. Make me not dependent upon others. Even if the seven seas were to amalgamate, if the world was to submerge in the huge expanse, even if the five great elements were to be destroyed, I shall not leave Thy company. Howsoever great the danger that may befall me, I shall never forsake Thy name, nor shall my determination move an inch. As a beloved is attached to her husband, so shall I be attached to Thee, says Bhānudāsa (Abg. 6). When these Abhaṅgas were composed, God is said to have showed himself to Bhānudāsa in as miraculous a manner as a dry piece of wood were to put forth sprouts, and as God came to relieve Bhānudāsa of his suffering, Bhānudāsa tells us he fell at His feet in utter submission (Abg. 7).

The Abhangas of Janardana Swami.

2. Janārdana Swāmī, the spiritual teacher of Ekanātha, tells us that he was initiated into the spiritual line by a Saint who lived at Ankalakop on the banks of the Kṛishṇā under an Audumbara tree. He does not mention Nṛisimha-sarasvati by name, but his description points to that Saint as being his Guru (Abg. 1, 2). He supplicates his Guru, because he had led a life of sin. He regarded his wife as the most beloved object of his love. He censured the Brahmins. He gave himself over to duties other than his own. He took pleasure in doing deeds of demerit. Being grieved in life, and being tormented by different kinds of calamities, he came to Audumbara. He describes himself, as verily a mine of sins, and he tells us that he went to his Guru, and sat at the threshold of his door, in order that he might relieve him of his sins (Abg. 2). If Thou wert not to relieve me from my misery, where else should I go ? or whom else shall I worship ? Dost Thou hide Thyself, because my sins are too strong for Thee, or art Thou gone to sleep ? Thy very silence increases my grief, says Janārdana (Abg. 3). Thou shouldst verily take pity on me. I did not know the way of spiritual illumination, and hence I wandered in various directions. I have suffered immense grief. Thou art known to afford succour to the fallen. I have come in submission to Thee, with the desire that Thou mightest relieve me (Abg. 4). These Abhaṅgas indicate the stage in which Janārdana was yet journeying as a spiritual pilgrim. When he reached his destination and became a full-fledged saint, and when later Ekanātha betook himself to him in order to receive spiritual illumination from him, Janārdana tells him not to care for this unreal world, but to follow the easy path of Pandharī (Abg. 7). There is no other remedy for spiritual knowledge than the utterance of God's name. What Puṇḍalīka achieved in his life-time, thou shouldst thyself achieve in thine (Abg. 8). Harbour no thought of otherness about other beings. Fall prostrate before the Saints, and give food to those who come to thee (Abg. 9). There is no greater merit than giving food to guests without consideration of caste or colour ; for, food indeed the Vedānta regards as God (Abg. 10). There is no use going to places of pilgrimage. If the mind becomes pure, God lives in our very house, and can be seen by the devotee wherever he may be (Abg. 12). Then Janārdana proceeds to describe certain mystical experiences. Wheels within wheels appear to the vision, says Janārdana, each as large as the sky. Therein seem to be set bunches of pearls. Light of the rubies, and lamps without wicks, appear before the vision, says Janārdana (Abg. 13). In the first stage of ecstasy, there is a dense form like that of a serpent, and pearls and jewels shine of themselves (Abg. 14). First, one sees white foam, and then the clear moon-light. Fire-flies, stars, the moon, and the sun follow one another. The swan presents itself in a state of steady contemplation. One should see straight into its eye, and should never leave the ecstatic state. Then the lord of souls who is of an imperishable nature shines forth : one should indeed regard him as the Self (Abg. 16). This, in fact, seems to be the essence of the spiritual experience which was communicated by Janārdana Swāmī to Ekanātha.

Ekanatha on his Spiritual Teacher.

3. Ekanātha's love for his Spiritual Teacher is as great as that of Jñāneśvara for Nivṛitti. Ekanātha has immortalised his teacher Janārdana Swāmī by coupling his name with his own in every Abhaṅga which he has composed. Ekanātha tells us that he first prepared a seat for his teacher in his purified mind. Then he burnt the incense of egoism at his feet, lighted the lamp of good emotions, and made over to him an offering of five Prāṇas (Abg. 2). Ekanātha felt greatly indebted to his teacher, because he had showed him a great miracle. He swallowed the egoism of his disciple. and showed him the light within himself, which had neither any rising nor any setting (Abg. 4). As the mind of a chaste woman is always fixed on the feet of her husband, similarly, the devotee has his mind always set on God. Janārdana, says Ekanātha, showed him the God within himself (Abg. 5). Is it not a matter of great wonder that he showed me the God in my heart without my being obliged to undergo any exertions for His attainment ? The real secret of the grace of the Guru is that a man should thereby see the whole world as God. Whatever one sees with his eyes, or hears with his ears, or tastes with his tongue, should all be of the nature of God (Abg. 8). Finally, he extols the Spiritual Teacher by saying that God Himself serves him who regards his spiritual teacher as identical with God (Abg. 9).

Ekanatha's moral and spiritual instruction.

4. Ekanātha excels in composing Abhaṅgas which have a didactic significance. Is it not wonderful, he asks, that the spiritual life, which is sweet in itself, appears sour to the man who has no belief in God (Abg. 10) ? Unless we repent, God's name shall not come to our lips. Repentance is the cause of ecstasy. If one sincerely repents, God is not far from him (Abg. 12). On the other hand, disbelief is the cause of many vices. It produces egoism, and destroys the spiritual life. One may say that disbelief is the crown of all sins (Abg. 14). People, who vainly seek their identity with God, forge new kinds of chains for themselves. They free themselves from the chains of iron to put on themselves the chains of gold (Abg. 15). Some people miss the spiritual life in the arrogance of their knowledge. Others abandon it because they cannot reach the goal. A few others always postpone their search, because they think they would give themselves over to the spiritual life some time later (Abg. 16). There are only two ways for the attainment of spiritual life : one is that we should not get ourselves contaminated with others' wealth ; the other is that we should not contaminate ourselves with others' women (Abg. 17). Seeking of wealth means losing of Paramārtha (Abg. 18). Even musk loses its odour if it is put alongside of asafœtida. Similarly, good men lose their virtue if they keep the company of the wicked. Even if we were to feed the roots of the Nimba tree with the manure of sugar, it would not fail to produce bitter fruits (Abg. 19). Ekanātha advises us not to leave away home and betake ourselves to a forest. Are there not many pigs who live in a forest, he asks us ? A man who betakes himself to a forest is like an owl that hides itself before sun-rise (Abg. 20). We should not have the dispassion of a goat, or the ecstasy of a cock. We should by all means avoid the pranks of a monkey (Abg. 22). Seeking of wealth is one sure road to ruin. If we were to add to it the seeking of women, we do not know what may come to pass (Abg. 24). Ekanātha is a great believer in the value of his Vernacular. Can we say that God created the Sanskrit language, and that the Vernaculars were created by thieves ? In whatever language we praise God, our praise is equally welcome to Him ; for God is Himself the creator of all languages (Abg. 27). Ekanātha discourses upon the power of Fate. Camphor, which is placed in a treasure, is destroyed by wind. A ship sinks in a great sea. Rogues come and pass counterfeit coin into our hands. Armies of enemies fall upon us, and take away money from subterranean places. Granaries of corn are destroyed by water. Sheep and cows and buffaloes are all destroyed by disease. A treasure placed undergound is reduced to ashes. Such, says Ekanātha, is the power of Fate (Abg. 28). He also tells us that people are afraid at the very word "Death". They do not know that it is sure to overtake us some day or other. The flower is dried up and the fruit comes in its place, and some time after even the fruit disappears. One goes before, another comes behind, and yet all pass into the hands of Death. Those who run away on hearing the name of Death are themselves placed some day on a funeral pile. The coffin-bearers, who regard a dead body as heavy, are themselves carried in a coffin to the cemetery some day. It is only those, who go in submission before God, says

Ekanātha, that do not come within the clutches of Death (Abg. 29). We should, therefore, live in life as mere pilgrims who come to a resort in the evening, and depart the next morning. As children build houses in sport and throw them away, similarly should we reckon this life (Abg. 30). As birds alight in a court-yard and then flow away, even so we should pass through this life (Abg. 31). Ekanātha tells us principally to observe one rule in life : we should never follow what our mind dictates to us. What the mind regards as happiness comes ultimately to be experienced as unhappiness (Abg. 32). We should thus always keep our mind imprisoned at God's feet (Abg. 33). Finally, sexual passion, says Ekanātha, has ruined many, and it is only those who conquer it that are able to consummate their spiritual life. The god of love, you may say, is like a powerful ram, or like a great lion. He jostled with Śankara, sent fear into the heart of Indra, threw himself against Nārada, destroyed Rāvaṇa, killed Duryodhana, caught into his meshes a great sage like Viśvāmitra. Only it was the sage Śuka, who by the power of his meditation, caught hold of this ram, brought him, and imprisoned him at the feet of Janārdana Swāmī, the spiritual teacher of Ekanātha (Abg. 35).

Bhakti and the Name of God.

5. Ekanātha defines Bhakti as the recognition of the divine nature of all beings. Remembrance of God is likeness of God, forgetfulness of God is illusion of life (Abg. 36). To utter the name of God is alone Bhakti (Abg. 37). Amongst all evanescent things, God's name is alone imperishable (Abg. 38). It fulfils all the desires of the mind (Abg. 39). He who has no devotion in his heart will regard the pursuit of God as a mere chimera. But he who gets spiritual experience will have the greatest value for it (Abg. 40). People vainly busy themselves in wrangling, without seeing that the name of God leads to the form of God (Abg. 41). If a man does not feel happy at heart at the utterance of God's name, we must take it that he is a sinful man. Even if we put the manure of musk at the basin of onion, its strong smell cannot be conquered. A man, who has high fever, does not find even fresh milk sweet. A man who is bitten by a serpent regards even sugar as bitter. Similarly, a man immersed in worldly life has no belief in the efficacy of the Name (Abg. 42). The Name of God gives us divine happiness. It puts an end to all diseases of body and mind. It enables us to preserve equanimity (Abg. 44). God runs to the help of the devotee, if he devoutly remembers Him. He thus came to the succour of Draupadī when a host of Brahmins had come to ask for dinner. He succoured Arjuna and protected him from deadly arrows. He saved Prahlāda on land and in water and in fire (Abg. 46). A man, who has no real devotion, even though learned, looks merely like a courtesan, who puts on different kinds of ornaments (Abg. 48). Bhakti is the root, of which dispassion is the flower, and illumination the fruit (Abg. 49). In the devoted performance of a Kīrtana, every time a new charm appears. The hearer and the speaker both become God. The devotees of God sound lustily the name of God. Even the sky cannot contain the joy of these Saints (Abg. 51). When a man devoutly performs the Kīrtana of God, God shows Himself before him. Great is the happiness of a Kīrtana when God stands in front of His own accord. He wards off all our calamities by taking a disc and a mace in his hands (Abg. 52). He who is impossible to attain by a life of Yoga, says Ekanātha, dances in a Kīrtana (Abg. 53). Ekanātha's sole desire is that he should be spared long to perform the Kīrtana of God (Abg. 54). A man who performs a Kīrtana and begs for money will go to perdition (Abg. 55). We should sing and dance in joy, and ask nothing of anybody. We should eat, if we get a morsel of food. Otherwise, we should live on the leaves of trees. We should determine not to leave a Kīrtana, even though the life may be passing away (Abg. 56). With great reverence, we should sing the acts of good men, and should bow to them with all our heart. In the company of the good, we should utter the name of God, and at the time of a Kīrtana we should nod in joy beside God. We should never waste our breath; and should talk only about devotion and knowledge. In great love, we should discuss the various kinds of dispassion. Saints perform a Kīrtana in such a manner that the form of God is thereby firmly set before the minds of men (Abg. 57). There have been various Saints who have performed various kinds of Bhakti. Parīkshit performed the devotion of the hearing of God's exploits. Śuka performed the devotion of Kīrtana. Prahlāda gave himself over to the uttering of the Name of God. Ramā did physical service of God. Akrūra performed the devotion of prostration. Māruti gave himself over to the service of God. Arjuna led a life of friendliness with God. And the great Bali performed the devotion of utter self-sacrifice for the sake of God (Abg. 58).

6. Ekanātha thinks that it is an extremely lucky event to meet with real saints. One may be able to know the past, the present and the future; one may be able to stop the Sun from setting; one may easily cross the ocean; but it is difficult to meet a real Saint (Abg. 59).

The Power of the Saints.

He alone is a real Saint who does not allow his peace to be disturbed, even if his body is tormented by another; or who does not shed tears of grief, even if his son is killed by enemies. He is not dejected, when all his wealth is taken away by thieves; and he does not become angry, even if his wife turns out unchaste (Abg. 61). He looks equally upon praise and censure (Abg. 60). He always sings the praises of God in the midst of difficulties. In poverty also, he remains equanimous (Abg. 63). Those, on the other hand, are false Saints, who assume sainthood only in order to fill their belly. They besmear their body with ashes, and tell people that they are the source of happiness. They deceive and rob innocent people, ask others to make them their spiritual preceptors (Abg. 66), and have no objection to take all kinds of service from their disciples (Abg. 67). Real saints are not like these counterfeit ones. God is at their beck and call, and Ekanātha implores them to show him the vision of God but once (Abg. 68). He regards it a matter of great joy, when the Saints come to visit his house (Abg. 72). He feels he should not be separated from them even for a moment (Abg. 73). Tears of joy flow from his eyes when he comes in contact with these saints (Abg. 74). The Saints are really more generous than even a cloud. They fulfil all desires. They turn away the minds of men from empty and insignificant things, and make them worthy of themselves. They rescue them from the clutches of Death (Abg. 76). There is no saviour except Saints when a calamity befalls a man (Abg. 77); for the gods become weary of the evil-doers, but the Saints accept them also (Abg. 80). As the Sun's light cannot be hidden in the sky, similarly, the greatness of a Saint cannot be hidden in the world (Abg. 82). All the treasures of heaven reside with these saints (Abg. 83). How wonderful is it, asks Ekanātha, that by means of Bhakti a devotee can himself become God (Abg. 84)? God forgets His divinity, and fulfils all the desires of his devotees (Abg. 87). If we place our burden on God, God shall certainly support us in the midst of difficulties (Abg. 89). He serves His devotees, as Kṛishna served Arjuna by being his charioteer (Abg. 90). God released Draupadī from calamities, and relieved Sudāman of his poverty; protected Parīkshit in the womb; ate of the morsels of cow-herds, and carried aloft the hill of Govardhana (Abg. 91); baked pots with Gorā; drove cattle with Chokhā; cut grass with Sāmvatā; wove garments with Kabīra; coloured hide with Rohidāsa ; sold meat with the butcher Sajana ; melted gold with Narahari ; carried cow-dung with Janābāī ; and even became a Pariah messenger of Dāmājī (Abg. 92). Devotion indeed makes the devotee the elder, and God the younger. The devotee is even the father of God (Abg. 95). God is impersonal, but the devotee is personal (Abg. 96). God and devotees are like the ocean and waves, like gold and ornaments, like flower and scent (Abg. 98). God even harbours the kick of his devotee on his breast (Abg. 100). Kansa hated Kṛishṇa, but honoured Nārada, and so went to heaven (Abg. 101). God is indeed the body, of whom the Devotee is the soul (Abg. 105). It is a matter of shame to God that His devotee should look piteous in the eyes of men (Abg. 107). God regards His life as useless, if the words of the devotee come untrue (Abg. 108). The Saints indeed take on a body when the path of religion vanishes, and when irreligion reigns. By the power of God's name, the Saints come to the succour of the ignorant and the fallen. By the force of their devotion, they destroy heresy and all pseudo-religion (Abg. 111).

The Mystical Experience of Ekanatha.

7. Ekanātha's mystical experience is of the highest order. He gives us all the physical and psychical marks of God-realisation. There are eight such marks to be found in a state of God-realisation : the hair stand on end ; the body begins to perspire ; a shiver passes through the system ; tears flow from the eyes ; the heart is filled with joy ; the throat becomes choked ; there is a mystical epokhē ; and there are long inspirations and expirations (Abg. 114). Through the ear, Ekanātha tells us in mystical language, he came to the eye, and ultimately became the eye of his eye. As he thus began to see the world, the world began to vanish from before him. His entire body, in fact, became endowed with vision (Abg. 115). He rose beyond merit and demerit. He left the three states of consciousness behind him. He dwelt in the light of the spiritual moon (Abg. 116). He was thus greatly indebted to his spiritual teacher, for he showed him the eye of his eye, which put an end to all doubt whatsoever (Abg. 117). Inside his heart, he saw Janārdana. The vision of self-illumination dispelled all his infatuation (Abg. 118). At the dawn of mystical experience, he saw that the whole world was clothed in radiance (Abg. 119). When the Spiritual Sun arose, he saw that there was neither noon, nor evening, nor morning. There was a constant rise of the Spiritual Sun before him. There was an

eternal end to all setting whatsoever. The East and the West lost their difference. Action and non-action both became as the Moon by day (Abg. 120). As he stepped inside water for bathing, he saw the vision of God even in water. By that vision, even the Ganges became sacred. To whatever place of pilgrimage Ekanātha went, it was rendered holy by his presence (Abg. 121). Ekanātha tells us that real Sandhyā consists merely in making obeisance to all beings with the feeling of non-difference (Abg. 122). As the cloud of Ekanātha began to rumble in the sky, the ocean of Janārdana began to overstep its limits (Abg. 124). Ekanātha tells us with warmth that he saw a four-handed vision of God, with a dark-blue complexion, with a conch and disc in his hands, a yellow garment over his body, and a beautiful necklace on his breast (Abg. 126). With one-pointed devotion, wherever the devotee may go, he sees the vision of God. He sees God in his meditation, in sleep, in the world, and in the forest (Abg. 128). Inside and outside, he sees God. Sleeping, and waking, and dreaming, he is always enjoying the vision of God (Abg. 129). Wherever such a one sees, he finds that God fills all directions and quarters (Abg. 130). God seems to be almost shameless, because there is no garment which he wears. God even becomes a white hog, says Ekanātha (Abg. 132). God becomes so happy in the house of the Saints, says Ekanātha, that He does not depart from their house, even though He is thrown out of the house. God enjoys the company of the Saints, and keeps returning to them even though He is driven away (Abg. 133). As one moves out to a foreign land, God moves with him. On mountains and precipices, wherever the eye is cast, God is seen. Ekanātha sat in the immaculate enjoyment of God, and so he did not move out into the world or into the forest (Abg. 134). His mind became engrossed in God, so much so, that it became God. As Ekanātha began to see God, the world began to vanish from him (Abg. 136). He did not care now whether his body remained or departed. A rope-serpent neither dies nor comes to life. We really did die, says Ekanātha, while we were living, and having been dead, yet lived (Abg. 138). The whole world became to us now full of the joy of God. Our mind rested on His feet (Abg. 139). The result of such a unitive devotion was that God and devotee became one. God forever stood before Ekanātha, and the distinction between God and Devotee vanished (Abg. 140). Now, asks Ekanātha, how would it be possible for him to worship God? All the materials of worship, such as scent, incense, light, and so on, were all the forms of God, with the result that there was no distinction between worshipper and worshipped (Abg. 143). So long as the world does not allow one to worship oneself, till then an ignorant man must appear better than a self-worshipper (Abg. 144). Now, says Ekanātha, I became one with Brahman. I became free from all the troubles of existence ; free from physical and mental torments ; I was left alone to myself with the result that all duality was at an end (Abg. 145). All that appeared to the vision was now to me the form of God (Abg. 147). All the directions became filled with God. There was thus no distinction between the East and the West. If God filled every nook and cranny of the universe, where was there any place left for Him to occupy (Abg. 149) ? I found out a suitable field for tilling, says Ekanātha. I sowed the seed of spiritual illumination. When the crop came out, the world was too small to contain the grain. Various Sciences have tried to take the measure of God, says Ekanātha, and yet God has remained immeasurable (Abg. 150).

CHAPTER XII.

The Bhagavata of Ekanatha.

1. The Bhāgavata of Ekanātha is a Marāthī Commentary on the eleventh Skanda of Shrīmat Bhāgavata. Ekanātha got his inspiration to open to the Marāthī-speaking people this treasure of divine love, hidden in the Sanskrit language, from Jñāneśvara, who had done pioneering work in this line by writing the Jñāneśvarī. Though Jñāneśvara and Ekanātha are separated from each other by nearly three centuries, Jñāneśvara's influence upon Ekanātha is so great that his Bhāgavata appears to be merely an enlarged edition of the Jñāneśvarī. In the works of Ekanātha, we meet with the same thoughts, the same similes, even the very words and phrases, which we meet with in the Jñāneśvarī. Ekanātha's greatness consists in using the old material with an addition of fresh stock for building a structure which wears a new yet old and familiar appearance. Following Jñāneśvara, Ekanātha, at the close of his work, mentions the place and date of composition of his work. He tells us that he undertook this work of commentation at Paiṭhaṇa, his own native place, and a great centre of pilgrimage on the banks of the Godāvarī, the longest and holiest river in the Deccan. There, however, he could finish five Adhyāyas only. The rest were completed in the Pañchamudrā Maṭha at Benares on the banks of the holy Ganges. Ekanātha is silent about the reasons which led him to discontinue his work at Paiṭhana, and to undertake a long journey to Benares to finish it. He simply proceeds to give the date of the composition according to the methods of calculation current in both parts of the country—the Deccan as well as the North. To state it according to Vikrama era current at Benares, it was the Vṛisha Samvatsara 1630 (*i.e.*, 1573 A.D.). In this year, it was in the auspicious month of Kārttika on the full-moon day on Monday that the work was completed. "Listen," he says, "to the year of composition according to the Śaka era established in my land. It was in the Śaka year 1495 that this wonderful commentary was completed through the grace of Janārdana" (E. B. XXXI. 527—28, 535, 552—56).

The Place and Date of Composition.

2. Ekanātha is one of those few saint-poets who have obliged the future generations by tracing their family ancestries at the beginning or end of their works. Unlike Jñānadeva, who is satisfied with tracing only his spiritual lineage, Ekanātha,

Family History.

in the beginning of his work, after he has offered salutations to the God and Goddess of Learning, proceeds to give an account of his family. He says that the family in which he was born, through good fortune, was a Vaishṇava family, that is, a family whose tutelary deity was God Vishṇu. He was the fourth in descent from Bhānudāsa, the illustrious devotee of the Sun Deity, whose birth in the family so endeared it to God. Ekanātha tells us that even when quite young, this servant of the Sun-god endeared himself to the luminous God by his unflinching devotion, and thus, through his grace, himself became the Sun of spirituality. Conquering the sense of conceit and pride, he made such a tremendous advance in spirituality that he now and then saw divine visions. His devotion and spirituality were so great that God Viṭṭhala once actually visited Paiṭhana in order to have a look at his feet, and in the dead of night, Bhānudāsa saw before him his own Ishṭam bedecked with precious ear-rings, and illuminating the whole surrounding world. Chakrapāṇi was the son of this widely renowned Bhānudāsa. Bhānudāsa named his grandson Sūrya, and expired. "Conceiving from this luminous Sūrya, Rukmiṇi his wife, gave birth to me." "Hence it is", he adds, "that Rakhumāī is my very mother" (E. B. I. 130—34).

Spiritual Lineage.

3. As is common with these Mahārāshṭra Saints, Ekanātha proceeds to trace his spiritual lineage. The originator of his line was God Dattātreya. The first to receive initiation from him was Sahasrārjuna, and king Yadu was the second. In this Kaliyuga, Janārdana alone had the good fortune to be accepted as disciple by Dattātreya. The divine discontent that Janārdana felt was so great, that in thinking of his Guru, he lost all outward sense. Seeing the divinely discontented state of Janārdana's heart, God Dattātreya, who expects only sincere faith from his devotees, approached him and favoured him by placing his hand on his head. Miraculous was the effect of this touch! Janārdana became the master of all spiritual illumination. He clearly felt the emptiness of this transitory world, and realised within himself the true nature of Ātman. Dattātreya taught him that faith which preaches inaction through action. Janārdana now understood the secret of living free, though embodied. The faith that was generated in Janārdana's heart through the grace of God Dattātreya was so determinate and fearless, that he never thought himself polluted even when he accepted the householder's life, and continued to perform the duties of that station. When his soul was thus overflowing with the spiritual possession bestowed by divine grace, it lost the very power of intelligence. Janārdana could not control the oncoming of this rapturous ecstasy, and lay on the ground motionless like a corpse. Dattātreya brought his mind down to the world of phenomena, and gently admonished him that even that kind of emotional surging was after all the work of the Sāttvic quality, and that the highest state consisted in suppressing the emotional swelling, and living a quiet life with the conviction of the realised Self. Having finished his worship, Janārdana wanted to prostrate himself before his Guru. But when he lifted his eyes, to his utter amazement he found that Dattātreya had vanished away. Ekanātha, at the end, offers an apology for going out of his way to give such a detailed account of his spiritual teacher. His apology consists in simply putting before his hearers his utter inability as compared with Janārdana. He says that even when he would like to be silent, his Guru would not allow him to do so. Thus, in spite of himself, he was forced to give an account of his spiritual lineage (E. B. IX. 430—439, 454).

Ekanatha's Humility before Janardana.

4. It was the sincere belief of Ekanātha that though, to all appearances it was his hand that was working to produce the Commentary, the real agency that worked was no other than that of Janārdana himself. It was his grace, he tells us, that enabled him to undertake and finish that gigantic commentary on the eleventh Skanda of Shrīmat Bhāgavata. Just as a father holds in his hand the tiny armlet of his child, and by means of it writes all the letters himself, so here it was Janārdana, who through him opened to the world the secret of the eleventh Skanda. As to his ability to perform the task, he says he must frankly state that he was a perfect ignoramus, that he knew not even how to proceed with the task, much less how to be true to the original. He was a perfect stranger to that kind of literary art. He was simply the mouthpiece of Janārdana. Ekanātha is not wearied to state that in getting this huge work done through a blockhead like himself, Janārdana had veritably performed a great miracle. To explain the meaning of every sentence in the Bhāgavata is a task beyond the capacities of even the great founders of philosophical systems. And yet here in this Marāthī commentary, all this has been achieved by Ekanātha. This is indeed due to the mercy of the omnipotent Janārdana. Such indeed is the extraordinary grandeur of Janārdana's grace! (E.B. XXXI. 496—504).

Ekanatha, an Enigma to his Neighbours.

5. So wonderful was the working of this grace that in spite of the authorship of this work, Ekanātha tells us that he continued to be an enigma to his neighbours. In the following words, he gives a very graphic description of popular notions about him. "Attend to the tale of Ekā Janārdana," he says. "Those that will perchance read his work will pronounce him to be an erudite Pandit; but if, by chance, they happen to meet him personally, they will surely find him an ignoramus. Some persons look upon him as a great devotee, yet some others believe him to be a Jīvanmukta. Some, on the other hand, conclude that Ekā is assuredly a worldly-minded man, attached to sense-pleasures. They declare that Ekā Janārdana knows nothing of Yogic postures, nor has he ever counted beads or practised meditation. He is not even found to be regular in the observance of a single rule, nor does he wear on his body any rosary or such other sectarian mark. Thus there is nothing with him that would characterise him as one walking on the path of devotion. To them, therefore, he is a great mystery. They therefore declare 'Who knows what sacred formula he possesses, and what he preaches to his disciples! He takes all possible care to keep his Mantra secret. He simply takes undue advantage of the blind faith of the poor innocent, and deludes them. He resounds the air with God's name, and hypnotises his hearers.' Such is the nature of the doubts that Janārdana himself kindles in their hearts. When Ekā tries to give an account of himself, Janārdana forces him aside, and begins to speak himself. Somehow, all trace of egotism in him is lost. The smallest movement of his tiniest finger is caused by Janārdana himself" (E. B. XXXI. 505—511).

Bhagavata, a Great Field.

6. We close this portion of the historical account by giving in the words of Ekanātha the history of the Bhāgavata itself. Ekanātha uses the simile of a field to trace the history of the Bhāgavata. "Śrī Bhāgavata," he says, "is a great field. Brahmā was the first to obtain seed. Nārada was its chief proprietor. And it was he who did this wonderful work of sowing the seed. Vyāsa secured protection for the field by erecting ten bunds about it, and the result was the unusually excellent crop of divine bliss. Śuka worked as a watchman to guard the crops: with simply discharging the sling of God's name, he made the sin-birds flow away. Uddhava thrashed the ears, heaped them together in the form of the eleventh Skanda, and winnowing the corn, separated the grains in the form of the weighty words of Śrī Kṛishṇa. From these were very skilfully prepared several dishes with an immortal flavour. Parīkshit succeeded Uddhava. He broke with the world to listen to the Bhāgavata from the lips of Śukadeva, and obtained divine bliss. Following in his footsteps, Śrīdhara illuminated the hidden meaning of the Bhāgavata in his Bhāvārthadīpikā, and brought blissful peace for himself. The favourite fly of Janārdana, namely, Ekanātha, with the two wings of the Marāthī dialect, flew straight upon that dish, and enjoyed it to its heart's content, as it was left there unmolested by any one. Or, otherwise, it might be said that Janārdana's favourite cat happened to see the delicious preparations through the light of the Bhāvārthadīpikā. Smelling the dish to be pure and delicious, it ventured and approached the plates. When it mewed, the merciful Saints were pleased to offer to it a morsel of the remnants of their dish. The favourite cat of Janārdana was simply overjoyed to lick the unwashed vessels of these Saints, and it enjoyed the dish as a heavenly ambrosia" (E.B. XXXI. 443—454).

I. Metaphysics.

Introductory.

7. In his metaphysical views, Ekanātha shows a distinct influence of Śankara, the eminent champion of Vedāntic Monism. It, however, appears that he appreciated and digested that great scholar's philosophy not only through his Sanskrit works, but also through the Marāthī works of Jñānadeva and Mukundarāja, especially through the works of the former. He expounds the spiritualistic monism of Śankara, using as is usual with him, the materials already prepared by Jñānadeva. For similes and ideas, it appears that he has laid under obligation not only the Jñāneśvarī but even the Amṛitānubhava. Ekanātha believes in Śankara's theory with all its deductions. It may therefore be truly said that his great contribution to philosophy consists in the popularisation of the Vedānta. Jñānadeva disappeared from this mundane world quite prematurely. Nāmadeva lived long and did a great deal of propagandist work by travelling on foot from South to North, and resounding the air with God's name ; yet he shows little trace of any acquaintance with Sanskrit scholars. Tukārāma who flourished after Ekanātha, carried on, with great success, the work of Nāmadeva. But he too lacked the close acquaintance with Sanskrit in which the treasures of Vedāntic philosophy were hidden. By his temperament, by his external environments like that of a birth at Paithana, then a great centre of Sanskrit learning, by his long term of life, and not the least, by his fortunate acquisition of divine grace quite early in life, Ekanātha was of all the fittest person to popularise the Vedānta. We give below a brief statement of the salient features of his metaphysical views.

Brahman alone is Real; the World is Unreal.

8. Ekanātha, as has been said above, advocates the theory of spiritualistic monism. But it is a monism proved through nescience. Ekanātha says: "Before its manifestation the world was not. After its disappearance it will not leave even a trace of its existence behind it. What therefore manifests itself during the middle state of existence is unreal, and manifests itself through the power of Māyā. Parabrahman or the Highest Being is the beginning of this world. It is that peerless Brahman that survives the destruction of the world. Naturally, even in the state of existence, when the world appears to possess a concrete existence, what really exists is not the world but Brahman. Only to the undiscriminating this illusory show appears as real." To illustrate what he means: "A mirage has no existence prior to the rays of the sun. And it dies without a trace when the sun sets. Naturally, during the middle state of existence what appears as flowing water is simply an illusion. Really, not a drop of real water can be found where such an amount of water appears to have flown." To take another illustration: "A rope is often confounded with a serpent. Prior to this confusion, a rope exists as a rope. When the misconception is removed, there is again the rope existing. Hence even when in the middle state, the illusion causes the confused perception of a serpent, the rope stands as a rope unchanged or unmodified." Ekanātha therefore concludes that if one were to think about the beginning and the end of the world, one will be convinced that Brahman alone is real, and the world is unreal (E. B. XIX. 87—91).

Four Proofs of the Unreality of the World.

9. The existence of this concrete world is the greatest stumbling block in the path of all the monists. Ekanātha therefore brings forth all possible arguments to prove the unreal character of this seemingly real world. "Brahman alone, without a second, exists. The world is only apparently real. It possesses an imaginary existence supported by the reality of Brahman." Ekanātha advances four arguments to prove the unreality of the world. First, the Scriptures can well stand witness to this. Secondly, we all of us perceive the transiency of body. Then, again, Mārkaṇḍeya and Bhuśuṇḍi have witnessed for millions of times the whole world reduced to ashes at the end of each cycle. This hear-say coming from the lips of the hoary venerable persons is the third proof, which may be called the historical proof. What is known as Inference in logic is the fourth proof to prove the unreality of the universe. It can be laid down in the following manner : "A rope is a rope at all times. But through misconception it is understood variously as a log of wood, a serpent, a garland of pearls, or a line of a water flow. Similarly, Brahman is existence itself, knowledge itself. But various mysterious theories discuss it as a mere void, or as being qualified. They range from pure nihilism to pluralism of an extreme type. Thus the fact that a variety of theories exists clearly shows that this world-experience is false." Ekanātha therefore asserts that in this case the Vedāntic theory alone expresses the truth. "As the cloth cannot be supposed to have an independent existence apart from the thread that goes to form it, so the world cannot be supposed to possess an independent existence apart from Brahman. Beyond the thread, which, woven into warp and woof, gives existence to the cloth, cloth is only a name. So the world beyond the Brahman which supports this misconception has existence only in name" (E. B. XIX. 197—205).

Avidya, Vidya and Maya.

10. In order to explain the existence of plurality, a monist of the type we are considering is required to think of a principle which will partake of both unity and plurality, and which without tampering in any way the purity of the One, will yet be the parent of the Many. The Śankarite Vedānta, with one important modification, accepts the Prakṛiti of the Sāmkhyas for such a principle. The Sāmkhyas believe in the eternity and independence of this principle. The Vedānta of Śankara just removes these two characteristics, makes it an existence dependent upon the Ātman, describes it as having its end with the rise of the knowledge of the Ātman, and steers clear of a rock upon which many monistic theories have suffered shipwreck. Ekanātha follows Śankara in the hypothesis of this explanatory principle. He first states the traditional meaning of Vidyā, Avidyā and Māyā and then proceeds to the important question of their futility. Vidyā, he says, can be defined as the experience which one has at the time of real knowledge. It expresses itself in the consciousness "I am Brahman". It is this experience which destroys Avidyā, which is the parent of all misery. The belief that 'I am sinful and ever unfortunate' is the clear expression of Avidyā, the mother of all doubts and miseries. Avidyā enchains the individual self, Vidyā delivers him from bondage. But these two are the eternal powers of Māyā, a great enchantress who is a perpetual enigma to men as well as to angels. She is a riddle because she cannot be proved to be real or unreal. She cannot be proved to be real, because she vanishes with the first ray of spiritual knowledge. And she cannot be proved to be unreal inasmuch as everyone feels her presence and power day and night. She has therefore been called the 'Indescribable', neither real nor unreal. It is she who spreads a net of allurement for the world. It is she who breeds and brings up under her fostering care the two powers, namely, Vidyā and Avidyā. But if one were to come closer and look at her carefully, it will be seen that this Enchantress is no other than the finite Self's own idea (E. B. XI. 98—100, 102—106).

As Maya is not, any question about it is useless.

11. Janaka, king of the Videhas, asked Antariksha a question about the nature of this Māyā. Thereupon, Antariksha said to the king, "Well, you have asked me a question about the nature of Māyā. But it is a question which is futile, as in this case the speaker has no support, or hold at all. All speech is at an end if a king demands from his servant the horoscope of a barren woman's son. Suppose some one was to build a shed for supplying water to the passers-by living in a town in the clouds ; suppose some one was to card the wind, roll it and light it at the flame of a fire-fly ; or suppose some one was to break the head of his shadow or take the skin off the body of the sky ; or suppose a son was born to the daughter-in-law of a barren lady, who was so graceful of figure that his very sight brought milk in the breasts of Bhīshma's wife. Grind the wind minutely in a windmill ; break open the heaven with the horns of a horse ; or let lamps be lighted with the lustre of a red berry to celebrate the marriage-ceremony of Hanumān. The story of Māyā can be told by those wiseacres who would make the above suppositions. Thus all discussions about Māyā would bring shame to the man who would venture to describe her" (E.B. III. 32—40).

There is no room for the world.

12. We have said in the beginning that Ekanātha's great work consists in the popularisation of the Vedāntic philosophy. If a further proof is necessary, it can be obtained from the various beautiful solutions which he offers of the problems he raises in his commentary. They show what a keen logical acumen this devotee of Paṇḍharapūr possessed. Let us hear what he says about his proof of the non-existence of the world. "It must be granted, he says, that there are two existences, the soul and the body. The question is, which of them supports Samsāra? It is no use saying that the Samsāra does not exist at all, for everyone of us feels its existence day and night. So, that it exists is a fact, and the question of its support must be solved. But the Ātman, which is ever free, and which is the principle of intelligence, cannot be its support; nor can Samsāra be supported by body which is dull and insensate. The eternal Ātman transcends all definition and description. It is his self-effulgence that helps the Sun and the Moon to send floods of light which alternately illumines the whole world. Such a self-effulgent Ātman could be fettered by the world-fetters, only if the Sun were to be drowned in a pool of mirage or to be burnt up by the fire of a fire-fly, or if the golden mountain Meru, which is considered to be the support of the three worlds, were to be drowned in a small pond, or finally if the heavens were to be blown up by the flutter of a fly's wings. We may go further and say that even if these impossibilities were to happen, the Ātman shall not be fettered by the world-fetter. As to body which is dull, stupid, and material, not even a fool will be prepared to regard it as the support of this world. If a stone were to suffer a stomach-ache, or if a mountain were to be affected with cholera, or if darkness were to be whitened by charcoal, then the body would support the Samsāra. Thus there is no room for the world either in the Ātman or in the Body (E. B. XXVIII. 122—133).

The Individual Self and the Universal Self.

13. Brahman has been declared by the Vedas to be indivisible. What then has divided it into two? Possibly he divided himself into two, after the fashion of a man looking in a mirror. But what a great contrast do these two selves present? When a man is before a mirror, his reflection stands before him, and appears to copy him exactly. But really it can be contrasted with the original in every way. For instance, if a man is looking in the eastern direction, his reflection in the mirror looks in the opposite, that is, the western direction. If so, how can it be regarded as the faithful copy of the original? So, in the case of Ātman, Māyā produces a wonderful difference. The Universal Self has his vision directed towards himself; while his copy, the individual self, directs his sight towards the world. Hence though it appears that they look at each other, they are entirely opposed to one another (E. B. XXIV. 90—93).

The Figure of two Birds.

14. Though opposed to each other, they are yet best friends. They can be very well compared to two birds who have nestled on the same tree, namely, the body. Both are equally intelligent, and in their eternal and undying love for each other excel the love of any other pair. At no time, whether by day or night, can they be seen separated from each other. On account of their close friendship and sincerity, they live together sportively. As the lamp never leaves the company of light, and *vice versa*, one cannot be separated from the other. Whatever the finite self desires, God never refuses but hastens to supply. God immeasurably satisfies all the desires which a man has in the last moments of his life. In return, the finite self also has surrendered himself to him completely. So great is the attachment between the two, that the finite self ungrudgingly obeys his friend, God, in the minutest detail, and even at the cost of life. When in great difficulty, the finite self prays to God for succour, and through mercy natural to Him, He runs to help him at the first call. Thus the finite self lives by God's grace, and in the end becomes one with Him. God also loves him to such an extent that He lives only for him. These reciprocal acts of love have but one exception. The finite self is greatly fond of tasting the sour, stringent fruits of the fig-tree. In spite of God's continuous warnings, he goes on tasting these fruits, and as a result suffers the miseries of birth and death. God Himself, never tastes these fruits, and thus enjoys eternal bliss (E. B. XI. 164—173, 199—205).

The essential unity of Jiva and Siva.

15. The two are the best friends because they are in essence one and the same. Here, there is no room for the smallest degree of difference. To continue the simile of a man looking into a mirror, when a man looks in this manner, he appears to double himself; but in reality he is one. The distinctness is only an appearance. The reflection of God in the dull mirror of Avidyā is Jīva or the finite self, in the mirror of Vidyā it is Śiva or the Universal Self. Thus the grandeur of unity remains undefiled, in spite of the appearance of duality (E. B. XXII. 111—113).

16. In this body, as their necessary background, the Ātman is an ever-present, changeless factor in all the varying states of body and mind. Living in a body, yet himself unsoiled by bodily changes, he is a continuously present witness to our changing states. This continuity of the Ātman can be very well inferred from the constant experience of every human being, that it is he who was once a young child, has become now a youth, and will, after a sufficient lapse of time, become a decrepit old man. In the state of wakefulness a man enjoys an infinite variety of objects. It is he who, in his dream, develops within himself the traces of the sense-enjoyments of the waking life. Again, it is he, who, without any vivid consciousness attached to him, witnesses sound sleep, where the mind is absorbed in ignorance and where there is neither waking nor dream. With the change of states, however, he does not change. He remains conscious that it is he who witnesses the waking state, the dream and the sleep. These things, says Ekanātha, are sufficient to prove the continuity of the Ātman (E. B. XIII. 481—483, 486, 490—491).

The Atman is present in all states of body and mind.

17. As the Ātman is a changeless witness to the varying states of mind and body, so he is an unmodified witness to the creation, existence, and destruction of the whole universe. What is true in the case of the microcosm needs only to be extended to the case of the macrocosm. Ātman is not born with the creation of the world, nor does he die with the destruction of the world. The world is born, grows, or is destroyed. Ātman is not born, nor does he grow, or die. He remains changeless all the while (E. B. XXVIII. 258—259).

The Atman remains unmodified.

18. If this is the true nature of the Self, where is there any room for the states of bondage and freedom? They have not the slightest room for existence in man's spiritual nature. It is all the working of the Qualities. The Self is in no way involved in them. Qualities are the creations of Māyā, and the true self transcends the influence of Māyā. If truth can be overcome by falsehood, or if a person living in *rerum natura* can be drowned in the flood of a mirage, then alone can the true Self be fettered by these Qualities and States. The all-pervading self-effulgent Ātman, man's true Self, alone exists and is ever free (E. B. XI. 29—32).

Freedom is an illusion, because bondage is so.

II. Ethics.

19. Ekanātha is very elaborate in giving gentle admonitions useful for spiritual life. The Bhāgavata of Ekanātha can be well called the best guide to an aspirant who is trying to explore the unknown region of Divine Bliss. But, as elsewhere, the chief merit of Ekanātha consists in his power of exposition rather than in absolute originality. We do not mean to say that there is nothing original in Ekanātha. It is impossible that there should be no originality. But it is a fact which even Ekanātha would have gladly admitted that he was so much influenced by Jñānadeva, that practically it was Jñānadeva who was explaining himself through Ekanātha. As for virtues, the cultivation of which forms a practical background for the development of spiritual experience, Ekanātha mentions the usual virtues, namely, purity, penance, endurance, celibacy, non-killing, equanimity, and such others. We quote here a few cases just to bear out what we have said.

Introductory.

20. The *sine quâ non* of spiritual life is purity, internal as well as external. The mind becomes impure by contact with evil desires. So long as it is not purified, all talk of spiritual life is useless. As gold purified in a crucible shines bright, so the constant meditation on the teachings of the Guru makes the mind pure, and bright with spiritual lustre. Thus if inside the mind is purified by the words of the Guru, that purity is sure to reveal itself through external activities. Mere bodily purity, without the purity of the heart, is absolutely useless. It would be a mere farce, like bathing a donkey. It is an empty show. It would be as ludicrous as a beautiful lady wearing on her head a garland of pearls, but all the while standing naked. What is absolutely necessary, therefore, is an internal purity of the heart coupled with the external purity of good actions (E. B. III. 380—399).

Purity.

21. Penance Ekanātha has described in various ways. Here also he distinguishes between the external appendages and the internal ore of penance. To emaciate one's body by fasting, or some such processes, is not true Penance. So long as there are evil passions in man, all external appliances are useless. For instance, a man may retire in a forest, and to all external appearances may be said to have forsaken the world, but in mind, all the while, he may be thinking of his own beloved. And then his stay in a forest proves to be absolutely useless. The true meaning of penance, therefore, is constant meditation on God (E. B. XIX. 451—454).

Penance.

22. To attain to God, it is necessary that a man must retire to solitude. He must lead a lonely life. Where there are two, Satan is always a third. This can be illustrated by the instance of a young girl to be married. Suppose, while alone in the house, her house was visited by the members of her would-be husband's family. Consistent with her modesty, she would offer hospitality through a window, thus showing that she was alone in the house. But she would now think that she must help her mother by pounding rice. When she would begin pounding, with the raising and lowering of her hand, her bangles would make noise. But that noise would carry an impression to the bridegroom's party that her family was poor. To avoid such an impression, she would take out one bangle after another. So long as there were more than one bangle in each hand, they would continue to make noise. She would therefore leave in each hand one bangle, so that all noise would come to an end. This illustration would show how an aspirant must retire from the world, and lead a lonely life for God (E. B. IX. 113—115, 87—102).

Retirement.

Bearing with the defects of others.

23. According to Ekanātha, another very important virtue which an aspirant must cultivate is the virtue of bearing with the defects of others. In the description of the virtues, but especially in the description of this and the next, the very life of Ekanātha seems to be reflected. To attend to the faults or defects in others is the worst of all faults in men. Virtue consists in not observing either the vice or virtue in others. If Brahman truly transcends the duality of vice and virtue, he who is prone to notice the faults or merits in others can be safely declared not to have attained to a true realisation of Brahman. Divine experience will forsake a man who attends to the vices or virtues in others. In a total solar eclipse, the stars become visible to the human eye even by day. Similarly, when this duality is visible, it can be safely inferred that the divinity is absent in men. The perception of duality can, therefore, be regarded as the sure sign of the prevalence of ignorance (E. B. XIX. 574—579).

Bearing with the slander of others.

24. For the attainment of the non-perception of this duality of virtue and vice in others, man must cultivate another but closely allied virtue of enduring abuse from others. Why should a man ever think of retaliation or revenge, when a man who slanders is but his own reflex ? Suppose a man's teeth were to press against his own tongue. With whom shall he be angry ? In a fit of anger, will he root out the teeth, or cut off his tongue ? Surely, nothing like this will be done, because a man understands that both the tongue and the teeth are after all a part of himself. He who suffers a fall by a sudden collision with another may easily have reason to be provoked against the latter. But suppose a man walks carefully, and his foot slips and he falls down. In this case with whom will he be angry ? A man in such a case simply looks down through shame, and resumes his course. A true Sādhu, similarly, suffers calmly the slanders of others, because he has realized his oneness with the universe. He will never allow himself to be over-ruled by the passion of anger or revenge (E. B. XXIII. 778—781).

One who is attached to woman and wealth is neglected by God.

25. So far, we have treated of positive virtues. We have said what virtues an aspirant must possess. We shall now discuss what vices he should avoid. The first thing, an aspirant must be free from, is attachment to wealth and woman. Let alone divine life ; even the ordinary and worldly life would become unhappy, if a man has a strong attachment to these. He is the seat of doubt, whose mind is maddened by attachment to wealth and woman. He becomes a stranger to worldly happiness ; what then of divine life ! He who loves money and is conquered by woman is shunned by God, who lives in the temple of the body (E. B. XXIII. 305—307).

An aspirant must not touch even a wooden doll by his foot.

26. A true aspirant, therefore, must be very careful in guarding himself against the evil influence of woman. So great and so many are the centres of influence in this case, that an aspirant will not know how and when the enemy has made entrance in his heart, and captured it. Ekanātha's injunction to an aspirant in this case is : "Let not an aspirant, while hurrying through the street, touch even a female doll by his feet, lest she should generate in him the sexual consciousness." How the society of woman serves as a check or a hindrance, how it more often than not produces a destructive influence upon the aspirant has been illustrated by Ekanātha by the example of an intoxicated elephant. So strong is this animal, that it is almost impossible to catch him and tame him. But even this huge animal is caught and tamed through his attachment towards the female of his species. To bear out his point, Ekanātha quotes from the Purānas a very interesting story. Ushā, the daughter of the demon Bāna, saw in her dream Aniruddha, the grandson of Krishna. Seeing him but once, and that too in a dream, she fell in love with him, and she managed through her female attendant to secure his attachment to her. So magical is the influence of sex. It is, therefore, absolutely necessary for an aspirant, who wants the divine presence in his heart to cleanse his mind of sexual attachment (E. B. VIII. 119—121, 126, 130—131).

A Sadhaka should keep himself away from the society of even Sattvic women.

27. It might well be urged that there is no danger to an aspirant if the woman is herself Sāttvic, that is, endowed with noble qualities. But Ekanātha advises an aspirant not to take a chance in this case, as the costs would be disproportionately heavy. The human mind is proverbially fickle, and so long as it is not completely lost in God's meditation, who knows what it may not love! It is very likely that an aspirant's mind may be softened by contact with a woman, as ghee melts in the vicinity of fire. An earthen jar that once contained ghee, say sixty years before, if kept near fire, would be moistened on account of the old remnants. Similarly, lust may rise even in old age. An aspirant must, therefore, keep himself aloof from the influence of woman (E. B. XXVI. 241—244).

Worse still is the company of the uxorious.

28. Worse, however, is the company of the uxorious, or men excessively fond of the company of women. We have heard of people, he says, who have been helped by women in their journey towards God, like Madālasā or Chūḍālā. But no one, who has kept company with those who are attached to women, has ever been saved. It is these who by their passionate glorification of the sexual life excite the passions that are slumbering in man. It is, therefore, highly essential that the company of these be avoided (E. B. XXVI. 302, 251).

Repentance is the greatest atonement.

29. The first step towards purification, the *sine quâ non* of spiritual life, is a searching self-examination culminating in repentance. For, that alone has the power to wash off all dirt generated in the human mind by the evil contact with sense-objects. A few moments of true repentance have the power to burn all sin. Repentance is, therefore, the true act of atonement, which washes off all sin. All other acts of atonement are simply a farce. When once a man truly repents for his follies, he is sure to feel disgusted for past life, and thus to renounce the old ways of life. The story of Purūravas is a standing example of this potency of repentance to break the tie of attachment in a single moment (E. B. XXVI. 17—20).

Mind can be conquered by mind.

30. Ekanātha gives us a formula as to how to bring the mind under control. Has not the mind already levelled to the ground many of the so-called great persons? All sādhanas are useless against this. Ekanātha proposes an easy way of bringing it under control. As a diamond can be cut only by a diamond, so mind can be conquered only by mind. But even that is possible only when the grace of the Guru is secured. This unconquerable mind is, as it were, a maid-servant of the Guru, and is at his beck and call. If, therefore, it is handed over to the control of the Guru, it shall give the aspirant the contentment and bliss which it alone can give. It is proverbial that the human mind is naturally full of many vices. But it has one saving feature. If it chooses to secure Divine Grace for man, it can certainly do so. Mind is its own friend or foe, as the bamboo is the cause of both its growth and destruction. The striking and rubbing of one branch of a bamboo against another produces a spark of fire that burns a whole forest of bamboos. Mind may destroy itself similarly, if it so thinks. The best means for its control is thus to make it our friend through the grace of the Guru, who alone can control it (E. B. XXIII. 684—691).

For different virtues, different models.

31. If a man wants to improve himself, he can find models worth copying everywhere, and at any time. Ekanātha makes Avadhūta narrate a very interesting account of his Gurus. For different virtues, Avadhūta takes different objects as his models. Avadhūta enumerates twenty-four such models. But he says that because it is possible to learn positively or negatively from almost everything in the world, in a sense, the whole world may be said to be full of Teachers. Only a man must have the will to learn (E. B. VII. 341—344).

Vedic injunctions are calculated to wean a man from sense-objects: the cases of (1) marriage, and (2) sacrifice.

32. Ekanātha is definitely of opinion that the Vedas want to preach the gospel, not of enjoyment but of renunciation. His argument may be briefly stated as follows. Men have an instinctive tendency towards sense-gratification. Who is there that does not love the world with all its enticements? Who does not like woman, or wealth, or sweets? Men have in-born tendencies towards flesh-eating, drinking, and copulation.

So strong is the attachment to these, that all the admonitions of the Saints prove absolutely futile in weaning a man from them. If this is so, what is the special feature of the Vedas, if they were to preach just this gratification of sense? They may as well not exist at all. Thus the existence of the Vedas can be justified only if it be supposed that they preach control or renunciation, rather than unrestrained enjoyment. That that is the Vedic ideal can be inferred from the two institutions of marriage and sacrifice, which they have introduced. The Vedic ideal of marriage means not a license to legal prostitution. It is established to restrain the sexual instinct, whose unlimited satisfaction may bring down the fall of man. The fact that it has introduced so many restrictions in the case of marriage is in itself a sufficient indication of the underlying motive. Similar is the case of sacrifices like Sautrāmani or Aśvamedha. They are introduced to put a restraint upon the unbridled instincts of man. Ekanātha thus concludes that the Vedas try to wean a man gradually from sense-objects, and in this wise gradation consists the importance of the Vedic Religion. It rightly understands human psychology, and therefore does not preach like some other religions a wholesale renunciation. The gradual detachment brought by the slow and sure path of control is the ideal which the Vedas place before the world (E. B. V. 208—210, 218—219, 236—239).

Limitations of Vedic commands.

33. But Ekanātha completely understands the limitations of these injunctions. So long as a mango-tree has fruits on it, it is not simply desirable but even essential that it must have a watchman to guard it. But once the fruits are ripe and are removed to the owner's house, the watchman may be safely dispensed with. Similarly, so long as a man is under the influence of Avidyā, it is binding upon him that he should obey the orders of the Vedas. But once a man has transcended body-consciousness, his soul being merged in Brahman, he may be said to have transcended also the limitations of Vedic orders (E. B. XIII. 474—75).

Persons qualified for knowledge, action and devotion.

34. He, who is completely unattached to the objects of enjoyment, either in this world or in the next, is the fittest man to betake himself to the path of knowledge. On the other hand, he who is attached to sense-objects and has never dreamt of non-attachment or renunciation, is the person qualified for the path of action (E. B. XX, 74—76). Ekanātha. however, treats at great length the qualifications of one fit for Bhakti. This Bhakta occupies a sort of a middle position. Having heard from the lips of the saints the greatness and mercy of God, a strong conviction is produced in him that the true goal of man's life is to secure God's grace. But unfortunately he has not the courage or the strength to free himself from the worldly bonds, and thus betakes himself to a solitary place to meditate on God. He is intellectually convinced of the emptiness of the world. But his attachment towards the world will not allow him to break with it. And he has therefore to stay on in the midst of a life which practically bores him. Suppose a child is attempting to lift up a heavy stone. When it has just raised it from the ground, suppose the stone slips from its hand and the child finds its hand heavily pressed under the weight of that very stone. The child then finds itself unable to throw off the stone unaided. It is impatient to extract its hand, but the heavy weight of the stone will not allow it to do so. As the child in that state simply chafes and frets but is all the while unable to withdraw its hand, similarly, the Bhakta finds the weight of the worldly affairs too heavy for him, and wants to get rid of them at once, but has no mental strength to throw them off, and be free at once. He lives a worldly life, but does not, and cannot enjoy it. In such a state, he prays to God day and night for succour. Such a man, who is neither completely free from desire, nor is completely attached to sense-objects, but is all the while praying to God, may be called a Bhakta. To him, God reveals Himself, pleased by his constant prayer (E. B. XX. 78—87).

The value of duly discharging one's duty.

35. Upon one who is attached to worldly objects nothing can confer greater benefit than the discharge of the duty of the station in which he may be placed. The performance of duty alone has the power to purify the mind. Ekanātha compares duty to a kind of philosopher's stone, which, if it is selflessly made to touch, will transform the whole world into the gold of Brahman. Or, he says, it can be called the Sun whose unselfish rise has the power to dispel the darkness of ignorance. A man who does not perform his duty is required to suffer the miseries of birth and death. The selfless discharge of one's duty pleases God. It can, therefore, be well called a boat which will help a man to cross the worldly ocean (E. B. XVIII. 380—387).

36. When a man's heart is thus purified by the discharge of duty, he becomes qualified for Bhakti. Bhakti has been defined and classified in several ways. The usual classification is the nine-fold one. But often it is classified under three, four, or even two heads. Following Nārada, the famous author of the Bhakti-sūtras, Ekanātha defines Bhakti as the deep and sincere love for God. To be widely known in the world as a great devotee is an easy task. But to be a true and sincere devotee of God is a very difficult one. He, upon whom God chooses to shower His grace, can alone be a true devotee. Sincere love for God may be said to have arisen in him, whose heart is seen panting after Him day and night. A lady, who is for all external purposes engaged in doing service to her husband, but is in the heart of hearts thinking constantly of her paramour, cannot be called a chaste and devoted lady; similarly, he cannot be called a true devotee, who is externally engaged in doing worshipful acts to God, and yet is inwardly expecting a worldly return for it. He is not a true devotee whose eye is set on worldly honours and worldly objects, and who simply externally engages himself in doing service to God. A true Bhakta is lost in the thought of God, and day and night remembers Him alone. He, who has through God's grace found the fountain of infinite love towards Him, need not perform his daily ablutions; for he has transcended the stage of action (E. B. XI. 1106—1109).

The meaning of Bhakti.

37. In the seventh Adhyāya of the Bhagavadgītā occurs the famous four-fold classification of the Bhaktas, the distressed, the seeker for knowledge, the lover of gain, and the knower of truth. Ekanātha tries to explain the classification further. He says that the distressed, in the discussion of spiritual knowledge, does not mean one afflicted with the pains of a disease. Here the suffering or disease is the intense excitement of the mind for God-realisation. The divinely distressed is so keen, and grows so impatient, that being unable to suffer the pangs of separation from God, he runs to a mountain-precipice to throw himself down, or rushes forth to throw himself in a burning fire. This impatience for God-realisation is the true characteristic of the spiritually distressed. Finding him prepared to commit suicide, the other, the seeker for knowledge, asks him to note that this human life is given to him by God not for self-destruction, but for patient work towards His attainment. He must look at the way by which the devotees of bygone times have been able to obtain God's favour. He says to him "What is the use of throwing away this golden opportunity? Suicide

The four kinds of Bhaktas.

will not bring you nearer God." Such an advice somewhat cools down the impatience of the divinely distressed man and he tries to understand how his predecessors on the spiritual path persevered in their attempts. This is the second stage, or the desire to know. Love of gain in this case does not mean love of money, for money is a definite obstacle in the path of the aspirant. The true love of gain means the expectation to find God everywhere. He is a true lover of gain, who tries to see God even when he meets an infinite variety of objects. The knower, of course, means not one who is well versed in the worldly affairs or scriptures, but he who has realised Brahman (E. B. XIX. 272—280).

Saguna easier of approach than Nirguna.

38. The religion of the Bhāgavata takes a special interest in the weak and the ignorant. Not that it neglects the strong and the wise, but it is true that it always puts before itself the many in number, namely, the weak and the ignorant. Looking to the frailty and instinctive tendency for ease in every man, the Bhāgavata always preaches an easy means to reach the Godhead. In several places, Ekanātha says that the Saguṇa or the Manifest is easier than the Nirguṇa or the Unmanifest. The apprehension of the Unmanifest is beyond the grasp of the intellect. Hence with discrimination and love, the aspirants concentrate their minds on the Manifest and save themselves easily. A mind can easily think of the visible rather than the invisible. Thus, idol-worship is meant for one who cannot realise His presence in all beings. Let a man begin somewhere, and by gradual steps he may be led to higher stages (E. B. XXVII. 251—352 ; 371).

The path of Knowledge.

39. He, whose mind is purified by the discharge of his duty and constant prayer to God, feels non-attachment to worldly objects. He then learns to discriminate truly the real from the unreal. This discrimination is knowledge. It is by this that the wise know that the true self is not the body, but the self-effulgent Ātman, who informs the physical and the subtle body. See through how many processes the sugar-cane has to pass before it can assume the pure form of a sugar-doll. First, the sugar-cane has to be squeezed in the juice-mill, thus producing a liquid juice. Thereupon, the juice is purified by heat and is exposed to cold to be congealed into a thick cake of sugar. But it has to be again melted before it can be moulded into the form of a sugar-doll. Similarly, the discriminating first realize the unreality of the seemingly solid physical body, then destroy the subtle body, while finally they annihilate egoism and become Brahman themselves (E. B. XXVIII. 221—224).

III. Mysticism.

Four means of God-realisation.

40. From Ekanātha's metaphysics and ethics, we now pass to his mysticism, the coping stone of his philosophy. Ekanātha gives Bhakti, Knowledge, Renunciation and Meditation as the four means of God-realisation. Bhakti he defines as intense love, and Knowledge as the firm belief in the identity of the finite self and the infinite self. Renunciation is defined as a feeling of strong disgust which contemptuously treats a damsel like Urvashī or a heap of jewels, as if they were like a blade of grass (E. B. XIX. 347—352, 355). In addition to these, he lays stress in various places on the path of 'meditation'. Let concentration be actuated by love, hate, or fear. If a man concentrates his body, mind, and speech upon one object, he is sure, in course of time, to be so transformed as to be one with the object. In order to prove the wonderful power of 'meditation', he gives the illustration of an insect and a bee. A bee catches an insect, and keeps it in the fissure of a wall and goes out in search of food. Between the bee's departure and return, the poor insect is practically lost in the thought of the bee. The insect expects the bee to come and peck at it every moment. As a result of this expectant concentration generated through fear, a wonderful transformation takes place in the insect. A day dawns when that crawling insect is itself transfomed into a flying bee, and in its own turn leaves the wall, and flies in the high air above. Ekanātha cleverly remarks that in this illustration both the insect and the bee are dull, and live only on the instinctive plane. If even an insect living on the instinctive plane is transformed into a bee through the strength of contemplation, will not the meditation of God, who is Self-effulgent, by a man, who is sentient and lives on the intellectual plane, transform him into God? (E. B. IX. 236—244).

One must make haste to realise God.

41. Ekanātha exhorts men to understand how precious this human life is. It is easy to be born either in hell or in heaven; because the former is the effect of the excess of demerit, while the latter is the result of excess of merit. A human birth on the other hand is possible only when merit and demerit balance each other. Coupled with this accidental character of human birth, if one were to note the impossibility of God-vision in any other life, one need not be told that one must make haste to realise the divinity in himself. If a man were to reason that he would try for spiritual life after he had gratified his sense, let him remember, says Ekanātha, that Death is certain, and no one knoweth the day and the hour when Death will lay his icy hand on us. As the soldier who has entered into the thick of a fight cannot take a moment's rest so long as he has not conquered his foe; or as a widower is most anxious to get himself wedded to a new bride; so let a man with all speed make ready to take up this new bride, more beautiful, and more chaste than can be imagined. As no moment is to be lost in the search of the lost child by a beloved monarch, so let no man waste a moment to start for the search after this divine bliss. Slaying sloth, conquering sleep, let a man watch and pray day and night, for "ye know not what hour your Lord doth come" (E. B. II. 22—30; IX. 334—344).

Esoteric Bhakti.

42. Ekanātha divides his discussion of Bhakti into two parts: Bhakti as end, and Bhakti as means. Ideal, or what we might call Esoteric Bhakti, is possible only on the highest plane of experience; and it is therefore possible only to a select few. In this highest form, the means and the end merge into each other. At this stage, with their minds purified by their faithful devotion, His devotees obtain the intuition of their true self through the grace of the Guru. From this view-point, they see that the hearts of all people are but temples for His residence. Thus they then see Him everywhere inside and outside. Then the devotee himself becomes God, who pervades the whole world. He now may be truly said to live, move, and have his being in Him. The perception of distinctions of kind, of names and forms, of conditions and actions, is now no bar to him for the true perception of divinity in all these. He is a true devotee whose conviction that God is everywhere is not in the least affected even when he sees before him an unmanageable variety of things and events. Ekanātha regards this as the acme of realisation, and is never wearied in describing the wonderful equality or even-mindedness in the experience of such a realised soul. The truest worship offered to God consists in realising divine presence everywhere. Realising His presence everywhere, such a Bhakta prostrates himself before men, women, and children, cows, asses, or horses. This kind of worship is possible only when God is pleased to illumine the heart of His Bhakta with the ray of His divine knowledge (E. B. XXIX. 275—280; 282—284).

The True Bhagavata Dharma.

43. The highest duty according to the Bhāgavata Dharma, therefore, consists in relinquishing one's affection for one's belongings and dedicating them all—wife, children, home, or even one's life—to the service of God. Ekanātha here tells us how all the eleven senses can be directed towards God. The Mind should always meditate on Him. The Ear should listen to the discussions of His greatness and mercy. The Tongue should always be active in uttering His holy name. The Hands should worship His image and the Feet should walk towards the holy temple, in which His image is installed. The Nose should smell the flowers and the "tulasī" leaves with which He is worshipped. The cast-off flowers of His worship should be placed on one's Head, and the water consecrated by the touch of His feet should be put inside the Mouth. Thus to direct towards God one's instinctive and purposive, religious and social actions, is the true Bhāgavata Dharma. As the bubbles on the watery wave are all the while playing on the water, so the Bhakta is in all of his actions engaged in worshipping his Ideal (E. B. II. 298—303, 346—347).

Three grades of the Bhagavatas.

44. We have up till now placed before our readers the highest kind of Bhakti and the truest nature of the Bhāgavata Dharma. We now discuss the different grades of the devotees, according as they remain faithful or unfaithful to their ideal. The best of the Bhāgavatas perceives God in all beings, and all beings in God. He sees one God pervading the whole universe. Not only this, he realises that he himself is this all-pervading God. He is the greatest of devotees, the greatest of the Bhaktas. The second type of Bhāgavata is he who makes a distinction between God, His saints, and the ignorant masses of men. As he regards God as the highest object of reverence, he loves Him. His devotees in His eyes are just inferior to Him; therefore he wants to make friendship with them. He pities the ignorant, as he considers them lowest in the scale; and he neglects the God-haters because they are sinful. He is said to be of an inferior type of Bhakta, because he has not completely understood the Lord as He truly is. The last type is represented by him whose dogmatic conviction would restrict divinity only to a stone-image. He never even bows before saints: what then of common people? He never even dreams of respecting them as divine: this is the lowest type (E. B. II. 643—645; II. 649—650; II. 652—654).

45. How the highest kind of Bhakta is merged in Divine joy has been well expressed by Ekanātha. When a man begins to repeat God's name, a Bhakta through divine grace, falls a victim to that divine madness, which, as it were, transfigures him completely. Tears flow from his eyes, the body trembles, and his breath becomes slow. When the mind is thus absorbed in its spiritual essence, his throat is choked with excess of joy, his hair stand on end, his eyelids become half-opened, and his look becomes stationary. The constant repetition of God's name results in his mind being overcome by divine love, and he begins to lament loudly almost in a frenzied manner. But somehow this lamentation results in an equally frenzied laughter, and thus he alternately wails and laughs. He feels excessive joy at the thought that the grace of the Guru has removed from him the last taint of egoism and ignorance. He exultingly dances because his teacher has returned to him his Self, who had been practically lost to him through his folly. With the exultation resulting from these, he begins to sing songs of God's praise. But then, he even leaves that, and cries aloud : "I am the singer as well as the hearer. I am my song. I alone exist in this world. There is no trace of duality to be met with " (E. B. III. 589—602).

The Bliss of the repetition of God's Name.

46. Thus it is the utterance of God's name that gives the blessed contentment to a man's heart. Bhakti may, therefore, be well called the great royal road, for God personally stands there to guard the wayfarer from the attacks of highwaymen. With the disc in His hand, God asks His devotee if He can do anything for him. Himself without enemies, He destroys with His weapons those who are the enemies of His devotees. With His disc also, He destroys His devotee's egoism, and with His mace, his attachment and ignorance. With His conch, He illuminates his mind with the spark of His knowledge, and with the lotus in His hand He worships His devotee. What fear of danger can there exist for a Devotee, when God has given him such an assurance of protection ? (E. B. II. 542—545).

Bhakti, a Royal Road.

47. Not only is the way of Bhakti easier than the path of knowledge, but it is by itself sufficient. As the Sun requires no help to dispel darkness, Bhakti requires no external help to destroy Avidyā. Intellectual knowledge is unnecessary. Ekanātha illustrates this by the example of

Intellect *vs.* Love.

the milk-maids of Vraja. Those ladies were manifestly ignorant of any scriptural knowledge. But by loving Him, and even acting against the injunctions of the Śāstras, they realised their spiritual goal. In his enthusiasm to show that the Gopīs could realise God simply through love, Ekanātha uses a phraseology which is likely to be misunderstood. He describes as if the Vraja milk-maids illegally associated themselves with their paramour, the young adolescent Kṛishṇa, while He was leading a pastoral life. Let it, however, be remembered that this is only imagery. Ekanātha expressly says in the 12th Adhyāya that the Gopīs loved him as a dutiful wife her husband. The above-mentioned immoral imagery is used just to put clearly two factors involved in the attempt towards the realisation of divine experience. The first is the extraordinary courage which will not be daunted to make a holocaust of everything, and the second is the forgetfulness of everything except God. As the paramour forgets everything beside the thought of the lover, so a devotee forgets all in thinking about God. That Ekanātha, though in word-painting he makes use of this loose language, did not mean any immorality, can be proved from two things. In the first place, he says that the Vraja ladies were not ordinary women: they were Śrutis or Vedic hymns incarnate. As hymns they were not able to obtain an intuitive, direct perception of God; hence they assumed a human form, and realised God through love. Secondly, he expressly lays down that they followed the Lord because they believed that He alone had the power to gratify the innermost craving of their heart. Thus it was not flesh but spirit that attracted them (E. B. XII. 191—192, 163—166).

The help of the Guru is invaluable.

48. In matters worldly as well as spiritual, says Ekanātha, the help of the Guru is invaluable, nay, indispensable. If an aspirant were to proceed in these spiritual exercises with a complacent self-reliance, his progress is sure to be obstructed by many obstacles. Not even God can guide him truly. Ekanātha illustrates this by quoting the case of Vasudeva, the father of Lord Kṛishṇa. Once it so happened that Nārada visited the palatial residence of Vasudeva. Vasudeva duly worshipped him and asked him the way to God. Nārada was simply amazed. He asked Vasudeva why he should ask him this question when Shrī Kṛishṇa was already his child. Thereupon Vasudeva told him his sad story. He said that he had formerly prayed to God, who was pleased to offer him a boon. But befooled by Divine

Māyā, he requested Him to be his son. Now He was his son, but He would not be his spiritual guide. He always pleaded ignorance before him, and then there was no help for it. The moral of the story is that even in matters of spiritual progress, one may please God; but unless one has understood from the Guru what should be asked of God, one is likely to go wrong and lose the golden opportunity (E. B. III. 806—807; II. 85—87).

If Divine Knowledge is communicated by the Guru, why worship God?

49. Here a little difficulty may arise. It might be objected that if the Guru is able to give everything that the disciple wants, there is no necessity of praying to God at all. Let it be remembered once for all, that without God's grace a true Spiritual Teacher can never be found. In a sense, it might be said that the Guru and God are one. And secondly, God confers His grace only upon those that have been favoured by Saints. This has been clearly expressed by Vasudeva to Nārada: "O Nārada, thou art the favourite of God. He saves those only that are favoured by you." Ekanātha has very finely described the anxious state of the disciple expecting every minute that some one, able to save, shall meet him. In his anxiety for such a one, he forgets all enjoyments, wanders from place to place to find him somewhere, worships him even before he has seen Him, and is lost day and night in the thought of a Guru. To such divinely discontented souls God reveals Himself in the form of a Guru (E. B. XXII. 97—100; X. 138).

God's meditation is a panacea for all evils.

50. Ekanātha tells us often that God's meditation is a panacea for all disturbances—physical as well as mental, material as well as spiritual. A single moment spent in meditating upon God can destroy tribulation, disease, obstacles, doubts, sin and egoism. All these things will vanish before the power of meditation. If it be not possible to find out a calm and quiet place, or to secure a good posture and meditate, even the constant repetition of His Name is able to ward off all calamities (E. B. XXVIII. 612—620).

Pitfalls in the path of meditation.

51. In the way of meditation, however, there are four pitfalls, against which an aspirant must guard himself. They are: dissipation, passion, fickleness and absorption. All these are the faults of an unsteady mind. To revolve in the mind the sweetness of sense-objects, when one is sitting in a meditative posture, is dissipation. To attend only to love-stories or descriptions of sexual unions, is passion. To pass from one field of consciousness to another, and thus to be every moment unsteady like a madman, is fickleness. To be inattentive through sad indifference to the chief object of meditation, and thus to be ultimately lost in sleep, or in blue or yellow colours, is absorption (E. B. XI. 706—711).

Experience of God-realisation.

52. If once God reveals Himself to the devotee in his heart, then that vision cannot be confined to the devotee's heart only. He sees God everywhere. God reveals Himself to him as the all-pervading Ātman, assuming various forms. Once He is thus revealed in His true universal form, a devotee becomes dead to all world-vision. Once He is revealed, the subtle body, the cause of all bondage, perishes without a stroke. A gust of strong wind dispels an array of clouds, so His spiritual light dispels all desires. With the destruction of desires, vanish all doubts and duties. As darkness cannot stand before the light of the Sun, qualities with their effects, Avidyā with ignorance, Jīva with Śiva, egoism with its ties of spirit and matter,—all vanish away. Even the constant repetition of the formula 'I am Brahman' is no more to be heard. All fear of birth and death disappears, and the stage is reached where the world is not, and God alone is. His devotees reach this stage by constantly praying to Him (E. B. XX. 374—381).

A True Samadhi.

53. This experience is true Samādhi. People have mistaken notions about this Brāhmic consciousness or Samādhi. Some believe that it is necessarily an actionless stage, characterised by stiffness of body and absence of speech and motion. But really it is not so. If stiffness of body is to be called Samādhi, any man who has an attack of apoplexy can well be said to have experienced Samādhi. Such a temporary loss of consciousness can be brought about by merely holding the breath for a few seconds, or even by hypnotism. That is, therefore, a mistaken notion of Samādhi. Yājñavalkya, Śuka and Vāmadeva are illustrations of perfect saints whose Brāhmic consciousness was in no way tampered with, even when they walked and talked and did all manner of things. Nārada used to cut all sorts of humourous jokes, and yet he was all the while living in Brāhmic consciousness. Yājñavalkya had two wives, but his Samādhi was proved real by the Sages of the Brihadāranyaka Upanishad. Why not take the most famous illustration of Arjuna ? Lord Kṛishna blessed Arjuna with Brāhmic consciousness, and made him fight against the Kauravas. In spite of his fight, Arjuna continued to occupy the level of Brāhmic consciousness. Thus a true Samādhi, resulting from the teaching of a true Spiritual Teacher, is entirely compatible with action. It is not a loss of consciousness, or motionlessness, but a constant divine experience (E. B. II. 423—432).

Description of a Soul that has realised God.

54. A devotee, who has been thus favoured has transcended the responsibilities of all the stages of life. Constant association with God is now his duty. Now neither good action, nor renunciation, nor discrimination can bring him any profit. He, who has surrendered himself to God, has paid all his debts to deities, sages, ancestors, and men. He, who has clearly understood his distinctness from body and senses, can have now no gain from the controlling of his senses. To him, who has truly realised God, no higher gain can be obtained by constant meditation on Him. He is merged in Brāhmic consciousness, even when he is enjoying all sense-objects (E. B. XVII. 389—391 ; XXVIII. 323—329).

Who can frighten a God's Servant ?

55. Who has the power to frighten this servant of God ? When, with His burning disc, God in person is ready to guard His devotee, who can attack him ? No obstacle can present itself before him. He, who saved Prahlāda from the clutches of his demoniac father, will never allow a hair of His devotee's body to be touched. If God Himself obeys His devotee, what can bring difficulties in his path ? All fear has left him for good. In him the very gods find a Tower of Strength (E. B. XXIII. 446—451).

Such men are rare.

56. Such perfect souls, however, are very rare. In this wide world, only by rare chance may it be possible for one to meet such a man. Equally rare is he who is gifted with the vision to recognise such a man, if chance but puts him in his way (E. B. XXII. 579—580).

CHAPTER XIII.

General Review.

There are certain characteristics which mark off the saints of this period from those of the preceding and the forthcoming ages. In the first place, there is to be seen among the saints of this period a unique reconciliation of worldly and spiritual life, unattained either before or afterwards. For example, as we have already pointed out, Janārdana Swāmī and Ekanātha were types of saints who did not extricate themselves from worldly life. Janārdana Swāmī was a fighter and a saint; Ekanātha was a householder and a saint. In this reconciliation of worldly and spiritual life, Ekanātha accomplished what had not been accomplished either by Jñānadeva or Nāmadeva before him, or by Tukārāma and Rāmadāsa after him. Jñānadeva and Rāmadāsa had no wives and children, and so we cannot say that they ever reconciled the worldly and the spiritual life. Nāmadeva and Tukārāma had wives and children, but, as in the case of Spinoza, God was to them a great lion's den to which all steps pointed, but from which none returned. They were so absorbed in God that nothing else was of any value to them. Not so with Ekanātha. He observed the Aristotelian mean in all things, was a man in whose life the principle of right judgment could be seen to have predominated at every moment. Ekanātha's life was unique, and he derived this tact in no small measure from his teacher Janārdana Swāmī himself. In the second place, at this period, we see a popularisation of Vedānta accomplished to an extent which was never known before. Jñānadeva's philosophy, like his language, was somewhat abstruse. It had also clothed itself in an antique garb, which prevented people from adjudging it at its proper value. Not so with Ekanātha. Ekanātha's teachings, whether in his work on the Bhāgavata, or in his heart-felt Abhangas, were such as could be appreciated by the populace. It was principally Ekanātha who made the ideas of Vedānta familiar to the men in the street. With Jñānadeva, philosophy had reigned in the clouds; with Ekanātha, it came upon the earth and dwelt among men. As we may see from the account of the various philosophical principles which he enunciates so lucidly in his great commentary on the Bhāgavata, Ekanātha had attained to a stage of exposition so simple, so lucid, and so popular, that nobody before his time, or nobody after him, has ever been equally successful in presenting

The Chief Characteristics of the Age of Ekanatha.

philosophy in such a popular manner. In the third place, the most distinguishing feature of Ekanātha as a Marāthi writer is his great love and respect for the language in which he wrote. It is the Saints of the Mahārāshṭra school, and most particularly Jñānadeva, Ekanātha and Rāmadāsa, who laid especial stress upon conveying their ideas in the simple vernacular, instead of in Sanskrit in which latter it was customary for the Pandits to clothe their thoughts. Jñānadeva first, Ekanātha afterwards, and Rāmadāsa last, broke away from this tradition of the erudite Pandits, took to the vernacular as a means of expounding their thoughts, and thus could appeal to the lowest rungs of the Marātha society. Prof. Patwardhan has stated the service which Ekanātha did to the cause of Marāthi literature in the following way: "The partisans of Sanskrit were still very powerful, and the contempt for Marāthi was still rank and rampant. But it was not for name and fame among the Pandits that Ekanātha wrote. It was for the diffusion of Truth and Light among the illiterate, among women and Śūdras, that Ekanātha wrote. He scorned the scorn of the learned, and championed the voiceless millions, espousing the cause of the vernaculars. He too had to fight the battle of the vernacular, as we in these days of greater enlightenment and consequent deeper darkness have to wage. Marāthi was the language of the illiterate and the vulgar, and one versed in Sanskrit lore ought not to have anything to do with it. It was degradation. That was the view of the learned in those days, just as nearly as of the so-called educated in these days. Ekanātha, like his great predecessor, cared not a jot for these considerations. His heart went out to the spiritually blind and mute, and he knew that the way to reach them was to approach them through their own mother tongue. He faced all opposition: answered the summons of the learned in Kāśī, endured his trial before that tribunal for the crime of rendering the sacred words of the Bhāgavata into the language of the Śūdras: and with his courage and powers of persuasion, he came out unscathed. Jñānadeva was proud of Marāthi. Prouder still was Ekanātha."

संस्कृत वाणी देवें केली । प्राकृत तरी चोरापासुनी झाली ।
असोत या अभिमान भुली । वृथा बोली काय काज ॥
आतां संस्कृता अथवा प्राकृता । भाषा झाली जे हरिकथा ।
ते पावनाचि तत्वतां । सत्य सर्वथा मानली ॥
देवासि नाहीं वाचाभिमान । संस्कृत प्राकृत तया समान ।
ज्या वाणी जाहलें ब्रह्मकथन । त्या भाषा श्रीकृष्ण संतोषें ॥
माझी मराठी भाषा चोखडी । परब्रह्मीं फळली गाढी ॥

Ekanātha asks very often "if Sanskrit was made by God, was Prākṛit born of thieves and knaves? Let these errings of vanity alone. Whether it is Sanskrit or Prākṛit, wherever the story of God is told, it is essentially holy and must be respected ......God is no partisan of tongues. To Him Prākṛit and Sanskrit are alike. My language, Marāthi, is worthy of expressing the highest sentiments, and is rich-laden with the fruits of divine knowledge." We can see thus how Ekanātha occupies not merely a high place among the saints of Mahārāshṭra, but also among its great poets.

PART IV.

The Age of Tukarama : Personalistic Mysticism.

CHAPTER XIV.

Biographical Introduction : Tukarama.

The date of Tukarama's passing away.

1. It is an unfortunate thing that, in spite of much research, there should still be a difference of opinion about the dates of the birth and death of a celebrated saint like Tukārāma. It may be said, however, that the date of Tukārāma's passing away is a little more definite than that of his birth. In an MS. of Tukārāma's Gāthā, which is preserved at Dehū, the place of Tukārāma's birth and death, the date of his passing away is given as 1649 A.D. (Śake 1571); while in the copy of Tukārāma's Gāthā written by Bāḷājī, the son of Santājī Jaganāḍe, the famous disciple of Tukārāma, the date of Tukārāma's passing away is given as 1650 A.D. (Śake 1572). It is to be noted, however, that the date on which Tukārāma passed off is generally recognised to be Phālguna Vadya 2, Thursday. Now Phālguna Vadya 2 does not fall on Thursday in 1649 A.D. (Śake 1571), but in 1650 A.D. (Śake 1572). Hence the greater probability of 1650 A.D. (Śake 1572) being the date of Tukārāma's passing away from this life.

Theories about the date of Tukarama's birth.

2. As regards Tukārāma's birth, there are four different theories: (1) Mr. Rājavaḍe relying upon the entry in an MS. of the Gāthā with a Vārkarī at Vāī, fixes upon Śake 1490 (1568 A.D.) as the date of Tukārāma's birth. Moreover, he quotes an Abhaṅga of one Mahipati that Tukārāma was initiated about thirty years after Bābājī's passing away. The main argument against Rājavaḍe's date is that if we are to suppose that Tukārāma was born in 1568 A.D. (Śake 1490), he must have been eighty-two years of age at the time when he passed away, that is, in 1650 A.D. (Śake 1572), and we know that it is a historical fact that when Tukārāma died, his wife, who was only seven or eight years younger than himself, was pregnant, and that later she gave birth to Nārāyaṇa, who was thus Tukārāma's posthumous son. Now we could not ordinarily suppose that a son could be born to a man at the age of eighty-two. Hence, Mr. Rājavaḍe's date cannot be regarded as very convincing. Rājavaḍe says that if his date were to be regarded as true, then we can very well explain how Tukārāma was

initiated in Śake 1520 (1598 A.D.) on Māgha Śuddha 10, which is a Thursday. (2) Mr. Bhāve argues from this date of Tukārāma's initiation, namely, Śake 1520 (1598 A.D.), Māgha Śuddha 10, which was a Thursday, backwards to about twenty-one years, when, according to him, Tukārāma was born, which gives us the date 1577 A.D. (Śake 1499). Bhāve thus relies upon 1598 A.D. (Śake 1520) as an absolutely reliable date of Tukārāma's initiation, and deduces all other dates from it. (3) Mr. Pāngārakar tries to prove that the famine referred to in Tukārāma's Abhaṅgas must be taken to be in 1629 A.D. (Śake 1551), and that very soon later Tukārāma was initiated, namely, in Śake 1554 (1632 A.D.) on Māgha Śuddha 10, which also was a Thursday. Also, Pāngārakar relies upon Mahipati's evidence that half of Tukārāma's life had been spent before the time of the famine, and the remaining half later, from which fact he goes back twenty-one years and comes to 1608 A.D. (Śake 1530) as the date of Tukārāma's birth. Now these dates, namely, Śake 1530, 1551, 1554 as the dates of Tukārāma's birth, of the famine, and of the initiation, are not impossible ones. But it must be remembered that Pāngārakar, on the evidence of Mahipati, conceives Tukārāma's life to be divided exactly into two half portions at 1551. Probably what Mahipati meant was that 'about' a half of Tukārāma's life and not exactly a half was spent at the time of the famine. Moreover, it must be remembered that Mahipati lived about 125 years later than Tukārāma, and that sufficient time elapsed between the two to allow some legends to grow about the life of Tukārāma. Moreover, if we take 1608 A.D. (Śake 1530) as the date of Tukārāma's birth, Tukārāma becomes a very short-lived man, that is, he was only forty-two years of age at the time of his passing away, and thus we cannot very well explain the reference to old age जरा कर्णमुळीं सांगों आली गोष्टी in Tukārāma's Abhaṅgas except in a vicarious fashion. (4) We thus come to a fourth date as not an improbable date of Tukārāma's birth. It is 1598 A.D. (Śake 1520) as given in the family chronologies of Tukārāma both at Dehū and Paṇḍharapūr. Now it is true that in these chronologies it is also told that the date of birth was Māgha Śuddha 5, Thursday. Now the fact that Māgha Śuddha 5, Thursday, does not occur in 1598 A.D. (Śake 1520) must not make us suppose, as Pāngārakar says, that Śake 1520 is an impossible date. The vagaries of calculation according to the Indian almanac are proverbial. Besides, if we are to give up either 1520 or Māgha Śuddha 5, Thursday, we had rather give up the second by all means. It must be remembered, however, that this date, namely, Śake 1520, is sanctioned by the family chronologies of Tukārāma both at Dehū and Paṇḍharapūr, and that it accounts for the reference in Tukārāma's Abhaṅgas to his old age, and yet does not make Tukārāma too old at the time of his death. As to the year again, when the famine took place and when Tukārāma was initiated, as we have pointed out above, we need not go to 1629 A.D. (Śake 1551) as the only year of famine. There are famines in India every now and then, and it is not impossible that some famine near Śake 1541 would have been meant. 1632 A.D. (Śake 1554) as the date of Tukārāma's initiation could then be brought back to 1619 A.D. (Śake 1541), on which there was Thursday on Māgha Śuddha 10. It thus seems probable that Tukārāma having been born in 1598 A.D. (Śake 1520), experienced a dire famine some time before 1619 A.D. (Śake 1541), when he lost his wife and trade, became sorrow-stricken, and gave himself up to the contemplation of God, when in Śake 1541 (1619 A.D.) on Māgha Śuddha 10, Thursday, he was initiated by Bābājī in a dream. Thus Tukārāma's earlier life of twenty-one years having been spent in Saṃsāra, the remaining thirty-one years, namely, from 1619 A.D. to 1650 A.D. (Śake 1541 to 1572) were spent in Paramārtha. Thus we can provide for a reasonably long time for the seed of Tukārāma's spiritual teaching to sprout, to flower, and to fructify. The 21 years before initiation and the 31 years after initiation do not balance against each other as half and half; but what we have to understand from Mahipati is that the life of Tukārāma was divided into two portions, the earlier and the later, the earlier having been given to worldly matters and the later to spiritual.

Incidents in the life of Tukaram.

3. The main incidents in Tukārāma's life may now be briefly recapitulated. Tukārāma was born in 1598 A.D. (Śake 1520), and about 1613 A.D. (Śake 1535), Tukārāma was married. It is well known that he had two wives: one Rakhumābāī, and the other Jijābāī. Soon afterwards his parents died. Tukārāma suffered a loss in trade. His first wife Rakhumābāī died for want of food in a dire famine. His son named Santu also died. Tukārāma now went to Bhāmbanātha and Bhaṇḍārā and other places, and gave himself up to spiritual reading. In Śake 1541 (1619 A.D.), on Māgha Śuddha 10, Thursday, he was initiated by his Guru Bābājī in a dream. We can see how Tukārāma must have experienced the dark night of the soul, and ultimately have come to God-vision. After having realised God, he taught others the same instruction in his Kīrtanas. He usually performed Kīrtanas at Dehū, Lohagaon and Poona. He was hated by Rāmeśvarabhatta, who, however, later became his disciple. He was also scornfully treated by Mambājī Gosāvī, who also later repented. Tukārāma's wife was a Xantippe, often quarrelled with her husband, told him that he was doing no work to maintain his family, and snarled when Tukārāma received all sorts of guests and gave himself to spiritual Kīrtanas. Tukārāma suffered all these things in patience. He continued to preach the secret of spiritual life to those who assembled around him. Before he died, Tukārāma probably met both Śivājī and Rāmadāsa. Śivājī had passed his teens at the time, and had already taken Toraṇā, and was trying to found a Marāthā kingdom. Tukārāma directed Śivājī to have the spiritual instruction of Rāmadāsa. Tukārāma also probably met Rāmadāsa when the latter had gone to Paṇḍharapūr to visit the temple of Viṭṭhala. Having led an intensely spiritual life, Tukārāma passed away in Śake 1572 (1650 A.D.), Phālguna Vadya 2. There is a story told that Tukārāma ascended to heaven with his body. This is to be credited only as little as or as much as the ascension of Christ. The story must have originated in the fact that there is no Samādhi of Tukārāma built anywhere. There is a Samādhi of Jñānadeva, there is a Samādhi of Rāmadāsa, there is a Samādhi of Ekanātha, there is a Samādhi of Nāmadeva, but there is no Samādhi of Tukārāma either in Dehū or at any other place. This is probably the reason why Tukārāma has been supposed to have ascended bodily to heaven. The philosophical meaning of the story seems to be that Tukārāma was liberated before death by virtue of his God-vision, or that his very body had become divine in the process of God-contemplation.

The making of Tukarama's Mind.

4. There are a few points in the life-history of Tukārāma which we must now disentangle with some care. The question has been asked as to who exercised the greatest amount of influence in the formation of the mind of Tukārāma. In the first place, it must be noted that the direct impulse to spiritual life must have come to Tukārāma from his spiritual teacher Bābājī. There are some historical things known about Bābājī and his line. Tukārāma himself tells us that his spiritual line may be traced from Rāghava Chaitanya to Keśava Chaitanya and to Bābājī Chaitanya. Bahiṇabāī, one of Tukārāma's greatest disciples, who had seen him and had lived under his instruction, tells us that Rāghava Chaitanya was a spiritual descendant of Sachchidānanda

Bābā, who was himself a disciple of Jñānadeva. From this, it may be seen that Tukārāma came directly in the spiritual line of Jñānadeva. Now, Bahiṇābāī's evidence in this respect must be considered as more authoritative than the evidence either of Niḷobā or Mahipati, as she lived in Tukārāma's presence, and Tukārāma must have probably told Bahiṇābāī that Rāghava Chaitanya was spiritually descended from Jñānadeva. Then, again, as regards the historical evidence for these Chaitanyas, there is a work called Chaitanya-kathākalpataru written in 1787 A.D. (Śake 1709), and based upon another work referred to in that book by Kṛishṇadāsa in 1674 A.D. (Śake 1596), *i.e.*, only twenty-five years after the death of Tukārāma. There, we are told that Rāghava Chaitanya lived in Uttama-nagarī, that is to say, in modern Otūra, on the banks of the Pushpavaṭī, known also as Kusumāvaṭī, which may be seen running into the river Kukadī. Rāghava Chaitanya initiated one Viśvanātha Chaitanya, and called him Keśava Chaitanya. Some people identify Keśava Chaitanya with Bābājī Chaitanya, while others say that they were two different persons. In any case, it is clear that Tukārāma mentions the name of his own spiritual teacher as Bābājī. Next in importance to the receiving of spiritual instruction from Bābājī, Tukārāma refers to four different persons as having peculiarly contributed to the formation of his spiritual life. There is a famous Abhaṅga of Tukārāma, to be uttered in tune with the sound of a Ṭiparī, where Tukārāma tells us reiteratingly चौघांची तरि धरि सोय रे—"at least follow these four". These four are, first Nāmadeva, the boy of a tailor, who played without faltering; then, Jñānadeva, who with brothers and sister danced around God; then Kabīra, the disciple of Rāmānanda, who was a worthy partner to these; and finally, Ekanātha, the child of a Brahmin, who gathered about him a number of devotees. These played, says Tukārāma, the game of spiritual life, and the game never affected them. Thus, we see, that Tukārāma calls our mind to the teachings of these four great saints, indicating probably that his own mind was specially influenced by them. We can see from the account we have given of the relation between Jñānadeva and Tukārāma in what high respects Tukārāma had held Jñānadeva. As regards Tukārāma's relation to Nāmadeva, the only meaning in the story that calls Tukārāma an incarnation of Nāmadeva is that the spiritual methods of the two were probably one. When Prof. Patwardhan says that Nāmadeva appears to put more sentiment in his Abhaṅgas, while Tukārāma surpasses him in logical consistency; that while Nāmadeva is more emotional, Tukārāma is more intellectual, we do not think that he represents the case accurately. Tukārāma is so much like Nāmadeva and both go so much by emotion, that we see that they leave no room whatsoever for philosophical argument. For that matter, we may say that Jñānadeva is more intellectual than either Nāmadeva or Tukārāma. But between Nāmadeva and Tukārāma, there is nothing to choose, so far as the life of emotion and the life of mystical experience which transcends all philosophical arguments are concerned. As regards Ekanātha, we know how Tukārāma had dived into the Bhāgavata of Ekanātha, and had committed the Bhāgavata like the Jñāneśvarī almost to memory. Thus, it is not untrue to say, as Mr. Pāngārakar has pointed out, that the Gītā, the Bhāgavata, the Jñāneśvarī, the Commentary of Ekanātha on the Bhāgavata, and the Abhaṅgas of Nāmadeva peculiarly moulded Tukārāma's spiritual life. When the influence of the thoughts of these writers was added to the spiritual instruction which he had received from his master, upon both of which he pondered in solitude, resigning his mind to God in the utterance of His name, it is no wonder that the outcome should be that of a very mature soul like Tukārāma, who not merely realised God himself, but brought God-realisation within the easy reach of all.

Tukarama, Sivaji and Ramadasa.

5. There is another point in the life-history of Tukārāma which is also well worth noticing, namely his meeting with Śivājī and Rāmadāsa. If we consider carefully the dates when Tukārāma passed away, namely 1650 A.D. (Śake 1572), when Rāmadāsa came to settle on the banks of the Kṛishṇā, namely 1634 A.D. (Śake 1556), and when Śivājī captured the Toraṇā Fort, namely 1649 A.D. (Śake 1571), thus bidding fair to become the king of Mahārāshṭra later on, it is not impossible that Tukārāma might have met both Rāmadāsa and Śivājī. If the tradition were merely a tradition unsupported by any documentary evidence, we would have consented to allow the meeting to be regarded as well-nigh legendary. But we have certain Abhaṅgas which are supposed to have been composed by Tukārāma for the sake of Śivājī, which will not allow us to regard the meeting as entirely unhistorical. Tukārāma performed his Kīrtanas at Dehū, as well as at Lohagaon. Now Poona is situated just between Dehū and Lohagaon, and Śivājī had already a lodgment at Poona. Hence, it is not impossible that Śivājī might have gone to Tukārāma, seen him, and expressed a desire to be initiated by him. But, Tukārāma with foresight probably sent Śivājī to Rāmadāsa. Some of the Abhaṅgas of Tukārāma addressed to Śivājī have been translated in the next chapter. Here, we may just give a glimpse of how Tukārāma once expatiated upon the theme of heroism, both worldly and spiritual, which was also, in all probability, meant for Śivājī. The Abhaṅgas are known as पाइकीचे अभंग, Abhaṅgas of soldiery or heroism. Tukārāma tells us that a hero is a hero both in worldly as well as in spiritual matters. "Without heroism, misery cannot disappear. Soldiers must become reckless of their lives, and then God takes up their burden......He who bravely faces volleys of arrows and shots and defends his master, can alone reap eternal happiness...... He alone, who is a soldier, knows a soldier, and has respect for him. They, who bear weapons only for the sake of bodily maintenance, are mere mercenaries. The true soldier alone stands the test of critical occasions." This Abhaṅga has been supposed to have been composed by Tukārāma with the object of comparing the worldly soldier with the spiritual soldier. Then, again, as regards Tukārāma having met Rāmadāsa at Paṇḍharapūr, it is true that we have no documentary evidence, as we have in the case of Tukārāma and Śivājī. But we know very well how Rāmadāsa had established himself on the banks of the Kṛishṇā in 1644 A.D. (Śake 1566), that is to say, about six years before Tukārāma's death, and how Rāmadāsa once visited Paṇḍharapūr and composed a song telling us that God Viṭṭhala and Rāma were identical. It would be a strange thing if Tukārāma and Rāmadāsa, being the two greatest saints of Mahārāshṭra at the time, should not have met each other. The 'story' is not entirely meaningless which tells us that Rāmadāsa and Tukārāma met at Paṇḍharapūr on the opposite banks of the river Bhīmā, the one weeping and the other bawling, and when their respective disciples asked them the meaning of these strange gestures, Tukārāma replied that he wept because people were so much merged in worldly matters that they would not know that the way out lay in the realisation of God ; while Rāmadāsa said that he bawled out because in spite of his bawling out, people would not hear his spiritual cry. The story only serves to rule out the improbability of the two of the greatest saints of Śivājī's time not having met each other, and it would be an irony of fate if the tender-minded and the tough-minded saints had not met, and exchanged their thoughts with one another.

6. Tukārāma had a distinguished galaxy of disciples, all absolutely devoted and full of admiration for him. Santājī

Telī, who was one of the greatest disciples of Tukārāma, was a writer of Tukārāma's Abhaṅgas, along with Gaṅgārāma Mavāḷa, who was another. The MS. of Santājī Telī has been preserved to this day, and has been published by Mr. Bhāve. Rāmeśvarabhatta, whose ancestors were residents of the Karnātaka, had come and settled in the district of Poona, and he worshipped his tutelary deity, namely, the Vyāghreśvara at Vāgholī. He was given too much to priestly pride and ritualism, but was later converted from this barren life to a spiritualistic life by Tukārāma. Śivabā Kāsāra, who lived in Lohagaon, first hated Tukārāma, but later became an ardent admirer of him. It was his wife, who, having been displeased with her husband for having become a disciple of Tukārāma, once poured hot water on the body of Tukārāma while he had once gone to Lohagaon. Mahādājīpant, the Kulkarni of Dehū, was a very honest and straightforward disciple of Tukārāma, who spent on the rebuilding of the temple of Viṭṭhala at Dehū every pie out of the extra proceeds of a farm which had been given to Tukārāma by his employer, but which he had refused to accept. Niḷobā, who was perhaps the greatest of Tukārāma's disciples, is said to have been initiated by Tukārāma in a dream in the year 1678 A.D. (Śake 1600). He lived at Pimpaḷaner, and continued the Vārkarī tradition of Tukārāma. Bahiṇābāī, whose Abhaṅgas have been recently discovered and printed, was a resident of Śiur, and had seen Tukārāma personally. Her account of Tukārāma's spiritual lineage has been already noticed by us as being of great historical value, and as Pāngārakar tells us, she later came under the influence of Rāmadāsa, who gave her an image of Māruti which is still worshipped in Bahiṇābāī's household. These constitute the greatest of the disciples of Tukārāma.

The disciples of Tukarama.

7. There are various collations called Gāthās of the Abhaṅgas of Tukārāma, of which we must quote here four of the most important. The exposition of Tukārāma's mystical career and teaching, given in the later chapters, follows closely the numbering of the Abhaṅgas in the edition of Vishṇubuvā Jog, who published his 1st edition of the Gāthā of Tukārāma in two volumes in 1909 A.D. (Śake 1831), which is in fact the first and the only attempt in Marāthi of presenting the original with a translation. Besides, Vishṇubuvā Jog spent his life in studying the Abhaṅgas of Tukārāma, and was well respected among the Vārkarīs at Paṇḍharapūr. He had an

Editions of the Gathas of Tukarama.

open mind, and was perhaps the greatest and the most enlightened among the Vārkarīs during the last quarter of the century. The second collection of Tukārāma's Abhaṅgas is the edition called the Induprakāsa edition, which was printed by the Government of Bombay with the help of Mr. S.P. Pandit in 1869 A.D. This is a very careful collation of the various recensions of Tukārāma's Gāthās based upon the MSS. at Dehū, Talegaon, Kaḍūsa and Paṇḍharapūr. Fraser and Marāthe's translation of Tukārāma's Gāthās follows this edition in point of numbering. A third edition is that of Mr. H. N. Apte, printed at the Aryabhushaṇa Press according to the MS. in the possession of the Baḍaves of Paṇḍharapūr. This is an edition which has got much traditional value, because the Vārkarīs perform their Bhajana according to the readings of that edition. Fourthly, Mr. Bhāve has recently published an edition of Tukārāma's "real Gāthā" as he calls it, which consists of thirteen hundred Abhaṅgas according to the MS. of Santājī Jaganāḍe. There is no doubt that this is a very authentic collection, but it is also likely that it is not a complete collection. The other editions of Tukārāma's Abhaṅgas which have been printed will not interest our readers very much, and so we refrain from giving any account of them. Our order of exposition* follows, for the sake of the numbering of the Abhaṅgas, the edition of Vishṇubuvā Jog which we have above referred to, and which we heartily recommend to our readers for the sake of the Marāthi original and the translation.

* Recently, a Source-book of Tukārāma's Abhaṅgas has been published by us, which gives *seriatim* the Abhaṅgas referred to in our exposition of Tukārāma in the next two chapters.

CHAPTER XV.

Tukarama's Mystical Career.

I. Historical Events in his Life.

Introductory.

1. A faithful account of Tukārāma's mystical development as traced through his Abhaṅgas is a subject hitherto unattempted, in the first place, because Tukārāma has left to us quite a large number of Abhaṅgas, and in the second place, because it is really a difficult thing to trace through his Abhaṅgas the order of his developing mystical experience. Yet an attempt has been made here to essay this difficult task with what success we leave our readers to judge. We shall try to present the account of Tukārāma's spiritual development in his own words, which will leave our readers free to form any conclusions they like in regard to the value of the data for the comparison of Tukārāma's spiritual experience with that of the great mystics of the West.

The occasion of Tukarama's initiation.

2. We shall begin by giving an account of Tukārāma's description of his own initiation. Tukārāma tells us that he was initiated by his spiritual teacher in a dream: "I imagined I met him while he was going to the river for a holy bath. He placed his hand upon my head, and asked me to give him some ghee for his meals. Unfortunately, being in a dream, I could not give it to him. An obstacle having thus apparently arisen, my spiritual teacher hastened away. He told me his spiritual lineage, namely, that it had come from Rāghava Chaitanya and Keśava Chaitanya. He told me also his own name which was Bābājī, and gave me the Mantra 'Rāma, Kṛishṇa, Hari' for meditation. As it was the 10th day of the bright half of Māgha, and as, moreover, it was a Thursday (a day sacred to the Guru), I accepted the Mantra with the whole of my heart" (Abg. 3427). Now this Bābājī, who was the teacher of Tukārāma, has his Samādhi at Otūr, and one does not know whether Bābājī was actually living at the time of Tukārāma. In any case; Tukārāma tells us that he got his initiation in a dream, and with that his spiritual career began: "Verily, my teacher being cognisant of the aspirations of my heart bestowed upon me a Mantra I loved so well, and a Mantra also which was so easy to utter. Verily, there can be no difficulty in the uttering of that Mantra. By that Mantra, have many, who have gone

from amongst us, crossed the ocean of life. To those who know, and to those who do not know, the Mantra has served as a raft to enable them to cross the ocean of life. Verily, I was put in possession of this raft —there is no limit to the grace of God Pāṇḍuraṅga!" (Abg. 3428).

Tukarama's family lineage.

3. Tukārāma was born of a poor family in the caste of the Kuṇabīs, that is to say, farmers. He feels glad that he was born a Kuṇabī; otherwise, he says, he would have died with arrogrance. "Well done, O God! Tukārāma dances and touches Thy feet. Had I been a learned man, I would have brought calamities on me; would have scorned the service of the saints;........would have been subject to pride and arrogance; would only have gone by the way by which other people have gone to the Hades. Greatness and arrogance would surely have brought me to hell" (Abg. 178). He tells us also that throughout his family lineage, he has been a Vārkarī of Paṇḍharī: "I have inherited this practice of going to a pilgrimage to Paṇḍharī from my ancestors. I recognise no other pilgrimage, and no other vow. My only vow is to make a fast on the Ekādaśī day, and to sing the name of God. I shall utter the name of God, which is verily what will last to the end of time" (Abg. 1599).

Tukarama's family difficulties.

4. As is often the case with the mystics, Tukārāma experienced every kind of difficulty in his life. "What shall I eat, and where shall I go? On whose support should I count and live in my village? The Patel of my village, as well as its other residents, have grown angry with me. Who will give me alms? People will say that I have lost touch with the world, and will drag me to the court. I have gone to the good people in my village, and have told them that these people are pursuing a poor man like myself. Verily, I am tired of the company of these people. I shall now go and find out Viṭṭhala" (Abg. 2995). Added to the forlornness in his village, Tukārāma experienced every difficulty within his family. His estate was all sold. Famine made havoc in his family. "By repentance, I am now remembering Thee. Life seems to me like vomit. Happy am I that my wife is a termagant. Happy am I that I have lost all reputation. Happy, that I have been disrespected by men. Happy, that I have lost all my cattle. Well it is that I have ceased to be ashamed among men. Well it is that I have come as a supplicant to Thee, O God! Well it is that I built a temple to Thee, and neglected my children and wife......" (Abg.

3941). Tukārāma's wife was so much exasperated at the demeanour of Tukārāma, and particularly at the very kind way in which he treated his saintly guests, that she began to exclaim: "Why is it that people come to our house? Have they no business of their own? For the sake of God, my husband has entered into relationship with the whole world. Indeed, he is put to no trouble for speaking mere good words." "My wife," says Tukārāma, "does not like any of these things, and runs after my guests like a mad dog" (Abg. 3489). "Verily, saints have no business here," says the wife of Tukā, "they can get food without doing any work. Every man that meets me beats the Ṭāḷa, and creates a spiritual hubbub. These people are as good as dead, and have bade good-bye to shame. They do not look so much as to the means of maintaining themselves. Their wives cry in despair, and curse these people" (Abg. 3491). The whole array of calamities now befell Tukārāma. His father died, and he probably began to experience anxiety for his maintenance, as he had never done before. One of his wives died of starvation, and Tukā believed that she got absolution. His child died, and Tukā was glad that God deprived him of the cause of unreal affection. His mother died, and Tukā bade good-bye to all anxieties forever. These incidents only served to increase the love of Tukā for God. "Between us two," says Tukā to God, "nobody now intervenes to create an artificial barrier" (Abg. 394). All these things he took to be the indications of God's favour on him. "God shall never help His devotee to carry on his worldly existence in an easy manner, but would ward off every source of affection. If He were to make His devotee fortunate, that would serve merely to make him arrogant. Hence it is that God strikes His devotee with poverty. Were He to give him a good wife, his affections would be centred on her. Hence God endows His devotee with a termagant. Verily, I have personally experienced all these things, says Tukā. Why need I speak about these matters to others?" (Abg. 2224).

Namadeva's command to Tukarama to compose poetry.

5. While he was experiencing such difficulties, Tukā had on another occasion another dream, in which Nāmadeva, the saint of Paṇḍharapūr, who had lived about three hundred years before the age of Tukārāma, appeared before him, and ordered him to compose poetry. "Nāmadeva aroused me in my dream and came in the company of God. He told me that I should not mis-direct my words, but should give myself to composing poetry. He told me to measure poems, telling me that God was counting the measure. He patted me on the back, and made me conscious of my mission. He told me also that the numbers of Abhaṅgas to be composed was a hundred crores all told. What part of this number had been unattempted by Nāmadeva, Tukā made good by his own composition" (Abg. 3937). We know how Nāmadeva had taken a vow that he would compose altogether a hundred crores of Abhaṅgas. But as he entered Samādhi before that number was reached, he entrusted the mission of composing the rest to Tukārāma. The number seems fabulous, but the meaning is that Tukā only carried on the mission of the spiritual elevation of Mahārāshṭra through literature, which Nāmadeva had set before him. Tukārāma felt glad that he saw God in a dream on account of Nāmadeva. "If thou allowest me, O God, I shall live in Thy company, or in the company of the Saints. I have left off a place, which otherwise I would have desired. Be not now indifferent to me, O God! Howsoever low my place, howsoever mean my vocation, I shall take rest on Thy feet. I have verily seen Thee in a dream on account of Nāmadeva, and shall ever consider it a blessing upon me" (Abg. 3938). In this way, Tukārāma was conscious of the great obligation which Nāmadeva had conferred upon him by bringing God along with him in his dream. It was also on account of this incident that Tukā was inspired to compose his lyrical poems. "I have composed poetry according to my lights," says Tukā. "Whether it is good or bad, God only knows. For whom and on whose behoof these Abhaṅgas have been created, God alone knows, because they are His own handiwork. I, for myself, extricate myself from egoism, throw my entire burden upon God, and rest content" (Abg. 3385).

Tukarama's great sorrow at his poems being thrown into the river.

6. When a number of poems had been composed, and when apparently Tukā was highly spoken of by the people of his village, he incurred the anger of those who were to all appearances more learned than he, and who therefore conspired to ruin the poetical reputation of Tukā. Once upon a time they caught hold of Tukārāma's poems, and threw them into the river Indrāyaṇī. Tukārāma felt extremely sorry at this sad turn which events had taken. He determined to try his luck, and invoked God to restore his poems to him, and in case this would not happen, he determined to commit suicide. "Why shall I compose poems any longer? Must I not be ashamed of doing so? Saints will verily laugh at me. Now has come the time when God must give the decision. Truth alone must prevail. Why should one undertake any work at all without having the backing of realisation ? I can no longer maintain courage. A great ruffle has been produced in me" (Abg. 3505). Tukārāma thus determined to make a fast, until he received an assurance from God that his work was appreciated by Him. He continued his fasting penance for thirteen days, and did not partake of even a drop of water. "It is thirteen days, O God, that I have remained without food and drink. Thou art yet so unkind as not to give me any assurance even after this long period. Thou art hiding Thyself behind a stone image. Now, verily I shall commit suicide and hold Thee responsible for it ; for long have I waited to receive an assurance ; but in its absence, I shall now destroy my life" ......(Abg. 1731). God could wait no longer and see the great agonies in which Tukā was merged. He made His appearance to him in the form of a youthful image, so Tukā tells us, and gave him comfort and assurance.

God's appearance and Tukarama's thanksgiving.

7. The Abhaṅgas which Tukārāma composed on that occasion have been left to us by Tukārāma himself, and we shall give them here in the very words in which Tukā has left them : "Thou, my God, who followest us poor men as the shadow the body, camest near me like a youth, and gavest comfort to me. You showed me your beautiful form, embraced me, and pacified my mind......Verily have I troubled you for nothing. Forgive me, my God. I shall never cause you trouble any more" (Abg. 3522). "I committed a great fault, because I have taxed your patience.... Mean creature that I am, I shut my eyes and went on fasting for thirteen days ......You saved my books in the river, and protected me against the calumny of the people. Verily have you come to succour your devotee' (Abg. 3523). "Let people put a scythe against my neck, or give trouble to me as they please. I shall no longer do anything which will give you trouble ......Forgive me for what I have done before ; I shall now guard myself against future events" (Abg. 3524). "What will you not do, O God, for the saints, if they keep patience ? I grew impatient, and without intelligence as I was, I nevertheless received favour at your hands"......(Abg. 3525). "Nobody had put a scythe on my neck, nor had anybody cudgelled me on my back, and yet I cried so much for your help. Compassionate as you were, you divided yourself in two places, near me and in the river, and saved both me and the books......There is nobody who can be compared to you in point of compassion. Verily, my words fail to describe your greatness" (Abg. 3526). "You are more affectionate than a mother. You are more delightful than the moon. Your grace flows like a river. What comparison can I find for your qualities, O God?......You, who have made nectar, are really sweeter than it......I place my head on Thy feet in silence. Forgive me, O God" (Abg. 3527) "I am a vicious and sinful man. Give me a place at Thy feet. Adieu to all worldly life which only moves the mind away from God's feet. The ripples of intellect change from moment to moment, and attachment ends in dislodging us from fixity of any kind. Put an end to all my anxieties, O God, and come to live in my heart" (Abg. 3528).

Tukarama and Ramesvarbhatta.

8. Tukārāma continued to be persecuted by the evil men in his native place, and Rāmeśvarbhatta, a learned Brahmin who did not know what spiritual life was, was probably one of the greatest of the persecutors of Tukārāma. Once upon a time, it is reported, some bad men threw boiling water on the body of Tukārāma as he was passing by. That put Tukārāma in a state of agony. "My body is burning; I feel as if I am actually burning in fire," says Tukārāma. "Run to my help, O God. My very hairs are aflame. The body is cremated unto death. It is bursting into two parts. Why do you wait any longer, O God? Run to my succour with water. Nobody else can help me. You are verily my Mother, who can save her devotee at the time of distress" (Abg. 3956). And as Nemesis would have it, Rāmeśvarbhatta himself, who was the cause of the above suffering, himself suffered great bodily distress on another occasion, and failing every resource to cure it, was ultimately obliged to go to Tukārāma for succour. Tukārāma, magnanimous as he was, composed an Abhaṅga for him, by which, it is said, Rāmeśvarbhatta was relieved from his suffering: "If the mind is pure, then verily even enemies become friends; neither tigers nor serpents can hurt them in any way; poison may become nectar; a blow may become a help; what ought not to be done may itself open for him the path of moral action; sorrow will be the cause of happiness; and the flames of fire will become cool; all these things will happen when one knows that there is the same immanent Being in the hearts of all (Abg. 3957).

9. Rāmeśvarbhatta tells us the way in which, after a life of hatred towards Tukārāma, he began to conceive a respect for him, and ultimately became his disciple. "As a result of my hatred towards Tukārāma," Rāmeśvarbhatta tells us, "I suffered great bodily anguish. Jñāneśvara appeared to me in a dream, and told me that I had contracted the disease, as I had censured Tukārāma who was the incarnation of Nāmadeva, and the greatest of all Saints. Jñāneśvara also told me to be submissive towards Tukārāma, and in that way, there would be an end to my sin. Believing in the dream, I made up my mind to attend his Kīrtana every day. It was in Tukārāma's company that my body became whole" (Abg. 4145). "However learned a man may be, and however well-versed in the Vedas, he can never equal Tukārāma. Neither those who read the Purāṇas, nor those who study the Bhagavadgītā, can come to know the secret of spiritual life. The Brāhmaṇas in this bad age have been spoilt by their arrogance about caste, and by the consciousness of their superiority. Tukārāma was a Bania after all, and yet he loved God, and therefore his words were as sweet as nectar. Tukārāma merely expounded the real meaning of the Vedas.... By his devotion, his knowledge, and his dispassionateness, he was without equal...... Many great Saints have lived in times of old, but it is only Tukā who took his body to heaven. Rāmeśvarbhatta says that Tukā took leave of all men, and went to heaven in a Vimāna" (Abg. 4144).

Ramesvarbhatta's description of his own conversion.

10. Tukārāma had by this time become fixed in God. As he had put his faith in the Name which his preceptor had imparted to him, meditated on it, and made it the stepping stone to God-realisation, he was able to say that he had crossed the ocean of life. In two or three different places, Tukārāma tells us how it was the name which had saved him through life. He gives us a piece of autobiography, which we narrate here in his own words: "Salutation to God, and salutation to the Saints ......Tukā is verily the servant of his teacher Bābājī. How will my words be able to please the Saints? I will at least try to please my own mind. Let my mind go after the Name of God, and sing His praises. My early life was embittered by calamities; but the Name gave me comfort. The happiness I derived by meditation on the Name was incomparable. The Impersonal took on a form. I found that God runs to the place where the Name is celebrated. Make haste to sing the praise of God. Everything else leads to sorrow......From

A piece of Tukarama's autobiography.

those who disbelieve in the Name, God stands at a distance. .... The Name is verily the pathway to heaven.... Those who have known tell us to meditate on the Name by leaving away all arrogance..... Those, who know and those who do not know, to them I say, meditate on the Name. In this way will you be saved. I have personally known how a sinner could be saved. There could be no greater sinner than myself: other people may have stored some merit at least. To me there was no other pathway except the Kīrtana. I found that the Saint need not be afraid of his sustenance: God will find ways and means for him. God will follow the Saint, look at his feet, and cleanse his path by his robe......God has really saved me. There is no limit to the kindness of God" (Abg. 3935, 1-23). "Verily, I am a great sinner," says Tukā in another place, "I wonder why I should be the object of your love, O Saints! I know in my innermost heart that I have not attained the goal of my life. But people say that I have attained it, and follow one another in saying so. I was greatly worried in my life. I tended the cattle, but that was not enough for my maintenance. What money I had, I spent on myself and did not give in charity to Brahmins and sages. I got wearied of my relatives, wife, children, and brothers..... I could not show my face to the people. Then I began to take recourse to the woods. Hence it was that I began to like solitude. I was greatly worried on account of family expenses, and I became very unkind. My ancestors worshipped this God, and I have inherited that worship from them. Do not suppose that I have got any high-strung devotion" (Abg. 3940). Yet, in another place, Tukārāma tells us at greater length and with more personal touches the story of his own conversion. "I was born a Śūdra, and was doing the duty which had fallen to my lot by the rules of caste. This deity Viṭṭhala has been worshipped throughout the history of my family. I should not have said anything about my personal life; but because you Saints have asked me about it, I say a few words. I was merged in much sorrow in my worldly life. My mother and father died. My wealth was all spent in a famine. I was dishonoured. My wife died, because there was no food to eat. I was ashamed, and got disgusted with my life. My trade became meagre. The temple which I wished to build fell to the ground. Originally, I fasted on the Ekādaśī day and performed a Kīrtana. My mind was not set on devotional practices originally. In full faith, and with full respect, I learnt by heart some sayings of the bygone Saints. With pure heart and devotion, I sang after the men who performed the Kīrtana. I tasted of the water on the feet of the Saints; nor did I allow any shame to creep into my mind. I conferred obligations upon others as far as lay in my power, not minding any bodily hardships. I took no account of what my friends said about me. I became entirely disgusted about my life......I never cared for the opinion of the majority. I relied only upon the instruction of my Teacher in the dream, and believed fully in the power of the Name. Then, I was encouraged to compose poetry, which I did with full faith in God Viṭṭhala. I was, however, obliged to drown my poems in the river, which greatly upset my mind. I sat fasting at the door of God, and He ultimately comforted me. The many incidents of my life will take me long to describe. I may say that I am content with what has happened. What is to happen further, God only knows. I know only this that God shall never neglect His Saint. I know how kind He has been to me. This is the treasure of my life, which God Viṭṭhala has made me give out" (Abg. 3939).

Some Miracles of Tukarama.

11. As a saint grows old, miracles inevitably gather round about him. Even so did it happen in the case of Tukārāma. Once upon a time, while he was engaged in performing a Kīrtana at Lohagaon, a woman brought her dead child, threw it before Tukā, and charged him that if he were a real Saint, he would raise that child; upon which, it has been related, that Tukārāma raised the child. There is an Abhaṅga of Tukārāma probably referring to this incident: "It is not impossible for Thee, O God, to bring to life a dead being. Have we not heard of Thy prowess in history? Why shouldst Thou not do a similar act at present? Fortunate are we that we call ourselves the servants of God. Pour a balm on my eyes, says Tukā, by showing the greatness of Thy power" (Abg. 3955). On one occasion, while Tukārāma was engaged in a Kīrtana and Śivājī was attending it, the enemies of Śivājī surrounded the place where the Kīrtana was going on, upon which, there was a hue and cry among the people that had assembled for Kīrtana; and, it has been related, that as Tukā began to implore God to ward off the danger, God appeared in the form of Śivājī, and tried to escape from the hands of the enemies. Whereupon, the enemies pursued him, leaving Tukārāma and the real Śivājī unmolested at the place of the Kīrtana. Tukārāma's Abhaṅga in this connection runs as follows: "How would it be possible for me to see this great disaster with my eyes? My heart is filled with sorrow to see others in calamity. Thou must not see the disaster happen to us! We have never heard that where the servants of God dwell, the enemies can come and molest them. Tukā says, my devotion has been put to shame. I shall be living only as a contemptible being in the eyes of others" (Abg. 3951). "I am not afraid of death. But I cannot see other people plunged in misery......That one's mind should be upset at the time of Kīrtana is itself a kind of death. Give me, O God, says Tukā, shelter at a place where there is no danger" (Abg. 3952). "Shall I believe what has been said about the Kīrtana of God, that where it is being celebrated, people are relieved of their miseries ? On the other hand, there is here a great danger : the enemies have almost laid a siege. I have come to know in person that without sin no sin can take place. How shall I now believe that Thou residest where Thy servants live ?" (Abg. 3953), upon which, it is said, that the enemies were put on a false scent by God, and Śivājī and Tukārāma escaped the danger. The meeting of Tukārāma and Śivājī does not seem to be unhistorical, and we must remember the famous verse which Tukārāma sent to Śivājī, in which he said that the ant and the king were to him alike. "My delusion and desires are at an end. They are verily the bait which death sets for us. Gold and clay are to me of equal consequence. The whole heaven has descended into my house" says Tukā (Abg. 3391); so saying, it has been said, that Tukārāma refused to accept the treasure which Śivājī had sent him.

Tukarama and Jnanesvara.

12. Once upon a time it so happened that a Brahmin went to the temple of Jñāneśvara at Āḷandī, and sat there in meditation with a desire that he might receive some spiritual illumination from him. After some days, the Brahmin dreamt a dream, in which he was advised by Jñāneśvara to go to Tukārāma, who was living at that time. The Brahmin came to Tukārāma and told him what had happened in the dream ; whereupon Tukārāma composed eleven Abhaṅgas, the substance of which is as follows : "Do not follow the lore of the learned books. Take a vow that you would seek the grace of God by emptying your heart of its innate desires......God will come to your rescue by the power of the Name, and take you across the ocean of life" (Abg. 3363). "God does not possess salvation ready-made, so that He may hand it over to His devotee. Salvation consists in conquering the senses and mind, and making them empty of the pursuit of objects"...... (Abg. 3364)......"Invoke the grace of God, asking His compassion on you, and make your mind your onlooker......

Tukā says that God is an ocean of compassion, and will relieve you of the thraldom of existence in a moment's time" (Abg. 3365). "If you meditate on the name of Govinda, then you will become Govinda yourself. There will be no difference between you and God. The mind will be filled with joy, and the eyes will shed down tears of love"......(Abg. 3366) ......"Why do you become small? You are really as large as the universe itself. Take leave of your worldly life, and make haste. Because you think yourself a small being, therefore you are merged in darkness, and are grieved" (Abg. 3370) ......"The king of learned men, and their spiritual teacher, you are worthily called Jñānadeva. Why should such a low man as myself be made great? A shoe on the foot must be placed only on the foot. Even gods themselves cannot be compared to you. How would then other people be compared to you? But I do not know your purpose, and hence I humbly bend my head before you" (Abg. 3372). "A child speaks any words it pleases. It behoves you, great Saint, to excuse its lisping. I have taken no account of my station. Keep me near your feet, O Jñāneśvara," implores Tukā (Abg. 3373).

The final scene of Tukarama's life.

13. Tukārāma had now reached the summit of his spiritual power. His fame as a Saint had spread far and wide. From the life of an ordinary Kunabī, he had risen to be the Spiritual King of the world. By performing Kīrtanas, and by spreading the glory of God's Name, he had been the cause of conferring infinite obligation on his devotees. He enjoyed every spiritual bliss in the world, and was waiting only for the final scene. When the time arrived, he tells us, God came in person to take him to heaven. "See, God comes there with the conch and the disc in His hands. The eagle, His favourite messenger, comes with ruffled pinions, and says to me 'fear not, fear not'. By the lustre of the crown of the gems on God's head, even the Sun fades into insignificance, God has a form blue like the sky, and is infinitely handsome. He has four hands, and down His neck hangs the garland called Vaijayantī. By the lustre of His lower clothes, the quarters are filled with light. Tukā is filled with gladness that the very heaven has descended into his house" (Abg. 3606). And when God Himself came to invite him, Tukārāma did not think it proper to live any longer in the world. He bade good-bye to the people. "I go to heaven. Compassion be on me from all of you." says Tukā. "Tender my supplications to all. God Pāṇḍuraṅga is standing up for a long time, and is calling me to heaven. At the last moment of my life, God has come to take me away, and Tukā disappears with his body" (Abg. 3616). As to whether Tukārāma did actually take his body to heaven, we have no other evidence from him to determine except this Abhaṅga, and the only meaning that we can make out of it is that his very physical existence had become divine as the time had come for him to ascend to Heaven.

II. Tukarama as a Spiritual Aspirant.

Introductory.

14. We have hitherto considered the incidents in Tukārāma's life as we gather them authentically from his works. Starting from the life of a Kuṇabī, we see how ultimately he merged in God. But though we have considered merely Tukārāma's external life-history hitherto, we have not taken any account of the history of his soul: how he commenced his spiritual life, what difficulties he met with on the way, what heart-rendings he had to experience in his lone journey, how ultimately a gleam of light began to shine on him, until finally how he realised God and became one with Him. The history of Tukārāma's soul, therefore, will occupy our attention for the three sections to come. In the first, we shall consider Tukārāma as a spiritual aspirant. Then, we shall go to consider the heart-rendings of Tukārāma when he was unable to find God. Finally, we shall consider how Tukārāma was able to realise God, and enter into union with Him. There is a sort of a Hegelian dialectic in Tukārāma's soul. In the first stage of his spiritual career, he seems to have resolved to withdraw himself from the life of the world with a determined effort to win spiritual knowledge. This is the stage of positive affirmation. Then comes the stage of negation, the dark night of Tukārāma's soul, a stage where Tukārāma is warring with his own self. Finally, there is the stage of a new affirmation, namely, the cancellation of the original determination and the middle negation into a final vision of the God-head, which supersedes them both. We shall first see how Tukārāma weaned his mind from the world with a determination to achieve his spiritual purpose.

Tukarama bids good-bye to the manners of the world.

15. Tukārāma began his spiritual career by girding up his loins against the life of sin "........... I have now determined to achieve the end. I shall never part with the treasure in my possession. Adieu now to all idleness which is the canker of the soul. Adieu to all forgetfulness which prevents one from harbouring God in his mind. Adieu to all shame, for it stands in the way of the attainment of God. Happy am I, that I have determined to find out God" (Abg. 2774). He imposes upon his mind an extreme severity in social relations. "How long shall I tell my mind not to run after everybody it sees? Idle affection is the cause of sorrow. Real happiness consists in leading a severe social life. Care not for praise or blame. Care not for compassion and affection. Care not for happiness and sorrow. Do not those who want to pursue God sit down at a place with a determined effort to find out God? Think about it, my mind, says Tukā, and be as hard as adamant" (Abg. 594). He expresses this same attitude elsewhere when he tells us that he had grown entirely indifferent to the amenities of social life. "Speak not with me" says Tukā. "Let people be as they are. My only business with them is to bid them good-bye as soon as I see them. Who can ever find time to mix with others? These people are merged in all sorts of fantastic activities. At a stroke, says Tukā, I have come out of the manners of the world" (Abg. 1514).

Tukarama invites deliberate suffering.

16. Tukārāma even craves deliberate misery in order that it might lead him to God. "Make me homeless, wealthless, childless" says Tukā, "so that I may remember Thee. Give no child to me, for by its affection, Thou shalt be away from me. Give me not either wealth or fortune, for, that is a calamity itself. Make me a wanderer, says Tukā, for, in that way alone I may be able to remember Thee night and day" (Abg. 2084). He elsewhere says also: "Let me get no food to eat, nor any child to continue my family line; but let God have mercy on me. This is what my mind tells me, and I keep telling the same thing to the people. Let my body suffer all sorts of calumnies, or adversities; but let God live in my mind. All these things verily are perishable, says Tukā; for God alone is happiness" (Abg. 247).

The evanescence of the human body.

17. "What use is there of this mortal body?" asks Tukā. "To feed on dainties and dishes is the life's ideal for the ignorant. People say that we should protect the body; but of what use is that? They do not know that ours is a perishable existence, and we will go out all of a sudden. Death will come and eat up our body like a ball of food. People have deliberately thrust scimitars in their bodies, have cut off pieces of their flesh, and like Śuka have betaken themselves to the forest. Did not king Janaka, asks Tukā, rule over his kingdom at the same time that he was placing one of his feet in the fire"? (Abg. 248). All this is as much as to say that as a spiritual aspirant, Tukārāma advises us to cease to take care of the body. He discants upon the infirmities of old age. "Old age comes and tells a tale in the ear that Death will soon pounce on the body. Why should not the mind grow alert at such a message ?......In no time shall the last scene take place......Think of the family deity, says Tukā, and leave away empty words" (Abg. 1914). Tukārāma tells people to put themselves in mind of Death when they see the cremation of others. Tukārāma probably whetted his own mind to spirituality at the sight of the cremation of others by fire. "You see the burning of other people's bodies. Why does it not make you alert ? Cry after God without fear, before death has caught hold of you. Death is verily a price which the body has to pay......Why do people vainly seek after various paths ? When death comes upon you, it shall not allow you to move even an inch" (Abg. 1006). In another place, Tukārāma asks : "Why do not people keep themselves awake when the robber is committing a theft in the neighbour's house ? Why do you merge yourselves in forgetfulness ? Your intellect has taken leave of you. Thieves are robbing everything that you possess, and are putting up a false appearance before you. You are entertaining a false idea. You never care to protect your inmost treasure : at least try to protect it now, says Tukā" (Abg. 1106).

Nobody can rescue one from the Clutches of Death except God Himself.

18. "It seems wonderful," says Tukā, "that people should rely upon anything except God to rescue them from the clutches of death. It is strange that people should not take thought of what would ultimately conduce to their benefit. Upon what do these people rely ? Who can help them at the final end ? What can they say to the messengers of Death ? Have they forgotten Death ? Upon what treasure do these people count ?........Why do not they remember God in order to get away from the bondage of life ?........" (Abg. 943). "People love you because you give money to them. But nobody would help you at the time of death. When your bodily power has gone, when your eyes and nose are sending down excreta, your children and wife will leave you in the lurch, and run away. Your wife will say, 'much better that this ass should die : he has spoilt the whole house by his spits'. Tukārāma says that nobody else can come to your rescue except God" (Abg. 2178). "Do not get yourself entangled", says Tukā, "in the meshes of worldly life; for Death is approaching you to make a morsel of you. When he pounces upon you, neither your mother nor your father can rescue you; neither the king, nor the governor of your place; neither your relatives, howsoever good. Tukā says that nobody can rescue you out of the clutches of death except God Himself" (Abg. 2035).

The spiritual value of mortal existence.

19. It was probably with a continual contemplation of the power of death that Tukārāma fortified his mind against any impending bodily calamities. But we must not say that he was not conscious of the great merit that belonged to the body if used well. "The body is verily a wish-jewel," he tells us. "It will yield you all desires if you put an end to all egoism, and if you make your mind as clear as a crystal by leaving away all censure, injury, and deceipt. Such a man need not go to a place of pilgrimage to get absolution. He will himself be a place of pilgrimage, and people will flock to him and get absolution at his sight. When the mind is pure, what is the use of those garlands and those ornaments? The Saint will himself be an ornament to all ornaments. He always utters the Name of God, and his mind is ever full of joy. He has given over his body and mind and wealth to God, and is entirely without desire. Such a man is greater than a touch-stone and is impossible to describe" (Abg. 28). From this, we see that, provided the body is used well, it may itself be an instrument for the revelation of God. "Even gods desire this mortal existence" says Tukā. "Blessed are we that we were ever born, and have become the servants of God. By means of this life, and in this very life, we can attain to the Godhead. We can make heaven the stepping-stone to divine existence" (Abg. 119).

Tukarama binds God with Love.

20. Tukārāma seems to have determined to turn his mortal existence to the best account possible. He prays to God to allow his mind to rest on His feet wherever his body may be. "This is my prayer to Thee, O God. I place my head on Thy feet. Let my body be where it likes, but let my mind always rest on Thy feet. Let me spend my time in meditating on Thee. Let me turn away from body, and mind, and wealth. Release me at the time of death from such dangers as phlegm, and wind, and bile. So long as my senses are whole, I have called upon Thee, in order that Thou mightest help me ultimately" (Abg. 2430). In the midst of his life's duties, Tukārāma's one interest was to remember the feet of God. "I do the duty which has fallen to me, but I always remember Thy feet. Why should I give expression to my love ? Thou knowest it already. I look at Thy form at all times, and somehow carry on my worldly existence. I have appointed my speech to sing Thy praise. My mind is anxious to have a vision of Thee without any craving for money or wealth. I am walking my worldly way, as a man must who has a burden to carry; but my mind is ever set on Thee......"(Abg. 2050). He says to God that he would never be afraid of Him, provided he can continue to have devotion for him. "To find out God, I know a remedy. We need not be afraid of God. What power can He have ? We should pray to Him in all humility, and then, we will be able to find Him. He will then do whatever He likes. Merely by the power of devotion, we may be able to attain to Him. Thus will I bind God by the cords of my love"......(Abg. 543). The same idea Tukārāma reiterates in another passage when he says that wherever God may go, He will find spread for Him the omnipresent meshes of Tukārāma's love. "Wherever Thou mayest go, Thou shalt see me. Thus, far and wide shall I spread my love. There will be no place which Thou canst then call Thine own. My mind, which is set on Thee, will watch Thee everywhere......"(Abg. 1064). Tukārāma also employs one or two metaphors to describe the manner in which to love God. He tells us in one place that he will enclose God within him, as a tortoise encloses its feet. "Thy secret I have come to know by the power of my devotion. I have enclosed Thy form within me, as a tortoise encloses its feet. I shall never allow Thy form to melt away" (Abg. 182). Again, Tukārāma says that he will be a bird on the creeper of God's Name. "The creeper of God's Name has spread far and wide, and has attained to flower and fruit. On it my mind will be a royal bird and eat to its satisfaction. The seed has shown its sweetness. Why should I not catch hold of the fruit ? As one allows time to pass by, one will surely miss the sweetness of the fruit" (Abg. 2401).

Tukarama pants for the company of the Saints.

21. The most important help, however, for the realisation of God is the company of the Saints, and Tukārāma expresses an earnest desire for the company of those who love God. "Let me meet people of my own kind, so that I may be satisfied. My mind pants to meet those who love God. My eyes keep a watch to see them. My life will be blessed only when I go and embrace those Saints. Only on that day shall I be able to sing God to my satisfaction" (Abg. 1316). It was with that view that Tukārāma prayed to God not to make him dependent on false prophets. "As I go to see God in the houses of the learned, I find only arrogance in those places. When I go to see those who recite the Vedas, I see that they only quarrel with one another. When I go to seek Self-knowledge, I find quite its opposite in those places. Those who have no control over their mind growl with anger, and falsely call themselves Gurus. Make me not dependent, O God, upon such false prophets" (Abg. 980). "I have left off everything and clung to Thy feet. I would much rather be the sands and pebbles in Paṇḍharapūr. I shall touch the feet of the Saints who go to Paṇḍharī. I shall even be the shoes and slippers on the feet of such Saints. I would not mind being even a cat or a dog in the possession of these Saints. I would even be a well or a stream, so that the Saints might come and wash their feet in it. If I am to be of any service to the Saints, I shall not be afraid of rebirth" (Abg. 3141). It was this spirit of Tukārāma which made the Saints reciprocate the feelings of Tukā. Tukārāma's obligations to the Saints knew no bounds. "How shall I express my obligations to the Saints? They keep me ever awake. How shall I be able to repay their kindness? If I sacrifice my life at their feet, that would be insufficient. They speak unconsciously, and yet impart great spiritual knowledge. They come to me, and love me, as the cow does the calf" (Abg. 2787). Thus in every way Tukārāma kept himself alert. He watched himself every moment, and became his own on-looker. He tenaciously clung to the feet of God. He became awake as he had previously experienced the fear of life's misery (Abg. 827).

III. The Dark Night of Tukarama's Soul.

"I have not seen Thee even in my dreams."

22. But not with all his determination to achieve the spiritual end would Tukā be so fortunate as to win God at once. The attainment of God involves infinite trouble and a perpetual racking of the soul. To the positive determination of the spiritual aspirant comes to be contrasted the negative psychology of the man who is in the throes of God-realisation. It was thus with Tukārāma. Not with all his efforts to know God would Tukārāma find that it was easy for him to reach God. "My heart tells me," he says "that I have not known Thee. A tin-plate cannot have the colour of brass. The child of a concubine cannot know its father. People will come to know that I am not as they have supposed me to be" (Abg. 1475). He tells us in another passage that it would be impossible for him to dance with joy, unless he has known God. "I have come to know the intentions of God," he says. "He deceives me and makes me serve, without bestowing His knowledge upon me......But He does not know that I am a Bania after all, and that I cannot be so easily cheated. How can I dance with joy unless I have known God?" (Abg. 1257). Tukārāma confes.. that he has not seen God even in dreams. "How am I not able to see Thy beautiful form even in dreams? I have not seen Thy four-handed vision, with a garland coming down Thy neck, and with a beautiful mark of Kasturi on Thy forehead.......Show me Thy form at least in my dream, O God, says Tukā" (Abg. 3257). He tells us furthermore that his desires have remained unfulfilled. He feels forlorn for not having had a fantasy of God even in his dream. "What I demanded of Thee has been of no avail. My trouble has remained. Thou hast never given comfort to me, nor fulfilled my wishes. I have not had even a fantasy of Thee even in my dreams......I feel ashamed of sitting in the company of the Saints. I have lost all courage. I think I am forlorn" (Abg. 2505).

Tukarama's desire to see the four-handed vision.

23. Tukārāma sets up as the ideal of his early spiritual life the vision of the four-handed Person, namely, God. He would be satisfied with nothing but that vision. "Honour among men, happiness of the body, all kinds of prosperity are merely a tantalising of the soul. Therefore come to me, O God...... What shall I do with mere argumentative knowledge about You?......It is merely a secondary consideration. Nothing can satisfy me except the vision of the four-handed God...... My Soul likes nothing but Your own vision, and pines for the realisation of Your feet" (Abg. 1161). "How shall I be able to know Thy intimate nature? The Sciences proclaim that there is no limit to Thy form. Take Thou on a spiritual form for me, and show me Thy four-handed vision. It would not be possible for me—a mortal being—to see Thy infinite form, which is above the heavens and below the nether worlds. I fully believe, O God, that Thou takest on a form according to the desire of Thy devotee" (Abg. 1719). "And I wish to see the same form which You have shown to bygone saints, Uddhava, Akrūra, Vyāsa, Ambaṛishi, Rukmāṅgada and Prahlāda. I am keenly desirous to see Thy beautiful face and feet. I am desirous to know in what shape You appeared in the house of Janaka, and how You ate the poor food of Vidura; how You favoured the Pāndavas in the midst of danger; how You saved Draupadī when her honour was being lost; how You played with the Gopīs; how You gave happiness to the cows and the cow-herd boys. Show me that form of Yours, so that my eyes may remain satisfied" (Abg. 1163). "Former Saints have described Thee. How, by the force of their devotion, Thou hast taken on a small form! Show me Thy small form, O God. Having seen Thee, I shall speak with Thee. I shall embrace Thy feet, shall set my eyes on them, and shall stand before Thee with my hands folded together. This is my innermost desire, which nobody else except Thee can satisfy" (Abg. 716).

Extreme restlessness of Tukarama's mind.

24. "I have become mad after Thee, O God. I am vainly looking in the various directions for Thee. I have left off all Samsāra and the worldly manners. My eyes pine after seeing Thy form, of which my ears have heard. The very foundations of my life are shaken, and I pant without Thee as a fish without water" (Abg. 2210). "Are You engaged elsewhere to attend to a devotee's call? Or, are You fallen asleep? You may have been caught in the meshes of the Gopis' devotion, and may be looking at their faces! Are You engaged in warding off some dangers of Your devotees? Or, is the way far off, that You have to cross? Do You see my faults that You do not come? Tell me the reason, O God. My life is really oozing out of my eyes," says Tukā (Abg. 1019). "My mind is fixed on Thee, as a beggar's mind is fixed on rich food. My heart is set on Thy feet, and my life-principle is dwindling. As a cat sits looking at a ball of butter ready to pounce upon it, so do I sit waiting for Thee, my Mother" (Abg. 3018). "As verily a young girl, who is going to her father-in-law's house, wistfully casts her glance at her home, similarly do I look at Thee and wish to know when I shall meet Thee. As a child that misses its mother, or as a fish that comes out of water, similarly do I pant after Thee," says Tukā (Abg. 131). "Shall I ever be fortunate to enjoy Thee without a moment's respite? When, O when, shall I enjoy that mental state? Shall I ever be so fortunate as to reap the divine bliss? Will ever God be pleased to give it to me?" (Abg. 2377). "I ask everybody I meet, will God help me? Will God have compassion on me, and save me from shame? Verily, I have forgotten everybody, and my only business is to think about God. Shall I ever be fortunate to see one who will be able to tell me when I may meet God?"

(Abg. 689). "Shall I ever be able to reach Thee like the Saints of old ? When I think how the Saints of old have known Thee, I suffer from extreme restlessness. I am a bondsman of my senses. They, on the other hand, were filled with happiness. I cannot curb a single sense. How shall I be able to curb them all ? If Thou leavest me at this stage, I shall be as good as nought" (Abg. 319).

Tukarama's constant warfare with the world and the mind.

25. Added to his extreme desire to see God and his inability to find Him, was the continual internal and external warfare which Tukā was carrying on in his life. "I am always warring," he says, "with the world and with the mind. Accidents befall me all of a sudden, and I try to ward them off by the power of Thy name" (Abg. 3140). "Yet, I am afraid on account of the darkness of the journey. All the quarters to me have become lone and dreadful, and I do not find anybody worth loving. I see herds of dangerous beasts and I lose all courage. The darkness prevents my journey, and I fall at every stump and stem. Alone, without a second, I find numerous paths opening out before me, and I am afraid to take to any one of them. My Guru has shown me the way no doubt, but God is yet far away" (Abg. 2504). As Tukā found desolation in the external world, so he found it also in the internal world. "Save me, O God," he says, "from the wanderings of my mind. It is always agile, and never rests for a moment. Be not now indifferent to me, O God. Run to the succour of this poor soul. Run before my various senses have torn off my mind into pieces. All my personal endeavour has been at an end : I am only waiting to have Thy grace" (Abg. 1136).

Tukarama's consciousness of his faults.

26. Tukārāma became at this stage keenly conscious of his own defects, as happens with all progressive mystics, and an introspective analysis of his mind put him in torments of self-calumny. Time and oft, Tukārāma calls in the help of God to save him from his faults. Any personal effort to remove the signs of sins and faults became insufficient, and an external help was invoked for the purification of his mind. "I know my own faults too well, O God. But I cannot help the wanderings of my mind. Now stand between myself and my mind, and show Thy compassion......I have solely become a slave to my senses. Be not indifferent to me, O God, however wicked I may be" (Abg. 2082). "My mind tells me that my conduct is wicked. I know my faults too well. Thou knowest everything, O God, and mayest do as Thou pleasest. I have now fallen on Thy compassion. Thou mayest do whatever Thou thinkest fit" (Abg. 1902). "I even think of the merits which I once possessed. I now feel I have lost all of them. My mind tells me that my capital has been lost. I think about the faults of others in order to make myself an object of praise. I have become like a cock which pecks ahead, and which while pecking loses its food" (Abg. 1454). "I have been verily ashamed of the spiritual life. I do not think that Thou mayest accept me. My mind does not stand still. It turns from object to object. I have been enchained by pseudo-greatness, and have given over my neck to be tied by the cords of affection. My body wishes to partake of dainties to which it is accustomed, and I do not like bad things. I have been a mine of faults, says Tukā ; my idleness and sleep know no bounds" (Abg. 2780). "I have assumed a saintly exterior, but have not bidden good-bye to the things of the world. I recall to mind this fact every day......My mind has not come out of the worldly life, and is persistently doing the same things over and over again. I have become like a Bahurūpi, and am never internally as I seem to be" (Abg. 465).

Tukarama's description of his own vices.

27. Tukārāma even goes to consider how his life has been a perpetual scene of vice and misery. "Cursed be my egoism. Cursed be my fame. There is no limit to my sin and to my misery. I have become a burden to this earth. How much have I suffered? My sorrow would break a hard stone. Men do not even so much as look at me. In body, speech, and mind, I have done evil things. My eyes, hands and feet have been the slaves of sin. Censure, hatred, betrayal, adultery: how much should I narrate my own defects? By the consciousness of my little wealth, I became arrogant. My house was rent on account of my having two wives. I have disrespected my father's words. I have been a thoughtless, crooked, duty-avoiding, censurable wrangler. How many more of my defects shall I enumerate? My speech is unable to mention them. My mind trembles to think of them. I showed no compassion to the poor, conferred no obligations on them, had no courage of words, have been entirely addicted to sex: I cannot even mention these things in words. Hear, O Saints, how my vices and thoughtlessness have increased my sin! Make me acceptable to God, O Saints! I have come in submission before you" (Abg. 2062). In another place, he tells us the same story: "Masterless as I was, I have been the source of many faults. No dutiful action has relieved my conduct. I have been a man of dull apprehension. I have never remembered Thee, O compassionate Lord! I have never heard or sung Thy prayer. I have entertained false shame. I have not known the way to realisation. I have never heard the Saints' stories. On the other hand, I have much reproached and censured the Saints. I have never conferred any obligations on others. I have shown no compassion in teasing others. I have done things which I should never have done. I have vainly laboured under the burden of my family. I have never gone to places of pilgrimage. I have fattened my hands, body and feet. I have never served the Saints. I have never given anything in charity. I have never worshipped any deities. I have hugged to my heart things which I should have avoided. I have done many unjust and unrighteous things. I have not known the way to real good. I cannot even speak or remember the things that I have done. I have been an enemy to myself, and have committed self-slaughter. Thou art an ocean of compassion, O God! Enable me to cross this worldly existence" (Abg. 4066).

Tukarama's sin stands between himself and God.

28. Tukārāma thinks that his constant sin stands between himself and God. "I pant after Thy vision and even seek Thy compassion—but it seems that my sin stands between Thee and me. I pursue the devotional path as if by compulsion...... I do not know when Thou mayest give composure to my mind" (Abg. 1486). "I came to Thee as a fond child, but my desires were not fulfilled. I follow Thee as under necessity, but my endeavour stops in the middle. It seems my sin has become powerful, and stands as an obstacle in my vision of Thy feet" (Abg. 2835). "New sins attack me while I try to surrender myself to Thee. Be Thou compassionate, O God. Why should anything have any sway over us, when we try to follow Thee?" (Abg. 2759). "Do not count my faults. I am sin incarnate. I am sinful, Thou art holy. I am a sinner, Thou art a redeemer. The sinner may do his deeds, but the redeemer must come to his help. If an iron hammer tries to beat down a Parisa, the Parisa will turn the hammer into one of gold. Nobody cares for a clod of earth; but it becomes valuable when it comes in contact with musk" (Abg. 1458). This same idea Tukārāma expresses elsewhere when he says that it may be his to sin, but it is God's to save him. "Do not fail to do Thy duty, O compassionate God! It becomes us to commit sins, but it becomes Thee to succour the unholy. I have done my duty, and it behoves Thee to discharge Thine. Do not fail to accomplish Thy traditional task, says Tukā" (Abg. 1223).

The reasons why probably God does not show Himself to Tukarama.

29. Tukārāma next goes on to discuss the reasons why probably God does not show Himself to him. In the first place, he says that he probably lacks sufficient endeavour, and the grit of body and mind which alone enables one to reach God. He is therefore thrown in a great doubt as to whether God may ever show Himself to him. "Whether Thou wilt ever accept me or not,—that gives me food for thought. Whether Thou wilt show Thy feet to me or not,—that makes my mind unsteady. Whether Thou wilt ever speak with me or not,—that puts anxiety into my mind. Whether Thou wilt remember me or not,—that puts me in a state of doubt. Probably, says Tukā, Thou dost not accept me, because I lack sufficient endeavour" (Abg. 3299). A second reason, probably, which, according to Tukā, makes God not to show Himself to him, is that God may suppose that he may ask something of Him when He has shown Himself to Tukā. Tukārāma tells God that he would ask nothing of Him, if God condescends to show Himself to him. "Anything which will put my Lord into difficulties,—what will that avail me? I shall not tease Thee, O God, or ask anything of Thee. I have from the bottom of my heart left off all ambition for power, or success, or wealth, or even absolution. I only want Thee to show Thyself to me but once, and clasp me to Thy bosom" (Abg. 3019). Probably also, says Tukā, God does not show Himself to him, because, he has not yet completely resigned himself to His will. "I have given over my body to Thee, and yet I entertain fear. So treacherous am I. Such a great mistake I have committed. What I speak by word of mouth, I have not experienced in my heart. I deserve a severe punishment at Thy hands, O God, for this impropriety" (Abg. 3061).

The humility of Tukarama.

30. Tukā's mind is tossed at the thought that people praise him for nothing. He invites God, to disillusion him when he regards himself as a great singer. "I think in my mind, O God, that there is no singer like me. Thou art omniscient and great. Shalt Thou not be able to dispel this illusion? Desire and anger have not yet lost their hold on my mind. They have taken a permanent lodgment in me. I have disburdened myself before Thee in order that Thou mayest know my mind" (Abg. 1476). "Of low caste though I may be, yet because Saints have praised me, I feel an internal arrogance. This, I am sure, will end by robbing me of my virtue. I feel internally that I alone am a wise man. Save me, says Tukā; or otherwise, I shall come to ruin" (Abg. 2072). Tukārāma questions God why He has brought fame to him when he did not deserve it. "What happiness will a man derive when his body is anointed with sandal, if he is feeling a severe ache in his stomach? Why hast Thou brought fame to me, O God? If dainty dishes are served before a man who has had fever, what relish could he have for them? If a dead body be adorned with ornaments, of what use would it be to the body?" (Abg. 1474). With humility, which is a natural product of mystical introspection, Tukārāma describes how with all his poetry he is forever away from God. "A parrot speaks as it is taught...... The happiness of a dream does not make one a king...... Why shouldst Thou have adorned my tongue with song? For, it takes me away from Thee. Of what use is gold reflected in a mirror? You look at it, but are unable to catch hold of it......A cow-boy tends cattle, but he does not own them" (Abg. 2850). "Good things," says Tukā, "are like poison to me. I do not want either happiness or honour. What should I do to these people who persist in giving that to me? When the body is being tended, I feel as if it were on fire. Good food is like poison. My heart is troubled when I hear my praise. Show me the way to see Thee, set me not to pursue a mirage, do what is ultimately good to me, and take me out of this burning fire" (Abg. 246). "When shall I be made an outcast, O God, in order that in repentance I shall remember Thy feet? Tears will trickle down my eyes, and I shall know no sleep. When shall I be able to enjoy solitude? Help me, O God, to achieve my object" (Abg. 1221).

A request to the Saints to intercede.

31. Tukārāma found, however, that not by merely living in solitude he would be able to reach God. He needed very much the company of the Saints, who would be able to give him the evangel of God. In a state of utter forlornness, Tukārāma says that there was no townsman for him in this life. His city was planted in heaven, while everybody who talked to him and met him spoke only of earthly things. "I see no townsman for me in this life. How shall I lead a lonely life in this world? I so much pant after spiritual company. Wherever I look, in whatever direction I cast my eyes, I find an empty space everywhere. I feel forlorn, and nobody tells me news of Thee," says Tukā (Abg.

741). If Tukārāma could not find God, he said he should be at least so fortunate as to live in the company of the Saints who would tell him the news of God. "Give me the company of those who have an incessant love towards Thee, O God. Then I shall no longer tease Thee. I shall live near the feet of the Saints and shall ask nothing of Thee. If Thou canst bestow upon me this boon, Thou wilt kill two birds with one stone. Neither Thou nor I shall be teased any longer. For this reason, I am standing like a beggar at Thy door" (Abg. 635). "When I remember the spiritual experience of the Saints, my heart burns within me. I shall offer my life to Thee as a sacrifice, so that Thou mayest make me worthy of the Saints. Words without experience are as valueless as a creeper without fruit......" (Abg. 2915). Moreover, "the Saints, who have seen Thee in bodily form, will laugh at me and count me as unworthy for spiritual life. It is this thought which makes me sad. They have described Thy form in this way and in that way. How shall I be able to describe Thee?...... Tell me what faults I have committed, and why Thou regardest myself as unworthy. Thou art known to have equal feelings towards all, being their common parent. Remove my ignorance, O God, by giving me this knowledge...... (Abg. 4092). Then, not being able to find God Himself, he appeals to the Saints to tell him whether God will ever favour him. "Shall I be relieved of this miserable existence? Will God favour me? Tell me, O Saints, and give composure to my mind. Can the actions I have done cease to bear fruit? ......How may I be able to know God's secret? Will my intellect be ever composed? Or will any obstacles come in the way? When shall I reach the end? When shall I be able to throw myself at the feet of God? When will these eyes rejoice at the blessed vision of God?......This is what is filling me with anxiety day and night, says Tukā. I cannot imagine that my unaided strength will ever make me reach the end" (Abg. 4072). "When shall I be able to rejoice in the vision of the God-head among all men? Then my happiness will know no bounds, and I shall merge myself in an ocean of bliss. Then will tranquillity and forgiveness and compassion make lodgment in my soul, and drive away my evil passions. Then shall I shine like a burning fire of dispassion and discrimination. Then shall I be a pattern of nine-fold Bhakti, the crown of all emotions......" (Abg. 1707). "When shall I be able to hear the words of the Saints that Thou hast accepted me? Then alone shall my mind rest at ease. I have made Thy face and feet the cynosure of my eyes. I shall fix myself firmly in the words of the Saints, and I shall do no other Sādhana for meeting Thee......" (Abg. 719). "Do me this charity, O Saints. You are compassionate and holy. Remember me to God, and tell Him the agonies of my heart. I am without a Lord. Faultful, fallen, throw me not away. God shall not leave me, if you but intercede on my behalf, says Tukā" (Abg. 1539).

The asking of grace from God.

32. Tukārāma tries yet another way. He approaches God direct, and feeling his great impotence in reaching God, requests Him to send down His grace on him. What cannot be done by human endeavour, may be accomplished by divine grace. "Throw me not away," says Tukā, "I am a dog at Thy door. I am sitting like a beggar before Thy house. Turn me not out of Thy mansion. I am like an evil thing before Thy presence. Save me by Thy power, O God" (Abg. 2722). "Save me," says Tukā again, "from these all-encompassing and never-ending meshes by Thy Divine power. As I think about it, I find my mind is uncontrollable, and runs after sense. I have taken the bait and cannot throw it out by my own power. Powerless as I am, I am waiting for Thy vision, O God" (Abg. 1452). "I have been verily pent up in this Samsāra as a serpent is pent up within a basket by the music of a juggler...... Save me by Thy power. I feel I am impotent to go beyond this enchantment. I have caught the bait like a fish which runs after food, and then kills itself by it. I am like a bird which tries to find its young one, but gets itself caught in a net. Like a fly sticking in a sweet substance, the more I shake my wings, the more I get myself inside. My very life is departing. Save me by Thy power, O God" (Abg. 639). Tukārāma takes resort to other analogies, and requests God to lift him up as a mother lifts up her child. "I have become wearied my Mother, and can walk no longer. Lift me up in Thy kindness and love. Put me to Thy breast, and ward off my hunger which has continued to give me trouble throughout life. I am wearied, and cannot even speak" (Abg. 1406). Then, again, Tukārāma regards himself as a Chātaka bird which is desirous of getting some drops of rain in its beak. It would not partake of any water on earth. It must have water from heaven to satisfy its thirst. "I feel thirsty like a Chātaka bird. Rain Thy grace on me, O God! I am directing my sight towards heaven, and Thou knowest it already. A sprout can grow into a tree only when it is watered from above" (Abg. 2863). "Let me have a vision of Thy feet, as a man after a long-continued fast may have of food. Let love spring in me, as it springs in a child when it sees its mother after a long time. Let covetousness rise in me about God, as it rises in a stingy man when he looks at a treasure," says Tukā (Abg. 1884). Indeed, says Tukārāma, there is no need for him to give vent to his thoughts by word of mouth; for God knows his thoughts already. His only business is to ask compassion of God......His own power is inadequate to reach God, and all sādhanas are useless. We must sacrifice ourselves to God, says Tukā, and cease to think of the end time and again (Abg. 1224). Finally, he invites God to help him, only if his words are a true index to his heart, and if his behaviour does not belie his internal feelings; for God knows all things already (Abg. 1084).

The Centre of Indifference.

33. Hitherto, Tukārāma believed it possible for him to have a vision of God. He waited long and tried various means to that end. But nothing would help him. He believed at first fully in his power to know God, but he now began to find it almost impossible for him to know Him. From the everlasting yea, he now began to pass through the centre of indifference. "How long shall I wait," he asks, "I see no sign of God's presence. It seems to me, O God that Thou and I shall have now to part. How long shall I wait? I do not see the fructification of Thy promises." Tukārāma thought that he was ruined both externally and internally. His family life was a failure, and it seemed that his spiritual life was equally so. So far as his family life was concerned, he was at his purse's end, and was so much in debt that nobody would give him any debt any longer. It was impossible for him to go to other men's houses. He had lost all reputation and honour among men for having followed the path of God (Abg. 1260). He was left by his relatives and friends......and it seemed that he had lost all shame...... He had disgraced himself. It seemed that an evil spirit had taken possession of his intellect, and would not give him any *ποῦ στῶ*. It was probable, says Tukārāma, that God had many devotees and left this one in the lurch" (Abg. 1757). Thus, Tukārāma seemed to have been ruined both in worldly and spiritual matters. His desire remained unfulfilled. His mind burned like a seed on a frying pan. Nothing gave satisfaction to his mind. He could not know what was in store for him. He went up and down as if caught in a whirlpool. He was incessantly going up and descending down the mountain of thought (Abg. 3540).

The Everlasting Nay.

34. Tukārāma did not stay for a long time in the centre of indifference. He saw no help coming. He began to call in question the omnipotence of God. He thought that even his Fate was more powerful than God. "I have lost all patience," says he, "and Thou hast not accepted me. I think my Fate is more powerful than Thee. I have grown powerless to wend on my way. My cries are of no avail. Tukā does not know how to sacrifice himself to God, and God has thus become indifferent to him" (Abg. 1485). "When people of old realised their spiritual end, they did so by their own power. They strained every nerve in realising Thee. Thou hast merely repaid the obligation which they had conferred on Thee. Thou hast never saved, O God, a powerless being like myself, ... says Tukā" (Abg. 1279). "God's impotence is now proved, says Tukā. His Name has no power. My love towards Thee is gradually diminishing. Enormous sin stands in the way. My mental agony increases. God has acquired the quality of impotence, says Tukā" (Abg. 1923). Then, again, Tukārāma tries another remedy for invoking the attention of God. He tells Him that He has forgotten what His devotees have done for Him. It is the devotees that have endowed Him with a form. "It is due to men like us that Thou art made to assume a form and a name. Who else might otherwise have cared for Thee? Thou hast lived in the great Void. Darkness brings lustre to the lamp. The setting brings lustre to the jewel. The patient brings the doctor to light......Poison makes nectar valuable. Brass makes gold have a value. It is due to us, says Tukā, that Thou art made a God at all" (Abg. 2527). In the same strain Tukārāma says, "Thou hast forgotten that our devotion has endowed Thee with Godhood. Great men are short of memory. They cannot remember unless they are put in mind of a thing. It is due to us that Thou art able to move. In Thine own impersonal form, Thou wouldst not be obliged to do anything of that kind......"(Abg. 2159). God taxed Tukārāma's patience to the utmost. Tukārāma now came to know that Godhood was a meaningless word. Who can now preserve that empty symbol? "Why has God punished me hitherto?" asks Tukā. "Now God and I are placed on an equality. Whatever I may say about Thee, whatever word of abuse I may utter, it all becomes Thee, O God. Thou art shameless, and without caste, and race. Thou art a thief, and an adulterer. Thou livest upon stones, and mud,......animals, and trees......I know that Thou art an ass, and a dog, and an ox, and bear all sorts of burdens. People in by-gone times have known that Thou art a liar. I have come to know the truth of the remark, says Tukā. Thou hast provoked me to a quarrel, and nobody can now gag my mouth" (Abg. 1531). Elsewhere, he says that God is verily a beggar, and His work a lie. "It is shameless beings like myself that have patience to put their faith in God......God does not speak, and yet accepts all service from His servants" (Abg. 1252). God is not merely a beggar, but makes His devotees beggars like unto Him. Woe to the company of God, says Tukā. "Thou makest Thy servant a beggar like Thyself. Thou hast no name and form. Thou makest Thy devotee even likewise. As Thou hast nothing in Thyself, Thou shalt reduce me to naught" (Abg. 1546). Tukārāma then goes on to shower every kind of abuse on God. He calls God timid, because He does not approach Tukā. "Nobody stands between Thee and me," he says. "Thou art timid to approach me........Being the support of the world, Thou seemest to be powerless. It is we, who give Thee support by uttering Thy name time after time. I have been verily caught, says Tukā, in the net of the elements" (Abg. 2662). He calls in question the generosity of God, and says that it is a shame to His generosity that He should have made him heter-dependent. "Thou hast made me dependent upon others......Thou art known to be generous, O God. There is an end to Thy generosity now. All my supplications are of no avail, and Thou knowest no charity. Why shouldst Thou have given birth to us at all, O God, asks Tukā ? Why shouldst Thou have made me an object of pity ? Does it not prove Thy impotence, asks Tukā ?" (Abg. 2776). "I am ashamed to call myself Thy servant. Events belie my words. Thou hast left unfulfilled the words of by-gone saints. Thou hast even made me sing. But that seems to be now merely a farce" (Abg. 3447). "How should I call myself Thy servant, if my wishes remain unfulfilled ? If Thou carest for my love, do not delay any longer. If Thou hast to show Thyself to me sometime, why dost Thou not do it now ? I can sing with justification only when I have seen Thee" (Abg. 1567). "How cruel must God be," asks Tukā, "that He should not have shown Himself to me even though He is reputed to be so near. Thou livest in my heart, and hast no compassion on me. Thou art cruel and impersonal. Thou knowest not the pangs of my heart. My mind knows no rest. My senses wander. My sin is not at an end. Thou art as angry as ever" (Abg. 243). "If Thou dost not show Thyself to me now," says Tukārāma, "Thou shalt receive a curse from me, Thy son. Why art Thou garnering Thy treasure and for whom, if not for us, Thy children? Thou allowest Thy children to cry with hunger......By our curse Thou shalt be ruined, O God. Being my father, Thou shalt be an object of my curse" (Abg. 3548). "I shall spoil Thy fair name, if Thou continuest to be indifferent......I shall refuse to utter Thy name, and shall drown Thy whole lineage" (Abg. 3549). "People will say that from our omnipotent Father we are born impotent. These abuses will be hurled in Thy face by the world, and Thy name shall be dishonoured......I feel my life to be a burden" (Abg. 3550). Tukārāma then went to call in question the very existence of God. He tells Him that he would not have grown mad after Him, had he known already that He did not exist. "Empty is the name that Thou obtainest in the world.........In my opinion, God does not exist......My words have fallen short of reality. I have grown hopeless. I have lost both the life of the world and the life of the spirit" (Abg. 3303). Tukārāma ends by saying that in his opinion God is dead. "To me, God is dead. Let Him be for whomsoever thinks Him to be. I shall no longer speak about God. I shall not meditate on His name. Both God and I have perished.......Vainly have I followed Him hitherto, and vainly have I spent my life for Him" (Abg. 1597). "Shall I now throw myself on a scimitar or into a flame of fire, or shall I lose myself in a forest and expose myself to the extremes of heat and cold, or shall I close my lips for-ever? Shall I besmear my body with ashes, or wander like a nomad over the world? Shall I give up the ghost by a long fast? Tell me, O God, the way to find Thee if Thou dost exist" (Abg. 457). And finally, not finding God, Tukārāma determines to commit self-slaughter. "Thou hast no anxiety for me. Why now should I continue to live?......I had lived in the vain hope that Thou mightest come to the succour of this sinful creature. Nobody will now accept me, and Thou hast adamantine cruelty. My hopes are shattered, and I shall now commit self-slaughter" (Abg. 2266).

IV. The Ecstatic and Post-ecstatic Experiences of Tukarama.

Tukarama's sudden vision of God.

35. God could wait no longer. The agonies of Tukārāma had reached an extreme stage, and his heart-rending cry was heard by God. The dark cloud on Tukārāma's heart was now suddenly illumined by the flashes of God's vision. As happens in the case of all mystics, the dark night was suddenly relieved by the great light that followed. Tukārāma saw God's vision and bowed at His feet. "I see God's face, and the vision gives me infinite bliss. My mind is riveted on it, and my hands cling to His feet. As I look at Him, all my mental agony vanishes. Bliss is now leading me to an ever higher bliss, says Tukā" (Abg. 1329). "Blessed am I that my effort has been crowned with success. I have attained the desired end. My heart is set on God's feet, and my mind is composed. The blessed omen has wiped off death and oldage......My body is changed. On it has fallen the light of God. I have now obtained limitless wealth, and I have seen the feet of the formless Person. I have obtained a treasure which has existed from times immemorial......For my very life, I will never leave it any longer. Let no evil eye affect my possession, says Tukā" (Abg. 4065).

Reasons according to Tuka for his Realisation of God.

36. When Tukārāma looked back to find out the reasons which had led him to realise God, he found, in the first place, that the company of the Saints had been mainly responsible for this happy consummation. "My fortune has brightened and my anxiety has been at an end on account of the company of the Saints. By their favour have I been able to find out God. I shall now enclose Him in the chest of my heart. That hidden treasure has been found out by my devotion" (Abg. 449). In the second place, Tukārāma says that the realisation of God was due entirely to the descent of God's grace on him without any merit on his own part. "Suddenly has the treasure been placed in my hands, and in fact, without any adequate service. My fate has become powerful, and I have seen God. Never more shall there be any loss to me, and my poverty is gone. My anxieties are at an end, and I have been the most fortunate of men......" (Abg. 1775). Tukārāma, however, is not entirely unconscious of the great effort that he had made for God-realisation. "In all ways, however, I tried to reach this consummation. I conscientiously did service to my Lord. I never looked back. I conquered time by utilising every moment. I did not disturb my mind by conjectures, nor did I allow any evil desires to come in the way....Now that fortune has smiled on me, I shall move on undaunted" (Abg. 1673). Lastly, Tukārāma says that God has accepted him, probably on account of his defects. "God accepted me seeing that I was a man of low birth, a man without intellect, a man of humble and mean form, and with other bad things about me. I have now come to know that whatever God does ultimately conduces to our good. I have enjoyed infinite bliss....Tukā says that God is proud of His name, and therefore comes to the succour of His devotees" (Abg. 691).

A Confession of Blessedness.

37. Tukārāma now feels satisfied that his long effort has come to an end, and that now he would be able to enjoy the company of God to his heart's content. "For long had I waited to see Thy feet. Time had parted us for a long time. Now shall I enjoy Thy company to my satisfaction. Desires hitherto had given me much trouble ......I was long moving away from the path......For long was I merged in mere semblance......Now the consummation has been reached, and I am merged in enjoyment" (Abg. 2322). Tukārāma asks God to stop and look at him. "I never cared for my relatives, I moved after Thee in order that Thou mightest speak with me. I had waited long to enjoy Thy company in solitude. Stand, O God, before me and look at me, says Tukā" (Abg. 1610). "How blessed am I that I have seen Thy feet to-day! How much have the Saints done for me, O God! To-day's gain is indescribable. Its auspiciousness is beyond measure. Tukā wonders how so great a fortune should have fallen to his lot" (Abg. 2005). "All the quarters have now become auspicious to me. Evil has itself been transformed into the highest good. The lamp in my hand has dispelled all darkness......The grief I hitherto felt will now conduce to happiness. I now see goodness in all created things" (Abg. 1310). "Blessed am I that my love has been fixed in Thy name. My blessedness is undoubted. I shall never be a creature to the onslaught of time. I shall now live on the spiritual nectar, and live always in the company of the Saints. Satisfaction is being added to satisfaction, and enjoyment to enjoyment" (Abg. 1098). Tukārāma now considers that everyday to him is a holiday. "Blessedness beyond compare!......We, who are mad after God, are sunk in blessedness. We shall sing and dance and clap our hands, and please God. Every day to me is now a holiday. We are full of joy, and the omnipotent God will vindicate us in every way......" (Abg. 3998). "I have become entirely careless of the objects of sense. Divine joy is seething through my body. My tongue has become uncontrollable, and ceaselessly utters the name of God. From greater to greater bliss do I go, as a miser goes from greater to greater riches. All my emotions have been unified in God, as the rivers in an ocean" (Abg. 975). "And no wonder that people will reckon me, says Tukā, as more blessed than any other being. Those who boast of self-knowledge, and those who boast of absolution, will both lose colour before me. My very body becomes divine when I sing the praise of God. Fortunate am I that God is my debtor. To a man who goes on pilgrimages, I shall bring weariness; and to one who seeks the enjoyment of heaven, I shall bring disgust ......Blessed will people call me, says Tukā; blessed are we, they will say, that we have seen Tukā" (Abg. 3598).

Tukarama is a photic as well as an audile mystic.

38. Tukārāma was a photic as well as an audile mystic, like all the other great mystics of the world. This is evident from the way in which he describes his light and sound experiences. "The whole world has now become alight, and darkness is at an end. There is no space for me to hide myself......The day of Truth has come, and its spread is now beyond measure. For the sake of his life, says Tukā, he has won his goal" (Abg. 2556). "God", he says, "shines like a diamond set in a circle of rich jewels. His light is like the light of a million moons......Tukā says that His vision is now satisfied, and refuses to return from its cynosure" (Abg. 4026). It is impossible for him, says Tukārāma elsewhere, to describe the bliss of unceasing illumination. "Thou art our kind and affectionate mother, O God, and bearest all our burdens. We know no fear, nor any anxiety......I cannot know the night from day, and the unceasing illumination exists at all times. How shall I be able to describe the great bliss I enjoy? I have worn the ornaments of Thy names, and by Thy power nothing is lacking to me" (Abg. 4083). Tukārāma also describes how he was hearing the mystic sound all the while. "God has really favoured me" he says. "My doubts and delirium are at an end. God and Self are now lying on the same couch in me. Tukārāma now sleeps in his own Form, and mystic bells lull him to sleep" (Abg. 3252). "I have been in tune with the Infinite, and psychical dispositions take time to emerge. I have become full of spiritual pride, and I cannot control my limbs. Another voice speaks through me, and happiness and sorrow have lost their difference. I can hardly find words to describe the happiness to these people. They may wonder at it, and say this is impossible. Both my exterior and interior are filled with Divine bliss, says Tukā" (Abg. 1039).

Tukarama's other mystical experiences.

39. Tukārāma elsewhere describes his other mystical experiences also. In one place, he tells us, "God is pursuing me outright. I have fallen in the hands of God", he says, "and He is using me as a menial without wages. He extracts work from me, not caring what condition it may bring me into. Wherever I go, God pursues me. He has deprived me of all my possessions," says Tukā (Abg. 2612). Elsewhere he tells us that God is moving all around him. "I have been pent up internally and externally by God. He has put an end to all my work, and has deprived me even of my mind. He has deprived me of self-hood, and has separated me from all things. In close connection with me, says Tukā, He is moving round and round" (Abg. 3810). Tukārāma orders God to stand before him, so long as he is looking at Him. "I like immensely this form of Thine; and my eyes are satisfied. My mind having caught the bait of Your vision, does not leave it on any account......" (Abg. 3111). Tukārāma tells us also that wherever he goes, God is there to walk by him, and help him on his way by taking up his hand. "It is by Thy support that I move on the way. Thou bearest all my burden. Thou puttest meaning into my meaningless words. Thou hast taken away my shame, and put courage into me......" (Abg. 1307). He tells us also that God and he himself are forever interlocked. "Thy hand is on my head, and my heart is on Thy feet. Thus have we been interlocked body into body, self into self. It is mine to serve, and Thine to favour, says Tukā" (Abg. 2761).

Tukarama's Self-vision.

40. The highest experience, however, of which a mystic is capable, occurs, as Tukārāma says in another passage, when the difference between Self and God has vanished. "I gave birth to myself, and came out of my own womb," says Tukā. "All my desires are at an end, and my end is achieved. When I became powerful beyond measure, I died at the very moment. Tukā looks on both sides, and sees Himself by himself" (Abg. 3944). When Tukārāma saw Himself, nothing remained for him to be achieved. "God is the giver, and God is the enjoyer. What else remains to be experienced? Or, how can we put it into words? By the eyes I see my own form. The whole world seems to be filled by Divine music, says Tukā" (Abg. 179). Finally, Tukārāma finds himself pent up all around by his own Self. "Deep has called unto deep, and all things have vanished into unity. The waves and the ocean have become one. Nothing can come, and nothing can now pass away. The Self is enveloping Himself all around. The time of the Great End has come, and sunset and sunrise have ceased" (Abg. 1815). In this way, Tukārāma describes how his Self had merged in God.

41. The very first effect of God-vision, says Tukārāma, is that God has made him mad. "He follows me wherever I go, and makes it impossible for me to forget Him. He has robbed away my heart which was all my treasure. He has shown Himself to my vision, and made me go mad after Him. My mouth refuses to speak, and my ears to hear.... My whole body has been filled by the heat of Divine passion, says Tukā" (1059). "My previous outlook," says Tukā, "has been entirely changed on account of the new possession. I find no life now in worldly life. A new possession of the soul has taken place. The former outlook has changed. My life has been filled with divine joy. The tongue has partaken of a new sweetness, God's name is fixed in my mouth, and my mind has become tranquil......Whatever I wish, shall now be fulfilled wherever I am, says Tuka" (Abg. 2623). God's vision has next deprived Tukā of solitude. "Where can I run, being afraid of this worldly life? Wherever I look, God is present. He has deprived me of solitude, and there is no place without Him. How shall I say that I am going to another place? When a sleeping man awakes, he finds himself in his home. What do I owe Thee, O God, that Thou hast penned me from all sides?" (Abg. 1197). Tukārāma tells us that God speaks to him whenever he wants an answer. "Look at my spiritual experience," says Tukā. "I have possessed God. Whatever I speak, God fulfils. Whatever I ask, God answers immediately. When I left off this worldly life, God became my servant. It is due to my patience, says Tukā, that I have been able to possess God" (Abg. 2260). Tukārāma asks God whatever his mind desires. "I shall now throw all my burden upon Thee. When I feel hungry, I shall ask for food. When I experience cold, I shall ask for clothing. Whatever my mind desires, I shall ask it of Thee at the very moment. Sorrow shall never attack our house. The great disc in Thy hand moves round about us, and wards off all evil. I have no care for absolution, says Tukā. I long for this worldly existence" (Abg. 2513). The mystic sees not, says Tukā, and yet he sees. "I have not seen anything, and yet I see everything. I and mine have been removed from me. I have taken without taking, I have eaten without eating, spoken without speech. Whatever has been hidden, has been brought to light. I never heard, and yet all things have sauntered into my mind, says Tukā" (Abg. 118). And thus it happens that Tukārāma is merely a looker-on. "There is now no work for me. All at once, every kind of work has been taken away. I will now sit silent at a place, and do whatever I like. The world vainly follows illusions. All of a sudden, says

The effects of God-vision.

Tukā, I have been out of the world" (Abg. 850). He has been free from all connections whatsoever. "I do not belong to any place; I belong only to one place. I do not move out, and come back......There is no difference to me between mine and thine. I do not belong to anybody. I am not required to be born and to die. I am as I am. There is neither name nor form for me, and I am beyond action and inaction, says Tukā" (Abg. 256).

The whole Universe becomes God.

42. "All men have now become God," says Tukā, "and merit and demerit have disappeared...... My mind has been filled with great happiness. When one looks into a mirror, it seems as if one is looking at a different object, and yet one is looking at oneself. When a brook runs into a river, it becomes merged in it" (Abg. 2281). "My country is now the universe," says Tukā. "I live in the whole world. All the people in the world have come to know that I am dear to my Father. There is nobody between Him and me; there is no chasm. My only resting place is the Name of God" (Abg. 1113). "If I mean to worship Thee," says Tukā, "such worship becomes impossible, as Thou art identical with all means of worship. Tell me, O God, how I may worship Thee. If I may give Thee ablution of water, Thou are that Thyself. Thou art the scent of scents, and the fragrance of flowers......If I am to place Thee on a couch, Thou art Thyself that. Thou art all the food that may be offered to Thee. If I am to sing a song, Thou art that song. If I sound the cymbals, Thou art those. There is no place whereon I could now dance. The scent and the light are now Rāma, Kṛishna, Hari" (Abg. 1128). "I see Thy feet everywhere. The whole universe is filled by Thee......Thou hast become everything to us, says Tukā. We have no taste for work or worldly life. We need not go anywhere or do anything. We utter Thy name and meditate on Thee. Whatever I speak is a recitation of Thy qualities......When I walk, I turn round about Thee. When I sleep, I fall prostrate before Thee ......All wells and rivers are now Thyself. All houses, and palaces have now become the temples of God. Whatever I hear is the name of God. Various sounds are heard," says Tukā, "we are the servants of God, and are ever filled with great joy" (Abg. 1228).

43. What are the marks by which a Saint may be known? "He to whose house God comes," says Tukā, "loses his manhood. When God comes to live in a man, He deprives him of everything except Himself. The marks of God's presence are that He allows no desires in a Saint, nor any affection....He, who has come to know God, becomes garrulous, and yet is never tainted by untruth ......All these marks may be seen in me, says Tukā" (Abg. 2583). He tells us furthermore that women to him appear as bears, and gold as a clod of earth. "I never like anything in this world except the Name of God. Mortal existence seems to me to be a vomit. Gold and silver are like a clod of earth. Jewels appear like stones. Beautiful women," says Tukā, "appear to us like bears" (Abg. 224). The Saint can know no fear, says Tukārāma. "Is it possible for a man to find out darkness by means of a lamp? Similarly, we, who are the servants of God, shall never be afraid of death and other mirages. An unfortunate man does not know that the Sun cannot be hidden by dust. Fire can never be hidden by grass," says Tukā (Abg. 258). A Saint in all his actions gives constant lodgment to God. "Whatever he sees is God, whatever he speaks is God......The whole body becomes filled by God, and passions forever take leave of me," says Tukā (Abg. 3942). Another mark is the utter self-surrender of the Saint. "I have for once surrendered myself at Thy feet. What more shall I surrender?......I do not see, O God, that there is anything else that I may surrender......" (Abg. 245). He need no longer ask compassion from God. "So long as I was not awakened to this spiritual life, I bore all kinds of grief. But because I am now wakened by the Saints, I know that all things are vain" (Abg. 192). No supplication is now needed, says Tukā. By the power of God, he has got control over events. "We, the servants of God, are not like other men to supplicate to others. By the power of God, the whole world looks dwarfish to us. Time and death are in our hands. God will justify us, His servants. We have surrendered ourselves to Him, and live at His feet. Whatever we now desire, God shall certainly fulfil for us" (Abg. 2296). Tukāram says he has conquered time by resigning all sorrow in God. "I shall meditate on Thee and play about Thee. My heart is set on Thy feet. Thou knowest my heart, O God; no false description of it would be of any use. We have resigned our happiness and sorrow in Thee. We have lost bodily egoism, and the distinction between self and not-self has been effaced" (Abg. 2647). Tukārāma tells us also that he has planted his foot on the forehead of Death. "Death eats up the world but we have planted our foot on his forehead. He will stand up when we shall dance with joy, and will himself

The signs of God's Presence in the Soul.

come to our help. He whose hunger could never be fulfilled, is now satisfied by God's name. Hot-burning as he was, he has now become cool" (Abg. 1393). Finally, he tells us that both night and sleep had become to him as good as non-existent. He feels that there is no night, because he sees the lustre of God at all times. He cannot sleep, because God's presence always keeps him awake. "Both night and sleep have now departed. I live in God in continual spiritual bliss. God is everywhere and 'me' and 'mine' have departed. God and myself shall now live together, and never shall we be separated" (Abg. 2866).

Tukarama sees his death with his own eyes.

44. Tukārāma speaks of having seen his death with his own eyes. This means that when he had realised God, his body was dead. "I saw my death with my own eyes. Incomparably glorious was the occasion. The whole universe was filled with joy, I became everything, and enjoyed everything. I had hitherto stuck to only one place, being pent up by egoism. By my deliverance from it, I am enjoying the harvest of bliss. Death and birth are now no more. I am free from the littleness of 'me' and 'mine'. God has given a place for me to live, and I am proclaiming God to the world" (Abg. 1897). In another passage, he speaks of the funeral pyre of the living body. "The living body is dead, and has been placed in the cemetery. Passions are crying that their lord is gone, and death is crying that he has lost his control. The fire of illumination is burning the body with the fuel of dispassion. The pitcher of egoism is whirled round the head, and is broken to pieces. The death-cry 'I am God' emerges vociferously. The family lineage has been cut off, and the body is delivered to Him who is its Lord. Tukārāma says that when the body was being reduced to ashes, the lamp of the Guru's compassion was burning on it" (Abg. 1896). This death, says Tukā, has brought on everlasting light. "When the body was emptied, God came to inhabit it......By my bodily death, the unending light began to burn. At one stroke, Tukā became non-existent, and his personality came to an end" (Abg. 2637). "When I died," he says elsewhere, "I made over my body to God. Whom and how shall I now serve? The doll throws out its hands and feet, as the wire-puller moves the thread. I speak as God makes me speak......Merit and demerit do not belong to me. They belong to God. Believe me, says Tukā, I am beyond this body" (Abg. 2160). "My end is gained, my heart is set on Thy name, and infinite joy springs from the remembrance of Thy feet. The purpose for which I had taken on a body has been achieved, and a future life is cut off. A sudden profit has now accrued, and nothing remains to be achieved" (Abg. 1314).

Tukarama's great Spiritual Power.

45. Tukārāma employs various images to describe his great spiritual power after God-realisation. He speaks of himself as the son of God, and God as his father, and as such he tells us the son must necessarily inherit the patrimony of his father. Then he speaks of himself as being the key-holder of the treasury of God. Thirdly, he speaks of God's grace as the harvest, and himself as the distributor of it. Lastly, he speaks of himself as the Spiritual King of the world. In all these ways he describes how he comes to have sovereign power. To quote Tukārāma, he tells us, in the first place, that he would no longer be a powerless, casteless, mean man. His father is God Pāṇḍuraṅga, and his mother is Rakhumāī. In both ways, he has descended of pure stock. He would no longer be of poor spirit or of dwarfish power. He would no longer be wicked or unfortunate. God would come to his succour ......He tells us, furthermore, that death would hide himself before him, and as the rich treasure has come to his lot, he would remain careless in mind (Abg. 1091). He asks in another place,—Who could prevent the son from obtaining the patrimony of his father? "All power and fortune seek the house of the Saints. Who could prevent the son from obtaining the treasure of his father? I would sit on the lap of God, says Tukā, and there remain fearless and content" (Abg. 859). "The father," he tells us yet in another place, "treasures riches merely for the sake of his son. He gives himself utmost trouble, bears the burden of his son, and makes him the master of his treasury. He puts ornaments on his son, and is satisfied by looking at him. He prevents people from troubling his son, and in so doing does not care even for his own life" (Abg. 2414). Secondly, Tukārāma speaks of himself as being the key-holder of God's treasury. "I shall now give and take by my own power. There is nobody who can prevent me from doing so. I possess, the key of God's treasury, and every kind of merchandise that may be asked for is with me. By the power of my faith, God has made me a free master, says Tukā" (Abg. 2386). Thirdly, he speaks of himself as distributing the rich harvest of God, and when the distribution is no longer needed, he would treasure up the remainder. "There is no deficit here," says Tukā, "All castes may come and take away to their satisfaction. The surface of a mirror shows a man as he is. Those who believe in God enjoy solitude even in company, and God comes upon us as a rich harvest. Tukā is the distributor of it, and gives to all as they like" (Abg. 3946). "And now I shall treasure up the harvest. I shall keep with me the seed of all existence from which all beings spring. I have blown off the chaff, and kept intact the rich grain. To my lot, says Tukā, God has fallen by the power of my desert" (Abg. 3947). Lastly, in almost the same strain, Tukā speaks of himself as being a crowned spiritual king. "My lineage has been found out, and (as at the coronation of a king) been proclaimed before all. In order to continue the spiritual tradition, I have been crowned king of the spiritual world. The white umbrella now unfurls itself; the banner of the super-conscious state flutters in the air; the mystic sound fills the universe. The Lord of Tukārāma places him on His own spiritual pedestal, and the whole world is filled with joy" (Abg. 3255). And as the spiritual king of the world, Tukā asks, is he not the master of all he wishes? "In the bosom of Bhakti, there are mines of rich jewels, and all things whatsoever are in God......When a king demands anything, nobody says 'nay'. By the power of his faithful service, a servant is himself raised to the position of a master......From his lofty throne, he can now look below upon the world. Tukā was at once placed on the spiritual throne by the power of his faith, and people regarded him as God himself" (Abg. 788).

The words of Tukarama are the words of God.

46. As a result of his identification with God, Tukārāma tells us in many places in his Abhangas that God is speaking through him, or that his words are mixed with divinity. "I know nothing, and what I am speaking are not my words, O Saints. Be not angry with me. These are not my words. God Pāṇḍuranga speaks through me, as He has filled every nook and cranny of me. How can a foolish man like myself have the power to speak what transcends the Vedas? I only know how to lisp the name of God. By the power of my Guru, God is bearing all my burden" (Abg. 1188). He invites people to believe in him though unlearned; because he bears the impress of Viṭṭhala. "If the holy waters of the Ganges flow past an idle man, should not the other people bathe in those waters? If the wish-cow stands in the court-yard of a pariah, should not the Brahmins make adoration to it? If a man, struck with leucoderma, holds gold in his hands, should not people touch it, considering it unholy ? If the Patel of a village is an outcast, should not his words be obeyed ? Tukā, in whom devotion has become strong, bears the stamp of Viṭṭhala, and those who do not listen to him, shall have their faces besmirched" (Abg. 3157). "People do not see," says Tukārāma, "that God is speaking through me. I am made to speak words of realisation by God Himself. Unbelieving and unintelligent men cannot know this. These unheard-of gracious words are the gift of God. People cannot come to believe this, even though I tell them so often and often" (Abg. 2353). "As for myself," he says, "I speak only as I am taught by my Master. I do not speak my words. My words are of my gracious Lord. The parrot speaks as it is taught by its master. What can an insignificant man like myself say, unless he is made to speak by the all-supporting Lord ? Who can know His ways, asks Tukā. He can make a lame man walk without feet" (Abg. 2163). "I have no intellect," Tukārāma tells us. "I speak straight on. I speak merely the words which have been used by the Saints......I cannot even properly utter the name of Viṭṭhala. What then do I know of spiritual knowledge ?......I was born of a low caste. I cannot speak much. The Lord makes me speak, and He alone knows the innermost meaning of my words" (Abg. 518). "Do not say that I am responsible for my poems. God makes me sing ......I am merely set to measure the corn : the corn belongs to my Lord. I am only a servant of my Lord, and hold in my hands His impress and authority" (Abg. 605). "My words are surely mixed with divinity. I do not grope in darkness. I go on sowing in faith. The treasure belongs to my Lord. What room is there for egoism here ? I go on awakening people to their duty," says Tukā (Abg. 771). "My speech," Tukārāma also tells us, "is like rain — universal in nature. The thief harbours perpetual fear in his heart...... What may we do to this ? My words touch the wounds in the hearts of people. He who has the wound will suffer from the probe" (Abg. 1939).

The mission of Tukarama.

47. Tukārāma had achieved the end of his life, and he now lived only for the benefaction of the world. He had realised, that, like God, he was smaller than an atom and larger than the universe. He had belched out the body and the universe. He had transcended the three stages of consciousness, and was living in the fourth, as a lamp may silently shine in a pitcher. He said that his only business now was the benefaction and betterment of the world

(Abg. 3340). His duty was only to spread religion. "To advance religion and to destroy atheism is my business now ......I take pointed answers in my hands, and send them like arrows. I have no consideration, says Tukā, of great and small" (Abg. 1445). Tukārāma is conscious that he has been doing this work through various lives. "Through various lives I have been doing this duty, namely, to relieve the oppressed from the sorrows of existence. I shall sing the praises of God, and gather together His Saints. I shall evoke tears even from stones. I shall utter the holy name of God, and shall dance and clap my hands in joy. I shall plant my foot on the forehead of death. I shall imprison my passions and make myself the lord of the senses" (Abg. 1585). He tells us that false prophets will have their sway only so long as they have not seen Tukā. "A jackal will make a noise only so long as he has not seen a lion. The ocean will roar only so long as it has not met the sage Agastya. Dispassion may be spoken of only so long as a beautiful maiden has not been seen. People will speak of bravery only so long as they have not met a born warrior. Rosaries and bodily marks will have their sway, only so long as their bearers have not met Tukā" (Abg. 2011). "Pebbles will shine only so long as the diamond is not brought forth. Torches will shine only so long as the Sun has not risen. People will speak of the Saints only so long as they have not met Tukā" (Abg. 2012). Tukārāma tells us furthermore that he has been a companion of God from of old. "We have been the companions of God from times immemorial. God has taken us along with Him. There has never been any difference between God and ourselves. We have never lived apart from one another. When God was sleeping, I was there. When God took Laṅkā, I was there. When God tended the cattle, I was there. Our business is the meditation of God's name without a moment's respite" (Abg. 1584). Tukā was present, he says, even when Śuka went to the mountains to attain Samādhi. "Spiritual arrogance pursued Śuka. Vyāsa sent him to Janaka in order to remove his pride. Janaka pointed the way to him and sent him to the peak of Meru. Tukā says that he was present even at the time when Śuka attained Samādhi" (Abg. 1717). Thus it happens, says Tukārāma, that he has been living through various incarnations, and as before, even in this life, has come to separate the wheat from the chaff. "I have come to illumine the ways, and to distinguish the true from the false. God makes me speak, being always in my company. By the power of the Lord, I have no fear in my heart. Before me, no tinsel can have any power" (Abg. 176). Tukārāma tells people that he has come in God's name to carry them over the sea of life. "I have girdled up my loins, and have found out a way for you across the ocean of life. Come here, come here, great and small, women and men. Take no thought, and have no anxiety. I shall carry all of you to the other shore. I come as the sole bearer of the stamp of God to carry you over in God's name" (Abg. 221). Tukārāma charges people to cease from doing wrong henceforth. "For whatever has happened hitherto through ignorance, I forgive you all. But do not commit any sins henceforth. He, who commits adultery with another man's wife, has made intercourse with his own mother. He, who does not listen to us, should never come to us. Be on your guard, says Tukā, and listen when I promise" (Abg. 146). "Your sins will be washed away if you do not commit them again. Utter the name of Viṭṭhala, and you will be free from your sins. Sins shall have no existence before the power of God's name. Millions of sinful acts will be burnt in the fire of God's name. Do not look backwards......I stand guarantee for your sins. Commit as many sins as you can name. Death will have no sway before the fire of God's name" (Abg. 106). "I enjoy this sweet ambrosia and distribute it among men. Do not wander among the woods. Come here and partake of my offer. Your desires shall be fulfilled, if your intellect is fastened on His feet. I come as a messenger from Viṭṭhala. Easy will be the Pathway by which you may go to God" (Abg. 198). Finally, Tukārāma tells us that having had his station originally in heaven, he came down to the earth, like the Saints of old, to pursue the path of Truth. "We will cleanse the path of the Saints. People have ignorantly gone to woods and forests......The true meaning of the Sacred Books has been hidden. Wordy knowledge has been the cause of ruin. Senses have stood in the way of Sādhana. We will ring the bell of Bhakti. It will send a threat into the heart of Death. Rejoice, says Tukā, in the victorious name of God" (Abg. 222).

CHAPTER XVI.

Tukarama's Mystical Teaching.

V. Preparation for Mystic Life.

Introductory.

48. Hitherto we have considered Tukārāma's mystical career as it is found in his own writings. Evidently, there is a personalistic colouring to the mystical development of Tukārāma as we have discussed it till now. We shall now proceed to consider the mystical teaching of Tukārāma. This is valuable as coming from Tukārāma when he had reached the stage of a full-fledged Saint. As we have hitherto discussed what Tukārāma said about his own mystical development personally, we shall now discuss what he says of mystical development in general. We shall first consider what preparation Tukārāma considers necessary for mystical realisation.

Rules for the life of the novice in Yoga.

49. In the first place, Tukārāma teaches how the novice in Yoga should modulate his life, so as ultimately to be able to reach God. He tells us that the novice in Yoga should always be indifferent to all things, should not get himself contaminated internally or externally by anything whatsoever. He should leave off greediness, conquer sleep, take a measured quantity of food, and should, in private or in public, avoid, on pain of death, conversation with women. He alone who believes in such a Sādhana, says Tukā, will ultimately reach the end of his endeavour by the grace of his Guru (Abg. 2068). Such a novice in Yoga should take only such clothing and food as would be sufficient for life, should live in a hermitage either in a far-off cave or in a forest,......should not sit talking among men, should carefully guard his senses by the force of his intellect, should make the best use of every moment of his life, and remember God (Abg. 933). It was for this reason that Tukārāma tells us that the Ṛishis of old avoided the world,. ....made subsistence on onions and roots of trees, lived in utter silence, shut their eyes, and meditated on God (Abg. 521). "If we carry on our spiritual practice regularly, what can it not achieve?" asks Tukā. "The wet root of a plant breaks even huge rocks. Practice can achieve anything whatsoever. Nothing can stand in the way of a determined effort. A rope can cut a hard stone. One can get oneself accustomed to poison by taking it in increasingly large doses. A child carves a place for itself in the mother's womb as time elapses" (Abg. 848). "Have not people taken large quantities of aconite," asks Tukā, "by gradually accustoming themselves to it? One can take a poisonous snake in his hands, striking terror into the hearts of the on-lookers. Through practice, says Tukā, even the impossible becomes possible" (Abg. 159). "Thus we should go to solitude and fix our mind on God, should not allow our mind to wander, should avoid all frivolity,........should set our heart on reality, and pierce it as an arrow pierces the mark. We should bid good-bye to idleness and to sleep, and live in the constant wakefulness of God" (Abg. 2865).

The worldly life of the spiritual aspirant.

50. Tukārāma's advice to the man who wishes to accomplish both Prapañcha and Paramārtha at the same time, that is to say, to seek the worldly and the spiritual life together, is, that by doing so, he would lose them both. "He who says that he would accomplish the worldly and the spiritual life together, shall accomplish neither. Between two stones he will only fall to the ground. He will be ruined on both sides, and will ultimately go to hell" (Abg. 3144). The novice in Yoga, therefore, should, in the first place, ward off all relatives, whether son or wife or brother. "When we have once known that they are ultimately of no use, why should we get ourselves contaminated by them? We should break a pitcher for them, as one breaks for a dead body......" (Abg. 81). "If our father and mother happen to create obstacles in our spiritual life, we should ward them off. Who cares for wife and children and wealth? They are merely a source of sorrow......Prahlāda left off his father, Bibhīshaṇa his brother, Bharata both his mother and kingdom. The feet of God alone, says Tukā, are our final resort; everything else is a source of evil" (Abg. 83). This is the negative social ethics which Tukārāma preaches for the initial stages of the spiritual life. "Such a man should take thought as to the real way of deliverance from mortal life. If one gets drowned in a boat made of stones, who can save him? One should not therefore destroy oneself like a fly jumping into a flame. If a man takes quantities of arsenic, he should not call for a doctor in his last moment" (Abg. 4002). "Such a man should throw away the frivolities of life, and follow the path by which have gone the Saints of old. He should gradually unwind the skein of worldly life. He should follow the foot-prints of those who have gone ahead...........He should think time after time about his past conduct, and take courage for the future. Tukā says that as a man speaks, so he must live" (Abg. 1399). "He should not fill his vision with the evanescence of the world. He should consider that the mortal body is destined to perish, and that Death is eating it up every moment. He should seek company of the Saints, and make haste for the spiritual life. He should not allow his eyes to be blinded by the smoke of worldly existence" (Abg. 2339). "He should eat the leaves of trees, and sing Viṭṭhala time after time. He should wear bark-garments, and leave off bodily egoism. He should consider honour among men as good as vomit, and live in solitude for the sake of God. He should not go in for complacency of conduct, but live in a forest. He, who determines to carry on his life in this way, says Tukā, will reach the goal of his life" (Abg. 2999). His final advice, so far as this kind of negative ethics is concerned, is that one should never hope to carry on Prapañcha and Paramārtha together. "When one goes to a menagerie of buffaloes, one gets only eaten-up straw. He who expects to get good sleep on a couch filled with bugs is a fool. A drunken man is sure some day to rave naked, says Tukā" (Abg. 1008).

Moral precepts for the spiritual aspirant.

51. Tukārāma advises the spiritual aspirant to regard another man's wife as his mother, to avoid censure of others, to throw away lust for other people's wealth, to sit at a place and meditate on God, to believe in the Saints, and to tell the truth. By these means, says Tukā, one can reach God (Abg. 36). He elsewhere enumerates the obstacles in the way of spiritual life as being the flattery of men, the bargaining of money for spiritual matters, lust for another man's wife and wealth, hatred towards beings, egoism of the body, and forgetfulness of God. These he asks God to prevent from attacking him (Abg. 1867). "Some people," he says, "tease their body uselessly for the sake of spiritual realisation. They wear brown clothes; but a dog is also brown. They bear matted hair; but a bear also has got matted hair. They live in caves; but even rats live in caves. These people, says Tukā, tease their bodies for nothing" (Abg. 2982). "The body is both good and bad. We should rise superior to the body, and think of God. If we look at it from one point of view, the body is a store-house of miseries, a mine of diseases, the birth-place of foulness, the unholy of unholies. From another point of view, the body is good and beautiful, the source of happiness, and a means of spiritual realisation. Yet, again, the body is merely a curdled product of menstrual blood, a net of desire and infatuation, and a prey to death. In another way, it is a pure thing, the treasure of treasures, the temple of God, the means for getting rid of worldly existence. We should give neither happiness nor unhappiness to the body. The body is neither good nor bad. We should rise superior to it, and think of God" (Abg. 4113). "He, who cares for the body," says Tukā, "cares for honour and repute, and thus becomes a prey to evil and suffering......Consciousness of honour puts a stop to further progress, and enthrals a man by tying a rope round his neck" (Abg. 2537). Tukārāma advises the spiritual aspirant to look upon pleasure and pain alike. "He may be a carrier of water at one time, and sleep on a costly couch at another. He may now eat dainties, and now again he may have to eat bread without salt. At one time, he may go in a palanquin, and at another he may be obliged to go bare-footed. Once, he may wear rich clothes, at another time, worn-out rags......The spiritual aspirant, says Tukā, should look upon pleasure and pain alike" (Abg. 2046). Tukārāma tells us not to tell a lie on any account whatsoever. "Even if a man were to help a marriage by telling a lie, he should not do it, because he would thereby merely go to hell. Dharma, the eldest of the Pāṇḍavas, lost his thumb for having told a lie. A man who has a lie in his heart, says Tukā, is bound to suffer" (Abg. 1021). He teaches that what is wanted is internal purity and not external purification. "Even if the body is purified outside, the mind is dirty inside......It is full of untruth and hypocrisy. Be thou thy own spectator. Wear the sacred cloth in the shape of freedom from passion. Only then wilt thou be really pure" (Abg. 1551). "Holy waters do not cleanse the wickedness within. They cleanse only the external skin. The bitter Vṛindāvana fruit will not lose its bitterness even if it be put into sugar. There is no use sobbing unless you have tranquillity, forgiveness, and compassion" (Abg. 1131). "We should empty the heart of its contents, and then will God live in it. No other remedy is required, says Tukā, to see God. We should nip all our desires in the bud. Where desires end, God comes to inhabit," says Tuka (Abg. 907). He tells us elsewhere that for reaching God, one is required to kill all one's desires. One need not look at a mark with concentration. One need not give anything in charity, or undergo penance. One need not forsake actions due to one's natural caste. One should only take leave of his desires, and then one would be able to realise God (Abg. 1405). In fact, if one meditates on God, Tukārāma allows him the enjoyment of all things whatsoever. "One need not leave food, nor go to a forest. One should meditate on God, and enjoy all things. A child sitting on the shoulder of its mother knows not the travail of walking. One need not consider what things to possess, and what things to abandon. One should only rest in God" (Abg. 816). Tukārāma does not even prevent a man from doing bad things, if by them one is able to reach God. One should not care for the preceptor's advice, if by that God may stand at a distance......The wives of the ancient Ṛishis disobeyed their husbands, and went food in hand to Kṛishṇa...... Prahlāda made enmity with his father for the sake of God......The wives of the cow-herds committed adultery with God. One should do even a bad deed, says Tukā, provided by it he reaches God ; and one should not do even a good deed by which God may stand at distance" (Abg. 680). "The spiritual aspirant must always live in the company of the Saints, for other company may take away his mind from God. If one goes to see anybody at all, he should go to see a Saint. If one lives in the company of anybody, it should be in the company of the Saints......The Saints are an ocean of happiness, says Tukā. God is their treasure. They speak no other language but of God. One should find rest only in the Saints" (Abg. 712). "One should not wait for a suitable opportunity to turn up to meditate on God. One should begin immediately. One can never hope to be so unperturbed as to give oneself unmolested to mere meditation on God. If a man says that he will meditate on God when matters are comparatively easy, that will never come to pass" (Abg. 1181). "Whatever be the difficulties in which one may be placed, one should offer prayers to God. One should call in the help of God, when calamities befall him. Then God will not wait, but ward off those calamities by his personal intervention. By meditation on God's name, obstacles will vanish away in different directions. One need only surrender his life to God" (Abg. 1625). "Thus God should be the sole object of the aspirant's meditation, even in dreams and in sleep. His mind should know no other object of contemplation. The natural bent of the senses should be in the direction of God, and the eyes should ever seek His vision" (Abg. 318).

VI. The Teacher and the Disciple.

52. In the opinion of Tukārāma, he alone deserves to be a Spiritual Teacher, who regards his disciples as gods. 'He, who does not accept service from his disciples and regards them as gods, is alone worthy of being a Teacher.......In him alone does knowledge live, because he is indifferent to self. I tell the truth, says Tukā, and care not for people who may become angry with me for saying so" (Abg. 881). "A spiritual teacher must not fatten his body. Unless the true mark of Sainthood has been generated in him, he is not worthy of making disciples. He who cannot swim himself should not make others catch hold of him in the waters......If an exhausted man goes to another exhausted man, both of them will perish," says Tukā (Abg. 3122). "A false teacher makes his disciples look uninterruptedly at a mark, and tells them to see the light by rubbing their eyes. He falsely teaches his disciples that he has thus enjoyed Samādhi, and deceives them..........He earns his livelihood by teaching any falsehood he pleases......He teaches his disciples to utter the name of the Guru himself" (Abg. 3431). "His disciples, on the other hand, go from bad to worse, and take no account of castes. They regard a holy man as a thorn in their way, and regard the pariah as a very spiritual man......This Guru gives spiritual advice to concubines, children, and some foolish Brahmins......They all eat together, and say that such inter-dining takes them to absolution. Such Gurus and disciples both go to hell," says Tukā (Abg. 3432). "A true Guru therefore should not be merely worthy of his instruction, but should see that his disciples are also worthy of his instruction. One should never force one's spiritual advice upon others. Does not a juggler keep a monkey with him? ......He, who wastes seed in a place which is not wet with water, is a fool. I distribute spiritual advice like rain, says Tukā" (Abg. 1714).

The teacher and the disciple.

VII. The Name.

53. The sole way to the realisation of God, according to Tukārāma, is the constant repetition of God's name. "Sit silent," says Tukārāma, "compose thy mind and make it pure, and then happiness will know no bounds. God will certainly come and dwell in thy heart. This will be the result of thy long effort. Meditate time after time on God's name,—Rāma, Kṛishṇa, Hari. I declare, says Tukā, that this will surely come to pass, if thou hast one-pointed devotion" (Abg. 1132). "The uttering of the name of God is indeed an easy way for reaching Him. One need not go to a distant forest. God will Himself come to the house of a Saint. One should sit at a place, concentrate

The celebration of God's Name as the way to realisation.

his mind, invoke God with love, and utter His name time after time. I swear by God's name, says Tukā, that there is no other way for reaching God : indeed, this is the easiest of all ways" (Abg. 1698). "If we only utter the name of God, God will stand before us. In that way should we meditate on Him. He, who does not present Himself to the vision of the gods, dances when His devotee sings" (Abg. 2021). There are always difficulties which intervene before God is reached. These are dispelled by the power of devotion. "The Name will lead to God if no obstacle intervenes. A fruit becomes ripe on a tree only if it is not plucked" (Abg. 695). "The ship of God's name," says Tukā, "will ultimately carry one across the ocean of life. It will save both the young and the old" (Abg. 2457). "All the different Sciences proclaim the supremacy of the Name. The Vedas tell us that nothing but the Name of God shall save us. The different Śāstras say the same thing. Throughout the different Purāṇas, says Tukā, the same message is preached" (Abg. 3128). He alone who knows the efficacy of the Name, says Tukā, may be said to have grasped the inner meaning of the Vedas. "We alone know the real meaning of the Vedas ; others merely bear the burden of knowing. The man who sees is not the man who tastes. The man who bears the burden is not he who owns the burden. The secret of the creation, preservation, and destruction of the world is with God. We have found out the root, says Tukā. The fruit will now come of itself to hand" (Abg. 1549). There are some occasions when one does not know what one's duty is. In such a case, says Tukārāma, we should utter the name of God. "We do not know what to do, and what not to do : we only know how to meditate on Thy feet...... We do not know where to go, and where not to go : we only know how to meditate on Thy name. By Thy making, says Tukā, sins become merits. By our making, says Tukā, merits become sins" (Abg. 3307). "Thus determinately and resolutely should one meditate on God by means of His Name. Let the head break off, or let the body fall, we should not leave off the celebration of God's Name. Even if we are fasting for a week, we should not fail to sing the Name of God. If the head breaks, or the body is cut in twain, we should not fail in the celebration of God's Name. He alone, who determinately utters the Name of God, says Tukā, will be able to find God" (Abg. 3258).

54. Tukārāma next goes on to discuss the physical and mental effects of meditation on the Name. "When I utter Thy name, my mind becomes composed. The tongue enjoys a stream of ambrosia. Good omens of all kinds take place. The mind is coloured in Thy vision, and becomes steady on Thy feet........One becomes as satisfied as if one has taken a dainty meal. Desires come to an end, and words come out of the mouth as of complete satisfaction. Happiness meets happiness, and there is no limit to blessedness" (Abg. 830). Tukārāma repeats the same idea elsewhere. "The whole body feels cool when one meditates on the Name. The senses forget their movements......By the sweet nectar-like love of God, one is full of energy and all kinds of sorrow depart immediately" (Abg. 1543). "The body which was hitherto unclean, becomes lustrous by the power of the Name, the mind is purified, and repentance puts a stop to one's accumulated Karma" (Abg. 3997). "......The evil passions are conquered ; all the impulses are nipped in the bud by the power of the Name. Tukā looks at God's feet, and waits for His answer" (Abg. 3302).

Bodily and mental effects of meditation on the Name.

55. The moral effects of uttering the Name, Tukārāma is never wearied of describing. The utterance of the Name, he tells us, brings with it exceeding merit. "He who utters the name of God while walking, gets the merit of a Sacrifice at every step. Blessed is his body. It is itself a place of pilgrimage. He who says God while doing his work, is always merged in Samādhi. He who utters the name of God while eating, gets the merit of a fast even though he may have taken his meals. He who utters the name of God without intermission receives liberation though living" (Abg. 3667). "Even if one were to give in charity the whole earth encircled by the seas, that cannot equal the merit of uttering the Name...... A repetition of all the Vedas cannot equal one Name of God. All places of pilgrimage have no value before God's Name. All sorts of bodily toils are useless before the Name of God" (Abg. 1581). "By the power of the Name of God, one shall come to know what one does not know. One shall see what cannot be seen. One will be able to speak what cannot be spoken. One shall meet what cannot be ordinarily met. Incalculable will be the gain of uttering the Name," says Tukā (Abg. 2220). Yet, again, Tukārāma says in another place: "Untold benefits will accrue if we sing the Name of God in solitude. We should pacify our desires, and should not give room to any passions. We should not waste words, but should utter the Name, which is as the arrow which

The moral effects of meditation on the Name.

will hit the mark" (Abg. 1093). The Name of God, says Tukārāma, will save us from all difficulties. "Enclose the Name of God in your mouth. Think constantly of what is valuable and what is not valuable. By meditation on God, all difficulties will vanish. We shall thus be able to cross the uncrossable ocean of life......The whole lineage will become pure, says Tukā, by the utterance of God's Name" (Abg. 3137). The medicine of God's name, we are told elsewhere, destroys the disease of life. "Drink the medicine of God's Name, and all your agonies will cease. Partake of nothing but the Name of God. Even the disease of life will thus vanish, not to speak of other small diseases" (Abg. 1384). Tukārāma tells us elsewhere that in this perishable life, the only rest is in the name of God. "The body is subject to all kinds of accidents, good and bad. Its happiness and sorrow are both evanescent. The only thing to be achieved in this life is love towards God......The only rest, says Tukā, in this mortal existence is in the constant remembrance of God's Name (Abg. 1859). One will even be able to confer spiritual obligations upon others by uttering God's Name. "One should not flutter about, but should remain steady, believing in the efficacy of God's Name. God will give you imperishable happiness, and the round of incarnations will cease. You will even be able to confer obligations upon others. That itself will be a great asset. The Name of God will save you in this life as well as in the next. If you leave off the pursuit of evanescent things, says Tukā, you will attain to incalculable bliss" (Abg. 670). "The sweetness of the Name is indescribable. The tongue soon gets averse to other kinds of flavours; but the flavour of the Name increases every moment. Other medicines lead you to death; but this medicine relieves you of death. God has become our constant food, says Tuka" (Abg. 1168). Tukārāma is so completely satisfied with the utterance of the Name that he is not desirous of anything else. He tells God that he has no desire for anything except His name. All kinds of powers which may accrue in contemplation are useless before the power of devotion. Tukā says that, by the power of the Name, he will easily go to heaven, and will enjoy complete bliss (Abg. 231). Finally, the sweetness of God's Name, Tukārāma tells us, cannot be known by God Himself. "Does a lotus plant know the fragrance of its flowers? It is the bee which tastes of its fragrance. The cow eats grass; but the calf alone knows the sweetness of her milk. The oyster shell cannot enjoy its own pearls; similarly, says Tukā, God does not know the sweetness of the Name, which only the devotees can experience" (Abg. 233).

VIII. The Kirtana.

Kirtana, as a way of realising God.

56. There is another way to the realisation of God—one closely related to the celebration of the Name. It is what may be called the "Kīrtana", or the singing of the praises of God, either in the abstract, or in His concrete manifestations in human life. Tukārāma was given to the celebration of the Kīrtana like many other Saints. "The Kīrtana," says Tukā, "is the meditation of God Himself...... There is no merit on earth which is equal to that of the Kīrtana. Believe me, says Tukā, God stands up where Kīrtana is being performed....A man who performs the Kīrtana not only saves himself, but also others. Without doubt, says Tukā, one can meet God by performing a Kīrtana" (Abg. 1604). Hence, anybody who disbelieves in the Kīrtana merely ruins himself. "The words of one who does not believe in the Kīrtana of God are unwholesome; his ears are like a rat's hole. Vainly do such people leave away sacred nectar, and follow after insignificant things. Vainly do people go astray, and become mad in their endeavour, says Tukā" (Abg. 3381). "He alone attends a Kīrtana who wishes to uplift himself. Nobody asks an ant to go where sugar is to be found. A beggar seeks out a donor of his own accord. He who is hungry goes and finds out food. He who suffers from a disease, goes of his own accord to the house of a doctor. He who wishes to uplift himself, says Tukā, never fails to attend a Kīrtana" (Abg. 1620). Tukārāma only prays that his body may be kept sound, in order that it might help him in the singing of God's praise. "A Kīrtana requires soundness of limbs. Do not allow my limbs to grow weak, O God. I do not mind if my life is cut short. But so long as I live, let me be sound, says Tukā, in order that I may pray to Thee" (Abg. 4023).

Kirtana is a river which flows upwards towards God.

57. Tukārāma often likens Kīrtana to a river. In one place, he tells us that it is a river which flows upwards towards God. "The Kīrtana is a stream of nectar flowing before God. It wends upwards, and is the crown of all holy things. It is the life-blood of Śiva and burns up all kinds of sins. The gods themselves describe its power, says Tukā" (Abg. 3382). In another place, he describes Kīrtana as a confluence of three rivers. "It is a confluence where God and Devotee and the Name meet together.

The very sands at the place are holy. Mountains of sins are burnt by its power. It spreads holiness among all men and women. Holy places come to it to be purified. It is more sacred than the sacred days. Its holiness is incomparable, and the gods themselves are unable to describe the happiness produced by it" (Abg. 1605).

Requirements of a man who performs Kirtana.

58. What, according to Tukārāma, are the requirements of a man who performs a Kīrtana ? "If I were to perform a Kīrtana by accepting money for it, let, O God, my body be destroyed. If I were to request anybody to arrange for my Kīrtana, let, O God, my tongue fall down, Thou art our helper, and there is nothing lacking before Thee. Why should I waste my words before others ? At Thy feet are all powers, and Thou art my Lord" (Abg. 3138). "Where one performs a Kīrtana, one should not take food. One should not have his forehead besmeared with fragrant scent. One should not allow himself to be garlanded by flowers. One should not ask for grain or for grass for a horse or a bullock. They, who give money, and they who accept money, says Tukā, both of them go to hell" (Abg. 2256). In this way, Tukārāma tells us that pecuniary bargains are an obstacle to spiritual progress.

Great is the power of Song.

59. Tukārāma tells us very often that the power imparted by a Kīrtana is indescribable. "Great is the power of Song," says Tukā. "This evidently is Thy grace. Allow me to consecrate my life to Thy service. Let my mind be so filled by Thy love that there may be neither any ebb nor any flow to it. Let my words be a mine of sweet nectar, says Tukā" (Abg. 309). He elsewhere tells us that the joy of Kīrtana is indescribable. "The Saints have told us an easy secret : they have asked us to dance with Tāla and Diṇḍī in our hands. The happiness of ecstasy is as nothing before this happiness of a Kīrtana. It continually grows, and one is merged in it by the power of his devotion. No doubts now harass his mind, the mind becomes tranquil, and all kinds of misery vanish immediately" (A[illegible]. 766). Tukārāma tells us that there is no entrance for the [illegible]sengers of Death where a Kīrtana is being performed. "D[illegible]h tells his messengers—Go not to the place where the Name is being celebrated. You have not power over that place. You do not go to the place where the Name-bearers live. Go not even to its outskirts. The great disc of God moves round and wards off all dangers. God Himself stands as a door-keeper at the place with a bludgeon and the moving disc in His hands...... The Saints are the most powerful beings on earth—so says Death to his servants" (Abg. 1608). While a Kīrtana is being performed, nothing can cause fear to the Saints. "God is before, and behind. Why need the Saints fear anything at all? Dance with the power of joy, and allow not your mind to be tossed by doubts. How can Death come and have power before God? When the all-powerful God is present, what can be lacking to the Saints?" (Abg. 350). Tukārāma tells us that he is always beating the cymbals, and dancing in joy for God. He has been telling people that there is really no fear before God. He has been singing and dancing in tune with Ṭāḷas and Bells. Fear can do nothing to us, says Tukā, for God comes before us" (Abg. 357). Finally, we are told that the merit of Kīrtana is superior to the merit of any penance, or the counting of beads. "For, in Kīrtana," says Tukārāma, "God is verily present. Believe these words of mine, and allow not your mind to wander. All ecstasy and all penance live, says Tukā, by the power of Kīrtana" (Abg. 2142).

IX. Bhakti.

God cannot be reached except through Love.

60. Generally speaking, meditation on the Name, or performance of a Kīrtana, are merely external marks of an internal devotion or Bhakti. Tukārāma tells us that when a man has this Bhakti, he may be said to have performed all religious functions whatsoever. "When a man has placed his mind, and words, and body at Thy service, there is no duty for him which he need perform. Why need he worship any stones?......Why need he bathe in the holy waters? What sins can he be relieved thereby? I have submitted all my desires to Thee, and have conquered all sin and merit......When the body has been made over to Thee, one need only rest silent in contentment" (Abg. 1183). "In this way, the Bhaktimārga," says Tukā, "is the only easy pathway in this age. All other ways have been useless. God Viṭṭhala stands up, raises his arm, and calls his servants to duty. Those who believe in Him will cross the ocean of life. Others, who do not believe, shall go to ruin" (Abg. 1582). Tukārāma tells us also that the transpersonal God cannot be reached except through love. "God has no form, nor any name, nor any place, where He can be seen; but wherever you go, you see God. He has neither form nor transformation; but He fills the whole world. He is neither impersonal nor personal; but is beyond all knowledge. This God, says Tukā, cannot be attained except through love" (Abg. 2148). In fact, God does not care for anything except love. He does not care for a sweet voice: he only looks to the heart within. "If God has not given us a sweet voice and if we cannot speak sweetly, let us not be afraid. God does not care for these attainments. Say Rāma, Kṛishṇa, Hari as you can. Demand of God a pure love for Him, and a belief in Him" (Abg. 7). "One need not worship stones, or brass, or any kind of images. What is required is pure devotion. That is the way to liberation. What is the use of these rosaries, and these garlands? Why need we care for a learned voice? Why need we care for a beautiful song? If we have no devotion, God will not care for us, says Tukā" (Abg. 2054). Let a man believe fully, and he will be saved by God. "He who attempts to know God at the cost of his life shall be saved by God. There is no doubt that he will reach the other side of existence. Blessed is he who believes; for in him alone God lives. God becomes the bond-servant of those, says Tukā, who blindly believe in Him" (Abg. 4028). Absence of real devotion makes God stand away from those who entertain doubt and fear......God stands away from those who cannot sacrifice their life for God. God stands away from those who speak vain words without any real sacrifice. God knows the hearts of all, and will reward them as they deserve" (Abg. 3874).

Images to describe the relation of Devotee to God.

61. Tukārāma employs various images to describe the devotee's love for God. In one place, he tells us that a devotee should throw himself on God, as a Satī on her husband. "When a Satī sees the cremation fire of her husband, her hair stand on end in joy......She does not look at her family, and her wealth. She does not weep. She only remembers her husband, and throws herself in the funeral pyre" (Abg. 1245). Even so must a devotee throw himself in God. In another place, he says, we should fall straight into Brahman, as a fly flies into a flame. "If we want to enjoy God, we should lop off our head from our body, and hold it in our hands. We should set all our belongings on fire, and should not look behind. We should be as bold, says Tukā, as a fly, which falls straight into a flame" (Abg. 3414). In a third place, he tells us that the devotee's spirit should rise to God like a fountain. "As a fountain rises upwards, even so must one's spirit rise to God. One should entertain no idea whatsoever, except that of God" (Abg. 801). Only then would we be able to reach God. Fourthly, he tells us that we should as much love to hear of God's praises, as a mother of her son's exploits. "As a mother is delighted to hear the good news of her son, even so must our mind be delighted to hear of God's praise. We must forget bodily consciousness like a deer which is infatuated by music. We must look up to God, as the young ones of a tortoise look up to their mother" (Abg. 3426). In fact, the mind that is engrossed in God should think only of God, and of nothing else. "One should know, and yet know not, being merged in the love of God. One should live in this life uncontaminated by it, as a lotus-leaf lives in water uncontaminated by its drops. Praise and censure must fall on his ears as if he were engaged in a state of ecstasy. One should see the world and yet not see it, as if he were in a dream. Unless this happens, says Tukā, whatever a man may do is of no avail" (Abg. 2179).

X. Castes.

Caste not recognised in God-devotion.

62. Tukārāma teaches us that the castes have no significance for God-realisation. A man may belong to any caste whatsoever. If he only devotes himself to the service of God, he will be regarded as holy. "Holy is the family, and holy the country where the servants of God are born. They have devoted themselves to God, and by them all the three worlds become holy. Pride of caste has never made any man holy, says Tukā. The untouchables have crossed the ocean of life by God-devotion, and the Purāṇas sing their praises......Gorā, the potter, Rohidāsa, the shoe-maker, Kabīra, the Muslim, Senā, the barber, Kanhopātrā, the concubine,......Chokhāmeḷā, the outcast......Janābāī, the maid......have all become unified with God by their devotion. The Vedas and the Śāstras have said that for the service of God, castes do not matter. Inquire into the various works, says Tukā, and you will find that unholy men become holy by God-devotion" (Abg. 3241). "Musk looks ugly," says Tukā, "but its essence is wonderful. The sandal trees present no good appearance, but their fragrance spreads all round. A Parisa is ugly to look at, but it creates gold. A sword when melted does not bring a pie; but by its own quality, it sells for a thousand coins. Castes do not matter, says Tukā, it is God's Name that matters" (Abg. 2194). "The cow eats all kinds of dung; but it is yet holy. The brooks that enter into a river become identified with it. The holy Pippala is born of the crow's excreta. The family of the Pāndavas was not a holy one......Ajāmela,

Kubjā and Vidura were not born of a high caste. Vālhā, Viśvāmitra, Vaśishṭha and Nārada cannot boast of a high lineage. Whatever unholy deeds are committed by men and women, when they remember God with repentance, they become free from sins" (Abg. 122). "A Brahmin who does not like the Name of God, is not a Brahmin. I tell you, says Tukā, that when he was born, his mother had committed adultery with a Mahāra......" (Abg. 706). "An outcast who loves the Name of God is verily a Brahmin. In him have tranquillity and forbearance, compassion and courage, made their home. When all the different passions have left a man's mind, he is as good as a Brahmin, says Tukā" (Abg. 707). Even though Tukārāma generally holds such opinions, he elsewhere respects a Brahmin because he is born a Brahmin. "Even if a she-ass gives milk, will she be equal to a cow? Even if a crow's neck is decorated by flowers, can it equal a swan? Even if a monkey bathes and puts a Tilaka on its forehead, can it equal a Brahmin? A Brahmin, says Tukā, even though he is fallen from his high station, must yet be respected" (Abg. 2223). Finally, Tukārāma tells us that we must recognise the difference of castes while we are living in this world. The difference, says Tukārāma, vanishes only in the ecstatic state. "I tell you, O Saints, that the different castes have been born of the same Being according to their merits and demerits......The mango tree, the jujube tree, the fig tree, and the sandal tree are different so long as they are not reduced to cinders in the same fire. The difference of castes must be taken into account, says Tukā, until it vanishes in the ecstatic state" (Abg. 920).

XI. The God of Pandharapur.

Description of the God of Pandharapur.

63. It cannot be gainsaid that Tukārāma for a long while looked upon Viṭṭhala, the God of Paṇḍharapūr, as the cynosure of his eyes. It was only later that he began to find that God was everywhere. Tukārāma, however, always tried to place before the mind's eye of the people some concrete object for worship, and this he succeeded in doing by calling them to the worship of Viṭṭhala. "My heart pants," he says, "for seeing the face of the God of Pandharapūr. The God who stands on a brick at Paṇḍharapūr with his beautiful form, has ravished my heart. My eyes can never be too much satisfied by looking at Him. My life-breath seems to take leave of my body if I am unable for a while to see the beautiful face of God. My mind has been ravished, says Tukā, by the son of Nanda, who has the Eagle for His banner" (Abg. 1700). Tukārāma tells us that neither any wealth nor any happiness pleases him. His mind is always set after going to Paṇḍharapūr. When shall the 11th day of Āshāḍha dawn, he asks, so that he may be able to go to Pandharī? It is only when a man is anxious to see God, says Tukā, that God is anxious to meet him (Abg. 1600). "The Saints have planted aloft the banner of God. I look at that banner as His ensign, and lose myself in His name. If you go by the path indicated by the banner of God, you will surely be able to find God" (Abg. 2871). "This is verily the pathway by which the Saints of old have gone. Mythologies tell us that we must not go by unbeaten paths. The way to God is so bright and straight, that nobody need ask any other man about it. Banners are flying aloft, and the eagle ensign is shining in the air, says Tukā" (Abg. 188). Hitherto many have walked by the way which leads to Paṇḍharapūr. "We have heard of many people who have harboured the Name of God in their minds. They have crossed the ocean of life, and have gone to the other shore. Let us go by the very same way as much as may lie within our power. The ferry which has carried them has been reserved for us, and there shall now be no delay. We need not pay even a farthing for it. We need only have devotion. The ferry is on the banks of the Bhīmā. Let us swim by it to where God is waiting and standing straight to receive us" (Abg. 2683). "The ferry is now on the banks of the Chandrabhāgā. Take away the infinite booty of God's wealth, O Saints! The banner of God's Name is flying aloft. Tukārāma is a porter on the ferry, but God carries his load" (Abg. 993). "When we reach the other shore of the Chandrabhāgā, God is standing there to exchange love for weariness. The poverty and hunger of the people shall disappear. The most generous of gods, the God of Pandharī, raises His arm, and makes you a sign to approach. He shall embrace the ignorant more than the wise......We are the helpless, we are the poor in spirit, says Tukā, and God will protect us" (Abg. 1427). When we go to the temple of Paṇḍharī, the image disappears, and infinite light takes its place. The God of Paṇḍharī is merely the external symbol of an all-immanent light. "The light within, which had remained hitherto hidden, will now begin to appear. The whole universe cannot contain the bliss of the moment. What happiness can be compared to it? The God, who is standing on the brick, is an external symbol of our devotion, though he is Himself impersonal, says Tukā" (Abg. 2069). "The God of Paṇḍharī is a manifestation of Krishna, who as a child lived in the house of Nanda, and who could show the whole universe within Himself. Him who gave satisfaction to the whole world, Yaśodā was trying to feed. Him who filled the whole universe, the cow-herd women were taking on their lap. Verily of various wiles is this God, says Tukā, Who keeps His celibacy intact in spite of His enjoyment" (Abg. 3747). "God Vitthala indeed is a great thief. He has taken the net of devotion in His hands, and has come to Paṇḍharī. He has deceived the whole world, and does not allow Himself to be seen. He raises His hand, and ensnares the eyes of those who wish to see Him. This thief has been brought by Puṇḍalīka to Paṇḍharī. Let us go, says Tukā, and catch hold of Him" (Abg. 442). Puṇḍalīka himself, says Tukārāma, has become arrogant by the power of his devotion, and has made Viṭṭhala stand up. "Thou hast become arrogant by the love of Viṭthala, O Puṇḍalīka! How audacious that you throw away a brick, and make Viṭṭhala stand on it. God is standing there for such a length of time, and yet you do not ask Him to sit down" (Abg. 2965). "The ghost of Paṇḍharī," says Tukārāma, "is indeed a powerful ghost, and possesses everybody who goes that way. Verily full of goblins is this forest, and the mind becomes possessed when it goes there. Go not there, says Tukā, for those who go there do not return. Tukā went to Paṇḍharī and never came back to life" (Abg. 3115). One need not aspire after going to heaven: one need only go to Paṇḍharapūr, says Tukārāma. "Go to Paṇḍharī, and become a Vārakarī. Why dost thou aspire after heaven, if thou goest to the sand-banks of Paṇḍharapūr? Tukārāma falls prostrate before the Saints who bear the banner of God on their shoulders, put on garlands of the Tulasī plant on their necks, and besmear their foreheads by the sweet scent that is sacred to God" (Abg. 2248).

XII. Tukarama's Theism.

The Personal superior to the Impersonal.

64. It is an easy passage from the worship of God in this manner to a theistic view of the God-head which does not allow formlessness to the object of worship. Tukārāma tells us often that he would not allow God to be formless. "Be formless as others desire; but for me take Thou on a form, O God!......I have fallen in love with Thy name. Do not suffer my devotion to wane. Thou mayest hold out for me the bait of liberation: but go and deceive the philosophers by that bait. I tell Thee that Thou shouldst not allow the stream of my devotion to grow dry" (Abg. 2410). "We have slighted liberation for this sake, and are content to re-incarnate again and again. The nectar of devotion only increases our desire from day to day. We have made God to take on a form, and shall not allow Him to become Impersonal" (Abg. 1116). Tukārāma tells us that God is obliged to take on a form in fear of His devotees. "A bee can pierce a hard tree; but it is enclosed by a little flower. Love is bound by love, and is encased in its bonds. A little child makes even an elderly parent powerless by its love. God, says Tukā, is obliged to take on a form in fear of His devotee" (Abg. 1282).

He who says he has become God is a fool.

65. As Tukārāma does not allow God to become formless, so he does not allow man, howsoever high and magnanimous he may be, to identify himself with God. "Thou shouldst be my Lord, and I Thy servant. Thy place should be high, and my place low......Water does not swallow water. A tree does not swallow its fruits. A diamond appears beautiful on account of its setting. Gold looks beautiful when it is transformed into ornaments......Shade gives pleasure when there is the Sun outside. A mother gives out milk when there is a child to partake of it. What happiness can there be when one meets oneself? I am happy, says Tukā, in the belief that I am not liberated" (Abg. 595). And thus he, who calls himself God, is a fool. "Some say that they have become gods; but these will surely go to hell. God has lifted up the earth: a man cannot lift even a bag of rice. God has killed great demons: a man cannot cut even a piece of straw. He who aspires to the throne of God, says Tukā, hides a mine of sins" (Abg. 3274). He who says that he has seen God is also a fool. "He is the greatest of rogues who says that he has seen God. How can the bonds of existence be unloosed by the advice of such a man? He drowns himself as well as others. There is no fool on this earth, says Tukā, comparable to him, who calls himself God" (Abg. 2064).

Service of God's feet superior to an Advaitic identification with God.

66. Tukārāma prizes the service of the feet of God more than an Advaitic identification with Him. "Advaitism pleases me not" says Tukā. "Give me the service of Thy feet...... Reserve for me the relation between God and devotee, and fill me with happiness" (Abg. 2884). He tells us also that he does not want Self-knowledge. He only wishes to be God's devotee, and talk with Him. "I do not want Self-knowledge. Make me a devotee of Thine, O God! Show me Thy form, and let me place my head on Thy feet. I shall look at Thee, shall embrace Thee, and shall sacrifice my body for Thee. When Thou askest, I shall speak with Thee good things in solitude" (Abg. 3308). Tukārāma repeats the idea elsewhere also. "I do not want Self-identity," he says, "I want the service of Thy feet. Let me be Thy servant from life to life. ......What value has Liberation for me which does not sustain the sweet relation between God and Saint? How shall the Impersonal please me, as I cannot see His face?" (Abg. 2709). Even Videhamukti Tukārāma identifies with the service of the Lord. "We shall always sing the Name of God, and keep our mind content. We dance with joy, and have no idea even of our own existence. We enjoy the Videha state even during life. We are verily made of fire, says Tukā, and shall dispel sin and merit alike" (Abg. 3229).

Rebirth superior to Absolution.

67. As Tukārāma supposes that the service of God is superior to unification with Him, so he also supposes that re-incarnation is superior to the state of liberation. "Hear my prayer, O God. I do not want absolution. For, the happiness that springs from devotion is superior to the happiness that can spring from absolution........ The happiness of heaven has an end; but the happiness of the Name is infinite. Thou canst not know the greatness of Thy Name, says Tukā; hence it is that Thy devotees long for re-incarnation" (Abg. 910). "Let me safely incarnate," says Tukārāma elsewhere, "if I can constantly sing the praises of God, and if I can always live in the company of the Good. Then shall I not mind the trouble involved in re-incarnation time after time" (Abg. 1589). Re-incarnation is also desirable, says Tukā, if one can become a Vārakarī. "I shall take on a new birth," says Tukārāma, "if I can become a Vārakarī of Paṇḍharī. This is what I have personally experienced. Hence it is that I have sacrificed all other things for Thy sake" (Abg. 1652).

The Omnipotence of God.

68. In fact, says Tukārāma, all things depend on God. With His great power, what can He not do? God indeed is the universal mover. He moves the body as well as the universe. "Who makes this body move? Who can make us speak except God Himself? It is God only who can make us hear or see......He alone can continue the mind in its egoism. He it is who can make even the leaf of a tree move....God has filled the Whole inside and outside. What can be lacking to Him in His universal presence?" (Abg. 3038). Man's business is only to rest in God, and to carry on his work without asking anything from Him. "Let the body be delivered over to God, and God will do as He pleases. He is the support of the whole world, and will bring about the proper thing at the proper moment. In this faith should we grow strong, says Tukā" (Abg. 2229). "We should have no other belief except this. God is all-powerful, and can achieve anything whatsoever. Why need a man care for anything at all? He who pervades the universe, and directs the will,—what can He not accomplish?" (Abg. 1174). What little power Tukārāma has, he says, is due to God. When the Saints had praised him for having possessed power, Tukārāma said that it was not his power, but God's. "Why do you burden me, O Saints, by attributing power to me? The doll cannot act in the absence of the puller. Could the monkeys have made the stones swim on the ocean in the absence of God? It is God who is the only mover. Everything else is inanimate in comparison, and God only uses it for His purposes" (Abg. 2057).

God favours people according to their deserts.

69. If God is omnipotent, man need ask whatever he desires of God alone. What is lacking to God, asks Tukārāma, that a man should beg of another? "In God, nothing is lacking, and the wandering beggar moves like a dog from door to door. He recites one passage after another only in order to gain a farthing. He praises some and censures others, and is full of anxiety at heart. The only fate which such a man deserves, says Tukārāma, is that his face should be burnt in fire" (Abg. 1391). "Let us therefore ask whatever we desire of God alone. What is lacking to Him, whom all Powers serve? We must sacrifice our mind and body and speech to God. He who supports the whole universe cannot help supporting us" (Abg. 1392). Only, God favours people according to their deserts. "Rain pours down of its own accord; but the earth brings forth fruit according to its quality. Like seed, like crop..... To a lamp, the master of the house and the thief are both alike. A crow feeds upon a bullock's bone; the Tittira bird feeds upon pebbles; while the swan feeds upon pearls....God indeed favours people according to their deserts" (Abg. 1320). "Nobody can withstand the will of God. King Hariśchandra and his wife Tārā served as drawers of water in the house of a pariah. The Pāndavas, who were the beloved of God, were dethroned from their place. Our business is merely to sit silent, and watch the progress of events" (Abg. 1031). And when it is said that God favours people according to their deserts, it follows that we must cultivate goodness and avoid evil. To Tukārāma, evil has a reality in this world. "The fire may serve to ward off cold; but you cannot gather it in the hem of your garment. Scorpions and serpents may indeed be God; but we must respect them at a distance, and not touch them" (Abg. 637). "From the same curds come out both butter and butter-milk; but the two cannot be priced at the same value. On the sky appear both the moon and the stars; but both are not of equal lustre. From the same earth come pebbles and diamonds; but the two cannot be priced equally. Similarly, says Tukā, Saints and Sinners are both men; but we cannot worship the two alike" (Abg. 1730).

XIII. God's Office for the Saints.

God's Office for the Saints.

70. God has a particular fascination for His Saints. They have made God the all-in-all of their life. True servants as they are, they are not be afraid of their Master. "Why need a true servant be afraid of his master? In arguing with his master, a true servant feels greater and greater delight. When one feels that he is in the right, he need not be afraid of anybody" (Abg. 283). Moreover, a true Saint has dedicated all his powers to God. "Whatever powers there may be with us, we shall place them at the service of the Lord. We have delivered over our life to God, and have wiped off considerations of life and death. What now remains is God only. He it is who eats, He it is who speaks, He it is who sings, and He it is who dances, says Tukā" (Abg. 795). "Shall not God who supports the whole world give support to a Saint in time of need? Why need not a Saint rest content in the belief that God will support him? Why should he not remember the kindness of the Lord who caters for the whole world, who creates milk in the mother's breasts for the child and makes the two grow together? Trees put forth new foliage in summer. Tell me now who waters them?...... Remember Him who is called the All-supporting, for He will certainly support thee" (Abg. 1593). "......In the bosom of a stone there is a frog. Who feeds this frog but God? The birds and the serpents do not lay by anything. Who finds food for them except God? When thou hast thrown all thy burden on God, Ocean of Compassion as He is, He shall not neglect thee" (Abg. 290). In this sure belief of the power of the all-supporting God, we should rest content and not beg before men. For begging before men means disbelief in God. "Shame to the man who takes the begging bowl in his hand. God should neglect such a fellow. He has no devotion for God in his heart, and shows merely a devotional exterior. Not to deliver over one's life to God is to commit adultery with Him. What a great misfortune and what a great disbelief in God, that in poverty of spirit a man should throw his burden upon the world!" (Abg. 858). God does not indeed neglect a devotee who is prepared to go to the uttermost extreme of penance for Him. "One should throw away all sense of shame, and invoke God by the power of one's devotion. One should catch hold of trees, partake of their leaves, and invoke God. One should sew together rags of cloth, cover one's loins with them, and invoke the grace of God. A man who goes to this length in seeking God shall never be neglected by Him" (Abg. 1729). "He who follows God, shall never be left by Him in the lurch. Near his body and near his mind, God stands as an eternal witness, and gives him as he deserves" (Abg. 3910). "And devotees wait upon God only because they firmly believe that no devotee can come to naught. They raise their hands and invoke God to come to their help ......" (Abg. 1073). "And God does really come to their rescue. What is, however, wanted is patience. God shall never leave His Saints uncared-for. Sing, O Saints, in joy, says Tukā. God's great power will turn away the predations of Death. Is not the mother prepared to go to the uttermost extreme in saving her child when it is attacked with a disease? God indeed is greater than the mother. I have personally experienced, says Tukā, that true devotion is ever crowned with success" (Abg. 665). Occasionally, God takes pleasure in throwing His devotees in the midst of difficulties. "God is very cruel," says Tukā. "He has no affection and mercy ......He deprived Hariśchandra of his kingdom,...... separated Nala and Damayantī,......tried King Śibi's generosity,..........asked Karṇa for charity at a critical occasion, ...deprived Bali of all his wealth,......and made Śriyāḷa kill his own son. Those who devotedly worship Thee, O God, Thou compellest to renounce all pleasure in life" (Abg. 105). "But, ultimately, God does ward off all evil from His Saints. He comes to their rescue all of a sudden. He seems to be nowhere, and yet comes all at once. He reserves happiness for His devotees, and takes for Himself their lot of sorrow" (Abg. 264). "His devotees need not, therefore, entertain any fear or anxiety......They should only maintain courage, bear courageously the buffets of fortune, and God will show Himself near them,......because, in fact, He fills the whole world" (Abg. 328). "When Death is before and behind, one should not run, for one's efforts will be of no avail. Onc should only invoke God, and God will come and take His devotee on His shoulders" (Abg. 781). "For, who shall kill him whom God saves ? Such a one may wander bare-footed in the whole forest, and yet not a single thorn may pierce his feet. He cannot be drowned in water. He cannot be killed by poison. He can never fall into the clutches of Death. When bullets and missiles are hurled at him, God will protect him" (Abg. 1017). "And God will attend upon His devotee with all happiness. It is the duty of His devotee to remember Him at every step, and then God will follow him with all happiness. He will hold His beautiful cloth as a cover to protect him from the sun" (Abg. 1048). "God has warded off the pecuniary difficulties of His Saints. He has helped Kabīra and Nāmadeva and Ekanātha" (Abg. 67). "When His devotees have sat in caverns, He has been their attendant. He has warded off their hunger and thirst when they have become indifferent to their body. Who else can be their friend who have no friend except God ? .....When God sends down His grace, even poison may become nectar" (Abg. 209). "All the Purānas bear witness as to how God fulfils the desires of His Saints. He has Himself become their Guru, has protected them before and behind, has held them by the hand and shown them the way, and has finally taken them to His heavenly home" (Abg. 472). "Their innermost desires have been fulfilled by God. For God knows the sincerity and earnestness of their desires. Only, the devotees should not be in a hurry, for nothing can avail them when time is out of joint" (Abg. 953). "Those especially who ask nothing of God, and bear disinterested love towards Him, God pursues outright in order that they may ask something of Him. He waits upon them as an attendant, is afraid of sitting down before them, and sacrifices Himself wholly for their sake" (Abg. 1411). "And when the Saints have sat down quietly in their places and have meditated on Him,......God on His part has been kind and has fulfilled their desires unasked" (Abg. 672). "He has lived with His devotees without minding their caste and creed. He has eaten with Vidura, the son of a concubine, has dyed skins with Rohidāsa, has woven silken clothes with Kabīra, has sold flesh with Sajana, has tilled the garden with Sāmvatā, has carried away dead cattle with Chokhā, has gathered cow-dung with Janābāī,......has moved the wall of Jñānadeva, has been the charioteer of Arjuna,......has been the door-keeper of Bali, has warded off the debt of Ekanātha,......has taken poison for Mirābāī, has been a Mahāra for Dāmājī, has borne earthen pots with Gorā,...... and has been waiting to this day for Puṇḍalīka on a brick in Paṇḍharapūr" (Abg. 2047). "He has done great miracles for His Saints. He has turned the temple at Āvaṇḍhyā, has cashed the cheque of Narasī Mehtā,......has brought to life the dead child of the Potter" (Abg. 3250). God's office for the Saints has been truly remarkable.

XIV. Saints and their Characteristics.

Real Saints are difficult to find.

71. The Saints, however, can rarely be met with. "We see many people calling themselves Saints. But who will believe everybody who calls himself a Saint? Sainthood is discovered only in times of trial. The brooks overflow in times of rain; but when the rainy season has passed, not a drop of water can be found in them. Pebbles look like diamonds only so long as a hammer has not tested them" (Abg. 251). "Many people indeed look like Saints, but they are not Saints. Saints are not those who can compose poetry. Saints are not those who are relatives of Saints......Saints are not those who hold the sounding gourd in their hands, or those who wear rags. Saints are not those who engage themselves in a sermon, or those who narrate mythological stories. Saints are not those who recite the Vedas, or those who perform caste duties. Saints are not those who go to a pilgrimage, or to a forest. Saints are not those who wear garlands and white marks on their body. Saints are not those who besmear their body with ashes. Until the consideration of the body is at an end, says Tukā, nobody can become a Saint by engaging himself in Samsāra" (Abg. 1588). "Pseudo-saints are like women, who show counterfeit pregnancy by creating a hollow of clothes under their wearing garment. They neither have milk in their breasts, nor a child in their wombs. Ultimately, the world finds them to be merely barren women" (Abg. 2244). Tukā indeed is not like the pseudo-saints. "He knows no wiles by which people may be deceived......He can never show any miracles. He has no long list of disciples with him. He does not go on instructing people who do not care for his advice. He is not the head of a Maṭha......He does not make the King of Ghosts work out his bidding......He is not a philosopher who can argue about trifles. He does not whirl round himself a fire-brand in ecstasy. He does not count beads and thus try to influence people about him. He is no Tāntrist who can use the black art for his purposes. Tukā indeed is not like these mad people who carve out a home for themselves in hell" (Abg. 137). Tukārāma tells us that the greatness of Saints cannot be estimated unless one has become a Saint himself. "Very difficult of understanding is the greatness of a Saint. Wordy knowledge is of no use there. Howsoever large the quantity of milk which a cow or a she-buffalo might give, can she be compared to the Milch-cow of heaven? We can know the greatness of Saints only when we have become like them, says Tukā" (Abg. 676). "The Saints incarnate in this world only in order to uplift the unholy, and to increase happiness and devotion to God. Just as a sandal tree can make other trees fragrant, similarly, a Saint makes other people holy in this world" (Abg. 2451).

Characteristics of Saints.

72. The first characteristic of a Saint is that he is calm and tranquil, and bears like a diamond the buffets of misfortune. "That diamond alone fetches immense value, which remains unbroken under the travail of a hammer. That gem is costly, which, when it comes into contact with a piece of cloth, does not allow it to be burnt by fire. That man alone is a great Saint, says Tukā, who bears imperturbably the buffets of the world" (Abg. 25). In fact, there is no other external mark of God-realisation except that a man be tranquil under God. "Thou tellest people that thou art God, and yet hast an inner desire for sense. Thou tellest others the sweetness of nectar, while thou art thyself being famished to death. That man alone, says Tukā, is equal to God, who is absolutely tranquil under the power of Self-realisation" (Abg. 1193). In the second place, a Saint cares not for the evil talk of the world, when he is following the ways of God. "The devotee of God is dear to God alone. He cares not for others. He cares for no friend or companion. People might call him a mad man ......He lives in forests, and woods, and in uninhabited places. When he besmears his body with ashes after having taken a bath, people look at him and blame him. When he sits alone to himself with a rosary of Tuḷasī beads on his neck, people ask—Why is it that he has been sitting apart? He is not ashamed of singing, nor of sitting anywhere he pleases, and his parents and brothers abuse him for his manners. His wife calls him names, and says that it would have been better if that impotent fellow had died......He alone can achieve the end of life, says Tukā, who has turned his back away from the world" (Abg. 1185). Thirdly, miracle-mongering, says Tukā, is no test of spirituality. "He who can tell what is going to happen in future, or can give news of the past and the present—I am entirely weary of these fellows! I do not like to see them. Those who follow after powers, and try to make reality square with their words—these, says Tukā, will go to hell after their merit is exhausted" (Abg. 948). It is only the unfortunates who care for the knowledge of the past, present and future. "We, the servants of the Lord, should only meditate upon Him in our mind, and allow fortune to take its own course. When a man keeps a shop of miracle-mongering, God keeps away from him. Bad indeed is Samsāra, but worse is the pursuit of power" (Abg. 638). In the fourth place, says Tukārāma, a servant of God is afraid of none. He entertains no fear of any person or thing. "He who has seen God stands as it were on an eminence. He who has seen God is afraid of none. He who has seen God will ask what he likes of God Himself. He who has seen God knows that God will fulfil all his wishes. He who has seen God knows that God cuts off his inner desires as with a pair of scissors" (Abg. 1267). And thus the Saint is not afraid of death at all. "The messengers of Death will run away when they see flocks of Saints. When the Saints come, Demons and Death shake with mortal fear. The whole earth rejoices by the spiritual ensign of the Saints, and Death takes to his heels when he sees that powerful army" (Abg. 1535). The fifth characteristic of a Saint is his absolute equality. "A Saint devotes himself entirely to the happiness of others. He worships God in helping his fellow-beings. When one troubles others, we may say, he hates God......This alone is Saint-hood, says Tukā; for, by this, man makes himself equal to the Self" (Abg. 2972). For such a Saint, no enemy can exist; because he himself has no feeling of enmity towards another. "To us there are neither friends nor foes; for wherever I see, I see the vision of God. Wherever I cast my eyes, I see God Pāṇḍuraṅga, and Rakhumāī, Rādhā, and Satyabhāmā. We have lost all shame and all anxiety, and happiness is wallowing at our feet. We, who are the sons of God, have become the fondlings of people in the world" (Abg. 1357). A Saint, says Tukārāma, is known by his compassion to humanity. "Those who are unhappy or sorrow-stricken, a Saint calls his own. Such a man alone deserves to be a Saint. God is present only with him. His mind is as soft as butter. The compassion which he feels for his son, he also feels for his servants and maids. It is needless to say, says Tukā, that such Saints are incarnations of God" (Abg. 201). Also, in such a Saint, opposite qualities like extreme mildness and extreme severity are to be simultaneously found. "The servants of God are softer than wax and harder than a diamond. They are dead though living, and awake though sleeping. They will fulfil the desires of all, and give them whatever they desire......They will be more affectionate than parents, and work greater wrong than enemies. Nectar cannot be sweeter, and poison more bitter than these Saints," says Tukā (Abg. 586). Sixthly, a Saint never leaves his spiritual practice in spite of calamities. "He alone is a servant of God, who loves God wholly. He cares for nothing else except God. When calamities befall him, he sticks to his spiritual practice" (Abg. 214). He is prepared even to sacrifice his life for spirituality. "Sainthood cannot be purchased in a market-place, nor can it be acquired by wandering in woods and forests. Sainthood cannot be bought by large quantities of wealth, nor can it be found in the upper and the nether worlds. Sainthood can be acquired, says Tukā, only at the cost of life. He, who is not prepared to sacrifice his life, should not brag of spirituality" (Abg. 677). Finally, the Saint goes beyond all dualities like sin and merit, death and life, and so on. "No room has now been left for sin and merit, or for happiness and misery......Death has occurred during life and the distinction between Self and not-Self has disappeared ....There is now no room for caste or colour or creed, or for truth and untruth......When the body has been sacrificed to God, says Tukā, all worship has been accomplished" (Abg. 3171). "The Saint has also gone beyond the influence of all sorts of actions: he cannot do any actions which can bear any fruit. God has taken the place of action, and has filled the inside and the outside of the Saint......Indeed, there has now remained no distinction, says Tukā, between God and the Devotee" (Abg. 155). And, "if God is now to be found anywhere, He is to be found in such Saints and not in the images. If one goes to a place of pilgrimage, one can find only stones and water. But in the Saints, one finds God ......Places of pilgrimage are useful to those who have devotion. In the company of the Saints, on the other hand, even rustics become good, says Tukā" (Abg. 89).

73. The spiritual power of Saints is indeed very great. "The sun and the lamp and the diamond show things which are visible. But the Saints show things which are invisible..........Parents are the cause of birth. But

Saints are the cause of the cessation of birth· ......It is for these reasons, says Tukā, that we should go to the Saints unasked, and cling to their feet" (Abg. 722). The Saints have indeed kept their shops open, and give to whomsoever goes to them with any desire. The Saints indeed are generous, and their treasure cannot be emptied. Those who beg will have their heart's content, and yet a large remainder will be left for others. When a bag is filled with God, says Tukā, it can never be emptied" (Abg. 1866). "Various people have taken away the contents of this mine, and yet it has never been emptied. The Saints of bygone ages have left this treasure for us. By the power of his devotion, Puṇḍalīka brought it to the notice of the world. Tukārāma was a poor beggar there, and received only a small quantity of it" (Abg. 2981).

The Spiritual Power of the Saints.

74. So far as their influence upon others is concerned, we may say that the Saints spread happiness all round. The very dust of their feet, says Tukārāma, brings happiness to people. "Immense pleasure is derived from the feet of the Saints. It is for this reason that people live at their feet. One cannot even so much as stir from that place, as all of one's anxieties come to an end. The whole body becomes cool, says Tukā, when the dust of the Saints' feet touches one's body" (Abg. 2528). "All sin and sorrow depart at the sight of a holy man. No holy place has the power of taking away sin and sorrow. God Himself bows to the pollen of the Saint's feet, and dances when he performs a Kīrtana. The Saint is indeed a boat by which one can cross the ocean of life uncontaminated by the stream of existence" (Abg. 990). "Sinful men must needs take care not to give trouble to the Saints. For thereby they only give invitation to death. The dog barks at the heel of the elephant, but is obliged to turn back in shame. When a monkey teases a lion, it is surely giving invitation to death. Sinful men who tease the Saints will have only their faces blackened," says Tukā (Abg. 2426). Finally, the Saints deprive everybody who comes into contact with them of all his possessions. "They are verily robbers, who on coming to the house, deprive the owner of his clothes and earthen pots. They rob him of everything in his possession, and take it away to a place from which there is no return" (Abg. 1904).

The Saints' influence upon others.

XV. The Identity of Saints with God.

Establishment of Identity between God and the Saints.

75. The Saints by their perfect morality and devotion raise themselves to the position of the Godhead. Tukārāma tells us that "Gods are Saints, and Saints Gods. Images are merely the occasional cause of worship......The impersonal God cannot satisfy our wants. But the Devotee satisfies all (Abg. 3993). God and Saint are merely the obverse and the reverse sides of the same spiritual coin. "God has to take on incarnation, and the Devotee engages himself in worldly life ......The Devotee derives happiness by God; and God derives happiness in the company of the Devotee. God gives the Saint a form and a name, and the Saint increases His glory......One should surely rest in the belief that the Saint is God, and God the Saint" (Abg. 3324). It is this identity which makes a Saint even enter into a quarrel with God. "Art Thou alone immortal, and am I not immortal? Let us go to the Saints, O God, and have their judgment on this point. Thou hast no name no doubt, but equally have I no name. Thou hast no form no doubt, but equally have I no form. Thou playest as in sport, equally do I play in sport. As Thou art true and false, equally am I true and false, says Tukā" (Abg. 1586). Thus it comes about that the distinction between God and the Devotee is an illusion. "We have now come to know Thy real nature. There is neither Saint nor God. There is no seed, how can there be a fruit? Everything is an illusion. Where is merit, and where is sin? I have now seen my own Self......I am celebrating the name of God only for the sake of others, says Tukā" (Abg. 1300). And yet, in a way, God and Saint *are* like seed and tree. "From the seed grows the tree, and from the tree comes the fruit. Thus art Thou and I like seed and tree. The waves are the ocean, and the ocean the waves. Image and reflection have now merged into each other, says Tukā" (Abg. 2242). And yet, even though the Saint has attained to identity with God, he manifests a difference for the sake of others. "The devotee alone can know the greatness of a devotee. It is impossible for others to know that greatness. By the power of the great happiness, the Saint knows and yet does not know; he speaks, and yet does not speak. He has become one with God, and yet shows a difference in order that the cause of devotion may prosper......It is only those who have realised God that can understand the meaning of what I say," says Tukā (Abg. 893). Indeed, in order to know God, one has to become God. "It is only he who has become God, that can understand that others are gods. Those who have not known this are only tale-tellers. He who has satisfied his hunger cannot know that others are hungry: he looks upon other people's happiness in the light of his own. What is wanted here, says Tukā, is experience, and not words" (Abg. 2065).

The Saint is even superior to God.

76. And yet in a way the Devotee is even superior to God. "God is required to provide for His creation, the Devotee has no anxiety even to provide for himself. God has to take into account the merits and sins of people: to the Devotee all are equally good. God has to create and to destroy the world; the Devotee is not called upon to undertake that onerous duty. God is always engaged in His work; the Devotee enjoys the satisfaction of not doing anything at all. Does not all this prove that the Devotee is superior to God?" (Abg. 1189). And the Devotee by his power can even rule over God. "Before the power of his devotion, no other power avails. Who can rule God except His devotee? Wherever the Devotee sits, all things come of their own accord, and nobody ever dares to do him wrong" (Abg. 1283). The Saint can even exercise authority over God, as Tukārāma did. "Go to my house with me, O God, and stand still until I place my head on Thy feet. Allow me to embrace Thee, and look at me with compassion. I shall wash Thy feet, and make Thee sit in my mid-house......I shall make Thee eat with me, and Thou darest not refuse. Thou hast hitherto prevented me from knowing the secret. Why may one now be afraid of Thee when one has come to know the truth? By the power of my devotion, I shall now make Thee do whatever I please, says Tukā" (Abg. 2582). And God in return will fold His hands before His devotee as He did before Tukā. "What can be lacking to us," asks Tukā. "All powers have now come to our door. He, who has imprisoned the demons of the world, now folds His hands before us. Him, who has neither name nor form, we have endowed with a name and a form. He, in whom the whole universe is enclosed, is to us now as good as an ant. We have really become more powerful than God, says Tukā, when we have once set aside all our desires" (Abg. 126).

XVI. Tukarama's Pantheistic Teaching.

77. The trend of all this teaching is a final pantheistic unification of the Personal and the Impersonal. The form which is worshipped by outward means, and the form which is experienced by an inner vision, are, according to this teaching, ultimately one. "What the Yogins visualise in their ecstasy is the same as what appears to our physical vision. The form of God, which stands before us with His hands on His waist, is the same as that Impersonal Existence which envelops all, which has neither form nor name,......which has neither end, nor colour, nor standing-place; which is familyless, casteless, handless, and footless. The Impersonal shines forth as the Person by the power of devotion, says Tukā" (Abg. 320). And all sciences proclaim the universal immanence of God. "The Vedānta has said that the whole universe is filled by God. All sciences have proclaimed that God has filled the whole world. The Purānas have unmistakably taught the universal immanence of God. The Saints have told us that the world is filled by God. Tukā indeed is playing in the world uncontaminated by it like the Sun which stands absolutely transcendent" (Abg. 2877). When such universal presence of God is realised, "who will care for all those paltry stone-deities which, when they are hungry, beg alms for themselves...... Why should one care for hospitality from the Maid-servants in the house? The Maid is powerless, and must go to her Mistress to dole out rations of food. The water in a pond can never give satisfaction to a thirsty man......These little deities hide their faces under the red ointment which besmears their bodies......He is a fool who calls them gods. The real God is the universal immanent God. Meditate on Him, says Tukā" (Abg. 4074). And it is due to the universal immanence of God that He acts as a thread through all the pearls of existence. He is verily the *vinculum substantiale* of all, and holds all things together. "By our relation to God, the whole world has become ours, as all pearls are threaded on the same string......The happiness and misery of others is reflected in us as the happiness and misery of ourselves is reflected in them" (Abg. 426). It is this experience which makes all people gods. It is this experience which makes a Saint look upon all beings as the incarnations of the immortal Godhead. "Immortal are ye all verily......Think not of your body as your own, and then you will realise the truth of my assertion. Why need fear anything at all, when all things are ours? Believe me, says Tukā, that all of ye are verily gods" (Abg. 849). And the true Saint is he who having realised the oneness of God, His immanence everywhere, and

A Pantheistic unification of the Personal and the Impersonal.

His ultimate identity with his own self, is enabled to say that there is no God beyond himself. "We should only say, says Tukā, that there is a God; but should realise in our minds that there is none. Love now meets love, body body. The internal becomes one with the external......The son has now met his parent. An inexpressible vision has been seen, and one now rejoices and is moved to tears" (Abg. 3208). And it is wonderful, says Tukā, that when such a real spiritual experience is within the reach of all, they should carry on their physical life as alone real. "They forget the memory of death......They forget that the body is merely a prey to death. They shut their eyes and grow deliberately blind" (Abg. 2625). "They do not know how the Self is playing with the Self; how the ocean has mingled with the rivers; how space is merged in space. The seed now points to the seed: the leaf and the flower are only an illusion" (Abg. 2692). "God indeed is an illusion. The Devotee is an illusion. Everything is an illusion. Only those who have got this experience, says Tukā, will come to know the truth of my remark" (Abg. 2524). The unreal Tukā is speaking unreal things with unreal men. Everywhere there is a reign of unreality. "One laughs vainly, and one weeps vainly......Vainly do people say that this is mine, and this is thine......Vainly does a man sing, and vainly does he meditate. Unreality meets unreality. The unreal man enjoys, the unreal man abandons. Unreal is the saint; Unreal is Māyā. The unreal Tukā, with an unreal devotion, speaks unreal things with unreal men" (Abg. 2096). To such heights are we carried by the force of Tukārāma's pantheistic teaching.

XVII. The Doctrine of Mystical Experience.

Knowledge as an obstacle in the way of reaching God.

78. Tukārāma's mystical experience is absolutely on a par with the experience of those who have preceded him, or those who have followed him. All mystics, it has been said, speak the same language, to whatever country they may belong; and if we collect together the various utterances of Tukārāma on the head of mystical experience, we will find that he is giving vent to the same feelings which have inspired other mystics. "Let us go," he says, "in the wake of those who have gone ahead of us; for they have been wiser than us......Let us gather together this great spiritual wealth......Meditation on the Name of God is alone sufficient to bring to us untold benefits. Life and birth would thus come to an end. Let us kill our individual self, says Tukā, and go to our original home" (Abg. 13). "In this path, consciousness of knowledge is a great obstacle. A mother indeed ceases to take care of the self-conscious child. When once the pearls are taken out of water, they can never again be resolved into water. When butter has been prepared, it is for all times severed from butter-milk" (Abg. 1705). "Of two children, the mother takes care of the younger one, and admonishes the other. It is consciousness which brings greater responsibility. Both the children are hers, and yet she behaves differently with either. She throws off her elder child, and puts to her breast the younger one when it begins to cry" (Abg. 111). "The cow-herd friends of Kṛishṇa were never conscious of their possession of God, and hence God liked them more than those who boasted of their learning. God turns away from boastful men, by creating in them egoism, difference, and censure" (Abg. 3865). In great humility, therefore, Tukā says merely 'Viṭṭhala', 'Viṭṭhala', and invites the learned to spit on him. "Tukā indeed is a thoughtless madman, and is given to bragging. He is given to the uttering of the Name of God, Rāma, Kṛishṇa, Hari forever......He finds that the Teacher's knowledge is all-pervading. He listens to nobody, and dances naked in a Kīrtana. He is weary of enjoyments, and wallows in uninhabited places. He cares not for advice, and says Viṭṭhala, Viṭṭhala. People criticise him variously, but he carries on his vocation. Spit on me, O learned men, says Tukā, for I am without learning" (Abg. 2090).

The importance of Realisation.

79. There is a great deal of difference between an intellectual conviction of God's omnipresence, and a mystical vision of Him. "The Anāhata sound is present in all. But, how can a man get liberation unless he utters the Name of God? God is indeed present in all beings. But nobody has yet been liberated without having seen Him. Knowledge is present in all. But without devotion it is incompetent to take one to Brahman. What is the use of all the different postures in Yoga, unless the ecstatic light shines? Feed not the body, says Tukā, for by that God could never be found" (Abg. 1187). Tukārāma hates all mythologies. What he wants is spiritual realisation. "I do not want the stories of old", he says. "What is the use of those dry words? I want experience, and nothing else. You talk of knowledge, but I know that you have had no mystical experience. The royal swan can distinguish between water and milk. What is wanted is a true coin, and not a counterfeit one" (Abg.

2277). It is this consideration of the inferiority of all merely intellectual knowledge to mystical realisation that makes the attainment of the end a very difficult task. "The blossom may be infinite, but the fruits are few. Fewer still are the fruits that ripen, and fewest come unspoilt from the fruit-store. Rare indeed is the man who has the satisfaction of having reached the end......Rare is the man who attains to victory in the midst of blazing swords. I shall call him my companion, says Tukā, who has been able to reach the end" (Abg. 752).

The Grace of God.

80. The greatest help, however, to realisation comes from the grace of God. Without the grace of God, says Tukārāma, no Sādhana is of any avail. "What is the use of all Sādhanas?" asks Tukā. "God's form will appear before us only if He takes compassion upon us. All our efforts would be of no use, unless they reach the final tranquillity" (Abg. 3165). "If only God wills, then alone can He endow us with spiritual vision. We need not go anywhere, nor bring anything from anywhere. If only God wills, these eyes shall have a spiritual vision, and our egoism shall disappear" (Abg. 3139). It was thus that God was attained by the Sages of old. "Śuka and Sanaka have borne witness that Parīkshit was able to attain to God in a week. Remember God's Name with all speed, and then God cannot hold Himself back. He will hasten as He did for the sake of Draupadī, and come ahead of His swift-winged Eagle. He cannot contain His love, and will run to the devotee's help" (Abg. 102).

Psychology of Mysticism.

81. Tukārāma's contribution to the Psychology of Mysticism is very clever and profound. He tells us, in the first place, that while we are contemplating God, both body and mind are entirely transformed. "When the Self has been transformed in God, and when the mind has been suffused in illumination, the whole of creation looks divine, and all of a sudden the influx of God fills the whole world" (Abg. 3133). Thus Tukārāma directs all Saints to sing the praises of God alone. "If I were to utter the praises of anybody except Thyself, let my tongue fall down. If my mind longs to think of anybody except Thyself, let my head break in twain. If my eyes have a passion for seeing anything except Thee, let them become blind at that very moment. If my ears refuse to hear Thy praise, they would be as good as useless. My very life would have no *raison d'être*, says Tukā, if I were to be oblivious of Thy presence even for a moment"

(Abg. 260). All the senses therefore, Tukārāma advises us, should be directed to the contemplation of God. "Your hands and feet must work for the sake of God. You have speech to utter His praise, and ears to hear His greatness. You have eyes to see His form. Blind men, and deaf men, and dumb men, and lame men, have hitherto gone without having an opportunity of serving God. He, who keeps himself in his house by setting it on fire, will soon cease to exist. Now at least, says Tukā, be awake, and do what is conducive to the highest happiness" (Abg. 511). "Let all the senses quarrel with one another," says Tukā, "for the enjoyment of God. My various organs are now at war with one another. My ears say that my tongue has been pleased. My hands and feet are pining for the service of God. My eyes are experiencing the dearth of His vision. Other senses are quarrelling with my ears, because they hear the praises of God, and with my speech, because it utters His greatness...... If Thou art kind, O God, create such a confusion among my senses" (Abg. 2593). "Let all the emotions be now transformed for the sake of God. Thou followest evanescent things. Why dost thou not follow God? As thou lovest another person, why dost thou not love God? Thou hast affection for thy son. Why dost thou not have that same affection towards God? Thou lovest thy wife, who ultimately robs thee of everything that thou hast got. Why dost thou not have that same tender affection for God? Thou worshippest thy parents in the consciousness of their obligation. Why dost thou not regard the obligation of God? Thou art afraid of other men. Why art thou not afraid of God? Dost thou suppose that thou hast come to life in vain?" (Abg. 2511). People, says Tukā, are ashamed of uttering the Name of God. "Bring Shame to the temple," he says. "We shall put herself to shame. I ring this cymbal in the Name of God. Give no shelter to Shame. This witch has spoilt good ways, and has taken people by the path of destruction. She shows herself off among men, and is crafty and mean. Bring her to the temple; we shall make her ashamed" (Abg. 2604). People do not experience tears in the contemplation of God, says Tukā. "Unless tears come out of our eyes in the contemplation of God, we cannot be said to have true devotion. Tears indeed are an index of love towards God" (Abg. 57). Also, spiritual contemplation has the value of stilling the mind. "Experience leads to experience. The mind gets stilled on the feet of God. The dross is burnt in the fire of God, and from the gold comes out a new ornament. Blissfulness alone remains. We conquer the worlds, says Tukā, by being the servants of God" (Abg. 783). And this beatification leads on to final spiritual silence. "Why now waste words? Whatever had been desired has been obtained. A union has been effected between Name and Form. Vain words have come to an end. As a dumb man eats sugar, so the mystic enjoys beatification. What now follows, says Tukā, is utter spiritual silence" (Abg. 262).

The manifold vision of God.

82. The immediate effect of carrying on a spiritual life is that the devotee is endowed with a new vision. "Red, and white, and black, and yellow, and other variegated colours fill the new spiritual vision. The spiritual collyrium opens out a divine eye. The vagaries of the mind stop automatically. Space and time cease to have any existence. The Self illumines the whole Universe. Physical existence comes to an end. The identity of God and Self takes place. 'I am Thou' is the spiritual experience which emerges in a state of beatification" (Abg. 3248). "When God shows Himself to the saints, the very monads are filled with light. Only those who have control over their senses, says Tukā, can understand this. This is what is called spiritual collyrium" (Abg. 495). "The mind should be placed on the feet of God. When it has been so placed, we should not lift it up again; for, God's form will melt away if it be moved but a little. God will now embrace the Saint, and will keep him beside Himself" (Abg. 1805). "And the form of God will be seen as pervading the whole universe. Society and solitude will cease to have any difference. Wherever a devotee looks, he will see God and His spouse. In the woods as in the city, all space will be pervaded by God. Happiness and sorrow will be at an end, and the Saint will dance in joy" (Abg. 24). "He will dance along with his spiritual companions......All peace, forbearance, and compassion, he will find in the Name of God. Why should he now grow indifferent to his body, when he has once found by it the stream of nectar? Why should he long for solitude? He would find that great bliss now in society. In fact, he would experience that God is constantly moving with him" (Abg. 470). And God indeed moves after the holy man. "His body is holy, and his speech holy. He utters constantly the Name of God. By meditating on the Saint, even sinful men will be relieved of their sin. God follows him, desiring to purify himself by the pollen of his feet. What can now be lacking to a Saint with whom God is ever present? We can now see the triple spiritual confluence of the Saint, God, and the Name" (Abg. 989). And if the Saint travels, God also travels with him. "Blissful in listening to the divine Kīrtana, God lives in the company of the Saint. A Saint like Nārada moves travelling and singing the Name of God, and God moves along with him. Nārada sings devotional music and God listens to it. God indeed loves no other thing so much as His own Kīrtana" (Abg. 3026). "God even dances before the singing Saint. That incarnate bliss, the form of God, stands in the court-yard of the devotee. The Saint does not care for liberation. Liberation cares for the Saint" (Abg. 301). "As the Saint sleeps and sings, God stands up to hear the song; as the Saint sits down to sing God's Name, God nods with pleasure; as the Saint stands up and utters the Name of God, God dances before him; as the Saint moves on his way singing the name of the Lord, God stands before him, and behind him. God indeed loves His Kīrtana as nothing else, and, for the sake of His Name, comes to the Saint's rescue at all times" (Abg. 1032). "God raises His hand and asks the Saint to choose whatever he likes. God is omniscient, God is generous, God is verily the father, and He supplies whatever the Saint wants" (Abg. 1403). "He does all the Saint's work unasked. He stands pent up inside his heart, and He stands outside with a beautiful form. He looks at His devotee's face in order that he may ask something of Him. Whenever the Saint desires anything, He fulfils it at once. But the Saint rests his mind on the feet of God, and asks for nothing" (Abg. 1343). Finally, the Saint becomes so unified with God, that it is impossible to distinguish between God and Saint. "Embrace meets embrace. Body is unified with body. The mind refuses to turn back in its enjoyment of God. Words mix with words. Eyes meet eyes. And as the Gopīs of old became merged in God, so does the Saint become one with Him in his inner contemplation" (Abg. 1614).

The life after God-attainment.

83. The Saint now goes about telling people that God has risen. He asks them to keep awake and arise from their sensual sleep. "Awake and arise", he says to the people, "God has arisen. All the Saints have been merged in happiness. The universe is full of spiritual joy. Now beat the cymbals, and blow the trumpets. Let all musical instruments make a chorus of God. Fold up your hands before God; look at God's face; and rest your head on God's feet. Tell God your sorrow, says Tukā, and ask of Him whatever you want" (Abg. 4044). "To a man who has become such a friend of God, the very creepers in the court-yard are as wish-trees. As he moves on his way, the very stones become wish-jewels. His very babbling is more significant, says Tukā, than the teaching of the Vedānta" (Abg. 2157). "And the Saint has undergone all this trouble in order that the final day might bring him the spiritual crown. His mind now rests in peace, and his desires are at an end. He wonders how he has had to wade through such a laborious process. But he is satisfied that it has at last landed him in the sure possession of God. He has now married Liberation, and will live with her a few happy days" (Abg. 787).

XVIII. Spiritual Allegories.

The allegory of the Crop.

84. Following the example of spiritual teachers like Ekanātha who had gone before him, Tukārāma makes free use of allegories for the expression of his spiritual ideas. In order to explain what we mean, we shall select three or four out of a number of allegories employed by Tukārāma. We shall first take the allegory of the Crop. We are asked by Tukārāma "to rear the crop of God's name on the land which has come in our possession. There is neither any Government assessment here, nor any external oppression......No thieves can come and attack this crop, and yet he who is anxious as to how this crop will grow is a fool...... The crop of God's love is vast and wide, and nobody has space enough to garner it" (Abg. 3327). "The keeper of the crop who does not guard it will ultimately lose all his grain, because the birds will come and feed upon it.....Those who deliberately shut their eyes in broad day-light will fall into a ditch. How can a man who keeps a barren cow be able to get milk and ghee from her?" (Abg. 3328). "Guard the four corners of the crop, and rest not until the crop is reaped from the fields. Let the Name of God serve as a stone in the sling of thy breath, so that the birds in the form of desires will fly away. Blow the fire of Self-realisation, and keep awake...... When you have gathered the corn, hand over to the elements their portions from the stock, and enjoy the rest" (Abg. 3329).

The allegory of the Dish.

85. Another allegory which Tukārāma employs is the allegory of the Dish. We are told to blow the chaff from the wheat, the Body from the Soul. Let the pestle of discrimination stop working when the wheat is separated from the chaff. The bangles in the form of the mystic sounds will now make a noise, and let the Name of God be sung in tune with the sounds......And when the Self will appear to us as in a mirror, at that moment the spiritual dish may be considered to be ready" (Abg. 3712).

The Fortune-teller.

86. Thirdly, we have barely to mention the allegory of the Fortune-teller, who comes and says that "he who says that all this is truth will go to hell. He who says that all this is a lie will enjoy happiness. Sleep therefore in your own places and believe in the thief who robs peoples' hearts. A chaste woman is handed over to the possession of five, and when she engages herself with the Supreme Person, she will enjoy happiness" (Abg. 3981).

The Supreme Power as Goddess.

87. Finally, we note Tukārāma's allegorical representation of the Supreme Power as Goddess. "Rajas and Tamas are burnt as incense before that Goddess. The ram of mind is killed with a fist, and in the rumbling of the Anāhata sound, the deity takes possession of the body and frees Tukā from disease" (Abg. 3958). "This deity," says Tukā, "dances along with the Saints. She is with you already; but you have mistaken her place. She gives eyes to the blind, and feet to the lame, and she makes the barren woman give birth to a child. Thus does that deity fulfil all desires" (Abg. 3959). "That deity lives on the banks of the Bhimā at Paṇḍharapūr. Call for her by a thousand names...... When the demon teased Prahlāda, she came out at once in all her fierceness. She helped Vasudeva, when his seven children were killed by the demon. She helped the Pāṇḍavas when they were wandering like madmen. She runs to the succour whenever her name is sung. She is verily our mother, says Tukā. Why need we any longer fear the messengers of Death?" (Abg. 3964). "This deity has now taken possession of me, and refuses to leave me. If you want to dispossess me of her, take me to the banks of the Chandrabhāgā, and place me at the feet of Viṭṭhala; otherwise, there is no hope of life for me" (Abg. 3966).

XIX. The Worldly Wisdom of Tukarama.

Tukarama's worldly wisdom.

88. The piercing insight which Tukārāma shows in the affairs of the world is extremely remarkable. Having penetrated the heart of reality, it was not difficult for him to understand the affairs of the world. We shall cite here a few illustrations to show what extraordinary insight he had in the affairs of the world. He tells us, in the first place, how a woman's beauty is the cause of sorrow. "Give me not the company of women," he says, ..."for by them I forget God's worship, and my mind goes beyond my control. A sight of them is spiritual death, and their beauty is the cause of hardship. Even if Fire were to become a Saint, says Tukā, he would be contaminated by their influence" (Abg. 3347). He tells us how "people avoid the sight of Saints, and look upon another man's wife with great regard. They become weary of the words of Saints; but their ears are satisfied when they hear the words of women. They sleep while the Kīrtana is being performed; while they are fully awake when women are being described. Be not angry with me, says Tukā, for I am only describing human nature" (Abg. 3237). Then, Tukārāma goes on to tell us that "real worth can never be hidden. One need not call together the different trees in a forest, and ask them whether the sandal tree has sweet scent. Real worth, though latent, cannot remain hidden. The Sun never orders his rays that they should awake people. The cloud of itself makes the peacocks dance with joy. It is impossible, says Tukā, to hide real worth" (Abg. 150). On the other hand, Tukārāma tells us that a counterfeit coin can never fetch any price. "A coin of copper can never fetch any price even if it is taken from place to place. The Good and the Old have no respect for the counterfeit. Pebbles shine like diamonds, but the connoisseur knows how to distinguish the one from the other. A painted pearl is never so valuable as a real pearl. Our mind tells us the real worth of things. There is no use mincing matters," says Tukā (Abg. 3146). Then, Tukārāma tells us that in this world smallness is preferable to greatness. "Make me small, O God, like an ant; for the latter gets sugar to eat. A great elephant is subjected to a goad. Those that stand high have many blasts to shake them; and if they fall, they shatter themselves to pieces" (Abg. 744). Smallness offers no occasion for rivalry to anything. "When the great flood sweeps away forests, the small grass subsists. The waves of an ocean cross past us if we humble ourselves down. If we hold a man by his legs, says Tukā, he will have no power over us" (Abg. 745). Then, Tukārāma tells us, that, under God, as under a Wish-tree, we should ask only for good things. "For the Wish-tree will yield anything that may be desired; and if we entertain good desires, good things will accrue; while if we entertain evil desires, ruin will be our lot" (Abg. 1381). Then, Tukārāma tells us how an ignorant man engages himself in devotion. "An ignorant man desires wealth and not knowledge. An ignorant man has no desire to see God. An ignorant man looks for the fruits of action. An ignorant man is prevailed upon by his senses. Burn the face of such ignorant people by a fire-brand, says Tukā; for they only increase the ignorance in the world" (Abg. 3150). "There is a very great difference," says Tukā, "between seeming and real affection. What seems is not reality. A shepherd used to attend the sermon of a priest, and he was so much moved by hearing the sermon, that he shed tears in seeming sorrow. People supposed that he was weeping for devotion. But what moved him to tears was really a different thing altogether. The priest once asked the shepherd why he was weeping, and the shepherd pointed to the two horns and feet, saying 'I am put in mind of my dead ram when I hear your voice. Thus it is that your sermon moves me to tears'. Seeming affection, says Tukā, is not real affection" (Abg. 91). Tukārāma then descants upon the uselessness of desire. "Man need only care for a seer of rice. Why need he waste words for other things?......His space is measured, which is just three and a half cubits. Why should he aspire after more land? To forget God, he says, is to put ourselves into all sorts of trouble" (Abg. 1326). Those who live in glass-houses, says Tukā, should not throw stones. "What is the use of the man who scratches the breasts of his own mother? A man who blames the Vedas is merely a Chaṇḍāḷa. Where can we live if we set our house on fire? People are sunk in illusion, and nobody knows the truth, says Tukā" (Abg. 793). Tukārāma next tells us that we must succumb to the power of Fate. "By fate, we obtain wealth. By fate, we obtain honour. Why dost thou waste thyself in vain? By fate, a man gets misery. By fate, a man is able to satisfy his hunger. Knowing this, Tukārāma does not complain of anything" (Abg. 2071). "An evil man," says Tukā, "is like a washerman. We are obliged to these washermen for washing away our faults. By the soap of their words, they take away our dirt, without charging us anything for it. They are coolies who work for nothing, and take our burden in vain. They carry us to the other side of the ocean of life, says Tukā, while they themselves go to hell" (Abg. 1122). Tukārāma supposes that "an evil-talker must have been either a washerman or a barber in his former birth. His words scratch like a razor. His mouth is like a cleansing vessel......He voluntarily takes on himself the business of washing the faults of others, says Tukā" (Abg. 1621). As regards initiation of disciples by a Teacher, Tukārāma tells us that a man should distribute his words in a general way like rain. For if he were to make a disciple, half the sins of his disciple would accrue to him......"We should never adopt a son, says Tukā. We should not sow on a rock...... We should talk about private things with the Saints. We should behave with our wife as with a maid-servant...... We should see what is pure and what is impure, and never accept anything that would involve us in a loss" (Abg. 1573). "We should instruct others," says Tukā, "only as they deserve. We should place only as much burden upon others as they could bear. What wisdom is there in covering an ant with an elephant's cloth? A clever huntsman is he, says Tukā, who employs nooses, and nets, and axes, as occasion requires" (Abg. 2460). Tukārāma next warns us not to live continually in the company of the Saints. "By living always in their company, we shall remember their faults; and when we remember their faults, our merit would come to an end. We should bow to the Saints from a distance, says Tukā, and should think of them respectfully" (Abg. 2587). At the fair of life, says Tukā, we should purchase only those things which would bring no loss. "Purchase not goods which would involve you in a loss. Call to your help the spiritual connoisseur, and think of the ultimate benefit. Whatever glitters, says Tukā, is not gold" (Abg. 1398). "We should never reveal the secret," says Tukā, "to anybody. For if we were to reveal the secret, people will run after us for nothing. They would never take to heart anything which we might teach them. Hence, unless they have Experience of their own, no words of ours would be of any avail" (Abg. 818). Finally, Tukārāma has no belief in omens, as the generality of mankind would have. "A true omen," says Tukā, "is the vision of God. When one remembers God, all benefits will necessarily accrue. By meditating on the Name of God, all speech will become holy, and the quarters full of auspiciousness" (Abg. 961).

CHAPTER XVII.

General Review.

Three points about Tukarama's Mysticism.

If we now review Tukārāma's Mystical Career and Teaching as a whole, we shall find that he supplies us with a typical illustration of what we have called Personalistic Mysticism. Tukārāma exhibits all the doubts and the disbeliefs, the weaknesses and the sufferings, the anxieties and the uncertainties, through which every aspiring soul must pass before he can come into the life of light, spirit and harmony. There is no other instance in the whole galaxy of the Maratha Saints, barring perhaps Nāmadeva, which can be regarded as illustrative of this human element which we find in Tukārāma. Jñānadeva is a Saint who appears to us from the beginning to the end of his spiritual career as a full-fledged Saint, a Saint not in the making but one already made. It is only rarely that we find in Jñānadeva and Rāmadāsa and other Saints the traces of a hazard towards the infinite life, which they must realize as the goal of their spiritual career. In Tukārāma, on the other hand, we find these traces from the beginning to the end of his spiritual career. Jñānadeva is a light that dazzles too much by its brilliance. Tukārāma's light is an accommodative, steady, incremental light which does not glitter too much, but which soothes our vision by giving it what it needs. It is for this reason that we say that the humanistic and personalistic element in Tukārāma is more predominant than in any other Saint. (2) A second question that arises about Tukārāma is whether we may regard him as having been influenced by Christianity. Mr. Murray Mitchell has no hesitation in saying that Tukārāma must be regarded as having been definitely influenced by Christian doctrine, inasmuch as the violence of the Portuguese in India in propagating their religious views must have attracted the attention of the Marathas to the Christian religion, as well as because we find in Tukārāma's life and teaching too much of a similarity to Christ's life and teaching. Dr. Macnicol gives an alternative, telling us that if Tukārāma could not be supposed as having been influenced by Christianity, he must at least be supposed as a remarkable instance of a *mens naturalter Christiana*. Mr. Edwards is more humble and says that his judgment must incline only in the latter direction (p. 282). To our mind, it appears that these are useless attempts to explain the parallelism between Christ and Tukārāma, which could best be explained on the hypothesis of a common mystical experience. All mystics of all ages have spoken almost the same language, and it is no wonder that in Tukārāma we find the reminiscences of Christ's life and thought. In this connection, we must prize very highly the attempt which Mr. Edwards has made in presenting the life and utterances of Tukārāma in Biblical fashion. Thus, for example, if we were to read the account which he gives of Tukārāma's ascension to heaven, we would think as if we are reading a Biblical passage. It were much to be wished that some day these students of Tukārāma were to present his Abhaṅgas to the world in Biblical terminology. But, if, for this reason, they venture to point out that Tukārāma ever knew anything of Christianity or was influenced by Christian doctrine, it would be, as the Maratha proverb goes, like extracting oil from sand. Even to-day, if we consider how very little even the most cultured minds of India know of Christianity, we might not wonder if a rustic saint like Tukārāma, in days of old, when no Christianity had ever penetrated the Mahārāshṭra, knew next to nothing about Christianity. And, as regards the judgment that Tukārāma's teaching is to be prized only so far as it complies with the teaching of Christ, we have only to remember that the teachings of both are to be valued only so far as they conform to a universal mystical experience. Hinduism cannot be tested by reference to the Christian ideal, as Christianity itself cannot be tested by reference to the Hindu ideal. Both Hinduism and Christianity must be tested according to the dictates of a universal mystical religion, which must absorb them both. (3) Finally, when people like Dr. Macnicol cannot understand how Tukārāma could be claimed both by theists and pantheists as an exponent of their views, and when they wonder that that inconsistency could be explained only by saying that Tukārāma was a poet, or that he was a Hindu (*Psalms of the Maratha Saints*, p. 21), they entirely ignore the fact that Tukārāma was a mystic, and that he was neither merely a poet nor merely a Hindu. Tukārāma was verily a citizen of the world, and for that matter, a citizen of the spiritual world. The discrepancies that we meet with in Tukārāma are not an outcome of his "ignorance of the divine dynamic" as Mr. Edwards puts it, but they are due to the fact that Tukārāma was a pilgrim who was wandering in a lonely and helpless world, and that it was not until he saw God that his words could be words of certainty and reality for himself, and of assurance and comfort for others. It was only when he went into the kingdom of God that he could see from aloft into the world below, and give them a message which they could not understand in their ignorance, but which was nevertheless real, because it was a definite echo of the majestic voice of God.

PART V.

The Age of Ramadasa : Activistic Mysticism.

CHAPTER XVIII.

Ramadasa.

Biographical Introduction.

The Vakenisi Prakarana.

1. The incidents in Rāmadāsa's life may best be chronicled by reference to a memorandum of events called the 'Vākeniśīprakaraṇa', which was set down on paper by one Antājī Gopāla Vākenavis according to the instructions of Divākara Gosāvī, one of the most beloved disciples of Rāmadāsa, just four days after Rāmadāsa's death on Māgha Vadya Navamī, Śake 1603 (1681 A.D.). It seems that Hanumanta Śwāmī, the writer of the Bakhara of Rāmadāsa, was mainly guided by this short memorandum of events. It is well known how Hanumanta Swāmī wrote a small biography of Rāmadāsa in Śake 1715 (1793 A.D.) and then enlarged it in Śake 1739 (1817 A.D.). The memorandum of events referred to was thus at least a century older than the biography by Hanumanta Swāmī. The credit of having discovered it belongs to Mr. Rājavāde, who had gone to Chāphaḷa a few years ago in search of certain papers relating to the life of Rāmadāsa, where he was fortunate to discover the memorandum of events we are referring to. Let us see how the main events in Rāmadāsa's life may be understood by reference to this memorandum.

A brief sketch of Ramadasa's life.

2. Rāmadāsa was born on Chaitra Śuddha Navamī, Śake 1530 (1608 A.D.), three years after his elder brother was born. While he was yet seven years old, his father Sūryājīpanta passed away. In Śake 1542 (1620 A.D.), that is, when Rāmadāsa was twelve years of age, he ran away from his house to Tākaḷi near Nasik. There are two stories connected with this incident. One story runs that Rāmadāsa had decided not to get himself married. His mother, however, pressed him very much to marry. For fear of disobeying his mother, Rāmadāsa apparently consented. But just at the time of the marriage ceremony, he ran away from the marriage hall. Thus he both obeyed his mother and fulfilled his intention. Another story tells us that Rāmadāsa ran away because his brother Gangādharapanta refused to initiate him into the spiritual life as Rāmadāsa was yet too young, and therefore Rāmadāsa ran away from his house to find out God for himself. Rāmadāsa practised severe religious austerities at Tākali for a period of twelve years, in the course of which

it seems Rāma appeared to him in a vision, and initiated him. Rāmadāsa says about his own initiation :—

साह्य आह्मांसी हनुमंत । आराध्य दैवत श्रीरघुनाथ ॥
गुरु श्रीरामसमर्थ । काय उणें दासासी ॥
दाता एक रघुनंदन । वरकड लंडी देईल कोण ॥
तें सोडोनि आह्मीं जन । कोणांप्रति मागावें ॥
ह्मणोनि आह्मीं रामदास । रामचरणीं आमचा विश्वास ॥
कोसळोनि पडो रे आकाश । आणिकाची वास न पाहूं ॥

After having finished his religious austerities in Śake 1554 (1632 A.D.), he devoted the next twelve years of his life to travelling all over the country, and in Śake 1566 (1644 A.D.), he came and settled on the banks of the Kṛishṇā. In Śake 1569 (1647 A.D.), Rāmadāsa obtained an image of Rāma from the deep places in the Kṛishṇā river at Angāpur, and in 1570 (1648 A.D.) he set up that image at Chāphaḷa and began to worship it. Then comes a very important matter. The Vākeniśīprakaraṇa tells us that Śivājī was initiated by Rāmadāsa in Śake 1571 (1649 A.D.) at Śiṅgaṇavāḍī on Vaiśākha Śuddha Navamī, Thursday, and Hanumanta Swāmī follows the memorandum in saying this. The same memorandum tells us that Rāmadāsa went to Paṇḍharapur in the month of Āshādha in Śake 1571 (1649 A.D.), and as Tukārāma did not pass away till about a year later, it is very probable that Rāmadāsa may have met Tukārāma, as we have already hinted in our chapter on Tukārāma. In Śake 1572 (1650 A.D.) Rāmadāsa came to live at Paraḷī. In Śake 1577 (1655 A.D.), so the memorandum tells us, Śivājī offered his whole kingdom to Rāmadāsa. In the same year Rāmadāsa went to Jāmba, his native place, to be present at the last scene of his mother's life. In Śake 1596 (1674 A.D.), Śivājī was crowned king, after which he came to Rāmadāsa at Sajjanagaḍa, lived there for a month and a half, and spent a large sum in feeding the poor. In the same year, Rāmadāsa spent the autumn at Heḷavāka where on account of the intense cold and damp climate, Rāmadāsa suffered from malaria and bronchitis, from which he was relieved only when he went from Heḷavāka to Chāphaḷa. When he reached that place, he sent a letter in his own handwriting, thanking his host Raghunāthabhaṭṭa at Heḷavāka, a letter which is preserved and reproduced in the Documents of the Rāmadāsī Sāmpradāya, published at Dhulia in 1915 A.D. Those who would be interested in seeing Rāmadāsa's autograph should consult that volume. Rāmadāsa's brother, Rāmīrāmadāsa, passed away in Śake 1599

(1677 A.D.). In Śake 1600 (1678 A.D.), Rāmadāsa ordered new images of Rāma, Lakshmaṇa and Sītā to be manufactured at Tanjore. The memorandum also tells us that Śivājī gave a Sanada to Rāmadāsa in the same year on Āśvina Śuddha 10, which is entirely corroborated by history, as may be seen later on. In the same year, Rāmadāsa sent Kalyāṇa to take charge of the Maṭha at Ḍomagaon. In the month of Pausha, Śake 1601 (1679 A.D.), Śivājī came to see Rāmadāsa, and then Rāmadāsa told him of his (Śivājī's) approaching death which took place in Chaitra, Śake 1602 (1680 A.D.) Then Sambhājī went with his minister Rāmachandrapanta to see Rāmadāsa in Jyeshtha during that year, and returned after living there for eight days. On Māgha Śuddha Ashtamī, Śake 1603 (1681 A.D.), the images of Rāma and Sītā were brought from Tanjore, and were duly set up at Sajjanagaḍa on Māgha Vadya Panchamī, only after four days from which date Rāmadāsa passed away, giving himself over wholly to meditation on God, on Māgha Vadya 9, Śake 1603 (1681 A.D.).

The connection of Sivaji and Ramadasa.

3. One of the points of greatest importance in the life-history of Rāmadāsa is, as we have already hinted above, his connection with Śivājī. The whole world knows that Rāmadāsa was a spiritual teacher of Śivājī; but at what time he actually became the teacher of Śivājī has been recently a matter of hot dispute. Tradition has hitherto said that Śivājī first met Rāmadāsa in Śake 1571 (1649 A.D.) in the garden at Śingaṇavāḍī, about a year after the establishment of the image of Rāma at Chāphaḷa. That Śivājī also contributed some money to the building of the temple in the early years of its progress is also known. That later on Śivājī offered his kingdom to Rāmadāsa which Rāmadāsa returned to him is also known. But what part Rāmadāsa actually played in the political achievements of Śivājī, and at what time the spiritual connection between the teacher and the disciple actually began, have been a matter of contention. Mr. Deva following the traditional account given by Hanumanta Swāmī has always argued for Śake 1571 (1649 A.D.) as the date of the first meeting of Śivājī and Rāmadāsa. Prof. Bhāṭe, who has availed himself of some material placed at his disposal by Mr. Chāndorkar, has argued for Śake 1594 (1672 A.D.) as the date of the actual connection. Now the point of greatest importance for the history of Mahārāshṭra is, that if Rāmadāsa initiated Śivājī in Śake 1571 (1649 A.D.), that is, just when Śivājī had passed out of his teens and was only beginning his political career, then the whole development of

Śivājī's political achievements must be traced to the inspiration that he received from his master Rāmadāsa. If, on the other hand, Rāmadāsa became the spiritual teacher of Śivājī in Śake 1594 (1672 A.D.), then the history of Śivājī's political achievements could only be very partially traced to the influence of Rāmadāsa, inasmuch as this date is just two years previous to when Śivājī crowned himself King in Śake 1596 (1674 A.D.), that is, only six years before his death. For long, people have held to the traditional date, namely Śake 1571 (1649 A.D.), as the correct date of the connection. But, quite recently, as pointed out above, Prof. Bhāte and Chāndorkar have argued for Śake 1594 (1672 A.D.). There is documentary evidence on both sides, and it is really very hard to come to a final conclusion about the date. Let us however see on which side the greater probability of truth would lie.

The recent view about the connection.

4. To begin with the presentation of the case by Messrs. Bhāṭe and Chāndorkar, we have to take account of an important letter to Divākara Gosāvī by Keśava Gosāvī dated Śake 1594 (1672 A.D.) which runs as follows :—

"I have duly received the information that Śivājī Bhonsle is coming to see Rāmadāsa. I was myself going to come, but as I have not been keeping good health, I am sorry I cannot come. I have written to Ākkā also ; but she also cannot come. Bhānājī Gosāvī may be there. This is the first visit of the Rājā. You must take to your help some people from the hamlet. They will be of great use to you as there is a dense thicket there. I shall send Trimbaka Gosāvī, Viṭṭhala Gosāvī and Dattātreya Gosāvī to-morrow. You may have received the two hundred coins from Dattājīpanta for the festival of God."

Now Chāndorkar and Bhāṭe argue that as this letter mentions that Śivājī is paying his first visit, it must be concluded that Rāmadāsa initiated Śivājī only at this time, namely, in Śake 1594 (1672 A.D.).

There is a second letter on which Chāndorkar and Bhāṭe mainly rely. This is dated Śake 1580 (1658 A.D.), and is a letter to Divākara Gosāvī from Bhāskara Gosāvī and runs as follows :—

"......Fifty coins have been hitherto sent with Bhānājī Gosāvī. I hope you will receive them duly. I went to Rājā Śivājī in my itinerary. He asked from what place I came and who I was. I told him that I was a Rāmadāsī, a disciple of Rāmadāsa. Then he asked me where he (Rāmadāsa) stayed and what was his original place. I told him that he originally lived at Jāmba on the Godāvarī and that at present he was living at Chāphaḷa and spending his time in the worship of God. He has ordered us to go out for alms and thus to celebrate the festival of God. It is for this reason that I am travelling ; upon which the Rājā sent a letter to Dattājīpant to contribute two hundred coins to the festival of God. ”

Now Bhāṭe and Chāndorkar argue that this letter is indicative of Śivājī's absolute ignorance of Rāmadāsa's existence in Śake 1580 (1658 A.D.), and that therefore we cannot, according to the traditional date, take Śivājī to have been a disciple of Rāmadāsa in Śake 1571 (1649 A.D.).

Then there are two other supplementary letters from Divākara Gosāvī which are undated, but in the post-script of both of which has been mentioned the fact that Śivājī obtained Paramārtha at Śingaṇavāḍī in the Indian year Paridhāvī. Now Bhāṭe and Chāndorkar argue that this year Paridhāvī comes only in Śake 1594 (1672 A.D.), and not in Śake 1571 (1649 A.D.), which year is named Virodhī. In general, it has been argued on this side that Rāmadāsa was only a religious man. He was hardly a politician. Instead of saying that Rāmadāsa helped Śivājī in the attainment of his political objects, we had rather say conversely that the influence came from the other side, and that Rāmadāsa was made aware of the political condition of the country through Śivājī's exploits (page 118).

The traditional view and its defence.

5. The main answer to these considerations has come from Messrs. Deva and Rājavāde. Rājavāde points out that the letters upon which Bhāṭe and Chāndorkar base their remarks are not genuine. They are after all only copies, and even thus the dates mentioned in them are open to doubt.

(1) When, in the first letter to Divākara Gosāvī we have referred to above, mention is made of the first visit of Śivājī, Mr. D. V. Apte has pointed out that the first visit must be interpreted as being the first visit to the Maṭha, especially as in close proximity to the mention of the Maṭha there is also the mention of a deep thicket, through which a way was to be prepared by the help of the people in the surrounding hamlet. It is thus that we have to explain Śivājī's order to Dattājīpant Vākenavis, dated 23rd July 1672, that is to say, immediately after Śivājī's return from the visit to the Chāphaḷa Maṭha, that he should protect by means of his police the people who went on a pilgrimage to the Matha at Chāphala from the

inroads of thieves and robbers who troubled the country. Śivājī also in that letter ordered Dattājīpant to remove the molestation of the Turks as well as to place himself at the service of Rāmadāsa in every way.

(2) As regards the second letter to Divākara Gosāvī, in which Śivājī inquires as to the whereabouts of Rāmadāsa, the question has been explained by saying that Śivājī was a very shrewd man, that he would not lend an easy ear to every beggar that came, that having inquired of the so-called disciple of Rāmadāsa who had come to beg in the name of the Saint he satisfied himself that he really was a disciple of Rāmadāsa, and that he thus convinced himself that any bounty given to him would be spent in the cause of Rāmadāsa. Śivājī is thus supposed to have merely feigned ignorance, and thus tested Bhāskara Gosāvī as to whether he was really a disciple of Rāmadāsa.

(3) As regards the two other letters from Divākara Gosāvī referred to in which mention is made of Śivājī having obtained Paramārtha at Śingaṇavāḍī, it has been pointed out that the mention of Śivājī's having accepted Paramārtha occurs only in the post-script of the letters which may consequently be a later addition, and that what actually happened in the year Paridhāvī referred to was not that Śivājī was initiated for the first time into the spiritual life by Rāmadāsa, but that he was given certain further instructions which would help him to go onward in his spiritual life. For these reasons it has been pointed out that we cannot rely too much upon the documents referred to, as helping us to fix Śake 1594 (1672 A.D.) as the first year of the meeting of Rāmadāsa and Śivājī and of the latter's initiation at the hands of the former.

(4) As regards the objection that Rāmadāsa had no political motive at all, and that his politics was influenced by the career of Śivājī, we have to note how strongly Rāmadāsa felt about the political condition of Mahārāshṭra. We can see from the opening sections of our review of the Dāsabodha in the next Chapter, how Rāmadāsa bewailed the condition of the Brahmins in his day, and how he bewailed the supremacy of the Mahomedans who destroyed Hinduism wherever they found it. We also know how Dāsabodha XVIII. 6 may be understood as constituting a piece of advice which Rāmadāsa gave to Śivājī. We are told how the name of Tuḷajā Bhavānī, the patron Goddess of Śivājī, has been mentioned there, and how it is said that she would always protect Śivājī: only he must be always on his guard. These references in the Dāsabodha are strongly supported by some of the other utterances of Rāmadāsa

in other places. We know very well that the establishment of the image of Tuḷajā Bhavānī in one of the greatest of Śivājī's forts, namely, Pratāpagaḍa, in Śake 1583 (1661 A.D.) at the hands of Rāmadāsa betokens very strongly the influence which Rāmadāsa must have exercised on Śivājī and his fort-keepers even at that time. If Rāmadāsa initiated Śivājī in Śake 1594 (1672 A.D.), as has been contended, the establishment of Tuḷajā Bhavānī at Pratāpagaḍa at the hands of Rāmadāsa would not have probably occurred. Moreover, if we look at the sentiment which Rāmadāsa expresses in the homage he pays to the deity at Pratāpagaḍa, we can see how he implores the Goddess just to advance the righteous cause of Śivājī: " I ask only one thing of thee, my Mother. Advance the cause of thy King in our very sight. I have heard often that thou hast killed the wicked in times past, but I now implore thee to show thy real power to-day." This shows how very strongly Rāmadāsa felt about the political condition of his time and how he wished the cause of his religion to prosper at the hands of Śivājī. To crown all these things, Rāmadāsa has left us a body of verses called Ānandavana-bhuvana, the " Region of Bliss ", in which he gives free vent to his political sentiments. The " Region of Bliss " is the Apocalypse of Rāmadāsa. He sees ahead of his times and sees the wicked being destroyed, the virtuous being supported, and the reign of Bliss coming into existence. Let us see what Rāmadāsa's vision was. " A great evil has fallen upon the Mlechchhas. God has become the partisan of the virtuous in the Region of Bliss. All evil-doers have come to an end. Hindusthan has waxed strong. Haters of God have been destroyed in the Region of Bliss....... The power of the Mahomedans is gone.........The Mother Goddess who had bestowed a boon upon Śivājī has come with a bludgeon in her hand, and has killed the sinners of old in the Region of Bliss. I see the Goddess walking in the company of the King, intent upon devouring the wicked and the sinners. She has protected her devotees of old, and she will again protect them to-day " (27-43). These utterances make evident how very strongly Rāmadāsa felt about the miserable condition of Mahārāshṭra in his day, and how instead of being influenced by Śivājī, he may have himself served as an inspiration to Śivājī's exploits.

(5) A very relevant Sanada which has been discovered by Mr. Deva in which Śambhu Chhatrapati, that is to say, Sambhājī, the son of Śivājī, has made over to Vāsudeva Gosāvī, one of the greatest disciples of Rāmadāsa, certain lands, is dated Kārttika Śake 1602 (1680 A.D.), in which a reference has been

made to another Inām Sanada to Vāsudeva Gosāvī by his father Śivājī dated चंद्र पंचवीस, जिल्हेज, सन इहिदे, सबइन अलफ़, that is to say, Vaiśakha Vadya 12, Śake 1593 (1671 A.D.), that is to say, about a year before ever, according to Chāndorkar and Bhāṭe, Śivājī was initiated by Rāmadāsa. Mr. Deva points out the very great improbability, nay even the absurdity, of supposing that Śivājī was not initiated by Rāmadāsa till Śake 1594 (1672 A.D.), while he had made over to Rāmadāsa's disciple Vāsudeva Gosāvī a piece of Inām land in Śake 1593 (1671 A.D.).

(6) Finally, that most important document in which Śivājī sums up his relation to Rāmadāsa, dated Śake 1600 (1678 A.D.) Āśvina Śuddha Daśamī, reference to which has been already made by us, goes also a very long way in pointing out that Śivājī must have been initiated by Rāmadāsa many many years before that date, thus making it highly improbable that he was initiated in Śake 1594 (1672 A.D.), that is, only six years before the Sanada, as Messrs. Chāndorkar and Bhāṭe suggest. The document reads as follows :—

"Obeisance to my most high Teacher, the father of all, the abode of all bliss. Śivājī, who is merely as dust on his Master's feet, places his head on the feet of his Master, and requests: I was greatly obliged to have been favoured by your supreme instruction, and to have been ordered that my religious duty lies in conquest, in the establishment of religion, in the service of God and Brahmins, in the relieving of the misery of my subjects, and in their protection and help, and that I should seek to obtain spiritual satisfaction in the midst of this duty. You were also pleased to say that whatever I wished from the bottom of my heart would be fulfilled for me.

Consequently, whatever business I applied myself to, whatever intentions I cherished in my mind, for example, the destruction of the Turks, the creating of fastnesses by spending enormous wealth in order to assure the continuance of my kingdom, have been fulfilled for me by the grace of your Holy Self.

Then, whatever kingdom I earned I threw at your feet, and bethought of applying myself all the while to your service. Then you ordered me that what you had already asked me to do by way of my religious duty was alone the service of your feet.

Then, when I implored that I should enjoy the close proximity of your company and should see you often, that somewhere a temple of God might be established and the spiritual tradition made to grow, you were pleased to live near about in the caves of mountains, to establish the image of God at Chāphala, and to spread your spiritual instruction far and wide,

Then, when I implored that now that the deity at Chāphaḷa had been established and that the Brahmins and the guests had been entertained, that buildings had been erected, and that ceremonies were being performed, I should be ordered to assign lands for the upkeep of these, you were pleased to say 'What is the use of this all ? But if you are really determined that you should serve God, then you might assign whatever lands you please according to your convenience, and should extend them only as your kingdom would grow.' Hence, wherever the images of God were established, therever I assigned my lands.

Then, when I again implored that I intended to make over wholly 121 villages to the temple at Chāphala, and eleven Viṭas of land in each of the other 121 villages, and when I said also that I intended to give eleven Viṭas of land for the continuance of worship in each of the places where God's image had been established, then you said that all these things might be done in course of time. Consequently, I have at present assigned the following lands for the service of God........I take upon myself punctually and without fail to present at the time of the annual religious festival of the Deity all the corn that may be grown on these lands, or else an equivalent amount of money in cash. Dated Rājyābhisheka Śake 5, Āśvina Śuddha 10." This letter is a formidable barrier to the interpretation of Śivājī's initiation as having taken place in Śake 1594 (1672 A.D.) Śivājī who passed such a Sanada in Śake 1600 (1678 A.D.), traces the whole history of his connection with Rāmadāsa, which scarcely could have taken place in the short period of six years that may be said to have elapsed from Śake 1594 to 1600 (1672 A.D. to 1678 A.D.). Moreover, it tells us that Śivājī had come into contact with Rāmadāsa since the foundation of the temple at Chāphaḷa, that is to say, since Śake 1571 (1649 A.D.). Thus, this letter presents a formidable difficulty to those who would push the date of the meeting of Śivājī and Rāmadāsa to about a quarter of a century later. The question arises—Shall we accept as true the letters of Divākara Gosāvī upon which the arguments for a later date of the meeting have been based ? It is highly probable that the earlier date is the more correct date ; but we shall await some new discoveries for the final decision in the matter.

The works of Ramadasa.

6. Of the works of Rāmadāsa, the Dāsabodha is, of course, the most important. It is the outcome of the fullest experience of the world by a person who had attained to the highest spiritual experience. It is prose both in style and sentiment ; but it is most highly trenchant in its estimate of worldly affairs. It seems that originally only seven Daśakas of the Dāsabodha were written continuously. This is evident from the way in which Daśaka VII. 10 ends. If we read the 42nd verse, we shall find that it says सरली शब्दाची खटपट । आला ग्रंथाचा शेवट । येथें सांगितलें स्पष्ट । सद्गुरुभजन ॥ This is almost a peroration of the work. If we examine the part of the Dāsabodha we have referred to, we shall find that VI. 4 was written in Śake 1581 (1659 A.D.). From a letter of Divākara Gosāvī to Bahirambhat Gosāvī from Chāphaḷa, we see that Rāmadāsa had retired to a solitary place in the valley of Śivathara in Śake 1576 (1654 A.D.). This letter also tells us that Rāmadāsa had determined to spend about ten years on this work. How many years he actually spent, we do not know. But just as VI. 4 can be seen to be written in Śake 1581 (1659 A.D.), similarly XVIII. 6 also refers to an incident in Śake 1581, namely, the death of Afazulkhan, as may be seen from the opening sections of our review of the Dāsabodha in the next Chapter. In any case Śake 1581 (1659 A.D.) seems to be a very important year in the composition of the Dāsabodha. There are two authentic editions of the Dāsabodha: one printed from the manuscript of Kalyāṇa at Domagaon Maṭha by Mr. Deva, and the other printed from the manuscript of Dattātreya, Kalyāṇa's brother, at Śirgaon, by Mr. Pāṅgārkar. This latter was discovered by Mr. Pāṅgārkar at Gwalior where the descendants of Dattātreya had repaired. This edition is dated Śake 1606 (1684 A.D.) *i.e.*, just three years after Rāmadāsa's Samādhi. The highest thanks of the Maraṭhi-speaking world are due to these gentlemen for their having discovered these two original manuscripts of Rāmadāsa's work. Mr. Pāṅgārkar claims that his manuscript may even be an earlier recension than the manuscript of Mr. Deva. The Pāṅgārkar edition reads डहुळेना ना वितुळेना, while the Deva edition strikes off वितुळेना and writes निवळेना instead. The Pāṅgārkar edition reads सकळ सृष्टीच वर्तती कळतो वायेा; the Deva edition strikes off everything after सकळ सृष्टी and writes instead ०ची वर्तती गती सकळ तेा वायेा. As the Deva edition is in possession of all the readings of the Pāṅgārkar edition and makes corrections here and there, Mr. Pāṅgārkar is inclined to argue that his edition may be taken to be an earlier edition. Howsoever this may be, we thank both these gentlemen for having given us the original texts. Of the remaining works of Rāmadāsa, the Pathetic Verses of Rāmadāsa (करुणाष्टकें), the Verses addressed to the Mind (मनाचे श्लोक), and the Pseudo-saints (जनस्वभावगोसांवी) are very important. The first shows in abundance of what a mild texture Rāmadāsa's mind was made. Very often he calls upon God from the very depths of his heart. As the Dāsabodha shows the rigorous logic of Rāmadāsa's intellect, his Pathetic Verses show at the same time that his heart was full of the highest devotion and emotion. His Verses addressed to the Mind are also very trenchant *bon mots,* full of the observations of the world, and full also of the highest spiritual advice, worthy in fact of a very high place in Mahārāshṭra literature. Janasvabhāvagosāvī, the Pseudo-saints, a work of about seventy verses, is also a very shrewd and trenchant work which probes into the nature of sainthood and exposes mercilessly all the weak points of the Pseudo-saints. "Vainly do people believe everything that they hear. They throw away jewels and gather dung-cakes ......Who can help these men if they wander like blind cattle? Wherever we see now, there are the so-called Saints, and in their company, people have mistaken the nature of real Sainthood......Some say that their Guru partakes of dung ......Others say that their Guru lolls on a dunghill......Some say that their Guru lives in a cemetery......Some say that their Guru makes the serpents dance......Some say that their Guru disappears at pleasure; and that he makes even inanimate objects walk like animate ones......Some say that their Guru rides a tiger, uses a serpent like a rope, and defies death for thousands of years......Some say that their Guru has lived for ever......Some say that their Guru turns earth into sugar......Others say that their Guru knows whether a pregnant woman is going to give birth to a male or a female child. ......Some say that while their Guru was sitting in Samādhī, he went from the east to the west......Some say that their Guru makes women of men, and makes them men again...... He eats food in quantities, and yet passes no excreta........ Some say that their Guru turns himself into a tiger and kills other tigers......Others say that their Guru was buried alive in sand, and woke up again from the sand after a number of days" (3—63). Thus in a very rationalistic manner does Rāmadāsa dispose of the ordinary notions of Gurudom. It may even be seen how in the passage, we have quoted above, there is a reference to the myth of Chāngadeva and Jñānadeva, one riding a tiger with a serpent in his hand, and the other making a stone-wall walk like an animate object. Miracles do not constitute spirituality, says Rāmadāsa, and such stories are not a true indication of spiritual greatness. Spiritual greatness lies only in the knowledge of the Self—Ātmajñāna—which Rāmadāsa is never wearied of praising.

7. Of the contemporaries of Rāmadāsa, Rāmīrāmadāsa, the elder brother of Rāmadāsa, was the most respected. He was

The Contemporaries and Disciples of Ramadasa.

born three years earlier than Rāmadāsa, and died also three years earlier. He has written the works entitled Bhaktirahasya and Sulabhopāya and some other miscellaneous poems. Even though he did not come actually into the Rāmadāsī tradition, we can say that Rāmadāsa must have influenced him. Kalyāṇa, the greatest of the disciples of Rāmadāsa, was sent to Domagaon to look after the Maṭha there, as we have already seen, in Śake 1600 (1678 A.D.), and he lived there supervising that Maṭha till Śake 1636 (1714 A.D.). After Rāmadāsa's death in Śake 1603 (1681 A.D.), Rāmadāsa's bones were preserved at Chāphaḷa for a number of years to be later taken over to the Ganges. One of the greatest miracles connected with the life of Kalyāṇa is that the very same day on which Rāmadāsā's bones were taken out from Chāphaḷa to be carried over to Benares *via* Domagaon, Kalyāṇa also left this world at Domagaon, so that those who brought Rāmadāsa's bones, when they came to Domagaon, found to their great surprise that Kalyāṇa was also dead, and therefore they carried the bones of both the teacher and the disciple together to Benares. Kalyāṇa never engaged himself in any controversies about the Maṭha at Chāphaḷa or Sajjanagaḍa. On the other hand, two of the other greatest disciples of Rāmadāsa, namely, Divākara Gosāvī and Uddhava Gosāvī, busied themselves in such a controversy. Divākara Gosāvī was asked by Rāmadāsa, even while he was living, to look after the affairs of the Maṭha after him ; while he asked Uddhava Gosāvī at the time of his death to do so. This was probably the reason of the quarrel between Divākara Gosāvī and Uddhava Gosāvī for the management of the Maṭha. The quarrel went to Sambhājī, who after calling in witnesses, gave his decision in favour of Divākara Gosāvī. Uddhava Gosāvī felt very sorry at this decision, went to Tākaḷi in Śake 1607 (1685 A.D.), and fasted and prayed there for fifteen years till Śake 1621 (1699 A.D.). Vāsudeva Gosāvī, whose name has been already mentioned in connection with the Sanads both from Śivājī and Sambhājī, was also a greatly respected disciple of Rāmadāsa. He was once beaten by Rāmadāsa for having disclosed certain secrets about the spiritual life. But Vāsudeva Gosāvī was so very obedient and respectful, that he threw himself before Rāmadāsa and would not stir an inch unless his Master had told him that he had forgiven him. Dinakara Gosāvi, yet again another disciple of Rāmadāsa, was a great poet and has written the 'Śvānubhava-Dinakara'. His Maṭha was at Tisgaon in the Ahmednagar District. It seems that he had studied many of the earlier writers of Marathi before him and his account of Yoga in the Svānubhava-Dinakara reminds us often of the 6th chapter of the Jñāneśvari. Veṇūbāī and Akkā were the two female disciples of Rāmadāsa. Veṇūbāī was the author of the " Marriage of Sīta " and had a Maṭha at Miraj. She died in the presence of Rāmadāsa, and has a Samādhī at Sajjanagada. Akkā, who lived forty years after Rāmadāsa, was instrumental in building the great temple of Rāma at Sajjanagaḍa. She also has her Samādhī at Sajjanagaḍa. Giridhara, who traces his spiritual lineage from Veṇūbāī and Baiyābāī, had the benefit of having seen Rāmadāsa. We know that he was about twenty-five years of age when Rāmadāsa took Samādhī. He was also told by Rāmadāsa to perform Kīrtanas. His Maṭha was at Bīḍa. His work, the Samarthapratāpa, which chronicles the events in Rāmadāsa's life, is very valuable, because it is a story of an eye-witness. It seems that this work was written about half a century after Rāmadāsā's death. It is in Giridhara's Samarthapratāpa, XVIII. 36, that we read the reference to " the death of Afzulkhan, the betterment of the Maṭha at Chāphaḷa, and the establishment of Tuḷajā Bhavānī at Pratāpagaḍa " in Śake 1583 (1661 A.D.) :—समर्थं आकारपूर्वक यवनास मारविलें । मग चाफळक्षेत्र उभें केलें । श्रीतुळजा माउलीसी संस्थापिलें । जाउनी पर्वतीं प्रतापगडीं ॥ According to Giridhara, it seems that the inspiration for the killing of Afzulkhan came to Śivājī from Rāmadāsa himself ; but we must remember that this statement was not made till after half a century after Rāmadāsa's death. In any case, it shows us the traditional way in which the relation between Rāmadāsa and Śivājī was understood. Finally, there is a work called Dāsaviśrāmadhāma bearing the authorship of Ātmārāma, which gives the story of the Sāmpradāya of Rāmadāsa. It is a huge work, though a late work. The narrations in this work naturally have not the authenticity of Giridhara's Samarthapratāpa. It is full of miracles about the life of Rāmadāsa. We should go to it not for the stories connected with Rāmadāsa's life, but for the traditional teaching in the school of Rāmadāsa, which it perfectly embodies. In any case, Rāmadāsa's Dāsabodha is itself a great history of the doings and thoughts of the Saint. It is a piece of Rāmadāsa's autobiography, as the Gāthā of Tukārāma constitutes his. A great man's life consists not of the miracles connected with him, but verily of his thoughts and utterances. It is from that point of view that the Dāsabodha is remarkably valuable as giving us the spiritual autobiography of Rāmadāsa.

CHAPTER XIX

The Dasabodha.

I. Introductory.

Internal evidance for the date of the Dasabodha.

1. There is an important internal chronological evidence in the Dāsabodha, which points to at least a portion of it having been written in the Śaka year 1581. In Dāsabodha VI. 4, we are told that the year of the Kali age, in which the work was written, was 4760, corresponding to the Śaka year 1581. Also, it must be remembered that Afzulkhan was killed by Śivājī in the very same year ; and in Dāsabodha XVIII. 6, we have, according to tradition, the advice which Rāmadāsa offered to Śivājī on this occasion. The reference to Tuḷajā Bhavānī, who was the patron Goddess of Śivājī, as well as the general tone of the advice which Rāmadāsa imparts, namely, the advice to a Ruler who had to carry on his kingdom in the midst of Mahomedan oppression, make it evident that the Samāsa must have been written by Rāmadāsa for the sake of Śivājī himself. One does not know, however, whether the whole stretch of the Dāsabodha from VI. 4 to XVIII. 6 was written during one year. Probably it was not so written. Most probably the original Dāsabodha was concluded at Daśaka VII. 10, as the 42nd verse of that Samāsa, as has been already pointed out, has a tone of peroration. If that be the case, the later Daśakas must be supposed to have been later on added to the original Dāsabodha either by Rāmadāsa himself or by his pupils under his direction.

Ramadasa's advice to Sivaji.

2. What is the advice which Rāmadāsa imparts to Śivājī in the Samāsa above referred to ? He tells him "to adorn his body not by clothes and ornaments, but by shrewdness and wisdom". He tells him that God feels proud of him, and particularly the Goddess Tuḷajā Bhavānī; but that he should undertake his enterprises with great care. He need not give advice to a man who is already on the alert. ....The Mahomedans have been spreading oppression throughout India for a long time, says Rāmadāsa ; hence Śivājī should be always on his guard. When God once calls a man His own, one cannot imagine what he may do. His justice, his forethought, his ready wisdom, and his knowledge of other peoples' hearts are all of them the gifts of God. His efforts, his alertness, his courage in the nick of time, his great prowess are all of them the gifts of God. His fame, his power, his greatness, and his incomparably rare qualities are all the gifts of God......A discrimination between matters which pertain to this world and those which pertain to the next, perpetual wakefulness about all matters, and forbearance with all are the gifts of God. To spread the cause of God, to protect the Brahmins, to help one's subjects, are all of them the gifts of God. Those, in fact, who re-establish the kingdom of God are all of them the incarnations of God (XVIII. 6. 9—20).

The miserable condition of the Brahmins in Ramadasa's time.

3. In a general way, Rāmadāsa was so much convinced of the bad condition of Mahārāshṭra at his time that he felt the necessity of a re-invigoration of religion in his own day. He bewails very much the bad condition of the Brahmins. He tells us that people of low character have acquired supremacy over those who were prized as spiritual teachers......The Brahmins have lost their intellect......They have fallen from the high pedestal of spiritual teachership, and have become the disciples of those who are worthy to become their disciples. Some follow after the Mahomedan deities. Some voluntarily embrace Mahomedanism..........The lower castes have attained to spiritual teachership : the Śudras are demolishing the social status of the Brahmins. The Brahmins, unable to understand this work of destruction, are yet retaining their social arrogance. The Mahomedans have robbed them of worldly kingdom on the fields of battle. The kingdom of the spirit has fallen to the lot of the base people in society, and the Brahmins are nowhere. They are vainly fighting among themselves.... We are verily the same Brahmins, says Rāmadāsa, and we have to reap the fruit of the actions of our ancestors. What have the Brahmins of to-day done, asks Rāmadāsa, that they should not get even food to eat, and he appeals to the people to say whether this is a matter of fact or not ? Finally, he tells us that we need not blame our ancestors in vain. "Let us lay all the blame at the door of the bad luck of the Brahmins," says Rāmadāsa, and he requests the Brahmins to forgive him if he has spoken harsh words to them (XIV. 7. 29—40). In a general way, he tries to exhort them to come to the standard of true Brahminhood, and to acquire supremacy both in worldly and spiritual matters.

4. One of the chief ways of accomplishing whatever one desires is to devote oneself to "Upāsanā," that is to say, to know the true way of meditation on God. "He, who does not know

God, is an evil man: he is a Durātman, says Rāmadāsa, that is to say, the Ātman is removed from him......When we become assimilated to God, then Prakṛiti begins to change her nature......Where God's knowledge is present, there also is success......One should think on God constantly in one's mind. How shall His spouse, the Goddess of Wealth, depart from one who always thinks on God? God is indeed immanent in the whole universe, and we should worship Him as everywhere.... This is my Upāsanā, says Rāmadāsa, which surpasses logic, and takes one beyond the phenomenal world to God Himself" (XV. 9. 18—29).

The way to get rid of difficulties is to meditate on God.

5. Rāmadāsa elsewhere describes at greater length and in more personal terms his devotion to Rāma. "Raghunātha is indeed my family deity ....He is the great God who has relieved the gods from their sufferings. We are His servants, and through service have attained to knowledge........Rāma does indeed kill evil men, and support His devotees. Such a miracle can be seen at every step in our life. Whatever we may desire from the bottom of our heart shall come to take place by the grace of God, and all obstacles will come to an end. By Meditation on God is acquired Illumination. By Meditation on God, Greatness is attained. Therefore one's first duty ought to be to meditate on God. This is indeed a matter of one's own experience. Set thyself to perform thy duty by meditating on God, and thou shalt surely succeed. Only thou shouldst suppose from the bottom of thy heart that God is the real agent and not thyself......If thou regardest thyself as an agent, thou shalt land thyself into many difficulties; on the other hand, if thou believest that God is the real agent, then shalt thou attain to fame, and to greatness, and to power" (VI. 7. 21—36).

Ramadasa's description of his own faith.

II. Metaphysics.

6. At the opening of the metaphysical section in Rāmadāsa, we have first to take into account what he does not regard as constituting knowledge. A man, who knows the past, the future, and the present to the smallest detail, is supposed to be a wise man, says Rāmadāsa; but really he is not a wise man. Knowledge of all the sciences is not real knowledge. To distinguish a good horse from a bad one, to know the various classes of animals, to have a knowledge of all the

What knowledge is not.

kinds of birds, is not knowledge. To know the various metals, to know the various coins, to know the various jewels, is not real knowledge. To know the various kinds of seeds, to know the various kinds of flowers, to know the various kinds of fruits, is not real knowledge. To know various words, to know various languages, is not knowledge. To speak straight away, to have ready wit, to compose poetry extempore, is not knowledge. To know the art of singing, to know the art of dancing, is not knowledge. To know the various kinds of pictures, to know the various kinds of instruments, to know the various kinds of arts, is not knowledge. All this is only skilfulness and not knowledge. It looks as if it is knowledge; but real knowledge is different from these. To know what is going on in another man's mind is regarded as knowledge, says Rāmadāsa; but really this is not knowledge. That knowledge, by which a man attains to liberation, is of a different kind altogether (V. 5. 3–37).

What knowledge is.

7. Then Rāmadāsa goes on to discuss what knowledge really is. Real knowledge, he tells us, is Self-knowledge—Vision of the Self by the Self. Real knowledge consists in knowing God, in cognizing His eternal form, in distinguishing the real from the unreal. Where the phenomenal world hides itself, where the "pañchabhautika" is at an end, there alone is knowledge. Knowledge goes beyond the mind, beyond the intellect, beyond all argumentation. It goes even beyond the Beyond, and beyond the highest stage of speech. It is good to give advice to others that they should meditate on the supreme sentence, "That art thou"; but this does not mean that they should take a rosary in their hands, and count the sentence in their minds. What is wanted is meditation on the substance of that great Sentence......Difficult indeed is that knowledge by which one attains to one's Self, to one's original Form, which is self-born and eternal. That indeed is the Form from which all this comes out. That is indeed the Form, by knowing which all ignorance comes to an end...... When we begin to know our Self, then indeed shall we be omniscient. All partial knowledge will then be at an end.... This is the great knowledge by which sages of the past have crossed the ocean of life. Vyāsa and Vaśishṭha, Śuka and Nārada, Janaka and Vāmadeva, Vālmīki and Atri, Śaunaka and Sanaka, Ādinātha, Matsyendranātha and Gorakshanātha—all these great sages have attained to this knowledge. By the happiness of that Knowledge, the great God Śiva sits nodding in bliss. That is the Knowledge, which has made saints and great men. That is the Knowledge which is immanent in the knowledges of the past, the present, and the future......Mythologists do not treat of this Knowledge. The Vedas fail to attain to it. But by the grace of the Guru, I shall tell you what that Knowledge is. I know neither Sanskrit nor Prākṛit. My Sadgurunātha alone resides in my heart. By his grace, indeed, I can dispense with all Sanskrit and with all Prākṛit. By his grace, I can dispense with the study of the Vedas, and the study of all kinds of Learning. My Guru's grace has fallen upon me without any effort on my part. Greater than the works in Marāṭhi are the works in Sanskrit. Greatest of all the works in Sanskrit is the Vedānta. Greater than the Vedānta itself, higher than it, and subtler than it, is the instruction of my Guru. By his instruction, I have reached contentment. The instruction of my Guru is my Vedānta. The instruction of my Guru is my final intellectual theorem. The instruction of my Guru is my personal conviction. By the words of my Lord, I have attained to complete contentment. This indeed is the secret of my heart. This I now intend telling thee if thou listenest to me for a while. The disciple here became confused. He fell at the feet of his Guru and then the Guru began to speak : Indeed the meaning of the expression 'I am He' is beyond all description. The teacher and the disciple become one in that meaning. Remember, my disciple, that thou art verily the Godhead. Entertain no doubt, no illusion, about it. Of all kinds of Bhakti, Ātmanivedana or Self-surrender is the best. When the elements have vanished, when the Prakṛiti and the Purusha have both been resolved in Brahman, when the phenomenal world has come to an end, the Self itself vanishes, being merged unitively in the Godhead. The sense of creation is then at an end. There is supreme Oneness. There is eternal identity between microcosm and macrocosm......If thou but forgettest thyself in thy Guru, why needest thou be anxious at all that thou wilt not reach this end ? Forget thy difference from the Guru, says Rāmadāsa. Now, in order that this experience of unison, says Rāmadāsa, should remain indelibly in thy mind, meditate on thy Guru. By that meditation, thou shalt attain to complete satisfaction. This indeed is Self-knowledge, my pupil ! By that, the fear of existence shall depart for ever. He who regards himself as identical with his body merely commits self-slaughter.......Nobody indeed is bound. People have been vainly deluded by the illusion of identity with body. Sit in a quiet place, and seek spiritual rest in thy Form. By that means, wilt thou grow in strength. When thou hast attained to Self-knowledge, then will complete dispassion fill thy mind. Do not vainly delude thyself by saying that thou art liberated, and give loose reins to thy senses. In that way thy spiritual thirst shall never be quenched......I tell thee, finally, says Rāmadāsa, that whatever thou searchest that thou shalt be (V. 6. 1—64).

Self-Knowledge puts an end to all evil.

8. Whatever sins a man may have committed, whatever miseries he may have been suffering from, Rāmadāsa tells us, that if he medidates on the Name of God, all his sins and miserise would come to an end. " The body is made of sin, as sin forever is its lot. If one entertains desires inside the body, what can external means do ? Let the body be shaved as many times as one pleases in places of pilgrimage ; let it be subjected to all kinds of compunctions in holy places ; let it be purified as much as you please by different kinds of clay ; let it be burnt as much as one wills by heated copper-signs ;........let a man eat as many balls of cow-dung as he likes ; let him drink as many pots of cow's urine as he pleases ; let him wear any kinds of rosaries and garlands he likes ; whatever holy costume he may put on, his mind is filled by evil and sin ; and in order that the evil and sin may be burnt, Self-knowledge is necessary. Self-knowledge is more powerful than all religious vows, than all religious charities, than the different kinds of Yoga, than the various kinds of pilgrimage. There is indeed no limit to the merit of a man who has seen the Self. For him, all sins are at an end. That eternal Form of God, which has been described in the Scriptures, is indeed a Form of the knower himself. When one reaches that, merit transgresses all bounds. These are matters of experience, says Rāmadāsa, and a man who does not attain to this experience, toils in vain. Oh ye men of spiritual experience, determine that this knowledge shall abide in you forever by the grace of God. Without it, there would be everywhere grief and sorrow " (X. 10. 59—68).

Images, not God.

9. Rāmadāsa with a true insight tells us that howsoever much images may satisfy the beginner in spiritual life, they cannot satisfy the advanced thinker : in fact, we have no right to call them God. "When an image made of stone breaks some day, his devotee feels sorry at heart, weeps, falls prostrate, and cries. Some gods are in this way destroyed even at home. Some gods are stolen away by thieves. Some gods are shattered to pieces by the iconoclasts. Some gods are dishonoured, others thrown into water, others made the foundation-stones of buildings. People cry in vain: 'The evil-doer has come and has disfigured the places of pilgrimage. We vainly believed that there was a great power in those places of pilgrimage. We do not know how this should happen.' People imagine that gods can be made by goldsmiths. Others think that they can be made by those who cast iron; still others suppose that they can be cut out of stones. Infinite thus is the number of deities that may be found on the banks of the Narmadā or the Gaṇḍakī. People do not know the real God. They worship the black round pieces of stone, or copper-pieces, or marble-pieces, and place them on the altars at home. The god that was made of silk has been now torn to pieces, and the devotee seeks after the god made of clay. He supposes that his god is a great Being who supports him in times of difficulty......This fool, who is under an illusion, does not know that the true God cannot be found in metals, in stones, in clay, in pictures, or in wood. These are all matters of imagination......The true God is to be found elsewhere" (VI. 6. 33—45).

Four ascending orders of the Godhead.

10. Rāmadāsa next proceeds to differentiate the conception of the Godhead into four different aspects. He tells us that people follow various paths, and worship various kinds of gods which could be classified under four general heads. In the first place, people worship images made either of clay, or of metal, or of stones. Secondly, people worship the incarnations of gods, meditate on them, worship them, and hear their praises. A third set of people worship the inner Self of all, who fills the world, who is regarded as the Seer, the Spectator, and the Intelligent. Finally, there are those who meditate on God as the Immaculate and the Changeless Being, and in that way try to become identical with that Being. Thus, says Rāmadāsa, there are those who worship the images, those who worship the incarnations, those who worship the Self, and those who worship the Absolute. He tells us finally that he who would worship the Immaculate, would himself become the Immaculate; while he who would worship the Changing, would himself undergo change. The real swans, he tells us, are able to distinguish water from milk. In that way shall we be able to find out the true God (XI. 2. 28—39).

11. After a criticism of the worship of images, Rāmadāsa goes on to tell us where the true God is to be found. When we become convinced that the real God is not to be found in clay-images, which are worshipped and forthwith thrown away, we should try to find out the God who cannot be thrown away, who inhabits all bodies, and leaves them at pleasure.... All people have an inner desire that they should be able to see God; but they do not know the way to Him. We cannot call any being God which does not stand the test of thought......When great men die, people make their images and worship them. It is impossible by manufacturing ink that a man may become a wealthy man. Blind faith is mere ignorance. By ignorance we shall never be able to reach God......We must throw over the illusion which prevents us from seeing God, and try in various ways to find Him out. We should go by the path of spiritual meditation and first-hand experience......Untruth is everywhere untruth, and cannot be compared with truth. Our mind naturally looks downwards. We should reverse the process and make it look upwards......That alone should be regarded as the final reality which persists when the body falls (XX. 9).

The true God is the pure Self who persists even when the body falls.

12. In a different place, Rāmadāsa reviews again the various kinds of gods, and tells us that knowledge of the true God could be imparted to us only by a great Spiritual Teacher. The true God, he says, is not made of gold, or silver, or brass, or copper. The true God is not a painting drawn on a wall. The true God is not the different kinds of stones found in rivers, or the moon-stone or the sun-stone. The true God is not copper pieces or gold pieces worshipped at home......The true God is indeed the Seer. He is One. From Him the many have sprung......People vainly worship deities in their households, or go hunting after the gods in places of pilgrimage, or yet try to find them in the different incarnations; but they do not know that these incarnations are dead and gone. Yet others regard Brahmā, Vishnu and Maheśa as gods; but they do not know that the true God is beyond all qualities. There is neither place nor measure of the true God, and any external worship of Him is useless......People vainly follow the various deities; and they do not know the Supreme God......He can be known only by the eye of spiritual vision. We should see Him, and abide in Him. We should become identical with Him by constant meditation on His name......This is indeed a subtle process and can be made known to us in an instant's time by a great Spiritual Teacher (XIX. 5).

Knowledge of the true God can be communicated to us only by the Spiritual Teacher.

13. This God, says Rāmadāsa, is indeed the Inner Self. Rāmadāsa dissuades people from vainly following after the many god .

God, identified with the Inner Self.

"Images take us back to gods in the places of pilgrimage. The gods in the places of pilgrimage take us back to incarnations. The incarnations take us to the three deities, Brahmā, Vishṇu, and Maheśa—the Creator, the Preserver, and the Destroyer of the world. But the highest God is only He Who presides over all these gods. He is the Inner Self ; He is the real Doer ; He is the Enjoyer ; it is by Him that the whole world is being moved. People miss this immanent God and follow vainly after other gods, and then they come to grief, because they are not able to find God in outer images. What is the use of mere wandering at random, they ask, and then they keep company with the good ; for, in the company of the good, has God been attained by many men (XVIII. 8. 1—13). It is this God who has transformed Himself into the various deities of the world. In Him are all powers centred. He is the real Enjoyer of the greatness and glory of the world ......People have vainly looked after the externals and have missed the God who is immanent in them. Indeed by incalculable merit alone can a man know the movements of this God. By meditating on Him, all sin would be at an end. They who have looked inside, have been saved. They who have looked outside, have all gone to perdition (XVIII. 1. 16—24).

The superstitious and the rationalistic in Ramadasa.

14. After all this philosophical discussion of the true nature of the Godhead, it seems somewhat strange that Rāmadāsa should have lent support to certain superstitious ideas. The whole of IX. 8 of the Dāsabodha is devoted to an exposition of the superstitions among men. Rāmadāsa tells us that even though people may die, they may come to birth again by being thrown down from heaven, whereas many we see born with their hands and feet hurt. When a man has been dead over three days from the effects of a serpent's poison, a conjurer can yet raise him up. Many people have raised the dead, says Rāmadāsa and have brought people back to earth from the kingdom of Death......Some have taken one birth after another and have consciously entered into other people's bodies......All gods and demons have indeed, says Rāmadāsa, windy forms. Deities and demons possess a man, and by proper spells can be driven out of the body. By calling up a spirit in the body of a man, one may know hidden treasures, one may know the solution of difficult problems. Of wind indeed are the different tunes in music constituted. By these tunes lamps are lit, and clouds are made to descend on earth......By the power of Mantras, deities may be made to manifest themselves. By the power of the Mantras, all sorts of magic can be made possible (IX. 8. 6—33). Elsewhere also, Rāmadāsa tells us that the deities exist as windy forms. Gods and goddesses, deities and spirits, are really innumerable, and they all exist in the shape of windy forms. Taking on a windy form, they enter into various bodies and become apparent to people's vision, or hide themselves at pleasure (X. 3. 9—10). If men can hide themselves and show themselves, asks Rāmadāsa, shall we deny that power to the deities ? Gods and deities, spirits and gods, show increasing power........The goblins also live in windy shapes and throw eatables in the midst of men. Do not suppose that all these stories are false. For almost all people in the world have had personal experience of them. If men can take on a new body, shall we deny that power to the Godhead ? Brahmā, Vishṇu, and Maheśa are indeed windy forms, and from them the whole universe has sprung (X. 4. 24—28). Rāmadāsa also tells us elsewhere that all these gods and goddesses, deities and ghosts, wander upon the surface of the earth in windy shapes and change their forms at will. They affect only ignorant men, he tells us, and they have no power over Saints, because the Saints have left no desire in them. It is for this reason, says Rāmadāsa, that we should attain to the knowledge of the Self (X. 9. 20—22). Over against this explanation of deities, including among them Brahmā, Vishṇu, and Maheśa as windy forms, Rāmadāsa elsewhere offers another explanation that they exist only in consciousness. Vishṇu, the preserver, he tells us, is only the principle of knowledge in us ; Rudra, the destroyer, is the principle of ignorance; while Brahmā, the creator, is a combination of knowledge and ignorance (X. 1. 26—31); from which the corollary is, as Rāmadāsa puts it, that Brahmā, Vishṇu, and Maheśa do not exist objectively but are only subjective embodiments of the principles of creation, preservation, and destruction (X. 2. 1—2). Experience tells us, says Rāmadāsa elsewhere, that Brahmā, Vishṇu, and Maheśa do not exist objectively, but that God alone exists, Who creates the Creator, preserves the Preserver, destroys the Destroyer (IX. 7. 10—12)—a sentiment which in his "Verses addressed to Mind" Rāmādāsa reiterates when he inquires as to Who must be the creator of the Creator, the preserver of the Preserver, and the destroyer of the Destroyer ? All these deities, says Rāmadāsa, must be sublimated into the one Godhead who alone is real, who alone is eternal, who alone is immanent in the whole universe.

The power of Untruth.

15. Indeed, the reason why we do not perceive this reality is that Untruth has a very great power over us. What is untrue appears to us to be true. What is true appears to us untrue. In this way does the whirligig of delusion deceive us. Many people have told us the way to get at truth, and yet untruth has fastened itself upon us. It has gone into our very hearts and has waxed strong. On the other hand, truth has hidden itself though ever present. The scriptures, the sciences, and the mythologies have narrated to us in various ways the nature of truth, and yet the Ātman who is the ultimate Truth, is hidden from us. The truth remains hidden though existing, and the false appears to us though it does not exist. In this way does the power of untruth deceive us (VII. 10. 1—5).

Creation is unreality: God is the only reality.

16. The way to get at truth from the region of untruth may be characterized as the way from Creation to God. The first illusion existed when this world did not exist, when creation had not been, when the Universe with its seven coverings had not come into being, when the gods Brahmā, Vishṇu and Maheśa did not exist, when the earth, the mountains and the oceans had not come into existence. The various worlds, the stars, the sun and the moon, the seven continents, and the fourteen heavens were created only later ....The thirty-three crores of gods did not exist then ....The twelve suns, the eleven Rudras, the nine serpents, the seven sages and the incarnations of God all came later. The clouds, and the first man, and the various beings, were created only later......The five elements which constitute the world, we should avoid as unreal, and then we can attain to Reality. As only when the threshold is crossed does one enter into a temple, similarly, when the phenomenal world is crossed, does one attain to the Real (VIII. 4. 47—58).

From the Cosmos to the Atman.

17. By the great power of his imagination, Rāmadāsa tells us how we must go from the contemplation of the Cosmos to the contemplation of the Ātman. Is it not by the power of God, he asks, that the Sun moves across the face of the sky ; that the mist in the universe showers immense rain ; that clouds as large as mountains rise up in the sky and hide the disc of the sun ; that the wind terribly moves through them ; that, like the servant of Destruction, it dispels the clouds and sets the sun free ; that thunderbolts shoot on the earth ; and that all beings in the world are filled with fear ?

Wonderful it is that God has set one element against another and thus restored equipoise to Creation. Infinite thus are the ways in which the Ātman expresses Himself. It is impossible to know them all. The mind reels in the contemplation of them. This indeed is my faith, says Rāmadāsa ; only those who have devotion in them can know what it is. Its infinite power surpasses the imagination of even the Creator (XX. 8. 23—29).

The cosmological argument for the existence of God.

18. Elsewhere, Rāmadāsa gives a true cosmological argument for the existence of God. "He indeed may be called God," says Rāmadāsa, "who is the Supreme Agent ; who creates rows of clouds and produces nectar from the disc of the moon ; who gives light to the sun ; who sets limits to the ocean ; who has appointed the great serpent for the sustenance of the world ; who has created the stars in the intermundane regions ;......who manifests Himself in the incarnations of the Creator and the Preserver and the Destroyer of the world. A godling on the altar of a house cannot possess the power of creating the world. Innumerable indeed are the deities on earth, none of which can create the sun and the moon and the stars......The true God is indeed He who creates the world out of waters, and who sustains it without a prop. God creates the earth, from the bosom of which the stones are produced; and these stones are regarded as gods by those who do not know. The true God is indeed He who lived before creation, just as the potter lived before the pot........We must remember that He who creates the world must necessarily exist before the world. He who pulls the strings of an idol cannot be identical with the idol itself.... Similarly, he who has created the Selves cannot himself be regarded as the Self. God is thus different from both the world and the Self......He is indeed the Supreme Ātman, who fills the whole world inside and outside. He is immaculate. He is changeless. That changeless Being should never be confused with the changeful Self. To say that God comes, and God goes, is indeed folly. God cannot be born, and God cannot die. God produced birth and death, and is different from either of them (VIII. 1. 8—50).

The relation of Body, and Soul, and God.

19. God is thus different from both body and soul. The body is made up of gross elements ; the soul is of changeful qualities ; the changeless Brahman is different from either. By intuitive experience we must come to distinguish between the changeless, the changeful, and the gross. When the Soul leaves the body, then indeed can we see how the gross body falls to the ground. What is gross falls to the ground; what is changeful passes away. The body comes to be inhabited by the soul, and thus creation moves on. What is due to the soul is wrongly attributed to Brahman. When the Saints who have attained to spiritual experience meet each other, they verily enjoy solitude, and their talk determines the nature of Brahman (XX. 7. 12—24).

The Four Atmans as ultimately one.

20. It is indeed through mistake that people suppose there are four different Ātmans. The Ātman is really one. It is supposed that the four kinds of Ātman are the Jīvātman, the Sivātman, the Paramātman and the Nirmalātman......That Ātman who fills the body is called the Jīvātman; that Ātman who fills the universe is the Śivātman; that Ātman who fills the space beyond the universe is called the Paramātman; while that Ātman who has no spatial connotation whatsoever, who is pure intelligence, and who is free from all taint of action, is called the Nirmalātman. It is on account of the difference of environment that the Ātmans are supposed to be different; but the Ātman is really one, and full of bliss (VIII. 7. 44—53).

The Highest Principle must be reached in actual experience.

21. Call the highest principle the Ātman or Brahman as you please, the real business of the spiritual aspirant is to apprehend that principle in actual experience. It is quality-less, and yet it fills every nook and cranny of the universe. It is a principle which remains eternal in the midst of change and destruction......It is a principle which is beyond all imagination, and which is untouched by any illusion whatsoever. What comes to be and what passes out of existence must never be confounded with what can never become or pass away......It is indeed a principle which is open to spiritual insight, and one who attains to it should remain alone to himself, and thus assimilate himself to the Divine. It is beyond what the eye sees and what the mind imagines. It is both beyond the physical and mental. That principle is both inside and outside. It is infinite. It is distant and near......As to our knowledge of this principle, we should depend upon our own spiritual experience. We must not be under compunction of another man's opinion; because another man's opinion is incompetent to lead us to God. If a doctor's medicine proves useless, we must give up the doctor; otherwise the patient will not survive. He who knows the King personally will never commit the mistake of calling another man a King. He who knows God, will himself become

God. The Brahman is indeed beyond all restrictions, and beyond all fatuities. Restrictions and fatuities are on this side; God is on the other side of existence (XIV. 9. 11—28). The practical way, according to Rāmadāsa, for the realisation of this God, we proceed to narrate in the next section.

III. Mysticism.

Exhortation to Spiritual Life, based upon the evanescence of the world.

22. Rāmadāsa begins by exhorting us to the spiritual life by calling our attention to the evanescence of all existence. "We do not know what accidents may befall us. As birds fly away in various directions, so our wealth and wife and sons will fly away from us......As soon as the body falls, the Self may migrate to a worse existence, for example, that of a hog or a pig......In thy previous existences, thou hast suffered immense pain, and it is only by exceeding fortune thou hast been relieved therefrom......One's mother is of no avail, one's father is of no avail, one's sister and brother are of no avail, one's friends and wife and sons are of no avail. All these follow thee, only if they derive happiness from thee.... Thou bearest their burden in vain for the whole of thy life, and they will ultimately abandon thee......If thou wert to die at this moment, thou shalt fall off from God as thou art centred in egoism. Thousands of mothers and fathers and sons and daughters thou hast had in thy former births......Thou followest after mean people for filling thy belly, and thou flatterest them and praisest them. Thou sellest thy body to him who gives food to thee. But thou forgettest God who has given thee birth......Sinful and mean are those who follow sensual enjoyment, leaving God......He who wishes to have eternal happiness should follow God, leaving away the company of men, which is the cause of sorrow" (III. 10. 39—63).

In this mortal fair, the only profit is God.

23. In the same strain, Rāmadāsa tells us elsewhere that in this mortal fair the only profit that we should seek is God. "Mortal things remain in this world and nobody can take them away for a future existence. Hence we should grow indifferent to all things, and give ourselves up to contemplation, by which the infinite profit of God will be attained. There is no greater profit than the vision of God, and one can attain to it even while carrying on the ordinary duties of life. Many meritorious men like King Janaka have lived and ruled erewhile. Similarly are there many meritorious men to-day. But death cares not for the King, and will not leave him even if he offers lakhs and crores of rupees. Life indeed is a dependent variable, and we have to suffer all kinds of pain and anxieties while living. In this mortal fair, the only profit is God, who alone compensates for all its sufferings" (XII. 8. 28—34).

Spiritual value of the body.

24. Rāmadāsa also elsewhere points out the great spiritual value of the body while it is yet living. It is only when the body is sound, that one can attain to God. The real end of bodily existence should be God-vision. "Blessed indeed is the body, for whatever true desire we may harbour while we are in this body shall come to fruition. By the help of the body, some have gone by the way of devotion, others of a more ascetic spirit have resorted to mountains and caves, some are undertaking pilgrimages, others are living with a full confidence in the power of God's Name......Some by teasing their body to an inordinate extent, and by the power of their devotion, have attained to the realisation of God......Some travel across the sky, some have been united with light or water in the Universe, others yet again have become invisible though living; some have assumed many forms, some while sitting are seen roaming in various places and oceans; some are able to sit on dreadful animals, others are able to move inanimate objects,—Rāmadāsa here probably refers to the incident of Chāṅgadeva and Jñāneśvara,—some by the power of their penance have raised dead bodies......Very many powerful persons have lived erewhile, who have been in possession of Siddhis......Some have gone by the nine-fold path of devotion; some by secret meditation have reached the highest heaven; some have attained to the world of the deity they have worshipped, others have lived near it, others have attained to its form, and yet others have become united with it. If these are the advantages of living in the body, how shall we adequately glorify its greatness?......Animals cannot have this open way to God; in the human body alone is one able to attain to God. It is only by taking on a human body that men have become saints and sages and devotees......We should utilize our body for the benefit of others, and should live only in the shape of fame. If the body is lame, or if the body is cripple, it cannot be of any service to others. If the body is blind or deaf, it can neither see nor hear;......if it is weak and diseased, it is as good as useless. If the body is subject to epileptic fits and possession by spirits, no good shall come out of it. Hence, if the body is strong and without any disease or defect, it should be forthwith utilised in the service of God" (I.10.1—32).

The extreme misery at the time of death.

25. If the great spiritual value of the body is an argument why man should turn it to good account for the purposes of God-realisation, the calling of our attention to the great misery at the time of death is another argument why people should rise from the contemplation of those miseries to a determination of turning it to good account. Rāmadāsa tells us that Death is a great leveller. There are innumerable miseries at the time of death. A man may enjoy all kinds of happiness during life, but the final torments he cannot suffer. The body is loath to give up the ghost, and the misery of death makes all people go a-panting. Howsoever broken-limbed he may be, he must live in that condition till he meets death......His beauty is of no avail; his bodily strength is of no avail; he must die in the midst of suffering. All people have equally to suffer at this final scene of life......The final scene is the most difficult one while a man is passing off like an extreme wretch (XVII. 6. 26—32).

The Power of Death.

26. Rāmadāsa tells us elsewhere how Death is all-powerful. The servants of Death keep striping every man, and take him to the home of Death. Nobody can indeed save another from the clutches of Death, and all people have some time or other to undergo the trial......Death does not take Power into account; Death does not take Wealth into account; Death does not take Fame into account. Death does not say this is a King; Death does not say this is an Emperor. ......Death does not say this is a learned man; Death does not say that this is a man of a higher caste. Death does not take proficiency in music into account; Death does not take knowledge of philosophy into account. Death does not say that this is a Yogi; Death does not say that this is a Samnyāsin; Death does not say that this is a Great Man......Some have just begun to tread the path of Death, others have gone half-way, others yet are about to reach the destination...... Death shall never leave you if you want to escape his clutches; you can indeed escape by no means whatsoever from Him. Death does not say this is a place of birth; Death does not say that this is a foreign land. Death does not say this man has given himself over to fasting. Death does not take the gods into account. Death does not take the incarnations of God into account......By carefully considering this, one should prepare himself for the realisation of the true end of life, and even though one may die, one should live in the form of fame....

Gone are the people of great glory; gone are the people who defied death for a long time; gone are the people of great fame; gone are the people of warlike exploits; gone are the people born of noble families. The protectors of men have passed away. Those who inspired the intellect of men have passed away. The philosophers who lived by logic have passed away......Gone are those who have weilded the sword; gone are those who have benefited others; gone are those who have protected people in all ways. Gone are the assemblies of men; gone are all the logicians; gone are all the ascetics.... All these are gone, says Rāmadāsa; only those have remained, who have realised the Self, and become united with Him (III. 9. 4—59).

Leave away everything, and follow God.

27. The outcome of all this teaching is that we should leave away all considerations of the body, of life, and of all things dependent thereon, and follow God; for God is the only good. " Leave away everything and follow Him. Then only will you come to realise the secret of life. God has created all happiness, but people forget Him, and hunt after the happiness He has created. God Himself has said in the Bhagavadgītā: 'Leave away everything and follow Me'; but people turn a deaf ear to what He has said. Hence it is that they suffer all kinds of grief. They long for happiness which they cannot get. Fools they that follow after other happiness except that of God......A wise man should behave differently, and should see God Who is beyond the world. What can be lacking to a man who has seen God? Discrimination leads to happiness; indiscriminateness leads to misery; choose whichever you will " (XIII. 7. 21—29).

God can be realised even in this life.

28. The justification for this exhortation to the pursuit of God consists in the teaching about the possibility of His realisation even during this life. " By discrimination is man able to encompass the end of his life without leaving the activities in the world. This is indeed a matter of experience, says Rāmadāsa. Vast is the difference between experience and logic, between credit and cash, between mental worship and actual realisation. We should never trust people when they say that God will be realised some day during the long evolution of our lives. God must be seen forthwith, and even while the body lasts. Immediately must a man be able to attain to God, and to free himself from the coils of doubt. In this life, one can get away from the world and attain to liberation by being united with the Godhead. He who doubts this shall go to perdition...... To be bodiless though living, to do and yet not to do, to be liberated even during life,—the secret of these things can be known only to those who have attained to that state" (VI. 9. 24—33).

The Bound man.

29. In general, says Rāmadāsa, mankind are really in a bound state. They pass their life without devotion, without knowledge, without meditation, without the company of Saints, without Self-knowledge. They hug worldly life to their heart and are disgusted with spiritual life. They give themselves incessantly to the censure of the Saints. They are bound by the chains of bodily affection. Their only rosary is the rosary of coins. Their only contemplation is the contemplation of women. Their eyes are given to see wealth and woman; their ears are given to the hearing of wealth and woman; their contemplation is given to the meditation on wealth and woman; their body and speech and mind, their intellect and wealth and life, are all given to the worship of wealth and woman. These alone make their senses steady. Wealth and woman are their places of pilgrimage. They are the end of their life, both spiritual and physical. They indeed waste not a single minute, and contemplate incessantly the cares of worldly life. These indeed, says Rāmadāsa, are the Bound (V. 7. 37—44).

The necessity of a Guru.

30. How can such men ever hope to have enlightenment? Rāmadāsa says this would be impossible in the absence of a Guru. "The Brahmins as Brahmins have efficacy in the social order; but without a great Guru we cannot attain to our intimate treasure. Without a Guru we can never attain to real knowledge ......He who has a desire to see God should move in the company of the good, for without the company of the good, God cannot be attained. One may practise any Sādhana one pleases; but it would be all useless without a Guru......Even though one may study the fourteen sciences and attain to all kinds of powers, both physical and mental, without the grace of the Guru one cannot realise the Self. Contemplation and concentration, devotion and worship, would be all useless without the grace of the Guru. Without the grace of the Guru, one moves on like a blind man, floundering and falling into pits and ditches as he wends his way. As one is able to see a hidden treasure when the proper collyrium is applied to the eye, similarly the light of knowledge shines only by the Word which the Guru imparts. Without a Guru, one's life would be useless. Without a Guru, one has only to sink in suffering. Without a Guru, the storms of the heart shall never be appeased. By the protecting hand of the Guru, God would reveal Himself......All the great men that have lived in bygone times, all the Saints and Sages of old attained to realisation only by the power of the Guru. Rāma and Kṛishṇa, and all the Saints and Sages of by-gone times, devoted themselves wholly to the service of their Master ......In short, those who wish to attain to liberation can attain to it only by the help of a Guru, and in no other way" (V. 1. 19—44).

The Guru gives the key of the spiritual treasure.

31. The efficacy of the Guru consists in the revelation to the disciple of the true way to God. He indeed gives us, as Rāmadāsa puts it, the key to unlock the door of spiritual experience. "What the mind cannot attain can be attained through the power of the Guru. The treasure-house may be full of treasure ; but it is all shut up, and one cannot go inside it unless one has the key in his hands. What this key is, is known to the disciple with the help of his Master. The Grace of the Master is indeed the key which illumines the intellect, breaks open the door of dualism, takes us to infinite happiness, and lands us for ever in the supersensuous state. That state is beyond the mind ; that satisfaction is beyond all desire. Imagination cannot imagine the superconscious condition. It is beyond what the most potent word can express ; it is beyond all mind and intellect ; it is beyond all things of the world. It is for this reason that one should dissociate oneself from the world, and reach spiritual experience. Only he who has attained to spiritual experience, will be comforted by these words of mine, says Rāmadāsa" (VII. 2. 12—19).

The Guru is greater than God.

32. If we compare the greatness of the Guru with the greatness of God, says Rāmadāsa, we shall arrive at the conclusion that the Guru is greater than God. "He who regards God as superior to the Guru is a fool. His mind is set merely upon power and glory. The Guru is immortal ; Godhood is evanescent. Before the greatness of the Guru, the greatness of God is as nothing. He must be a bad disciple who regards his Guru and God as of equal count. In his heart, delusion dwells. God is made God by men by the power of Mantras ; but the Guru cannot be made even by God. The power of God is the power of illusion ; the power of the Guru carries every thing before it" (V. 3. 40—46).

33. If the Guru is so great, it follows that no words can be adequate to his praise. "The greatness of the Guru cannot indeed be described. It is beyond the power of everybody. The Vedas themselves have said 'Neti, Neti'. How then can a fool like myself be adequate to know the nature of the Guru ?....If one cannot know God actually, one has to make an image of Him ; similarly if I cannot really praise the Guru, I will praise him by illusion. The Guru is indeed superior to the sun. The sun dispels darkness, which yet comes back again ; but when the Guru has swept off the rounds of birth and death, they do not recur......The Guru is indeed superior to the touch-stone. The touch-stone makes gold of iron, but cannot turn it into a touch-stone itself ; while a disciple of the Guru becomes the Master himself. In respect of the greatness of the Guru, we cannot cite an ocean in comparison, because it is full of salt water ; the mountain of gold, because it is after all stone ; ether, because the Guru is more subtle than ether ; the earth, because it will vanish in the great conflagration ;......nectar, because nectar cannot prevent the circle of birth and death ; the wish-tree, because the Guru's grace is greater than whatever wish can accomplish......All the gods are ultimately subject to annihilation ; but the Guru can never be annihilated......My only adequate praise of the Guru is thus that he cannot be praised. The subtle conditions of the mind, the subtle mind alone can know" (I. 4. 1—31).

The ineffability of the greatness of the Guru.

34. Even though, thus, theoretically the greatness of the Guru is ineffable, yet Rāmadāsa tries to characterise it in positive terms. "The miracle-monger is called a Guru," says Rāmadāsa, "but he alone is a real Guru who leads to liberation......He who instils into our mind the light of the Self and dispels the darkness of ignorance, he who brings into unison the Individual and the Universal Selves —he alone is entitled to be called a Guru. He alone who relieves people of the sufferings of existence, and takes them out of the meshes of illusion, is entitled to be called a Guru......He who does not bend the mind of his disciples Sādhanaward, who does not teach them to control their senses, should be avoided even though he may be had at a pie's cost........One who is able to speak with cleverness on the Advaita doctrine, and yet is sensual, can never deserve the title of a Guru...... Hence he alone can be called a Guru who has no desires left in him, and whose determination is as steady as a mountain. The primary characteristic of a Guru is that he possesses immaculate Self-knowledge, and the satisfaction of a determinate life

The Characteristics of a Guru.

in the Self. To add to these, he must have extreme dispassion, and his actions should be beyond censure. With him, spiritual discussion must be a constant pastime; for him, the distinguishment between the false and the true must always take place. He uplifts the world and becomes an exemplar for the various kinds of Bhakti. He who leads people Sādhanaward and establishes Sādhana on a firm footing—he alone can be called a Guru. Inwardly, there must be Self-illumination; outwardly, there must be devoted Bhajana, whereby alone he leads his disciples to spiritual happiness......Hence knowledge, dispassionateness, devotion, rightful conduct, Sādhana, spiritual discussion, meditation, morality, justice, and the observation of the mean constitute the chief Characteristics of a Guru" (V. 2. 44—53).

The Characteristics of a Saint.

35. From the consideration of the Characteristics of a Guru, let us pass on to what Rāmadāsa regards to be, in general, the Characteristics of any great Saint. "When a man has tasted of the sweet spiritual nectar, his very body begins to shine. But what is his internal condition? How shall we know that a man has reached Self-knowledge? He alone may be said to have reached the end of Sādhana who has attained to the realisation of the Self......When the Self is attained in direct vision, the body seems to work in a region of phantoms. There are, however, certain characteristics of a Saint which we must mention. The first characteristic of a Saint is that he is always looking at the Self, and he is outside the world even though he happens to be in it. When the Self is seen, he ceases to care for worldly life and engages himself in teaching others the knowledge of the Self. Another characteristic of the Self-realiser is that his Sādhana is a Sādhana without any scope for doubt. His mind becomes motionless, and is one with God...........Whether his body rests motionless in a place or moves away, his Self is always motionless. He alone is entitled to the name of a Sādhaka, whose heart is fixed on God......When a person sits upon a throne, kingly qualities come to him of themselves. Similarly, when a man has seen the Self, the qualities of a Siddha come to him of themselves. No amount of mere practice is able to produce these qualities. But the aspirants obtain them only when they have reached the Self......A Saint is he who has left no desires in him, and has no anger in him; his desires are centred in the Self, and his treasure is the Name. When one is shut up on all sides by one's own Self, one is always merged in bliss, and no arrogance is possible in such a man. A Saint has no reason for logic-chopping, nor does he show hatred, jealousy, or hypocrisy towards others......What value has he for the world, if the world is to him ultimately unreal? When he has seen the Self, he has no reason for grief, or infatuation, or fear. God indeed is beyond these, and the Self becomes assimilated to God. His egoism comes to an end, and his heart is set upon the eternal......A Saint never cares for what is going to happen; for living as he does in the Self, he knows that all will be well for him. A Saint is a man of supreme insight, for his vision is set upon God. He is immaculate, because he holds in vision the spotless Brahman. In fact, the Saint has attained to the highest of all qualities, namely, the abiding life in God. That indeed is the primary characteristic of the Saint" (VIII. 9. 1—54).

The Saints confer a vision of God upon their disciples.

36. The Saints have in them the power of giving what nobody else can give. The esoteric knowledge of the Godhead, which is impossible to be attained by men, becomes possible only by contact with Saints. Nothing really stands between us and God, and yet we are not able to see Him, because our sight is not properly directed towards Him. Those who have sought to understand the nature of God have failed. Those who have prided themselves on their power of observation are deceived in the case of God-vision. God, indeed, cannot be shown by a lamp, nor can he be found out by means of light. For God's vision, there is no collyrium that can be applied to the eye to make Him visible. Nor can God be revealed in the searchlight of the Sun, or in the pleasing light of the Moon....Such a God can yet be shown by the Saint to the Seeker. The Saints indeed teach us the way to God, who is beyond the region of illusion......They are the abode of bliss. They are the root of satisfaction. They are the source of rest. They are the end of devotion......They are the home of ecstasy. The Saints indeed are truly the rich; for they possess in their hands the keys of the spiritual treasure. The spiritually poor have been made by them spiritual Kings of men......Emperors and kings have lived erewhile, but none of them has been able to make a grant of God. The Saints confer a boon which nobody else can confer. There is no limit to the greatness of the Saints, for it is on account of them that God reveals Himself (I. 5).

37. In a famous passage, in the first Daśaka of the Dāsabodha, Rāmadāsa gives us a mystic description of an Assembly of Saints. "I bow to that Assembly," he says, "where God stands in joy. God does not live in the heaven or in the heart of the Yogins, but only where the devotees sing His praise. Blessed is that Assembly, where the devotees are filling the heaven with the sounds of God's name. Blessed is that Assembly where the devotees are singing the greatness of God, and sounding their cymbals in praise of God, and narrating His great qualities and exploits. Blessed is that Assembly where satisfaction of various kinds accrues, where all doubts are set at rest, where God's form stands motionless before the mind. Blessed is that Assembly where Saints have attained to the knowledge of the Self, and the knowledge of God. Blessed are they, for they know the future, as they have known the past. In them is all peace, and forgiveness, and compassion......The beloved of God are indeed gathered together in that Assembly, irrespective of their worldly or ascetic lives, irrespective of their being young or old, or men or women. Their central bond is devotion to God. I forever bow to that place, says Rāmadāsa, where this Assembly is singing the praises of God" (I. 8).

Description of an Assembly of Saints.

38. As to whether the Saints can perform miracles or not, Rāmadāsa is of opinion that we cannot attribute to the Saints any miracle-mongering. It is not they who perform the miracles: it is rather God who performs them for the Saints. "Incarnations of God, and Men of great spiritual illumination have lived erewhile. They were indeed liberated after passing away from this mortal existence, and yet there is a power which we may say lives after them. If it were to be objected that these great Saints thus manifest a desire *post mortem* for the fulfilment of their disciples' wishes, Rāmadāsa says that the power which is thus exhibited is yet not due to any physical desire. We must consider how it is that miracles take place even after the Saints have left off their body. What wonder is there if the miracles happen after the death of these Saints, if they have happened during their life?......The Saints have not moved from their places, and yet people have seen them away from their places. What shall we say to miracles of this kind? The only answer is that it is the devotional character of the people themselves that enables them to perceive these miracles. The great Saints of old have been liberated, and they do not live in their astral bodies to fulfil their disciples' wishes. Their power spreads around simply because they have led a life of merit. It is therefore that we should lead a life of

The Saint does not perform miracles: God performs them for him.

meritorious deeds, and devote ourselves to the worship of God. We should not forsake the right to follow the path of what is not right" (X. 7. 1—12).

Power and Knowledge.

39. But it is not for the sake of miracles that spiritual knowledge is to be prized. It is not right to set one's heart upon power; for spiritual illumination is something different from power. "When we hear of the powerful actions of ancient Saints who had become one with God, we think that our bare spiritual illumination is of no avail, as no strength or power is connected with it. Those who harbour a desire for power in this way are only hunting after an illusion. They have not yet become desireless. Many intelligent men of old have been led astray by this desire for power. Rare indeed is the Saint in whose mind no desire whatsoever reigns. His mind is set upon something which others cannot reach. That eternal treasure, which ought to be open to the vision of all, is yet not seen by them; for they love their body, and are thus led astray from the path of God. Considerations of power and prosperity fill their mind with egoism. They leave off the pursuit of eternal happiness, and vainly follow after the ideal of power. ......Whatever desire there may be in man, except the one for God, will only contribute to his ultimate ruin. When the body falls off, the considerations of power will also cease, while God will have ever kept Himself away from the aspiring soul" (V. 2. 33—43).

Characteristics of a Disciple.

40. The true disciple is therefore he, whose heart is not set upon power; who has a firm belief in the words of his master; who has merged himself in the personality of his master; who is pure and spotless; who is of an ascetic temper, and observes the mean in all matters; who is distinguished by a capacity for effort; who is endowed with great insight, as he has been able to visualise the invisible Ātman; who devotes himself to the service of humanity; who is jealous of none; who has great courage and moral determination; who does not spare himself any pains in the pursuit of the spiritual life; who knows the ways and means of the development of Paramārtha; who has suffered great pains, physical, mental and moral; who by the power of the pain has set his heart upon the Eternal in an utter disgust of the evanescent world;......for whom considerations of wealth and prosperity are of no significance; who has his heart purified by repentance; whose mind has been made tranquil by the words of his master; finally, whose pure devotion knows no back-turning, even though the heavens might fall upon him (V. 3. 19—51).

The causes that contribute to Liberation.

41. It is indeed the qualities of a disciple that ultimatey bring liberation to him from the turmoil of the worldly life into a vision of the Spirit. If the question be asked—What time does a disciple take to attain to liberation in the company of the good, Rāmadāsa tells us that the disciple attains to liberation instantaneously by the grace of his Teacher, almost as instantaneously as iron becomes gold under the influence of the touch-stone, or a drop becomes one with the ocean. Men of insight attain to liberation in a moment's time. It is the quality of the intellect of the disciple which leads him on to liberation. To add to his intellect, he must have an unmitigated faith in his master, and must have renounced all bodily egoism. Those indeed need not enter upon a great Sādhana who are naturally clever, or have a firm intellect, or an attitude of trust (VIII. 6. 41—50).

When Sattva predominates.

42. In general, we may say that a man who wishes to reach God, must have within him the predominance of Sāttvika qualities ; for they alone lead a man Godward. How shall we know that the Sāttvika qualities predominate in a man ? Rāmadāsa tells us that "when Sattva predominates, a man feels greater and greater love for God. He forgets all the miseries of the worldly life. He comes to know the way of devotion. He has an intense desire to engage himself in the spiritual life......He loves the narration of God's works. He transforms his original qualities for the service of God......He loves the Saints more than himself, and is not ashamed of doing small things for the sake of God. ......He leaves aside everything else, and engages himself in devotion to God. His heart is filled with intense devotion. His body experiences horripilation through intense spiritual emotion. His eyes stare at God. He always utters the name of God, and beats his hands like cymbals......He becomes weary of all, and loves only the spiritual life ; and in times of great calamity, his heart rises with great courage. For enjoyment, he has no inclination. He is indifferent to everything for the sake of God. He never allows any guests to walk away without being properly cared for. His mind is not disturbed by the accidents of worldly life. He has left off all happiness for the sake of God. His mind may move in the direction of sense, but he has forever within him the ballast of Spirit. His determination stands unvanquished by adversities, or by hunger, or by thirst......His one desire is to live after death by fame......He devotes himself to the service of others, and gladly undergoes all the trouble for the funeral ceremony of a man who dies in a foreign land......His heart rises within him when he sees a Saint......and by his grace he becomes capable of showing to others the Pathway to God" (II. 9—79).

The power of the Name.

43. Hitherto, we have merely considered the moral preparation of the spiritual aspirant. The driving power, however, for spiritual life is given by meditation on God. All Saints, both Indian and Christian, have laid stress upon the efficacy of the Name in fulfilling the ambitions of the spiritual aspirant. "We should always meditate on God," says Rāmadāsa, "and utter His Name; for satisfaction lies in the uttering of God's Name. We should never forget to meditate in the morning, at mid-day, and in the evening, and should at all times give ourselves to the uttering of God's Name. We should never forget God's Name, whether we may be merged in happiness or in sorrow, in dejection or in anxiety. At the time of joy and at the time of calamity, ...at the time of rest and at the time of sleep, we should always utter the Name of God. Whenever difficulties overtake us, whenever we are down with the worries of life, we should meditate on the Name of God. While walking or talking or doing our business, while eating or enjoying, we should never forget the Name of God. During prosperity and adversity, in days of power and greatness, at all times, we should never forget the Name of God. If prosperity succeeds adversity, or if adversity comes after prosperity, at all difficult times, we should not leave the Name of God. By the Name of God are all our difficulties dispelled, and all our calamities swept away. The demons and goblins, the spirits and ghosts, have no power before a devout meditation on God's Name. Poisons have no effect, nor are any magical practices of any utility, before the Name of God. The Name of God takes us to an excellent state after death. In childhood or in youth, in old age or at the time of death, we should always remember God......The great sage Vālmīki was liberated even though he uttered the Name of God contrariwise, and he was able to predict the life-work of Rāmachandra. By meditation on God's Name, Prahlāda was saved and was rescued from all calamities. The outcast Ajāmila was made holy by the Name of God. Even stones have been saved by the Name of God. Innumerable devotees have crossed the ocean of life by the power of the Name. Sinful men have become holy. There are a thousand

and one names of God. It matters not which name we utter. If we only utter it regularly and continuously, Death shall have no power over us. If a man does nothing but only utter the Name of God, God is satisfied and protects His devotee. Holy indeed is the body which is given to the utterance of God's Name. By the power of the Name, mountains of sins are destroyed. The power of the Name is ineffable, while numerous persons have been saved by the power of the Name. The great god Śiva himself has been relieved from the torments of poison by the power of the Name. There is no distinction of caste in the utterance of God's Name. Small men as well as great men, the dull as well as the intelligent, have been saved by the power of the Name. Finally, we must take care that while we utter the Name of God, God's Form is also present before us" (IV. 3).

We should meditate on God, for God holds the keys of success in His hands.

44. In a general way, Rāmadāsa commends the meditation on God, as God, he says, ever holds the keys of success in His hands. "God is the protector of all beings, and of all worlds......Where God is not, nothing can be, and all the beings on earth would be as good as ghosts. Where God is not, one would meet with Death. Without God, there can be no life......Hence it is, that one should always meditate on God. Meditation gives us great support. Without it, we cannot get victory in any work that we undertake. Where God is not present to support us, we would be routed by anybody whatsoever. Hence the necessity of Upāsanā" (XVI. 10. 23—33). Elsewhere, Rāmadāsa tells us that no undertaking can succeed unless it is backed up by the presence of God. "When we recognize that God is the real doer in the world, Egoism cannot possess us......God is the only reality; the self is an illusion......Only he who has ascended to the top of experience can testify to the truth of this" (XX. 4. 26—30).

The power of Disinterested Love of God.

45. There is another side to the problem of the love of God. We may love God not only because He may crown us with success in our undertakings but because He is Himself worthy of our highest love. "There is no comparison whatsoever to a disinterested love for God. It also requires great worth in us to be able to love disinterestedly. Desire indeed may bring the realization of the fruit; but disinterested love brings God Himself nearer to us. One may choose, as he likes, between the fruits of one's actions and the realisation of God! God can bring any fruits to us whatsoever ; but a desire for fruits stands between ourselves and God. Hence the necessity of a disinterested love of God. Great power comes out of a disinterested love for God which slights the realisation of any fruits. What the devotee has in mind, God brings to fruition of His own accord. There is no necessity for the devotee to take any thought about the matter. When the devotee's disinterested love is coupled with the great power of God, Death itself cannot stand the onslaught of the combination " (X. 7. 19—26).

Sravana as a means of spiritual development.

46. In order, however, that a man's mind may be set on God, it is necessary that he should give himself to the reading, or hearing, or meditating of spiritual literature. Śravaṇa is indeed a very important means of spiritual development. "Śravaṇa creates devotion. Śravaṇa creates dispassion. Śravaṇa purifies the mind. Śravaṇa produces mental determination. Śravaṇa wards off egoism. Śravaṇa gives internal satisfaction. By Śravaṇa, our doubts are resolved. By Śravaṇa, our difficulties come to an end. By Śravaṇa a man's mind craves for God. Śravaṇa keeps off bad company. Śravaṇa drives away all infatuation. Śravaṇa creates spiritual insight. Śravaṇa endows us with tranquillity......Śravaṇa creates repentance. Śravaṇa leads the aspirant onwards in the path of God...... Where there is no Śravaṇa, the spiritual seeker should not remain even for a single moment. He who does not love Śravaṇa—how can he love the realisation of God ? By regularly devoting ourselves to Śravaṇa, we would be able to reach the goal of our life. As we take food and water day after day, so we should devote ourselves to Śravaṇa time after time. He, who disregards Śravaṇa on account of idleness, shall surely miss the end of his life. To give scope to idleness is verily to cut at the root of all search after God " (VII. 8).

Requirements of a true Kirtana.

47. Like Śravaṇa, Kīrtana is another means of spiritual realisation. Only, we must know the requirements which a true Kīrtana must possess. A man who engages himself in Kīrtana should not give himself to a description of beautiful women, or to a narration of sexual passion. When a man describes the beauty of a woman, he is at that very moment affected by the sexual appetite and loses his moral courage. The contemplation of a woman is indeed a great obstacle in the path of the aspirant. Man's mind is capable of harbouring all sorts of sentiments. If he harbours the sentiment of love engendered by the contemplation of the beauty of a woman, how will he be able to meditate on God? ......On the other hand, a man whose mind is fastened on God can fill his Kīrtana with spiritual bliss, if he but meditates on God for a moment. When his mind is fixed on God, he will have no sense of the presence of people about him, and he will fill his Kīrtana with delight by dancing with composure and without sense of shame. The knowledge of Rāgas and the knowledge of Tālas, the knowledge of languages and arts, and a musical voice, are one thing; and true devotion is another. A true devotee meditates upon nothing except God. While he is giving his mind to the contemplation of the arts, he cannot give it to God......The arts indeed stand between him and God, if pursued for their own sake. Just as a serpent may stand between a man and a sandal tree, or a ghost between a treasure and a seeker, similarly a practice of music without meditation on God is an obstacle in the path of spiritual progress. On the other hand, twice blessed is he who keeps his mind on God, as well as performs Kīrtana according to its rules" (XIV. 5. 21—37).

A devotional song is an inspired song.

48. Rāmadāsa elsewhere describes how a man, whose mind is devoted to God, engages himself in Kīrtana. "He looks upon prosperity, woman, and gold as vomit, and contemplates God alone. His love of God increases from moment to moment. He does not allow a single minute to be wasted without the contemplation of God. At all times, his heart is full of the fire of devotion. When God has taken secure lodgment inside a man's heart, whatever he does is indeed the worship of God. The mouth merely gives out the inner love of his heart, and he dances in joy for the sake of God. His bodily consciousness is at an end, and his doubts and shame vanish......He sings and dances without reserve. He is not able to see men, for wherever his eye is cast, he sees only God......What words come out of an intense devotion in such a man's heart may alone be regarded as words of true inspiration" (XIV. 3. 22—34).

The use of Imagination in Spiritual Life.

49. Śravaṇa and Kīrtana are, however, the external manifestations of a heart full of love. But the method that Rāmadāsa prescribes for him who wishes silently to carry on a meditation on God may be set down as follows. The first obstacle in the path of every one who tries in silence to reconcile himself to God is the up-springing of variegated mental impulses, which destroy the one-pointedness of Yogic endeavour. Rāmadāsa duly recognises the power of Imagination, and tells us that when it grows powerful, it creates objects which never exist. "All of a sudden, it brings fear in our mind ; all of a sudden, it makes our mind steady......Imagination is the cause of rebirth ; Imagination is the cause of liberation......The way to the conquest of Imagination lies in a determinate endeavour to reach God. In that way, all doubts will come to an end, and the riddles of Imagination will be automatically solved......One kind of Imagination kills another, as by the help of one deer we are able to catch another deer......Pure imagination is that which is centred upon one Reality. Impure imagination is that which reflects upon duality" (VII. 5. 21—38). In another place also, Rāmadāsa tells us the same story. "The only way to get rid of Imagination is to go beyond Imagination. Before the eternal Reality no illusion can exist, and self-experience is able to put an end to all Imagination. This is at least a relieving feature of Imagination, says Rāmadāsa, that it can be made to imagine God, and when it is led Godward, it loses itself in the Unimaginable. When we imagine the Unimaginable, Imagination evidently comes to an end. God is not like an external object, so that He can be made perceptible to sense. The knowledge of God, says Rāmadāsa, comes to us only through the medium of a Spiritual Teacher" (VII. 3. 47—52).

False meditation and true meditation.

50. In a famous place, in the 14th Daśaka of the Dāsabodha, Rāmadāsa tells us the nature of true meditation. True meditation is a meditation on God ; false meditation is a meditation on any other thing except God......People vainly concentrate their mind on an image, says Rāmadāsa, for their spiritual development. Whether one should meditate on the Self or the not-Self, on the Immutable or the Mutable, one should clearly take thought beforehand. The body is verily a temple, and the Self is the image therein. Considering these two, which would you prefer to fix your mind upon ? No imagination of an image would be of any use whatsoever unless one knows the inner way of devotion. Imagination leads to new Imagination and people become vexed by a contemplation of gross objects...... The spiritual aspirant thus becomes disturbed in his mind. The only index to true meditation is, that the mind in the process of meditation should be affected by no doubts whatsoever. What is the use of that meditation which is carried on by a broken mind on a decomposable object ?...... True meditation consists in the unification of him who meditates, with Him who is meditated upon......This is a matter of experience, says Rāmadāsa ; but people vainly follow the beaten path. Fools they that do not know the truth from the untruth. They raise vain cries and talk about useless matters. When a man was engaged in meditation, and when, in the process of meditation, he found the head of the image he was meditating upon a little too tall, he was advised by his spiritual teacher to remove the crown from the head of the image, and thus to put the garland round the neck of the image. Fools both the teacher and the disciple, says Rāmadāsa ! They could not imagine that the garland itself could be made so extensive as to include both the crown and the head, so that it could be thrown easily round the neck of the image. The flowers were imaginary flowers, and the garland was an imaginary garland. Why should we not imagine the garland to be as long as we please ? What need for arguing with these fools? They have no intellect, says Rāmadāsa......It is unfortunate that these quacks administer vain nostrums to patients, and murder them in silence. There is only deception, and no knowledge with these men. It behoves us, says Rāmadāsa, to go to the root of the matter, and to rely upon Self-experience alone " (XIV. 8. 24—49).

The Aspirant.

51. Rāmadāsa has indeed a very high opinion about a Spiritual Aspirant. From the beginning of his spiritual pilgrimage to even the attainment of God, a man, according to Rāmadāsa, leads only the life of an Aspirant, or a Sādhaka, as he calls him. " An Aspirant is indeed he who has gone in all submissiveness to his Teacher and has been instructed by him on the path to God. When his Spiritual Teacher opens out to him the pathway to Ātman, the shackles of his worldly existence are destroyed ; and yet he performs Sādhana in order to be convinced of his liberation. He seeks the company of the Saints in order that his doubts may be dispelled, and he tries to bring his spiritual experience on a par with the teachings of the Śāstras, as well as with the teachings of his Spiritual Teacher......He throws off his bodily egoism and centres his heart upon Ātman......The Aspirant indeed is he who revives the lost tradition of Ātmajñāna. He has once for all bade good-bye to evil actions, and has been multiplying virtuous actions in order that he might ultimately get lodgment in the Form of God......With a firm determination, he tries to merge himself in the Ātman......What the eyes of ordinary people cannot visualise, what their mind cannot imagine, he tries to realise in his own experience. What cannot be expressed by word of mouth, what would ordinarily dazzle the eye, the

Aspirant tries to realise on his own account......Where the mind comes to a standstill, where logic is of no avail, that the Aspirant tries to apprehend by the power of his own spiritual experience. The Aspirant tries to become one with God......He has found out the root of both God and Man, and has immediately become one with the Ideal......In a superconscious state, he has seen the Self for all time, and brought the Aspirant's life to completion......When this mental attitude is firmly fixed in him, he begins to lead a different life in his outward actions. He leaves away all passion and anger, all vanity and jealousy, all shame and pride of family. He has dispelled all doubts,......cut off the shackles of death, and has once for all destroyed the round of births and deaths" (VI. 9. 3—41).

The Friend of God.

52. Higher than an Aspirant Rāmadāsa regards what he calls the Friend of God. "The Friend of God binds his love with God's love, and behaves only in a manner which would be approved of by God. In that way, indeed, the friendship between him and God grows. God likes the devotion of men, their narration of His exploits, and their loving songs. We should behave exactly as God wishes us to behave........We should give up our happiness in order to attain the friendship of God, and must not mind sacrificing ourselves for His sake. We should forget the pain of worldly life, and should always engage ourselves in meditation on God........In order to secure the friendship of God, we should not mind even if we were to lose our nearest relatives. We should ultimately sacrifice everything to God, including even our own life. It matters not if we lose all in order to gain the friendship of God......When the devotee so intimately loves God, then God becomes anxious for the welfare of his devotee, and rescues him as he rescued the Pāṇḍavas from the burning fire-house. That God may remain in a friendly way with us depends upon our own way of behaving with Him ; for, the echoes of our words come in the very manner in which we utter them. If we solely devote ourselves to God, God becomes solely devoted to us. If the cloud does not send drops into the beak of the Chātaka, the Chātaka does not give up longing for the cloud. If the moon does not rise to give nectar to the Chakora, the Chakora would nevertheless be longing after the moon......We should never relax our affection to God. We should call God our Friend, our Mother, our Father, our Learning, our Wealth, our All-in-All. People say that there is nobody to help them except God ;

but they do not really believe this from the bottom of their heart. Our affection towards God must be a real affection, and we should hold God fast in our mind. We should not get angry with God, if what we desire is not attained. We should always succumb, without grumbling, to the will of God. Then easily will God have compassion for us. Can we compare the compassion of our mother with the compassion of God ? The mother may kill her child in times of adversity ; but we have never heard or seen that God has killed His devotee. God has ever been a protective adamant to those who have submitted themselves to His will. God will justify the devotee. God will save the sinful. God will come to the help of those who have no protector......God will succour men from all calamities, and will run to their help as He did to the help of Gajendra...... God knows how to maintain His friendship, and we should only seek after His affection. The friendship of God is unbreakable, and the love of God is undiminished........Hence we should be friends of God, and communicate to Him our innermost desires.......In the same way in which we love God, we should also love our Spiritual Teacher" (IV. 8).

Atmanivedana : Self-surrender.

53. There is a type of devotion to God which Rāmadāsa calls Ātmanivedana, which implies the entire surrender of the Self to God. This he regards as the highest kind of Bhakti. "At the time of the Great Worship, they even sacrifice one's head to God : even so intimate is the Bhakti called Ātmanivedana. There are really few devotees who attain to this state ; for God would save them in an instant's time........Ātmanivedana consists in finding out who the Devotee is, and then what is meant by God. Ātmanivedana is attained when we have properly investigated the nature of Self and God. When the Devotee realises God, he becomes one with Him, and the distinction between God and Devotee vanishes. A Devotee is called a 'Bhakta', because he is not 'Vibhakta', that is, separate from God......He alone, among the Saints, is worthy of bestowing salvation upon others, who regards God and Devotee as one. When the Devotee sees God by being His Devotee, then all the qualities of God are immediately seen in him" (VIII. 8. 9—24). The first step to Ātmanivedana is the study of spiritual literature. The next step is the service of the feet of the Guru. Then, by the grace of the Guru, Ātmanivedana takes place. When this kind of Bhakti is attained, God begins to shine in His native purity, and a Devotee knows himself to be Ātman. By virtue of that knowledge all griefs of the worldly life vanish. The Devotee leaves off for ever all considerations of birth and death. The round of his births and deaths comes to an end. God and Devotee become one, and the contact with the Good ends in a first-hand knowledge of God" (VI. 2. 39—45).

Four different kinds of Liberation.

54. As regards the doctrine of Liberation, Rāmadāsa teaches us that there are four kinds of Liberation possible. "The first kind of Liberation is called Salokatā; that is to say, a Saint is supposed to obtain this kind of Liberation when, after the death of his body, he is lifted up to the region of the deity whom he worships. Secondly, when the Devotee, after death, lives in close proximity to the Deity, that kind of Liberation is called Samīpatā. Thirdly, when the Devotee reaches the Form of God without, however, acquiring the ornaments Śrīvatsa and Kaustubha, and without Lakshmī, then he may be said to have attained Sarūpatā. There is, however, an end to all these three kinds of Mukti; for as soon as one's merit is exhausted, the Devotee is thrown down from above to be reborn on earth. Hence, the fourth kind of Liberation alone is real Liberation, namely, what may be called Sāyujyamukti. When the world will come to an end, when the earth with its mountains will be reduced to ashes, when the gods will disappear, when the three different kinds of Liberation will cease to exist, then God alone will remain to be united to the Godhead, and that state alone would be called Sāyujyamukti" (IV. 10. 23—29).

The Saint is already liberated during life.

55. The Saint, however, need not care for any of these kinds of Liberation. He attains to Jīvanmukti, that is to say, he is liberated even during life. The Saint has seen his own Self, and has thus reached the end of his spiritual endeavour. "This has filled his heart with satisfaction, and his mind has become one with God......He has thrown his body in the stream of fate. Illumination has dispelled his doubts, and he cares not whether his body lives or dies. He has realised that his body is a fatuity. Holy is the ground where his body falls down. Places of pilgrimage become purified when the Saint enters them. Other people think that their body should fall on the bank of a holy river. But the saint is eternally liberated. He does not care whether the time of his death falls in the Uttarāyaṇa or the Dakshiṇāyaṇa. This is indeed a delusion for which he does not care. He cares not whether he leaves his body during the bright half of the month or not; whether he dies in the presence of a light or not; whether he will die by day or not; or even whether he may remember the Name of God at the time of death or not. All these things are of no avail to him, for he has been liberated during life......Foolish people say that he alone is a blessed man who meets with a 'euthanasia'. They falsely imagine that God meets a man at the time of his death. They never turn their life to good account, and they expect to see God! A man who does not sow corn should not expect to reap it......Hence a man who does not give himself in his life to the contemplation of God shall never reach a holy end. Even if he meets an easy death, he will really go to hell, as he has never entertained devotion towards God......Blessed is the body of the Jīvanmukta, whether it falls in a desert or in a cemetery. People foolishly imagine that the Saint has not met a good end, if his body lies suffering at the time of death, or is eaten up after death by dogs......The Jīvanmukta has never been born at all. How can he then suffer death? By the power of his discrimination, he has destroyed forever the round of births and deaths. By the power of his contemplation on God, his illusion has come to an end......He is dead while living. He has killed even Death itself. Birth and death do not touch him. He appears like other men while behaving with them; but he is really different from them. For, he is that immaculate Ātman who is untouched by anything sensible" (VII. 10. 7—31).

Sadhana necessary at all stages.

56. As to the question whether Sādhana is necessary after God-realisation, Rāmadāsa gives two different answers. In the first place, he tells us that Sādhana is necessary at all stages, and that even though a man may have reached the end of spiritual life, it is still necessary for him to continue his Sādhana. At another place, he tells us that Sādhana is unnecessary after God-realisation. According to the first, he says that a man who questions whether he should perform Sādhana after God-realisation is subjecting himself to a delusion. "Sādhana indeed is a necessity of the body, and so long as the body exists, it must be subjected to Sādhana. A man who wishes to continue in Brahman without Sādhana is only giving scope to bodily egoism and idleness. As those who pretend to seek the spiritual end are in fact seeking the material end; as those who pretend to give themselves to meditation are in fact giving themselves over to sleep; similarly, those who consider themselves to be liberated are giving scope merely to idleness and arrogance. Hence, to suppose that it is not necessary for one to perform Sādhana is only to cut one's own throat by one's own sword. Such a man, though liberated, is yet bound. He arrogantly feels that if he performs Sādhana after God-realisation, he would be called merely a Sādhaka. That fool does not know that even the great gods perform Sādhana " (VII. 7. 54—71).

Sadhana unnecessary after God-realization.

57. In opposition to this statement, we are told elsewhere by Rāmadāsa that Sādhana is really unnecessary after God-realisation. " If a man has attained to the ideal of Sādhana, what can Sādhana now do for him ? If a potter has become a king, why should he keep asses ? ......If a Saint has become one with God, why should he now subject himself to Sādhana any more ?......The poor man has become a King ; why should he now speak of poverty? ....How should the Vedas obey the order of the Vedas ? How should the sciences study the sciences ? What is the place of pilgrimage for pilgrimage itself ? Nectar cannot taste nectar. The infinite cannot comprehend another infinite. God cannot visualise another God......Of what use is the practice of Sādhana after the attainment of the end ? How should the object of meditation itself meditate ? How should a superconscious mind take cognisance of mind ? " (IX. 10. 17—26.)

The criterion of God-realisation.

58. What now, asks Rāmadāsa, is the criterion of God-realisation ? How may one know that he has reached God in his spiritual experience ? Rāmadāsa tells us that "only then can a man be supposed to have reached the end of his spiritual life, when he has personally known that all his sins have come to an end ; when he has known that the round of births and deaths has come to a stop ; when he has known both God and Self, and when he has experienced the extreme surrender of Self to God ; when he has known the stuff out of which the world is made ; and when he has known who has been responsible for the creation of it. When a man still entertains doubt about these matters, then his pursuit of the spiritual life has been in vain. He has merely merged himself in doubt without any experience. This indeed is the secret of the realisation of spiritual life. He who says this a lie is a vile man. He who believes this is a lie is still viler. God alone stands sponsor to what I say. The glory of my Upāsanā consists, says Rāmadāsa, in teaching this knowledge. If you call this a lie, you might as well call God a lie. Hence, I say again that the end of spiritual life will be attained only when one comes to know who the All-doer is " (X. 8. 21—28).

The Spiritual Wealth.

59. Rāmadāsa now proceeds to give us certain characteristics of mystic experience. "The wealth of the spiritual seeker is indeed a hidden wealth. Servants cannot know the entire extent of a treasure. They only know the external appearances. Real wealth has been hidden inside, while what appears is merely tinsel......Spiritual experience is indeed like wealth deposited inside a lake which is filled with water. People only look at the water, but are unable to get at the treasure. It is only the Sages who know the value of spiritual experience. Others give themselves over to visible things. It is a law of nature that some carry merely logs of wood, while others wear rich jewels......The Sage is in possession of the inner spiritual treasure; others, who want to satisfy their appetite, follow after philosophical opinions. The treasure which cannot be seen by the physical eye can yet be seen when the proper collyrium is applied to it. Similarly, God, who is hidden to the sight of ordinary men, can be attained only in the company of the Good. When a man is allowed to come in the presence of a King, he becomes a rich man; similarly, when we enter the company of the Good, we immediately attain to God" (VI. 9. 1—20).

Contradictions of Spiritual Experience.

60. Indeed it is in the nature of all mystical experience to appear contradictory. "As soon as we begin to be aware of it, we forget it. But as soon as we forget it, it comes within the ken of our consciousness......When we go to see God, we miss Him. But we see God without going anywhere to meet Him. This indeed is the virtue of spiritual Epochē. When we try to realise God, He cannot be realised. When we try to leave Him away, He cannot be left. We are connected with God forever, and the connection is unbreakable. God always is, and when we begin to see Him, He moves away from us. But when we do not look at Him, He immediately appears before us. The means for His attainment are only the means for His disappearance, and the means for His disappearance are really the means for His attainment. Only that man can know the meaning of this, says Rāmadāsa, who has attained to spiritual experience himself" (VII. 7. 19—23).

61. A spiritual seeker, however, has only to depend on himself for the attainment of God. For "according as his inner emotion is, similarly does God manifest Himself to him. He knows the inner feelings of men. If a man tries to cheat God, God will first cheat him. God behaves with men only as they deserve. He gives satisfaction to His devotees only according to the quality of their devotion. But as soon as there is any deficit in their sentiment, He also moves away. The image of our face that we see in a mirror is exactly like our face. If we stare at the image, that also stares at us. If we bend our brow, that also bends its brow. If we laugh, that also laughs. According as our sentiments are, similarly God behaves with us, and He rewards us only according to our worth" (III. 10. 13—19).

God rewards His devotee according to his deserts.

62. In various places in the Dāsabodha, Rāmadāsa gives us descriptions of mystic reality in different aspects. "Mystic experience is a sealed book to many, for verily they do not know the secret of the company of the Good. The mystic way is not like other ways. These only promise and never fulfil. The mystic way points out the inner secret of the revealed scriptures......Only the Sages can know the secret path in the heavens which leads to God...... No thieves can take away the treasure of spiritual experience. There is no fear to it from a king, nor any danger from fire, nor can a cruel beast ever pounce upon it. God cannot move, and will never miss His place. He is unmoved, and remains at His place for all time. This inner possession shall never change if time changes, and shall never increase or diminish during æons of time......It cannot indeed be seen except by the grace of the Guru......Before spiritual experience, everything that comes within the ken of the five elements appears as false and mean......When this spiritual experience gets secure lodgment in us, our doubts will be dispelled to the confines of the universe, and the visible world will cease to exist. ......It is impossible accurately to describe the worth of this spiritual experience. By this experience the greatest sages have attained to inmost satisfaction......He who attains to this experience can save other beings....He is a King of the spiritual world. He who has it not is a beggar......This spiritual experience can be obtained only on the strength of the merit during the whole course of our lives, and then shall the supreme God reveal Himself to us" (I. 9. 2—24).

Mystic reality as a solace of life.

63. Mystic reality is elsewhere described by Rāmadāsa in the manner of the Bhagavadgītā as "that which the weapons cannot pierce, which the fire cannot burn, which cannot be moistened by water, which cannot be blown away by wind, which can neither fall down nor wear away, which cannot be manufactured,

Reality beyond the influence of the Elements.

and which cannot be hidden. Reality, says Rāmadāsa, has no colour. It is different from everything that we can mention, and yet it exists at all times. It may also be seen that it is omnipresent. It fills the universe and yet is subtle. Physical vision can scan whatever is presented to it; but what is subtle cannot be open to vision. The Guru tells us that what is sensible is useless, and what is hidden is valuable.... What the Sages and Gods fail to attain, the Sādhaka tries to accomplish......This Reality can be attained only by spiritual meditation. It is neither earth, nor water, nor fire, nor wind. That indeed deserves the name of God. But ordinary people have each of them a god in their village" (VI. 2. 15—27).

Mystic description of Brahman.

64. Elsewhere also, Rāmadāsa devotes a whole Daśaka to the description of the immaculate Brahman. "Brahman is more spotless than the sky. It is as formless as it is vast.... It extends above all heavens. It exists below all worlds. There is not the smallest part of the universe which it does not occupy......It is quite near to us, and yet it is hidden. We live in it, and yet we do not know it......It penetrates the earth, and yet it is not hard. In fact, there is no comparison to its softness. Softer than earth is water; softer than water is fire; softer than fire is wind; softer than wind is ether; and softer and subtler than ether is Brahman. It pierces the adamant, and yet retains its softness. It is indeed neither hard nor soft. It does not perish with the earth; it is not dried up with water; it is not burnt in fire; it does not move with the wind; it exists in the sky, and yet cannot be known......Wherever you cast your glance, it is before you. You in fact see within it. It is both inside and outside. Where we feel it is not, it immediately manifests itself...... Whatever object we may take in hand—it is nearer to us than the object. Only he can know this secret, says Rāmadāsa, who has had spiritual experience himself......One sees it while reading. It enters into the very alphabets of a book. It enters into our eyes and lives softly. When we hear words, it is there. When our mind thinks, it is there. It indeed fills our mind inside and outside. As we walk, we feel it at every step. When we take anything in hand, the Brahman stands between us and that object......It can be seen by intuitive and not by physical vision. Only those who have had inner experience can understand what I say......Their ignorance is at an end. Their knowledge is at an end. Their superconsciousness is at an end. That is the Eternal Brahman which puts an end to all imagination, and which can be experienced in solitude by those who have devoted themselves to it" (VII. 4).

65. Finally, we have that excellent description of Brahman in the last Samāsa of the Dāsabodha. "If we try to catch hold of Brahman, we cannot catch it. If we wish to throw it away, we cannot throw it. Brahman is anywhere, and everywhere. As we turn ourselves away from it, it presents itself before our face. By no means whatsoever could we turn our back on it......Wherever a being goes, he will find himself circumscribed by the sky. It would be impossible for him to go beyond the limits of the sky. Similarly, wherever one may go, one is inside Brahman......In order to visit places of pilgrimage, we undertake long journeys. But we need not go anywhere to see God. We can see Him wherever we are. When we stand or when we run away, Brahman is with us. As the bird, which soars up in the sky, is surrounded on all sides by the sky, similarly does Brahman envelop all beings ......The Brahman is always before all beings. It is inside and outside. It fills the whole universe. To its immaculateness, there is no comparison. In all heavens, in the celestial worlds, from Kāśī to Rāmeśvara, it fills every nook and cranny. It fills all this space at once. It touches all, and abides in all. It cannot be soiled by clay. It cannot be carried away by the flood even though it may appear on it. Simultaneously, it is before us and behind us. Simultaneously, it is to our right and to our left. Simultaneously, it is above and below......It is a refuge of solace to all saints, to all good men, to the gods ......How can we reach its end ?......It is neither gross nor subtle. There is nothing which can be cited in comparison to it, and it cannot bring solace unless it is seen by intuitive vision. It is all-enveloping, and yet it is not all-enveloping ; because there is nothing outside it which it can envelop" (XX. 10. 1—23).

Final characterisation of Brahman.

IV. Activism.

66. We now come to Rāmadāsa's ideal of the practical life of a Saint. In fact, all the previous discussion was undertaken to prepare the way for Rāmadāsa's description of the Ideal Saint. Rāmadāsa tells us often in his great work that he has practised the virtues which he is preaching to others, and that the ideal of life which he sets forth before others is the ideal which he had realised for himself. According to Rāmadāsa, the Ideal Man is a practical man. "The fool looks only in one direction, but the wise man

The Ideal Man is a practical man.

looks in all......He has indeed identified himself with the Ātman, and cannot therefore be regarded as limited. He looks all round, and is famed everywhere. He is known to young and old alike. He does not put on only one kind of dress. The ornament of dress he does not regard as an ornament at all. The ornament of fame he regards as the only true ornament. The Sage does not allow even a single minute to be wasted in vain. He moves away from people of his acquaintance, and finds out new men every day. People test him to see whether he entertains any desire ; but he has none. He does not look at anybody for any length of time. He does not speak much with anybody. He does not live long at any place. He does not tell people whither he goes. He does not go where he says he will go. He does not allow his condition to be imagined by others. What people think about him he tries to falsify......What people have a desire to see, he does not care to see......He does not allow his heart to be searched. He does not live without the service of God for a single moment. People, who form wrong notions about him, are in course of time led to correct their notions themselves. The Sage has done a great thing indeed, when people examine him and he stands the test of all. He lives in solitude, always gives himself to meditation, and spends his time usefully in the service of God along with other men. He cultivates in himself the best of qualities, and teaches them to the people. He collects men together, but in secret. He always has some work to do, and leads people to the service of God. People then submit themselves to him, and ask him what they should do. Unless we undergo a great deal of trouble first, we cannot realise any great end......We should examine various people, should know for what things they are competent, and then either hold them near or keep them at a distance. It is only when we assign proper work to proper persons that it is well accomplished. Unworthy men cannot accomplish any work at all......We should believe in people only when they do their duties heartily. We should always reserve something which we can call our own. This is a matter of experience, says Rāmadāsa. I have first done all these things, and then have advised others to do them. You may accept any of these things if you think they are good. A great man must be able to create great men. He should fill them with wisdom, and spread them broadcast through various lands " (XI. 10).

67. " An Ideal Man, who has regulated his life, becomes known to all. All people will now try to please him......A man should never allow his peace to be disturbed by the evil words of others. Great indeed is the Saint who mixes with evil men......If we pursue fame, we cannot get happiness; and if we pursue happiness, we cannot get fame. We should never injure the hearts of others ......If we forgive them, our greatness is not mitigated.......A Saint should give himself to intense devotion, and should cultivate the highest qualities. Then will people come searching for him. Such a great-souled man alone should gather people in the name of God. If he were to die suddenly, who would carry on the service of God after him ? I have determined, says Rāmadāsa, not to ask anything from my disciples. I ask only this thing of them—that they should worship God after me......In order that we might be able to gather people together in the cause of devotion, we should have two qualities: in the first place, we should have the power of illumination by which other peoples' hearts might be conquered; secondly, we should act exactly as we speak, for it is only then that our words would have any value ......We should take people along with us, should teach them gradually, and lead them to the realisation of the end of spiritual life" (XII. 10. 14—41).

The spiritual man demands only the service of God from his disciples.

68. Then, again, Rāmadāsa goes on to tell us certain other characteristics of the Ideal Man. "The Ideal Man loves to put forth effort, enters boldly on any enterprise, and does not shun work. He can live in the midst of difficulties, bear the brunt of action, and yet keep himself away from contact with it. He is everywhere, and yet nowhere. Like the Ātman, he hides himself. Nothing can take place without his mediation; yet he is not himself seen. He makes people act without himself being seen. ......Those who follow the instructions of a wise man themselves become wise. That is the justification of the existence of a wise man. He always supports the right cause, and never gives himself to unrighteousness. In the midst of difficulties, he knows the way out. A man of courage is a great support to all. This indeed is what he has become through the grace of God" (XI. 6. 12—19).

The Ideal Man moves all, being himself hidden.

69. One further characteristic of the Ideal Saint is that he never displeases anybody. "He tells the truth, and behaves in the right way. Great men, as well as small—all have a regard for him. If the Ideal Man were not to forgive people for their ignorance, he would merely

The Ideal Man does not displease anybody.

bring himself on a level with them. If pieces of a sandal tree are not rubbed on a sandstone, they would not produce a fragrant scent, and then they would be on a par with pieces of other trees. What can people know, so long as they have not known the superior qualities of the Ideal Saint? When these qualities come to light, the whole world is filled with good feelings towards him.. When the world is pleased, that is to say, when God in the world is pleased, nothing can be wanting to the Ideal Saint......Good behaviour with others leads to happiness. If we speak bad words, they are echoed back on us. We need not teach other people how to behave ; we should teach ourselves. If we meet a bad man, and if the limits of forgiveness are reached, then we should leave the place in silence. People have various kinds of knowledge, but they do not know the hearts of others. It is thus that they make themselves miserable. We must remember that we have to die some day. Hence it is that we must try to please all" (XII. 2. 15—26).

The Ideal Man pleases all.

70. Rāmadāsa does not give merely a negative rule that we should not displease anybody, but he tells us positively that we should try to please everybody. "What is censurable we should avoid. What is praiseworthy we should practise. We should fill the world with good report.... We should avoid evil qualities, and cultivate the good...... The one rule of life should be that we should try to please all, and gradually make them holy. Just as one tries to please a child, similarly, we should try to please the people. Wisdom consists in giving satisfaction to the hearts of men......We should never call a fool a fool. We should never point out his defects. Only then can a Saint conquer the world. There are various situations in which a Saint may find himself placed. He should always try to assimilate himself to the hearts of all beings. He alone is a great Saint who gives satisfaction to the minds of people ; for, it is only then that people flock to him in numbers" (XIII. 10. 20—29).

The Active Saint should retire, should set an example, should be courageous.

71. Then Rāmadāsa proceeds to give further characteristics of the Ideal Saint. "The Ideal Saint is known everywhere by the power of his devotion. People know him, but they do not find him, and they do not know what he is doing. People from various lands come with a desire to see him. The Ideal Saint pleases all, and fills the minds of all with discrimination and good thoughts.

There is no limit to the disciples he makes. All of these he leads on the spiritual pathway........Whatever he knows, he teaches the people, and makes them wise. Whenever they get into a difficulty, he is ready to help them. He makes the minds of all pure and holy. What one can do oneself one should do immediately. What one cannot do oneself, one should get done by others; but on no account whatsoever should the service of God be relaxed. We should first do, and then get everything done by others. We should first discriminate, and then should ask others to do it. If the Saint grows weary of people, he should go to a new place......His Sainthood would come to an end if he does not practise spiritual meditation every day......So far as he can engage himself in activity, he should do it. But as soon as he cannot, he should wander anywhere he pleases in contentment......If he cares for fame, he cannot get happiness. If he wants happiness, he cannot get fame......One should never lose courage in the midst of activity: how would one be able to reach the end of his life in that way? Life is indeed a miserable affair. By the power of discrimination, however, one can make it good; and as soon as one makes it good, it fades away......The greatest thing of all is that the Saint should never give up courage" (XIX. 10. 8—29).

The Master is found nowhere.

72. Rāmadāsa insists from time to time that the Active Saint should not meddle much with the affairs of society. He should hide himself, and let other people talk about him. He who wants to gather people together should always take resort to solitude. There, one gets to know the internal condition of men......Whatever people have in mind, the Saint knows already. Hence nobody can come, and deceive a Saint......He should engage himself regularly in various forms of devotion, thus never leaving any scope for inferior kinds of work......He who depends on another spoils his work. He alone is a good man who depends on himself......One should take the central thread in his hands, and get details done by others. If one wants to collect a number of men, one should have great strength of mind.....One should know what people are wicked, but should not say openly that they are so. They should be given even greater importance than good men...... An Ideal Saint should not be seen anywhere, and yet people must talk about him from place to place. In order to meet a fool, one must set a fool. In order to meet a dullard, one must set a dullard......In order to meet a fool-hardy man, one must set a fool-hardy man. In order to meet an arrogant person, one must depute an arrogant man. A boisterous man must be met by a boisterous man. When equals meet equals, then a splendid encounter takes place. All this should be done, but the Master should be found nowhere" (XIX. 9.)

Activity should alternate with Meditation.

73. One of the most important teachings of Rāmadāsa about his ideal Sage is that his activity should alternate with meditation. He should lead an intensely active life for some time, and should immediately engage himself in intensive meditation. In that way, both his meditation and his activity become strengthened. "He who cannot undertake active work should not engage himself in active work. He should compose his mind and remain silent......If by his activity he only brings grief to other people, he should not engage himself in that activity at all......Indeed, activity leads to good results as well as bad results. When people have an element of devotion in them, we must support it. We should never expose their hypocrisy......The place of complete rest is only the Ātman ......There, all anxieties come to an end. The mind becomes content, and the unapproachable life of God becomes ours by the force of meditation. Indeed, the Self is not affected by any environment. People come together by accident, and part from each other by accident......We should spend some time in intense activity, and some in silent devotion. In that way, the mind becomes tranquil and powerful" (XIX. 8. 19—30).

Further characterisation of the Active Saint.

74. "Wherever the Active Saint goes, he is liked by all. He has indeed the fire of devotion in him, and nobody can withstand him...... When people are eagerly waiting for him, he presents himself suddenly before them ......Wherever the wise man is, no quarrel can arise. He does not say one thing to a man's face, and another behind him. All people are ever anxious to meet him. He never troubles the hearts of people......He always engages himself in conferring obligations on others. He is pained by other peoples' sufferings, and becomes happy in their happiness. He desires that all people should be happy. As a pater-familias cares for all the members of his family, similarly the Sage cares for all......If his body is reproved, it does not matter to him; for he never identifies himself with his body ......When people know that he forgives their faults, then they come and support him. All people regard themselves great but the Saint alone is a great man. He is courageous, and he is noble ; and the depth of his mind cannot be measured" (XIX. 4. 5—31).

The Active Saint must fill the world with God.

75. As the Saint has pledged himself to the service of God, his one business is to fill the world with God. "If he should ask anything of anybody, he should ask him to continue his devotion to God......People would be spoilt if one has a Turk for his Guru and Chamārs for his disciples. Hence, one should collect together Brahmins, should respect the assemblies of Devotees, should search after the Sages......One should become famous on earth by desiring nothing......One should always merge oneself in the narration of God's exploits, so that people may always be attracted towards Him. The light that one spreads must be like the light of the Sun. The Sage should know the inner motives of men. Men who live in his company should immediately mend their manners, and those who are round about him should engage themselves in incessant meditation. Wherever he goes, he should behave like a guest ; people should desire that he should stay with them. He should, however, not stay there for fear of becoming too familiar...... No fame is attained without intense virtue of some kind...... One does not know when the body may fall. One does not know what calamities may befall us. Hence, we should always be on the alert, should do all that we can for spiritual life, and fill the world with the holy name of God. What we can do soon, we should do immediately. What we cannot do soon, should be done after mature thought. There is nothing that does not come within the ken of reflection. Hence, we should give ourselves to incessant thought, and always find new remedies. Unless a man retires to solitude, he cannot find the way out. In utter silence, we should reach the Ātman, and then no difficulties will present themselves before us" (XIX. 6. 11—30).

Autobiography of the Active Saint.

76. Finally, Rāmadāsa supplies us with a piece of an autobiography for the life of an Active Saint. He tells us how in his time the Mahomedans had oppressed the whole land ; how he gave himself up to the life of a Saint, and became the support of all on account of his great spiritual power. "Many people have now become Mahomedans ; some have fallen on the field of battle ; many have lost touch with their native language, and have become proficient in foreign tongues. The bounds of Mahārāshtra have been curtailed. People are engaging themselves in politics,

They do not find time even to take their food. Many engage themselves in a life of warfare, and by the pride natural to that life, they engage themselves day and night in war topics. The merchant is carrying on his commerce, and cares for nothing but his belly. Various sorts of philosophical opinions have prevailed. Many kinds of atheistic schools have sprung up. Wherever you go, you find false teachers. Others have divided themselves as followers of either Śankara or Vishṇu. Confusion reigns everywhere. People are merely following the bent of their desires. They cannot distinguish right from wrong......Many people attend Kīrtanas, but nobody cares for mystical experience. Mystical knowledge has been hard to get at......It can be attained only by him who has a piercing insight, and who does not waste a single minute. A man of insight as he is, the Sage is respected by all. He knows many passages by heart, and with the power of his memory makes straight the path of spiritual life. He knows the hearts of all, and knows various ways of illuminating them. He says little; and saying little, he attracts the hearts of all. On the strength of his own mystical experience, he levels down all philosophical opinions, and compels the people to leave their beaten paths. He speaks pointed words, and by the power of his indifference, immediately takes leave of the assembly. When he has gone away after speaking words of spiritual experience, people naturally feel attracted towards him. They leave away all beaten paths, and go in all submission to him. But he cannot be found in any particular place; and as regards his dress, he looks like a beggarly man. His great power lies in his work in silence. Indeed, his fame and name and power know no bounds. He engages people in spiritual service from place to place, and himself goes away from their midst......He goes and lives in mountain valleys where nobody can see him, and there he meditates for the good of all. In difficult places and among peculiar men, he always maintains the regularity of his spiritual life. All people in the world come to see this spiritual Saint. His motives cannot be fathomed. He determinately engages people in a politico-religious life, and multiplies disciples through disciples, so that they ultimately grow numberless. What power he exercises on earth is exercised in silence. Wherever he goes, he finds numberless men believing in him, and he engages all in spiritual life. Whatever place he visits, he makes people sing aloud the greatness of God, while he brings his own spiritual experience to their help. The end of human life consists in realising such an ideal, says Rāmadāsa. I am describing it to you in a few brief words." (XV. 2. 3—30).

God, the Author of the Dasabodha.

77. We might conclude this survey of Rāmadāsa's teaching in the same words in which Rāmadāsa concludes his great work, the Dāsabodha. Rāmadāsa is convinced that it is not he who has composed the Dāsabodha, but that he is only an instrumental cause for the display of God's activity. He thanks himself that he has been able to reach the end of spiritual life. "The end of my spiritual life has been attained. The purpose of my life has been fulfilled. The Impersonal Brahman has been reached. All illusion has come to an end. The nature of the phenomenal world has been traced...... What I had seen as in a dream has been dispelled in the state of spiritual wakefulness. The secret of spiritual life has been ineffable......The round of births and deaths has come to a close. The completion of this work, the Dāsabodha, has been due to the grace of my Lord, the son of Daśaratha, who is proud of His devotees. This work has been divided into 20 Daśakas, and 200 Samāsas. He, who meditates on them, will gradually come to know the secret of spiritual life. There is, however, no need of praising this work; for what matters is first-hand experience. The body is made up of elements, while the Ātman is the All-doer. How shall we credit a man with the production of this work ? God indeed does all things. ......The body is made up of elements, and these disappear in the final resort. We should leave off all delusion, and take recourse to the thought that it is God who does all things" (XX. 10. 26—37).

CHAPTER XX.

General Review and Conclusion.

God-realisation and Activism.

1. The most characteristic feature of Rāmadāsa's teaching may now be seen to be activism. Rāmadāsa, more than any other Saint of the Maratha School, called peoples' minds to the performance of duty, while the heart was to be always set on God. Rāmadāsa tells us time and oft that the first thing that a man should do is to believe in God, and the next thing is to do his duty to himself and to the nation. For, Rāmadāsa tells us that it is only when our efforts are backed by devotion, that they are likely to succeed : समर्थाची नाहीं पाठी । तयास भलताच कुटी । याकारणें उठाउठी । भजन करावें ॥. No wonder that, with this teaching, he helped the formation of the Maratha kingdom as no other Saint had formerly done before. It is indeed true, as the late Mr. Justice Ranade said, that even pacifist Saints like Nāmadeva and Tukārāma laid the moral foundations on which Rāmadāsa later reared his politico-religious edifice. It is not given to each and every one to achieve all things on earth. While Nāmadeva and Tukārāma went one way, Rāmadāsa went another. While the first called back the attention of men from irreligion to religion, the other raised upon the foundation of religious faith an edifice of national greatness. For that matter, we are not to suppose that Rāmadāsa alone is of any consequence so far as the political destiny of Mahārāshṭra was concerned, and that Tukārāma and Nāmadeva preached only a pacifist doctrine which ruined the kingdom. The controversy is a very old one, dating from the days of the Bhagavadgītā, as to the value of knowledge and works. Such conflicts can be resolved only when we cancel them in a higher synthesis, as the great German philosopher Hegel said. We want both knowledge and works as we want both religion and national greatness, and it is from this point of view that Tukārāma and Nāmadeva were of as much use to the Maratha kingdom as Rāmadāsa himself. It is merely exhibiting bad blood to discard any one for the sake of the other.

Ramadasa and Christianity.

2. A very painstaking writer has recently produced a work on "Rāmadāsa and the Rāmādāsis" in the English language, and we cannot commend his assiduity and earnestness, and, on the whole, his fairmindedness too highly. Mr. Deming has utilised his opportunities of a stay at Satara, and has produced a book in the "Religious Life of India" Series, in which he has gone into the smallest

details about the life and history of Rāmadāsa and his school. Though, however, the book is, on the whole, praiseworthy, in the last Chapter, Mr. Deming harks back to a comparison between Rāmadāsa and Christianity, and as is usual with his class of writers, ends his volume by pointing out the superiority of the teachings of Christianity over the teachings of Rāmadāsa. In the first place, he tells us that Rāmadāsa makes a confusion between a personal and an impersonal view of the Godhead (p. 200), and that even though in modern times a justification has been given for a reconciliation of the personal and the impersonal by saying that the first concept belongs to the sphere of Religion while the second belongs to the sphere of Philosophy, Mr. Deming inclines the beam in favour of the first and rejects the second, all the while oblivious of the fact that a Philosophy of Mysticism might concern itself neither with the Personal nor with the Impersonal, but with the Trans-personal, meaning thereby that the category of personality has no place in a Philosophy of Mysticism. Secondly, as is again usual with his school, Mr. Deming points out that Rāmadāsa's conception of salvation was negative instead of positive (p. 204), meaning thereby that Rāmadāsa dwelt too much upon the ills of life rather than upon the joy consequent upon a life in God. Now, any man who will read Rāmadāsa's works carefully will see how time and oft he insists upon the beatific element in life, thus giving the lie direct to the theory that he takes merely a pessimistic view of salvation. In the third place, Mr. Deming points out that Rāmadāsa's view of Incarnation is only a plausible one, in which God merely seems to become man instead of becoming man in reality, meaning thereby that God in the Hindu scheme plays merely the dramatic rôle of an actor instead of actually personifying himself in the world of men (p. 207),—a view with which no writer on the Philosophy of Hinduism can agree, inasmuch as, throughout Hinduism, Incarnation is regarded as a verity and a fact, and not as a mere appearance. For, are we not told in the Bhagavadgītā that God incarnates himself time and oft in the world of men whenever religion comes to an end and irreligion prevails? In the fourth place, we entirely agree with Mr. Deming when he points out that the Ethics of Rāmadāsa and the Ethics of Jesus were absolutely on a par, for "like Rāmadāsa, Jesus spoke of purity, unselfishness, truthfulness, sympathy, patience, humility, the forgiving spirit, and other motives in the heart,—traits, which, like Rāmadāsa, Jesus actually personified in his own life" (p. 210). In fact, the teaching of both Jesus and Rāmadāsa seems to be absolutely alike in this respect, inasmuch as both of them practised the virtues which they preached, and preached them only after they had practised them. Fifthly, we may also agree with Mr. Deming when he says that with Rāmadāsa the ideal of caste was yet predominant, while Jesus preached "a Christian brotherhood of the most democratic type, regardless of colour, race, wealth, culture, or any other distinction" (p. 212). Rāmadāsa's justification, however, would be that spiritually all people were equal in the eyes of God, while socially there might be differences owing to traditions of racial evolution. Sixthly, when Mr. Deming speaks of the difference between the Svāmi and the Christ, inasmuch as the Svāmi seemed to enjoy prosperous circumstances at the close of his life, while Jesus bore the Cross, we have only to remember that these are accidental circumstances over which man has no control, and that each was playing out his rôle where God had chosen to place him. Finally, when Mr. Deming speaks of the narrow geographical outlook of the Svāmi and the mere contemporary background of his vision, while Christ's message was timeless and universal in its nature (p. 216), he is entirely mistaking the fact that all mystics, of whatever lands they may be, preach a message which is timeless and universal, and that if Rāmadāsa's teaching as outlined in the previous Chapter seems evidently to be of the mystical type according to the criteria of Mysticism to be elsewhere discussed, then his message can never be only either localised or of mere contemporary value. In fact, Rāmadāsa's mystical teaching, like that of the other mystics of the Maratha School, was as timeless and as universal in its nature as the teaching of any other mystics of any other lands or times.

Bhakti and Rationalism.

3. The doctrine of Bhakti which these Saints of the Maratha School taught in their Spiritual Literature has been held in such high esteem by rationalistic writers like Prof. Patwardhan, that one wonders how these could keep to their rationalism, while applauding the Bhakti doctrine of the Saints. "Here we have a literature that takes us from the bewildering diversity of the phenomenal world to the soul-consoling kinship of the ultimate realities. Here is a literature that subdues all the bestial instincts of man, and reminds him of what he truly is and what he is to seek......If to discover the uncommon in the common, the unfamiliar in the familiar, the unknown in the known, the supernatural in the natural, the infinite in the finite, and the one in the many, be an element of the Vision Romantic, unmistakably we have it in the literature of the

Bhakti school......Here we have the Romance of a Light that never was on sea or land ; of a Dream that never settled on the world of clay ; of Love that never stirred the passion of sex......Here is the romance of piety, of faith, of devotion, of the surrender of the human soul in the Love, the Light, and the Life of the Ultimate Being. " If all rationalism could be so eloquent of the merits of Bhakti, one would by all means be such a rationalist.

The Philosophy of Mysticism.

4. The philosophic aspects of mysticism we have hardly any time to enter into in this volume. It has been a matter of very great difficulty to those who entertain a barely theistic view of the world how at the same time a mystical view could be sustained. It is no wonder, therefore, that we find that many an acute critic has landed himself into contradictions when the question of the reconciliation of theism and mysticism has arisen. Thus, while Dr. Macnicol calls into question " the audacity of that pantheistic speculation which makes God feel the necessity of a devotee, as it makes the devotee feel the necessity of God ", he is at the same time led elsewhere to recognise the claims of Mysticism where both dualism and monism become one. Thus, though he says that " the resonant note of thankfulness which throbs in the 103rd psalm is outside of the knowledge of Maratha Saints who venture on the contrary to say that God is their debtor, " and that "such an audacity is beyond the reach of the Hebrew or Christian penitent, unless his conscience is overlaid with pantheistic speculation as that of Eckhart ", he also feels it necessary to recognise elsewhere that " not in the Monism of Sankarāchārya, nor in the Dualism that is satisfied to remain two, but in a Spiritual Experience that transcends and includes them both, is peace to be found ". This is exactly the problem of the Psychology and Philosophy of mysticism. It is too wide a problem to be attempted in this historico-analytical work. For that, another time and another place may be necessary. How the mystic criterion of reality compares with the idealist, the realist, and the pragmatist criteria, how the mystical faculty of intuition compares with intellect and feeling, how we may reconcile the phenomenal and the noumenal elements of human experience, showing man simultaneously to be a denizen of two worlds, the one human and the other divine,—which alone can make it possible for him to realise the divine in the human,—shall form the subject of a forthcoming work on the " Pathway to God ".

INDEX OF NAMES AND SUBJECTS.

A.

Abhangas, as out-pourings of the soul (p. 166).

Abhangas of Jnanesvara, as raising a problem which is the crux of Jnanadeva scholarship (p. 38); the comparative modernness of their style, as due to their being learnt by heart, and reproduced from memory (p. 39); as possessing the entire repertory of old words with Jnanesvari (p. 39); as brilliant in ideas as the Jnanesvari (p. 40); as bespeaking the very heart of Jnanadeva (p. 40); as the emotional, while the Jnanesvari, the intellectual garb of Jnanadeva (p. 40); the extreme similarity of ideas between, and Jnanesvari and Amritanubhava, proved by a number of quotations (p. 40).

Abhangas of Namadeva, characterised by his pantings for God (p. 192).

Abhanga literature, as corresponding to the religious lyric of English Literature (p. 166); used for criticising social customs (p. 166).

Absolute Existence, as the upward root of the Asvattha Tree (p. 59).

Absolute, the conception of the, as an intellectual ideal for logical purposes (p. 69); as all-pervading (p. 69); as immaculate and eternal (p. 70); as the Creator, Preserver and Destroyer (p. 70); as the Great Void (p. 70); as formless and yet having form (p. 70); as not admitting of the distinction of subject and object (p. 159); the natural condition of, as lying between the destruction of the seer and seen, and their new revival (p. 160).

Absolution, as opposed to the transmigrating process (p. 57); reached by men who go beyond the three psychological qualities (p. 57); reached by men who by their devotion have attained to identity with God (p. 57); as absolute transcendence of the qualities (p. 105).

Action, gospel of (p. 99); excess of, is actionlessness (p. 99); necessary until one is fixed in the knowledge of the self (p. 99).; wears away internal impurity (p. 100); as an antidote to the evil effects of action itself (p. 100); to be done without any attachment (p. 101); offering of, to God, as the highest means of securing actionlessness (p. 102).

Actionlessness, not to be preached to the incompetent, not even in sport (p. 99); four kinds of helps to secure (p. 103).

Actions, as flowers by which to worship God (p. 103).

A—*Contd.*

Activity, to alternate with meditation (p. 418).

Adinatha (p. 377).

Advaita, the philosophical ground of Jnanadeva (p. 178).

Advaita Bhakti, of a man of realization (p. 163).

Advaitic identification *vs.* the Service of God (p. 330).

Ahamkara, of the Samkhyas (p. 5).

Aikantika doctrine, identical with Bhagavatism (p. 3).

Aisvarya, a power of the Godhead in Pancharatra (p. 4).

Ajagara, as adopting the Serpent and the Bee as his teachers (p. 9).

Ajamila, the perfect sinner, getting liberation by uttering the name of God (p. 9); reference to, made by Kanhopatra (p. 208); not born of a high caste (p. 326); the outcaste, made holy by the name of God (p. 399).

Ajnanavadins, those who argue for the existence of ignorance in the Atman (p. 154); the arguments of Jnanadeva against the (p. 154); as gone mad according to Jnanadeva (p. 157).

Akbar, receives Jesuit missions (p. 16).

Akhandesvara, as more of a moralist than a mystic (p. 18).

Akka (p. 364); died forty years after Ramadasa; instrumental in building the temple at Sajjanagada; Samadhi at Sajjanagada (p. 373).

Akrura, as reaching God through devotion (p. 109); referred to by Tukarama (p. 287).

Akshara, the immutable, as described in the Jnananesvari (p. 54); as absolutely formless (p. 55); as what appears as Ignorance (p. 55); as psychologically corresponding to the state of Deep Sleep (p. 55); as the root of the tree of Existence (p. 55).

Alandi, made a place of pilgrimage by the passing of Jnanadeva (p. 35).

Allauddin Khilji, as come to Ellichpur in 1294 (p. 27); invading the Deccan in 1294 A.D. (p. 185).

Allegories, spiritual, in Tukarama (p. 350).

Allegory, of the Crop (p. 350); of the Dish (p. 351); of the Fortune-teller (p. 351); of Goddess as Supreme Power (p. 351).

Alvars, as heading and heralding the Tamil Vaishnavites (p. 17); established in the country in the 6th century A.D. (p. 17).

Ambarisha, referred to by Tukarama (p. 287).

A—*Contd.*

A—*Contd.*

B.

B—*Contd.*

B—*Contd.*

B—*Contd.*

D.

Dama, mentioned both in the inscriptions at Besanagar and Ghasundi, and in the Bhagavadgita (p. 3).

Damajipant, as living about either 1458, or 1468 to 1475, the dates of the dire famine in the Deccan (p. 213); God as becoming a pariah for (p. 336).

Damaseta, Namadeva's father, a tailor, living at Narasingpur (p. 186).

Damsels of Psychological States (p. 128).

Dark Night of the soul, of Western Mysticism, as partially experienced by Namadeva, as fully experienced by Tukarama (p. 192).

Dasabodha, the close of the Seventh Dasaka of (p. 370); the date of the first part of (p. 370); the two authentic editions of (p. 370); Pangarkar edition, dated Sake 1606 (p. 370); a great history of the doings and thoughts of Ramadasa; remarkably valuable as giving the spiritual autobiography of Ramadasa (p. 373); date of, internal evidence for (p. 374); date of a part of, Sake 1581 (p. 374); date of the, reference to Tulja Bhavani as an aid to determine, (p. 374); original, written in 1581 Sake; the seven dasakas theory (p. 374); the completion of the, as due to the Grace of God (p. 421); divided into 20 Dasakas, and 200 Samasas (p. 421).

Dasavisramadhama, by Atmarama, describing Ramadasa, as having a number of names (p. 45); gives the story of the Sampradaya of Ramadasa (p. 373); full of miracles about the life of Ramadasa (p. 373).

Dattajipanta, giving 200 coins for the festival of God (p. 364).

Death, signs of approaching, according to Jnanadeva (p. 173); the thought of, should always be present in one's mind (p. 196); the messengers of, not entering a place where the Kirtana is being performed (p. 323); Tukarama planting his foot on the head of, (p. 307); a great leveller (p. 389); the innumerable miseries at the time of, (p. 389); not considering wealth, power, or even incarnations of God (p. 389); as powerless before God's Name (p. 400).

Deep, calling unto deep (p. 169).

Dehu, place of Tukarama's birth, and death (p. 261).

Delhi, visited by Jnanadeva and Namadeva (p. 34).

Deliverance, Maiden of, as adorning the neck of the dispassionate (p. 91).

Deming, Mr., the work of, on 'Ramadasa and Ramadasis' (p. 422); on Ramadasa and Christianity (p. 423); the view of, that Ramadasa makes a confusion between a personal and an impersonal view of the Godhead, considered

D—*Contd.*

(p. 423); on Ramadasa's conception of Salvation as negative instead of positive (p. 423); regarding Ramadasa's view of Incarnation as only a plausible one (p. 423); the Ethics of Ramadasa and the Ethics of Jesus as absolutely on a par (p. 423); on Ramadasa's advocacy of caste and Christ's advocacy of democracy (p. 424).

Democratic Mysticism, and the Vernaculars (p. 16).

Demoniac Heritage, a heritage of vices (p. 86); consisting of the six vices, hypocrisy, pride, arrogance, anger, harshness, and ignorance (p. 91); including 'harshness' which makes a man's sight like the discharge of arrows (p. 92).

Deva, S. S., on the first meeting of Shivaji and Ramadasa (p. 363); and Rajavade, answering the arguments of Bhate and Chandorkar (p. 365).

Devagiri, kings of, as supreme (p. 25); the kingdom of, as confiscated in 1318 A.D. (p. 27).

Devala, as talking of God to Arjuna (p. 112).

Devotee, as superior to the Philosopher (p. 69); meditating on the form of Guru in his heart (p. 75); regarding a moment without Guru as greater than a world-cycle (p. 75); having his Guru's residence as his only cynosure (p. 75); worshipping his Guru with the flowers of his emotions (p. 76); regarding his Guru as a mother (p. 76); regarding his Guru as a cow, and himself a calf (p. 76); imagining himself as the young one of a bird (p. 76); desiring, after death, to dissolve himself into the elements for the service of his Guru (p. 76); feeding on the love of his Guru (p. 76); having his Guru as his sole place of pilgrimage (p. 76); filling his mouth with the Mantra of his Guru (p. 77); as God, of whom Knowledge is the devotee (p. 77); true, enters into my being and becomes one with me (p. 112); knows no distinction between king and pauper (p. 114); his love towards other devotees (p. 129); spoken of by Jnanesvara as Beloved (p. 130); description of a true, (p. 130); as an object of worship to God (p. 130); dearer to God than even Lakshmi (pp. 129, 131); as the object of God's adoration (p. 132); the recipient of particular grace from God at the time of death (p. 133); absolute identity of, with God even before his departure from life (p. 134); the father of God (p. 225); has not his eyes set on worldly honour (p. 246); one on whom God chooses to shower His grace (p. 246); his spirit should

D—*Contd.*

E.

E—*Contd.*

F.

F—*Contd.*

G.

G—*Contd.*

G—*Contd.*

G—*Contd.*

G—*Contd.*

H.

H—*Contd.*

I.

I—*Contd.*

J.

J—*Contd.*

J—*Contd.*

J—*Contd.*

K.

K—*Contd.*

L.

M.

M—*Contd.*

M—*Contd.*

M—*Contd.*

N.

N—*Contd.*

N—*Contd.*

N—*Contd.*

N—*Contd.*

O.

P.

P—*Contd.*

P—*Contd.*

P—*Contd.*

Q.

R.

R—*Contd.*

R—*Contd.*

the body (p. 388); referring to the incident of Changadeva and Jnanesvara (p. 388); giving a mystic description of the Assembly of Saints (Dasabodha I. 8) (p. 395); his description of the Ideal Saint (p. 413); determined not to ask anything from his disciples, except the worship of God after him (p. 415); giving us a piece of autobiography (p. 419); activism, the most characteristic feature of the teachings of, (p. 422); telling us that our efforts succeed only when backed up by God (p. 422); unlike other saints, helped the formation of the Maratha Kingdom (p. 422); contrasted with Namadeva and Tukarama (p. 422); insisting upon the beatific element in human life (p. 423); regarding all people as spiritually equal in the eyes of God, but socially different (p. 424); the message of, as much universal and timeless as that of Christ (p. 424).

Ramadevarao, the Yadava king of Devagiri mentioned at the end of the Jnanesvari (p. 25); a great patron of learning (p. 25); the devotee of the god of Pandharpur (p. 25); giving a ransom to Allauddin to save his kingdom (p. 27); taken as prisoner to Delhi, and returning to his kingdom to die in 1309 A.D. (p. 27); Kingdom of, as enjoying all prosperity so long as Jnanadeva lived (p. 27); the support of all arts and sciences (p. 47); as visiting the temple of Vitthala in 1276 A.D. (p. 184); as giving a large subsidy to the temple of Vitthala (p. 184).

Rama, Krishna, Hari, the mantra given to Tukarama for meditation (p. 270)

Ramananda, as a philosophical descendant of Ramanuja (p. 15); settling at Benares (p. 15); the three great mystical schools of Tulasidasa, Kabir and Nabhaji, as springing from, (p. 15); the teacher of Jnanadeva's father (p. 19); and Maharashtra Mysticism (p. 19); and Kabir and Tulasidasa (p. 19); as supplicated by Siddhesvarapant and Rakhumabai (p. 30).

Ramanuja, opposed to Maya (p. 15); his influence as dwindling in his birth-land (p. 15); his influence, as reappearing with greater force in Upper India (p. 15); the philosophical descendant of Yamunacharya (p. 18); building a system intended to cut at the root of both monism and dualism (p. 18); the predecessors of, as given more to devotion than to philosophy (p. 18); the arguments of, against the Maya Doctrine, utilised by Jnanadeva (p. 179).

Ramanuja and Madhva, not understanding how mysticism can reconcile theism and pantheism (p. 15); and Christianity (p. 16).

Ramesvarabhatta, first a hater, and later a disciple, of Tukarama (p. 264); from Karnatak, as worshipping Vyaghresvara at Vagholi (p 268); suffering pain when Tukarama was troubled (p. 275); asked by Jnanesvara to submit to Tukarama (p. 276); conversion of, as a disciple of Tukarama (p. 276); his references to Tukarama's life (p. 276).

Ramiramadasa, passing away in Sake 1599 (p. 362); author of Bhaktirahasya and Sulabhopaya (p. 372).

Ranade, Mr. Justice, on Ramadasa as rearing his politico-religious edifice on the moral foundations laid by pacifist saints like Namadeva and Tukarama (p. 422).

Realisation of God, the terrific nature of, (p. 126); incomparable with the knowledge of the three worlds (p. 101).

Realisation, the joy of, (p. 126).

Realisation of the Self, as different from that of the Visvarupa (p. 119).

Realiser of Brahman, pays all his debts to deities, sages, ancestors, and men (p. 255).

Reality, as having no colour (p. 412); eternal, omnipresent, and subtle (p. 412).

Reincarnation, phenomenally real (p. 57); noumenally an illusion (p. 58); superior to liberation (p. 331).

Religion, as living by the words of a sage (p. 123).

Renunciation, as a means for securing actionlessness (p. 102); of actions into a mere void, as advocated by Jnanesvara (p. 102); as disgust even for Urvasi, or a heap of jewels (p. 248).

Repentance, *raison d'être* of, destroyed by the celebration of God's name (p. 114); the cause of ecstasy (Ekanatha) (p. 220); the true act of atonement (p. 242).

Resignation to God, as submission to God and complete union with Him (p. 98).

Retirement, the value of, described by Ekanatha, by the metaphor of a bride (p. 240).

Rigveda, the development of Indian thought traced from the dimmest beginnings in, (p. 1).

Rishabhadeva: his utter carelessness of the body as a mark of God-realisation (p. 9); living as a dumb, deaf and blind man, in towns and forests (p. 9); as wandering lone and naked, in Karnatak and other provinces (p. 9); offering his body as a holocaust to God (p. 9).

Rohidasa, referred to by Tukarama (p. 326); God as dyeing the skins of (p. 335).

Rukmangada, referred to by Tukarama (p. 287),

S.

S—*Contd.*

S—*Contd.*

S—*Contd.*

S—*Contd.*

S—*Contd*

S—*Contd.*

S—*Contd.*

T.

T—*Contd.*

T—*Contd.*

T—*Contd.*

T—*Contd.*

U.

U—*Contd.*

V.

V—*Contd.*

V—*Contd.*

W.

X.

Y.

A SHORT BIBLIOGRAPHICAL NOTE ON COMPARATIVE MYSTICISM.

I. Indian Mysticism.

THE aim of the present work being to show the place which Indian Mysticism and, particularly the Mysticism of Maharashtra, occupies in the Mystical Literature of the World, it would be necessary here to give a comparative view of Maharashtra Mysticism along with the Mystical literature of the other Provinces of India as well as of the general Mystical literature of Christianity and Islam, together with recent works, historical, psychological, devotional, and philosophical, on the Philosophy of Mysticism in general.

The details of the works of the Mystics treated in the present volume have been already given in the body of the book. Before, however, one can arrive at a comparative estimate of this Mysticism along with others, it would be necessary to have in a nutshell a general knowledge of the great lights of Maharashtra Mysticism for the benefit of a comparative study.

The Jnanesvari, the greatest work in Marathi on mystical philosophy, composed by the Saint Jnanesvara, has been edited by various writers, prominent among whom are Sakhare, Kunte, Madgaonkar, Rajwade and Bankatswami. Sakhare's edition of the Jnanesvari gave the first Marathi translation of that great work, and appeared in a revised form in 1915 from the Indira Press, Poona. Kunte's edition printed at the Nirnayasagar Press, Bombay, and revised in 1910, is a very handy edition, and though it does not contain any translation of the work as a whole, it has still some good footnotes and is very serviceable for original study. Madgaonkar's edition, 1907, was planned on a more ambitious scale. The different readings were cited in the work in the footnotes, and an attempt at a Glossary of the terms appearing in the Jnanesvari was made by the Editor after a comparative review of the meanings of the same words appearing in different contexts in different parts of the said work. Rajwade's edition (Dhulia, 1909), which was intended to give us a redaction of the Jnanesvari earlier than that revised by Ekanatha, contains a good introduction on grammar, and a second attempt was made by him for the Glossary of the difficult words occurring in the Jnanesvari on the aforesaid pattern. The latest work on the Jnanesvari is that of Bankatswami, who, in collaboration with a number of scholars, has produced a Marathi translation of the Jnanesvari which will necessarily repay close study. A complete English translation of this greatest work in Maharashtra Mysticism, the Jnanesvari, is badly necessary, and let us hope that it is produced at no very distant date. In that way, the entire Jnanesvari may be made available to English readers, as Manikkavachagar and Tulsidasa have been rendered available to English readers by Pope and Growse respectively.

The Abhangas of Jnanesvara, being his heart-pourings, are also exceedingly valuable from the point of view of Mysticism. An accurate, close, and well-thought out edition of these Abhangas is absolutely necessary. When such a one is produced and translated, we might feel the real heart-beat of Jnanesvara, and see his inner aspirations towards God-attainment.

As regards the Abhanga Literature of many other Mystics treated in the present volume, such as Nivritti, Sopana, Muktabai and Changadeva; Namadeva and a host of his contemporaries; Janardan Swami, Bhanudasa and Ekanatha, we have to commend to the attention of our readers our Four Source-books of Maharashtra Mysticism (Poona, 1927). They contain relevant excerpts arranged in terms of the internal psychological development of these great Mystics, and may prove a valuable incentive to all aspirants after God-realisation. We only note in passing, as we have said in the body of the book, that a good and authentic edition of the entire repertory of Namadeva's Abhangas is absolutely necessary, and should be taken up by some scholar at no very distant date.

Ekanatha's Commentary on the Bhagavata appears in the classical edition of Pangarkar, Nirnayasagar Press, 1909. This, however, is a Vedantic presentation of his Philosophy, but his real Mystical utterances are to be found in his Abhangas, the best of which, as we have noted above, have been included in our Source-books.

Tukarama's Abhangas, again, have found very able editors. The Induprakasha edition published by the Government of Bombay under the editorship of Mr. S. P. Pandit, 1869–1873, has long been a standard work, though now not very available. Vishnubuva Jog's edition (1909) might be regarded as a modern standard presentation of Tukarama's Abhangas, especially as it contains a Marathi translation of all the Abhangas of the Saint. It has recently appeared in a second edition (Poona, 1927). Mr. H. N. Apte's edition of Tukarama's Abhangas (Arya Bhushan Press, Poona) is also very serviceable and is regarded as traditionally valid. Bhave published (Thana, 1919) another edition of what he regarded as the original Abhangas of Tukarama from the notebooks of Santaji Jaganade, one of the personal disciples of Tukarama. A discussion of the meaning of Tukarama's Abhangas attempted by the late Prof. W. B. Patwardhan with the co-operation of the late Dr. R. G. Bhandarkar has been recently brought out under the editorship of Prof. G. H. Kelkar (Ganesh Press, Poona, 1927).

The most standard edition of Ramadasa's Dasabodha is, of course, the Dhulia edition of Mr. Dev, first published in 1905. Amongst its consecutive five editions, the latest to appear was in 1925. Mr. Dev is not yet satisfied with the editions which he has produced and wants some day to produce a better one still, possibly the best after his heart, which, let us hope, may not be long in coming.

We need not detail here all the works in English on the Maratha Saints which have been mentioned in the body of the present work. We might only recapitulate by saying that those who want to make an acquaintance with Marathi Religious Literature through English might do well to give a perusal to Prof. W. B. Patwardhan's Wilson Philological Lectures (which we incidentally call upon the Bombay University to publish separately on account of their intrinsic value), Macnicol's "Psalms of the Maratha Saints", Rawlinson's "Shivaji" (Oxford University Press, 1915, the appendix of which contains some translations from "Tukarama", and "Ramadasa" by Prof. R. D. Ranade), Edwards' "Life of Tukarama", Fraser and Marathe's English Translation of Tukarama's Abhangas, Deming's very assiduous work on Ramadasa, and so forth. Particular mention, however, must be made of the indefatigable and zealous attempt that is being made in the cause of Marathi Religious Literature by Mr. Justin E. Abbott of America, whose translations it was not possible to mention in the body of the book, as they came to hand too late for recapitulation and survey, but which we earnestly recommend to the readers of Marathi Literature. Mr. Abbott has been devoting his green old age to a series of publications in that field, 5 volumes having already appeared, thus proving his very great love towards that Literature. His published works in English include "A Life of Ekanatha", "Autobiography and Verses of Bahinabai", a life of "Dasopant Digambar", "Stotramala", a garland of Hindu prayers culled from various sources, "Bhikshugita" or the Mendicant's Song, while a number of others are to follow. We only wish that Mr. Abbott is spared for a long while yet to exhibit in further detail the remaining parts of the panorama of Marathi Literature.

The Mysticism of the Maharashtra Saints is on all fours with the Mysticism of the Saints in the various Provinces of India outside Maharashtra. We have contemplated, that as companion volumes to the present one, at least five other volumes on the teachings of the Mystics of the other Provinces of India could be very easily produced by scholars who have devoted their life to a study of the Original Sources, combined with a Philosophic understanding and a Mystical insight. Of such volumes we might say that at least the following five could be produced immediately: (1) a volume on Hindi Mysticism, (2) a volume on Bengali Mysticism, (3) a volume on Gujerathi Mysticism, (4) a volume on Tamil Mysticism, and (5) a volume on Canarese Mysticism. When these five volumes have been written *pari passu* with the present one, and on the lines indicated here, the world at large might have a fair knowledge of the teachings of the great Mystics of India.

It is impossible to give within a short space any reasonable account of the vast literature in the original of the Saints who have written in the various languages aforementioned. Though, however, the original literature of these great Mystics of the various Provinces of India is vast, English literature on them is comparatively slight. Unless and until the Mystics of these Provinces of India have been interpreted into English, it may not be possible for people outside India to understand the peculiar contribution which has been made by the Saints of each Province to the development of the World's Mysticism. It would behove us in the present place, however, just to make a short mention of the more important English works that have been written on these great Saints of the various Provinces of India, remembering that space here may not allow us to enumerate the originals.

Hindi Literature has been best studied of all the Provincial Literatures of India by writers in the English language. Mr. Grierson's "Modern Vernacular Literature of Hindustan" (Calcutta, 1889) gives a good account of the teachings of the Hindi Saints. Mr. Grierson is also responsible for a large number of articles in the *Royal Asiatic Society's Journal*, London, on such great Hindi Mystics as Ramananda, Tulsidasa and Nabhaji. Particular mention might be made here of essays on Hindi Mystics in the *J. R. A. S.* for 1903, 1909, 1910, 1912, 1913, 1914, 1916 and 1920. Westcott's "Kabir and Kabir Panth" is an excellent appreciation as to how even a Christian missionary might look at the teachings of an Indian Saint. Growse's translation of the "Ramayana" of Tulsidasa is another illustration in point. Carpenter's "Theology of Tulsidasa" (Madras, 1918) is a general review of the teachings of Tulsidasa from the point of view of Indian Christianity. The Rev. Ahmad Shah's English translation of Kabir's Bijak (Hamirpur, 1917) is also worth while noticing. Dr. R. G. Bhandarkar in his "Vaishnavism and Saivism" has given a running summary of the teachings of the Mystics in the different Provinces of India, to which also reference might be made with advantage. Dr. Bhandarkar writes accurately, and succinctly, and we are almost tantalized by the account that he has given of these great Saints.

The Literature of the Bengali Saints is very vast. In the originals, a study of it is formidable, and must be attempted by a Philosophic scholar who knows the original Sources, as well as the general principles of Mysticism. Mr. Sen's "Vaishnava Literature of Mediæval Bengal" (Calcutta, 1917), his work on "Chaitanya and his Companions" (Calcutta, 1917), as well as his "History of Bengali Language and Literature (Calcutta, 1911) would surely repay perusal. Mr. Sarkar's "Chaitanya's Pilgrimages and Teachings" (Calcutta, 1913) is also worth while studying, as it comes from a historical writer who is interested in his language and religion. Dr. Estlin Carpenter's "Theism of Mediæval India", like Dr. Bhandarkar's "Saivism and Vaishnavism", is another work of importance which considers in passing the teachings of Chaitanya, as it does also of Tulsidasa and Kabir. Unfortunately Dr. Carpenter's life was not spared, otherwise we would have had the benefit of further work from him so far as the Mystics of India are concerned.

The Literature of Gujerathi Mystics, though not so vast in the original, is nevertheless acute and penetrating from the mystical point of view. Narasi Mehta and Mirabai's songs in Gujerathi, and Hindi or Braj, must excite the interest of everybody who cares for mystical knowledge in any part of the world. Of English books on the great lights of Gujerathi Literature might be mentioned Jhaveri's "Milestones of Gujerathi Literature" (Bombay, 1914) Tripathi's "Classical Poets of Gujerat" (Bombay, 1894), and Scott's "Gujerathi Poetry" (Surat, 1911). There has been, however, a new consciousness in Gujerat about the contribution which the Literature of that Province has made to the development of Indian Literature, and it seems, in course of time, research might be instituted on other great mystical poets of Gujerat, and other able books might be produced on the Mystics that have written in that language.

So far we have discussed the Mystics who have come under the spell of Aryan influence. Of those mystics who have come more or less under the spell of Dravidian influence might be mentioned the Tamil, the Telugu, and the Canarese Mystics.

Tamil Literature, again, would not yield either to Hindi or to Bengali in its width or intensity. The name of the mystical writings in that language is legion, though at the same time it must be mentioned that not many English works have been produced on the writings of these Saints, one of the principal reasons for this probably being that English writers take to a study of Hindustani, and therefore there are greater opportunities for them for the study of the Hindi poets instead of the Tamil poets, whose language it is very hard and difficult for them to learn. It is for this reason highly creditable for Mr. Pope to have produced a monumental translation of the "Tiruvasagam" (Oxford, 1900) with introduction, text, translation and notes. This, in fact, ought to be the type after which the writings of other great mystics of India such as Jnanesvara might be produced with advantage in the English language. Kingsbury and Phillips' "Hymns of the Tamil Saivite Saints" (Heritage of India Series, 1920), though a small book, yet gives us an insight into the teachings of those great Tamil Saints. K. Aiyangar's "Ancient India" (1911), and S. Aiyangar's "Tamil Studies" (Madras, 1914) might also be mentioned in connection with the great writers of the Tamil land. We hope, however, that some scholar takes up at an early date the work of Tamil Mysticism as a whole, and brings out an edition which would tell the world of what stuff these Tamil Saints were made.

Of the Telugu Saints, not many are accessible from the viewpoint of mysticism, though the Literature itself is vast. Vemana, the Heracleitus of the Telugu language, has produced beautiful *bon mots*, which have a mystico-psychological tenor, and have at the same time a didactic and exhortative value. Mr. Brown is responsible for the translation of the Verses of Vemana (Madras, 1911), while a few translations might also be found in Barnett's "Heart of India" (London, 1908). A scholar of the calibre of Prof. Radhakrishnan might easily take up the work of writing a work on Telugu Mysticism.

Of the Canarese Mystics, again, it might be said as of the Bengali, Tamil, and Hindi Mystics, that their Literature is so vast that a different volume would be necessary for an adequate presentation of it. There are two different streams of thought running in Canarese Mystical Literature, the Vaishnavite and the Saivite, the first represented more or less by Brahmins, and the second represented more or less by the Lingayats, and each has got its own contribution to make to the Literature of the World's Mysticism. It would be impossible to enumerate here the many original works of writers like Purandardas, Jagannatharaya, Basava, Akhandeshvara, and so forth, who have enriched the mystical literature of the world. English literature, however, as before, is again scanty about these writers. A few translations may be found in Gover's "Folk-Songs of Southern India", (London, 1872). The sprightly little volume of Mr. Rice on Canarese Literature (Calcutta, 1918) would be a good sign-post for a brief indication of the great works in this language. Mr. Pavate has recently produced a work on "Virasaiva Philosophy" (Hubli, 1928), and Mr. P. G. Halkatti is responsible for the very valuable translation of the "Vachanas of Basava", which he contributed to the Indian Antiquary a few years ago. Much further work, however, remains to be done in this field, and let us hope that some Canarese scholar soaked in the principles of the Philosophy of Mysticism takes it up at an early date.

II. Christian Mysticism.

For a proper understanding of the teachings of these Indian mystics, we must compare them somewhat to European and Islamic mystics. In fact, a proper apprehension of the works of these great Saints can take place only when they are studied in connection with those of the great Saints of Christianity and Islam. On a general survey of the spiritual experience attained by these mystics, it might be found that the kernel of Mysticism is at bottom one, though Indian Mystics may ring the changes upon one chord, the Christian Mystics on a second, and the Islamic yet on a third. All these Mystics constitute the musical band of God, and each contributes his note in such a way that the whole becomes a harmony, and a symphony wonderful.

The Literature of European Mystics is as vast as the one we have indicated above, and the European mystics are scattered through all such countries as Greece, Germany, France, Italy, Spain and England. For the last two thousand years and more, they have continued a mystical tradition which is still powerful, and which is still the breath of European civilization to-day. *Pace* the Rev. Dean Inge, who tells us that so far as Mysticism is concerned, "we shall not find very much to help us in the Old Testament, the Jewish mind and character, in spite of its deeply religious bent, being alien to Mysticism" ("Christian Mysticism", p. 39), we have to remember that wherever people have walked with God, there has been a veritable mystical experience, and we can scarcely deny to people like Moses, Isaiah, Jeremiah, and so forth, a direct mystical experience of God. So far as Jesus Christ himself is concerned, we regard him as one of the greatest of mystics that ever lived. "The account of the Transfiguration, his Agalliasis (Luke, x. 21) which is so characteristic of his mystical rapture, his choice as his nearest companions of men like Peter, James, John and Paul, to whom the vision-state was familiar, his appreciation of those who were child-like in heart, and his teaching, in the Sermon on the Mount, about a direct vision of God for people who were pure in heart, are illustrations to show what radical hold mystical experience had on his mind" (Fleming, "Mysticism in Christianity"). In fact, it is experiences like this which make the Bible one of the world's text-books of Mysticism. One of Christ's nearest disciples, St. John, merely voices the sentiments of his Master, when he teaches that God is Love, God is Light, God is Spirit. The Gospel of St. John has been appropriately called by Dean Inge the "Charter of Christian Mysticism".

St. Paul is, again, yet another great mystic of Christianity. The appearance in the sky which immediately preceded his conversion was responsible for his spiritual rebirth. His entire disparagement in the "Epistles" of the forms and externalia of religion, his doctrine of the pre-existence of Christ in "the Form of God", his description of Jesus as well as all created beings as the Images of the Invisible God who is mirrored in them, and his characterization of Christ as the principle of creation in the universe have all the fundamentals of a mystical philosophy writ large upon them.

Plotinus (A.D. 205–270), the greatest of the Neoplatonists, exhibits no influence of Christianity whatsoever, and his "Enneads", which were so called because Porphyry arranged them in 9 groups of 6, are an embodiment and a visible manifestation of his mystical, literary and philosophical powers, and must be studied by everyone who wishes to understand the Philosophy of Mysticism.

"The Confessions" of St. Augustine (A.D. 354–430) constitute another great landmark in the history of Mysticism. His greatness is already adumbrated for us when St. Ambrose told his mother Monnica who was weeping for his derelictions that the son of those holy tears would never perish.

Dionysius, the Areopagite, (A.D. 475–515) is another great name in the history of Mysticism. In fact, it is probably the first greatest name among Christian writers who have described the workings of the mystical consciousness. His works later made a profound impression upon the development of Mysticism, and included "the Angelic Hierarchy", the "Ecclesiastical Hierarchy", "the Names of God", and "Theologia Mystica", the last of which was translated into English by the anonymous author of the "Cloud of Unknowing" (14th century). Dionysius himself,—and the name seems to be an assumed name,—is responsible for the description of God as "the super-essential Essence, the irrational Mind, the absolute Not-Being above all existence", comparable to the Upanishadic description of God as the "Neti, Neti".

After Dionysius, we have two women mystics in the persons of St. Hildegarde (A.D. 1098–1179) and St. Gertrude (A.D. 1182–1226). The point of contrast between them is that while the one combined mysticism with practical life, the other busied herself in her subjective experiences. "The Letters" of St. Hildegarde, and the "Exercises" and the "Revelations" of St. Gertrude are well worth studying.

St. Francis of Assisi (A.D. 1182–1226) is another great name in the history of Mysticism. So far as his ethical qualities are concerned, he reminds us of the great Buddha. He wedded "Lady Poverty", and much to the wrath of his father, who was a rich merchant, went out into the world a poor man. He left a large number of works, of which two at least are available in English translation: "The Mirror of Perfection" (Temple Classics, London, 1903), and "The Little Flowers of St. Francis" (Temple Classics, London, 1903). We are told how he would preach to his little sisters the birds, and once undertook the conversion of the "ferocious wolf of Agobio". He saw God in all things, and in an oft-quoted passage, we are told how "he would remain in contemplation before a flower, an insect, or a bird; how he was interested that the plant should have its sun and the bird its nest; and how he supposed that the humblest manifestations of creative force should have the happiness to which they are entitled".

Angela of Foligno (A.D. 1248–1309) was converted from a sinful life to a spiritual life, and in the "Book of Divine Consolations" we are told how she congratulated herself on the deaths of her mother, husband and children, who were to her great obstacles in the way of God.

Thomas Aquinas (A.D. 1226–1274) is known more for his Philosophy than for his Mysticism, though from the undoubted influence that he left upon Dante, we cannot deny to him a niche in the temple of Mysticism. His "Summa Theologica" (Paris, 1880), and "Summa Contra Gentiles" are his great monumental works on Philosophy. In English translations, he is available to us in Rickaby's "Moral Teachings of St. Thomas", and "God and His Creatures".

Dante (A.D. 1265–1321) is one of the greatest names in the history of Mysticism. He combined extraordinary powers of rhythm, imagination, and spiritual experience, so as to be able to unfold the pathway through the Inferno and the Purgatorio to the Paradiso, where one might enjoy the Beatific Vision of God.

We now come upon the trio of the great German Mystics, Meister Eckhart (A.D. 1260–1329), Tauler (A.D. 1300–1361), and Suso (A.D. 1300–1365). Meister Eckhart (A.D. 1260–1329) had as great intellectual power as he has mystical insight, and was condemned for having taught "Pantheism and other Heresies" by the Church. His "Mystische Schriften" (Berlin, 1903), and "Sermons" translated by Claud Field (London, 1909) must be read by every student of Mysticism. His was the doctrine of the "Fünkelein", or the Divine Spark, which was the "apex" of spirit by which the human mind was in direct communication with God.

Tauler (A.D. 1300–1361), whom we have quoted in our Preface, is another great mystic, whose "Inner Way", which is a selection of 36 of his Sermons, is available to us in the Library of Devotion, London, 1909.

Suso's (A.D. 1300–1365) "Autobiography" is a very remarkable document, as we have seen in his comparison with Tukarama in our Preface. As Miss Underhill points out, mysticism to him is not so much a doctrine to be imparted to other men, as an intimate personal adventure. His Autobiography is a standard record of his "griefs and joys, pains and visions, ecstasies and miseries", and is available in English translation, London, 1865. His "Little Book of Eternal Wisdom" (London, 1910) might also be read with advantage. He seems to have been a Visionary, and saw Angels, the Holy Child, and even his blessed master Eckhart. As a token of devotion, he "cut deep in his breast the name of Jesus, so that the marks of the letters remained there all his life about the length of a finger-joint".

Under the influence of these three great German Mystics was produced a very valuable tract of Mystical Theology called "Theologia Germanica" by a Member of the "Friends of God". In its English form, it is available in the Golden Treasury Series. Luther said about it, that next to the Bible and the Confessions of St. Augustine, there was no other book which influenced him so deeply. It was first edited by Luther, and has since passed through several editions in German and various other languages.

Ruysbroeck (A.D. 1293–1381), the mystic of Flanders, is another great name in the history of Mysticism, and in him we find a happy combination of the "metaphysical and personal" aspects of Mysticism. In English translation he is available to us in his "Flowers of a Mystic Garden" (London, 1912), and in Miss Underhill's monograph on him (Quest Series, London, 1915). He was informed through and through by the doctrine of love, and was exceedingly fond of using the image of Espousal with the Divine Bridegroom.

Richard Rolle (A.D. 1290–1349) starts the line of English Mystics; but his interest in Mysticism is not philosophical, but practical. He regards Mysticism not as philosophy, but as a mode of life. His "Form of Perfect Living" (London, 1910) and his "Mending of Life" (London, 1896) show us the entirely practical bent of his Mysticism. It was Rolle who, among all the mystics, was peculiarly characterised by his Experience of God as Music, and he tells us how the burning Love for God is later on changed into Divine Song, "Calor into Canor".

The Anonymous Author of "The Cloud of Unknowing" (14th century), who also translated Dionysius' "Theologia Mystica" into English, makes an acute analysis of the Psychology of Mysticism from a universal standpoint which makes the whole world kin, and which therefore deserves to be studied by every student of Mysticism.

Lady Julian of Norwich (A.D. 1343–1413) is one of the greatest of English female mystics, and her "Revelations of Divine Love" (Methuen, London, 1901), "Sixteen Revelations of Divine Love" (London, 1902), "Visions and Voices vouchsafed to Lady Julian" (London, 1911) show us of what stuff she was made. In one of her visions of the Lord, we are told how she saw three things: "game, scorn and earnest; game, in that the fiend was overcome; scorn, in that he was scorned of God; and earnest, in that he was overcome by the blissful passion and death of the Lord Jesus Christ, which was a very earnest affair indeed".

About the merits of Thomas à Kempis (A.D. 1380–1471) as a mystic, opinions vary. Inge's judgment about Thomas à Kempis' "Imitation of Christ" is that it cannot be regarded as a mystical treatise, but only as a moral one. It cannot be taken, he says, as a safe guide to Christian life as a whole. It only offers to us the defence of the life of a recluse. His indifference to human interests, and his utterance that 'whenever he had gone among men he returned home less of a man', provokes Dean Inge to call him, in Platonic terminology, a 'Shell-fish'. Asceticism is an important phase of Mysticism, and if Francis has depicted that in his work prominently, we need not quarrel with him, as we do not think that he regards it as the be-all and end-all of the life spiritual.

Two great Italian female Mystics now catch our vision: Catherine of Siena (A.D. 1347–1380), and Catherine of Genoa (A.D. 1447–1510). Both of them reconciled the active life with the ecstatic life, and in their respective works "The Divine Dialogue" (London, 1896), and the "Treatise on the Purgatory" (London, 1858), we have two masterpieces of mystical literature. Catherine of Siena (A.D. 1347–1380) suffered from acute ill-health; but she had the good fortune to wear a ring of pearls as a symbol of her marriage with God. St. Catherine of Genoa (A.D. 1447–1510) has been honoured by Hügel in his great work on "The Mystical Element of Religion", which faithfully describes her mysticism, and that of her friends (London, 1908).

We have now a trio of great Spanish mystics, who were at the same time actives of a high order. Ignatius Loyola (A.D. 1491–1556), founder of the Society of Jesus, has his mystical greatness hidden on account of the active propagandist work that he did. His text of the "Spiritual Exercises", translated from the original Spanish, London, 1880, must be read by everybody who wishes to know how Mysticism could be reconciled with active life.

St. Teresa (A.D. 1515–1582) is again one of the greatest of the mystics of all ages. In translation, she is available in her "Autobiography" (London, 1904), "The Interior Castle" (Baker, 1902), and the "Way of Perfection" (Baker, 1902). The most remarkable passage in her Autobiography is where she describes the four kinds of prayer by an allegory: "it has been always a great delight to me to think of my soul as a garden, and the Lord as walking in it. Our soul is like a garden, out of which God plucks the weeds, and plants the flowers which we have to water by prayer. There are four ways of doing this: first, by drawing water from a well; second, by a water-wheel; third, by causing a stream to flow through it; and fourth, by rain from heaven. It is only in the last stage that the soul labours not at all; all the faculties are quiescent, and it is no more the soul that lives, but God." Max Nordau has the veritable audacity to call such a great active mystic as Teresa a "degenerate"!

St. John of the Cross (A.D. 1542–1591), who was the greatest of St. Teresa's disciples, is available to us in English translation in the "Ascent of Mount Carmel" (Baker, 1906), "The Dark Night of the Soul" (Baker, 1908), "The Spiritual Canticle" (London, 1911), all translations from the Spanish. In St. John of the Cross, we read how all visions are at best "childish toys". "The fly that touches honey cannot fly"; and hence St. John of the Cross recommends to us a flight from all mystic phenomena, such as those of sight, hearing, and others, without examining whether they are good or bad. To our mind, he appears as the one of the most powerful descriptive mystics that have ever lived, and his apostrophe to "Touch" and his description of the "Balsam" of God are beyond all comparison.

The German shoe-maker, Jacob Boehme (A.D. 1575–1624), is the type of a mystic who was sprung from a lower class and has analogues in Chokhamela, Raidas, and others from the Indian Mystics, though in intellectual power he surpasses them. His "Theosophia Revelata" were published in 7 volumes (Amsterdam, 1730–1731). In English translation he is fairly well available in the "Three-fold Life of Man" (London, 1909), "The Three Principles of the Divine Essence" (London, 1910), "The Forty Questions of the Soul" (London, 1911), "Dialogues on the Supersensual Life" (London, 1901), and the "Signatures of all Things" (London, 1912). The two central points of his teaching were the "Doctrine of the Microcosm", and the "Law of Antithesis", as a corollary of the latter of which the World was supposed to be created from God.

We have now to take note of two great contemplatives of the Quietistic school in France. With Francis de Sales (A.D. 1567–1622), Mysticism was a cult of the inner life. He was a voluminous writer, as might be seen from his "Oeuvres Completes" published in 16 volumes (Paris, 1835); but his "Introduction to the Devout Life" and his treatise on the "Love of God" are available in English translation in the Library of Devotion, 1906 and 1901.

Madame Guyon (A.D. 1648–1717), the second great Quietistic mystic, was again a prolific writer, her "Oeuvres Completes" having been published in 40 volumes (Paris, 1729–1791). She was the centre of a group of Quietists, and was therefore "involved in the general condemnation of the passive orison". She suffered through her life from mortifications of ill-health, as well as an unhappy married life. Her beauty was shattered by small-pox, and her books were burnt in the market-place. In English translation, she is available in her "Autobiography" translated by Allen (London, 1897), and "A Short Method of Prayer and Spiritual Torrents" (London, 1875).

John Smith (A.D. 1616–1652) is a typical Cambridge Platonist, who in his "True Way of attaining to Divine Knowledge" tells us how faith must become vision, and how a consciousness of sins produces in one the workings of an Aetna or a Vesuvius. He speaks of how he had enjoyed the delights of "mysterious converses with the Deity", and how to him every place was holy ground. His "Select Discourses" were published by the Cambridge University Press, 1859.

Bunyan, the great Puritan writer (1628–1688), describes in his "Grace Abounding" how he passed through a soul-shaking experience, which entitles him to the name of a mystic. A voice would exclaim within him "Sell Him, Sell Him, Sell Him", but Bunyan replied "I will not, I will not, for ten thousands of worlds". So far as his Mysticism is concerned, his "Grace Abounding" is more valuable than his "Pilgrim's Progress". While the first is a marvellous autobiography of struggle and conversion, the second is a valuable manifestation of his fruitful toil.

George Fox (1624–1690), the founder of the school of the Quakers, made a crusade against mere formality in religion, and trusted to the 'Inner Light' alone. It has been said about him by Emerson that an "Institution is the lengthened shadow of a man, as Quakerism of George Fox". He wandered in a suit of leather, calling on all people to trust in the

'Inward Light', which is the main article of his preaching, "the disuse of sacraments, the abandonment of liturgy, silent worship, unpaid ministry, and so forth, being merely consequences of that central doctrine".

Two English gentlemen who now come under the direct influence of Boehme are William Law, and William Blake. William Law (A.D. 1686–1761) was a full-fledged disciple of Boehme. In his earlier "Serious Call", he had given the traditional view of Christianity, but in his "Spirit of Prayer" (1750), and his "Spirit of Love" (1759), he approaches the standpoint of spiritual mysticism, and "is not ashamed to be an enthusiast".

William Blake (A.D. 1757–1827), painter, poet and mystic, made a remarkable combination of colour, rhythm, and spiritual experience. He is known for nothing so much as for his childlike simplicity in everything that he produced. Though a "determined foe of conventional Christianity", we see in his "Jerusalem", his "Songs of Experience" and his "Songs of Innocence", how he is at the same time a true Christian of a deeply mystical type.

Of recent English mystics we might mention John Keble; Wordsworth, Browning and Tennyson; Carlyle and Emerson. John Keble (1792–1866) was the author of the "Christian Year" (1827), which has been "accepted and studied by religious people of all shades of conviction". He was as well the author of the "Lyra Innocentium", and along with Newman and others of "Lyra Apostolica", and has the honour of having a monograph written on him by Lord Irwin. It would be needless to go into details here about the merits of Wordsworth, Browning and Tennyson as poetical mystics. A full description of them belongs to another sphere; but we cannot forbear remarking here that the essential difference between them seems to be that "while Wordsworth was a poet of Nature, Browning was a poet of the Soul, and Tennyson was a Cosmic poet and seer". Tennyson particularly is valuable for Mysticism on account of his experience of the Waking Trance which he used to have from his childhood onwards by contemplation on his name alone. Emerson has been accused by persons like Dean Inge of having preached a Mysticism of the Oriental type, but his "Oversoul" and other essays must be read by every student of Mystical Philosophy. His description of himself as a "transparent eye-ball", and of his "being nothing, and seeing all", as well as his description of "the currents of Universal Being circulating through him" mark him out as a mystic of a high order. Carlyle's "Vision of the Flaring Flame", his doctrine that "all things are the Symbols of God", and his description that "the true Shekinah is Man" make us understand of what mystical fibre he was made.

It is needless to enter upon the merits of contemporary mystics. They are yet in the process of history, and time alone would enable us to pronounce a judgment upon their value and worth.

III. Islamic Mysticism.

In India we are rent by schisms and sects, as well as racial and religious differences. These can vanish only when a firm mystical philosophy gains ground all round. Mysticism as the Philosophy of Spiritual Experience can be the only possible ground for a World-religion. It is only under its influence that differences of all shapes might disappear.

We have thus to consider briefly along with Indian and European Mysticism the contribution which the Mystics of Islam have made to the world's mystical literature. If we study their work carefully, we shall see that they have the same message as the above-mentioned Indian and European Mystics.

The greatest lights among Mahomedan Mystics are Al Ghazzali in the 12th century, Sadi and Jalaluddin Rumi in the 13th, Hafiz in the 14th, and Jami in the 15th century.

As regards the works in the original of these great Saints available for English readers, we have to mention Al Ghazzali's "Confessions" translated by Claud Field (Wisdom of the East Series, London, 1909), and the "Alchemy of Happiness" translated by the same scholar (Wisdom of the East Series, London, 1910).

Sadi's "Gulistan" is available in the English translation of Mr. E. B. Eastwick (Hertford, 1852).

Jalaluddin Rumi, one of the greatest of Mahomedan mystics, in fact of the mystics of all ages and countries, has had the honour of having his "Selected Odes from the Divani Shamsi Tabriz" edited by Prof. R. A. Nicholson (Cambridge, 1898), with Persian text, introduction, English translation and notes. Selections from Rumi are also available in Hadland Davis' translation (Wisdom of the East Series, London, 1908). Mr. E. H. Whinfield has also given us an abridged translation of the "Masnavi" (2nd edition, London, 1898).

The "Divan" of Hafiz has been translated into prose by H. W. Clarke in two volumes, with a note on Sufism, (London, 1891). "Ghazels" from his Divan have been done into English by J. H. McCarthy (London, 1893).

Whinfield and Mirza Kazvini have been responsible for translating Jami's Lawa'ih, a treatise on Sufism (Oriental Translation Fund, 1906), while Selections from Jami are available in Mr. Davis' translation (Wisdom of the East Series, London, 1908).

As a specimen of the mystical utterances of these Saints, we take the liberty of quoting a typical passage from Jalaluddin Rumi, which would show our readers how these mystics would make the whole world kini The theme of the selection is the virtue of Epoche or Mystical Silence: for we have often been told by the mystics that 'he who knows God becomes dumb'. To quote from the "Masnavi" of Jalaluddin Rum (Whinfield's translation):—

"The story admits of being told up to this point,
But what follows is hidden, and inexpressible in words.
If you should speak and try a hundred ways to express it,
'Tis useless; the mystery becomes no clearer.
You can ride on saddle and horse to the sea-coast,
But then you must use a horse of wood (*i.e.*, a boat).
A horse of wood is useless on dry land,
It is the special vehicle of voyagers by sea.

Silence is this horse of wood,
Silence is the guide and support of men at sea."

As regards expository and critical works in English on the writings of these Saints, we have principally to mention the works of Prof. R. A. Nicholson of Cambridge, and especially his brilliant little treatise on the "Mystics of Islam" which must be in the hands of everybody who cares to know not merely what Islamic Mysticism is, but also what all Mysticism is.

Among German writers, we have to mention Von Kremer's "Geschichte der herrschenden Ideen des Islams" (Leipzig, 1868), and Goldziher's "Vorlesungen uber den Islam" (Heidelberg, 1910), both of which contain brilliant accounts of Sufi Mysticism.

Shaikh Muhammad Iqbal's book on "The Development of Metaphysics in Persia" (London, 1908), as well as his recent "Lectures on the Reconstruction of Religious Thought in Islam", would surely repay perusal.

IV. General Works on Mysticism.

Hitherto we have given a Bibliography of Indian, European and Islamic Mysticism. It would now behove us for a brief while to enumerate the most important works bearing on Mysticism in general, in its historical, psychological, contemplative, and philosophical aspects. Literature in all these fields is growing, and is based on the sure foundation of the study of the sources we have indicated above.

From the point of view of the History of Mysticism, one of the best small essays on the subject is to be found as an Appendix to Miss Underhill's "Mysticism", to which our own Bibliography is not a little indebted. Inge's "Christian Mysticism" is another very important work bearing on the lives and teachings of the great Christian Saints, and covers in detail the ground occupied in a small compass by Miss Underhill's essay above-mentioned. Mr. Inge is also responsible for writing another historical treatise on an allied subject in his "Studies of English Mystics" (John Murray, 1921), wherein, after a general survey of the psychology of Mysticism, he goes on to discuss the contribution made by Julian of Norwich, Hilton, Law, Wordsworth, and Browning to the general theory of Mysticism. Vaughan's "Hours with the Mystics" is also a historical account of the great mystics, but his point of view is vitiated by his definition of Mysticism as "a form of error which mistakes for a divine manifestation the operations of a merely human faculty". Rufus M. Jones' "Studies in Mystical Religion" is again another historical account of the great Mystics, and contains, in particular, a good account of the 'Friends of God'. One of the most lucid introductions to a general history of Mysticism in Christianity comes from the pen of Mr. W. K. Fleming (Robert Scott, 1913), which also covers the same ground as is occupied by the works of Underhill and Inge above-mentioned, and to which also as to the two others we are equally indebted. Dom Cuthbert Butler's brilliant and penetrating work on Western Mysticism, as opposed to the Mysticism of the West, contains a studied account of the contribution which SS. Augustine,

Gregory, and Bernard, as well as St. John of the Cross, made to the general theory of Mysticism. Its full extracts from the originals are very pleasant reading. As regards treatment of particular authors and the schools they founded, we might mention a book like Hügel's "Mystical Element of Religion", which is a study of the teachings of St. Catherine of Genoa and her friends. We have also books like "Masters of the Spiritual Life" by Mr. F. W. Drake (Longmans, 1916) which contains a study of the writings of certain great mystics, for example, Augustine's "Confessions", Julian's "Revelations", à Kempis' "Imitation", Francis de Sales' "Devout Life", and so on. A brief historical study of the works indicated above would, we suppose, be sufficient to ground the student of Mysticism in a general knowledge of the subject.

As regards the Psychology of Mysticism, James' "Varieties of Religious Experience", of course, occupies the first place. It is an exhaustive and, on the whole, an unbiassed account of the rise and growth of mystical consciousness. Joly's "Psychology of the Saints" is another contribution in the same line, but with more of devotion in it. Of modern works on Religious Consciousness, we might mention particularly Selbie's "Psychology of Religion" (Oxford, 2nd Edition, 1926), which is a very valuable contribution to the subject. Pratt's "Religious Consciousness" (Macmillan, 1924) is a good analytical account of mystical psychology, while Thouless' "Introduction to the Psychology of Religion" (2nd Edition, Cambridge, 1924), is a reasonable defence, as against Leuba, of possible transcendent causes in mystical experience against mere psychological laws. We have also special treatises on such subjects in the Psychology of Religion as Conversion. Mr. Underwood's "Conversion, Christian and Non-Christian" (George Unwin Allen, 1925) gives first a historical account of the phenomena of Conversion in Judaism, Christianity, Hinduism, Buddhism, Islam, and so forth, and later enters into a psychological study of the phenomena by discussing the relation of Conversion to Adolescence, its Accompaniments, its Mechanism, and finally its Fruits. De Sanctis' "Religious Conversion" (Kegan Paul, 1927) is a bio-psychological study, and finds the possibility of Conversion in certain natural tendencies of the individual such as the presence of religiosity, a habitual tendency to absolute convictions, the tendency to extend one's attention beyond the realities of the senses, a richness of affective potential, and, finally, constant recurrences of the experience of pain. The French mind is particularly engaged in a psychological study of mystical phenomena, and we might make particular mention of the following works in that line: Leuba's "Psychological Study of Religion" (Macmillan, 1912), and "Psychology of Religious Mysticism" (Kegan Paul, 1925); Récéjac's "Essai sur les fondements de la Connaissance Mystique" which appears in English translation as "Essay on the Bases of the Mystic Knowledge" (London, 1899); Delacroix's "Ètudes d' Histoire et de Psychologie du Mysticisme", which contains a detailed account of St. Teresa, Madame Guyon, and Suso. In all these works on the Psychology of Mysticism, it is the element of the subliminal consciousness and its upshot into the normal waking consciousness which is the central theme, and all mystic phenomena are thus explained on the hypothesis of the subliminal consciousness. As an acute critic points out, it is this very subliminal consciousness which we might equate with the Soul, and hence all the phenomena which these try to explain from the point of view of Psychology may even be explained metaphysically and mystically in terms of the workings of the Soul.

Of works on the contemplative and devotional side of Mysticism, there have been an infinite number of books on hymns, songs, religious lyrics, and so forth, which express the passion of the aspiring Soul after God. So far as the mystics themselves are concerned, we need here only mention one book, Inge's "Life, Light, and Love", being selections from the German Mystics (Library of Devotion). Of books more on the contemplative side, we might mention works like those of Arthur Chandler, whose "Ara Coeli" (5th Edition, Methuen, 1912) is an excellent essay on Mystical Theology, containing very readable articles on such subjects as Disillusionment, Detachment, Meditation, Union, and so forth. Another of his works, "The Cult of the Passing Moment" (5th Edition, Methuen, 1922) is again a very valuable contribution to religious and contemplative life, in which he tells us how "we have our place in the transitory, striving, agonizing world. We do our bit of work, pass, and are forgotten........ By receiving, however, each moment as from God, and offering it to His service, we shall find that we have wrought in us an Eternal Life reflecting the supreme reality of God" (pp. 216–217). Hodgson's "In the Way of the Saints" (Longman's, 1913) is another work of the same kind, and has a brilliant last chapter on the "Direct Vision of God". Nicoll's "Garden of Nuts" (Hodder and Stoughton, 1923) is again another very beautiful production of the same kind, containing very excellent sermons on such subjects as "The Stages of the Inward Way", "The Doctrine of the Holy Assembly", "The Lighting of the Lamps", and so on. Poulain's "Graces of Interior Prayer" (London, 1910) is an excellent exposition of Mysticism from the Catholic standpoint, and contains a well-selected body of extracts at the end of every chapter. Waite's "Studies in Mysticism" (London, 1906) is based upon the existence of a Secret Tradition, and his translation of Eckhartshausen's "The Cloud upon the Sanctuary" (London, 1909) contains an exposition of the doctrine of the Holy Assembly. Otto's "Idea of the Holy" is another work of the same kind,—a brilliant characterisation of the nature of the Numinous, which is the spiritual counterpart of the Etwas or the Ding-an-sich of Kant, and which compels our admiration and fascination, love and worship, fear and awe, by its overpowering energy and its non-moral and non-rational holiness, even though it exists outside of us as the wholly Other, and thus as an entirely transcendent Object which exercises influence merely from the beyond.

Of works pertaining to the philosophical side of Mysticism, the most brilliant is, of course, Underhill's "Mysticism", which has passed through several editions since its first appearance in 1911. Her "Mystic Way" which is an interpretation of the earliest documents of the Christian Church is not so brilliant, being more historical than philosophical. Herman's "Meaning and Value of Mysticism" is yet another brilliant work on Mysticism, and offers a challenge to the intuitionism of Miss Underhill in her intellectual defence of Mysticism. A. V. Sharpe's "Mysticism, its True Nature and Value", which contains a translation of the Mystical Theology of Dionysius the Areopagite, maintains a distinction between the eternity of beatific experience "post mortem" and the transiency of mystical experience during life. Hügel's "Eternal Life" is a classical exposition of the doctrine of the life ever-lasting, from both the historical and the philosophical points of view. Dyson's "Studies in Christian Mysticism", though written primarily, as the author tells us, for his own guidance, and to give definiteness to his own thoughts, is a brilliant production, which contains many new and original ideas, and is securely based on the teachings of the great Mystics. Waite's "Way of Divine Union", and his work on the "Holy Graal" have been praised as being great works on Mysticism; but their style is uncouth, though there is a certain directness about them. Dean Inge's Gifford Lectures on "Plotinus", though intended primarily to discuss the Mystical Philosophy of the great Alexandrian Philosopher, is a vindication of the mystical point of view in general in the light of Contemporary Philosophy. His "Personal Idealism and Mysticism" (1st Edition, 1907; 3rd, 1924) is intended to offer a challenge to the doctrine of the so-called Personal Idealists, whose influence in psychology he commends, but whose influence in theology he regards as mischievous. Personality, according to Dean Inge, is an abstraction, and the highest ideal is not to remember Personality, but to forget it. "There is but one virtue", as Fichte would say, "to forget oneself as a person; one vice, to remember oneself" (p. 106).

This discussion takes us into the domain of Contemporary Philosophy in general, represented especially in the Gifford Lectures of the great savants of the West. The validity of Mystical Experience must be judged by a criterion, and it would be the business of a study of Contemporary Philosophy to afford such a criterion. Of course, this criterion may change from philosopher to philosopher, but unless we are in sure possession of a criterion, we shall be without a compass and a rudder on the mystic sea. Bradley's "Appearance and Reality", the greatest recent pronouncement on Philosophy allied to Mysticism, did not appear in the Gifford Series, having been published before that series was probably conceived. Most of the other great books, however, on Contemporary British Philosophy were delivered as Gifford Lectures. Bosanquet's "Principle of Individuality and Value" (1912) and "Value and Destiny of the Individual" (1913) were delivered as Gifford Lectures, and they afford to us a criterion in their own way for the judgment of mystical experience. Ward's "Realm of Ends", which is more pluralistic than absolutistic, is for that reason more theistic than mystical, and yet its Theism would place us in a position to discuss whether we might not pass beyond mere Theism to Mysticism, as its author first passed from Naturalism to Spiritualism, and then from Pluralism to Theism. Royce's "The World and the Individual", which was also delivered as Gifford Lectures many years ago, is not entirely unsympathetic to Mysticism, though he has a critico-monistic philosophy of his own, which, in his opinion, surpasses the mystical point of view. Of modern works on the Philosophy of Religion in the Gifford Series, we need only mention Pringle Pattison's "Idea of God", and "Studies in the Philosophy of Religion", Sorley's "Moral Values and the Idea of God", and Webb's "God and Personality", which enable us to discuss the nature of the Person and to discover his relation to God. Alexander's "Space, Time, and Deity", Fawcett's "The World as Imagination", Lloyd Morgan's "Life, Mind, and Spirit" and works of that kind, again, enable us to discover the nature of God each in its own way. There is no end, in short, to philosophical construction, and each philosopher has his own favourite theory about the nature of Reality. The Mystic may be a Philosopher, but is not necessarily so. His mystic experience is sufficient for his own elevation into Divinity; but if he philosophises, he may raise thinking humanity into a Divine Kingdom of Ends.